0223985

SM02004140
4.03.

D1460685

International Trade

Second Edition

...st date shown below.

This new edition of *International Trade* has been rewritten to provide an up-to-date, clear and comprehensive account of the most important developments currently taking place in the world economy. The topic-driven text introduces the reader to the major economic theories and models with an emphasis on changes within the world trading system and how governments respond. Features include:

- An expansion of chapter three to include some formal models of intra-industry trade under imperfect competition.
- A restructuring of the text to create two separate chapters on Japan and newly industrialising countries, up-dating and incorporating new material.
- New sections on Strategic Trade Policy and on the Political Economy of Protectionism.
- A new chapter to provide a more extensive treatment of the institutional aspects of world trade in particular to discuss the deliberations of the World Trade Organisation in the period leading up to Seattle and the Millennium Round.
- Extra pedagogical content in the form of background boxes, comprehensive suggestions for further reading and glossary.

Nigel Grimwade is Principal Lecturer in Economics and Head of Economics Division in the Business School at South Bank University. He is the author of *International Trade Policy: a Contemporary Analysis*, published by Routledge in 1996 and has written extensively on aspects of International Trade and International Trade Policy.

HAROLD BRIDGES LIBRARY
ST. MARTINS SERVICES LTD.
LANCASTER

0415156262

International Trade

New Patterns of Trade, Production & Investment

Second Edition

Nigel Grimwade

London and New York

First published 1998. This second edition published 2000
by Routledge
11 New Fetter Lane,
London EC4P 4EE

Simultaneously published in the USA and Canada
by Routledge
29 West 35th Street, New York, NY 10001

Reprinted 2001

Routledge is an imprint of the Taylor & Francis Group

© 2000 Nigel Grimwade

Typeset by Thomson Press (India) Limited, New Delhi
Printed and bound in Great Britain by TJ International Ltd, Padstow, Cornwall

All rights reserved. No part of this book may be reprinted or reproduced or utilised in any form or by any electronic, mechanical, or other means, now known or hereafter invented, including photocopying and recording, or in any information storage or retrieval system, without permission in writing from the publishers.

British Library Cataloguing in Publication Data

A catalogue record for this book is available from the British Library

Library of Congress Cataloging in Publication Data

Grimwade, Nigel, 1949-
International trade : new patterns of trade, production & investment / Nigel Grimwade.— 2nd ed.
p. cm.
Includes bibliographical references and index.
1. International trade. 2. International economic relations. 3. Investments, Foreign.
I. Title.

HF1379.G75 2000
382—dc21 00-032175

ISBN 0-415-15626-2(hbk)
ISBN 0-415-15627-0(pbk)

Contents

Figures

Tables

Preface to the Second Edition

The first edition of this book was published in 1989, pre-dating a number of important developments in the world trading system. In view of the major changes that have taken place in international trade since then, it has been necessary to re-write most of the original text. The basic structure of the original text has been retained with one or two alterations. Chapter 2 in the first edition, entitled *The Changing Structure of World Output and Trade*, has been moved to Chapter 1 and Chapter 1 in the first edition, entitled *Basic Theories of International Trade and Production*, has been moved to Chapter 2. At the same time, the content of Chapter 2 is now purely concerned with theories of trade, while the discussion of tariffs and international economic integration has been shifted to later chapters. The treatment of trade theories in Chapter 2 has also been made a little more formal and rigorous than in the first edition, so as to reduce the need for the reader to supplement the theoretical sections with reading from another, more conventional text.

Chapter 3 has been kept in much the same form as in the first edition. However, the section dealing with trade under imperfect competition has been expanded. Some formal models of intra-industry trade under imperfect competition, which were not dealt with in the first edition, are now included. Again, this should enable the reader to gain a much more complete picture of new trade theory than was previously possible, reducing the need to supplement the text with additional reading from another source. The title of Chapter 4 in the original text has been changed, but the content is much the same as in the first edition. Chapter 5, also, has much the same content as in the first edition.

Chapter 6 in the first edition, which was entitled *The Growth of Japan and the Emergence of the Newly Industrialising Countries*, has been split into two separate chapters. The need to include some new material, as well as up-date the rest, necessitated breaking the chapter into two. There are also sound pedagogical arguments for treating the two issues separately. Although the newly industrialising countries have to some degree followed in the wake of Japan, the factors causing their growth have been different. Moreover, the problems created by Japan's current account surplus for the western industrialised countries differ from those resulting from the rise of the newly industrialising countries.

Chapter 8 differs in a major way from the original Chapter 7 in the first edition, which was entitled *The Growth of the New Protectionism and the Adjustment Problem*. The section on the adjustment problem has been moved into Chapter 7 as it makes better sense to discuss this problem in the context of the rise of the newly industrialising countries. At the same time, I have moved the brief discussion of tariffs, which was found in the first chapter of the original edition, to Chapter 8. It seems more logical to discuss tariff protectionism within the same chapter as non-tariff protectionism. However, I have used the opportunity to broaden the content of this chapter to provide a more formal presentation of the arguments for and against free trade. Chapter 8 also contains a completely new section on Strategic Trade Policy and on the Political Economy of Protectionism.

Chapter 9 is an entirely new chapter written to provide a more extensive treatment of the institutional aspects of world trade. Although the first edition contained a brief section on the General Agreement on Tariffs and Trade (GATT), there was a need for a larger section on this subject. Moreover, there is the need for any new text on International Trade to discuss the results of the Uruguay Round and the work of the newly created World Trade Organisation (WTO), which has replaced the GATT. The first edition also contained nothing on regional economic integration. However, this has clearly become an important issue in the years since then, with the creation of the European Single Market, the North American Free Trade Area (NAFTA) and the spread of regional trading arrangements in the developing world.

Chapter 10 retains much the same content as did Chapter 8, entitled *Trade in Services*, in the first edition. However, the data have been substantially up-dated and a section included on the new General Agreement on Trade in Services (GATS) and the agreement on trade-related intellectual property rights (TRIPs) set up after the Uruguay Round.

All of these changes have been motivated by an awareness of some of the deficiencies of the original edition and in response to feedback received from academics and students alike. In particular, I have become aware that, if the book is to be adopted as a core text for a course in International Trade, a fuller treatment of some subjects is needed than is the case in the original edition. I hope that these changes go a substantial way towards satisfying these requirements.

Introduction

The aim of this book is to provide undergraduates and post-graduates, who are studying International Trade as part of their degree, with an intermediate text which provides a clear and comprehensive account of the most important developments currently taking place in the world trading system. The book is written for students who have at least a first-year knowledge of Economics, but prefer a topic-driven approach to the model-driven style of more traditional texts. In particular, students studying Trade as part of a degree other than Economics (e.g. Business Studies, International Business or International Relations) may find this approach more helpful. Although this book seeks to set out most of the major theories needed for an understanding of the subject, the emphasis is more on the changes that are taking place in the world trading system and how governments are responding to these changes. The student who wishes to probe more deeply into the various models used by economists to explain trade flows can seek out one of the large number of more conventional texts that are now available. My experience is that many students, especially those who are not Economics specialists, need a text that is a little more friendly and is couched more in reality than is often the case with conventional theoretical texts. Hopefully, having had a taste of the subject and acquired an interest in some of the models referred to, they will develop an interest in probing more deeply into the theoretical side of the subject matter.

A further consideration in writing this book was to provide a text on International Trade, which attached a greater importance than is often the case in the teaching of International Trade to the role that is played by the multinational company in world trade. More conventional texts tend to treat the multinational company as being of secondary importance only. Students who are interested in the factors motivating the decisions of the multinational company generally have to seek out other books. Indeed, it is still the convention in most universities to separate the study of trade from that of the firm, creating what is, largely, a false dichotomy. Today, multinational companies are the main players in the world trading system. Attempts to explain trade without giving the multinational company a prominent place leave a feeling of dissatisfaction. For students, especially students of International Business, the failure of trade economists to pay due attention to the firm is rightly regarded as naïve. As a consequence, the study of International Trade comes to seem increasingly unrealistic.

Fortunately, one of the most encouraging developments within the subject of International Trade that has taken place in recent years has been a recognition of the valuable role that theories of industrial organisation can play in explaining trade. Trade economists have discovered that many of the theoretical tools used in the study of industrial organisation are extremely useful for explaining trade. As a result, many of the newer models of trade that have sprung up in recent decades, borrow important concepts and techniques from the tool box of the industrial organisation economist. The result has been that trade economists can now explain more fully than ever before some of the forms of trade which are known to take place, but which contradict the predictions of more conventional models of trade. Unfortunately, much of the literature that has grown up as a consequence of this development, is not easy for the untrained mind to understand. Largely, this is because the level of mathematics involved is beyond what most students (and even some academics!) are able to cope with. As a result, some of the valuable insights of these models are missed.

This book tries to tackle this difficulty by presenting the models in a more 'user-friendly' manner. Although some students may still feel that they would rather abandon the exercise altogether, they are encouraged to persevere as the models in question can provide many useful insights in to why countries trade in particular products and what effects government intervention in trade can have. On the other hand, some students of Economics may wish that the book provided a more formal and rigorous presentation of the models with more use of mathematics. I understand this concern. However, my excuse is that there already are many excellent texts that have been written for this purpose. The diligent Economics specialist will not have to search too far to find a book that will suit their requirements. However, the concern of this book is rather different. It is to introduce students of International Business, as well as Economics, to some of the new developments taking place in trade theory, that help explain some of what can be observed as actually taking place in the world economy.

Texts that are concerned with explaining trade in a more formal way, relying mainly on expounding complex models of trade making much use of mathematics, can sometimes make for dry reading, especially for non-Economics specialists. Largely, this is because the models seem rather abstract and distant from the world that they observe. In particular, students of Business, International Business or Management Studies, are interested in what is actually happening in the world that they observe through books, newspapers and television. It is a pity if the study of International Trade is reduced to making laborious and often time-consuming journeys through complex and often abstract theoretical models. Students will find it hard to make the connection between the world described in the texts which they use and the world in which they work, live and play. There are other dangers, too. An excessive focus on model building may lead to students neglecting the more descriptive side of the subject matter. Policy issues, too, may get squeezed out, with the result that the student is poorly equipped to understand the big issues generating trade conflict between countries. Students will emerge from academia seeking a career in business or government badly prepared to grapple with the decision making responsibilities that face them.

For these reasons, this book tries to pay more attention than is often the case in more conventional texts to what is actually taking place in the global trade system. It does so in several ways. First, a greater prominence is given to the firm as a key player. The actions of firms affect trade flows between countries in a number of very important ways. How multinational firms organise their global operations has major implications for patterns of regional and global specialisation. Also important are the precise ways in which they engage in trade with other firms across borders. Trade theory tends to neglect these issues, assuming that all trade takes place on an arms-length basis between independent buyers and sellers. In fact, this is probably the exception rather than the norm. Students of International Business want to know why different firms may choose different ways to trade their goods internationally, not just the effect of changed assumptions on the predictions of models that sometimes lack much realism in other ways also.

Second, this book provides a more policy-focused approach than conventional theoretical texts, with particular consideration given to the role played by international institutions in trade. It asks what problems the expansion of trade creates for different players, including domestic producers, consumers and the public authorities. This necessitates a contemporary approach, as the specific problems that are relevant at one point in time may be very different at another. Moreover, the response of those affected, whether positively or negatively, by these changes varies as the structure of the industries in which they operate changes. If the study on Trade is to be worthwhile, it must consider how and why firms and governments respond in particular ways to the various changes that confront them at any moment in time. For firms, the task is how best to maximise profits or sales in a global environment, characterised by rapid technological change, globalisation and the emergence of new sources of competition and growing constraints on their actions. For governments, a major concern is the appropriate commercial policy that it is best to pursue in the face of new opportunities and new challenges taking place in the global trading system. At both the regional and multilateral level, the institutions that govern relations between countries must decide what changes are needed to the rules governing world trade in the context of a more open trading system and changing national and international priorities.

My hope is that this book will provide students of International Trade with a satisfying alternative to the more traditional style of other books covering the same subject matter. At the same time, I hope that it will, sufficiently, whet their appetite for the subject of International Trade so that they will choose to pursue some of the subject matter at a deeper and more advanced level. The level of knowledge presumed should not be beyond that of a second-year undergraduate who has successfully completed first-year courses in Micro- and Macro-Economics. Third-year under-graduates and post-graduates should be able to read the text without difficulty. However, the book contains a glossary of terms, which should be helpful if and when the reader finds himself/herself confronted, suddenly, with a concept with which they are unfamiliar. Students will find the book more beneficial if they read it in the order in which the chapters are set out. Often, later chapters build on ideas developed in earlier chapters, such that failure to understand material contained in earlier chapters may make later chapters less easy to follow. However, the more topic-driven approach of this book means that, to some extent, the chapters can be read selectively, especially by students with a good knowledge of Economics.

With regard to the contents of the book, it is obviously not possible even in a text of this length to address all topics of major importance in International Trade at the present time. There are bound to be particular topics, which different observers would wish were included. In part, this reflects the particular areas of interest of different individuals. However, I have sought to include those issues that I consider to be of primary importance at the present time and that fit into the overall theme of this book. One major omission is any specific reference to monetary/financial matters. Thus, this book does not specifically address the determination of exchange rates, balance of payments policy or the subject of international capital flows, although these are, obviously, topics of major importance at the present time. It would not have been possible to do so in the space of a single book. It is also conventional in universities to teach the subject of International Monetary Economics/International Finance separately from that of International Trade, although it is clear that, in modern business, the two areas are intimately bound together. At times, the book does discuss issues pertaining to exchange rates and the balance of payments. In this case, it is assumed that the reader will have covered these areas at other times in the course of their studies.

The structure of this book is as follows. First, Chapter 1 examines the main ways in which the structure of world output and trade has changed over the past half century. The chapter examines detailed output and trade statistics to identify the most important trends that have occurred. One of the most important developments has been the fact that, throughout this period, world trade has consistently grown faster than world output. This reflects a deepening specialisation among countries. One consequence of this has been that most of the major industrialised economies of the world have become more open. At the same time, there has been some tendency for world trade to become more 'regionalised' or geographically biased. This chapter examines the methods used by economists to measure these trends. At the same time, the geographical and commodity structure of world trade has altered in a number of important ways. This chapter examines these changes and the factors underlying them.

The next two chapters are concerned with the theories which economists have put forward to explain the pattern of world trade and specialisation. Chapter 2 sets out basic or orthodox theories of trade that have been used to explain both why trade is beneficial and the factors which shape the products in which countries specialise. Most students of Economics will be familiar with the classical theory of comparative advantage. The chapter provides a formal statement of the theory and some reference to attempts made to empirically test the theory. However, the theory of comparative advantage fails to provide an explanation for why differences in comparative costs exist between countries. It was left to the neo-classical school to fill this gap. Writing in the late 19th and early 20th century, the neo-classicists developed what has come to be known as the factor proportions theory of trade. Although this provides a relatively simple, and, therefore, highly attractive explanation, based on differences in the factor proportions required to produce different goods, it is not well supported by empirical research. Especially when explaining patterns of trade in manufactured goods, a more promising approach is to examine the differences that exist in consumer preferences (on the demand side) or technological 'know-how' (on the supply side). Yet a further possibility is to relax the assumption made by most neo-classical models that average costs increase with output. However, this opens up the possibility that markets for goods will be dominated by one or a small number of firms, rather than being perfectly competitive as assumed in most orthodox theories of trade.

Chapter 3 examines some of the consequences of relaxing the traditional assumptions about markets being perfectly competitive. One consequence of doing so is that the simple predictions of neo-classical trade theory break down. Rather than each country specialising in the activities in which it enjoys a comparative cost advantage, countries end up both exporting and importing products belonging to those industries. This is known as intra-industry trade and specialisation. Much of the trade that takes places between western industrialised countries is of this kind. In this chapter, some explanations for why countries simultaneously export and import products belonging to the same industry are examined. The results of empirical tests carried out to test the reliability of these explanations are then surveyed. The question is asked as to whether or not there are particular characteristics of individual industries or countries that can account for why intra-industry rather than inter-industry trade predominates.

Alongside the expansion of world trade over the past half century, there has occurred a parallel growth of foreign direct investment (FDI). This investment in productive capital is carried out by firms that wish to expand their operations internationally. This chapter sets out the main trends that have occurred in FDI over the post-war era and that have resulted in the emergence of the multinational enterprise. It asks what theories best explain these trends. It will be seen that firms may expand internationally by various different means (exporting, overseas production, licensing agreements) and that any theory of the multinational enterprise must account for why overseas production is the preferred route. One of the consequences of the expansion of the multinational enterprise is that a growing volume of world trade now takes the form of trade between different parts of the same multinational company. This is known as intra-firm trade. Mainly this occurs because, for certain transactions, internalised markets have efficiency advantages over external markets. This, in turn, constitutes one explanation for the expansion of the multinational company. However, a further possible advantage of internalisation is that it creates opportunities for transfer-price manipulation. In this chapter, the various motives for transfer-price manipulation are examined alongside the internal and external constraints that exist on doing so in practice. The chapter concludes by asking the question whether theoretical explanations for FDI can be integrated with trade theories to provide a single theory of international production capable of predicting both forms of international expansion.

Chapter 5 examines some of the forms of international economic involvement, other than FDI that have become common in recent decades. Almost in parallel with the growth of intra-industry trade, growth of intra-industry FDI has occurred. FDI between two countries may occur in both directions within an individual industry or sector. This may reflect the oligopolistic nature of the competition that takes place between large firms in the markets for many manufactured goods. A particular feature of much of the FDI that has taken place in recent decades is that it is not concerned with an exporter seeking to gain greater access to the overseas market for its product. Rather, it is motivated by the need to reduce costs by rationalising production on a regional or global basis. While local market-oriented FDI tends to act a substitute for trade, rationalised FDI is trade-enhancing. In this chapter, the reasons for rationalised FDI and its consequences are discussed. However, FDI is not the only way in which firms expand internationally. A trend in recent decades has been for multinational firms to use a wide range of different methods of international involvement. These include several non-equity modes of expansion, such as joint ventures, licensing agreements, franchising agreements, international sub-contracting, turnkey contracts and strategic alliances. In this chapter, some of the most important alternatives to FDI are examined and the factors which influence the choice that firms make between these alternatives are considered. Finally, the chapter examines the growing importance of counter-trade as a method that firms are increasingly using with developing countries and state-planned economies in particular. This chapter describes the various forms of counter-trading that exist and examines the factors that give rise to counter-trading. It asks the question whether or not the rise of counter-trading with its emphasis on achieving a bilateral balance on trade flows between countries is damaging to global economic efficiency.

Chapters 6 and 7 address two of the most important developments that have occurred in the geographical structure of world trade in the post-war era. The first has been the rise of Japan, which, in the course of a few decades, grew from being a semi-industrialised country with a relatively low per capita income to becoming one of the world's most industrialised and leading exporters of manufactured goods. Although, in the last decade, the Japanese 'miracle' has turned sour, Japan may yet recover her former pre-eminence. In this chapter, the reasons for her post-war success are discussed. At the same time, the impact of the rise of Japan on the western industrialised world is examined. Beginning in the early 1970s, Japan began to enjoy a large current account surplus on her trade with the western industrialised countries, which has created considerable friction between Japan and her western trading partners. In this chapter, some of the micro- and macro-economic explanations for that phenomenon are considered.

Chapter 7 examines the impact of the rise of the so-called 'other Japans', the newly industrialising countries of the East Asian region. In fact, the term 'newly industrialising country' is broader than just the economies of the East Asian region. It includes a wide range of developing countries in Central and Southern America, Eastern Europe and the Mediterranean region and South Asia that have managed to break through into rapid economic growth, often based on export expansion. In this chapter, some of the reasons for the success of these economies are discussed, taking into account that the expansion in the East Asian region came to an abrupt halt just at the time when this book was nearing completion. The chapter also examines the impact of the rise of these countries on the advanced industrialised countries of the world, especially on the traditional manufacturing sectors and the regions on which they depend. It asks the question whether or not the high levels of unemployment experienced by these countries can be explained as a consequence of increased competition from the newly industrialising countries. If increased imports from newly industrialising countries have contributed to increased unemployment in the western industrialised world, there is a need for a policy response, which addresses the problem of how resources can be shifted out of the sectors adversely affected and into new faster growing areas of the economy.

Increased competition from Japan and the newly industrialising countries is one of the reasons why western industrialised countries place barriers or restrictions on imports. In Chapter 8, the effects of different forms of protection are examined. The standard economic arguments in favour of free trade are presented to show why most economists prefer free trade to protection. The damaging effects of tariffs and the different kinds of non-tariff barriers that have emerged in recent years are analysed. On the whole, over the past fifty years, governments have realised that freer trade is better and have lowered or eliminated the formal barriers which impede trade. Thus, tariffs on industrial goods are now out at their lowest level ever. However, there remain important exceptions. Moreover, many governments have found other more subtle ways of restricting imports. If free trade makes countries better off, why do governments deny their citizens these benefits? In this chapter, we shall see that there are few sound economic arguments for protection, so many of the reasons for protection are clearly based on non-economic considerations. However, there are some possible cases where government intervention can be beneficial. One is the strategic trade policy argument for intervention in oligopolistic industries that are dominated by a small number of firms and where entry barriers enable each producer to earn excess profits in the long run. However, economists are not agreed that strategic trade policy arguments provide a robust case for widespread interference by governments in free trade. If we are to explain why governments are so willing to inflict welfare losses on their own citizens by interfering with trade, we need to give more careful consideration to the political process whereby trade policy is determined. This chapter finishes by examining the political economy model of protection, which employs some of the tools used by modellers in the discipline of political science to construct a model of trade policy determination.

Chapter 9 examines how trade policy is determined at the global and regional level. Trade policy may be used not merely to secure economic or non-economic advantages for a country by curtailing imports or subsidising exports, but also as a negotiating ploy to secure improved access for a country's exporters to foreign markets. Since the Second World War, the main forum for conducting such negotiations was the General Agreement on Tariffs and Trade (GATT). Since 1995, the role of the GATT has been taken over by the World Trade Organisation (WTO). Both the GATT and the WTO provide a means whereby countries can gain domestic acquiescence for welfare-increasing reductions in tariffs and/or non-tariff barriers. In recent years, however, many countries have preferred to achieve freer trade on a regional basis by entering into regional trade agreements with countries, with whom they trade a great deal. This so-called 'regionalism' has not always been intended as an alternative to the multilateralist approach of the GATT/WTO. Nevertheless, it has posed a potential threat to the GATT/WTO. This chapter explains why this might be the case and considers if anything needs to be done to control the growth of regional trading blocs. The chapter also discusses why countries negotiate such arrangements and what benefits they hope to gain by doing so.

Finally, Chapter 10 addresses the subject of trade in services. In this chapter, it is argued that there are differences between trade in goods and services, although it is often difficult to distinguish between them. Over the past half century, the service economy has grown in all the advanced industrialised economies. So, too, has trade in services, although services are often more difficult to transport across borders in the same way as goods. Important technological developments, however, have made it increasingly possible to separate the production of a service from its consumption. This chapter asks the question as to whether or not the trade theories examined in earlier chapters can be applied to trade in services. It also examines some of the problems involved in liberalising world trade in services. The Uruguay Round of multilateral trade negotiations established a new General Agreement on Trade in Services (GATS), which has created a framework for further liberalisation in the future. This chapter examines the main features of the new GATS and discusses the prospects for achieving more open markets for services. The chapter concludes with a brief discussion of the role of intellectual property rights in world trade and new TRIPs agreement reached in 1993 as part of the Uruguay Round.

Abbreviations

ACP	African, Caribbean and Pacific countries
AFTA	ASEAN Free Trade Area
AMS	Aggregate Measure of Support
ANZCERTA	Australian and New Zealand Closer Economic Relations and Trade Agreement
APEC	Asia Pacific Economic Co-operation
ASEAN	Association of South East Asian Nations
CACM	Central American Common Market
CAP	Common Agricultural Policy
CET	Common External Tariff
CIS (C15)	Commonwealth of Independent States
CMEA	Council for Mutual Economic Assistance
COMECON	See CMEA
CU	Customs Union
DSB	Dispute Settlements Body
DME	Developed Market Economy
EC	European Community
ECSC	European Coal and Steel Community
EEA	European Economic Area
EEC	European Economic Community
EFTA	European Free Trade Area
EMS	European Monetary System
EMU	European Monetary Union or Economic and Monetary Union
EPZ	Export Processing Zone
FDI	Foreign Direct Investment
FTA	Free Trade Area
CATS	General Agreement on Services
GATT	General Agreement on Tariffs and Trade
GDP	Gross Domestic Product
GNE	Gross National Expenditure
GNP	Gross National Product
GSP	Generalised System of Preferences
G5	Group of Five
G7	Group of Seven
IMF	International Monetary Fund
LAFTA	Latin American Free Trade Association
LDC	Least Developed Country
LTA	Long-Term Cotton Textile Arrangement
MFA	Multi-Fibre Arrangement
MFN	Most Favoured Nation
MITI	Ministry of International Trade and Industry (Japan)
MNC	Multinational Company or Corporation
MNE	Multinational Enterprise
NAFTA	North American Free Trade Area
NEC	Newly Exporting Country

NIC Newly Industrialising or Industrialised Country
NIDL New International Division of Labour
NTB Non Tariff Barrier
OAP Offshore Assembly Provision
OECD Organisation for Economic Co-operation and Development
OEEC Organisation fort European Economic Co-operation
OMA Orderly Marketing Arrangement
OPEC Organisation of Petroleum Exporting Countries
PTA Preferential Trading Agreement or Area
SCTA Semi-Conductor Trade Agreement
SEM Single European Market
SII Structural Impediments Initiative
SITC Standard International Trade Classification
STA Short-Term Cotton Textile Arrangement
TNC Transnational Company or Corporation
TRIM Trade-related Investment Measure
TRIP Trade-related Intellectual Property Right
UN United Nations
UNCTAD United Nations Conference on Trade and Development
UNCTNC United Nations Centre on Transnational Corporations
UNIDO United Nations Industrial Development Organisation
VER Voluntary Export Restraint
VIE Voluntary Import Expansion
VRA Voluntary Restraint Agreement
WIPO World Intellectual Property Organisation
WTO World Trade Organisation

Chapter 1

The Changing Structure of World Output and Trade

CHAPTER OUTLINES: Introduction. The Growth of World Output – historical perspective, post-war trends in world output, the 1973–74 Oil Crisis, the 1979–80 oil crisis, the 1990–93 downturn, the East Asian financial crisis. The Growth of World Trade. Changes in the Commodity Composition of World Trade – primary products: food, agricultural raw materials, ores and minerals and non-ferrous metals, fuels; manufactures. Changes in the Geographical Composition of World Trade. The Regional Structure of World Trade. Conclusion.

Introduction

The fifty years or so that have passed since the ending of the Second World War have been a period of extremely rapid economic growth. On average, *world output* has grown at a faster rate than in any other period of history. A major cause of the growth in output has been the rapid growth of *world trade*. Throughout this period, world trade consistently grew faster than world output. This, in turn, was the result of a major increase in the degree of international *specialisation* between countries. An increase in the degree of specialisation would result in an increase in world trade even with no increase in world output. Hence, the fact that trade has been growing faster than output implies an increase in the degree of specialisation. Although this has taken place in all sectors, the trend has been most pronounced for manufacturing.

The much faster expansion of trade relative to output has also meant that those countries that have shared in the process, have become increasingly interdependent. The proportion of output that is traded has increased in most regions of the world. This means that 'shocks' in one part of the world economy are much more quickly transmitted to other parts. For example, a downturn in the level of economic activity in one country is likely to cause a similar downturn in those countries that depend on the former for export markets. It has also meant that it is more difficult than ever before for governments to pursue independent macroeconomic policies.

At the same time, the growth of world trade has brought important changes in the structure or composition of world trade. First, there have been some important changes in the *geographical composition* of world trade. This shows the share of world trade accounted for by different countries or regions. Secondly, structural shifts have also taken place in the *commodity composition* of world trade. This shows the share of different product groups in world trade. For example, the share of primary products has tended to fall while that of manufactures has increased. One important development has been the growth in the importance of *services* in world trade.

The chapter begins with an analysis of trends in world output. This is followed by a close look at the growth of world trade and the relationship between world output and world trade. Attention is focused on merchandise trade. The increasingly important area of trade in services is discussed in a later chapter. The next section of the chapter sets out the major changes that have occurred in both the geographical and commodity composition of world trade. This is followed by an analysis of the changing regional structure of world trade and the evidence examined for any tendency towards a 'regionalisation' of world trade. The chapter concludes with some observations about likely future trends in world trade.

The Growth of World Output

A Historical Perspective

Over the past half century, world output has grown at a faster rate than in any previous period in history. Table 1.1 compares post-war growth with previous periods of history for which growth rates have been calculated.

Between 1950 and 1990, world output has increased at an average annual rate of 3.9%. This compares with 2.8% for the forty-three years immediately preceding the First World War (1870–1913) and 2.1% for the inter-war period from 1924 to 1937. However, the five-year period from 1924 to 1929 witnessed a growth rate of much the same order before growth was interrupted by the 1929 Wall Street Crash and the ensuing Depression. The table also shows that growth was somewhat slower in the seventeen years after 1973 than in the preceding twenty-three years.

Table 1.1 The Growth and Volatility of World Output, 1870–1990

Period	*Average annual growth rate (%)*	*Standard deviation (%)*	*Coefficient of variation*
Pre-World War I			
1870–1913	2.8	2.1	0.75
Inter-War:			
1924–37	2.1	4.8	2.26
1924–29	3.7	0.8	0.22
1929–37	1.3	5.9	4.53
Post-War:			
1950–90	3.9	1.8	0.45
1950–73	4.7	1.6	0.34
1973–90	3.1	1.6	0.53

Source: Kitson and Michie (1995).

Growth has also been more stable since the Second World War than in earlier periods. Growth is never even. Rather, output tends to oscillate between periods of rapid growth (booms or upswings) and periods of slow or even negative growth (recessions or downturns). Annual variations can be measured by calculating either the standard deviation or coefficient of variation for the period in question. Both measures were lower for the post-war period than for the pre-World War I period or the inter-war period. Much more violent fluctuations in output were apparent for the inter-war period, especially the period after 1929.

Post-War Trends in World Output

The growth in world output is usually measured by the average annual rate of increase of *real gross domestic product (GDP) measured at market prices*. Real GDP is to be preferred to nominal GDP because a rise in nominal GDP may be the result simply of a rise in the price of final goods and services. Real GDP is calculated

Table 1.2 Annual Average Growth Rates of Real Gross Domestic Product (GDP) at Market Prices by Region, 1960–1998 (percentage)

Countries/ Territories	*1961–70*	*1971–80*	*1981–90*	*1991*	*1992*	*1993*	*1994*	*1995*	*1996*	*1997*	*1998*
ADVANCED ECONOMIES, of which:	4.8	3.1	3.1	1.2	2.0	1.3	3.2	2.6	3.2	3.2	2.2
United States	4.5	2.8	2.9	−0.9	2.7	2.3	3.5	2.3	3.4	3.9	3.9
Germany	4.4	2.6	2.3	5.0	2.2	−1.1	2.3	1.7	0.8	1.8	2.3
United Kingdom	2.9	2.0	2.7	−1.5	0.1	2.3	4.4	2.8	2.6	3.5	2.2
Japan	12.4	4.3	4.0	3.8	1.0	0.3	0.6	1.5	5.0	1.4	−2.8
France	5.7	3.2	2.4	0.8	1.2	−1.3	2.8	2.1	1.6	2.3	3.2
Newly industrialised Asian economies	n.a.	n.a.	8.2	8.0	6.0	6.3	7.5	7.3	6.2	5.8	−1.8
DEVELOPING COUNTRIES, of which:	5.9	5.3	4.2	4.9	6.7	6.5	6.8	6.1	6.6	5.8	3.2
Oil exporters	7.5	4.6	0.9	n.a.	n.a.	n.n.	n.a.	n.a.	n.a.	n.a.	n.a.
Major exporters of manufactures	5.6.	7.3	4.2	n.a.	n.a.	n.a.	n.a.	n.a.	n.a.	n.a.	n.a.
Heavily indebted poor countries	n.a.	n.a.	2.5	0.9	1.4	1.7	2.6	5.5	5.7	5.0	4.1
Least developed countries	3.5	2.2	3.0	2.2	2.4	3.6	3.1	6.3	5.6	5.0	4.4
COUNTRIES IN CENTRAL AND EASTERN EUROPE	6.7	5.4	2.8	−9.9	−8.5	−3.7	−2.9	1.6	1.6	3.0	2.2

Source: UNCTAD (1993), IMF (1999).

Table 1.3 Annual Average Growth Rates of Real Groups Domestic Product (GDP) per Capita at Market Prices, 1960–1998 (percentage)

Countries/ Territories	*1961–70*	*1971–80*	*1981–90*	*1991*	*1992*	*1993*	*1994*	*1995*	*1996*	*1997*	*1998*
ADVANCED ECONOMIES, of which:	3.6	2.2	2.4	0.4	1.3	0.6	2.5	1.9	2.5	2.6	1.6
United States	3.2	1.7	1.9	−2.0	1.6	1.2	2.5	1.3	2.5	3.0	3.0
Germany	2.3	2.6	2.0	4.2	1.5	−1.8	2.1	1.4	0.5	1.7	2.3
United Kingdom	2.3	1.9	2.5	−2.2	−0.3	2.1	4.0	2.4	2.3	3.2	2.0
Japan	11.3	3.1	3.4	3.4	0.7	–	0.4	1.3	4.6	1.2	−3.0
France	4.6	2.6	1.9	0.4	0.8	−1.7	2.4	1.7	1.2	1.9	2.8
Newly industrialised Asian economies	n.a.	n.a.	6.8	6.9	5.0	5.3	6.1	5.8	4.8	4.9	−2.6
DEVELOPING COUNTRIES, of which:	3.2	3.0	1.9	2.9	4.1	4.5	4.9	4.4	4.9	4.2	1.5
Oil exporters	4.4	1.8	−1.8	2.3	−0.5	n.a.	n.a.	n.a.	n.a.	n.a.	n.a.
Major exporters of manufactures	2.8.	4.9	2.3	1.3	3.1	n.a.	n.a.	n.a.	n.a.	n.a.	n.a.
Heavily indebted poor countries	n.a.	n.a.	n.a.	n.a.	n.a.	n.a.	n.a.	n.a.	n.a.	n.a.	n.a.
Least developed countries	5.5	−0.4	−0.5	0.0	0.5	n.a.	n.a.	n.a.	n.a.	n.a.	n.a.
COUNTRIES IN CENTRAL AND EASTERN EUROPE	5.5	4.5	2.9	−15.7	−8.4	n.a.	n.a.	n.a.	n.a.	n.a.	n.a.

Source: UNCTAD (1993), IMF (1999).

by measuring GDP at constant prices (i.e. assuming no change in prices since the base year). To compare increases in living standards in different countries, however, it is more meaningful to measure the average annual rate of increase of *real gross domestic product per head of population (GDP per capita) measured at market prices*. Real GDP per head is real GDP divided by the size of the population. Tables 1.2 and 1.3 show the rates of growth in real GDP and real GDP per capita over the past three and a half decades for different regions of the world.

The figures in Table 1.2 show that real GDP in the advanced economies grew at a rate of 4.8% in the 1960s, slowing to 3.1% in the 1970s and 1980s. In the 1960s and 1970s, the most impressive growth was recorded by Japan and the least impressive by the UK. In the 1980s, the U.K. economy performed a little better, but Germany and France both experienced slower growth. The most impressive growth rates, however, were recorded by the newly industrialised countries of East Asia (Taiwan, Hong Kong, Singapore and South Korea). In 1991, all the advanced economies, except for Germany and Japan experienced a sharp downturn, with GDP falling in the United States and UK. In the following two years, growth in the US and UK was resumed, but Japan, Germany and France suffered a severe downturn. By the mid-1990s, most countries had recovered from the recession, with the single and notable exception of Japan. By 1995, growth in Japan appeared to be back to normal, but, in the following three years, another recession ensued from which the Japanese economy has yet to recover. In the newly industrialised economies, only a modest slowing down in growth was apparent in the early 1990s. However, following the financial crisis in the East Asian region of 1997, these countries did experience a severe recession in 1998, with real GDP falling by 1.8%

In the developing world, GDP has grown faster than in the advanced economies throughout the period since 1960. However, as developing countries started from a lower base, faster growth rates were to be expected. Since these countries have also experienced faster population growth, what is more important is the growth of real per capita GDP. This is shown in Table 1.3. This shows that, in the 1960s, per capita GDP grew more slowly in developing countries than in the advanced economies. However, in the 1970s, developing countries out-performed the advanced economies. In the 1980s, the situation was once again reversed with the developing countries lagging behind the developed countries. This is disappointing, given that per capita GDP needs to grow faster in developing countries simply to prevent the gap between rich and poor countries in the world from widening. The recession experienced by the developed countries in the early 1990s, however, did not affect the developing countries as severely, so that per capita GDP was once again growing faster in developing countries.

The developing countries constitute a very broad group of countries ranging from the poorest, least developed countries through to the richer, oil-producing states and countries that are in the process of achieving rapid industrialisation. Thus, in the 1970s, although developing countries as a whole enjoyed fast growth in per capita GDP, the least developed group actually experienced a decline. Again, in the 1980s, although per capita GDP grew at a modest rate in the developing countries, this was mainly concentrated on the Asian region. In Africa, where many of the poorest countries are located, GDP per head fell. The same was true in the 1990s, with GDP per head in the African region barely rising at all.

Economic growth since the Second World War was subject to cyclical swings with periods of rapid growth giving way to periods of recession followed by a new upswing. Up until the early 1970s, interruptions to growth in the developed countries were relatively minor. At worse, these countries experienced a slowing down in their rate of growth. However, in 1973–74, the first major slump in world output took place, largely the result of a sudden quadrupling of world oil prices. A second severe downturn occurred between 1979–82, also initiated by another sharp rise in world oil prices. More recently, the early 1990s witnessed a third major recession with output falling first in the United States and the United Kingdom, then somewhat later in continental Europe and Japan. Unlike the two previous downturns, however, this was not brought about by a rise in oil prices. Finally, in 1997–98, the increasingly important region of East Asia experienced a major financial crisis, which resulted in an extremely severe reversal of the economic growth enjoyed by the region in the preceding decade. Below, the reasons for each of these recessions are discussed.

The 1973–74 Oil Crisis

The post-war period, in fact, witnessed no serious downturn comparable with that of the inter-war period up until 1973. Between 1973–74, there occurred the first major interruption to this process of more or less continuous growth. The immediate cause was a sharp rise in world oil prices brought about by the oil-producing countries that were members of the Organisation of Petroleum Exporting Countries (OPEC). The rise was preceded by a period of oil shortage caused by the oil embargo, which certain Middle Eastern states had imposed on countries that supported Israel in the Yom Kippur War. In 1973, the price of a barrel of oil rose roughly fourfold from $3.30 to $11.59. The effect was to cut real incomes in the advanced industrialised countries, all of which had become dependent on imports of oil mainly from the Middle East for their energy requirements. The fall in real incomes caused a fall in the aggregate demand for goods and services in these countries leading in turn to a decline in output and employment. As workers tried to secure wage increases to offset the fall in their real incomes, prices rose. As the rise in oil prices coincided with a rise in world commodity prices, the effect was a serious increase in inflation in all the advanced industrialised countries. This limited the scope for governments to expand aggregate demand by fiscal and monetary means to combat the deflationary impact of higher oil prices.

It is debatable whether or not the crisis was caused by OPEC. There were signs that growth in the advanced industrialised countries was slowing down even before 1973. Moreover, the ability of OPEC to force up world oil prices was only made possible because of a serious supply–demand imbalance in the world oil market. Over the course of the two preceding decades, oil consumption had expanded rapidly due in large measure to a fall in the real price of oil. The cheapness of oil had encouraged the advanced industrialised countries to substitute oil for other forms of energy. At the same time, the low price of oil discouraged oil companies from exploring and developing new higher cost oilfields in other parts of the world. As a result, oil production failed to keep pace with demand. The imbalance was further aggravated by the transformation of the United States, which consumed about one-third of the world's supply of oil, from a position of self-sufficiency to dependence on imports to meet fuel requirements. By the early 1970s, conditions on the world oil market were favourable to an enforced rise in oil prices. Because a large proportion of world oil production was controlled by members of OPEC, they were able to maintain a high price by limiting supply. At the same time, the low price elasticity of demand for oil meant that, in the short run, the rise in price resulted in higher oil revenues for the oil-producing states.

After 1974, growth was resumed. In part, this was due to recycling of the so-called 'petro-dollars' accumulated by the oil-producing states of the Middle East. Recycling happened in two ways. First, oil-producing states spent some oil revenues on importing more goods and services from the West. Second, oil revenues not spent on buying more goods and services from the West were either invested in physical or financial assets in the West or deposited with western banks. This inflow of capital enabled the western industrialised countries to finance their current account deficits induced by the rise in the cost of oil imports. Petro-dollars placed with banks in the West were in some cases re-loaned to other countries faced with oil-induced current account deficits and were used to sustain demand. Between 1975 and 1978, growth was particularly rapid in the United States. Because of the size of the U.S. market, rising real incomes created additional demand for goods and services in other developed market economies. At the same time, the advanced industrialised countries responded to higher oil prices by cutting their demand for oil. As oil consumption fell, oil production rose as higher oil prices made it profitable for oil companies to open up new, higher cost oilfields. The improvement in the demand–supply balance on world oil markets helped stabilise oil prices.

The 1979–80 Oil Crisis

A second major downturn occurred between 1979 and 1981, following another sharp rise in world oil prices. Once again, the background was a global shortage of oil. On this occasion, it was brought about by a massive stockpiling of oil as oil consumers feared that the revolution in Iran would lead to a sharp drop in world oil supplies. By 1981, the price of a barrel of oil had reached $34.41. Much the same effects on real incomes, demand and output in the advanced industrialised countries resulted as with the first oil crisis. Most countries experienced an actual fall in output, at a time when unemployment rates were already at a high level. (Only Japan among the developed market economies was able to maintain positive growth during this period, mainly through reliance on export growth.) Once again, all countries experienced a sharp acceleration in their rates of inflation. Most countries responded by pushing up real interest rates, which served further to cut aggregate demand. At the same time, the option of borrowing to finance oil-induced balance of payments deficits was no longer available to certain countries which had already incurred overseas debts that they were having difficulty servicing. Since these debts were in most cases denominated on U.S. dollars, these countries experienced a double 'whammy' on account of the rise in U.S. interest rates. Even had these countries wanted to borrow more, western banks were increasingly reluctant to lend more for fear that loans would not be repaid.

As with the first oil crisis, growth was eventually resumed. Tight monetary policies in the advanced countries succeeded in reducing inflation. The situation was helped by a fall in world commodity prices, although this added to the difficulties of developing countries heavily dependent on primary commodities for export earnings. In addition, after 1982, the price of oil began to fall. By 1987, the price of a barrel of oil had reached $18 or one-half the price of 1981. The drop in the real price was even greater. Slower growth in the western industrialised countries helped reduce oil consumption. De-stocking by oil consumers also played an important role. Demand for oil was further reduced by the success achieved in the western industrialised countries in reducing their dependence on oil as a source of energy. Energy conservation programmes combined with a shift away from energy-intensive forms of production further contributed to reducing demand. At the same time, new oilfields had been opened up in certain countries that were not members of OPEC (e.g. Norway and the United Kingdom). This undermined the ability of OPEC to control the level of oil production and thereby enforce high oil prices. This meant that, if OPEC countries cut their output, non-OPEC countries merely increased their share of the world market. This made some OPEC countries reluctant to agree production limits.

Higher real incomes in the western industrialised countries led to an increased demand for goods and services, higher output and some fall in levels of unemployment. After 1983, output was once again growing fast in most developed countries although growth remained sluggish in Western Europe for most of the next four years.

The 1990–93 Downturn

In 1989, the developed market economies of the world experienced a third major economic downturn although the fall in output was less dramatic than that following the two oil crises. Moreover, it was not caused by any rise in world oil prices, but rather was the consequence of the inflationary boom, which immediately preceded it. A major cause of this boom had been the decision of the monetary authorities in the developed world to lower short-term interest rates in the wake of the sudden decline of share prices on the Wall Street market in the United States in the autumn of 1987. Although this was intended to ensure adequate liquidity to prevent a sudden sharp downturn in the economy, the effect was to add to the problems of excess demand. In the end, too rapid a rate of inflation compelled the authorities to put a break on expansion by raising short-term interest rates, resulting in a sharp drop in demand. Growth declined first in the countries of North America, with the region experiencing falling output between 1990–91. The downturn in Western Europe and Japan followed a year later with output falling between 1992–93.

The recession was particularly acute in the United Kingdom with GDP falling by 2.5% over the two-year period from 1990 to 1992. In Japan, growth began to fall roughly one year later. The economy remained nearly stagnant between 1993–95. Likewise, the recession arrived in continental Europe about one year later than in the Anglo-Saxon economies. Growth declined sharply in 1992 and turned negative in 1993. The slowdown in growth in the advanced economies also saw a rise in unemployment with the average rate of unemployment climbing to 7.5% by the mid-1990s. Worst hit of all were the EU economies where the average unemployment rate peaked at 11% in 1993. Even in Japan, where unemployment rates averaged a mere 2.5% throughout the 1980s, the rate rose to 4% in 1998.

Nevertheless, by the mid-1990s, the recession had ended. Growth was resumed at levels equal to or higher than in the 1980s. Among the major industrial countries, growth was strongest in the United States, with growth reaching almost 4% in 1998. The U.S upswing has provided one of the longest periods of growth in the post-war era, with more or less consistent expansion for eight years in succession. By way of contrast, growth in Western Europe remained more subdued (although impressive growth rates were recorded in some of the smaller states such as Ireland and Luxembourg). One reason was the discipline imposed on the European economies in public sector borrowing by the need to meet the convergence criteria to qualify for entry to the Euro in 1999. In Japan, after a short-lived recovery in 1996, growth rates fell again and turned negative in 1998, signalling that the Japanese post-war miracle was weak and truly over. One reason for this second fall in GDP was the financial crisis that ensued in the East Asian region, to which we now turn.

The East Asian Financial Crisis

As noted above, throughout the last two decades, the fastest rates of economic growth in the world have been recorded among the newly industrialised economies of the East Asian region. In the 1980s, these economies enjoyed rates of economic growth in excess of 8% per year. Some modest deceleration occurred in the early 1990s in the most advanced economies of the region (Hong Kong, Taiwan and South Korea). However, this was more than counterbalanced by faster growth in the so-called 'tiger economies' such as Thailand, Malaysia,

Indonesia and the People's Republic of China. One consequence of this rapid growth (but also a cause) was an influx of foreign capital, much of it in the form of investment funds placed by western financial institutions as deposits with banks. An important factor in this process was the high return on capital that could be obtained by investing in these countries and a judgement that the risks from doing so were minimal. Investors believed that the boom being enjoyed by the region would continue for some while to come and that, should any bank get into financial difficulty, the public authorities of the country concerned would bail out the investors.

To some extent, this optimism was justified by an examination of the economic 'fundamentals'. Growth rates were high, unemployment was lower and inflation was under control. On the other hand, a number of these countries were faced with large current account balance of payments deficits, the counterpart to their large capital account surpluses. On the other hand, the cause of these deficits was not, as in other developing countries, excessive borrowing by the public sector. Rather, it was due to large inflows of private capital from abroad. However, what was not, perhaps, fully understood was that much of this money was being invested unwisely. Much of it was being used by financial institutions not to make investments in productive capital, but to take advantage of rising asset prices. Many banks loaned funds to individuals simply for the purpose of buying securities or real estate. When the prices of these assets ceased rising, investors began to panic. Funds were withdrawn from banks, already faced with an increase in the number of their bad loans. Withdrawal of funds by western investors added to the sense of panic by forcing down the external value of local currencies. As several countries operated pegged exchange rates, reserves had to be used to support the currency. However, as speculative pressure mounted, this became difficult to sustain.

The first country to be affected was Thailand in the summer of 1997. By this stage, the Thai baht was coming up intense pressure, because foreign investors feared the possibility of a devaluation. They were proved right. On July 2, 1997, the Thai authorities were forced to concede defeat and the baht was set free to float. It promptly went into free fall. Shortly afterwards, speculative pressure switched to other Asian currencies, including the Korean won, the Malaysian ringit and the Indonesian ruppiah. This was the phenomenon referred to as contagion, whereby a crisis in one country in the region spread quickly to other countries. In a similar manner to the Thai baht, governments in these countries were forced to abandon any attempt to peg their currencies. The result was a sharp depreciation, such that between June 1997 and December 1998, the currencies of Thailand, Korea, Malaysia and the Philippines managed to fall by between 30–35% and that of Indonesia by 70%. As devaluation reduces the real incomes of consumers, the effect was to cause a severe fall in demand in these economies. Output and employment declined sharply. At the same time, as a condition for borrowing from the International Monetary Fund (IMF), most of these countries were forced to make big cuts in public spending and the level of public sector borrowing. This accentuated the fall in demand and hence the recession in these countries, although it was intended as a measure to restore the confidence of western investors.

The crisis in the East Asian economies had spill-over effects on the Japanese economy, which was experiencing problems of its own. The rise in the value of the yen meant that Japan could no longer rely on export growth for rapid expansion. However, domestic demand was depressed due to the unwillingness of Japanese consumers to spend. Confidence had also been rocked by a series of financial crises caused by banks acquiring too many non-performing loans. The East Asian economies were important markets for Japanese goods, so when the recession occurred in these countries the Japanese economy was badly hit. In 1998, GDP fell in the newly industrialising countries of the region, with particularly steep falls in Indonesia (13%), Thailand (9%) and South Korea (6%). The recession in the East Asian region remained a regional crisis, despite the importance of these countries in the world economy. A modest slowdown in economic growth occurred in the advanced economies in 1998, although this was mainly accounted for by negative growth in Japan and the continuing sluggish growth in some of the EU economies (notably, Germany and Italy). By 1999, however, the worst of the crisis appeared to be over. Growth was resumed in most of the East Asian economies, with forecasts for a still bigger improvement in 1999. Only the Japanese economy remained in a rut of zero growth.

The Growth of World Trade

One of the main reasons for the rapid growth in world output over the period since 1945 has been the growth of world trade. Over the post-war period, world trade has grown at a rate roughly one and one-half times that of world output. Over the period between 1950 and 1990, whereas output grew by 3.9% per annum, world trade measured in volume terms grew by 5.8% per annum (Kitson and Mitchie, 1995). This represents the fastest recorded growth of world trade in history. In the period from 1870 to 1913, which just preceded the outbreak of the First World War, the volume of world trade is estimated to have grown at a rate of 3.5% per annum (i.e. roughly 1.3 times the growth in world output). However, during the inter-war period, world trade grew at a much more modest rate of only 2.2% a year, roughly the same as world output. In the 1930s, the volume of trade was almost stagnant (Kitson and Mitchie, 1995).

Table 1.4 sets out the growth in world trade over the period from 1960 onwards. During the 1960s, world exports grew in volume terms at a rate of 8.5% a year or roughly 1.4 times world output. The 1970s and early 1980s saw a significant slow down in the expansion of world trade which accompanied the fall in the growth of output in the world as a whole. However, the ratio of trade to output growth was roughly stable. After 1985, trade growth was resumed and the ratio of trade-to-output growth also rose. In the first half of the 1990s, trade grew at a rate four times that of world output. Thus, in recent years, there has been a noticeable increase in the rate of trade expansion relative to output growth, although it is probably too early to conclude that a permanent shift has taken place in the relationship between the two. We can conclude that post-war economic growth has been essentially *trade-led growth*, that is, the expansion of trade has led the growth in output rather than following it.

Table 1.4 shows that the leading role in the expansion of trade has been played by *manufactures*. Throughout the period shown, trade in manufactures has grown faster than world merchandise trade as a whole. Moreover, for manufactures, the ratio of trade-to-output growth has been consistently higher, rising from 1.4 in the 1960s, to 1.7 in the 1970s, to 1.8 in the 1980s and more recently reaching 6.5. This increase in the ratio of trade-to-output growth in manufactures clearly reflects a process of increasing specialisation that was taking place in the world. If trade grows faster than output, it means that countries are increasing the degree of their specialisation either in particular

Table 1.4 The Growth of World Production and Trade, 1960–1996

	1960–69	*1970–79*	*1980–85*	*1985–90*	*1990–95*
Average annual percentage change in volume					
Production					
Total	6.0	4.0	1.5	3.0	1.5
Agriculture	2.5	2.5	3.0	2.0	2.5
Mining	5.0	3.5	−2.5	3.0	2.0
Manufacturing	7.5	4.5	2.5	3.5	1.0
Exports					
Total	8.5	5.5	2.0	6.0	6.0
Agriculture	4.0	3.0	1.0	2.0	4.5
Mining	6.5	2.5	−2.5	5.0	4.5
Manufacturing	10.5	7.5	4.5	6.5	6.5
Ratio of export growth to production growth					
Total	1.4	1.4	1.3	2.0	4.0
Agriculture	1.6	1.2	0.3	1.0	2.0
Mining	1.3	0.7	1.0	1.7	2.3
Manufacturing	1.4	1.7	1.8	1.9	6.5

Source: GATT, various issues.

industries in products in which they enjoy a comparative advantage. The fact that the ratio of trade-to-output growth has been rising would suggest that specialisation has been increasing at an accelerating rate especially in recent years, although it is not yet clear whether this is a permanent or transitory change.

By way of contrast, trade in *primary commodities* (mining and agriculture) has grown more slowly. Except for the last five years, exports of *agriculture* have grown at a rate no faster than the growth of output of all products in the world as a whole. In other words, trade in agricultural goods has essentially *followed* the rise in world incomes. The same has been true of *mining* products although in the last ten years trade has risen faster than world output. Nevertheless, trade in primary products has grown faster than output of primary products for most of the time reflecting some increase in international specialisation.

What have been the reasons for this rapid growth in world trade? A major factor has been the success that has been achieved since the Second World War in bringing about *a gradual reduction in the level of trade barriers* both at a global and a regional level. In bringing about multilateral trade liberalisation (i.e. liberalisation on a global scale), the major role has been played by the General Agreement on Tariffs and Trade (GATT) and its recent successor, the World Trade Organisation (WTO). The General Agreement was signed in 1947 initially by a small group of 23 nations but later by most of the leading trading nations of the world. It introduced a set of rules to govern world trade that gave stability and certainty of access to world markets for exporters and created a framework through which countries could negotiate freer trade. The result was a very large reduction in the level of tariffs, particularly in relation to industrial goods, and, more recently, some regulation of the use of non-tariff barriers.

In addition, a still higher level of trade liberalisation has been achieved at the regional level in certain parts of the world through *the formation of regional free trade areas and customs unions*. In Western Europe, the creation of the European Communities (EC) in 1958 and the European Free Trade Area (EFTA) in 1960 resulted in the elimination of tariffs on trade between the member states. More recently, intra-European trade has been a given a fillip through the creation in 1993 of the Single European Market (SEM). In North America, the formation of the North American Free Trade Area (NAFTA) in 1994 provides for free trade in goods and services between the United States, Canada and Mexico. In recent years, there have been a number of other regional trading arrangements established between developing countries such as MERCOSUR in South America and the Asian Free Trade Area (AFTA) in South East Asia. Some of these arrangements are discussed in more detail in Chapter 9.

Second, the period since the Second World War has seen *a gradual relaxation of exchange controls and restrictions on capital flows*. Immediately after the War, most countries operated strict controls on the purchase of foreign currency for both current and capital account transactions and some countries also placed restrictions on capital inflows. Later these were gradually dismantled. The West European economies initially achieved this on an intra-European basis under the auspices of the Organisation for Economic Cooperation (OEEC). Full convertibility with the dollar in respect of current account transactions was not achieved until the later 1950s. Controls on capital inflows and outflows, however, remained subject to control, although these were gradually relaxed. In 1979, the UK abolished all controls on the outflow of capital. In Western Europe, the SEM has also resulted in the ending of controls on intra-European flows of capital.

One effect of capital liberalisation has been to bring about a dramatic increase in the movement of both short-term and long-term capital between countries. Since settlement of debt arising from trade requires a movement of funds between different countries, the increased ease with which money can be moved has directly facilitated trade. However, capital liberalisation has also helped stimulate long-term investment by companies in the setting up of subsidiaries or affiliates in other countries. This has resulted in *the rise of the multinational or trans-national corporation (MNC or TNC)* with operations abroad, which often exceed the scale of its domestic operations. More recently, we have witnessed the growth of 'globalised production' with MNCs planning their production of different goods and services on a regional or world-wide basis. This phenomenon is discussed more fully in Chapter 4. One result of this has been a big increase in trade in intermediate goods (goods used as inputs in the production of other goods) between different branches of the same company each located in a different country.

Third, trade has been stimulated by *technological change* particularly in the area of telecommunication and transportation. In recent decades, the so-called 'information revolution' has spawned the growth of private computers, the fax machine, the Internet and satellite technology to name just a few of the products which have facilitated international communication. In the earlier part of the post-war period, trade was directly stimulated by the containerisation revolution in international shipping. Faster and cheaper air travel and improvements in different forms of inland transport have increased the international mobility of people as well as of goods.

A major consequence of the fact that trade has grown faster than output has been that economies have become more open and economically more interdependent. *Openness* is generally measured by the ratio of country's exports and imports to its GDP. (It is customary

Table 1.5 The Percentage Share of Gross Domestic Product (GDP) Traded, 1928–1990

	Percentages						
Region	*1928*	*1938*	*1948*	*1958*	*1968*	*1979*	*1990*
Western Europe	33	24	35	33	34	48	46
Eastern Europe	30*	25*	25*	25*	40*	40*	41
North America	10	8	11	9	10	19	19
Latin America	45*	30*	30*	30	21	27	28
Asia	32	27	25	26	21	27	29
Africa	60*	50*	50*	58	37	56	53
Middle East	60*	50*	50*	46	38	48	49
World total	24	19	22	22	22	35	34

Source: Anderson and Norheim, 1993.
Note: *means that these are guestimates.

to take exports *plus* imports rather than just exports or imports because otherwise the ratio may be distorted by any change in the export–import balance.) Table 1.5 shows the percentage share of GDP traded for different regions of the world for the period from 1928 to 1990.

It is interesting to note that in 1928 the trade-to-GDP ratio for the world as a whole was higher than in the early part of the post-war period. However, after 1968 it rose, and by 1990 had reached 34%. The Middle Eastern and African regions were the most dependent on world trade followed by Western and Eastern Europe. The North American region was noticeably less open with a ratio of trade-to-GDP of only 19%. However, over the period since the Second World War, the ratio rose steadily in all regions with the possible exceptions of Africa and Latin America.

A consequence of greater openness is increased *interdependence*. This means that external economic shocks are more quickly transmitted from one country to another. For example, an economic downturn in one of the major economies of the world more quickly leads to a fall in incomes and output in other countries because imports from these countries are adversely affected. At the same time, policy measures adopted by countries to stabilise their economies more quickly spill over into the economies of trading partners. This increased interdependence has made it more difficult for countries to ignore events that occur in other parts of the world and has made the pursuit of an independent economic policy more difficult to achieve. One possible response to this change is for governments to cooperate more closely to ensure consistency of policy.

Changes in the Commodity Composition of World Trade

The growth of world trade over the period since 1945 has brought major changes in the commodity composition of world trade. This refers to the change in the share of world trade accounted for by different groups of products. Table 1.6 sets out the main changes that have taken place in the share of world trade accounted for by different product groups.

Changes in the share of world trade accounted for by any particular group may be due to either:

1. A faster (or slower) growth in the *volume* of trade taking place in the products in question relative to other products, or

Table 1.6 The Commodity Composition of World Merchandise Exports, 1955–1995

	1955		*1978*		*1985*		*1995*	
	$bn	*%*	*$bn*	*%*	*$bn*	*%*	*$bn*	*%*
Primary Products								
Food	20.42	21.9	162.60	12.5	199.20	10.4	444	9.1
Raw materials	12.13	13.0	52.05	4.0	65.70	3.4	135	2.8
Ores and minerals	3.44	3.7	24.5	1.9	33.80	1.8	59	1.2
Fuels	10.26	11.0	223.60	17.2	356.40	18.5	349	7.1
Non-ferrous metals	3.62	3.9	27.80	2.1	36.80	1.9	104	2.1
Total	49.87	53.5	490.60	37.7	691.90	36.0	1091	22.3
Manufactures								
Iron and steel	4.25	4.6	57.15	4.4	69.30	3.6	149	3.0
Chemicals	4.91	5.3	100.60	7.7	163.40	8.5	467	9.6
Other semi-manufactures	4.47	4.8	65.20	5.0	86.40	4.5	386	7.9
Engineering products*	19.59	21.0	439.05	33.7	682.0	35.5	1900*	38
A. Machinery specialised*	6.43	6.9	117.45	9.0	150.60	7.8	–	–
B. Office and telecom equipment	5.82	0.9	38.80	3.0	97.90	5.1	595	12.2
C. Road and motor vehicles*	3.32	3.5	99.45	6.9	158.30	8.2	456*	9.3*
D. Other machinery and transport equipment*	7.72	8.3	147.90	11.4	216.30	11.3	849*	17.4*
E. Household appliances*	1.30	1.4	35.40	2.7	58.90	3.1	–	–
Textiles	4.72	5.1	40.70	3.1	55.40	2.9	153	3.1
Clothing	0.80	0.9	28.35	2.2	49.20	2.6	158	3.2
Other consumer goods	3.00	3.2	57.50	4.4	91.60	4.8	428	8.7
Total	41.73	44.7	788.50	60.5	1197.3	62.3	3640	74.4
Total Exports	93.30	100.0	1303	100.0	1921.5	100.0	4890	100.0

Source: GATT, various issues.
Note: *means that the product group was defined differently for 1995. Road and motor vehicles became automotive products. Machinery specialised and other machinery and transport equipment became other machinery. Household appliances disappeared as a separate *product group* and was subsumed under other consumer goods.

2. A faster (or slower) rise in the *unit values* (i.e. the prices) of the products in question relative to other products, or
3. Both.

As we examine the most important changes that have occurred since 1955 we shall see that both factors explain the shifts which have taken place.

Merchandise trade is divided into *primary products* and *manufactures*. We shall discuss each of these categories in turn.

Primary Products

Primary products are any products which has been extracted from the earth or sea or from crops grown on the earth or from animals but which have not been processed or only subject to minimal processing. Broadly speaking, there are two main types of primary products, namely, *agricultural products* and *mining products*. Agricultural products include both foodstuffs (including processed food products, live animals, beverages and tobacco, animal and vegetable

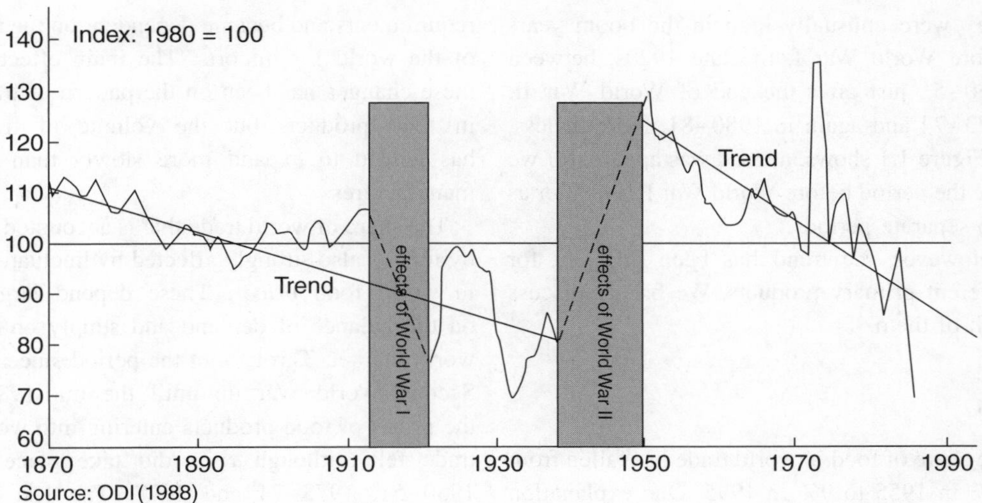

Figure 1.1 Real commodity prices deflated by price of manufactures: 1870–1986

oils, fats and waxes, oilseeds and fruit) and agricultural raw materials (such as raw hides, skins and fur-skins, crude but not synthetic rubber, cork and wood, pulp and waste paper, textile fibres, etc.). Mining products comprise ores and minerals (iron ore, crude fertilisers, etc.), fuels (including petroleum) and non-ferrous metals (copper, tin, zinc, etc.). Apart from foodstuffs, primary products consist essentially of raw materials. In 1995, primary products accounted for just over 22% of world trade, compared with nearly 50% in 1955. This fall is due to both a slower growth in the volume of world trade in primary products and a fall in the price of primary commodities in world trade relative to the price of manufactures.

One of the most important trends apparent over the last hundred years has been for the *prices* of primary commodities to fall relative to the price of manufactures. This is illustrated by Figure 1.1, which shows the trend in real commodity prices deflated by the price of manufactures. In other words, the price of primary commodities is measured relative to the price of manufactures. Considerable problems are involved in the measurement of prices of commodities over such a long period. The normal practice is to estimate changes in the unit value of a basket of commodities with each product being assigned a weight that reflects its importance in world trade. However, the relative importance of different commodities tends to change over time, the more so the longer the period that the index seeks to cover. Moreover, changes in the prices of different goods may reflect changes in quality. For example, some of the increase in the prices of manufactures reflects improvements in quality. Furthermore, because commodity prices tend to fluctuate from year to year, a problem is created by the years chosen to compare prices. For example, if the starting year was one in which prices were abnormally low and the finishing year one in which prices were abnormally high, it may seem as if commodity prices have risen relative to the prices of manufactures! This can be seen from Figure 1.1. Commodity prices were exceptionally low in the first few years after World War I, during the Depression years of the 1930s and then again in the mid-1980s.

They were unusually high in the boom years before World War I, the late 1920s, between 1950–51 just after the end of World War II, 1973–74 and again in 1980–81. Nevertheless, as Figure 1.1 shows, a trend was apparent if we take the period before World War II and after as two separate periods.

However, the trend has been different for different primary products. We briefly discuss each of them.

Food

The share of food in world trade has fallen from 22% in 1955 to 9% in 1995. One explanation lies in the relatively slow growth in the *volume* of trade in food products over this period. Within the advanced industrialised countries, the demand for food tends to be relatively income-inelastic that is, the demand for food increases less than proportionately with per capita income. This means that imports of food by these countries are unlikely to grow at a rate faster than per capita income. In addition, throughout the past fifty years most of the advanced industrialised countries have adopted highly protectionist policies in an effort to boost domestic production of food and reduce dependence on imports. On the other hand, because these policies have resulted in massive overproduction of food, these countries have resorted to subsidies to boost their exports of surplus food to the rest of the world. Thus, the advanced industrialised countries have shifted from being net importers to becoming net exporters of food products. By way of contrast, because food production in the developing countries has often not kept up with population growth, many of these countries have had to import more food than they export to feed their growing populations. Furthermore, many of the so-called Eastern Bloc countries failed to produce sufficient food to meet their requirements and became dependent on the rest of the world for imports. The main effect of these changes has been on the pattern of trade in food products but the volume of trade has tended to expand more slowly than for manufactures.

The share of world trade that is accounted for by food is also strongly affected by fluctuations in world food *prices*. These depend largely on the balance of demand and supply on the world market. Throughout the period since the Second World War up until the mid-1980s, the prices of food products entering into world trade fell, although rises did take place in 1950–51, 1973–74 and 1977. The last ten years, however, have seen some reversal of that trend. After reaching a new low in 1986, world food prices began rising strongly reaching a new peak in 1995. Sharp declines in food prices, however, occurred once again in 1997 and 1998. The reason for the secular decline in the earlier decades was the massive overproduction of food in the advanced industrialised countries which was not offset by food shortages in the developing world and Eastern Bloc countries. In the 1970s, however, food prices along with other primary commodity prices began to rise and there was much talk of a Malthusian world food crisis which might lead to a permanent rise in world food prices. In the early 1980s, however, food prices renewed their downward decline. The reversal of this trend in the last ten years suggests that it is too soon to rule out the possibility that the concerns expressed in the 1970s might still prove warranted. A combination of climatic changes which had adversely affected global production of certain products and some reduction in levels of agricultural support in the advanced industrialised countries can be expected to keep world food prices somewhat stronger in the coming decades than has been the case until now.

Agricultural Raw Materials

The share of raw materials in world trade has fallen from 13% in 1955 to just under 3% in 1995. Again, this is due to both a relatively slow growth in the volume of trade in raw materials and a secular decline in the unit value of imports. The *volume* of trade in raw materials is essentially a function of the level of industrial output in the world. For much of the past half century, this has been governed by industrial output in the developed market economies of the world. Unlike food, imports of raw materials have been subject to relatively low tariffs. However, the demand for raw materials can never grow faster than output in the developed market economies. Given that trade has grown faster than output, it follows that, all other things being equal, the share of raw materials in world trade must fall. However, another tendency has been at work, which has caused the demand for some raw materials to grow more slowly than output. This has been the tendency for manufacturing industry to substitute synthetic for natural materials. For example, synthetic fibres such as nylon and rayon have replaced natural fibres such as cotton and wool and synthetic rubber has replaced natural rubber. These factors have meant that trade in raw materials has grown relatively slowly in volume terms.

However, to a greater extent than food, raw material *prices* have fallen in real terms over the period since the Second World War. They have been subject to strong cyclical swings with peaks in 1951, 1955, 1960, 1969, 1973, 1984 and 1990 but the trend has been imperceptibly downwards. Raw material prices are highly sensitive to fluctuations in the demand for raw materials, which is largely determined by the level of economic activity in the advanced industrialised countries. Because the output of most raw materials cannot be immediately raised to meet increased demand, prices rise sharply. Supply tends to respond to demand only with a time lag such that, by the time increased supplies have become available on the world market, demand may have fallen back to its 'normal' level causing prices to fall. Such price fluctuations conform to the 'cobweb cycle' well known to students of price theory. The long-run secular decline in raw material prices, however, is largely the consequence of the tendency for synthetic substitutes to displace natural materials in the manufacturing production process discussed above. Although the revival of world economic activity in the mid-1990s has witnessed an increase in agricultural raw material prices, there are no grounds as yet for expecting a permanent change in the trend of long-run decline in the prices of these commodities measured in real terms.

Ores and Minerals and Non-Ferrous Metals

The shares of ores and minerals in world trade have fallen from 3.7% in 1955 to 1.2% in 1995. Likewise, the share of non-ferrous metals has fallen from 3.9 to 2.1% of world trade over the same period. Trade in these products has been subject to much the same influences as agricultural raw materials. The *volume* of trade in these products cannot grow faster than the level of world output. At the same time, technological changes in production methods have enabled manufacturers to use metals and ores more intensively. This has also contributed to the downward trend in *prices*. Again, prices fluctuate a great deal depending on the level of economic activity in the advanced industrialised countries. Prices of metals and minerals measured in real terms peaked in 1952, 1956, 1966, 1969, 1974, 1983 and 1988–89. A new low point was reached in the mid-1980s since when a strong recovery has occurred. It cannot be ruled out that, as industrialisation spreads to the developing world, higher levels of industrial production, combined with finite global reserves, could in the future causes prices to rise. When metal and mineral prices peaked in the late 1960s and early 1970s, precisely such a scenario was envisaged in reports such as the now-famous 'Club of Rome' Report. As it turned out, these warnings of global shortages proved unduly pessimistic. One reason was that higher prices induced producers to seek ways of substituting cheaper synthetic materials for metals (e.g. optic fibres in place of copper wires in telecommunications). Much will depend on the extent to which new technologies permit further substitutions of this kind in the future.

Fuels

Fuels have been the only category in the primary commodities sector whose share in world trade rose albeit for a brief period of time. Between 1955 and 1985, the share of fuels in world trade rose from 11 to 18%. However, by 1995, the share had fallen back to 7.1%. The main reason for the increase was the sharp rise that took place in world oil prices in the early 1970s. For much of the post-war period, world fuel prices remained roughly constant in real terms. However, in 1973, they roughly doubled. The reasons for this are now well known. In 1960, the world's main oil-producing countries set up the Organisation of Petroleum Exporting Countries (OPEC). Their purpose was to obtain a better price for their oil and reduce the share of the price that was taken by the western, multinational oil companies which dominated both the production and distribution of oil. In time, OPEC developed into a classic producer cartel. Controlling as they did well over one-half of world petroleum output, the OPEC countries were able, by placing restrictions on supply, to force up the world oil price. They were helped by the fact that, in the preceding decade, largely because of low oil prices, oil consumption had grown at a rate faster than that of production. In particular, the United States had moved from a position of self-sufficiency to being a net importer of oil.

In 1973, the posted price of a barrel of Saudi Arabian crude oil rose from $3.30 to $11.59. This vastly exceeded what was needed to restore balance to world markets. The effects of real incomes, the level of economic activity, prices and the balance of payments of the western industrialised countries and oil-importing developing countries have been discussed above. However, as with most cartels, their success was short-lived. Higher prices made it profitable for oil companies to develop new oilfields which it was previously not worth doing, thereby increasing world supplies. At the same time, high oil prices encouraged consumers to substitute other cheaper sources of energy for oil in so far as they were able. Both trends took place but only over a comparatively long period of time. Some easing of prices did take place between 1973 and 1978 due in part to slower growth in output in the western industrialised economies. However, by 1979, a renewal of economic growth combined with a revolution to overthrow the Shah of Iran led to fears of another world oil shortage. Large-scale stockpiling of oil caused many of these fears to be realised. The OPEC countries responded by implementing a further massive increase in the price of oil. By 1981, the posted price of a barrel of Saudi Arabian crude oil had reached $34.41 or roughly seven times the 1970 price measured in real terms.

Thereafter, oil prices began to fall for the reasons given. New sources of oil that had been opened up in the North Sea came on stream. The United Kingdom and Norway were major beneficiaries. Large-scale de-stocking of oil further weakened prices. Divisions opened up within OPEC about how to respond. Some of the poorer OPEC countries became increasingly unwilling to accept production limits to enforce high prices. In addition, investment in new energy-saving measures combined with increased reliance on renewable sources of energy had served to lower demand. From 1982 onwards, crude petroleum prices fell. By 1988, they had reached a new low roughly 60% below the 1982 level. A significant rise in world oil prices did occur in 1991, following the outbreak of the Gulf War when the spot price rose to over $20 a barrel. However, this was short lived. The ending of the War saw another sharp drop in prices, such that by December 1998, spot prices had fallen to less than $10 a barrel. In March 1999, however, OPEC showed that it had not entirely lost its ability to force up world oil prices. Members of OPEC in conjunction with some other non-OPEC states succeeded in bringing about a sharp reduction in output. As a result, oil prices rose roughly threefold. At the time of writing, a barrel of oil costs nearly $30, the highest level for nearly ten years. It remains to be seen whether this will be sustained or whether more moderate member states within OPEC will engineer another fall.

This recent rise in oil prices shows that OPEC is still able to bring about a rise in prices through reductions in output. However, much depends on its ability to persuade non-OPEC oil producers to cut their output, otherwise cuts imposed by OPEC are unlikely to succeed. Almost certainly, however, the effects of higher oil prices on oil-consuming states are less than in the past. The price of crude oil now accounts for a smaller share of the price of petrol in developed countries, mainly as a result of higher petrol taxes. In addition, most developed countries are less dependent on oil than they were. There has been a shift towards other sources of fuel and a decline in the relative importance of energy-intensive industries within their economies. On the other hand, energy-intensive industries have become relatively more important in the newly industrialising countries. These countries could, therefore, be adversely affected by permanently higher oil prices. In the developed countries, however, the effects are likely to be less severe than in the 1970s. To the extent that OPEC countries accumulate larger revenues due to higher oil prices, they are more likely to spend these revenues than in the 1970s, as many of these countries have large current account deficits today and so need additional revenues to pay for increased imports. To the extent that revenues are spent on imports from developed countries, the deflationary impact of higher oil prices is reduced.

Manufactures

Essentially, a manufactured good is a product that has been subject to some element of refining or processing from its raw material state. In practice, some refined or processed goods (e.g. some food products) are classified under primary products. A distinction is often drawn between *finished manufactures* and *semi-finished manufactures*. The latter are products which have been subject to a degree of processing but which must pass through further stages of manufacturing before the good is in a condition for sale to the ultimate buyer. The term *intermediate goods* is used to refer to goods which enter into the production of other goods. In Table 1.6, the first three categories of manufactures – iron and steel, chemicals and other semi-manufactures – might be regarded as intermediate products. In 1995, they accounted for about 20% of world trade compared with about 15% in 1955. Final manufactures are sometimes divided into *consumer goods* and *capital goods*. Consumer goods are those which satisfy the wants of consumers, while capital goods are goods which are used to assist the production of other goods. The distinction between consumer and capital goods is not clear cut as the same product can serve both purposes. For example, a personal computer may be a consumer good to a household but a capital good to a business.

In 1995, manufactures accounted for 74% of world trade, compared with 45% in 1955. The rise in the share of manufactures is accounted for both by the more rapid increase in the volume of trade in manufactures and a rise in the unit value of manufactures relative to primary products. As we saw above, the volume of world exports of manufactures has grown significantly faster than for non-manufactures. At the same time, the prices of manufactures have tended to rise relative to the price of non-manufactures. Within the manufacturing sector, the biggest increases in trade shares have occurred for engineering products whose share rose from 21% in 1955 to 38% in 1995. In particular, office and telecommunications equipment increased its share from just under 1% in 1955 to over 12% in 1995. The share of road and motor vehicles also rose from 3.5 to 9.3% over the same period and of other machinery and transport equipment from 8.3 to 17.4%. Although the share of textiles has fallen, that of clothing rose. Finally, other consumer goods saw their share rise from 3.2 to 8.7% over the period covered.

Changes in the Geographical Composition of World Trade

Next, we consider the changes in the shares of world trade accounted for by different regions of the world. Table 1.7 shows the main trends. It should be borne in mind that some of the changes shown in the table may reflect changes in the way in which different regions are defined. However, these are unlikely to have made a substantial difference to the figures. As with the commodity composition of world trade, changes in the share of a particular region in world trade reflect either (a) a faster (or slower) growth in the volume of its exports compared with other regions or (b) a faster (or slower) growth in the average price of its exports compared with that of other countries.

The table shows that well over two-thirds of world trade is accounted for by the developed countries, a share that has been broadly stable over the past thirty years. The share of the developing countries in world trade has increased from 21% in 1963 to 28% in 1995, while the share of the former Communist countries of Eastern Europe has declined, especially in the last ten years. With regard to the *developed countries*, several important changes have occurred. Firstly, there has been a relative decline of the North American region (United States plus Canada) although this was partially reversed after 1983. Secondly, the share of Japan has risen strikingly from a mere 3.4% in 1963 to 9.2% in 1995. Western Europe's share has been broadly constant. However, within this total, the share of the EC has risen (matched by a decline in EFTA's share) although some of this reflects an expansion in the size of the EC from six members in 1963 to fifteen in 1995. Australia, New Zealand and South Africa have seen a small decline in their share of world trade.

The *developing countries* include a wide range of countries, in some cases, at very different stages of development. An obvious contrast exists between the rapidly growing 'newly industrialising countries' of South and East Asia and the poorest countries of the African continent which, in some cases, have little or no industrial base. In part, the figures bring out these differences. The share of the South and East Asian countries has risen dramatically although the 1995 figure is somewhat

Table 1.7 The Geographical Composition of World Trade, 1963–1995

	1963		*1973*		*1983*		*1985*		*1995*	
Region	*$bn*	*%*	*$bn*	*%*	*$bn*	*%*	*$bn*	*%*	*$bn*	*%*
North America	29.6	19.1	95.5	16.6	267.0	14.8	290.8	15.1	668.5	15.9
Japan	5.3	3.4	36.9	6.4	146.8	8.1	176.0	8.1	386.3	9.2
W. Europe of which	66.1	42.8	258.9	45.1	709.6	39.2	771.2	40.1	1772.3	42.2
EC	52.6	34.0	211.8	36.9	570.3	31.5	613.8	31.9	1621.6	38.6
EFTA	9.7	6.2	37.5	6.5	103.9	5.7	114.4	6.0	126.0	3.0
Australia, New Zealand and S. Africa	5.1	3.3	15.4	2.7	34.0	1.9	37.0	1.9	84.1	2.0
Developed countries	**104.1**	**67.3**	**406.7**	**70.8**	**1157.4**	**64.0**	**1275.0**	**66.4**	**2911.2**	**69.3**
Latin America	11.3	7.3	29.5	5.1	104.5	5.8	103.0	5.4	189.0	4.5
South and East Asia	8.4	5.4	31.6	5.5	159.0	8.8	176.0	9.2	739.72	17.6
Middle East	5.3	3.4	27.5	4.8	123.0	6.8	98.0	5.1	121.9	2.9
Africa	6.6	4.3	20.9	3.6	59.0	3.3	61.0	3.2	81.3	1.9
Developing countries	**31.9**	**20.6**	**110.4**	**19.2**	**447.1**	**24.7**	**440.0**	**22.9**	**1160.98**	**27.6**
Eastern trading area	**18.7**	**12.1**	**57.2**	**10.0**	**204.0**	**11.3**	**206.5**	**10.7**	**130.3**	**3.1**
World Total	**154.7**	**100.0**	**574.3**	**100.0**	**1808.5**	**100.0**	**1921.5**	**100.0**	**4202.48**	**100.0**

Source: GATT, various issues.

inflated by a change in definitions. By way of contrast, the other regions have experienced a fall in their share of world trade, most dramatically the African region. The share of the Middle Eastern states has tended to fluctuate with the price of oil, rising noticeably after 1973 but falling back after 1985.

Since *manufactures* have constituted the most dynamic component of world trade, it may be useful to examine the shares of different countries in world manufacturing exports. This is shown in Table 1.8.

While in 1963, 77% of world exports of manufactures were accounted for by the top ten countries, by 1995 their share had fallen to 58%. The share of world trade accounted for by the advanced industrialised countries has fallen due, largely, to the rise of a growing number of newly industrialising countries (NICs) in the developing world. In Table 1.8, the biggest increases in export share are found to have occurred in the countries of South and East Asia, in particular Japan (which ranked third in the world in 1995), Hong Kong, China, the Republic of Korea, Chinese Taipei, Singapore and Thailand. By way of contrast, the United States' share of world exports has fallen by 5%, although she is still the largest exporter. Germany's share has also fallen by roughly the same amount, while that of the United Kingdom by 6%. If, however, the members of the European Union are treated as a single entity, the EU (fifteen member states) accounted for the largest share of world trade in 1995 (44.4%) although this compared with 52% in 1963.

Table 1.8 World's Leading Exporters of Manufactures, 1963–1995

Country	Percentage shares of total world trade of manufactures			
	1963	*1973*	*1983*	*1995*
United States	17.4	12.8	12.4	12.4
Germany	–	–	–	12.3
Former FRG	15.7	17.0	13.6	–
Former GDR	2.8	1.7	1.7	–
Japan	6.1	10.0	13.4	11.6
France	7.1	7.3	6.4	6.0
Italy	4.7	5.3	5.9	5.6
United Kingdom	11.4	7.0	5.5	5.4
Hong Kong*	0.9	1.3	1.9	4.4
Belgium–Luxembourg	4.3	4.9	3.4	3.5
China**	–	0.6	1.2	3.4
Canada	2.6	3.5	3.7	3.3
Republic of Korea	0.0	0.8	2.1	3.1
Netherlands	3.3	3.9	3.0	3.0
Chinese Taipei	0.2	1.1	2.1	2.9
Singapore	0.4	0.5	1.0	2.7
Switzerland	2.7	2.4	2.2	2.1
Spain	0.3	0.9	1.3	1.9
Sweden	2.7	2.6	2.0	–
Mexico	0.2	0.3	0.7	1.7
Malaysia	0.1	0.1	0.3	1.5
Austria	1.2	1.2	1.2	–
Thailand	0.0	0.1	0.2	1.1
Finland	0.8	0.8	0.9	–
Ireland	0.1	0.3	0.5	0.9
Denmark	0.9	1.0	0.8	0.8
Indonesia	0.0	0.0	0.1	0.7
Brazil	0.1	0.4	0.8	0.7
India	0.8	0.5	0.5	–
Former USSR	4.1	3.1	2.8	–
Portugal	0.3	0.4	0.3	0.5
Turkey	0.0	0.1	0.3	0.4
Poland	–	1.2	0.7	0.4
Australia	0.3	0.6	0.3	0.4
Former Czeck Rep. and Slovakia	0.3	0.6	0.3	0.4
South Africa	–	–	0.3	0.3
Norway	0.6	0.8	0.5	0.3
Finland	0.8	0.8	0.9	0.3
Percentage top ten	76.8%	74.3%	58.0%	67.9%
Value $billion	80.8	346.4	1049.7	3639.9

Source: GATT, 1996.

The Regional Structure of World Trade

Table 1.9 sets out the regional structure of world merchandise exports. The regions defined are those used by the WTO in its annual trade statistics. The first section of the table shows the value of merchandise exports from the major regions of the world to other regions. Out of total world merchandise exports of $4890 billion, Western Europe accounted for $2191 billion or 45%. The Asian region (which includes Pacific Rim countries such as

Table 1.9 The Regional Structure of World Merchandise Exports, 1995 (billion dollars and percentages)

	Destination							
Origin	North America	Latin America	Western Europe	C/E Europe/ Baltic States/ C15	Africa	Middle East	Asia	World*
A. Values								
North America	***279***	100	148	6	11	19	211	777
Latin America	108	***47***	39	2	3	2	22	224
Western Europe	162	53	***1510***	96	61	58	211	2191
C/E Europe/ Baltic States/C15	7	3	88	***29***	2	3	20	153
Africa	15	2	56	1	***10***	2	14	103
Middle East	17	3	32	1	4	***11***	67	141
Asia	310	29	214	13	18	31	***662***	1301
World total	897	237	2086	149	111	127	1206	***4890***
B. Shares of Intra- and Inter-Regioal trade flows in each region's total exports								
North America	***36.0***	12.9	19.0	0.8	1.4	2.4	27.2	100.0
Latin America	48.0	***20.8***	17.6	0.8	1.4	1.1	9.9	100.0
Western Europe	7.4	2.4	***68.9***	4.4	2.8	2.7	9.6	100.0
C/E Europe/ Baltic States/C15	4.8	2.2	57.3	***18.9***	1.4	2.2	12.8	100.0
Africa	14.2	1.7	54.6	1.4	***10.0***	1.6	13.5	100.0
Middle East	11.7	2.1	22.9	1.0	3.2	***8.0***	47.6	100.0
Asia	23.8	2.2	16.4	1.0	1.4	2.4	***50.9***	100.0
World total	18.4	4.8	42.7	3.1	2.3	2.6	24.7	***100.0***
C. Shares of intra- and inter-regional trade flows in world merchandise exports								
North America	***5.7***	2.0	3.0	0.1	0.2	0.4	4.3	15.9
Latin America	2.2	***1.0***	0.8	0.0	0.1	0.0	0.5	4.6
Western Europe	3.3	1.1	***30.9***	2.0	1.2	1.2	4.3	44.8
C/E Europe/ Baltic States/C15	0.2	0.1	1.8	***0.6***	0.0	0.1	0.4	3.1
Africa	0.3	0.0	1.1	0.0	***0.2***	0.0	0.3	2.1
Middle East	0.3	0.1	0.7	0.0	0.1	***0.2***	1.4	2.9
Asia	6.3	0.6	4.4	0.3	0.4	0.6	***13.5***	26.6
World total	18.4	4.8	42.7	3.1	2.3	2.6	24.7	***100.0***

Source: WTO, 1996.
*Includes unspecified destinations. Exports to unspecified destinations are important in the case of Africa.

Australia and New Zealand) accounted for a further \$1301 billion or 27% and North America for \$777 billion or 16% of the total. A comparison of these shares with 30 years earlier shows that the share of the Asian region has increased significantly from roughly 15 to 27% today. That of the West European region has increased from 43% while the share of all other regions has declined.

The second section of Table 1.9 gives the share of a region's exports, which pass to other countries in the region (intra-regional trade) and the share going to countries outside the region (inter-regional trade). The diagonal column written in bold print gives the intra-regional share. It is noticeable that a higher proportion (68.9%) of West European exports is intra-regional than for other regions. 50.9% of the exports of the Asian region but only 36% of the North American region are intra-regional. The shares are even lower for the Latin American, Central/Eastern Europe/Baltic States/C15, African and Middle Eastern regions. The final section shows the share of a region's total exports (intra- and inter-regional) in world exports. Once again, the bold diagonal shows the share of intra-regional exports in world exports. Trade between countries belonging to Western Europe accounts for just under one-third of world merchandise trade.

One question that has attracted some interest in recent years concerns the extent to which trade has become more 'regionalised'. This may be defined as a tendency for different regions of the world to do proportionately more trade with themselves (intra-regional trade) and less with the rest of the world (inter-regional trade). A simple way of measuring any geographical bias in world trade is to observe the trend in the share of intra-regional trade in a region's total trade. This is given in the second section of Table 1.9. However, there is a need to compare the trend over time. This is shown for various regions of the world in the first section of Table 1.10.

Taking all regions of the world, it is clear that intra-regional trade has been increasing since 1948 after falling in the inter-war period. Intra-regional trade was highest in Western Europe and has risen faster than in any of the other regions. In Eastern Europe, the intra-regional share rose sharply after 1948 but has been falling since 1968. In North America, the intra-regional share also rose significantly after 1948 but fell between 1968 and 1979. From 1979 to 1990, it was roughly constant. In Asia, there has been a similar increase in the share since 1968 but over the period as a whole it has been less stable than in other regions. In Latin America, Africa and the Middle East, the intra-regional share is much lower and no sustained upward trend is discernible.

However, one problem with using the intra-regional trade share as the measure of geographical bias is that it is affected by the region's share in total trade. If the latter increases over time, the intra-regional share will also increase. For example, suppose that there are two regions each made up of two countries, A and B in Region 1 and C and D in Region 2. A, B and C each account for 20% of world trade and D for 40%. Each country exports an amount to each other country in proportion to the importer's share of world trade. As Region 2's share of world trade is greater, its intra-regional trade share is higher (46%) than for Region 1 (25%). To correct for this distortion, Andersen and Norheim (1993) have proposed the use of an intensity of intra-regional trade index. This is obtained using the following formula:

$$I_{ij} = X_{ij}/M_j$$

where i and j are two countries making up a region. X_{ij} is the share of country i's exports

Table 1.10 Measures of the Regionalisation of International Trade, 1928–1990

	1928	1938	1948	1958	1968	1979	1990
A. Intra-regional trade share							
Western Europe	51	49	43	53	63	66	72
Eastern Europe	19	14	47	61	64	54	46
North America	25	23	29	32	37	30	31
Latin America	11	18	20	17	19	20	14
Asia	46	52	39	41	37	41	48
Africa	10	9	8	8	9	6	6
Middle East	5	4	21	12	8	7	6
World total	39	37	33	40	47	46	52
B. The intensity of intra-regional trade index							
Western Europe	1.13	1.14	1.21	1.38	1.51	1.57	1.60
Eastern Europe	4.36	2.61	10.22	7.62	7.30	7.88	10.88
North America	2.59	2.91	2.39	3.07	3.57	3.63	3.50
Latin America	1.37	2.30	1.71	1.95	3.55	3.80	3.53
Asia	2.61	2.83	2.74	3.15	2.84	2.77	2.31
Africa	2.37	1.73	1.27	1.38	1.91	1.24	2.48
Middle East	7.56	3.47	9.55	4.25	3.00	1.17	2.23
World total	1.85	1.92	2.43	2.65	2.81	2.64	2.62
C. The percentage share of GDP traded							
Western Europe	33	24	35	33	34	48	46
Eastern Europe	30*	25*	25*	25*	40*	40*	41
North America	10	8	11	9	10	19	19
Latin America	45*	30*	30*	30	21	27	28
Asia	32	27	25	26	21	27	29
Africa	60*	50*	50*	58	37	56	53
Middle East	60*	50*	50*	46	38	48	49
World total	24	19	22	22	22	35	34
D. The index of propensity to trade extra-regionally							
Western Europe	0.30	0.21	0.31	0.26	0.21	0.28	0.23
Eastern Europe	0.25	0.23	0.14	0.11	0.16	0.20	0.24
North America	0.09	0.06	0.09	0.07	0.07	0.15	0.14
Latin America	0.43	0.27	0.27	0.27	0.18	0.22	0.25
Asia	0.21	0.16	0.18	0.18	0.15	0.19	0.19
Africa	0.56	0.48	0.49	0.45	0.37	0.48	0.47
Middle East	0.57	0.49	0.41	0.52	0.35	0.56	0.51
World total	0.21	0.16	0.19	0.16	0.15	0.23	0.21

Source: Adapted from Andersen and Norheim, 1993.
*In the absence of reliable estimates, it was necessary to make guestimates of the trade-to-GDP ratio for these regions in some years.

going to country j (i.e. intra-regional trade) and M_j is the share of country j in world imports. If the index gives a value greater than one, this would indicate a geographical trade bias. Section B of Table 1.10 gives the results for different regions. Taking the world as a whole, the index has increased since 1928 although it has fallen somewhat since 1968.

This would suggest that world trade has become more geographically biased. In Western Europe, the index rose steadily throughout the period. In North America, the index rose after 1948 before falling slightly after 1970. The index for the Asian region has fluctuated a great deal but has been on a declining trend since 1958.

Although trade does appear to have become more regionalised, this has in part been offset by a tendency for countries and regions to become more 'open'. As was discussed above, openness is usually measured by the proportion of Gross Domestic Product (GDP) that a country trades. This is shown in Section C of Table 1.10. This shows that a high degree of openness existed in the period following the end of World War I illustrating that the current high levels of openness are not unprecedented. In the inter-war period, regions became less open. However, after 1948, this was reversed for all the developed regions and, from 1968 onwards, for all other regions. Western Europe, which also had the highest intra-regional share, was the most open region measured in this way except for Africa and the Middle East. It follows that, whereas trade does appear to have become more regionalised, this has not yet been achieved by regions doing less trade with the rest of the world. Global trade has expanded as regions have become more open, but this has been accompanied by an increased geographical bias in world trade.

Andersen and Norheim's fourth index, the index of propensity to trade intra-regionally, adjusts for changes in the degree of openness of particular regions. This is given by the formula:

$$P_{ij} = t_j \cdot I_{ij}$$

where t_j is the ratio of country i's total exports to i's GDP (measuring its openness) and I_{ij} is the index of intensity of intra-regional trade defined above. Since the level of t_j is always less than one, P_{ij} will always be less than I_{ij}. However, the higher the degree of openness, the higher will be the adjusted index of propensity to trade intra-regionally. However, Section D in Table 1.10 measures the index of propensity to trade *extra-regionally* which is the more interesting case to examine. As is to be expected, the index has a low value indicating geographical bias in trade. It is also the case that the index fell in the inter-war years. However, it is noteworthy that, over the post-war period as a whole, the index rose from 0.19 in 1948 to 0.21 in 1990. This suggests that the tendency to greater openness in trade may in part have offset the tendency towards greater regional bias.

Conclusion

In this chapter, we have seen that the period since the Second World War has been a period of unprecedented global expansion. The developed market economies have experienced faster and generally more stable economic growth than any other period in history for which records exist. The exceptions to this were the two global recessions, which followed the oil crises of 1973–74 and 1979–80. To varying degrees, the developing world shared in this growth. Most successful were the newly industrialising countries of East and South East Asia. At the other extreme, per capita GDP grew more slowly in the poorest, least developed countries, particularly in the African continent and West Asia.

Economic growth in the developed countries has been largely export-led. A characteristic of the post-war expansion was that trade grew consistently faster than output. This reflected an increase in the degree of international specialisation between countries, particularly in the manufacturing sector. By way of contrast, trade in primary commodities tended to follow the growth in output in the developed market economies. An important cause of increased trade has been the willingness of countries to lower their barriers to trade both at the multilateral level through GATT and through the creation of regional trading arrangements such as the EU, NAFTA, *Mercosur* and AFTA.

Globalisation has also brought about important changes in the composition of trade. In terms of commodities, the major shift has been from primary to manufactured goods. Geographically, the most important change has been the increase in the share of world trade accounted for by the developing countries and the decline in the share accounted for by the advanced industrialised countries. Among the developed market economies, however, a major development has been the emergence of Japan as a major trading nation. In the developing world, the biggest increases in export share belonged to the newly industrialising economies of South and East Asia. These trends were particularly apparent if attention is focused on trade in manufactured goods.

The chapter concludes by observing that the trend towards greater openness of economies has been, in part, offset by a tendency towards increased geographical bias in trade. Although intra-regional trade is generally more important than inter-regional trade, there is some evidence that geographical bias has increased in recent decades. Does this mean that the world is polarising into increasingly exclusive trading blocs? This question is addressed in more depth later on in the book. However, it is important to examine whether or not increased intra-regional trade has been at the expense of extra-regional trade or whether it constitutes newly created trade. To date, the evidence favours the latter. Although intra-regional trade has grown relative to intra-regional trade, regions have become more open such that extra-regional trade has not fallen in proportion to GDP.

There is much debate about the costs and benefits that increased globalisation has brought to the world. On the one hand, by making possible a more efficient use of resources, trade increases global economic welfare and makes it possible for countries to enjoy a higher standard of living. On the other hand, globalisation makes countries more interdependent. Not only are they more affected by developments in other countries or regions, they may well enjoy less power to determine their own economic policies. However, globalisation is now a reality. There is unlikely to be any return to the more sheltered existence of previous eras. The important question for countries is how they can reap the maximum benefits from globalisation, while retaining some control over their own destiny.

Notes for Further Reading

The main sources of statistical information about economic growth are the World Bank's annual *World Development Report* and the International Monetary Fund's annual *World Economic Outlook*. Summaries of these reports are available free on the Internet. For trends in world trade, the main source of information is the World Trade Organisation's *Annual Report*. Again, a summary of this report and some statistical information is available free on the Internet. For a good overview of the growth of world output and trade in a historical perspective, the interested reader will find the following a useful reference:

Kitson, M. and Michie, J. Trade and growth: A historical perspective, Chapter 1 in Michie J. and Grieve Smith J. (eds), *Managing the Global Economy* (Oxford: Oxford University Press, 1995).

One of the best historical sources on economic growth remains:

Angus Maddison, *Dynamic Forces in Capitalist Development* (Oxford and New York: Oxford University Press, 1991).

On world trade, the World Trade's Annual Report contains analytical comment in addition to statistical information.

On primary commodity prices and trends in the global terms of trade, the reader should see:

Sapsford, D., The debate over trends in the terms of trade, Chapter 7, Greenaway D. (ed), *Economic Development and International Trade*, London: Macmillan, 1988.

The IMF's *World Economic Outlook* provides statistical information about primary commodity prices.

On the regionalisation of world trade, the interested reader should consult:

Andersen, K. and Norheim, H., History, Geography and Regional Economic Integration, Chapter 2 in Andersen K. and Blackhurst R. *Regional Economic Integration and the Global Trading System*, Hemel Hempstead: Harvest Wheatsheaff, 1993.

Chapter 2

Basic Theories of International Trade

CHAPTER OUTLINES: Introduction. Classical Theories of Trade – absolute advantage, comparative advantage, the empirical evidence. The Terms of Trade. The Factor Proportions, Heckscher–Ohlin Theory of Trade – the Leontieff Paradox, other empirical evidence. Increasing Opportunity Costs. Indifference Curves. General Equilibrium. The Factor Price Equalisation Theorem. Demand-Side Theories of Trade. Economies of Scale. Technology-Based Theories of Trade – technology-gap trade, the product life-cycle model of trade. The Case of Monopoly. Conclusion.

Introduction

Why do countries engage in trade? What benefits does trade bring to countries? What products will a country export and what will it import? What determines the pattern of its trade? And, since trade is the result of specialisation, what determines the products in which a country specialises? Moreover, how does a country's pattern of specialisation and trade change over time? These are some of the questions which have pre-occupied trade theorists for over two centuries. In this chapter, we shall identify some of the theories which economists have developed (and the various theoretical tools which they have used in the process) in an attempt to answer these questions.

This chapter is primarily concerned with the basic or more conventional theories which set out the gains which countries can expect from specialising in those activities in which they are relatively efficient. These constitute necessary 'building blocks' for understanding the more esoteric models which have been developed in recent years, which take into account some of the complexities of trade in today's world. These newer trade theories are not considered until Chapter 3. Usually, the term 'conventional' is restricted to the theory of trade expounded by the Classical and Neo-Classical schools of economic thought. However, this chapter also discusses some of the attempts of post-war economists to explain patterns of international trade and specialisation in a world where consumer preferences cannot be assumed to be identical and where technological innovation plays an important role.

Essentially, the basic theory of trade is concerned with answering two questions. The first seeks to explain how and why countries may gain from trade. The second seeks to explain the pattern of trade and specialisation, that is, why certain countries export particular goods and import others. An answer to the first question was provided by the Classical economists writing in the late 18th and early 19th centuries. An initial attempt at answering the second question was made by the Neo-Classical School in the late 19th and early 20th centuries. Differences in relative efficiencies were seen to be the result of differences in the amounts of the different factors of production with which each country was endowed. This, however, attaches primary importance to differences on the cost side and ignores the influence of demand-side factors in determining patterns of trade. It also fails to give sufficient weight to differences in the availability of newly created knowledge in shaping international specialisation and in affecting changes in specialisation over the course of time.

Classical Theories of Trade

Absolute Advantage

The main concern of the classical economists in their writings on the subject of international trade was to debunk popular misconceptions about trade that had arisen, largely, due to the writings of a group of scholars known as the Mercantilists. Mercantilism was premised on the mistaken notion that exports are *per se* 'good' because they earn a country gold, while imports are *per se* 'bad' because they result in an outflow of gold. (In those days, gold was the currency normally used to finance trade.) Consequently, a country should strive to reduce its dependence on imports by producing as much as it could itself. Such a policy is often referred to as one of autarky or self-sufficiency. In practical terms, it suggested that government policy should seek to reduce imports by imposing duties on imports and restricting the amount of foreign goods that are allowed into the country. At the same time, every effort should be made to boost exports by whatever means. An obvious objection to such a policy is that it can only ever work for one country at a time. This is because one country's export surplus is another country's import deficit. If one country succeeds in achieving a large export surplus, it can only do so if other countries run an equivalent trade deficit. It follows that, if all countries pursue such a policy, the result will be conflict among them. Either one country will succeed at the expense of the rest or else all will fail to achieve their objective.

However, Mercantilism is wrong for another reason. The accumulation of a large hoarding of gold through running an export surplus does not make a country materially better off, although it may impart a feeling of economic strength. Indeed, the opposite may be true. A country may be able to achieve a large export surplus by denying its citizens goods which could satisfy their wants, that is, by deliberately under-consuming. It is only by earning the foreign currency with which to pay for imports that trade makes a country prosperous. For this reason, there is nothing inherently 'good' about exporting. Nor are imports themselves 'bad' for a country. Thus, trade is not a 'zero-sum game' in which one country's gain is another country's loss as was implied by the Mercantilist view. On the contrary, trade is able to benefit all countries by enabling them to enjoy more goods at lower cost than could be obtained in the absence of trade.

Writing in his famous book, *The Wealth of Nations*, in 1776, Adam Smith argued that trade is beneficial because of differences between countries in the costs of producing different goods. Like all of his contemporaries, Smith held to a labour theory of value, according to which the cost of producing a good was given by the labour time required to produce it.

Therefore, differences in the costs of producing a certain good in different countries reflected differences in labour efficiencies in each country. However, rather than each country striving to produce all the products which they could, each should concentrate on those products in which they enjoy a cost advantage over other countries. The result will be that all are better off.

To see this, consider a simple numerical example of the kind used by Smith to illustrate this principle. Imagine two countries, A and B, which possess identical labour resources which they divide equally between the two activities, cloth and wheat. (It may be helpful to think of cloth as representing manufacturing and wheat as representing agriculture.) The following figures give the amount of the two goods which each country is able to produce if all its workers are fully employed.

	Cloth 000s	Wheat 000s
Country A	100	200
Country B	250	160
Total	350	360

Clearly, A is more efficient at producing wheat and B at cloth. Therefore, it pays A to specialise in wheat and B in cloth. Hence, A switches all its resources into wheat and B into cloth. Smith assumed that production of both products took place under conditions of constant costs. That is to say, the use of twice as many resources to produce a particular good resulted in a doubling of output. As a result of specialisation, both countries can produce more of the two products with the same resources as before, as is shown below.

	Cloth 000s	Wheat 000s
Country A	0	400
Country B	500	0
Total	500	400

However, does this mean that both countries will gain? Yes, provided they trade at the right terms of trade. The terms of trade are the rate at which cloth exchanges for wheat or vice versa. Clearly, producers in each country will require a price for their good which is better than the price which they could obtain domestically for trade to be worthwhile. In country A, 200 units of wheat have the same value as 100 units of cloth, since they require the same amount of labour time to produce. Therefore, before specialisation, wheat producers would have got 0.5 units of cloth for every unit of wheat they sold. Therefore, the terms of trade must be greater than 1 wheat = 0.5 cloth for A to be willing to trade. In Country B, before trade, 250 units of cloth are worth 160 units of wheat. This means that cloth producers would get 1 cloth = 0.64 wheat in the absence of trade. It follows that they will require a price below 1 wheat = 1.56 cloth for trade to be worthwhile. It follows that the terms of trade must lie somewhere between these two limits for both countries to derive some benefit.

For the moment, let us just assume that the rate at which the two countries trade is 1 unit of wheat trades for 1 unit of cloth. Let us further assume that Country B decides to exports half its cloth output, that is, 250 units and to exchange this for 250 units of wheat. Likewise, Country A exports 250 units of wheat in exchange for 250 units of cloth. The following will be their position after trade.

	Cloth 000s	Wheat 000s
Country A		
Production	0	400
Consumption	250	150
Exports	0	250
Imports	250	0
Country B		
Production	500	0

Consumption	250	250
Exports	250	0
Imports	0	250

It is clear that Country B has gained as it can now consume more wheat while consuming the same amount of cloth as before. Country A has more cloth but less wheat, which might suggest that she is no better off. However, since 150 units of cloth are worth more than 50 units of wheat, she clearly gains. Thus, specialisation and trade have benefited both countries. It should be borne in mind that how much each country consumes and produces of each of the two goods after trade will depend on the preferences of consumers in each country for the two goods.

Comparative Advantage

Smith's theory of trade identified differences in absolute costs as the basis for trade. What, however, if one country has an absolute cost advantage in the production of both goods? Is it still worthwhile for the two countries to specialise? The answer provided by classical political economist, David Ricardo (1772–1823), was that it may still be so, because the basis for trade is comparative and not absolute advantage. In his text, *Principles of Political Economy* written in 1816, Ricardo demonstrated that the reason why it pays countries to trade is the existence of different relative or comparative costs in the production of different goods. So long as each country possesses a comparative advantage in at least one activity, it pays to specialise in that activity and engage in trade.

Differences in comparative costs are given by comparing the relative cost ratios existing in the two countries before trade. These express the cost of producing one unit of a particular good in terms of the number of units of the other good that must be forgone in order to do so. If we assume that all labour is employed in one or other activity, an extra unit of one good can only be produced by reducing output of the other. This way of expressing cost is what economists call 'opportunity cost' or the cost of something expressed in terms of opportunities foregone. We can see this by considering an example of two countries similar to that used to illustrate the principle of absolute advantage. Once again, each country is considered to have the same labour resources and to divide these equally between two activities.

	Cloth 000s	Wheat 000s
Country A	100	200
Country B	80	100
Total	180	300

In this case, Country A is more efficient at both activities. If, however, we measure the opportunity cost of producing each product in both countries, it will be apparent that A has a comparative advantage in wheat and B has a comparative advantage in cloth. In A, the production of an extra unit of wheat requires sacrificing 0.5 units of cloth, whereas in B, it requires sacrificing 0.8 units of cloth. Thus, A has a comparative advantage in wheat production. Turning next to cloth, the cost of producing an extra unit of cloth in A is 2 units of wheat and in B 1.25 units of wheat. So, B has a comparative advantage in cloth production. Note also that these pre-trade cost ratios for each country will give the pre-trade relative price ratios.

Now, let us see what happens if both countries specialise in the product in which they enjoy a comparative advantage. Assuming once again constant costs, the output of each product will double:

	Cloth 000s	Wheat 000s
Country A	0	400
Country B	160	0
Total	160	400

In order for both countries to benefit from trade, the terms of trade must lie somewhere between each country's pre-trade relative price ratio, that is, between 1 cloth = 2 wheat and 1 cloth = 1.25 wheat. At anything less than 1 cloth = 1.25 wheat, cloth producers in B will have no incentive to exchange cloth for wheat internationally as they could get a better price domestically. Likewise, at anything less than 1 cloth = 2 wheat (1 wheat = 0.5 cloth), wheat exporters in A will have no incentive to export wheat for the same reason. For the moment, let us assume that 1 unit of cloth exchanges for 1.5 units of wheat. Suppose that B keeps half its cloth output for domestic consumption and exports the other half. In this case, it will export 80 units of cloth in exchange for 120 units of wheat. If A exports 120 units of wheat, it will be left with 280 units of wheat for domestic consumption. In addition, it will buy 80 units of cloth from B. The following situation results:

	Cloth 000s	Wheat 000s
Country A		
Production	0	400
Consumption	80	280
Exports	0	120
Imports	80	0
Country B		
Production	160	0
Consumption	80	120
Exports	80	0
Imports	0	120

Country B is better off, having more units of wheat but the same amount of cloth. Country A has 80 more units of wheat but 20 less units of cloth. However, she is still better off because 80 units are equivalent to roughly 53 units of cloth at the terms of trade of 1 cloth = 1.5 wheat. Her net gain is 33 units of cloth equivalent.

The above example can be illustrated with the aid of a *production possibility* or *transformation* line drawn for each of the two countries. This is shown in Figure 2.1a,b. This shows different combinations of the two products which each country can produce with the labour resources at their disposal. Point P shows the combination of the two products which each country produces before specialisation. Using

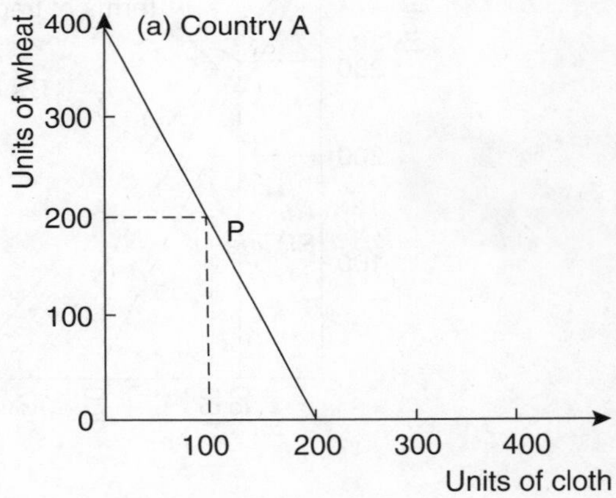

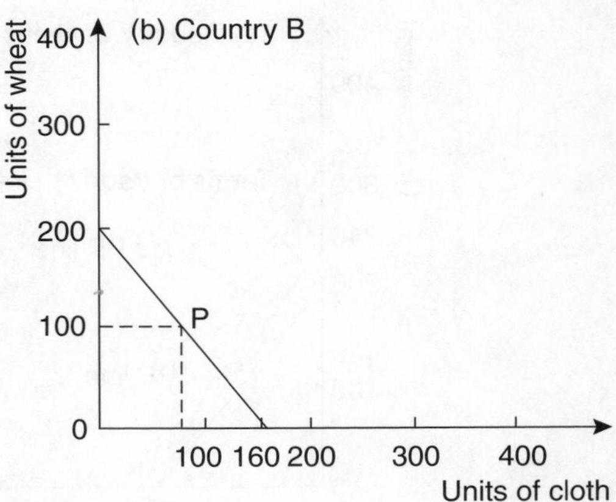

Figure 2.1 The production possibility line under constant opportunity costs

the concept of opportunity costs, the slope of the line measures the costs of producing cloth in terms of wheat (or of wheat in terms of cloth) and, hence, the relative price ratio of each good in both countries. The fact that the PP line is straight reflects the fact that opportunity costs are assumed to be constant. Later, we shall consider what happens if costs either increase or decrease with output. An important feature of the PP line is that, in the absence of trade, no country can reach a point beyond its PP line. (Of course, in the long run, an increase in its labour resources and increases in labour efficiency will result in this line pushing outwards.)

In order to show the gains from trade, it is necessary to redraw the PP line for each country as starting from the same point on the axis for the product in which each country specialises. This is shown in Figure 2.2a,b. Consider first the case of Country A. In this case, the PP line of each country is drawn from

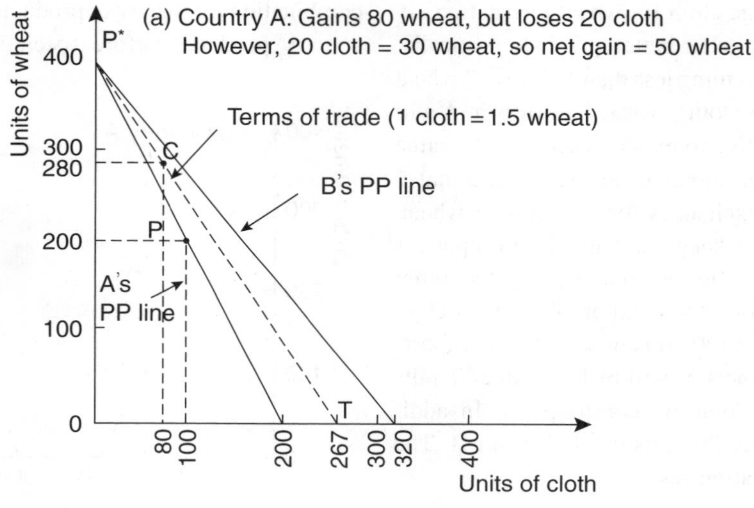

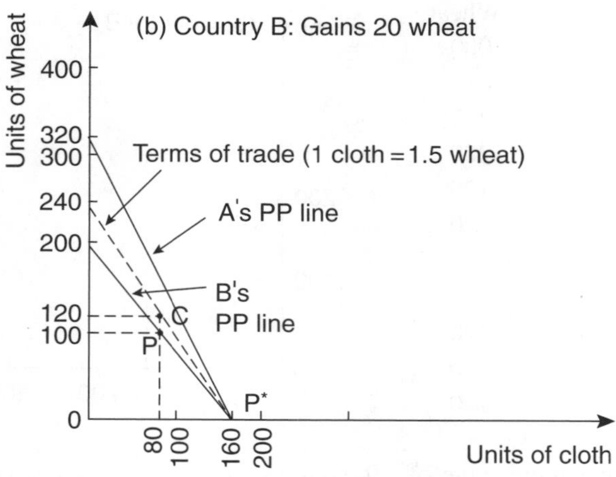

Figure 2.2 The gains from trade under constant opportunity costs

the vertical axis to show the relative costs of producing wheat in the two countries, as this is the product in which A has a comparative advantage. Country A's PP line is steeper than Country B's reflecting the fact that A can produce wheat at lower opportunity cost than B. Before trade, Country A was producing at P. It now specialises completely in wheat production and so production shifts from P to P*. The terms of trade are drawn as a line starting from P* and crossing the horizontal axis at T. The slope of this line is equivalent to 1 cloth = 1.5 wheat. Note that this is between A and B's PP line, the slope of which shows each country's pre-trade cost ratio. By exchanging some wheat for cloth, A can consume at point C, that is, at a point beyond its PP line. This means that it is able to obtain a bundle of the two goods that exceeds what it could have obtained in the absence of trade. At C, it consumes 280 units of wheat and 80 units of cloth, which leaves her better off than before trade.

Next consider the case of Country B. In this case, the PP line of each country is drawn from the cloth axis to show the relative price of producing cloth in the two countries. Now B's PP line is flatter than A's because B can produce cloth at lower opportunity cost than A. As B specialises in cloth, production shifts from P to P*. P*T is the terms of trade line drawn as starting from P* on the cloth axis. By exchanging 80 units of cloth for 120 units of wheat, B is able to move from P to point C beyond its PP line where it can consume 120 units of cloth and 80 units of wheat. This represents more than it could obtain in the absence of trade as is apparent from the fact that C is beyond B's PP line. Thus, both countries gain from trade. The gain is measured by the movement from a point on a country's PP line to a point beyond it.

The Ricardian model is important for demonstrating the benefits from two countries engaging in trade. First, it demonstrates that the basis for trade between any two countries is the existence of differences in comparative, not absolute, costs. This means that trade is still beneficial even where one country is superior at producing everything providing that its advantage is greatest in at least one activity. Second, providing that the terms of trade lie within the limits set by each country's pre-trade cost ratios, both countries will gain from trade. Thus, trade is not a zero-sum game in which one country gains at the expense of the other. However, the terms of trade will determine how these gains are distributed between countries. Third, the model predicts the pattern of trade that will, in the absence of barriers to trade, take place among different countries. Countries will tend to specialise in those products in which they enjoy low relative costs. These will be the industries in which their labour efficiency is highest relative to that of their trading partner. This provides a reasonably straightforward prediction that can be subject to empirical testing to see how well the theory fits the facts.

The Empirical Evidence

Despite the fact that the Ricardian theory of trade was first set out in the early 19th century, it was another 134 years before anyone sought to test the theory to see whether its predictions were borne out in practice. The first formal test was performed by MacDougall in 1951 (MacDougall, 1951). MacDougall sought to determine whether or not the trade of both the United States and the UK with the rest of the world conformed with the predictions of the Ricardian theory. The theory predicts that countries will specialise in those products in which they have a comparative costs advantage. In the Ricardian model, comparative costs are determined by the relative efficiency of labour.

Strictly speaking, the model is applicable only to bilateral trade between two countries. However, bilateral trade between the US and UK was at that time too small relative to each country's total trade and too distorted by tariffs for such an exercise to be usefully performed. Instead, MacDougall focused on each country's trade with the rest of the world. He sought to test the following hypothesis. Since wage rates in manufacturing were roughly twice as high in the US as in Britain, the US should be the dominant exporter in third markets of products in which her labour productivity was more than twice as high as in Britain. Likewise, Britain should be the dominant exporter in products in which U.S. productivity was less than twice as high as in Britain.

The study covered some twenty-five manufactured product groups for the year 1937. His results appeared to confirm the theory. The ratio of U.S. to British exports was mostly higher in those industries where her ratio of labour productivity was higher. The coefficient of correlation was estimated at 0.8. This supports the Ricardian thesis that it is comparative and not absolute advantage that governs trade. Although the methodology used by MacDougall was subsequently criticised by Bhagwati (1964), there has been no serious challenge to MacDougall's results. Indeed, subsequent attempts to test the theory for later years and using more extensive data generally confirm his findings (e.g. Stern, 1962).

The Terms of Trade

It is clear that the terms of trade are of considerable importance for determining how the gains from trade are distributed. In Figure 2.2, the terms of trade were roughly half way between the pre-trade price ratios of both countries. This ensured that both countries enjoyed some gain from trade. However, it is self-evident that the closer are the terms of trade to the pre-trade price ratio of a country, the smaller the gain from trade for that country and the bigger the gain for the other country. Thus, it is important to ask the question: what determines the terms of trade? The English Classical economist, John Stuart Mill, answered this in terms of the so-called *Law of Reciprocal Demand.* Reciprocal demand refers to a country's demand for a product in which another enjoys a comparative advantage in exchange for the product in which the former enjoys a comparative advantage. Thus, in Figure 2.2, where A enjoys a comparative advantage in wheat, A exercises her reciprocal demand for cloth when she offers wheat in exchange for cloth. Likewise, B exercises a reciprocal demand for wheat when she offers cloth in exchange for it. The Law of Reciprocal Demand states that the terms of trade will depend on the relative strength of each country's reciprocal demand for the product which the other country supplies. If both countries are of roughly equal size, it is likely that their reciprocal demands will be in approximate balance. In this case, the terms of trade will lie roughly half way between the pre-trade prices of the two countries. If, however, one country is larger than the other, the terms of trade will be closer to the pre-trade prices of the larger country. Interestingly, this will mean that the larger country will gain less than the smaller country from trade. This is what has been referred to by Kindleberger (1968) as 'the importance of being unimportant'.

Now, it is possible to give greater precision to this explanation of how the terms of trade are determined by making use of the technique of *offer curves* developed by two neo-classical economists, Alfred Marshall and F. Edgeworth. An offer curve expresses the demand for a product in terms of how much of the other product a country is prepared to offer in exchange for it. As with demand for any good,

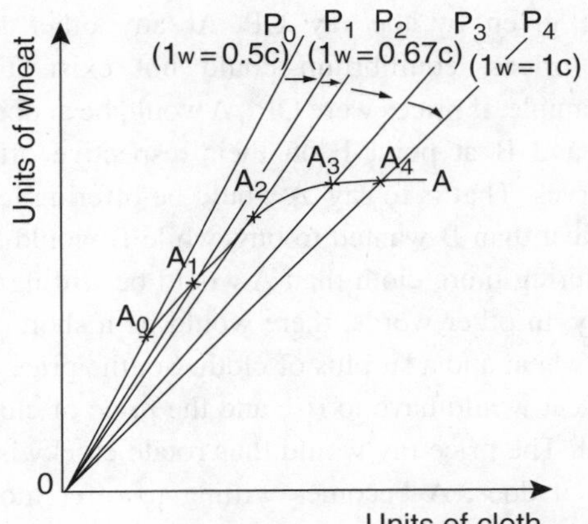

Figure 2.3a Country A's offer curve of wheat for cloth

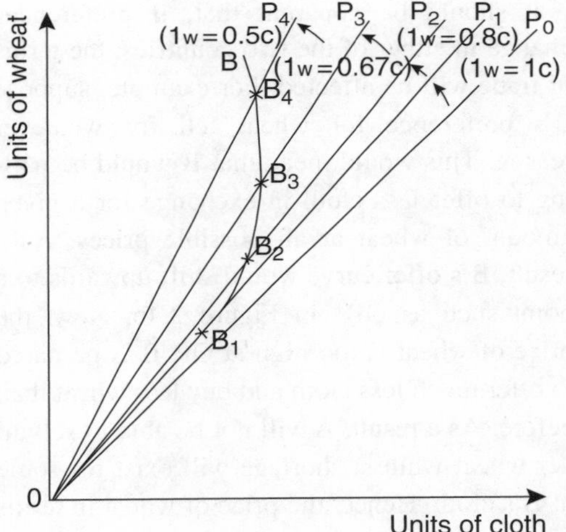

Figure 2.3b Country B's offer curve of cloth for wheat

this will vary with the price of that good expressed in terms of units of the other good. An offer curve is, in effect, both a demand and a supply curve. To see this, consider Figure 2.3. Both diagrams contain a series of rays from the origin, the slope of which shows the relative price of cloth (wheat) in terms of wheat (cloth). As the rays rotate clockwise, the price of cloth in terms of wheat falls. As they rotate anti-clockwise, the price of cloth in terms of wheat rises. Consider Figure 2.3a. At a price of 1 wheat = 0.5 cloth, which is the pre-trade price of cloth, A is unprepared to offer any wheat in exchange for cloth because it cannot gain by doing so. However, as the price of wheat rises (i.e. the price of cloth falls), it is prepared to offer increasing amounts of wheat in exchange for an extra unit of cloth. In brief, its demand for cloth rises as the price of cloth falls. However, as the price of cloth continues to fall (and the price of wheat to rise), the offer curve becomes flatter, implying that A is prepared to give up smaller and smaller amounts of wheat in exchange for cloth. This is because, as A enjoys more and more units of cloth and parts with more and more units of wheat, the benefit from having further units of wheat diminishes. Every student of Economics knows that a basic law of demand is that, the more units of a commodity which consumers possess, the less value they attach to an extra unit. It is also the case that, as A parts with more and more units of wheat, the value of an extra unit of wheat increases. Hence, the offer curve must become flatter and will indeed eventually turn inwards. At this point, the country is no longer prepared to offer any wheat in exchange for further units of cloth.

Next, consider Figure 2.3b. This shows Country B's willingness to offer cloth in exchange for wheat. At the pre-trade price of 1 cloth = 1 wheat, B is unwilling to offer any cloth in exchange for wheat. However, as the price of cloth rises, B becomes willing to offer increasing amounts of cloth in exchange for extra units of wheat. However, the more units of wheat that B enjoys, the less value it attaches to extra units of wheat. Also, the more units of cloth, which it parts with, the more wheat it requires in exchange for an extra unit of cloth. Hence, B's offer curve becomes steeper, the more wheat it offers and the more cloth it buys

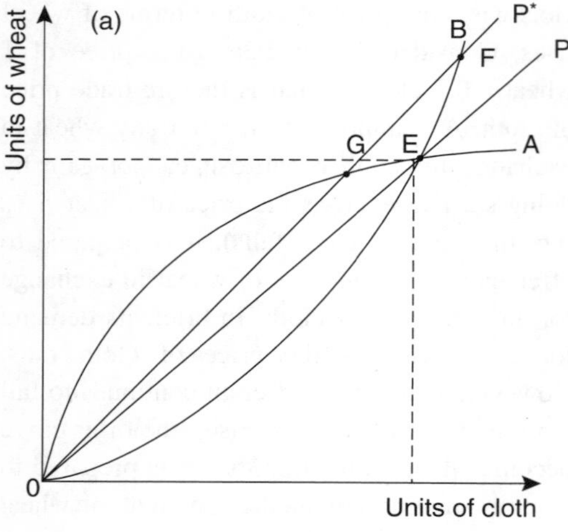

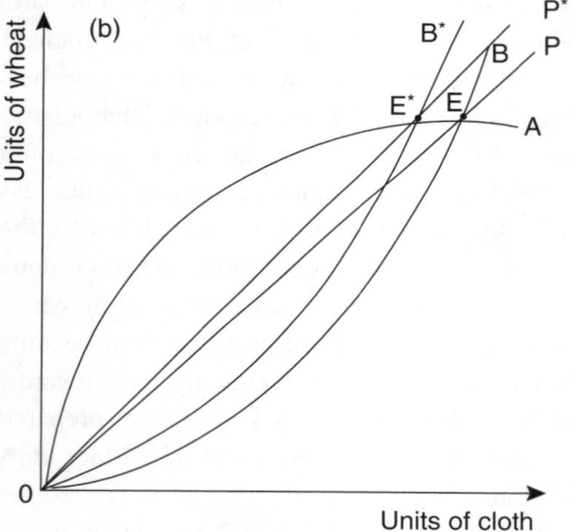

Figure 2.4. The equilibrium terms of trade

in exchange. Now, if we put the two offer curves on to the same diagram, we can see how the terms of trade are determined. This is illustrated by Figure 2.4.

In Figure 2.4a, the offer curves intersect at point E. At this point, A is prepared to offer exactly the same amount of cloth in exchange for wheat as B is prepared to buy and B is prepared to offer the same amount of cloth as A is willing to buy. At this point, the terms of trade are given by the ray OP. At any other set of prices, equilibrium could not exist. For example, if prices were OP*, A would be at point G and B at point F on their respective offer curves. That is to say, A would be offering less wheat than B wanted to buy, while B would be offering more cloth than A would be willing to buy. In other words, there would be a shortage of wheat and a surplus of cloth. So, the price of wheat would have to rise and the price of cloth fall. The price ray would thus rotate clockwise. As it does, A becomes willing to offer more wheat and B becomes less willing to supply cloth. Eventually, when prices reach OP, demand and supply for both commodities are equal.

It should be apparent that, if preferences change in either of the two countries, the terms of trade will be affected. For example, suppose B's preference for wheat fell for whatever reason. This would mean that B would be willing to offer less cloth in exchange for a given amount of wheat at all possible prices. As a result, B's offer curve would shift upwards to a point such as OB* in Figure 2.4b. Now, the price of wheat is too high at OP. B is prepared to offer much less cloth and buy less wheat than before. As a result, A will not be able to sell all her wheat while a shortage will exist for some of B's cloth. Hence, the price of wheat in terms of cloth will have to fall, that is, the price ray will move anticlockwise. It will do so until a new equilibrium is reached at E* where B is now prepared to buy all the wheat which A offers and B is prepared to buy all the cloth which A offers. The new terms of trade are represented by OP*. Thus, the terms of trade change in the same way as any set of prices in response to changes in demand and supply. However, as they change, they have important effects on countries, redistributing the gains to be reaped from trade. Of course, no country will trade unless it can enjoy some gain. However, the terms of trade will determine how much of the gain goes to each country.

The Factor Proportions, Heckscher–Ohlin Theory of Trade

One of the weaknesses of the classical theory of trade is that it provided no explanation for why relative efficiencies and, hence, comparative costs should differ between countries. It was left to the Neo-Classical school to suggest an explanation. This was provided simultaneously, but independently, by two economists, namely, Eli Heckscher (1879–1952) and a Swedish economist, Bertil Ohlin (1899–1979), writing in the early 20th century. They explained differences in comparative costs in terms of differences in the amounts of different factors with which countries were endowed and differences in the *factor proportions* required for the production of different goods. Different goods require for their production different proportions of the various factors of production (land, labour, capital). At the same time, countries possess different amounts of these factors. Some countries are well endowed with land, others with labour and still others with capital. This means that the relative prices of these factors will differ in different countries. Because factor prices differ, the costs of producing the same good will vary between one country and another. For example, the cost of producing labour-intensive goods will be lower in countries where labour is relatively abundant. In brief, countries will enjoy a comparative advantage in the production of those goods, which use relatively large amounts of the country's most abundant factor of production. Thus, countries in which labour is abundant will possess a comparative advantage in labour-intensive goods. Other countries in which capital is the most abundant factor will enjoy a comparative advantage in capital-intensive goods.

It is important to state the assumptions on which the theory is based. These may be listed as follows:

1. Trade takes the form of an exchange of two goods, which use just two factors in their production, between two countries (a so-called $2 \times 2 \times 2$ model of trade).
2. Products are homogeneous so that there is nothing to distinguish the product of one seller from that of another, that is, no product differentiation.
3. Each country has the same production function for a particular good. That is to say, the proportions within which factors are combined (so-called *factor intensities*) are the same regardless of where that product is produced. (A production function is an equation that describes the proportions of different factors that are required to produce a given amount of any product.)
4. All countries enjoy equal access to the same body of technological knowledge and any new knowledge, which is created, about how to produce a particular product is instantly diffused internationally.
5. Consumer preferences are assumed to be broadly identical in all countries. That is to say, consumers are assumed to spend broadly the same proportions of their incomes on different products in all countries.
6. All factors of production (except land) are perfectly mobile 'within' countries, but immobile 'between' countries.
7. Both product and factor markets are assumed to be perfectly competitive.
8. Transport costs are non-existent.
9. There exist no tariffs or other barriers to trade.

Clearly, many of these assumptions do not hold in the real world. However, this is not sufficient ground for rejecting the theory. All theories must, to some degree, make assumptions that may not always apply in practice. The important point is whether or not the predictions of the theory (viz., that countries will specialise in those products which use proportionately large amounts of the country's most abundant factor) are found to be true when the theory is subjected to empirical testing. This is the ultimate test for the validity of any theory.

The Leontieff Paradox

One of the attractions of the HO theory is that it provides us with set of fairly simple and readily testable predictions. One of the first attempts made to test the theory was made by a Russian-born economist, Wassily Leontieff (b.1906) in 1954. Using the 1947 input–output tables for the United States, he sought to test the proposition that the US had a comparative advantage in capital-intensive goods and therefore traded these goods for imported labour-intensive products. Leontieff measured the factor intensity of U.S. exports and *import replacements* using the input–output tables. The reason for taking import replacements (U.S. produced goods that are substitutes for goods imported) rather than imports was that information about factor intensities could not be obtained for all the products which the US imported or for all the countries from whom she imported. If the factor intensities for these products are the same in other countries, the use of import replacements need pose no major problems. Interestingly, Leontieff's results showed that U.S. imports were more capital-intensive than U.S. exports, the exact opposite of what the theory predicted (Leontieff, 1954)!

The *Leontieff Paradox*, as it came to be known, seemed to prove that the HO theory was wrong. Subsequently, a variety of explanations were put forward for Leontieff's results.

1. One possible explanation was that the year chosen, 1947, was not very representative given that trading patterns may still have been distorted by the ending of the Second World War. However, attempts to carry out the same test for later years reproduced the same result and thus appear to refute this explanation (Leontieff, 1956).
2. A second explanation focused on the use of import replacements rather than imports. If products imported by the US were produced by different methods in other countries to those adopted in the US, factor intensities will differ and the use of import replacements as a proxy for imports will render the theory invalid. Specifically, it is possible, given the scarcity of labour in the US, that goods that are produced by labour-intensive methods abroad, are produced by capital-intensive methods in the US. This is known as *factor-intensity reversal* (Ellsworth, 1954). The important question is: to what extent does factor-intensity reversal occur in reality and is it of sufficient importance to render the HO theory invalid? If factor-intensity reversal is a common occurrence then the HO assumption that all countries face identical production functions for the same good is not valid and the theory breaks down. Empirical research has established that factor-intensity reversal does, indeed, take place (Minhas, 1963). However, it appears that, in most cases, it is not sufficient to account for the result obtained by Leontieff. (See Leontieff, 1964, Moroney, 1967, Bhagwati, 1969.)
3. A third explanation is that the assumption of identical consumer preferences is invalid. Specifically, it was argued that, in 1947, on account of their higher per capita income, U.S. consumers had a greater preference for capital-intensive goods. Higher quality consumer goods are generally more capital-intensive than lower quality ones (see

Valvanis–Vail, 1954, Robinson, 1956, Jones, 1956). It is important to note that such a bias is not inconsistent with the HO assumption that consumer preferences are identical. Identical consumer preferences means that consumers in different countries spend their incomes on different goods in broadly similar 'proportions'. However, given that the income elasticity of demand for different goods is in some cases more than unity and in other cases less than unity, different levels of per capita income must mean that demand will be biased towards goods with a high income elasticity of demand in those countries with high per capita incomes and vice versa in countries with low per capita incomes. If U.S. demand were biased towards capital-intensive goods and on the assumption that average costs increase with output (i.e. a concave transformation curve), the relative prices of capital goods could be higher in the US than other countries although the US is relatively well endowed with capital. In this case, the US might be a net importer of capital-intensive goods. This possibility is discussed below. However, the bias on the demand side would need to be sufficiently strong to counter the effect of factor endowments on the supply side for this result to obtain. Moreover, it would need to be demonstrated that demand patterns do, indeed, differ markedly between countries. So far, the available evidence suggests otherwise although the results are not conclusive (see Houthakker, 1957).

4. The explanation preferred by Leontieff was that U.S. labour was superior to that of other countries. Quite arbitrarily, he gave a figure of three to one as the difference between the efficiency of U.S. labour and that of other countries. In that case, labour could not be described as relatively scarce and the fact that U.S. exports were more labour-intensive than U.S. imports was hardly surprising. The main problem with this argument is that it is by no means apparent why this should be true of labour alone. There is every reason to suppose that U.S. capital was also more productive than that of other countries, in which case the capital–labour ratio would be unaffected and the presumption that labour was relatively scarce would still hold. No empirical evidence has been forthcoming to contradict this.
5. A further explanation has emphasised the failure of Leontieff to distinguish human from physical capital. Human capital finds its embodiment in the skills and education of a country's labour force. If allowance is made for this, it would be the case that U.S. exports are more capital-intensive than Leontieff found. In a later work, Leontieff himself found that the average level of skill of the labour force in the U.S. was higher in the export than the import replacements sector (Leontieff, 1956). Subsequently, Kenen (1965) has shown that, once human capital is included, the Leontieff Paradox is reversed but only just. On the other hand, using a different method of estimating human capital, Baldwin (1971) found that, while the inclusion of human capital was sufficient to weaken the Paradox, it was not enough to reverse it. In fact, since physical and human capital are hardly perfectly substitutes, it is more appropriate to treat human capital as a separate factor of production. Since human capital and not capital in aggregate is most probably the United States' most abundant factor of production, the right test to perform is to measure the relative human capital intensity of U.S. exports.
6. The next explanation concerns natural resources that are omitted as a factor from the model used by Leontieff. The HO model becomes more complex if a third factor

of production is introduced. Attention was drawn to the fact that, on account of her rapid industrialisation, the US had become relatively deficient in natural resources such that much of what she imported consisted of resource-intensive goods. The possibility, therefore, existed that natural resources and not labour were her relatively most scarce factor. Therefore, the US had become an exporter of both capital- and labour-intensive goods in exchange for resource-intensive goods. In a later study, Leontieff excluded certain resource imports which were non-competitive with U.S. production (i.e. they could not be produced anywhere in the US) and found that the original Paradox disappeared. Work by Vanek (1963) confirmed that U.S. imports were more resource-intensive than her exports. He also found some evidence that capital and natural resources were complementary in U.S. imports but not in U.S. exports. If so, this would impart a capital-intensive bias to U.S. imports.

7. Finally, it was argued that trade restrictions might have distorted U.S. trade. Specifically, if tariffs were higher on labour-intensive imports, this could explain why the proportion of such goods was low in total U.S. imports. This begs the question why other countries should trade with the US if the outcome was to force them to produce goods at which they were relatively inefficient. If, however, natural resources are included, this argument breaks down and it is conceivable that protectionism could explain the result. A study by Kravis in 1954 did indeed find that the most heavily protected industries in the US were the labour-intensive industries (Kravis, 1954).

Box 2.1 below summarises the main explanations given that could account for the Leontieff Paradox.

Other Empirical Evidence

Subsequent attempts to test the HO theory, incorporating some of the factors discussed above, have not wholly resolved the problem. As referred to above, Baldwin (1971) found

Box 2.1 Major Explanations for the Leontieff Paradox

1. The year chosen (1947) was unrepresentative. Evidence: Leontieff (1956)
2. The methodology was wrong because import replacements were used as a proxy for imports. Evidence: Minhas (1963), Leontieff (1964), Moroney (1967) and Bhagwati (1969)
3. United States consumption was biased towards capital-intensive goods. Evidence: Valvanis–Vail (1954), Robinson (1956), Jones (1956) and Houthakker (1957)
4. United States labour was superior to that of other countries
5. No attempt was to include human capital in the measurement of factor content. Evidence: Kenen (1964), Keesing (1966), Baldwin (1971), Stern and Maskus (1981)
6. Natural resources should have been omitted from the calculation. Evidence: Vanek (1963), Baldwin (1971)
7. United States trade restrictions were biased towards capital-intensive imports Kravis (1954)

that, if human capital is included as a separate factor of production and natural resource products are excluded, the paradox is nearly eliminated but not reversed. On the other hand, using multiple regression analysis, Baldwin also found U.S. net exports to be negatively related to capital intensity, thus supporting the Leontieff Paradox. Stern and Maskus (1981) found that, for 1958, the paradox held but that U.S. exports embodied more human capital than U.S. imports. This, however, was reversed in 1972, and could be explained by the fact that other countries had caught up with the US in levels of education and skill. Havrylyshyn (1984) found that the HO theory better fitted the trade of less developed countries. This, perhaps, reflects the fact that these countries do most of their trade with industrialised countries, which possess markedly different factor endowments. Similar tests have been carried out for other countries and yield similar results.

Box 2.2 summarises the results of the empirical work carried out to test the Heckscher–Ohlin theorem.

What conclusions can be drawn from this? There is widespread agreement among trade economists that, in its simple form, the HO theory is unsatisfactory as an explanation for trade. At best, it may provide some explanation for trade between developed and less developed countries, which is not surprising given the fact that these countries differ greatly in factor endowments. If the theory is adapted to include a larger number of factors, especially if human

Box 2.2 Major Empirical Tests of the Heckscher–Ohlin Theory of Trade

Leontieff (1954) used 1947 U.S. input–output tables to estimate the factor-intensity of U.S. exports and 'import replacements'. He found that, contrary to theoretical expectations, U.S. exports were more labour-intensive and less capital-intensive than U.S. exports.
Conclusion: the evidence appeared to contradict the predictions of the theorem.

Vanek (1959) found the natural resource content of U.S. exports was approximately one-half that of U.S. imports. He suggested that capital and natural resources were, to some degree, complementary in U.S. trade, so that U.S. importation of natural resources necessarily meant that U.S. imports were relatively capital-intensive.
Conclusion: natural resources should be excluded from any test of the theory.

Minhas (1963) found evidence that factor-intensity reversals was fairly prevalent. He studied 24 industries in 19 countries and found factor-intensity reversals in five cases. A bilateral comparison of 20 industries in the US and Japan found a low correlation in capital–labour ratios between the two countries.
Conclusion: factor-intensity reversal is not uncommon, in which case relative factor endowments may fail to predict patterns of trade.

Kenen (1964) made the first attempt to include human capital. It was estimated for U.S. exports and imports and added to physical capital requirements. Using 1947 data, he found that, even including natural resource-based products, the paradox was eliminated.
Conclusion: if capital is broadened to include human capital, the evidence appears to support the theory for U.S. trade.

Continued

Keesing (1966) found that U.S. exports were more skill-intensive than the exports of nine other industrial countries for the year 1957.
Conclusion: the inclusion of human capital shows U.S. exports to be relatively capital-intensive.

Baldwin (1971) examined the factor content of U.S. trade for 1962, using a wider range of factors and distinguishing between physical and human capital. He found that the inclusion of human capital significantly weakened the Leontieff Paradox, but was not sufficient to reverse it. He also found that the exclusion of natural resource-based products almost eliminated the paradox.
Conclusion: the inclusion of a wider range of factors achieves a better result, but still fails to confirm the theory.

Leamer (1980) adopted a different approach by comparing the capital-to-labour ratio is U.S. production with U.S. consumption rather than U.S. exports compared with imports. He found that the capital–labour ratio was indeed higher in U.S. production than U.S. consumption and concluded that there was, therefore, no paradox.
Conclusion: the use of a different methodology gives a different result.

Stern and Maskus (1981) also incorporated human capital using a single measure based on rates of pay as reflecting the skill of the labour involved. They found that the paradox remained for U.S. trade in 1958, but disappeared in 1972. They also estimated the factor content of production and consumption to be equal for all three factors used.
Conclusion: the inclusion of human capital eliminates the paradox, but leaves the theory saying very little.

Havrylyshyn (1984) tested the Heckscher–Ohlin theory for a sample of trade between developed and developing countries (i.e. North–South trade). He found that the exports of developing countries to developed countries were less capital-intensive than their imports, including both physical and human capital.
Conclusion: the Heckscher–Ohlin theory works better in predicting trade patterns between developed and developing countries.

Bowen, Leamer and Sviekauskas (1987) used data for 27 countries to see how well relative factor abundance predicted actual patterns of trade. Data for 12 factors were used. Relative factor abundance was measured by the share of different factors in a country's national income (factor income) and factor intensities by the factor content of exports and imports. They found that, for two-thirds of the factors, trade flows ran in the direction predicted less than 70% of the time.
Conclusion: the empirical evidence fails to provide support for the Heckscher–Ohlin theory.

capital is separated from physical capital, its explanatory power is strengthened in respect of trade in non-resource-based products. Even then, the results of empirical work still fail to confirm the predictions of theory in all cases. This suggests that the determinants of trade are more complex than the HO theory maintains. In particular, the theory breaks down entirely when countries with similar resource endowments and at a similar stage of development trade with each other. Yet, the fastest growth in world trade in the past half century has occurred in trade in manufactured goods *between* developed market economies (see Chapter 1).

Increasing Opportunity Costs

Classical trade theory assumed constant opportunity costs. However, it is more probable that, in most activities, as resources shift out of one activity and into another costs increase. In short, a doubling of the resources used in the production of a particular good leads to something less than a doubling of output. One reason for this is that not all the resources used in the production of one good will be equally suitable for use in the production of another. For example, labour employed in wheat farming may be unsuitable for employment in cloth production. Then, as labour leaves wheat farming and enters cloth production, the efficiency of labour will decline. As cloth production expands, it will be necessary to switch increasingly unsuitable units of labour from wheat to cloth production with the result that the costs of producing an extra unit of cloth (measured in terms of wheat foregone) will rise.

However, a further reason why costs may increase with output is that some of the resources used in a particular activity may be specific to that sector, that is, incapable of being used in any other sector. (Neo-Classical economists recognised the existence of more than one factor of production.) This is true of much land and capital. For example, the site used for locating a factory producing cloth may be incapable of being turned over to growing wheat. Likewise, machinery used in agriculture clearly has no alternative use in manufacturing. This means that some resources simply cannot switch out of one activity and into another. Then, as production of cloth (or wheat) expands, the proportions in which factors (say, labour and capital) are combined in production will change. More and more of the non-specific factor (labour) will have to be combined with a more or less constant amount of the specific factor (capital). It is a well-established principle of economics that, if increasing amounts of a variable factor (such as labour) are combined with a given amount of a fixed factor (say, capital), the average and marginal productivity of the variable factor will decline. This is called the *Law of Diminishing Returns*. Another way of putting this is to say that, as cloth (or wheat) output expands, the costs of producing an extra unit of cloth (or wheat) measured in terms of wheat (or cloth) will increase.

For both these reasons, it is more appropriate to assume that production takes place under conditions of increasing, rather than constant, opportunity costs. In this case, we can no longer assume that the production possibility schedule is linear. Instead, if the costs of producing an extra unit of one product in terms of another rise as more is produced, the production possibility schedule will be a curve which is concave to the origin. This is illustrated by Figure 2.5.

A curve such as AD shows various combinations of wheat and cloth that a country can produce with the resources at its disposal. It can

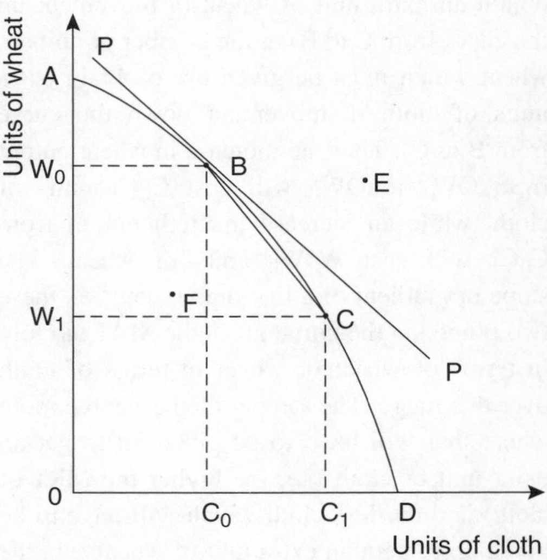

Figure 2.5 A country's production possibility (transformation curve under increasing opportunity costs)

produce anywhere on the curve such as points B or C but not outside it (e.g. point B). Although it can produce at any point inside the curve such as C, it would not be efficient as the country would not be making full use of her available resources. The exact point along her transformation curve where she will locate will depend on the relative prices of cloth in terms of wheat or wheat in terms of cloth prevailing at any point in time. These, in turn, will depend on the relative preferences of consumers in that country for cloth as opposed to wheat. As a country moves from one point on the curve to another (e.g. from B to C), it shifts resources out of one activity (wheat) and into the other (cloth). In effect, it transforms units of one commodity (wheat) into units of the other (cloth). Hence, the curve is sometimes known as a *transformation curve*.

The rate at which one commodity is 'transformed' into another by this process is known as the *marginal rate of transformation (MRT)*. It may be measured as either the number of units of cloth which must be given up to obtain an extra unit of wheat (a movement up the curve from C to B) or the number of units of wheat which must be given up to obtain extra units of cloth (a movement down the curve from B to C). Thus, an increase in wheat output from OW_1 to OW_0 will cost C_0C_1 units of cloth, while an increase in cloth output from C_0C_1 will cost W_1W_0 units of wheat. The slope or gradient of a line drawn between these two points on the curve gives the MRT of cloth in terms of wheat or wheat in terms of cloth over this range. The steeper the curve, the more wheat that will have to be given up to get an extra unit of cloth (i.e. the higher the MRT of cloth) and the less cloth which will have to be given up to gain an extra unit of wheat (i.e. the lower the MRT of wheat). The flatter the curve, the lower the MRT of cloth in terms of wheat and the higher the MRT of wheat in terms of cloth. At any given point on the curve, the MRT will be given by the slope of a line drawn tangent to the curve at this point. (Starting from any point on a curve, as smaller and smaller changes between the two product are considered, the line between these two points will approximate towards a line drawn at a tangent to the curve at that point.) Thus, the line PP measures the MRT of cloth in terms of wheat or wheat in terms of cloth at point B. The MRT is the same thing as the marginal cost of producing one more unit of a product but measured in terms of the units of the other product which have to be forgone as a result (rather than in monetary terms). So marginal costs are given by the slope of the transformation curve at any point. Now, if costs are assumed to be constant (as in the Classical model), the curve would be a straight line. However, since costs are assumed to increase with output, the curve must be concave to the origin. This is because, as we move down the curve (say, from C to D), we have to give up increasing amounts of wheat to get more cloth. Likewise, as we move up the curve from B to A, we have to give up increasing amounts of cloth to obtain increasing units of wheat. Thus, a concave transformation illustrates the case of where marginal costs (the costs of producing one extra unit) increase with output.

Next, we need to consider where producers will produce, if the structure of demand in the market is assumed to be given. We shall deal with consumer preferences shortly. For the moment, we assume that consumers express their preference for different goods through relative prices. That is to say, the relative price of cloth in terms of wheat or wheat in terms of cloth is determined by the strength of consumer demand for each good in each country. Let us further assume that markets are perfectly competitive, in which case all producers will produce up to the point at which price equals marginal costs since this is when profits are maximised. So long as the price of one good exceeds the marginal cost of producing that good, producers will have an incentive to expand their output (as, by doing so, they will add more to their revenues than to their total costs). As they do so, marginal costs will increase until they eventually reach a point where price equals marginal cost. Now, if price exceeds marginal cost in one activity, it must be less than marginal cost in the other (as both prices and marginal cost are expressed in terms of units of the other commodity). In the activity where marginal costs exceed prices, producers will have an incentive to reduce their output (as they will reduce their total costs by more than the fall in total revenue). As they do so, marginal costs will fall. However, they will go on reducing output until price equals marginal cost, at which point no more profit can be earned by reducing output further. Equilibrium will be achieved where the following condition is satisfied:

$$P_{CLOTH}/P_{WHEAT} = MRT_{CLOTH}/MRT_{WHEAT}$$

That is to say, producers in both industries are perfectly satisfied that they can make no more profits by making further changes in output.

We can illustrate the nature of such a point of equilibrium if we represent relative prices by lines or rays, the slope of which measures the price of cloth in terms of wheat or wheat in terms of cloth. The steeper the line, the higher the price of a unit of cloth measured in terms of units of wheat and the lower the price of a unit of wheat measured in terms of units of cloth. At any given time, the exact slope of the price line will depend on consumers' preference for cloth over wheat or wheat over cloth. If these preferences change, the price line will change. For example, if consumers' preference for wheat increases, the price of wheat in terms of cloth

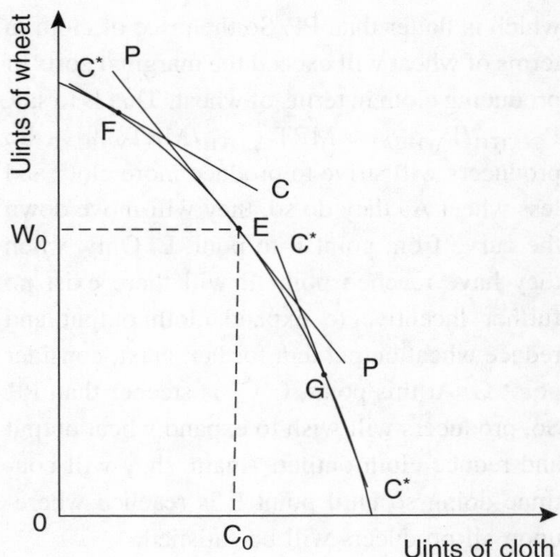

Figure 2.6 The nature of pre-trade equilibrium under conditions of increasing opportunity costs

will rise and the price line will become flatter. Conversely, an increased preference for cloth would cause the price of cloth to rise in terms of wheat and the price line would become steeper. Now, suppose that, in the absence of trade, prices are represented by the line PP in Figure 2.6.

The PP line could have been drawn anywhere on Figure 2.6 provide it had the same slope. However, we need to draw a line such that it will just touch the transformation curve at a particular point. This is because equilibrium occurs where price equals marginal cost in both activities and because the slope of the curve at a particular point measures marginal cost. (We assume that a country will produce at a point on its transformation curve and not inside it.) Point E in Figure 2.6 is the only point on the curve where the equilibrium condition is satisfied, because the line PP measures both relative prices and marginal costs. To see this, consider another point such as F. At point F, marginal costs are given by the slope of CC which is flatter than PP. So the price of cloth in terms of wheat will exceed the marginal costs of producing cloth in terms of wheat. That is to say, $P_{CLOTH}/P_{WHEAT} > MRT_{CLOTH}/MRT_{WHEAT}$. So producers will strive to produce more cloth and less wheat As they do so, they will move down the curve from point F to point E. Only, when they have reached point E will there exist no further incentive to expand cloth output and reduce wheat output anu further. Next, consider point G. At this point, C*C* is steeper than PP. So, producers will wish to expand wheat output and reduce cloth output. Again, they will continue doing so until point E is reached whereupon all producers will be satisfied.

Indifference Curves

So far, we have taken consumer preferences as given. If we can model preferences in some way, it will be possible to provide a complete picture of how trade brings welfare gains to a country. A technique widely used in Neo-Classical theory is that of the *indifference curve map*. Consumers are assumed to be rational beings who make choices about whether to spend money on different goods weighing up the value which an extra unit of a good will bring them compared with the price which they pay for it. They are assumed to adjust their spending in such a way that, for every good which they purchase, this condition is satisfied. In this way, they maximise their total utility, that is, the amount of satisfaction that they can derive from a given level of income. Since the 'satisfaction' that consumers derive from a good is a difficult concept to measure, one solution is to measure the value of an extra unit of one good in terms of the number of units of the next best alternative that must be foregone. For example, if I spend £10 on a theatre ticket on Saturday night and my next best alternative was to enjoy a meal out, I can say that the value of a theatre ticket is equal to the meal that I have thereby sacrificed. If, now, the price of theatre tickets should rise (say, to £12), I have to decide whether I still wish to spend my money in this way. In reality, consumers are making a multitude of such choices at any given time. However, we can represent their choices by employing the concept of indifference curves. This shows the various combinations of any two goods that yield a constant degree of satisfaction such that the consumer is indifferent between different points on the curve. Consider Figure 2.7 which measures the consumer's preference for cloth over wheat.

Any point on an indifference curve such as II yields the consumer the same amount of satisfaction. Thus the consumer is indifferent as between points a and b. However, a point such as x or y is superior because it takes the consumer on to a higher indifference curve and, therefore, a higher level of total utility. Note that indifference curves are always drawn convex to the origin. The reason for this is that, as a consumer enjoys more and more units of one commodity (e.g. cloth) and, therefore,

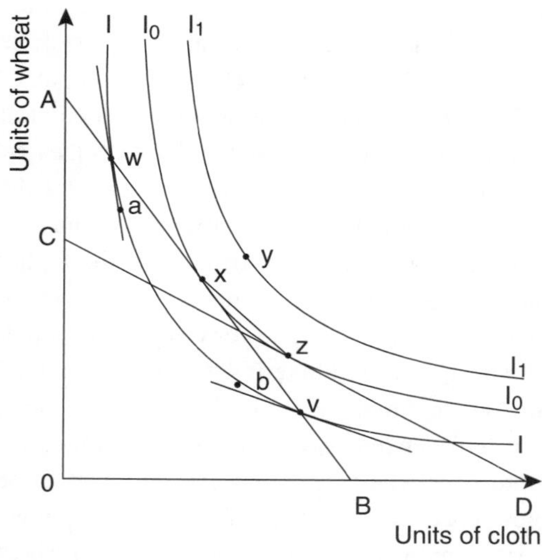

Figure 2.7 Consumer indifference curves

less and less units of the other (wheat), he/she derives less satisfaction from an additional unit of that commodity (cloth) and becomes less willing to give up further units of the other (wheat). Another way of putting this is to say that they experience *diminishing marginal utility.* Eventually, the indifference curve will become parallel to the horizontal and vertical axis as the consumer will no longer be prepared to sacrifice any more units of the other commodity to get more of the commodity which he/she now possesses in large amounts. Note, too, that no indifference curve can intersect another indifference curve since, by definition, a higher curve yields more satisfaction than a lower one.

Now, where the consumer will locate will depend on (a) his/her real income and (b) the relative prices of the two goods. A rational consumer will wish to get on to the highest indifference curve possible with the real income at their disposal. Suppose that the consumer's income will enable him to buy either OA units of wheat or OB units of cloth or a combination of both. Then, we can draw a line AB, which shows what he can buy with the resources at his disposal. Now, if each indifference curve represents higher levels of utility, he will wish to get on to the highest possible indifference curve achievable with his income. Such a point is x. Points such as w and v are attainable, but leave the consumer on a lower indifference curve. Now suppose the relative prices of the two goods should change. For example, suppose the price of cloth should fall in terms of wheat. This will enable him to buy more cloth but less wheat with the same amount of money income as before. This could be represented by a change in the slope of AB to CD. Now, he cannot reach point x. However, he can move to point z which enables him to enjoy the same amount of satisfaction as before. Such a move involves substituting some cloth for wheat. The opposite would happen if the price of wheat should fall relative to the price of cloth.

The significance of point x is that, at this point, the consumer is equating the marginal utility (the utility derived from an extra unit of the good) of each good to the price of the good. This is because the line tangent to the indifference curve I_0I_0 at point x measures both the marginal utility of each good, expressed in units of the other good, and relative prices. Thus, we can say that, at point x:

$$P_{CLOTH}/P_{WHEAT} = MU_{CLOTH}/MU_{WHEAT}$$

Consumers get as much satisfaction from an additional unit of each good as the price that they pay for an extra unit. This would not be true at any other point on AB. Thus, at point w, the price of cloth in terms of wheat is less than the MU of cloth measured in terms of wheat. Hence, the consumer will buy more units of cloth and less units of wheat. As he does so, he moves down AB towards x. As he does so, the MU of cloth in terms of wheat falls until, eventually, the purchase of an extra unit of cloth yields as much satisfaction as the price that he pays for it. This equilibrium is achieved at x. Likewise, at a point such as v, the price of cloth in terms of wheat exceeds the MRS of cloth. This means that he can improve his economic welfare by buying more units of wheat and substituting these for units of cloth. As he does so, he moves up AB towards x. Only, when he reaches this point, will it pay to cease substituting wheat for cloth. At this point one more unit of wheat adds as much to his total welfare as the price which he is paying for it.

For the purposes of analysing trade, however, we are not interested in the decisions of the individual consumer but of consumers as a whole. We could envisage the community as facing an indifference curve map analogous to that of the individual consumer. However, that would only be true if all consumers had identical tastes. In Figure 2.7, if individual consumers have different tastes, it does not follow that a movement from z to y, for example, leaves the community as a whole better off. Since this means that the community has more units of wheat and less units of cloth, some consumers may consider this improvement and others a deterioration in their situation. Who is to say that the gain of the one group compensates for the loss of the other? Even then, there is a problem if the distribution of income within the country were to change as this would affect the combination of the two goods which the community would wish to consume at any given level of income. Suppose the distribution of income changes in favour of higher income groups. If higher income consumers have a preference for cloth, while lower income consumers would have a preference for wheat, the slope of the indifference curve will change. Basically, the community indifference curve will become steeper, as consumers will want more units of wheat as substitutes for fewer amounts of cloth. Then, a movement from z to y may well increase economic welfare because the community now values extra units of cloth more than before. One solution is to assume that all consumers have identical tastes and to assume that the distribution of income does not change. However, even this is not sufficient. Even if tastes are assumed the same at a particular moment in time, they will change as income increases. This is because the income elasticity of demand is not the same for all goods. For some goods (mainly, luxury goods) demand increases faster than income. For other goods (mainly necessities), demand increases more slowly than income. So, changes in income may affect preferences and hence the shape of the indifference curve. Then, the only solution is to make the even more drastic assumption that tastes are 'homothetic', that is, all goods have an income elasticity of demand of one. Only by making these assumptions can we make the transition from the individual to the community indifference curve. Clearly, community indifference curves have major conceptual problems. However, they do constitute a convenient device for showing the effects of trade on economic welfare.

General Equilibrium

We are now in a position to show what happens when two countries with different factor endowments but identical preferences engage in trade. One the one hand, each country will have a transformation curve showing what it can produce of the two goods with the resources at its disposal. This will have a different shape in each case reflecting the differences in factor endowments. Thus, in Figure 2.8, A is land-abundant and B is labour-abundant, so A's curve is steeper than B's. The indifference curve map of each country is assumed the same, reflecting identical tastes. Equilibrium before trade exists at point E in both diagrams, because, at this point, each country is on the highest possible indifference curve that it can reach with its productive resources. At this point, consumers are satisfied because:

$$P_{CLOTH}/P_{WHEAT} = MU_{LOTH}/MU_{WHEAT}.$$

and, therefore, have no incentive to substitute cloth for wheat or wheat for cloth. At the same time, producers maximise profits because:

$$P_{CLOTH}/P_{WHEAT} = MRT_{CLOTH}/MRT_{HEAT}.$$

Now, if markets are perfectly competitive, it can be shown that each country will reach this point of equilibrium. Producers will adjust their production until profits are maximised and consumers will arrange their consumption such

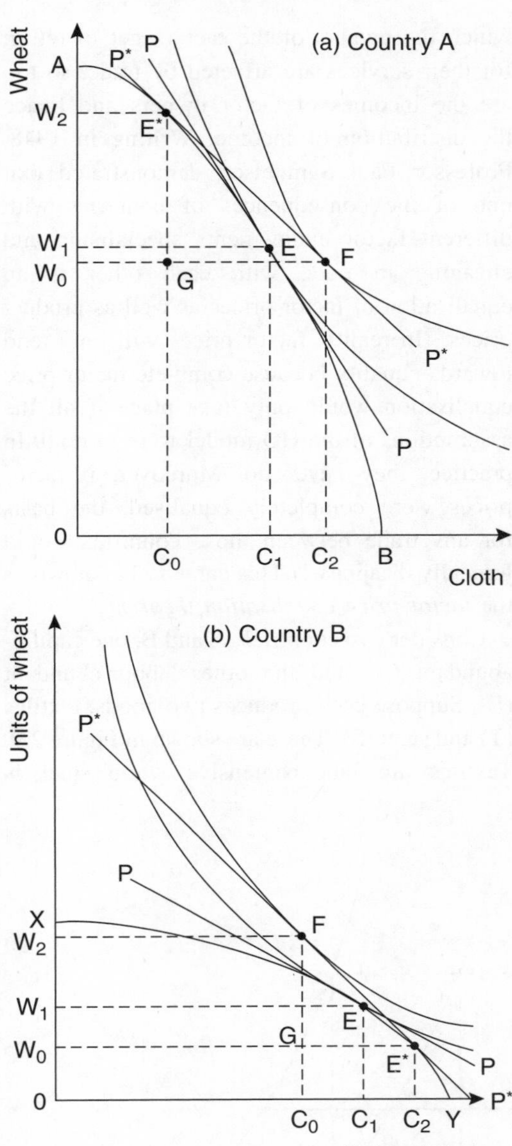

Figure 2.8 General equilibrium before and after trade

that their total welfare is also maximised. Such a point is known as one of *Pareto efficiency* where resources are allocated between alternative uses in such a way that community welfare is maximised. Consequently, consumers as a whole cannot be made better off by re-allocating resources in any way among different activities. In the absence of trade, however, a country cannot get to a point beyond its transformation curve. The only way, in the short-run, that it can do so is by engaging in trade. By specialising in the production of goods in which it has a comparative disadvantage and exchanging these for goods in which other countries have a comparative disadvantage, it can place itself on a higher indifference curve. In Country A, the price of cloth (in terms of wheat) is higher than in Country B, whereas, in Country B, the price of wheat (in terms of cloth) is higher than in Country A. Thus, it pays A to export wheat to B and B to export cloth to A. The prices, at which they will do so, will depend on the international terms of trade. Suppose these are represented by a price line P^*P^*, which lies somewhere between the pre-trade prices of the two countries. Country A now shifts from point E to point E^* on the transformation curve. At the new set of prices, it pays to produce more wheat and less cloth. Only when point E^* is reached can producers make no further additional profits by shifting resources out of cloth and into wheat. The opposite is true of Country B. At point E, extra profits can be made by shifting resources out of wheat and into cloth. Eventually, point E^* is reached where this is no longer the case. Thus, in both diagrams, a new point of production equilibrium is achieved, with A specialising in wheat and B in cloth, although neither country specialises completely in one product.

Now what happens when they trade? Consider Country A. By exporting W_0W_2 ($=E^*G$) wheat, it can buy C_0C_2 ($=GF$) cloth. This is because the slope of the price line, P^*P^*, measures the rate at which wheat exchanges for cloth internationally. This enables A to consume at point F on a higher indifference curve, giving more cloth but less wheat than before trade. Because F is on a higher indifference curve than E, A has gained from trade. Likewise, Country B can export C_0C_2 (=GE*) cloth and obtain in exchange W_0W_2 (=GF) wheat. This enables B to reach point F on a higher indifference curve than before. Thus, both countries gain from trade. Note that trade has equalised product prices in both countries.

The Factor Price Equalisation Theorem

Before leaving Neo-Classical trade theory, we need to consider another important extension to the Heckscher–Ohlin model that addresses the important question of how trade affects the distribution of income within a country. General equilibrium analysis shows that trade increases the total income of a country. However, does this mean that all income groups gain? The answer is not necessarily. This is because trade affects the prices of the factors used in production and not just the prices of products entering into trade. Since the prices which the owners of the factors get in return for their services are affected by trade, so too are the incomes of factor owners and hence the distribution of income. Writing in 1948, Professor Paul Samuelson demonstrated that one of the consequences of countries with different factor endowments specialising and engaging in trade with each other is an equalisation of factor prices as well as product prices. (In reality, factor prices will only tend towards equality because complete factor price equalisation would only take place if all the assumptions of the HO model were to hold. In practice, they never do. Moreover, if factor prices were completely equalised, the basis for any trade between those countries would logically disappear!) This came to be known as the *factor-price equalisation theorem.*

Consider two countries, A and B, one capital-abundant (A) and the other labour-abundant (B). Suppose each produces two goods, textiles (T) and steel (S). These are shown in Figure 2.9. Textiles are labour-intensive while steel is

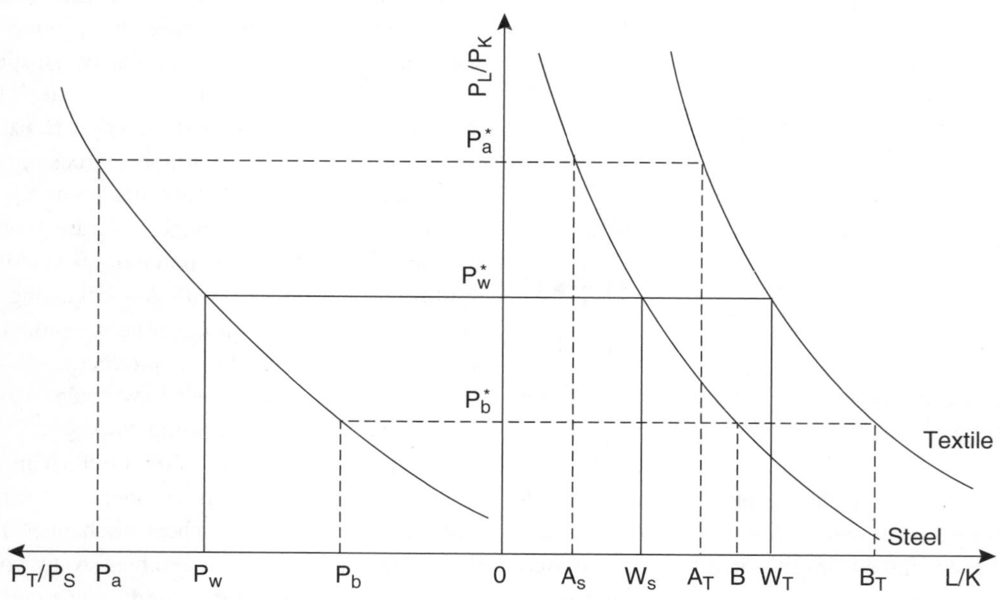

Figure 2.9 Factor price equalisation

capital-intensive. In the absence of trade relative goods prices and relative factor prices will differ in the two countries. In A, capital will be relatively cheap and labour expensive; in B, labour will be relatively cheap and capital expensive. If P_K is the price of capital (the rate of profit) and P_L is the price of labour (the wage rate), let P^* represent $P_L P_K$ which is measured on the vertical axis. We can see that, in the absence of trade, $P^*_a > P^*_b$. If, now, we move across to the left-hand quadrant of the diagram, we can read off the relative prices of the two goods in each country. Let P stand for the price of textiles relative to the price of steel. Now, because labour is relatively expensive in A, textiles, being a labour-intensive good are relatively more expensive in A, that is, $P_a > P_b$. Finally, we move across to the right-hand quadrant to determine the the ratio of labour-to-capital in each of the two sectors. Because textiles are labour-intensive and steel capital-intensive, the schedule for textiles lies to the right of that for steel. In A, the labour–capital ratio is A_S in steel and A_T in textiles; in B, because labour is cheaper, the labour–capital ratio is higher in both sectors, B_S in steel and B_T in textiles.

Next, consider what happens if both countries trade. A specialises in steel and B in textiles. Trade equalises product prices in the two countries. Suppose the terms of trade are denoted by P_W. As A shifts resources out of textiles and into steel, the demand for capital rises and the demand for labour falls. Consequently, P_L/P_K falls. As it does, producers in both sectors substitute some labour for capital. Hence, the L/K ratio rises in both sectors. The opposite happens in B. Eventually, factor prices are equalised at P^*_w. At this level of factor prices, both countries will use the same amount of labour to capital in both sectors, namely, W_S in steel and W_T in textiles. Since B is a labour-abundant country, will this not mean some unemployment since less labour is being used relative to capital in both sectors than before trade? No, because B is producing more of the labour-intensive good, textiles, and less of the capital-intensive good, steel, than before. Indeed, if the labour market is a perfect market, the wage rate will fall to whatever level is required to ensure that producers provide jobs for all workers seeking employment. The changes in relative factor prices are the mechanism whereby specialisation ensures changes in the labour-capital ratio in different sectors of the economy such that all resources are fully-employed at the new post-specialisation levels of production. However, the important point here is that trade has not only equalised product prices; it has also equalised factor-prices.

Now, what follows from this is that, although trade should increase the economic welfare of both countries, not all factors within the two countries benefit equally. In A, the price of labour has fallen relative to the price of capital. So, labour loses out relative to the owners of capital. In B, the price of labour has risen relative to the price of capital. So, labour has gained relative to the owners of capital. Indeed, the theorem predicts that trade will always worsen the relative position of the owners of the country's scarce factor and improve the relative position of the owners of the country's abundant factor. Of course, a fall in relative prices need not mean that factor owners are worse off in *absolute* terms. As we saw above, trade enables a country to obtain goods at more favourable prices than those which prevailed before trade. If the prices of consumer goods fall, the 'real' wage-rate (money wage rate divided by the average price level) may still rise even if 'money' wage rates are lower. However, it is possible that trade will leave the owners of a country's scarce factor worse off in absolute terms also. In an earlier paper, Stolper and Samuelson (1941) gave a formal demonstration of how this might happen. If the wage rate were to fall by more than the prices of consumer goods, real wage rates will fall. This does not negate the case for a country entering into trade since trade still leaves countries as a whole better off. Income groups who gain from trade could compensate those groups that lose and still be better off. In practice, however, this may not happen in which case factor owners who stand to lose from trade are likely to oppose the opening up of trade and to call for trade restrictions. This can help explain why pressures exist within countries for protectionism even when trade theory says that trade makes countries better off. Since some income groups stand to lose both in a relative and possibly an absolute sense, they oppose a lowering of trade barriers.

In recent years, there has been a revival of interest in the Stolper–Samuelson Theorem. Evidence of a widening gap between the wages of skilled and unskilled workers in the United States and, to a lesser extent, other western industrialised countries has emerged at a time when imports from Third World countries have risen. Since Third World countries have plentiful supplies of unskilled labour while the developed countries enjoy plentiful supplies of skilled labour, one might expect the latter to trade skill-intensive goods in exchange for simple manufactures. Conceivably, this could reduce the relative and even absolute wages of unskilled workers in countries such as the United States. Taking the period from 1979 to 1989, Lawrence and Slaughter (1993) found that the real wages of blue-collar workers had fallen not only in relative but in absolute terms also. However, this may not have been due to trade. During this period, there was a trend towards increased employment of skilled relative to unskilled workers in nearly all industries. If trade were the cause of greater inequality of wages, one would expect employers to 'reduce' their demand for skilled labour in all industries as a response to the increased cost of employing skilled labour. As we saw above, it is only through a rise in the wages of skilled workers that the output of the skill-intensive sector of the economy can rise within the economy as trade takes place. Instead, they concluded that technological change was the cause of the reduced demand for unskilled labour. However, this does not prove the Stolper–Samuelson theorem wrong. It may simply have been the case that the trade effect was weaker than the technology effect. As we shall see in Chapter 7, trade with Third World countries still accounts for only a small proportion of the trade of most western industrialised countries. However, this is likely to change in the future, in which case trade may exert a more marked effect on wage differentials within the advanced industrialised countries.

Demand-Side Theories of Trade

One major assumption on which the HO theory rests is that consumer preferences are identical among countries. What if we relax this assumption? We have already noted that, even with this assumption, demand conditions might still differ if the levels of per capita income are different in the countries in question. However, the assumption is too restrictive anyhow. Preferences clearly do vary among countries, although whether or not they differ sufficiently to materially affect the pattern of trade is less clear. If tastes differ between countries, it is not too difficult to show that a basis for trade can exist even between countries with identical factor endowments. This is because relative product prices will be different in the absence of trade. Figure 2.10 illustrates the case of two countries, A and B, each of which possesses identical factor endowments but different tastes, engaging in trade.

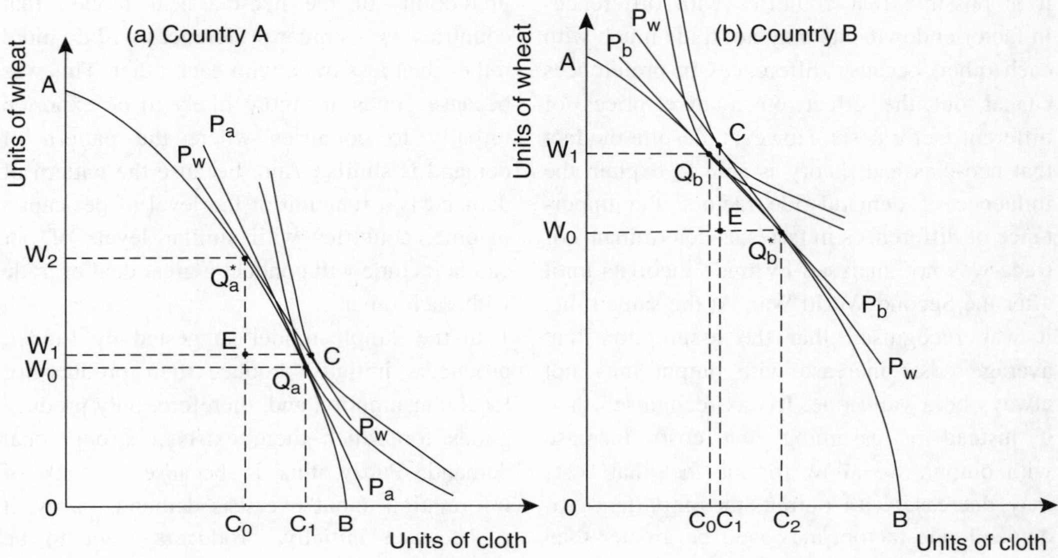

Figure 2.10 Trade between two countries with identical factor endowments but different tastes

Both countries have the same transformation curve, AB. However, the indifference curve map for each country differs. Consumers in Country A have a stronger preference for cloth, while consumers in Country B have a stronger preference for wheat. Pre-trade equilibrium in Country A exists at Q_a and prices are represented by the relative prices line P_aP_a. Pre-trade equilibrium in Country B occurs at Q_b and prices are represented by the relative prices line P_bP_b. Note that the price of cloth is evidently higher in A than in B because the demand for cloth is relatively stronger in A. However, the price of wheat is higher in B because the demand for wheat is relatively stronger in B. As a result of these differences in prices, a basis exists for trade between the two countries despite the fact that they have identical factor endowments. Each country will specialise in the good for which prices are lower than in the other country. Thus A will specialise in wheat and B in cloth. Let us see how this happens. Trade establishes a new set of prices at P_wP_w which lies between the pre-trade prices ratios. A moves up her transformation curve to Q_a^*, producing more wheat and less cloth. B moves down her transformation curve to Q_b^* where it produces more cloth and less wheat than before.

Now what happens when they trade? At the new set of prices, A can exchange wheat for cloth and reach a higher indifference curve. By exchanging W_1W_2 for EC, A can reach point C which lies on a higher indifference curve than was attainable without trade. Likewise, B can exchange C_1C_2 cloth for EC wheat and reach point C on a higher indifference curve. Thus, trade benefits both countries. It follows that neo-classical trade theory can be readily modified to introduce demand-side factors as a determinant of trade. This would suggest that countries with similar factor endowments may, indeed, do much trade with each other, if there exist large differences in preferences. Equally, it is possible that countries with differences in factor endowments may not trade much with each other, because differences in preferences cancel out the effect on relative prices of different factor costs. However, despite the fact that neo-classical theory is able to explain the influence of demand-side factors, the importance of differences in tastes as determinants of trade was not analysed by trade theorists until after the Second World War. At the same time, it was recognised that the assumption that average costs increase with output may not always be a valid one. It was recognised that, if instead of assuming that costs increase with output, we allow for the fact that costs may decrease with output, the importance of demand-side factors may well be greater than was often assumed.

In this regard, a major contribution to our understanding of how demand-side factors can influence trade was made by the Swedish economist, Staffan Linder, writing in 1961 (Linder, 1961). Linder argued that, while factor endowments play the major role in determining patterns of trade in primary commodities, consumer preferences are the more important for trade in manufactures. One reason for playing down the role of factor proportions in manufacturing trade is the observation that much trade in manufactures seems to take place among countries with similar factor endowments. More precisely, Linder argued that it is the structure of demand that determines the pattern of trade, that is to say, the proportion of average income which households spend on different products. This was seen by Linder to be, primarily, a function of the level of a country's per capita income. The higher per capita income, the greater the demand for high-quality or sophisticated manufactures. Conversely, demand in low per capita incomes is skewed towards low-quality or unsophisticated goods. Now, Linder argued, contrary to the predictions of the neo-classical model, that countries with similar preferences will do more rather than less trade with each other. This was because goods are more likely to be exported initially to countries where the pattern of demand is similar. And, because the pattern of demand is a function of the level of per capita income, countries with similar levels of per capita income will conduct a great deal of trade with each other.

In the simple model suggested by Linder, producers initially produce their product for local consumption and, therefore, only produce goods for which there exists a strong local demand. Partly, this is because of lack of information about overseas demand. Partly, it is because, initially, producers want to be close to the consumer in order to identify any adaptations to the product considered necessary in the light of buyer feedback. Eventually, however, the domestic market becomes satiated and producers are compelled to seek new outlets for the product abroad. At this point, exporting takes place. To which countries is the product first exported? A key consideration is the existence of a similar structure of demand. This will exist in countries that have a similar level of per capita income. To illustrate this, Linder introduced the notion of *overlapping demand*, which may be defined as products of a certain quality or degree of sophistication, for which there exists a common demand in both of the countries engaging in trade. Figure 2.11 illustrates the notion of overlapping demand.

The vertical axis measures some imaginary index of quality or product sophistication. Products of high quality appear further up the vertical axis, while products of low quality appear further down. The horizontal axis measures per capita income. The ray, OR, shows that the higher the per capita income of a country, the more sophisticated the type of

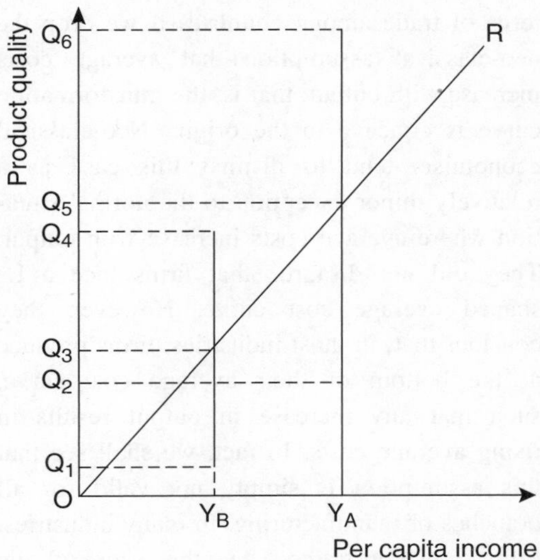

Figure 2.11 The influence of product quality and per capita income on the pattern of trade

product bought by the average income earner. Country A has a high per capita income, Y_A. At this level of income, income earners prefer the variety Q_5. Country B has a low per capita income, Y_B. At this level of income, income earners prefer the variety Q_3. However, within each country, household incomes will vary around the average. This means that there will exist a demand for a variety of products having different quality indices. The spread of demand will be determined by the spread of incomes above and below the average. In Country A, a demand exists only for products within the range Q_2 to Q_6. In Country B, a demand exists for products within the range Q_1 to Q_4. However, both countries have a common demand for products within the range Q_2 to Q_4. This is what Linder called overlapping demand. The closer the level of average income in the two countries, the greater the extent of overlapping demand. What follows is that producers of products within the range of overlapping demand will be able to export their product to the other country. Trade will, therefore, take place in products within this range. It follows that, since countries with similar per capita incomes will enjoy more overlapping demand than countries with very different levels of per capita income, trade will be greatest between countries with similar levels of per capita income.

This accords with what we know to be the case in reality. A large amount of trade in manufactured goods occurs among developed countries with similar factor endowments and similar levels of per capita income. We also know that much of this trade involves exchanging different varieties of the same product, an issue which is addressed more fully in Chapter 3. As Linder explained, other factors will also affect the directional flow of trade. Since culture exerts a strong influence on consumer preferences, trade might tend to be greatest among countries sharing a similar culture. Distance raises the cost of trade so that countries are more likely to trade with other countries in close geographical proximity. Furthermore, where countries are separated by a long distance, producers are more likely to be ignorant of market opportunities in the foreign market. In its simple form, however, Linder's theory of overlapping demand falls short of being a theory of trade. This is because, unlike the Heckscher–Ohlin model, it cannot tell us what products a country will export and what products it will import when trade takes place. In other words, it cannot account for the actual pattern of trade that occurs among countries. This also makes it very difficult to test, as there is no simple prediction against which we can compare the facts. Such attempts as have been made to test the model have focused on the prediction that countries with similar levels of per capita income will do more trade with each other than countries with different levels of per capita income. Early attempts to verify the hypothesis were largely unsuccessful (Ellis, 1983; Kohlhagen, 1977). However, the models used in these studies have been criticised as being wrongly formulated and for using poorly defined variables giving rise to a prejudiced outcome (Hoftyzer, 1984; Greytack and Tuchinda, 1990). An attempt to test the hypothesis using a better specified model applied to trade among forty-eight continguous states within the United States found some positive support (Greytack and Tuchinda, 1990).

On the positive side, however, it is clear that the Linder hypothesis is saying something important about the determinants of trade in manufactures. Countries with similar factor endowments may do a great deal of trade with each other, especially if they have similar levels of per capita income. Moreover, this trade will tend to take the form of an exchange of products with similar factor-intensities and which differ very little in substance from each other. If we observe much of the trade that takes place among advanced industrialised countries in manufactured goods, it is clear that it is of this kind. These countries often exchange very similar products, in some cases different models or varieties of the same product. The factor-intensities of these products are often very similar. Moreover, countries with similar factor endowments and similar levels of per capita do engage in a great deal of trade with each other. All of this is the exact opposite of the kind of trade predicted by the neo-classical model. This predicts that only countries with very different factor endowments will trade with each other and these will tend to be countries with different levels of per capita income.

Economies of Scale

We may get a great deal closer to understanding how demand-side factors may influence patterns of trade among countries if we drop the neo-classical assumption that average costs increase with output, that is, the transformation curve is concave to the origin. Neo-classical economists tend to dismiss this case as a relatively minor exception to the normal situation where average costs increase with output. They did not disagree that firms face a U-shaped average cost curve. However, they consider that, in most industries, firms produce at the bottom of their average cost curve, such that any increase in output results in rising average costs. In fact, we shall see that this assumption is simply not valid for all branches of manufacturing. In many industries, firms are constrained by the size of the domestic market from achieving the optimum level of output. However, neo-classical theory assumed that most markets were perfectly competitive. If average costs fall with output, large firms would soon succeed in eliminating small firms and markets would become concentrated in the hands of a small number of sellers. In certain cases, this could lead to the entire output of the industry falling into the hands of a single large seller.

However, the Neo-Classicists did recognise the importance of a second type of scale economy – namely, economies external to the firm or so-called *external economies of scale*. These arise whenever the expansion of a particular industry results in a downward shift in the average cost curves of 'all' producers within that industry. These are often associated with the concentration of an industry in a particular region or district. As many firms are attracted to the region, all firms enjoy certain benefits. Ancillary firms supplying important components and parts or vital services get drawn to the region. A pool of skilled labour is created from which all firms can draw. Banks and other financial institutions with a specialist knowledge of the

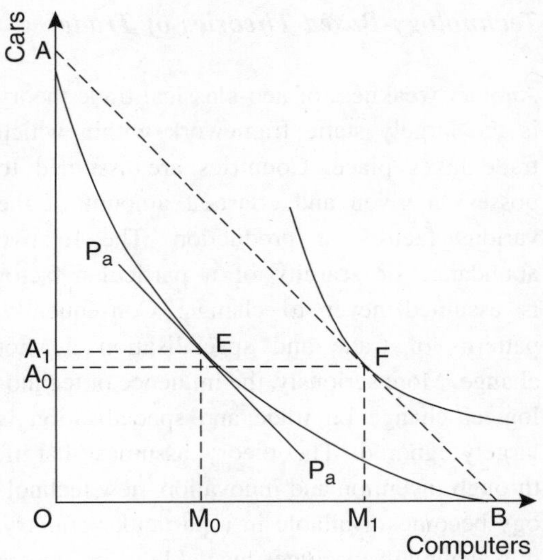

Figure 2.12 Trade under decreasing costs

industry and experience in lending to firms in the industry are set up. Universities and colleges provide courses of training for those working in the industry. As a consequence, as the industry expands, unit costs may well fall.

In this case, the transformation curve facing a particular country will be convex to the origin and not concave as in the case of increasing costs. This case is illustrated by Figure 2.12. We assume just two industries, cars and computers. The further down the transformation curve a country proceeds, the flatter the transformation curve becomes; that is to say, the fewer the units of one good (say, cars) that must be given up to get an extra unit of the other (computers). Pre-trade equilibrium occurs at point E where the price line, $P_a P_a$, is tangential to the transformation curve. However, the smallest disturbance to prices will set in motion a movement towards a new equilibrium that will take the country either all the way up or all the way down the transformation curve. Suppose it enters into trade with another country with identical factor endowments but different preferences. Suppose that preferences in the other country are slightly biased towards cars. Relative prices will, therefore, differ in the two countries and pre-trade equilibrium will occur at different points on AB. A basis will, therefore, exist for trade. Which product will each country specialise in? The answer is the product for which demand is greatest. Thus, if consumers in the foreign country have a stronger preference for cars, cars will be cheaper in that country. The reason is that average costs will be lower because costs fall with output. This is, surely, more realistic than the neo-classical prediction that countries will export the product for which there is little local demand.

However, as these countries enter into trade, a process is set in motion that leads each country all the way to complete specialisation in one product or the other. In Figure 2.12, the country is assumed to be selling computers more cheaply than its trading partner. However, trade enables this country to exchange computers for cars at a much better set of prices than in the absence of trade. In short, $P_a P_a$ becomes steeper. However, because price now exceeds the MRT at point E, the country will move down its curve towards B. As it does so, the MRT of producing computers falls, which means that it pays to continue expanding the output of computers and reducing the output of cars. Instead of moving towards a new equilibrium where the relative prices line is tangential to the transformation curve, it is clear that we are moving further away. The process will only stop when the country has reached B, at which point it can no longer expand output of computers any further by reducing output of cars. At this point, it has specialised completely in computers. Likewise, the other country will have specialised completely in cars. How may it gain from trade in this case? In the same way as under increasing costs, by exchanging its export product for units of the imported product at a more favourable set of prices than could have been obtained internationally. For example, if the terms of trade are given by AB (which is steeper than $P_a P_a$ but flatter than the pre-trade relative prices line for the trading partner), it could exchange M_1B computers for OA_0 ($=FM_1$) cars and consume at a point such as F which lies beyond its transformation curve and on a higher indifference curve than before trade.

Thus, the existence of decreasing costs (or increasing returns) can explain why countries specialise in particular products when they trade with countries with identical factor endowments. Preferences differ. At the same time, because costs fall with output, countries will enjoy a cost advantage in producing particular goods for which there exists a strong local demand. Hence, when they start trading with other countries, they tend to specialise in these goods. Moreover, trade is likely to lead to complete specialisation in these activities. The existence of external economies of scale leads also to the prediction that specialisation may be the result of some chance event which gives producers in one particular country a head start on producers in other countries. Because an industry happened to be established first in a particular country or region, producers were able to move further down their long-run average-cost curve. This meant that they enjoyed lower costs compared with producers in other countries who entered the industry much later. Then, when trade took place, producers in the country with lower average costs were able to knock out rivals in other countries. As a result, they moved to complete specialisation in the industry in question.

Technology-Based Theories of Trade

Another weakness of neo-classical trade theory is the largely static framework within which trade takes place. Countries are assumed to possess a given and constant amount of the various factors of production. The relative abundance or scarcity of a particular factor is assumed never to change. Consequently, patterns of trade and specialisation do not change. More seriously, the influence of technological change on trade and specialisation is largely ignored. The theory assumes that if, through invention and innovation, new technology becomes available in a particular country, this eventually becomes available to producers in other countries through the process of international diffusion. Hence, technological change cannot in the long run give any country a source of comparative advantage in a particular product or activity. These assumptions are clearly unsatisfactory. There is plenty of superficial evidence to show that technology and the process of its creation and diffusion internationally exerts a strong influence on patterns of trade. For example, for much of the early part of the post-war period, the United States enjoyed a comparative advantage in certain branches of manufacturing that were grounded in technological superiority. Other countries were not immediately able to imitate U.S. producers and thereby match U.S. production methods and costs. Eventually, much of this knowledge became available to other countries. Producers in other countries either bought the ideas from the original innovator or succeeded in copying the ideas once these ideas became universally known. At the same time, as U.S. companies set up subsidiaries or affiliates in other countries, many of the new ideas got transferred to other parts of the world. In some industries, as a result of this process, the US actually lost its original comparative advantage and became a net importer of the products in question.

Technology-Gap Trade

One of the first economists to address the issue of how technological change can influence patterns of trade was Michael Posner (Posner, 1961). In Posner's model, innovating countries may enjoy a temporary advantage in the manufacture of a particular product because of time lags in the diffusion of knowledge internationally. Posner clearly had in mind the United States as the country, which, at that time, enjoyed the most advantage from superior technology. Posner considered the case of where a U.S. manufacturer discovered a new and cheaper method of producing a particular product. The innovation gives the United States a temporary cost advantage in the production of those goods. United States' exports of the product accordingly increase. Because the knowledge about how to produce the product more cheaply is not immediately available to producers in other countries, the United States may enjoy technological superiority for a considerable period of time. Posner identified two kinds of time lags in the diffusion of knowledge. First, there is a *demand or reaction lag*, which is the time it takes for consumers to respond to the emergence of new, lower cost supplies of the product. The quicker they respond, the faster will U.S. exports of the product grow and the more producers in other countries will be forced to react to the competition posed by the innovation. Second, there is an *imitation lag*, which is the time it takes for foreign producers to imitate the innovating firm in the United States. This will depend partly on the extent to which the innovator is protected by patent law in his own and the foreign country. The occurrence of these lags gives rise to *technological gap trade*, so-called

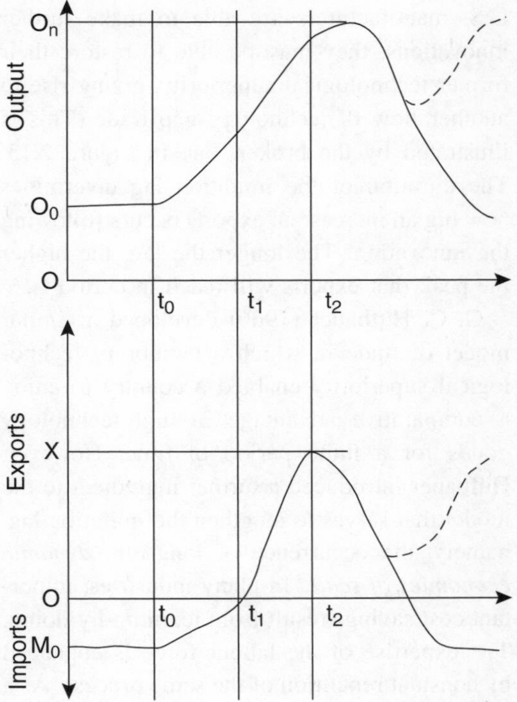

Figure 2.13 Technological-gap trade

because a temporary gap exists in the diffusion of technological knowledge to producers in other countries. Figure 2.13 illustrates the nature of such trade.

To begin with the United States is a net importer of the product in question. The discovery of a new method of producing the good occurs in period t_0. Production expands, imports decline and eventually the country becomes a net exporter of the product. The reaction or demand lag will determine how quickly exports expand in the period between t_0 and t_2 when the innovation is copied by other producers. Once the innovation has been copied, production falls in the US and exports decline. Eventually, they may disappear altogether and the innovating country may become a net importer of the goods. On the other hand, if

U.S. manufacturers are able to make further innovations, they may be able to restore their former technological superiority, giving rise to another flow of technology gap trade. This is illustrated by the broken line in Figure 2.13. The duration of the imitation lag determines how big an increase in exports occurs following the innovation. The longer the lag, the higher the peak that exports will reach in period t_2.

G. C. Hufbauer (1966) developed a similar model of trade in which a temporary technological superiority enabled a country to enjoy a comparative advantage in high-technology goods for a finite period of time. However, Hufbauer introduced a further ingredient to the model that serves to lengthen the imitation lag, namely, the occurrence of long-run, *dynamic economies of scale*. In many industries, important cost savings result from learning-by-doing. The expertise of the labour force is enhanced by constant repetition of the same process. As a result, average costs fall as the cumulative volume of output increases. Consequently, the innovator is able to hold on to his comparative advantage for much longer even after the new method of production has been copied by producers in other countries. Like Posner, Hufbauer attached importance to the factors that cause innovation to occur more in some countries than in others. Hufbauer advanced the hypothesis that technological advances are more likely to occur in high-wage economies because high wages create an incentive for both producers and consumers to find ways of economising on labour. Producers must seek out ways of introducing labour-saving techniques of production, while high wages increase the opportunity cost of leisure for households and generate a demand for goods that save time (e.g. washing machines, spin dryers, vacuum cleaners, microwaves, etc). This leads to the prediction that technology-gap exports will tend to flow from high-wage to low-wage economies. In his article, Hufbauer provided some empirical support for the technology gap hypothesis for trade using the example of synthetic materials.

The Product Life-Cycle Model of Trade

A similar, but nevertheless different, approach to the analysis of trade patterns in the context of technological change was provided by Raymond Vernon (1966). Vernon was concerned with innovations, which give rise to new products. In industries where product innovation is important (e.g., pharmaceuticals), products have a limited market life. Their life span depends on the time that it takes for producers to develop a new and superior substitute. During their life span, products pass through various phases giving rise to the notion of the *product life cycle*. Vernon distinguished three distinct phases:

1. *The New Product Stage*. During this phase, all production is located in the innovating country for several different reasons. First, most (if not all) production will be for the home market. Exports will begin to take place but will initially be subordinate to domestic sales. Second, the manufacturer will seek to be as close to the consumer as possible to receive any feedback about the product and to make any alterations or adaptations to the product as may be considered necessary. Third, during the early years in the life of the product, the demand for the product is price-inelastic reflecting the fact that the innovator faces little or no competition. Patent laws will protect the innovator from his product being copied or replicated by rivals. This means that the higher costs involved in locating production in the home country can be passed on in price to the consumer.

2. *The Maturing Product Stage*. By the time the product has reached maturity, the degree of competition facing the innovating firm both at home and abroad will have increased. Patents will have expired and the product copied by producers in other countries. Demand will be more price-elastic meaning that the producer must find ways of holding down costs. At the same time, a higher proportion of output will now be exported to expanding markets abroad, mainly in other developed countries. Consequently, the innovating firm finds it profitable to set up factories abroad to service the foreign market, thereby eliminating transport costs and getting behind any tariff or non-tariff barriers erected in the importing country. As a result, exports of the product from the innovating country begin to taper off and even fall.
3. *The Standardisation Stage*. By the time the product has reached standardisation, the demand curve for the product facing the individual firm will be highly price-elastic. That is to say, the product will sell largely on the basis of price and the degree of price competition will be intense. This places a premium on producers seeking out the lowest cost location for producing the product. Low wage costs in developing countries favour shifting most production to these countries. As a result, production in the innovating country and other industrialised countries begins to fall. Exports from the innovating country decline and imports increase until, eventually, the innovating country becomes a net importer of the product.

Figure 2.14 illustrates this process.

Like Posner and Hufbauer, Vernon predicted that most product innovations will occur in high-wage economies. High wage rates encourage producers to develop products which save

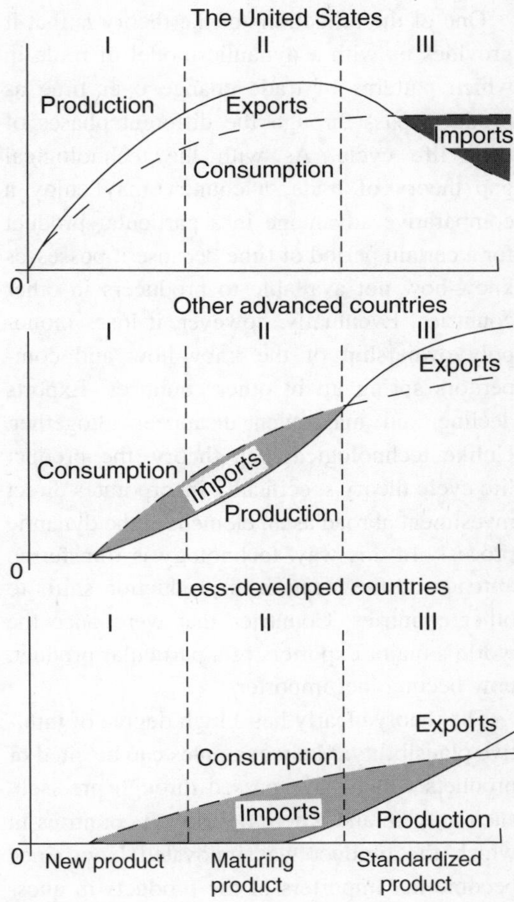

Figure 2.14 The product life-cycle model of trade
Source: Vernon (1981)

on labour time. At the same time, the large market that exists in these countries for sophisticated products and the rapid growth in demand for new products creates an environment highly conducive to product innovation. The existence of a larger pool of qualified scientists and engineers will also favour innovation occurring there. One conclusion which follows from the theory is that high-wage economies will tend to be net exporters of new products, while developing countries will specialise more in known products.

One of the attractions of the theory is that it provides us with a dynamic model of trade in which patterns of trade change over time as products pass through the different phases of their life cycle. As with the technological gap theory of trade, a country may enjoy a comparative advantage in a particular product for a certain period of time because it possesses know-how not available to producers in other countries. Eventually, however, it loses monopoly ownership of the know-how and competitors spring up in other countries. Exports decline and may even disappear altogether. Unlike technological gap theory, the product life cycle theory specifically incorporates direct investment abroad as an element in the dynamic process. In this way, technology is transferred abroad and the location of production shifts to other countries. Countries that were once the world's major exporters of a particular product, now become net importers.

The theory clearly has a high degree of intuitive plausibility. Many examples can be cited of products which have passed through precisely such a cycle and where developed countries in which the product was innovated have since become net importers of the products in question (washing machines, radios, TVs, etc.). One of the most often cited examples of the product life cycle is the case of the semi-conductor industry. Semi-conductors or transistors were first invented in the United States but over the 1950s and 1960s production spread to Western Europe and Japan. Faced with increased competition from producers in other developed countries, U.S. manufacturers began to shift production to new locations in the developing world. Then the South-East Asian economies became major producers of semiconductors. In some industries, products pass through a series of product life cycles. High-wage economies may first lose and then regain the comparative advantage in a particular product as a new wave of innovation restores their former technological superiority. Thus, the development of the silicon chip did much to re-establish U.S. leadership in semiconductors, before once again the technological advantage passed to manufacturers in the developing world. There is also some evidence for this in the case of TVs first as monochrome TV sets were replaced with colour TVs and now as high-definition TV (HDTV) restores the advantage to producers in the developed countries.

However, the theory is open to some obvious criticisms:

1. First, it best describes the world as it was in the 1960s rather than as it is today. In the 1960s, most new products were first launched in the U.S. market before being exported to other advanced industrialised countries. Subsequently, exports were displaced by local production as U.S. multinationals set up subsidiaries in Western Europe and other developed countries. Nowadays, new products are as likely to originate in Western Europe or Japan as in the US. This opens up the possibility of much two-way trade between developed countries in high-technology goods.
2. Second, most of the largest companies in the world are already multinationals with subsidiaries in all the major regions of the world. This means that when a new product is discovered it is more or less immediately sold through the various overseas subsidiaries of the company in all the major regions of the world. As most large companies already have a global presence, the production of a new product can from its inception be planned on a global basis.
3. Third, the fact that many large multinational companies already have assembly plants in the developing world means that it is possible to shift the final stages in the pro-

duction of many goods to the developing world at a much earlier stage. At the same time, the production of components and parts may be concentrated in large specialist plants in the developed world. This kind of global rationalisation of production is discussed further in Chapter 5.

4. Fourth, where the rate of product innovation is rapid, products may never reach the standardisation or even maturity phase. Improvements to the product may mean that the technological lead remains with the innovating country for an indefinite period of time.
5. Last, the theory may be criticised for the emphasis that it places on the need to conserve labour as the primary incentive for innovation. While labour-saving may have been the major incentive to innovate in the United States, the need to conserve energy and to reduce dependence on imported raw materials have at times been the more important spur to innovation in Western Europe and Japan. The need to develop new ways of producing goods which impose lower pollution costs or satisfy consumer demand for environmentally friendly goods may serve as a further incentive to innovate. It follows that technology gap trade need not originate only in high-wage economies as technology-based theories tend to assume although environmental factors may still favour innovation taking place in the most developed countries of the world.

In 1974, Vernon modified the Product Life Cycle model to give greater emphasis to the oligopolistic behaviour of firms (Vernon, 1974). In the later version, he distinguished three, slightly different phases through which products pass–*innovation-based oligopoly, mature oligopoly* and *senescent oligopoly.* Because of the existence of scale economies creating barriers for entry to new firms, technology-intensive industries are often dominated by a small number of large firms. Such firms behave in the manner described in oligopolistic theories of the firm. However, this is affected by the particular phase in the life of the product at which the firms are selling. In the innovation phase, production is located mainly in the innovating country. However, in this newer version of the theory, innovations are no longer confined to the US, but may occur in Europe or other advanced industrialised countries and in response to a variety of different factors (e.g. scarcity of land and natural resources in Europe). In the maturity phase, however, the locational decisions of firms are based more upon the actions and reactions of their rivals. However, because of the uncertainty that tends to characterise oligopolistic markets, the strategies of each firm are motivated by the desire not to allow rivals to gain an advantage. For this reason, Vernon argues, firms tend to follow each other into particular foreign markets in order not to be caught out. This may lead to a concentration or 'clustering' of production in particular markets. In the final stages of senescent oligopoly, entry barriers become weaker and competitive pressures become greater. Decisions about where to locate production become more influenced by cost considerations than oligopolistic reactions.

The Case of Monopoly

Earlier we said that neo-classical trade theory considered the case of decreasing unit costs to be a rare exception. Although external economies of scale may result from the expansion of an industry particularly if it is concentrated in a certain region, internal scale economies were considered to be unimportant. Such cost reductions as did occur could be achieved at a modest level of output, such that most firms were able to reach the lowest point on their long-run average cost curve. What if this is not true? What if firms in a particular industry face falling average costs over a substantial range of output? We shall explore this issue in more depth in the next chapter. However, for the time being, it is important to take note of the possible consequences. If average costs 'go on' falling with output, then the industry will become dominated by a single seller or monopolist. This gives rise to, what the neo-classical economists regarded as an exception, the case of 'natural monopoly'.

How will the existence of a monopoly in one or more countries affect trade? Every student of Economics knows that a profit-maximising monopolist will produce where marginal costs equal marginal revenue because, at this level of output, any increase in output will add as much to costs as to revenue. However, unlike the perfectly competitive firm, marginal revenue does not equal price. This is because the production of more units of the good drives down the price such that marginal revenue is always less than price. Under perfect competition, an individual seller is too small for his output to affect the price, so price is constant in which case marginal revenue equals price. We can summarise as follows. Under perfect competition, $P = MC$; under monopoly $P > MC$. The extent to which P exceeds MC is a measure of the degree of monopoly power enjoyed by the seller.

Now, if a monopolist is exposed through trade to competition from producers in other countries, then he will become like a perfectly competitive firm. He ceases to be a monopoly and as a result his demand curve becomes flatter (i.e. more elastic). His demand curve (and hence his MR curve) will also move inwards to the left. Profits will now be maximised at a lower level of output. Price also falls. Gradually, the monopolist's excess profits are competed away until eventually price is sufficient only to cover average costs. As demand becomes more elastic, price moves closer to marginal costs. Eventually, a point is reached where $P = MC$ as under perfect competition. Indeed, the effect of trade is to transform the market from a monopoly into one of perfect competition. In such industries, trade plays a benign role in bringing down prices to consumers and eliminating the excess profits of the monopolist. At the same time, by exposing the monopolist to increased competition, trade forces the monopolist to seek out ways of lowering costs by making efficiency gains. Consumers will enjoy further gains so long as these savings are passed on in a lower price.

However, what happens if the monopolist remains protected from foreign competition by import barriers? In other words, he remains a monopolist at home, but faces competition should he wish to sell some of his output abroad. In effect, this means that the monopolist faces two demand curves–a downward-sloping demand curve on the domestic market where there is no competition but a horizontal demand curve on the world market where there are many sellers. Figure 2.15 illustrates this case. If he wishes to maximise his profits, he needs to produce at a point where MC equals MR for both export and domestic sales. This is achieved if he produces output OB where marginal costs equal BE. Then, if he sells OA on the domestic market and AB on the world market, he will have equalised MC and MR in both markets. (This is because his marginal costs are the same regardless of where he sells the product, but marginal revenue differs in the two markets.) However, prices are different in the two markets. The quantity OA will sell on the domestic market at the price OP_1, but the quantity AB that is exported will be sold at the world price of OP_w. The logic behind this is that the existence of a downward-sloping demand

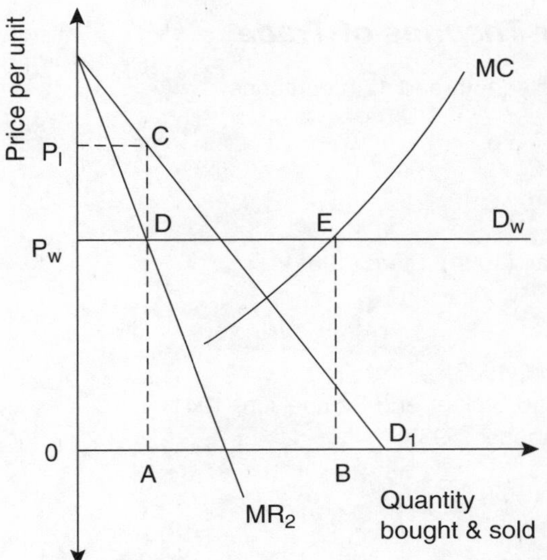

Figure 2.15 Export policy under monopoly

curve at home means that it pays to restrict domestic sales. If all his output were sold domestically, the price would be driven down on every unit sold. By restricting domestic sales, he can maintain a high domestic price. However, sales abroad have no effect on the world price so that he can he sell as much as he likes.

The charging of a lower price for the same product when exported than when sold domestically is known as *dumping*. Dumping is a common occurrence in industries where the domestic market is monopolised by a single seller. It is also widely considered to be unfair competition. As a consequence, the likely outcome is that importing countries will retaliate against any foreign producer engaging in such a strategy. Many countries have anti-dumping laws that provide for the imposition of anti-dumping duties on any foreign producer found to be dumping if dumping causes injury to domestic producers. International trade law requires that the rate of duty should not exceed the difference between the two prices, the so-called margin of dumping. If this happens, the monopolist will not be able to dump the produce in this way. Indeed, it is not uncommon for the importing country to persuade the monopolist to raise his export prices as an alternative to duties being imposed. In fact, it is by no means obvious why such dumping *per se* should be regarded as damaging. The losers would appear to be consumers in the exporting country who pay more for the product than consumers in the foreign market! Nor is it true that the monopolist is undercutting producers in other markets, although he may seek to do so. For example, he could use some of the excess profits earned domestically to sell products abroad at a price below OP_w. One reason for doing so might be a desire to drive out foreign competitors. Then, having gained control of the foreign market, he could raise prices above OP_w and act like a monopolist in the foreign market. Such so-called predatory pricing is not uncommon and is clearly harmful if it results in less competition. However, for such a strategy to work, the monopolist must be sure of success. Otherwise, he will quickly use up the profits earned on domestic sales and soon find that instead he is making losses.

Conclusion

This chapter has explained the main theoretical explanations put forward by economists for how and why countries trade with each other and the factors that determine the products in which they will specialise and trade. Box 2.3 summarises the major theories discussed in this chapter.

The chapter began with a discussion of the classical theory of trade with its emphasis on comparative advantage as the basis for trade. This identified differences in comparative costs as the basis for trade. These, in turn, were regarded as the result of differences in the

Box 2.3 A Summary of the Major Theories of Trade

Pre-Classical Theories of Trade – the Mercantilists (16th and 17th centuries)

Classical Theories of Trade
- Absolute Advantage (Adam Smith, 1776)
- Comparative Advantage (David Ricardo, 1816)
- Law of Reciprocal Demand (John Stuart Mill)
- Empirical Tests – MacDougall (1951), Bhagwati (1964), Stern (1962)

Neo-Classical Theories of Trade
- Offer Curves (Marshall, Edgeworth)
- Factor Proportions (Heckscher, 1919 and Ohlin, 1933)
- Factor Price Equalisation (Samuelson, 1948 and Stolper and Samuelson, 1941)
- General Equilibrium (Marshall, Edgeworth, Haberler, 1937)
- Empirical Tests – Leontieff (1954) and others

Post-Neo-Classical Theories of Trade
- Overlapping demand (Linder, 1961)
- Economies of Scale (Young, 1928)
- Technology-based theories (Posner, 1961, Hufbauer, 1966 and Vernon, 1966 and 1974)
- Monopoly (Viner, 1923 and Corden, 1974)

amount of labour-time required to produce these goods. Leaving to one side the problem of value, the classical theory of trade left unanswered the question of how and why such differences arise and, therefore, the basis for differences in comparative costs. It was left to the Neo-Classical school to provide an explanation. It did so in terms of differences in factor endowments among countries and differences in factor proportions required to produce different goods. However appealing this explanation is, it fails to gain the necessary support in empirical research. In particular, trade flows among advanced industrialised countries possessing broadly similar factor endowments appear to have little to do with differences in factor endowments.

Hence, the need to search for other explanations for specialisation and trade. One approach has been to explore the role of demand-side factors. Differences in consumer preferences appear to be especially important in explaining patterns of trade in manufactured goods. Linder's theory of overlapping demand shows that, where consumer preferences determine trade flows, trade is more likely to occur between countries with similar levels of per capita income. This is consistent with the observation that the fastest growth has occurred in trade between advanced industrialised countries, not between countries with different factor endowments. Another approach has been to examine the influence of technology on patterns of trade. Innovation clearly plays an important role in many branches of manufacturing. It is clear that the advantage enjoyed by certain countries in many high-technology industries is due largely to technology. Technology-based theories of trade help explain how comparative advantage can shift over time such that countries may lose an advantage that they once enjoyed and even become net importers of those products.

Although all these explanations are useful as explanations for why countries specialise in particular products, a common weakness is the assumption that production takes place under increasing or constant costs. The assumption conflicts with the reality observable in many branches of manufacturing that average costs typically fall over a wide range of output. If the possibility of decreasing costs is incorporated, some useful insights can be gained as to why countries have gained cost advantages in particular industries or even products. If preferences are not the same, producers in countries where there exists a strong preference for a particular good will enjoy a cost advantage over rivals abroad. The country will then become a net exporter of these goods due to considerations quite unrelated to differences in factor endowments or factor proportions. However, the relaxation of the assumption that costs increase with output has other implications. In particular, if firms can cut costs and hence prices simply by producing more, markets will become increasingly concentrated. The assumption that markets are perfectly competitive is as a consequence no longer tenable. As a result, much of the edifice on which neo-classical trade theory rests falls down. Although cases of where a single producer accounts for all of the domestic production of a good are rare, a small group of firms may behave like a monopolist by jointly restricting production and raise the price. Such cartels, however, are often illegal and firms which enter into such agreements risk prosecution. A more realistic situation, which we shall consider in the next chapter, is where a small number of firms dominate an industry yet act independently.

A further weakness of conventional models of trade is that they assume that the products that are traded internationally are homogeneous. Indeed, this assumption is necessary if the assumption that markets are perfectly competitive is to be upheld. However, it clearly conflicts with the reality that is apparent in many branches of manufacturing, particularly finished consumer goods. Products are not homogeneous but differentiated. As with the case of a monopoly, this means that firms are not passive price-takers, but face downward-sloping demand curves (although their demand curve is more elastic than under monopoly). As under monopoly, they can choose the price at which they will sell their products. This means that, in the short run, price will exceed marginal cost and firms will earn abnormal profits. In the long run, however, new entrants will be drawn into the industry and long-run profits will be competed away. As we shall see in the next chapter, this type of market may give rise to patterns of trade that are rather different to those predicted by more conventional models.

Notes for Further Reading

Most of the subject matter of this chapter is covered extensively by the large number of traditional International Economics/International Trade texts. The following have excellent sections on trade theories:

Winters, A. *International Economics*, 4th ed. (London: Harper Collins, 1991).

Brenton, P., Scott, H., Sinclair, P. *International Trade: A European Text* (Oxford: Oxford University Press, 1997).

Mikic, M. *International Trade* (Basingstoke and London: Macmillan, 1998).

Markusen, J., Melvin, J., Kaempfer, W., Maskus, K. *International Trade: Theory and Evidence* (New York: McGraw-Hill, 1995).

These books provide a more thorough and rigorous treatment of trade theory than has been possible in this chapter.

Chapter 3

Intra-Industry Trade and Specialisation

CHAPTER OUTLINES: Introduction. Definitions. Measurement – the Grubel–Lloyd index, the Balassa index, the Aquino formula, the Bergstrand method, the Glejser approach. The Aggregation Problem. The Level of Intra-Industry Trade. The Theory of Intra-Industry Trade – trade in functionally identical products, trade in differentiated commodities. The Determinants of Intra-Industry Trade: the Empirical Evidence – country differences, industry differences, vertical and horizontal intra-industry trade. Conclusion.

Introduction

In the theories of trade examined in the previous chapter, each country specialised in goods in which they enjoyed a comparative advantage and exchanged these products for those in which other countries enjoyed a comparative advantage. Normally, these were the products of different industries, for example, wheat and cloth. This is to be expected where trade is based on differences in comparative costs. If a country has a comparative advantage in one product, it is likely to enjoy a similar advantage in all the products belonging to that industry. Where countries exchange products belonging to different industries, this is called *inter-industry trade.* Likewise, the kind of specialisation giving rise to such trade is called *inter-industry specialisation.* However, much of the trade which takes place in the world is of an entirely different kind. Countries exchange products which belong to the same industry. This suggests that countries engage in a narrower form of specialisation, specialising in particular products within a given industry and exchanging these products for other products belonging to the same industry. As a consequence, their exports and imports of products belonging to the same industry increase simultaneously. Such trade is known as *intra-industry trade* and the kind of specialisation leading to such trade is called *intra-industry specialisation.*

This distinction is an important one for two reasons. First, it suggests that conventional trade theories are deficient in some respects. Why do countries simultaneously export and import the products of the same industry? An explanation cannot be found within the framework of classical or neo-classical trade theory. The latter predicts only inter-industry specialisation and trade. However, as we saw towards the end of the last chapter, a weakness of conventional trade theory is that it assumes markets are perfectly competitive. What if they are not? Two aspects of perfect competition are important in this regard: the assumption that there are many sellers of a product each of whom is a price-taker and the assumption that the product of any one seller is identical in the eyes of the consumer to that of another. If these assumptions are dropped, it will be seen that trade between countries with similar factor endowments is more likely to take the form of intra- than inter-industry trade. This conclusion is also reinforced if we drop the assumption that costs increase with output.

Second, where countries engage in intra- as opposed to inter-industry specialisation, the expansion of trade has different consequences. In the previous chapter, we saw that the main gain from increased inter-industry specialisation was higher real incomes. Countries were able to consume a greater bundle of the two goods after than before trade. More precisely, the country as a whole was able to move to a higher indifference curve. We shall see that, although intra-industry specialisation may equally bring lower prices and hence higher real incomes, the gains from such trade come more in the form of an increase in the number of varieties of goods from which to choose. However, increased trade also has different consequences for producers. Under inter-industry specialisation, each country experiences a decline of some industries matched by an expansion of others. Under intra-industry specialisation, all that happens is that producers change the range of products which they produce, concentrating on only certain types while importing the others. One result of this is that the adjustment pressures caused by the expansion of trade are likely to be less where intra- rather than inter-industry specialisation takes place.

In this chapter, the first of these two issues is examined in depth. Later chapters discuss the consequences for exporting and importing countries where specialisation is of the intra-industry type. The chapter will begin by considering more closely the distinction between inter- and intra-industry trade. This is followed by a survey of the different measures proposed for measuring the extent of a country's intra-industry trade and of some of the problems involved in doing so. Some of the formulae are then applied to see how important intra-industry trade is as a component of the trade of different countries and for different industries. We, then, turn to a discussion of the theory of intra-industry trade. Why does intra-industry trade take place? A distinction is drawn between trade in identical or homogeneous goods belonging to the same industry and trade in differentiated or heterogeneous goods. The predictions of theory are then contrasted with the results of empirical research into the determinants of intra-industry trade.

Definitions

We begin with some definitions. Intra-industry trade is the simultaneous export and import of products belonging to the same industry. Inter-industry trade is the exchange of products which belong to different industries. *Intra-industry specialisation* is the specialisation of a country in a narrow range of products within a given industry. *Inter-industry specialisation* involves a country specialising in an entire industry or activity. Inter-industry specialisation leads to inter-industry trade and intra-industry specialisation to intra-industry trade. However, it is possible for intra-industry trade to take place between two countries without either country undergoing intra-industry specialisation. Some of the reasons for this are given below. Therefore, not all of the increase in intra-industry trade in recent decades is attributable to intra-industry specialisation. However, it is true that most intra-industry trade results from intra-industry specialisation. Hence, thoughout this book, the terms are used interchangeably.

If intra-industry trade is the export and import of products belonging to the same industry, the question arises as to what constitutes an industry. Does the term 'industry' have any economic meaning? If it does not, the distinction between inter- and intra-industry trade is largely meaningless. Clearly, economists do mean something specific by an 'industry' but they do not always mean the same thing! Three different criteria are frequently used to group products together as belonging to the same industry:

1. *Substitution in production*, which means that each product is produced with roughly similar proportions of inputs or factors even though their end-use may be different (e.g. automobiles and tractors)
2. *Substitution in consumption*, which means that each product has broadly similar uses such that consumers could readily substitute one for the other in use even though they were made using different proportions of inputs (e.g. rubber-sole and leather-sole footwear)
3. *Identical technology intensity*, which means that products are grouped together because the technology employed in their manufacture was roughly the same.

Clearly, each of these criteria will result in a different classification of products. Products, which have high substitution in consumption (e.g. leather and rubber-sole footwear), may have a low or non-existent substitution in production. One must therefore choose which criteria are to be adopted. To some extent, this will depend on the purpose for which data are required. Thus, if the concern is to test the predictive powers of the Heckscher–Ohlin model of trade, substitution in production is clearly the most suited. On the other hand, if we wish to evaluate the role of differences in consumer preferences in determining patterns of trade, substitution in consumption will be the preferred choice. However, there is some evidence to show that technology intensities best explain actual trade flows in which case the last criteria may be the most appropriate.

As there is no consensus on how products should be classified as industries, the concept of intra-industry trade necessarily suffers from a degree of ambivalence. It may therefore be difficult to distinguish some inter- from some intra-industry trade. Some trade flows might have to be categorised as hybrids of both inter- and intra-industry trade (Dunning and Norman, 1985). Moreover, as we shall see below, the problem is compounded by the fact that published trade statistics employ methods of classification based more on statistical convenience than economic logic. Attempts therefore to accurately measure intra-industry trade are thwart with hazards.

Measurement

Leaving aside these conceptual problems of definition for the moment, how is intra-industry trade measured? Various alternative formulae have been proposed by different economists. The following section considers five alternatives.

The Grubel–Lloyd Index

Grubel and Lloyd were among the first economists to measure the extent of intra-industry trade (Grubel and Lloyd, 1975). They measured intra-industry trade as the percentage of a country's total trade (exports plus imports) which was matched or balanced, that is exports equal imports. For an individual product group or industry i, the formula is:

$$B_i = \frac{(X_i + M_i) - |X_i - M_i|}{(X_i + M_i)} \times 100 \qquad (1)$$

where X_i and M_i stand, respectively, for the exports and imports of product group i. The straight brackets around the expression $X_i - M_i$ denotes that the sign of the trade balance is ignored. If all trade was balanced, B_i would equal 100. If all trade was one-way, B_i would equal zero. Thus, the closer B_i is to 100, the greater the importance of intra-industry trade. The closer B_i is to zero, the greater the importance of inter-industry trade. For convenience, the simple G–L formula above may be rewritten as follows:

$$B_i = \left\{1 - \frac{|X_i - M_i|}{(X_i + M_i)}\right\} \times 100 \tag{2}$$

To obtain the average level of intra-industry trade for a country, Grubel and Lloyd proposed calculating a weighted mean, using the relative size of exports and imports of a particular product group as weights. The formula is as follows:

$$B_j = \frac{\sum B_i(X_i + M_i)}{E(X_i + M_i)} \times 100 \tag{3}$$

The Σ sign is the Greek capital letter 'sigma' and is used to denote 'the sum of'. It means that we must add together all the terms like the one following, that is, all the B_is weighted by total trade (exports plus imports) of that product group. The j means that the formula is for the jth country and the i means the ith of n industries. For convenience the Grubel and Lloyd summary measure may be written in one of two ways:

$$B_j = \frac{\sum(X_i + M_i) - \sum|X_i - M_i|}{\sum(X_i + M_i)} \times 100 \tag{4}$$

or

$$B_j = \left\{1 - \frac{\sum|X_i - M_i|}{\sum(X_i + M_i)}\right\} \times 100 \tag{5}$$

for n set of industries.

Table 3.1 sets out a simple example of how the Grubel and Lloyd summary formula may be used to obtain a measure of a country's average level of intra-industry trade.

There are assumed to be just five industries–A, B, C, D and E. B_i is calculated for each. The average level of intra-industry trade, B_j, is obtained using the above formula and comes to 64%. To have taken the average of all the B_is would have given a misleading average because

Table 3.1 An Example of How to Calculate Intra-Industry Trade Using the Grubel and Lloyd Indices

Product groups	X_i	M_i	$[X_i - M_i]$	B_i
A	40	30	10	86
B	80	40	40	67
C	10	60	50	29
D	70	70	0	100
E	200	60	140	46
Σ	400	260	240	

$$B_j = \frac{(660 - 240)}{660} \times 100 = \frac{420}{660} \times 100 = 64$$

$$C_j = \frac{(660 - 240)}{(660 - 140)} \times 100 = \frac{420}{520} \times 100 = 81$$

the importance of some products is clearly greater than others. The Grubel and Lloyd formula is a weighted mean.

One problem with B_j is that it makes no allowance for any imbalance in a country's total trade. When a country has a large trade imbalance (surplus or deficit), B_j will be biased downwards and the true extent of intra-industry trade will accordingly be underestimated. To tackle this problem, Grubel and Lloyd proposed an alternative formula, which adjusts for any trade imbalance:

$$C_j = \frac{\sum(X_i + M_i) - \sum|X_i - M_i|}{\sum(X_i + M_i) - |\sum X_i - \sum M_i|} \times 100 \qquad (6)$$

Compare (6) with (4). It can be seen that the denominator in (4) has been reduced by the amount of country j's overall trade imbalance. Accordingly, the greater a country's trade imbalance, the greater the difference between C_j and B_j. Clearly, whenever a country's total trade is unbalanced, C_j is the preferred formula. This can be seen from Table 3.1. The C_j formula gives a mean level of intra-industry trade of 81% compared with 64% for the B_j formula.

The Balassa Index

In estimating the extent of intra-industry specialisation in the European Community, Bela Balassa adopted an alternative formula (Balassa, 1974). He measured intra-industry trade by taking the sum of the ratios of trade balance (exports less imports) to total trade (exports plus imports) for each product group and then dividing by the number of product groups:

$$E_j = \frac{1}{n}\sum\frac{|X_i - M_i|}{(X_i + M_i)} \qquad (7)$$

Here j stands for country j and i for product group i out of n industries. In the Balassa formula, E_j tends towards zero when all trade is intra-industry trade and towards one when all trade is inter-industry trade. Thus, Balassa took a fall in E_j as evidence for intra-industry specialisation.

The Aquino Formula

Aquino criticised the Grubel and Lloyd formula for failing to fully correct for an imbalance in a country's overall trade (Aquino, 1978). He argued that, as a result, Grubel and Lloyd underestimated the true extent of intra-industry specialisation. His argument is that C_j is itself a weighted average of the individual product group ratios, B_i. However, these are also downwardly biased whenever a country's total trade is unbalanced. Therefore, it is not enough to correct the summary formula B_j by the overall trade imbalance to obtain C_j. Each B_i needs to be adjusted for the trade imbalance, not just the summary formula, B_j.

The easiest way of understanding Aquino's argument is by means of an example. Consider Table 3.2.

Two hypothetical cases are shown. In both cases, the overall trade surplus is the same. The unadjusted Grubel and Lloyd formula, B_j, gives an average level of 66.7% in both cases. However, because of the imbalance in total trade, B_j gives a downwardly biased estimate of the true level of intra-industry trade. If, however, we apply the adjustment proposed by Grubel and Lloyd to obtain C_j, we obtain a level of 100% in both cases. However, while Aquino agrees that this is correct in the first case, he argues that it is incorrect in the second case. In the first case, all trade is clearly intra-industry trade as the ratio of exports-to-imports is the same for all product groups. Therefore, it is appropriate to adjust the average level of intra-industry trade by the size of the overall trade balance. However, in the second case, this is clearly not so. Rather,

Table 3.2 An Example of the Trade-Imbalance Distortion Effect of Using the Grubel and Lloyd Summary Intra-Industry Trade Index

	Case 1			Case 2		
Product group	X_i	M_i	$[X_i - M_i]$	X_i	M_i	$[X_i - M_i]$
Chemicals	20	10	10	10	10	0
Textiles	10	5	5	40	5	35
Machinery	40	20	20	20	20	0
$\sum$	70	35	35	70	35	35

$$B_j = \frac{105 - 35}{105} = 66.7 \qquad B_i = \frac{105 - 35}{105} = 66.7$$

$$C_j = \frac{105 - 35}{105 - 35} = 100 \qquad C_j = \frac{105 - 35}{105 - 35} = 100$$

there is a tendency towards specialisation in textiles relative to chemicals and machinery. Yet C_j is the same in the second as in the first case.

Therefore, Aquino proposed adjusting each B_i whenever a country's total trade is unbalanced and then estimating the overall average for the country using the adjusted B_i ratios. He proposed estimating hypothetical export and import values for each product group I on the assumption that total trade is balanced. The formulae for calculating these hypothetical export and import values are:

$$X_i^e = \frac{X_i \frac{1}{2} \sum (X_i + M_i)}{\sum X_i} \tag{8}$$

$$M_i^e = \frac{M_i \frac{1}{2} \sum (X_i + M_i)}{\sum M_i} \tag{9}$$

These hypothetical values may then be inserted into formula (4) to obtain a trade-imbalance-adjusted summary measure of intra-industry trade:

$$Q = \frac{\sum (X_i + M_i) - \sum |X_i^e - M_i^e|}{(X_i + M_i)} \times 100 \tag{10}$$

Table 3.3 gives an example of the Aquino method for adjusting for trade imbalance. The data used are those contained in Table 3.2.

Q_j equals 100% in the first case and 57% in the second case. In this particular example, the Aquino method gives a lower estimate of intra-industry trade than the Grubel and Lloyd formula. However, when a country's total trade is unbalanced, the Grubel and Lloyd formula may also underestimate the true extent of intra-industry trade.

Aquino's approach has been criticised on a number of grounds. First, it implicitly assumes that any trade imbalance is equi-proportionately spread across all industries. Thus, in Tables 3.2 and 3.3 it is assumed that the imbalance of $70/35 = 2/1$ is evenly spread across chemicals, machinery and textiles. The validity of this assumption is questionable. Thus, a country may have moved strongly into surplus on account of a uniquely good performance in just one of the three sectors (say, textiles in the second case). Is it then appropriate to apply accordingly an adjustment to the B_i ratios for the other sectors (chemicals and machinery)? Does this not create a new

Table 3.3 An Example of the Aquino Trade-Imbalance Adjusted Method of Measurement of Intra-Industry Trade

	Case 1			*Case 2*		
Product group	X_i^e	M_i^e	$X_i^e - M_i^e$	X_i^e	M_i^e	$X_i^e - M_i^e$
Chemicals	15.0	15.0	0	7.5	15.0	7.5
Textiles	7.5	7.5	0	30.0	7.5	22.5
Machinery	30.0	30.0	0	15.0	30.0	15.0
$\sum$			0			45.0

$$Q = \frac{105 - 0}{105} = 100 \qquad Q = \frac{105 - 45}{105} = 57.1$$

kind of distortion to the measurement of intra-industry trade? Second, it fails to allow for cyclical or other exceptional influences on a country's overall trade imbalance. The basis for the adjustment is the country's trade balance for the year in question, but this might not be a normal year. The trade balance is subject to cyclical fluctuations in the level of economic activity. Periods of upswing tend to correspond with a deterioration in the country's external balance. If the year in question is one such year, over-adjustment will result. However, it is not clear how this problem can be overcome. Ideally, we would have some estimate of a country's trade balance adjusted for cyclical influences, but this is rarely available.

The Bergstrand Method

A criticism of all of the above methods of measuring intra-industry trade is that they seek to measure intra-industry trade as a proportion of a country's total trade with all other countries, that is, the country's multilateral trade. Bergstrand (1983) has argued that, instead, intra-industry trade should be measured as a proportion of a country's bilateral trade, that is, the country's trade with each of its trading partners. For example, in measuring intra-industry trade in the European Community, intra-industry should be estimated in relation to each bilateral trade flow between every pair of member states. Practically, this may be complex and time-consuming. For example, with 15 member states in the EC, that would necessitate making 210 estimates of intra-industry trade. However, there surely exist strong theoretical grounds for preferring such an approach? In particular, if our concern is with the validity of the Heckscher–Ohlin theory of trade and its ability to predict trade flows between countries, the appropriate level for evaluating the theory is that of bilateral trade between any pair of countries. As Bergstrand argues

> …in a multi-country, multi-commodity, two-factor, factor price non-equalised world, the commodity version of the H–O theorem need not hold for a country's multilateral trade, but will hold for any pair of countries. The inability of this generalised commodity version of the H–O theorem to hold for multilateral trade suggests that the existence of multilateral IIT (intra-industry trade) is not unexpected; hence, the prominence of multilateral IIT is uninteresting. The holding of this H–O theorem's commodity

version for bilateral trade suggests that the presence of bilateral IIT is interesting (because this version of the theorem precludes it) (Bergstrand, 1983).

Thus, Bergstrand has proposed the adoption of a bilateral intra-industry trade index. The question arises as to how such an index should be corrected for trade imbalance in a country's overall trade. Should we take the imbalance in a country's multilateral trade or her trade with the partner in question? Bergstrand favoured the first of these alternatives. He proposed the following *bilateral* intra-industry trade index adjusted for each country's *multilateral* trade imbalance:

$$G_{ij}^{k*} = 1 - \left| \frac{|X_{ij}^{k*} - X_{ji}^{k*}|}{X_{ij}^{k*} + X_{ji}^{k*}} \right| \tag{11}$$

where

$$X_{ij}^{k*} = \frac{1}{2}\left| \frac{(X_i + M_i)}{2X_i} + \frac{(X_j + M_j)}{2M_j} \right| \times X_{ij}^{k} \tag{12}$$

$$X_{ji}^{k*} = \frac{1}{2}\left| \frac{(X_j + M_j)}{2X_j} + \frac{(X_i + M_i)}{2M_i} \right| \times X_{ji}^{k} \tag{13}$$

In this formula, X_{ij}^{k} refers to the value of bilateral exports from country i to country j (or bilateral imports of country j from country i) in industry k. Conversely, X_{ji}^{k} refers to the value of bilateral exports from country j to country i (or bilateral imports of country i from country j) in industry k. If country i's overall trade is balanced and $X_{ij} = X_{ji}$, all trade between country i and country j in industry k will be intra-industry trade and the intra-industry trade index for industry k, G_{ij}, will be equal to one. However, when country i's total (i.e. multilateral) trade is unbalanced, adjustment must be made. Equations (12) and (13) involve the calculation of hypothetical export and import values, X_{ij}^{*} and M_{ij}^{k*}, respectively, for each flow of bilateral trade in industry k between each pair of countries involved, utilising the adjustment formula proposed by Aquino. However, Bergstrand's method is subject to the same criticisms as Aquino's. It is, arguably, inappropriate to distribute the multilateral balancing proportionately between industries in the manner which Aquino and Bergstrand both do for the reason discussed above. The multilateral imbalance for any one particular year cannot be used as a measure of long-term disequilibrium in a country's overall trade since it is too strongly influenced by cyclical factors. On the other hand, Bergstrand is surely right in his insistence that intra-industry trade should be measured only in relation to the bilateral trade between any two trading partners.

The Glejser Approach

An important break with the conventional approach to the measurement of intra-industry trade was made by Glejser and applied to the measurement of intra-industry specialisation in the European Community (see Glejser, Goossens and Vanden Eade, 1979, 1982 and Glejser, 1983). Their concern was to compare changes in the degree of intra-industry specialisation in different countries over time. They were critical of the conventional approach (i.e. Grubel and Lloyd and Balassa) on several grounds. First, the conventional approach made no distinction between specialisation on the export (supply) side and specialisation on the import (demand) side, yet it is desirable to distinguish between them. Second, when changes in the degree of intra-industry specialisation over time are being measured, there is a need to statistically test for the significance of measured changes in a way that is not possible with a conventional formula.

The Glejser index for export (supply) specialisation at time period t is as follows:

$$\varepsilon_t = \frac{1}{n}\sum \log\left\{\frac{X_{ij}}{\sum X_{ij}} \bigg/ \frac{\sum X_j}{\sum X}\right\} = \frac{1\sum \varepsilon_{jt}}{n} \quad (14)$$

where

X_{ij} = exports of industry j by country i to a particular group of countries (e.g. the EC)

$\sum X_{ij}$ = total intra-area exports (across all industries) of country i

$\sum X_j$ = total intra-area exports of industry j, excluding country i

$\sum X$ = total intra-area exports by a particular group of countries (across all industries) excluding country i

The expression $X_{ij}/\sum X_{ij}$ therefore measures the share of industry j in country i's exports to the EC. The expression $X_j/\sum X$ measures the share of industry j in total intra-area imports excluding country I). So, dividing the former by the latter gives a measure of the strength of country i's export specialisation in product j within the EC. Basically, if it is more than one, country i could be said to have a degree of export specialisation in product j within the EC.

For import (demand) specialisation, the index is as follows:

$$\mu_t = \frac{1}{n}\sum \log\left\{\frac{M_j}{\sum M_{ij}} \bigg/ \frac{\sum M_j}{\sum M}\right\} = \frac{1}{n}\sum \mu_{jt} \quad (15)$$

with corresponding definitions.

Next, they proposed calculating the variance (which is the average of the squared deviations from the arithmetical mean) of the export specialisation (and import specialisation) index to test for intra-industry specialisation using the following formula:

$$\frac{1}{n}\sum(\varepsilon_{jt} - \varepsilon_t)^2 = S_{et}^2 \quad (16)$$

The larger the variance of individual values around the mean value, the greater the degree of inter-industry specialisation, distinguishing exports from imports. The lower the variance, the greater the degree of intra-industry specialisation. A decrease in the variance over time would provide evidence for increased intra-industry specialisation. Glejser has argued that the particular properties of these two formulae make it possible to further test for statistical significance. In surveying the statistical evidence on intra-industry specialisation below, the results obtained by Glejser for the member states of the European Community will be discussed. Despite the complexity of the Glejser formulae, they clearly provide a much more satisfactory approach when the aim is to measure the degree of intra-industry specialisation taking place over time. On the other hand, sole reliance on the Glejser indicator may be dangerous, as Greenaway (1986) has shown, because it focuses too much on comparative performance. Essentially, the formulae measure changes in the trade levels of any one country relative to those of the group of countries with whom they trade rather than in relation to domestic production or sales.

The Aggregation Problem

One of the greatest problems involved in accurately measuring the extent and importance of intra-industry specialisation is the aggregation problem. The problem arises because of the way in which products are grouped together for the purposes of compiling international trade statistics. If products which belong to essentially different industries are grouped together, the true amount of intra-industry trade will be exaggerated. Trade data are published according to an agreed international system of classification known as the Standard International Trade Classification (SITC). This groups products together at various different levels of aggregation. The level of aggregation is shown by the number of digits in the number used in the product classification. The highest level of aggregation is the one-digit level, which is followed by the second-, third-, fourth- and fifth-digit levels representing successively higher levels of disaggregation.

The need is to choose the appropriate level of aggregation to use for the purpose of measuring intra-industry trade. The three-digit level is often taken as being broadly equivalent to an economist's definition of an industry. However, this may still result in a high degree of aggregation bias when measuring intra-industry trade. One of the problems is that the product groups used by statisticians are often based more on statistical convenience than economic meaningfulness. Even where an attempt is made to use economically meaningful categories, there is the problem discussed above of agreeing on the appropriate criteria for grouping products together. In other cases, the product groups used make sense but, even at the three-digit level, over-aggregation is present. In this case, a solution would be to use four- or even five-digit product groups. This, however, is not going to be appropriate in all cases, as it would result in separating products that are essentially products of the same industry. Accurate measurement of intra-industry trade is likely to require using a mixture of three- and four-digit product groups. There is also a need to omit the various 'miscellaneous' product groups that have no relevance for intra-industry trade. A further possibility is for individual researchers to rearrange trade statistics to produce new, more economically meaningful product groupings.

The problem of aggregation – often referred to as *categorical aggregation* (Greenaway and Milner, 1983) – sometimes leads to a tendency to dismiss intra-industry trade as being largely a statistical phenomenon. Intra-industry trade is thought to be merely the result of grouping together essentially different products and treating them as belonging to the same industry. If these products require different factor intensities in their production, then what appears to be intra-industry trade is in fact inter-industry trade. It is, however, important to realise that aggregation will not always lead to an overestimation of the true extent of intra-industry trade. Following Gray (1979), aggregation can be regarded as giving rise to two quite different effects: (1) an 'opposite sign' effect and (2) a 'weighting' effect. Suppose that a product group, X, has two sub-groups, X1 and X2, both of which have different input requirements or factor intensities and which, therefore, are outputs of different industries. When these two subgroups have opposite signs, a trade surplus in one and a trade deficit in the other, aggregation bias will result. This is because the surplus in one product group wholly or partly offsets the trade deficit in the other resulting in high level of matched trade. Indeed, at the extreme, where the trade surplus in one product (say, X1) exactly equals the trade deficit in the other (say, X2), there will be a zero trade balance in X and all trade in X will appear to be intra-industry trade. A conventional measure of intra-industry trade will record a level of 100% as the amount of intra-industry trade. Where, however, the two products, X1 and X2, both have the same signs – whether a surplus or deficit – there will be no opposite sign effect and intra-industry trade will not be overestimated despite the fact that the products are wrongly aggregated. This is because a conventional Grubel–Lloyd formula has the highly desirable quality that it estimates a weighted average level of intra-industry trade in the two sub-groups, X1 and X2. Thus, the weighting effect assists in the accurate measurement of intra-industry trade.

The important test is whether or not intra-industry trade tends to disappear when lower levels of aggregation are used. Greenaway and Milner (1983) calculated the average level of intra-industry trade for the United Kingdom at the third-, fourth- and fifth-digit levels of the SITC. The average level of intra-industry trade was found to fall from 56 to 47 to 46.5% as the level of aggregation fell from the third- to the fourth- to the fifth-digit level. The fact that 46.5% of trade was found to be of the intra-industry type shows that aggregation bias is not as great a problem as is often assumed. Greenaway and Milner (1983) conclude that it is posssible to be reasonably confident that measurement at the three-digit level is predominantly recording true intra-industry trade and not mere categorical aggregation.

Greenaway and Milner (1983) have proposed another way of testing for the degree of aggregation bias. Suppose a third-digit product group, j, is made up of four four-digit sub-groups, A,B,C and D. The levels of exports and imports for each product group are shown in Table 3.4.

A conventional Grubel–Loyd formula for measuring intra-industry trade, B_j, gives the level of intra-industry trade for product group j to be 86.7%. It is apparent that some aggregation bias exists because product group, D, has a different trade balance sign to groups A, B and C. If the factor intensities of all four product groups are different, the level of intra-industry trade will be overestimated. The extent of aggregation bias may be calculated by using the following formula to measure intra-industry trade:

$$C_j = 1 - \frac{\sum[X_{ij} - M_{ij}]}{\sum(X_{ij} + M_{ij})} \times 100 \qquad (17)$$

where j is the jth set of n industries and i is the component sub-group categories for the jth industry. This differs from B_j in that the numerator uses the sum of the trade balances 'regardless of the sign'. It can be seen from Table 3.5 that the use of this formula yields a measure of intra-industry trade of 66.7%, somewhat lower than B_j. The difference measures the degree of aggregation bias. If all four product groups had the same trade balance sign, then B_j would equal C_j. Greenaway and Milner (1983) applied this test to United Kingom and

Table 3.4 An Example of How to Test for Categorical Aggregation in the Measurement of Intra-Industry Trade: the Greenaway–Milner Method

	The jth of n industries		*Trade balance sign*	
Product subgroups	X_i	M_i	$X_i - M_i$	
A	20	20	0	0
B	60	40	20	+
C	40	30	10	+
D	10	80	70	−
$\sum$	130	170	100	−

$$B_j = \frac{300 - 40}{300} = 86.7$$

$$C_j = \frac{300 - 100}{300} = 66.7$$

Table 3.5 Intra-Industry Trade Ratios for Trade in Manufactures Among OECD Countries, 1964, 1967, 1974

Country	*Change 1964–74*	*1964*	*1967*	*1974*
France	+7	74	77	81
Netherlands	−1	73	72	72
United Kingdom	+9	68	71	77
Belgium-Luxembourg	+11	68	71	79
Italy	+3	58	58	61
West Germany	+6	52	55	58
United States	+8	46	49	54
Canada	+8	40	41	48
Japan	+8	46	49	54
Australia	+3	26	26	29
All countries	+6.7	53.7	56.5	60.4

Switzerland trade statistics for the year 1977. They found that, as was to be expected, values for C_j were typically less than those for B_j, confirming that aggregation bias was indeed present, but the differences were surprisingly small. An interesting finding was that aggregation bias was greater in foodstuffs and raw materials (SITC 0–4) than in semi- and finished-manufactures (SITC 5–8).

We can conclude that the problem of aggregation bias is probably not as serious as might be expected. Although some recorded intra-industry trade is probably purely statistical, the bulk of recorded intra-industry trade is real. Moreover, we can use trade flows measured at the three-digit level to obtain reasonably good estimates of the true extent of intra-industry trade. Clearly, a higher level of disaggregation is often to be preferred. However, collecting data at this level is usually time-consuming. Moreover, there is the added problem that, for some product groups, this may represent too low a level of aggregation, such that intra-industry trade is underestimated! It should also be noted that aggregation bias cannot explain why the level of intra-industry trade appears to have been increasing over time. Although this could, in some cases, be due to a proliferation of products having different factor intensities but remaining within a given statistical classification, it seems unlikely that this could explain the extent of increased intra-industry trade that is apparent.

The Level of Intra-Industry Trade

A large number of studies have been carried out to measure the level of intra-industry trade in different countries. One of the first comprehensive studies of intra-industry trade was carried out by Grubel and Lloyd in 1975 (Grubel and Lloyd, 1975). This measured the average level of intra-industry trade in ten OECD countries covering some 160 product groups at the three-digit level of the SITC. The formulae used were those discussed above. They found that the average level of intra-industry trade rose from 36% in 1959 to 48% in 1967. The highest levels of intra-industry trade were obtained for trade in manufactured goods. The average level of intra-industry trade for these products rose from 54% in 1964 to 57% in 1967. An updated estimate using the Grubel–Lloyd measure found that, by 1974, the level of intra-industry trade for manufactures had risen to over 60% (Lassudrie-Duchene and Muchieli, 1979).

Tables 3.5 and 3.6 summarise these results.

Table 3.5 shows that the level of intra-industry trade increased steadily in all countries except the Netherlands over the period from 1964 to 1974. The highest levels of intra-industry trade were recorded for the West European countries. A noticeably much lower level of intra-industry trade was found for the United States, Canada, Japan and Australia. Table 3.6 shows that the level of intra-industry trade increased in all product groups. However, the highest levels of intra-industry trade were to

Table 3.6 Intra-Industry Trade Ratios and Growth in Total Trade for OECD Countries, 1959–1967

	Intra-industry trade ratios				*Increase in total trade*
SITC Section Code	*1959*	*1964*	*1967*	*1974*	*1959–67*
(0) Food and live animals	22	25	30	–	72
(1) Beverages and tobacco	40	42	40	–	68
(2) Crude materials	36	28	30	–	49
(3) Mineral fuels	30	29	30	–	80
(4) Oils and fats	41	39	37	–	23
(5) Chemicals	56	60	66	63	122
(6) Manufactures	43	49	49	58	325
(7) Machinery	43	53	59	62	202
(8) Misc. maufacturing	45	53	52	58	149
(9) Commodities, n.e.s.	34	45	55	–	180

Source: Grubel and Lloyd (1975), Lassudrie-Duchene and Muchieli (1979), UNCTAD Secretariat (1980).

be found in manufactures (SITC Codes 6–9), in particular chemicals and machinery.

As we saw earlier in the chapter, Grubel and Lloyd's formula was criticised by Aquino for failing to fully adjust for an imbalance in a country's overall trade (Aquino, 1978). Using a different formula, Aquino measured the level of intra-industry trade for twenty-five manufacturing product groups in twenty-six countries. Although Aquino's study covered a smaller range of product groups, he used a mixture of three- and four-digit groups in an attempt to overcome aggregation bias. Aquino's results are shown in Table 3.7.

Table 3.7 Levels of Intra-Industry Trade as a Proportion of Total Trade in Manufactured Goods by Country, 1972

Country	*IT Ratio %*	*Country*	*IT Ratio %*
France	87.4	Australia	58.5
United Kingdom	81.9	United States	57.3
Netherlands	78.7	Yugoslavia	55.3
Sweden	76.3	Japan	54.8
West Germany	76.0	Mexico	54.8
Austria	75.0	Brazil	49.8
Canada	73.5	Spain	49.1
Norway	72.5	Portugal	40.9
Italy	72.3	Korea Republic	39.2
Singapore	71.4	Hong Kong	39.2
Denmark	70.3	Greece	35.7
Belgium	70.1	India	22.9
Ireland	64.5		
Switzerland	60.9		

Source: Aquino (1978).

The figures show an even higher level of intra-industry trade than found by Grubel and Lloyd. In line with Grubel and Lloyd, intra-industry trade was highest for the West European countries (over 80% for France and the United Kingdom) and lower for the United States, Australia and Japan. The fact that Japan's ratio was lower than other western industrialised countries despite the fact that the measure was fully adjusted for trade imbalance would suggest that Japan's trade surplus (see Chapter 6) was not the primary cause. A noteworthy feature of Table 3.6 is that intra-industry trade is generally higher for the advanced industrialised countries than for developing countries. However, quite high levels of intra-industry trade were apparent for certain newly industrialising countries (NICs) listed in the table. The high ratio recorded for Singapore must have been due in part to the level of her entrepôt trade.

Using the Grubel–Lloyd adjusted summary measure, Culem and Lundberg found that, by 1980, intra-industry in most countries had increased further (Culem and Lundberg, 1986). This is illustrated by the first columns of Tables 3.8 and 3.9.

The study covered trade in manufactured goods calculated at the four-digit level of the

Table 3.8 Shares of Intra-Industry Trade in Total Trade and in Trade with Certain Groups of Countries in 1980

	Trade with							
Country	*World*	*South Europe*	*Asian NICs*	*Latin America*	*Other LDCs*	*All LDCs*	*All DCs*	*CPEs*
Australia	35.8	16.3	26.9	19.4	22.9	29.2	22.7	5.5
Belgium	79.7	54.1	29.8	11.4	33.4	40.1	77.6	28.0
Canada	58.5	30.6	15.7	25.0	11.0	33.0	56.7	18.1
France	80.4	64.4	29.7	16.3	31.4	44.2	79.2	40.0
West Germany	65.4	42.3	24.4	13.0	28.9	34.6	74.1	31.6
Italy	65.4	55.1	36.0	19.8	28.1	44.3	58.8	40.2
Japan	28.8	14.8	27.2	10.6	10.1	17.6	33.6	11.8
Netherlands	74.2	43.0	24.8	17.7	35.5	45.5	70.3	22.6
Sweden	66.5	29.2	15.1	7.6	8.8	17.4	72.5	30.7
United Kingdom	79.1	50.7	27.4	24.0	38.6	44.2	77.5	30.9
United States	60.7	33.8	26.5	29.6	25.8	35.0	66.7	37.9

Definitions. *South Europe*: Greece, Portugal, Spain, Cyprus, Gibraltar, Israel, Malta, Turkey, Yugoslavia; *Asian NICs*: Hong Kong, Macao, Singapore, Taiwan, South Korea; *CPEs*: European centrally planned economies.

Table 3.9 Change in the Share of Intra-Industry Trade Between 1970 and 1980 (percentage units)

	Trade with							
Country	*World*	*South Europe*	*Asian NICs*	*Latin America*	*Other LDCs*	*All LDCs*	*All DCs*	*CPEs*
Australia	5.4	−0.7	−8.3	2.8	3.8	0.1	4.2	−10.6
Belgium	4.1	15.3	10.7	−1.1	17.1	16.3	5.2	−17.7
Canada	−3.4	19.6	7.9	13.0	−8.4	11.6	−5.4	−6.5
France	3.6	29.4	9.2	1.5	11.0	19.0	6.4	4.0
West Germany	6.6	14.5	7.5	4.9	14.1	15.1	7.4	−4.2
Italy	6.6	26.8	1.1	9.3	7.5	20.5	0.3	8.7
Japan	−7.3	7.3	10.3	2.9	−2.5	1.9	−4.6	−21.5
Netherlands	5.5	7.8	11.3	−9.1	−1.2	7.0	5.7	−18.8
Sweden	4.1	9.3	9.0	2.7	−1.2	4.8	5.8	−0.6
United Kingdom	18.3	21.1	−0.8	7.3	12.7	12.8	12.3	−3.4
United States	1.4	8.1	2.4	6.3	1.1	4.3	5.8	6.9

Source: Culem and Lundberg (1986).

SITC of the eleven most industrialised countries of the world. Only in Japan and Canada had the ratio falling over the period from 1970 to 1980. The figures also show that the highest levels of intra-industry trade are to be found for trade between the developed countries (DCs). Intra-industry trade ratios are much lower when the industrialised countries trade with less developed countries (LDCs) and centrally planned economies (CPEs). Certain regional patterns are also apparent. Thus, high levels of intra-industry trade existed for Japan's trade with the Asian NICs. Western Europe's trade with South Europe also involved much intra-industry trade, as did the United States' trade with Latin America. This would suggest that intra-industry trade is greatest between countries in close geographical proximity to each other. An interesting feature of Table 3.7 is that, although intra-industry trade was lower when developed countries traded with developing countries, it grew faster over the period than trade between developed countries. With a few exceptions, the fastest growth in intra-industry trade occurred in trade between the western industrialised countries and the NICs of Southern Europe, Asia and Latin America. We discuss this point further in Chapter 7 when we consider the implications of the rise of the NICs for the western industrialised countries.

In an important paper written in 1990, Globerman and Dean (1990) found evidence that, during the 1970s and 1980s, intra-industry trade had begun to level off. Taking a sample of OECD countries, using an unadjusted Grubel and Lloyd measure and focusing on manufactured products only, they found that the trend towards intra-industry trade that had been apparent in previous decades, began to slow down for most countries by the late 1970s. In some sectors for certain countries, there was even evidence of an absolute reversal of the previous trend during the early 1980s. However, Greenaway and Hine (1991) consider the sample of countries used by Globerman and Dean to be too small and the periods compared as misleading. During the period 1980–85, the intra-industry trade share fluctuated a great deal, while the growth of trade in manufactures slowed down. Slow overall trade growth, they argue, served to retard the expansion of intra-industry trade. Furthermore, Globerman and Dean failed to adjust their measure for trade imbalance at a time when both the United States and Japan experienced major increases in their trade imbalance.

Greenaway and Hine used two separate measures of intra-industry trade to analyse trends in intra-industry trade for twenty two OECD countries over the period 1970–85. Table 3.10 shows the results using the Grubel–Lloyd index.

The figures show that the average level of intra-industry trade continued to rise during the 1980s although the upward trend was weaker. Only eight out of twenty two countries experienced an actual reduction in intra-industry trade over the period. There is, however, some evidence of a levelling off of intra-industry trade in the original EC countries where intra-industry trade had already reached very high levels by 1980. Although intra-industry trade fell in the United States and Japan between 1980 and 1985, a probable explanation was the rise in the overall trade imbalances of these two countries during this period (see Chapter 6 for a discussion of the reasons for this development).

The Theory of Intra-Industry Trade

We turn now to the theoretical explanations that have been given for why countries engage in intra-industry trade. In doing so, a distinction is made between trade in homogeneous or identical products and trade in heterogeneous or

Table 3.10 The Grubel–Lloyd Index for Intra-Industry Trade in Manufactures, OECD Countries, 1970–1985

Country	*1970*	*1978*	*1980*	*1983*	*1985*
Canada	0.663	0.687	0.645	0.737	0.764
United States	0.680	0.716	0.682	0.705	0.665
Japan	0.406	0.281	0.308	0.301	0.293
Australia	0.211	0.286	0.296	0.279	0.306
Belgium	0.800	0.835	0.841	0.875	0.867
Denmark	0.630	0.679	0.674	0.721	0.726
France	0.814	0.828	0.861	0.855	0.855
Germany	0.607	0.641	0.554	0.687	0.682
Ireland	0.444	0.600	0.685	0.723	0.703
Italy	0.617	0.614	0.696	0.662	0.695
The Netherlands	0.741	0.759	0.779	0.776	0.763
United Kingdom	0.620	0.807	0.808	0.832	0.843
Austria	0.707	0.777	0.766	0.802	0.792
Finland	0.411	0.569	0.567	0.630	0.664
Norway	0.613	0.634	0.647	0.632	0.621
Sweden	0.630	0.653	0.681	0.706	0.719
Greece	0.283	0.415	0.396	0.462	0.463
Portugal	0.457	0.410	0.453	0.514	0.546
Spain	0.570	0.644	0.504	0.677	0.682
Turkey	0.154	0.120	0.223	0.359	0.468
Yugoslavia	0.638	0.647	0.688	0.700	0.700
Mean	0.546	0.590	0.598	0.639	0.645
Standard deviation	0.185	0.195	0.184	0.175	0.169
Coefficient of variation	0.339	0.330	0.307	0.274	0.262

Source: Greenaway and Hine (1991).

differentiated goods. Although there are some important cases where intra-industry trade will take place in homogeneous goods, most intra-industry trade tends to take place in differentiated goods. Nevertheless, we need to discuss both cases. Box 3.1 provides a summary of the main theories that help explain different forms of intra-industry trade.

Box 3.1 Theoretical Explanations for Intra-Industry Trade

Intra-Industry Trade in Identical Products

- Aggregation bias
- Cross-border trade in weight-gaining products
- Differentiation in time

Continued

- Joint production and consumption
- Entrepôt (re-export) trade
- Cross hauling by multinational companies (offshore processing)
- Reciprocal dumping (trade in oligopolistic markets) – Brander (1981), Brander and Krugman (1983)

Intra-Industry Trade in Differentiated Products

- Horizontal Differentiation
  The Core Property Model – Lancaster (1966, 1980)
  The Helpman Model – Helpman (1981)
  The Love for Variety Model – Dixit and Stiglitz (1977)
- Vertical Differentiation – Linder (1961), Falvey (1981), Falvey and Kierzkowski (1984)

Trade in Functionally Identical Products

Functionally identical commodities may be defined as commodities that have perfect substitutability in use. Another way of putting this is to say that they have a high positive cross-elasticity of demand. In the extreme case of where consumers are indifferent between any two products, the cross-elasticity of demand will have a value of infinity. That is to say, a rise in the price of one good will cause an infinite increase in the demand for the other as consumers switch all their purchases over to the product which is now cheaper. In neo-classical trade theory, the products belonging to an industry are usually assumed to be homogeneous. For example, in the cement industry, buyers are indifferent as between one bag of cement made by a producer in one country and another bag of cement made by producers in another country. In reality, there are few industries where perfect substitutability in use exists. However, there are some industries that approximate towards such conditions. For a variety of reasons, intra-industry trade may occur in products that are functionally identical. Some of these are listed below.

1. *Aggregation bias.* We have already discussed this problem earlier in the chapter. It is possible that products may be grouped together that are produced using different factor proportions or input requirements. Because factor proportions differ, the different products may be produced in different countries and exchanged through trade. This is really inter-industry trade, but it may show up statistically as intra-industry trade. This will most likely happen when products are classified according to substitutability in use rather than substitutability in production.
2. *Cross-border trade.* Intra-industry trade may occur in functionally identical products that are produced by so-called *weight-gaining industries* where the two countries share a common border. Weight-gaining industries are industries in which the ratio of the weight of the product relative to its unit value increases with the degree of processing. Examples are bricks, coal or glass bottles. Production of the final product must therefore be located as near as possible to the market in order to minimise transport costs. The costs of transportation will set limits on the extent of the market in which it is profitable for producers to sell the good. In Figure 3.1, the market in which it is worthwhile for producer A to sell is given by a circle around A and likewise for B. It

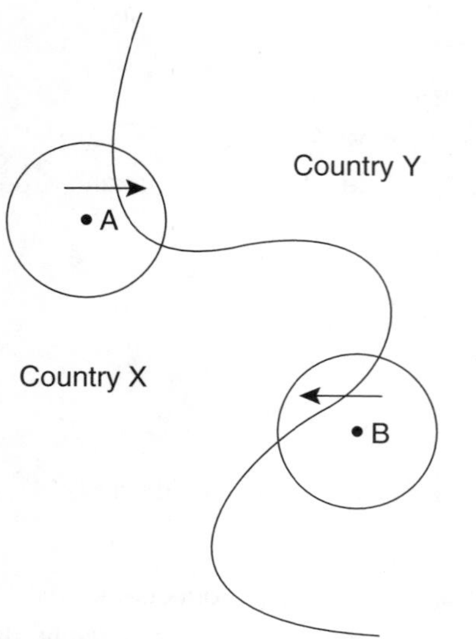

Figure 3.1 An example of intra-industry trade occurring in weight-gaining products across borders

follows that, in the absence of trade barriers, the two countries will both export and import the product in question. Producer A will export to buyers in Country Y and producer B will export to buyers in Country X. If such trade is restricted by the existence of trade barriers, trade liberalisation will clearly lead to increased intra-industry trade. There is evidence to show that, following the establishment in 1952 of the European Coal and Steel Community (ECSC), which removed barriers on trade in coal and steel products between six West European countries, increased intra-industry trade occurred between countries sharing a common border for this reason.

3. *Differentiation in time.* Some so-called 'seasonal goods' (e.g. fresh fruit, vegetables, etc.) are only available at certain times of the year. At these times, a country that produces these goods will export some of its output to the rest of the world. However, out of season, it will import these goods from other parts of the world. This will show up in the country's annual trade statistics as intra-industry trade. The same happens when the demand for a good fluctuates yet domestic production cannot be readily adjusted to match the change in demand. This is the case in the electricity supply industry where it is costly to run an electricity generating plant at a level substantially below full capacity. At peak times, producers may be unable to meet demand and will therefore supplement domestically generated power with imported electricity. However, at off-peak times when domestic demand is inadequate to ensure full utilisation of capacity, electricity will be exported to neighbouring countries. Once again, intra-industry trade is the result.
4. *Joint production and joint consumption.* Some products (e.g. petrochemical products such as benzene, toulene, ethylene, etc.) are produced jointly. At the same time, the proportions in which they are produced cannot readily be altered. Unless domestic demand for these products exactly corresponds with the proportions in which they are produced, the result will be excess supply of some products and excess demand for others. The result may be that some of the output of certain products is exported, while demand for other products has to be supplemented by imports from plants in other countries. The result will be intra-industry trade. The same situation may arise where products are jointly consumed. Unless domestic producers are able to supply the goods in exactly the right proportions, home production may have to be supplemented by imports, while some of the output of other products is exported.
5. *Entrepôt trade.* Entrepôt trade (sometimes called re-export trade) involves a country importing a product not for the purpose of sale on the domestic market but, for more

or less, immediate re-export. The entrepôt country provides a specific service by enabling the good to be stored in a warehouse, providing finance to enable the good to be purchased by a wholesaler or distributor and ensuring the good is properly packaged and labelled before it is exported to the country of destination. Such trade is an important source of income to countries such as Singapore and Hong Kong which for both historical and geographical reasons have developed an expertise in this kind of trade. Much of this trade shows up statistically as intra-industry trade.

6. *Cross-hauling by multinational companies.* This refers to the practice of multinational companies relocating the final assembly stages involved in the production of a good at an offshore site in a developing country in order to take advantage of lower labour costs. The final assembly stage is frequently the most labour-intensive and the type of labour relatively unskilled. Components and parts made in factories located in the home country are exported to the assembly plant in the foreign country and the finished product is then re-exported back to the home country for sale to domestic consumers. Examples of this kind of trade are to be found in both the clothing and textile industry and the consumer electronics industry. The phenomenon is discussed in more depth in Chapter 5. To the extent that components and parts (e.g. television tubes) are classified as belonging to the same product group as the finished product (e.g. television sets), the result is intra-industry trade. In fact, however, such trade more closely resembles the inter-industry trade of the Heckscher–Ohlin theory as it is based on differences in factor proportions. The factor proportions required differ at the various stages of production. Hence, it is more economical for producers to locate the different stages in different countries because factor endowments (and hence the relative cost of factors) differ between countries. Nevertheless, it may well appear as intra-industry trade in trade statistics and so could be treated as a special type of intra-industry trade.

Trade in Oligoplistic Markets

One special case where trade in functionally identical goods may take the form of intra-industry is the case of oligopoly. It can be shown that, where, in each of any two countries, the domestic market is monopolised by a single seller and the two countries engage in trade, the result will be intra-industry trade. This is the special case of *duopoly* in which just two producers control the market for a product. A model of trade based on these assumptions, and which predicts intra-industry trade as the outcome, has been proposed by Brander (1981) and Brander and Krugman (1983). The model assumes that the two countries are identical in all respects, that is, equal size, identical factor endowments and identical preferences. In the absence of trade, there exists just one monopoly producer of the good. The model analyses what will happen if both countries engage in trade.

An important feature of the model concerns the assumptions made about firm behaviour. A major problem with analysing oligopolistic markets is that, unlike perfect competition, firms are not passive price-takers concerned merely with choosing the output level at which profits are maximised and whose decision about how much to produce has no impact on market price. Each seller is sufficiently large so that the decisions it makes about how much to sell has a major impact on the market and, in particular, on its rivals. For example, any decision to cut price or sell more has implications for its rivals that cannot be ignored. Firms, therefore, cannot act without taking into account how rivals might react. For example, any decision to cut price will result in increased sales if rivals fail to follow suite but will lower profits if they do. How rivals will react is, therefore, a consideration of major importance to each seller. For this reason, firms in oligopolistic industries engage in strategic behaviour constantly seeking to outwit their rivals. (This, of course, assumes that they do not, instead, engage in collusive behaviour in an effort to eliminate the uncertainty which the high degree of interdependence existing between firms creates. If, however, they choose to collude, their actions become equivalent to those of a joint monopoly and the model of monopoly considered in the previous chapter becomes relevant). However, where firms' decisions are based upon an assessment of how they think their rivals will react, it becomes extremely difficult to arrive at a determinate solution as to the amount that each firm will produce and the price they will charge.

One way round this problem is to make certain assumptions about firm behaviour in such markets. A relatively simple assumption is to suppose that firms do not engage in any kind of guessing game. Instead, they take the output of their rivals as given and choose whatever output level will maximise their profits on the basis of this assumption. Writing in the early 19th century, the French mathematical economist, Augustine Cournot, attempted to construct a model of firm behaviour in an oligopolistic market based on this assumption (Cournot, 1838). The Brander–Krugman model of trade makes Cournot assumptions about firm behaviour. The advantage of this approach is that it gets round the problem of indeterminacy, which arises if no such assumption is made. On the other hand, it is subject to the objection that firms in oligopolistic markets simply do not act in this way. It seems unlikely that firms ignore the likely reactions of their rivals when deciding how much to produce or at what price to sell. It may also be open to question whether they engage only in quantity competition in the manner assumed by this model. That is to say, they fix output at the most profitable level and treat price simply as the outcome of that decision. An alternative assumption would be to assume that price is treated as the target variable and quantity is merely the outcome. In other words, firms fix the price at whatever they consider the most profitable level and sell whatever they are able to do at that price. Where firms fix their price at the most profitable level taking the price of their rivals as given, this is called *Bertrand competition.* On the other hand, it may not be unrealistic to assume that firms are more likely to engage in *Cournot competition*. Since firms have to plan their production levels over long periods of time, it may, indeed, be the case that they set output at the most profitable level and, having done so, charge whatever price consumers will pay for that amount.

We begin by assuming no transport costs. It can be shown that, if the two countries are assumed to be identical in all respects, each producer will sell exactly half his output on the home market and export the other half to the exporting country. This is illustrated by Figure 3.2. To see why this is so, it is necessary to consider how each firm will react to the output decisions of its rivals using Cournot-type assumptions about how firms behave. Each producer may be considered as facing a *reaction function* or *best-reply function* of the kind shown in Figure 3.3. The horizontal axis shows how much output producer 1 (the home producer) will supply to the home market (country 1), Q_1^1, and the vertical axis shows how much producer 2 (the foreign producer) will supply to the home country market (country 1), Q_2^1. Each producer's reaction function shows how they will react to the output

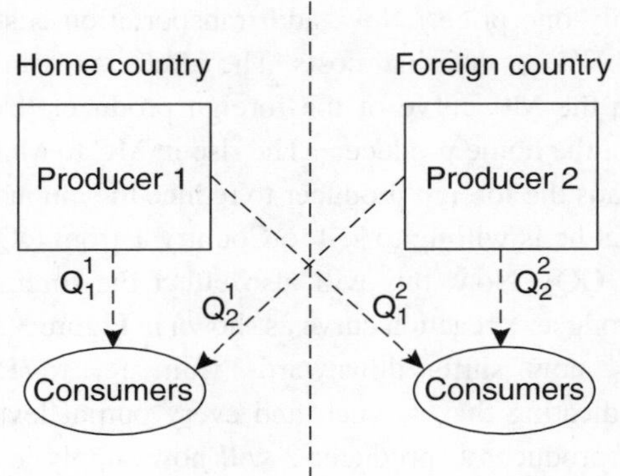

Figure 3.2 The Brander–Krugman duopoly model

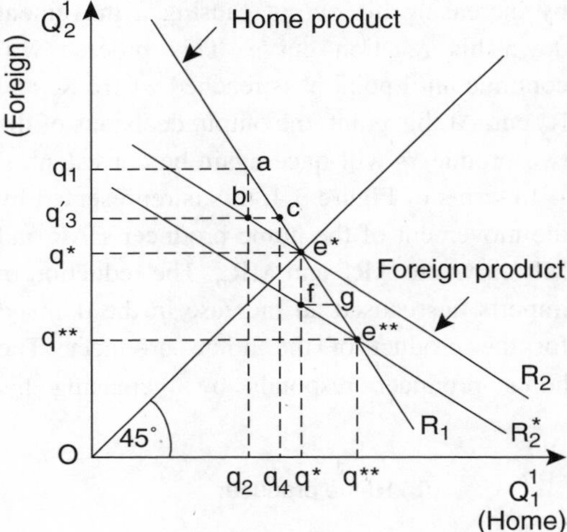

Figure 3.3 Oligopoly equilibrium under Cournot assumptions about firms' behaviour

decision of their rival. Thus R_1 shows how producer 1 (the home producer) will react to changes in output by the foreign producer R_2. R_2 shows how the foreign producer will react to changes in output by R_1 (the home producer). Each producer's reaction curve slopes downwards because the more output the rival decides to sell, the less output it is profitable for the other firm to supply. For example, as producer 1 supplied more, the market price of the product in the home country will fall (and hence the MR curve of both producers will shift inwards). Producer 2 will find that his marginal costs now exceed his marginal revenue. Accordingly, he will choose to reduce his output until he reaches a point where marginal revenue again equals marginal cost. So, the reaction of producer 2 to the decision of producer 1 is to supply less output to country 1's market. Graphically, this is represented as a movement down R_2 (the foreign producer's reaction curve). Likewise, if producer 2 decided to supply more to country 1's market, the effects would be the same. Price would fall, marginal revenue would decrease and producer 1 would respond by supplying less. Graphically, this would express itself as a movement up R_1 (Country 1's reaction curve). Why is R_1 steeper than R_2? Because the effects of a change in the output of the home producer on the foreign producer (R_2) are assumed to be stronger than those of the foreign producer on the home producer (R_1).

Equilibrium exists at point e* where the two reaction curves intersect. To see this, suppose that the foreign producer, 2, initially chooses to sell output O_{q1} to the home market of producer 1. The home producer will react by supplying output O_{q2}. However, this will cause the foreign producer to reduce his output to O_{q3}. This, in turn, will cause the domestic producer to expand output to O_{q4}. This game will continue until point e* is reached where neither producer has an incentive to revise his level of output. At this point, it can be shown that each producer will supply exactly half the market in each country. This is shown by the 45 degree line passing through point e*. The trade which results is two-way trade or intra-industry trade in a product which is functionally identical.

Next, let us assume the existence of transport costs for exports but not domestic sales. In this case, both producers will once again sell part of their output to consumers in their own country and part to consumers in the partner country.

However, each producer will supply less to the foreign market than before. Moreover, they will sell the product to the foreign market at a lower *ex-factory price* than, the price that they receive at home. In the previous chapter, we saw that this situation is termed 'dumping'. However, in this model, dumping takes place in both directions. Each producer sells the product on the foreign market at a lower *ex-factory* price than at home. Brander and Krugman termed this *reciprocal dumping*. How can this be? Consider Figure 3.4. In this figure, the left-hand diagram shows the position of the foreign producer in respect of his sales to Country 1's market. The right-hand diagram shows the position of the home producer in respect of his sales to Country 1's (i.e. his own) market. Each producer produces where MC equals MR. (We assume constant average costs so that marginal costs equal average costs.) Thus, the home producer produces at A selling OQ_1 at the price OP_1, while the foreign producer also produces at A selling OQ_1 at OP_1. (Note that OP_1 is the same for both producers as the product is a homogeneous product and there is only one price.) Now, add transportation costs of VW to marginal costs. The effect is to shift up the MC curve of the foreign producer (but not the home producer). The rise in MC to MC_g leads the foreign producer to reduce the amount that he is willing to sell to Country 1 from OQ_1 to OQ_2. Now, this will also effect the foreign producer's reaction curve as shown in Figure 3.3. R_2 now shifts downwards from R_2 to R_2^* indicating that, at each and every output level of producer 1, producer 2 will now supply less than before. Now, there is no longer equilibrium at point e. At point e, producer 2 is now supplying less. Hence, producer 1 will respond by increasing his output causing a movement down his reaction curve. This process will continue until point e^* is reached where R_1 and R_2^* cut. At this point, the output decisions of the two producers will once again be consistent.

In terms of Figure 3.4, this is represented by the movement of the home producer's AR and MR curves to AR_0' and MR_0'. The reduction in imports has caused an increase in the demand for the product of the home producer. The home producer responds by increasing his

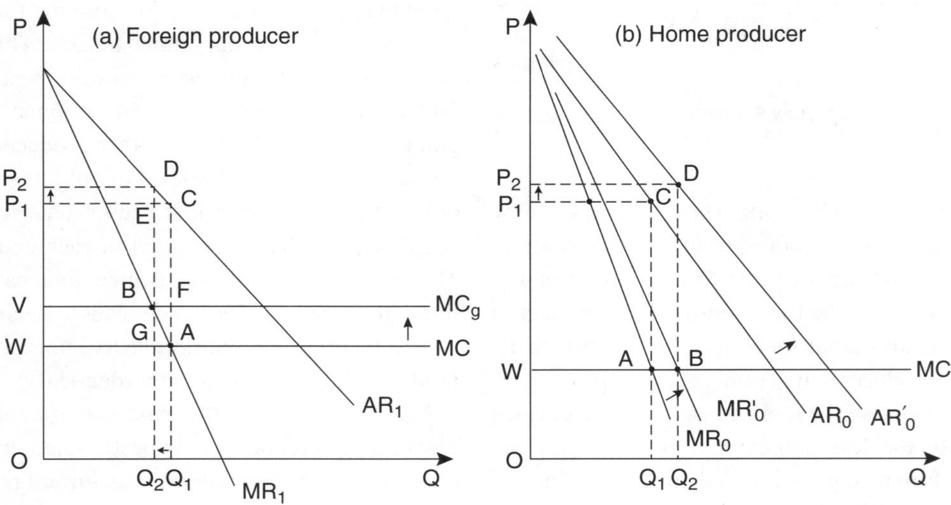

Figure 3.4 Reciprocal dumping in the Brander–Krugman duopoly model

output from OQ_1 to OQ_2. Price also goes up for both the foreign and home producer from OP_1 to OP_2. It can be seen that the foreign producer now supplies less to Country 1's market and the home producer more. Exactly, the same changes will take place in Country 2's market as the inclusion of transport costs pushes up the MC curve of producer 1 in Country 2. At first sight, it appears that the price of the product is the same for each producer's export sales as for its home sales. However, the *ex-factory* price is clearly lower for export sales. This is because the ex-factory price does not include any costs incurred after a product has left the factory gates whether for domestic or export sale. Since transport costs have risen by more (VW) than the price of the good in the foreign market, each foreign producer must have experienced a fall in the ex-factory price for export sales. However, the domestic price has risen. In effect, part of the costs of transport costs is borne by the exporter and only part passed on to the consumer in a higher price. Thus, dumping has occurred. Because it happens in both directions, the term 'reciprocal dumping' is appropriate.

Thus, we can see that where markets are dominated by a single dominant seller, trade can result in intra-industry or two-way trade in identical goods. At first sight, it may seem as if such trade is wasteful. Unnecessary transport costs are incurred which result in consumers paying more for the good than they would otherwise. On the other hand, trade injects an element of competition into the domestic market where previously the entire market was controlled by a single seller. Providing the two firms do not collude, consumers will gain as competition drives down the market price. (The AR curve will become more elastic and price will converge closer towards marginal cost.) Increased competition will also spur firms to seek out ways of cutting costs and eliminating X-inefficiency. (See Chapter 8 for a fuller discussion of these effects). Provided that pro-competition effects exceed the costs of transportation, the net welfare effect should be favourable. However, if transport costs are large, consumers may lose.

Trade in Differentiated Commodities

Differentiated commodities are products that are close, but not perfect, substitutes for each other. Hence, they have a high, but not infinite, positive cross-elasticity of demand. Differentiation can take the form of either *horizontal* or *vertical differentiation*. In the case of *horizontal differentiation*, products differ mainly in style or appearance and perhaps marginal performance characteristics. This type of differentiation is common in many non-durable consumer goods industries such as soap detergents, soft drinks, breakfast cereals, cigarettes, sports shoes, paints etc. Competition typically takes the form of non-price competition in which each producer strives to differentiate his good from that of his rival. Firms in such industries tend to spend relatively large amounts on advertising and sales promotion. In the case of *vertical differentiation*, products differ in quality as measured by their performance capabilities. Such differentiation is more common in durable consumer goods industries such as automobiles, motor cycles, personal computers, electronic games, television sets, CD players, etc. Competition in these industries is characterised by product development and product innovation. (The term *technological differentiation* is sometimes used where firms develop new products that are substitutes for existing ones.) Firms seek to increase their market share by making quality improvements to their products or developing new superior versions of their products. Typically, firms in these industries will face high levels of expenditure on research and development (R&D). It can be shown that both forms of differentiation may result in intra-industry trade with consumers exchanging different varieties of the same good. Let us consider each case in turn.

A. Horizontal Differentiation

Trade economists have developed at least two types of models for analysing the kind of trade that takes place when goods are horizontally differentiated. Both types assume that the market for the product traded is a monopolistically competitive one, in which there exist many sellers of a horizontally differentiated product. The first type of model is referred to as 'the core property model' and builds on the work of Kelvin Lancaster (1966, 1980). Lancaster viewed horizontally differentiated goods as goods that possess the same core attributes but combine these in different proportions. This can be illustrated with the aid of a 'variety specification'. Suppose a good possesses two core attributes, x and y. A variety specification shows the different combinations of each of these two attributes which any given variety of the good contains as illustrated below.

x--y

At either extreme, a good will possess only one of these varieties. Between the two extremes, there will be varieties that combine these attributes in different proportions. The closer it is to x, the more x and the less y will be contained in the product. The closer it is to y, there will be more y and less x. Each consumer is assumed to have a preferred variety of the differentiated good. However, he may be persuaded to buy another variety if he receives adequate compensation in the form of a lower price. However, the further a particular variety is located in the variety specification from the consumer's preferred variety, the more compensation he will require if he is to be persuaded to buy it. This may be illustrated by using a 'compensation function' such as is shown in Figure 3.5. Suppose V^* is the consumer's preferred variety. As the consumer moves in either direction, compensation is required. The

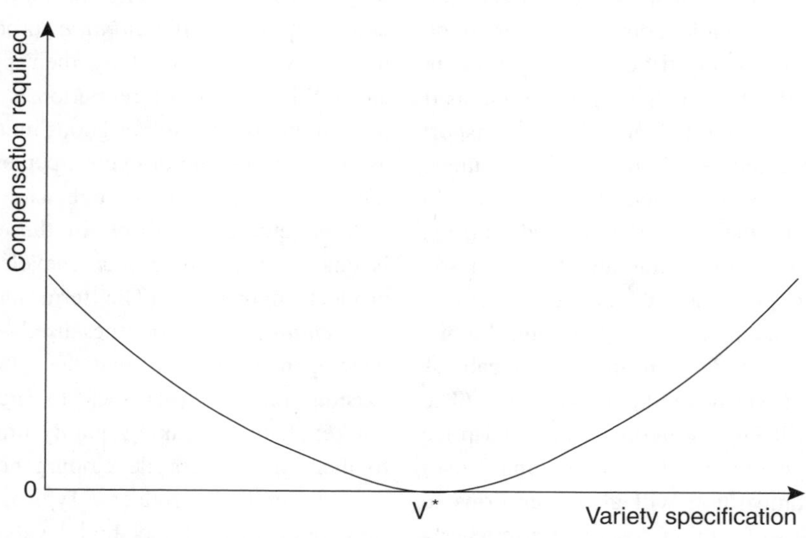

Figure 3.5 A consumer's compensation function

further he moves in either direction, the greater the compensation that must be paid. Hence the 'compensation function' assumes a U-shape. As the two extremes are approached, the function may become vertical, indicating that no amount of compensation is sufficient to persuade the consumer to substitute this particular variety for his preferred one.

Suppose that the preferences of consumers are, uniformly, distributed over the various types such that a demand exists for each type. It is unlikely, however, that producers will supply all of these varieties because the demand for any one variety will be insufficient to enable them to recover the fixed costs that must be incurred before any units of the good are produced. In the production of most differentiated goods, average costs tend to fall with output because fixed costs on advertising and sales promotion account for a high proportion of total costs. It follows that producers must produce a large amount of each variety if they are to reach the lowest point possible on their average cost curve. If demand is uniform over the full range of different varieties, it is possible to show that each producer will produce just one variety and no producer will produce the same variety as the other. Moreover, the varieties will be evenly spread over the range of types for which a demand exists. One way of illustrating this is to regard each different type of the good as a different point on the face of a clock. There may be sixty different varieties for which a demand exists equivalent to the sixty minutes on the clock. How many varieties producers will supply in the absence of trade will depend on the demand for each variety (itself a function of the size of the market) and the slope of the average cost curve of each producer. Suppose producers find that, in the absence of trade, it is worthwhile supplying only four types. These are represented by the four points, A_0, A_3, A_6 and A_9, in the Figure 3.6.

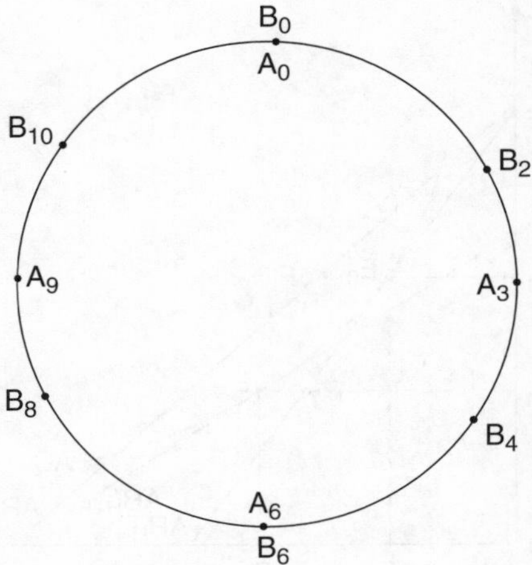

Figure 3.6 The Lancaster core-attributes model of horizontal differentiation

Clearly, any consumer whose preference is for one of these types will be perfectly satisfied. However, any consumer whose preferred variety lies in between any of these four types will be dissatisfied. The further their preferred variety is from any of the ones actually available, the more dissatisfied they will be.

Now, suppose this country engages in trade with another identical country in which producers produce exactly the same four types but no more. Each producer now faces a market that is potentially double the market in which he previously sold. However, to begin with, he faces competition from another producer producing a variety of the good that is exactly identical. If, however, one of the two producers of each type can gain an increased market share at the expense of their rival, they can move to a lower point on their average-cost curve, cut prices and drive out their rival. It follows that, one producer of each of the four types is likely to get knocked out. In this case, the number of varieties does not change. However, the number of producers in the two countries combined will fall. On the other hand, because each producer now faces a greater demand for his variant of

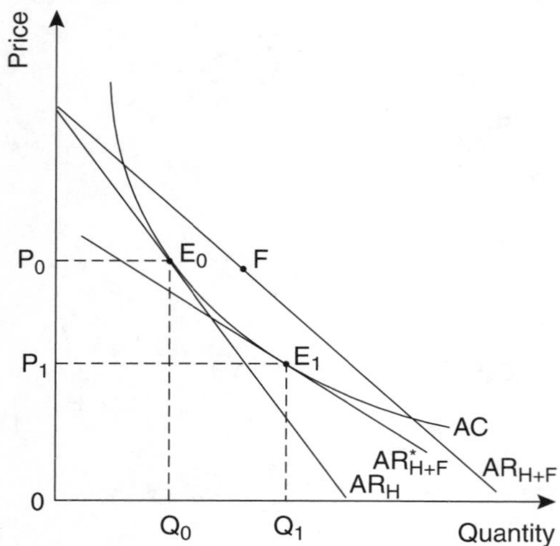

Figure 3.7 Trade under monopolistic competition

the product, his profits will increase. This is illustrated by Figure 3.7.

Figure 3.7 shows the equilibrium position of a firm under monopolistic competition both before and after trade. Under monopolistic competition, all producers produce where MR equals MC. If, however, they earn excess profits (i.e. $p > \text{AC}$), new firms will enter the industry. As they do, the demand curve (AR) facing the individual firm will shift downwards until price is just equal to AC at the point where profits are maximised ($\text{MC} = \text{MR}$). Such a point is E_0, where the AR curve is tangential to the AC curve. As a result of trade, however, the demand for each firm's product doubles. AR_H becomes AR_{H+F}. (MR is not shown in the diagram but that too will increase.) Producers will respond by increasing output. Production will expand to a point such as F where excess profits may now be earned. (Excess profits are given by the distance between AR_{H+F} and AC.) Because the producers who have remained in the industry are now making excessive profits, two consequences will ensue. First, new producers will enter the industry and commence production of other varieties of the product. However, they will not produce the same varieties of the product as existing producers as this would be less profitable. Second, some existing producers (those knocked out of the market in the initial bout of competition) will switch to producing other varieties. This will cause the demand (AR) curve of existing producers to shift to the left to AR^*_{H+F} and to become less steep (i.e. more elastic). The latter occurs because existing producers now face more competition from a greater number of varieties and so their product becomes less differentiated. New firms will continue entering the industry until there are no further excess profits which may be earned. This will occur when the demand (AR) curve is once again tangent to the AC curve at the point where $\text{MC} = \text{MR}$. In Figure 3.7, AR^*_{H+F} is the new demand curve and long-run equilibrium is established at the point E_1 where AR is again tangential to AC.

In terms of Figure 3.6, these changes manifest themselves in an increase in the number of varieties available. Suppose that instead of four varieties before trade, six varieties are now available. How many varieties will be available after trade is impossible to say. This will depend on consumer demand for each variety and how sharply average costs fall with output. However, the number of varieties must be larger because each producer now faces an increased market. It is important to realise that no one producer will produce exactly the same variety. Instead, each will strive to differentiate his good from that of competitors. If consumers' preferences are assumed to be equally distributed around the clock, each producer will produce a variety equally spaced around the clock, such as at B_0, B_2, B_4, B_6, B_8 and B_{10}. However, consumers as a whole have clearly gained from the expansion in the number of varieties available. Some will lose because their preferred variety is no longer available.

For example, consumers located at A_3 or A_9. However, these are outnumbered by those who can now buy a product that is closer to their preferences. It should also be noted that the prices of existing varieties are lower than before (see Figure 3.7). Once again, the kind of trade that takes place is intra-industry trade in which each country exchanges different varieties of the same good.

Helpman (1981) has carried the model a stage further and demonstrated how and why both inter- and intra-industry can take place between the same pair of countries. Suppose two countries with different factor endowments engage in trade. Suppose, further, that, in each country, there exists one homogeneous goods sector and one differentiated goods sector. However, in the homogeneous goods sector, production takes place under conditions of constant returns to scale, while, in the differentiated goods sector, there are falling average costs (decreasing returns). For the reasons given above, both countries will simultaneously export and import different varieties of the differentiated good. However, because their factor endowments are different, they will also engage in inter-industry trade. The country which is capital-abundant will enjoy a comparative cost advantage in differentiated goods and will, therefore, be a next exporter of these goods, while the capital-scarce country will be a net importer. However, for their trade to balance, it is an additional requirement that the labour-abundant country be a net exporter of the homogeneous product. Helpman shows that, as the differences in factor endowments increase between the two countries, the share of intra-industry trade in total trade will fall and that of inter-industry trade will rise.

An alternative approach to analysing demand for horizontally differentiated goods has been suggested by Dixit and Stiglitz (1977). Rather than consumers preferring one variety to another, consumers have a desire to consume many different varieties because they value variety for its own sake. For example, rather than consumers preferring French wine to Spanish wine or Italian wine, they may prefer to consume all three types at different times because they want variety. Several trade theorists have developed models of trade which adopt such an approach to differentiation (Krugman, 1979, 1980, 1982; Dixit and Norman, 1980; Venables, 1984). An important feature of this model is the assumption that is made about the demand side. All consumers are assumed to be alike and to have their taste patterns represented by a utility function of the following type:

$$U = \sum v(c_i) \qquad v' > 0, \quad v' < 0$$

where c_i denotes consumption of the ith good by the representative consumer and v is the share of consumption accounted for by each good. It is further assumed that all varieties enter into consumers' utility functions symmetrically. The utility of consumers is increased not only by consumers enjoying more of each good, but also by an increase in n, the number of varieties. It is also true that, even if the consumer has less of each good, if he has more goods his utility increases. On the supply side, it is assumed that each good has an identical production function (so there is no basis for trade based on factor proportions), using a single factor of production labour as in the Ricardian model. Goods are assumed to be produced under conditions of increasing returns (decreasing costs) because a proportion of the total costs are fixed costs. Because of the existence of fixed costs and the symmetrical nature of the utility function, each producer produces only one product and there are as many producers as there are products. In other words, no producer will seek to produce the same variety as other producers. Each producer seeks to maximise profits by equating marginal costs to marginal revenue. However, it assumed that there is freedom of entry to (and exit from) the industry. So, if individual producers earn non-zero profits, new firms will enter the industry, driving down the price, until there are no extra profits to be made.

If we assume that, under autarky, there is just one monopolistically competitive sector, market equilibrium will be determined by two relationships. First, the more firms there are in the industry, the higher will be their average cost. This is because each firm will produce less. Since all firms have the same production function, they will all charge the same price. The relationship between the average price and the number of firms is shown by CC in Figure 3.8. Second, the more firms there are, the more intense the competition and, as a result, the lower the prices they charge. This relationship between price and the number of firms is shown by PP in Figure 3.8. Equilibrium occurs where CC_1 and PP intersect. The logic behind this is that, at this point, the profit-maximising price, P_1, is equal to average costs such that no firms have any incentive to enter or leave the industry. If the number of firms were less than N_1, the price charged by firms would have been above average costs, so new firms would have an incentive to enter the industry. The opposite would be true if the number of firms were more than N_1.

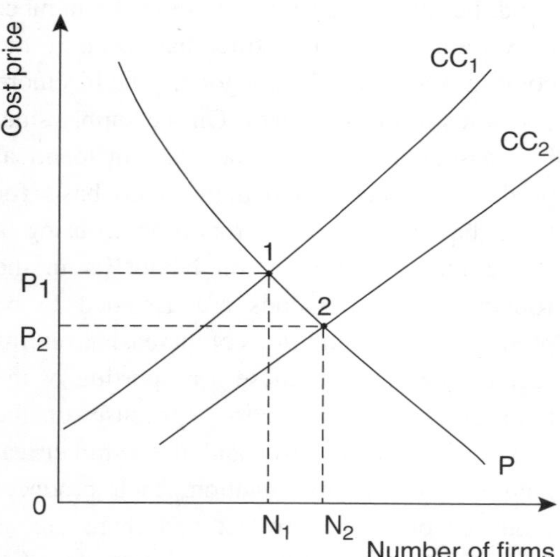

Figure 3.8 Market equilibrium in the Dixit–Stiglitz model

Now, what happens if this country enters into trade with another exactly identical country having the same cost structures and consumption patterns? Since all variants of the product are assumed to have the same utility value, in the absence of trade both countries produce identical variants at the same prices. The effect is to increase the size of the market. The CC curve defines the relationship between the number of firms and average costs for a given level of consumption. If now the level of consumption doubles, CC will shift outwards to CC_2. Average costs will fall and profits of existing firms will increase. New firms will enter the industry causing a movement down PP until a new equilibrium is established at point 2. However, since the number of firms in each country has increased, the number of varieties of the good has also risen. This is ensured because of the stipulation that no new firms will produce the same variety. In other words, each variety will be produced in one country only. As in the Lancaster model, intra-industry trade is the result. Consumers gain because they have more varieties of the same good from which to choose and an increase in the number of varieties increases total utility in the particular type of utility function used in this model. However, consumers also gain because average costs and hence prices are lower.

B. Vertical Differentiation

Attempts to develop models of trade where products are *differentiated vertically* have fallen back on neo-classical, factor endowments differences as the main determinant of specialisation. The most well-known example of such a model is that of Falvey (1981) in which quality is determined by the amount of capital relative to labour that is used in the production process. Thus, labour-abundant countries will have a comparative advantage in low-quality goods and capital-abundant countries in capital-intensive goods. This, of course, ignores the role of demand-side factors. In the previous chapter, we discussed the model of trade put forward by Linder in which different countries exchanged manufactured products having different degrees of sophistication. If the products are different varieties of the same good, Linder's model predicts intra-industry trade in vertically differentiated goods. However, in this model, demand-side factors play the crucial role. In countries with high per capita incomes, demand is biased towards high-quality varieties, while, in countries with low per capita incomes, the preference is for low-quality varieties of the same type. What happens if these differences in demand are incorporated in the model? Falvey and Kierzkowski (1984) have shown that a demand-side framework of this kind can indeed be incorporated into the model to provide a determinate solution. The demand-side and supply-side factors work together to determine the level of pre-trade prices and hence the determination of comparative advantage. However, the two sides may conceivably work in opposite directions, demand-side factors reducing the scope for trade which supply-side factors open up. For example, if per capita income is higher in the capital-abundant country, this may mean that the pre-trade price of high quality varieties is no lower (and even conceivably higher) in the capital-abundant compared with the labour-abundant country thus reducing the opportunity for trade. Where trade does result, since the products belong to the same industry, the resultant trade is of the intra-industry type, as with horizontal differentiation. Interestingly, however, these conclusions are derived from a model, which, largely, uses a Heckscher–Ohlin framework although without the assumption that products are identical.

The Determinants of Intra-Industry Trade: the Empirical Evidence

A considerable amount of empirical work has been carried out to test the various possible explanations for both *inter-country* and *inter-industry* differences in levels of intra-industry trade. How well do the theoretical explanations for intra-industry trade considered in the previous section stand up to empirical testing? Let us discuss the results of empirical work for each of the cases.

Country Differences in the Level of Intra-Industry Trade

One set of empirical studies has been concerned with explaining differences between countries in levels of intra-industry trade. In general, the advanced industrialised countries have higher levels of intra-industry trade than developing countries, but there are also significant differences within these categories. For example, the members of the European Union appear to do more intra-industry trade than the countries of North America. Econometric studies have been carried out to test the explanatory power of different variables designed to capture the role of different factors in determining a country's average level of intra-industry trade. The factors which appear to best explain country differences in the level of intra-industry trade are summarised in Box 3.2. with an explanation following.

Box 3.2 Summary of the Econometric Evidence on the Determinants of Intra-Industry Trade

Determinants of Inter-Country Differences

- The higher the level of a country's per capita income, the higher the proportion of IIT to total trade. Evidence: Balassa and Bauwens (1987)
- The greater the degree of income equality between any two countries, the higher the proportion of IIT to total trade. Evidence: Balassa (1986), Culem and Lundberg (1986), Balassa and Bauwens (1987)
- The higher the stage of development, the higher the proportion of IIT to total trade. Evidence: Havrylyshyn and Civan (1983)
- The greater the difference between countries in the level of economic development, the lower the level of IIT
- The larger the size of a country as measured by GDP, the higher the level of IIT. Evidence: McAleese (1979), Glejser (1983), Balassa (1986), Balassa and Bauwens (1987)
- The higher the degree of economic integration between countries, the higher the proportion of IIT to total trade. Evidence: Grubel and Lloyd (1975), Kreinin (1979), Greenaway (1987), Balassa (1979), Balassa and Bauwens (1987), Ezram and Laird (1984)
- The greater the geographical distance between countries, the lower the level of IIT. Evidence: Balassa and Bauwens (1987)
- The greater the imbalance in the level of trade between two countries, the lower the level of IIT

Determinants of Inter-Industry Differences

- The higher the degree of product differentiation, the higher the level of IIT. Evidence: Caves (1981), Greenaway and Milner (1984), Balassa (1986), Balassa and Bauwens (1987)
- The greater the importance of decreasing average costs (increasing returns), the higher the level of IIT. Evidence: Caves (1981), Greenaway and Milner (1984), Tharakan (1984), Balassa (1987)
- The more oligopolistic the market structure (the smaller the number of firms), the lower the level of IIT. Evidence: Greenaway and Milner (1984), Balassa (1986), Balassa and Bauwens (1987), Greenaway, Hine and Milner (1995)
- The greater the importance of foreign direct investment in an industry, the higher the level of IIT. Evidence: Caves (1981), Balassa (1986), Balassa and Bauwens (1987), Greenaway, Hine and Milner (1995)
- The higher the degree of product innovation, the higher the level of IIT. Evidence: Greenaway (1986)
- The greater the variability of tariff rates within an industry between countries, the lower the level of IIT. Evidence: Caves (1981), Balassa and Bauwens (1987)

Continued

- The inclusion of offshore assembly provisions in tariff schedules makes for a higher level of IIT. Evidence: Balassa (1986), Balassa and Bauwens (1987)
- The greater the importance of transport costs relative to the unit value of the product, the higher the level of IIT. Evidence: Balassa (1986), Balassa and Bauwens (1987)

1. The Level of a Country's Per Capita Income

The higher the level of a country's per capita income, the greater the demand for variety. As per capita income rises, so consumers demand more variety. The demand for variety leads to an increase in the degree of product differentiation. This promotes intra-industry trade and reduces the component of inter-industry trade in total trade. The fact that intra-industry trade has increased with the rise in per capita incomes in the western industrialised countries would lend support to this view. On the other hand, it should be borne in mind that other factors were at work, which also served to increase the importance of intra-industry trade, in particular global and regional trade liberalisation. Balassa (1987) found that the extent of average intra-industry trade was positively correlated with average per capita income.

2. The Degree of Income Equality between any Pair of Countries

In the previous chapter, we saw how in Linder's model of overlapping demand, the more equal the level of per capita income of any two countries, the greater the amount of trade that will take place between them. Moreover, this mainly takes the form of intra-industry trade. The level of per capita income is known to exert a strong influence on the pattern of demand. It follows that the pattern of demand will be similar in countries with a similar level of per capita income. Therefore, it is likely that products initially developed to meet local tastes will sell best in countries with similar per capita incomes. The Linder hypothesis enjoys strong empirical support. Balassa found that inequality of per capita income had a significant negative effect on the United States' level of intra-industry trade with different trading partners (Balassa, 1986). Culem and Lundberg also found that differences in per capita GNP had a significant negative effect on bilateral intra-industry trade between countries (Culem and Lundberg, 1986). In a model comprising thirty-eight countries and 152 product categories, Balassa found that intra-industry trade was negatively correlated with differences in income levels as measured by per capita GNP (Balassa, 1987).

3. The Stage of Economic Development

We have already seen that the importance of intra-industry trade tends to increase with the level of a country's per capita income. Closely related to this is the stage that a country has reached in its economic development. Less developed countries tend to have lower intra-industry trade ratios. Fast developing countries (so-called newly industrialising countries) have quite high ratios, while the advanced industrialised countries tend to have the highest. One reason for this is that intra-industry is highest in manufacturing products so countries that are relatively industrialised will have higher intra-industry trade ratios. The other reason is that their per capita income is likely to be higher which makes for more intra-industry trade. However, it is possible for a country to have a high per capita income but remain at a relatively low stage of economic development (oil-producing states such as Kuwait or the

United Arab Emirates might be examples). Ideally, therefore, we need to distinguish between these two factors.

4. The Difference in the Level of Economic Development of any two Countries

When any two countries at different stages of development trade with each other, the result is more likely to be inter- rather than intra-industry trade. This is because the stage of development affects the ratio of capital-to-labour in a country. The more economically advanced a country, the greater the ratio of capital-to-labour. As we have seen, the level of intra-industry trade is lower for trade between developed and developing countries than for trade between developed countries. However, it is also the case that the level of intra-industry trade is greater between newly-industrialising countries and developed countries suggesting that, as developing countries grow, more of their trade with developed coutries takes the form of intra-industry trade.

5. The Size of a Country

There are grounds for expecting the level of intra-industry trade to be greater for large than for small countries. What matters is the size of a country's gross domestic product (GDP) not its geographical size or the size of its population. The larger the GDP, the larger the market in which producers can sell their goods. Since most differentiated goods are produced under conditions of decreasing average costs (increasing returns), producers in large countries will enjoy lower average costs than producers in small countries. These countries are therefore more likely to specialise in differentiated goods in which intra-industry trade is more important than inter-industry trade. For standardised goods, however, producers in small countries will face no disadvantage since most available economies of scale can be reaped at a relatively low level of output. However, trade in standardised goods is more likely to take the form of inter-industry trade. This is not readily apparent from comparing the levels of intra-industry trade of different countries. Thus, we find that a fairly small country like Belgium has quite a high intra-industry trade ratio, while a large country like the United States has quite a low one. However, this may be because other factors offset the influence of country size. On the other hand, it may be the case that the smallness of Norway contributed towards her relatively low intra-industry trade ratio and the largeness of France to her relatively high one.

One interesting study which lends some support to this hypothesis was carried out by McAleese for the Republic of Ireland (McAleese, 1979). He found support for the view that Ireland's size was a reason for its relative specialisation in standardised goods and its relatively low intra-industry trade ratio. Following Ireland's entry to the EC in 1973, unlike the other member states, Ireland appeared to undergo inter- rather than intra-industry specialisation (see Glejser, 1983). A factor that may offset the tendency for large countries to have high levels of intra-industry trade is the role played by natural resources. Trade in natural resources is generally of the inter-industry type and large countries are often well endowed with these. Undoubtedly, this is one reason why Australia, a very large country, has a low intra-industry trade ratio. In a model comprising thirty-eight countries and 152 product groups, Balassa found empirical support for the hypothesis that the extent of intra-industry trade is positively correlated with the average size of a country as measured by GNP and negatively correlated with differences in country size (Balassa, 1987).

6. The Degree of Integration Existing between Countries

There is strong empirical support for the hypothesis that countries that are in close geographical proximity and that have lowered or eliminated their barriers on trade with each other relative to their trade with the rest of the world, will have relatively high levels of intra-industry trade. Thus, Grubel and Lloyd found that the average level of intra-industry trade for the member states of the EC rose from 54% in 1959 to 67% in 1967. This compared with a rise from 36 to 48% for the OECD countries over the same period (Grubel and Lloyd, 1975). Building on and extending earlier work by Balassa, Kreinin (1979) showed how the establishment of the EC and its subsequent enlargement in 1973 led largely to intra-industry specialisation. However, using the Grubel–Lloyd index, Greenaway (1987) found that in several EC countries, the average level of intra-industry trade fell in 1980 although in most cases the ratio remained high. Using a different approach, Glejser (1983) found that intra-industry specialisation generally increased between 1973 and 1979, although export specialisation appeared to have increased in France and import specialisation in Ireland. As we have already noted, Ireland's experience of entry to the EC was somewhat different resulting in more inter- than intra-industry specialisation.

It is not only among the member states of the EC that regional integration has led to intra-industry specialisation. The same has been true of regional integration schemes involving developing countries. Thus Balassa (1979) found that the level of intra-industry trade taking place between the members of the Latin America Free Trade Area (LAFTA) and between members of the Central American Common Market (CACM) was higher than trade between these countries and the rest of the world. Balassa also found econometric support for the hypothesis that the formation of the EEC, EFTA and LAFTA had a positive and highly significant effect on the extent of intra-industry trade (Balassa, 1987).

Another study by Ezran and Laird (1984) examined intra-industry trade as a component of trade between the members of the Association of South-East Asian Nations (ASEAN). In 1980 nearly 50% of the trade of the ASEAN countries with each other was intra-industry trade, compared with 43% for their trade with other developing countries, 36% for their trade with principal developing-country exporters of manufactures (PEMs), 29% for their trade with developed countries and 12% for their trade with the socialist countries.

7. Geographical Closeness

The greater the geographical distance between any two countries, the smaller the level of intra-industry trade likely to take place between them. Although distance acts like an artificial barrier to trade in reducing all trade between the countries in question, intra-industry trade is especially promoted by closeness. One reason is the scope for two-way border trade in weight-gaining products which exists between countries in close proximity. Balassa found that both distance and the existence of a common border had a positive and significant effect on the level of intra-industry trade (Balassa, 1987).

8. The Existence of Large Trade Imbalances between Countries

As we have seen, some methods of measuring intra-industry trade fail to adjust fully for imbalances in a country's overall trade. In this case, countries with very unbalanced trade will have low intra-industry trade ratios. As we observed earlier, this partly accounts for Japan's low intra-industry trade ratio.

Industry Differences in the Level of Intra-Industry Trade

Another series of empirical studies has focused on why levels of intra-industry differ across industries within the same country. Substantial differences among product groups in the level of intra-industry trade have been shown to exist. Generally, intra-industry is higher in manufactured than primary commodities. However, even within the manufacturing sector, significant differences are apparent. This provides economists with the opportunity to conduct tests to see which factors can best explain such cross-industry differences in the level of intra-industry trade. Again, the approach is one of estimating the extent to which inter-industry differences in the levels of intra-industry trade can be explained by different factors. Equations are constructed containing different variables each designed to capture the effects of different causes of intra-industry trade. The task is then to use econometric techniques to estimate the equations.

The following is a summary of the factors which appear to provide the best explanation of such differences:

1. The Degree of Product Differentiation

The greater the degree of product differentiation, the higher the level of intra-industry trade. The more standardised the product, the greater the likelihood of inter-industry specialisation. Econometric research lends qualified support to this hypothesis. A number of different variables have been used as proxies for product differentiation. These have included:

(i) The number of sub-groups within a single three-digit product group (which is a measure of the degree of product heterogeneity)
(ii) The variation of the unit values of exports within the product group (the so-called Hufbauer index)
(iii) The ratio of selling costs (advertising, sales promotion, market research) to total costs
(iv) The ratio of research and development (R&D), expenditures-to-sales (as a measure of the degree of product innovation)

Although results differ according to the particular study undertaken, most of these variables have been found to have a positive influence on the level of intra-industry trade. However, there is some ambiguity concerning the influence of advertising intensity (as measured by selling costs) on the level of intra-industry trade. Caves (1981) has argued that advertising expenditures exert a negative influence on the level of intra-industry trade. He distinguishes between two prototypes of differentiation, namely, complexity' and 'information'. In the first case, products are technologically complex combinations of different attributes (e.g. automobiles) that are typically produced under conditions of increasing returns to scale (decreasing average costs). This means that producers cannot profitably produce all the varieties that consumers want and hence high levels of intra-industry trade are common. In the second case, however, the products are physically much alike but are differentiated in the eyes of consumers by small differences in appearance (e.g. different brands of soap detergent or cigarettes). This kind of differentiation is largely subjective arising from the fact that consumers lack useful 'objective' information to guide them in choosing between alternative types. Industries, which produce these kinds of products, are usually characterised by exceptionally high levels of promotional expenditures relative to sales.

However, levels of intra-industry trade are generally lower in these products because foreign direct investment is generally preferred to trade as a means of reaching the consumer in overseas markets. Why? Because of the nature of advertising, which tends to be highly cultural-specific favouring production close to where the consumer is situated. Caves found empirical support for this hypothesis. However, other studies have obtained different results. Balassa found that both of his measures of product differentiation – namely, the dispersion of prices and the ratio of marketing expenditures-to-total costs – were positively related to the extent of intra-industry trade (Balassa, 1987).

2. The Extent of Economies of Scale

There is a theoretical expectation that the level of intra-industry trade will increase with the importance of economies of scale. As we have seen, it is not product differentiation per se that gives rise to intra-industry specialisation. Rather, it is a high degree of product differentiation and the tendency for average costs to fall with output (increasing returns) that lead to intra-industry specialisation. The latter is the reason why producers cannot produce all the varieties that consumers want. It is, therefore, at first sight rather surprising that econometric research appears to refute this hypothesis. Most studies show a negative relationship between economies of scale and the level of intra-industry trade. For example, Caves found strong support for the opposite relationship, namely that the level of intra-industry trade falls with the extensiveness of scale economies (Caves 1981). Balassa also found that intra-industry trade was negatively correlated with economies of scale (Balassa and Bauwens, 1987).

However, this is because most studies have tested the relationship between the level of intra-industry trade and the economies of large plant size. The relationship between the minimum efficient scale (MES) and the size of the market is the variable frequently used to capture this effect. However, industries in which such scale economies are important are generally standardised goods industries (e.g. petrochemical production, steel production, etc.) in which inter-industry trade is more important. The types of scale economies which lead to intra-industry specialisation are those associated with long production runs. Long production runs may be achieved in quite small specialist plants. These types of scale economies are therefore more common in differentiated goods industries and are not properly accounted for by variables that measure economies of plant size. One way of dealing with this is to use different measures of market structure, such as the number of firms in an industry, the importance of economies of scale and the degree of market concentration. Using this approach, Greenaway, Hine and Milner (1995) found that intra-industry trade was positively related to the number of firms, negatively related to scale economies and negatively related to the degree of market concentration. This would suggest that high levels of intra-industry trade are more likely to be found in industries where there are a large number of firms and where there exists ease of market entry. Where product differentiation also exists, such industries conform with the monopolistically competitive market structure discussed above.

3. The Type of Market Structure

The relationship between market structure and intra-industry trade is ambiguous. As we have seen, some models predict that high levels of intra-industry trade will be found in oligopolistic industries dominated by a few sellers even when the product is an identical one. However, it is equally true that intra-industry trade is the outcome of competition among a large number of firms producing a differentiated product (monopolistic competition). Econometric research provides little evidence for a positive relationship between intra-industry trade and conventional measures of oligopoly. For example, the degree of oligopoly may be measured by the level of industrial concentration. The share of total sales accounted for by the top five firms – the so-called five-firm concentration ratio – is one frequently used measure of industrial concentration. The level of barriers to entry to an industry is another widely used gauge of the degree of oligopoly power present. However, measures such as these often fail to capture the extent to which an industry is dominated by a small number of firms at a global level (the degree of international oligopoly power present) which is what counts in generating high levels of intra-industry trade. One solution is to divide the domestic concentration ratio by the share of imports in the output of an industry so as to allow for competition from abroad. The higher the share of imports in output, the lower the adjusted concentration ratio.

However, even using an adjusted concentration ratio, Balassa found only a negative but statistically signficant relationship between industrial concentration and the level of intra-industry trade. This might suggest that the degree of oligoply is not an important determinant of the level of intra-industry trade contrary to the predictions of certain theoretical models. However, the problem may be that a high internationally adjusted concentration ratio does not properly measure the degree of actual oligopolistic rivalry prevalent within a particular industry. On the contrary, as rivalrous firms situated in different countries succeed in penetrating each other's markets with their product, the internationally adjusted concentration ratio will fall! Then, a falling ratio is the better measure of the type of oligopolistic competition, which leads to intra-industry trade according to theoretical models which predict such a relationship.

4. The Importance of Foreign Direct Investment

The relationship between intra-industry trade and the level of foreign direct investment in a particular industry is similarly ambiguous. As we shall see in Chapter 5, direct investment abroad may be a substitute for or complement to trade. The establishment of a subsidiary in a foreign country to produce a product may in some cases displace exports, while, in other cases, it may lead to higher exports. The latter will take the form of components and parts exported from the parent company to the foreign subsidiary, or of raw materials or semi-finished goods from the subsidiary to the parent company for further processing or of finished goods for sale in some third country. Clearly, where foreign direct investment acts as a substitute for trade, high levels of such investment will be associated with low levels of intra-industry trade. Where, however, direct investment acts as a complement to trade, a positive relationship will be found between such investment and the level of intra-industry trade. Indeed, where components and parts are treated as belonging to the same product group as the finished product (e.g. automobiles and automobile parts), this is to be expected (so-called vertical, as opposed to horizontal, intra-industry trade).

Caves (1981) has argued that where the 'information' aspect in product differentiation predominates (as in industries such as tobacco manufacturing, soap detergents, household goods, etc.), foreign direct investment will tend to substitute for trade. This is for the reasons discussed above, namely, that advertising plays an important role in these industries and this favours producing goods as close as possible to the consumer to fashion the product to best suit local tastes and culture. However, where the 'complexity' aspect is predominant (e.g. automobile production), it is better to concentrate production in large, specialist plants located in only a few countries so as to reap all available economies of scale. This will make for high levels of intra-industry trade. The former leads to geographically dispersed production and the latter to geographically concentrated production. Caves has claimed econometric support for this hypothesis. He found that advertising expenditures and the level of foreign direct investment were strongly correlated. At the same time, advertising expenditures had a negative effect on the level of intra-industry trade. In other words, where the degree of advertising intensity was high, foreign direct investment had a negative influence on the level of intra-industry trade. Balassa and Bauwens (1997) also found that high levels of foreign direct investment were negatively correlated with the level of intra-industry trade. However, several studies have found evidence for a positive relationship between the degree of offshore processing – which often (but not always) follows the establishment of a processing plant in a foreign country using components and parts supplied by the parent company – and the extent of intra-industry trade. Caves (1981) found evidence for a positive linkage of this kind as did Balassa and Bauwens (1987) and Greenway, Hine and Milner (1995).

5. *The Degree of Product Innovation*

In industries characterised by rapid rates of product innovation (e.g. pharmaceuticals), product differentiation takes the form of technological differentiation. As we have seen, this may be expected to result in high levels of intra-industry trade because production typically takes place under conditions of increasing returns to scale. One proxy for product innovation is the ratio of R&D expenditure to total sales (although this only measures innovation from the input rather the output side). Greenaway (1986) found weak support in econometric testing for such a relationship.

6. *The Importance of Tariff Rates*

There exists no evidence for the view that the level of intra-industry trade is higher in industries where trade barriers (whether tariff or non-tariff) are lower. This is not surprising since lower trade barriers are as likely to increase inter- as intra-industry trade. However, the variability of tariff rates within an industry as between countries may be expected to influence the level of intra-industry trade. Both Caves (1981) and Balassa (1987) found some support for this hypothesis. In addition, the inclusion of offshore assembly provisions (OAPs) within tariff schedules will further enhance intra-industry trade. These allow imports of finished products to enter a country at a reduced tariff rate to the extent that they embody components and parts supplied by the importing (home) country. Such OAPs have encouraged vertical specialisation in the production of certain products and have in some cases resulted in vertical intra-industry trade (see Chapter 5 for a more detailed discussion of this phenomenon).

7. *Transport Costs*

Intra-industry trade will be greater in products which are costly to transport and where transport costs increase with the degree of processing (so-called weight-gaining industries). As we have seen, the products of weight-gaining industries are sometimes subject to considerable amounts of border trade. Econometric studies lend some limited support to the hypothesis.

Distinguishing between Vertical and Horizontal Intra-Industry Trade

One weakness of much of the empirical work carried out to test for the importance of different variables in the determination of cross-industry differences in levels of intra-industry trade is that it fails to distinguish between horizontal and vertical intra-industry trade. Yet, there are theoretical grounds for supposing that the determinants of each are different. Greenway, Hine and Milner (1995) sought to disentangle the two forms of intra-industry trade in estimating the determinants of industry differences in the level of intra-industry trade. They did so by using unit value dispersion criteria to distinguish vertical from horizontal intra-industry trade and applying this to the U.K. multilateral trade at the five-digit SITC level. Large differences between the unit value of exports and imports at the five-digit level were taken as demonstrating the prevalence of vertical over horizontal intra-industry trade. Separate equations for the two kinds of intra-industry trade, but containing the same variables, were then estimated. Their results show that *total* intra-industry trade is positively related to the number of firms in the industry, negatively related to the degree of market concentration and negatively related to the existence of scale economies. However, somewhat surprisingly, attribute diversity was found to have a negative effect on intra-industry trade.

If, however, horizontal and vertical intra-industry trade are separately estimated, some important differences emerge. As theoretical expectations suggest, horizontal intra-industry trade is positively related to attribute diversity (a proxy for horizontal differentiation) and vertical intra-industry trade to skill intensity (a proxy for vertical differentiation). Vertical intra-industry trade is found to be positively related to the number of firms in an industry and negatively related to the importance of multinational enterprises in an industry. By way of contrast, horizontal intra-industry trade is found to be positively related to the importance of multinational enterprises in an industry, although the authors caution that transfer pricing (see Chapter 4) may have distorted the unit-value dispersion measure. Surprisingly, the attribute diversity variable was not found to be significant and did not show a consistently positive relationship. Scale economies had the expected negative effect on horizontal intra-industry trade but the number of firms in an industry had the opposite effect.

These results suggest that the determinants of the two types of intra-industry trade are different and that, therefore, it is important in econometric work to distinguish between them. In the case of the UK, it would appear that vertical intra-industry trade has been relatively more important than horizontal. Since different factors affect the two types of intra-industry trade, any attempt to measure the explanatory power of different theoretical determinants is likely to give misleading results unless this distinction is made.

Conclusion

A large and growing proportion of world trade now takes the form of two-way trade in products belonging to the same industry. This is especially true of trade in manufactured goods between advanced industrialised countries. While some of this may result from counting within the same industry products that have different factor intensities, a surprisingly large amount of intra-industry trade remains even when product groups are broken down into high levels of disaggregation. This suggest that intra-industry is a real and not merely a statistical phenomenon. From a theoretical point of view, the growth in the importance of intra-industry trade cannot be explained using a neo-classical, factor proportions framework. The latter predicts inter- not intra-industry trade. This would seem to further emphasise the limitations of the Heckscher–Ohlin model for explaining much of the trade that is taking place in the world, especially trade between advanced industrialised countries.

In recent decades, several different models have been developed by trade theorists to explain the phenomenon of intra-industry trade. All require relaxing one or more of the assumptions of perfect competition on which neo-classical trade theory largely relies. First, models in which the global market is dominated by a small number of sellers (oligopoly) show that intra-industry trade can take place in identical products. Second, models in which there are a large number of firms but where the product of each producer differs somewhat from that of other producers (horizontal differentiation) also predict that intra-industry trade will result. Finally, in industries where there exist large differences in the quality of different goods (vertical differentiation), intra-industry trade will result, although the determinants may be much the same as in the Heckscher–Ohlin model because factor intensities change over the product spectrum. Attempts to test how well these different theories explain intra-industry trade have generated results that largely conform with expectations.

One of the most important results of these models is that they show that trade may benefit countries not merely because it results in an improved allocation of resources. Where markets are dominated by firms with a high degree of monopoly power, two-way trade in the same product may force producers to reduce prices closer to marginal costs. Intra-industry trade in horizontally differentiated goods may also result in lower prices, as each producer is able to get further down their falling average cost curve. However, consumers also gain because they are able to enjoy a greater variety of a particular good or acquire a variety closer to their preferred type. Under autarky, producers supply fewer varieties because it is not profitable for them to produce all the varieties that consumers want. Vertical intra-industry trade is more likely to bring conventional efficiency gains, depending on the assumptions that are made about the number of firms and the nature of the long-run average cost curve.

However, the observation that much trade is of the intra-industry type is interesting for another reason. Where the expansion of trade leads to intra-industry specialisation, there is no need for resources to move between industries. In short, adjustment to increased trade may be easier where intra- as opposed to inter-industry specialisation results. This may explain why the advanced industrialised countries have, generally, been more prepared to lower barriers on their trade with each other than on their trade with developing countries. Trade between industrialised countries is mainly intra-industry trade, whereas trade between developed and developing countries is, more commonly, of the inter-industry type. Furthermore, because factor intensities vary less within than between industries, increased intra-industry trade has less of an effect on relative factor prices than inter-industry trade. In Chapter 2, we saw that, because inter-industry trade leads to a tendency towards factor-price equalisation, the owners of a country's scarce factors of production tend to oppose freer trade. For this reason, too, intra-industry specialisation is likely to meet with less resistance from within the importing country than inter-industry specialisation. Moreover, the gains to producers in the export sector are potentially greater because of decreasing average costs, so that strong support for lower barriers to trade can be expected. These issues are explored in more depth in Chapter 8.

Notes for Further Reading

There now exists a large and growing theoretical and empirical literature on the subject of intra-industry trade. One of the earliest works on this subject was:

Grubel, H. and Lloyd, P. J. *Intra-Industry Trade – The Theory and Measurement of International Trade in Differentiated Products* (London and Basingstoke: The Macmillan Press, 1975).

An excellent, more recent text covering the entire subject matter is:

Greenaway, D. and Milner, C. *The Economics of Intra-Industry Trade* (Oxford: Basil Blackwell, 1986).

On the theory of intra-industry trade, the most important contributions remain the following:

Brander, J. 1981. A Intra-Industry Trade in identical commodities, *Journal of International Economics*, **11**, pp. 1–14.

Brander, J. A. and Krugman, P. 1983. A reciprocal dumping model of international trade, *Journal of International Economics*, **13**, pp. 313–21.

for the reciprocal dumping model. For models of horizontal intra-industry trade, the most important contributions are the following:

Lancaster, K. 1980. Intra-industry trade under perfect monopolistic competition, *Journal of International Economics*, **10**, pp. 151–76.

Helpman, E. 1981. International trade in the presence of product differentiation, economies of scale and monopolistic competition, *Journal of International Economics*, **11**, pp. 305–40.

Dixit, A. K. and Stiglitz, J. 1977. Monopolistic competition and optimum product diversity, *American Economic Review*, **67**, pp. 297–308.

Krugman, P. 1979. Increasing returns, monopolistic competition and international trade, *Journal of International Economics*, **9**, pp. 469–79.

Krugman, P. 1980. Scale economies, product differentiation and the pattern of trade, *American Economic Review*, **70**, pp. 950–59.

Krugman, P., Trade in differentiated commodities and the political economy of trade liberalisation, in Bhagwati, J. (ed.), Import Competition and Response (Chicago: University of Chicago Press, 1982).

Venables, A. J., 1984. Multiple equilibria in the theory of international trade with monopolistically competitive industries, *Journal of International Economics*, **16**, pp. 103–21.

Dixit, A. K. and Norman, V., *Theory of International Trade* (Cambridge: Cambridge University Press, 1980).

For vertical intra-industry trade, the interested reader should refer to the following:

Falvey, R. E. 1981. Commercial policy and intra-industry trade, *Journal of International Economics*, **11**, pp. 495–511.

Falvey, R. E. and Kierzkowski, H., Product quality, intra-industry trade and imperfect competition, Discussion paper, Graduate Institute of International Studies, Geneva, 1984.

Chapter 4

Multinational Companies and World Trade

CHAPTER OUTLINES: Introduction. Definitions. The Growth of Foreign Direct Investment since the Second World War. The Rise of the Multinational Corporation – the regional distribution of MNC activity, the sectoral distribution of MNC activity. The Determinants of Foreign Direct Investment – Horizontal FDI, vertical FDI, conglomerate FDI. The Importance of MNCs in world trade: intra-firm trade – industry variations. Transfer Pricing – motives for transfer pricing, constraints on transfer price manipulation, empirical evidence on transfer pricing, the control of transfer pricing. Integrating Multinationals into Theories of Trade – international production in the neo-classical framework, the Dunning eclectic approach, recent attempts to integrate trade and FDI, Porter's approach. Conclusion.

Introduction

Accompanying the increase in world trade over the period since the Second World War, there has been an equally rapid growth of private foreign investment. Much of this has taken the form of companies setting up or acquiring a controlling interest in overseas subsidiaries/affiliates. Today, most large companies and many medium-sized firms operate in more than one country. Such companies have come to be variously referred to as *multinational companies* (MNCs), *multinational enterprises* (MNEs) or *transnational corporations* (TNCs). The largest among them have overseas operations that match or exceed the size of their domestic operations. (Ranked by foreign assets, Royal Dutch Shell, part Dutch and part British, is ranked as the world's largest company with assets of $102 billion, closely followed by Ford, Exxon, General Motors and IBM, all of the USA.) Such companies invariably operate on a global basis, planning their activities on a regional or international scale. One consequence is that the production of many goods has become transnational.

Overseas investment by companies to set up a new overseas subsidiary or acquire a controlling interest in another company is referred to as *direct investment abroad* or *foreign direct investment* (FDI). This is different from investment by individuals and financial institutions in the purchase of interest-bearing securities, which is called *portfolio investment*. Direct investment abroad is one way in which companies can expand their operations internationally. In this chapter, the motives for firms engaging in this kind of investment are discussed. It may be that producing abroad is viewed as an alternative to exporting. Much investment by United States MNCs in the first two decades after the Second World War in Western Europe was undertaken for this reason. However, direct investment may equally well be undertaken for efficiency-seeking reasons. A company may shift its production of a particular good or just a particular stage in the production process to another country to take advantage of differences in costs or a more favourable environment. In industries dominated by a small number of sellers, the decision to invest abroad may be dictated merely by the need to prevent rivals from securing an advantage.

In this chapter, we first discuss the growth of the MNC over the past half-century and ask what factors best explain the decision of firms to invest abroad. However, our primary concern is with the impact of MNCs on world trade. In the second half of the chapter, the importance of MNCs in world trade is, therefore, discussed. We shall see that a growing proportion of world trade now constitutes so-called *intra-firm* or *in-house trade*. This may be defined as trade between a parent company and its overseas affiliates. In this chapter, the importance of intra-firm trade as a component of world trade is discussed. We shall see that a close relationship exists between the incentive of firms to internalise their markets for intermediate goods and services through FDI and the importance of intra-firm trade in total trade. One of the reasons why firms internalise markets for intermediate goods and services is because of the opportunities it creates to manipulate so-called *transfer prices*. Transfer prices are the prices that are used when a MNC transfers goods or assets from one part of the company to another. We shall see that reasons exist why MNCs might choose to use prices for internal sales that differ significantly from market-determined prices used for equivalent transactions that are conducted on an arms length basis.

Finally, the chapter concludes by discussing whether or not new models of trade are needed to take into account of the growing importance of MNCs in world trade. Reference is made to some recent attempts made by theoretical economists to develop models of trade which incorporate FDI.

Definitions

Although the era since the Second World War has witnessed a rapid growth of overseas investment, this should not be thought of as a unique occurrence. High levels of overseas investment have occurred at similar times in the past. The half-century before the First World War saw a similar dramatic growth in the level of overseas investment. However, most of the investment that took place during this period was portfolio investment. It involved investors in the rich, colonial countries of that time acquiring interest-bearing financial assets (shares or government bonds) in the colonies and dependencies of these countries. The UK was the most important creditor nation. In 1913, she accounted for over 40% of all overseas credits. Nearly half of all her investment overseas went to countries which were part of the British Empire (Canada, Australia and New Zealand and India were the main recipients.) Over 40% of investments went into railways, although investment in government bonds issued by governments in the colonies and dominions was also important. At its peak, capital exports from Great Britain amounted to as much as 9% of national income (see Thomas, 1967).

Unlike direct investment abroad, portfolio investment is motivated purely and simply by the desire for financial gain. This comes in the form a dividend or fixed interest payment payable on the asset held and/or a rise in the price of the asset during the time in which it is held. It takes place because differences exist between countries in the rate of yield obtainable on equivalent assets. This, in turn, takes place because there are differences between countries in the demand for loanable funds (for purposes of fixed investment) and the supply of loanable funds (by households and companies which have accumulated surplus funds through saving). In the period before the First World War, a higher return on capital could be obtained by investing in the colonies because the demand for funds needed to build railways, create public utilities and extract raw materials vastly exceeded any savings which these countries were able to generate themselves. Hence, capital flowed, in the manner predicted by the neo-classical theories of the time, from the capital-abundant to the capital-scarce countries of the world. It played an important role in the economic development of these regions, while at the same time creating new markets and sources of raw materials for producers in the colonial countries.

In the period after the Second World War, however, an important shift took place towards direct investment undertaken by companies. For example, between 1951 and 1964, an estimated four-fifths of gross long-term investment overseas was direct as opposed to portfolio investment. Unlike portfolio investment, direct investment is not undertaken by individual investors or financial institutions in search of a higher return on the funds invested. Rather, it is carried out by companies whose main motive is to establish production operations in another country. Indeed, if the motive were purely financial, portfolio investment would be preferred to direct investment as the risks are much lower. Instead, the company is anxious to expand its operations internationally and prefers to do so by producing its product overseas rather than by exporting or any other means. This may entail the establishment of an entirely new, subsidiary in the foreign country – a so-called *greenfield venture*. Alternatively, it may acquire a controlling interest in another, existing overseas company, by buying shares in the foreign company, through a merger with a foreign company or by means of an acquisition. In recent decades, mergers and acquisitions (M & As) have, in certain parts of the world, come to account for a major proportion of FDI activity. Although definitions vary between countries, a controlling interest is usually taken to be a minimum of 10% of equity capital. (Some countries set the figure higher including the UK, which uses a 20% threshold.)

One of the main differences between direct and portfolio investment concerns what is transferred between the home and host country. While portfolio investment involves merely the transfer of financial or money capital from one country to another, direct investment transfers a package or 'bundle' of resources, of which money capital is only one of the ingredients. This package is made up of several components, which include ownership of the foreign company, the exercise of control over the foreign company, the provision of some management expertise and the possible transfer of some technology. Thus, direct investment is potentially more beneficial to the recipient country than portfolio investment. Portfolio investment is beneficial in providing the recipient country with additional funds which can be used to finance productive investment. However, direct investment provides the host country with additional resources, which will raise the country's rate of economic growth. Both benefit the balance of payments of the host country. However, direct investment may do so more, if the some of the output of the foreign company is exported or if the output in part substitutes for imports.

Our concern in this book is with direct and not portfolio investment. However, in recent decades, largely as a result of a gradual lowering of controls on international capital movements, the growth in the range of different financial assets available and the growth of markets for buying and selling such assets, the growth of portfolio investment has exceeded even that of direct investment abroad. The desire of investors to spread risk by diversifying the portfolio of assets held combined with the search for higher returns and quicker financial gain has led to a growth in the volume of financial flows taking place between countries. Increased volatility of exchange rates has also encouraged holders of surplus funds to shift their funds around to take advantage of expected changes in exchange rates or to cover themselves against the risk of unexpected movements. Prior to the financial crisis of 1997–98, much of this investment took the form of a flow of funds from the developed countries to the so-called emerging markets of the world, located mainly in East Asia, Latin America and (following the collapse of Communism) Eastern Europe. Also important was the flow of funds from the world's biggest creditor nation, Japan, to the world's biggest debtor nation, the United States. As we shall see in Chapter 6, this was directly stimulated by the existence of a large differential in the rate of return on long-term financial assets between the two countries.

The Growth of Foreign Direct Investment since the Second World War

The growth of FDI over the period since the Second World War can be measured in one of two ways: a rising *flow* of investment abroad or an increased *stock* of direct investment held abroad. The *flow* of direct investment abroad is a measure of the amount of *new* direct investment activity taking place each year. A country's *net* flow of capital abroad – the difference between *gross* outflows and *gross* inflows – is recorded as part of the country's balance of payments. Although practices vary among countries, this usually includes the unremitted profits of overseas affiliates, that is, earnings of overseas affiliates that are not distributed as dividends to shareholders or remitted to the parent company and which are assumed to be reinvested in the affiliate. In other words, if an overseas affiliate reinvests profits, this is treated as direct investment by the parent company, since the company is effectively adding to its stock of investment abroad. However, unremitted profits are not always included. The figure should also include any borrowing by the affiliate from the parent company. However, if a MNC expands abroad by raising funds on the capital market of the host or some third country, this will not normally be included in any measure of the flow of investment abroad, although it adds to the stock of investment held abroad. Indeed, the more established a company is in the foreign country, the less likely are its overseas affiliates to depend on the parent company for additional funds. Thus, figures showing the flow of direct investment abroad are likely to underestimate the extent of actual FDI taking place, the more so for companies that are already well-established overseas.

The *stock* of direct investment abroad measures the money value of assets held abroad. Since this includes any increase in assets financed by capital raised on the capital markets of the host or some third country, it provides a more complete measure of the growth of FDI. On the other hand, stock measures of FDI are often unsatisfactory because company assets are frequently valued on a historical and not current cost basis, that is, assets are valued on the basis of the price paid for them when they were first bought rather than their current value. The use of historical costs underestimates the worth of a company because it fails to take sufficient account of inflation. Table 4.1 shows the growth of FDI using both stock and flow measures for the period from 1960 to 1994 and compares these with the growth of world trade, GNP/GDP and gross fixed capital formation.

The percentage rate of increase refers to the growth in the value of these flows measured at current prices and therefore takes no account of inflation. In the period from 1960 to 1970, inflows of FDI grew at a rate equal to that of world trade but significantly faster than domestic fixed investment and GNP. However, in the 1970s, inflows of FDI slowed, growing at a slower rate than world trade and about the same rate as domestic fixed investment and GNP. In the decade after 1986, this was reversed with inflows of FDI growing considerably faster than world trade, domestic fixed investment and GDP. The FDI growth rate using the stock figure is somewhat slower for the period since 1986 but still shows FDI as growing faster than domestic investment or trade.

Table 4.2 shows the *geographical distribution* of both the inflow and outflow of direct investment for the period since 1983.

Table 4.1 Rates of Growth of GNP, Trade and Investment at Current Prices in the World's Market Economies, 1960–1994 (percentage)

	1960–70	*1970–80*	*1986–90*	*1991–94*
Inward FDI flows	10.2	15.0	24.7	12.7
FDI outward stock	n.a	n.a	19.8	8.8
GNP/GDP*	8.4	15.2	10.8	4.3
Gross fixed capital formation	9.6	15.3	10.6	4.0
Exports**	10.4	19.9	14.3	3.8

*GNP up to 1980 and GDP after 1980.
**Includes non-factor services after 1980.
Source: UNCTC (1985), UN (1996).

Table 4.2 FDI Inflows and Outflows by Region, 1983–1995 ($ billion)

	Inflows		*Ouflows*	
	1983–87	*1988–92*	*1983–87*	*1988–92*
Developed countries	58.7 (76)	139.1 (78)	72.6 (95)	193.3 (93)
Developing countries	18.3 (24)	36.8 (21)	4.2 (5)	15.2 (7)
Central and Eastern Europe	0.02 (0.02)	1.36 (0.07)	0.01 (0.01)	0.04 (0.02)
All countries	77.1 (100)	177.3 (100)	76.8 (100)	208.5 (100)

Source: UN (1996).
Note: Figures in parentheses show percentages of total FDI.

Ninty-three percent of all FDI outflows originated with the developed countries although the importance of the developing countries as FDI exporters has been growing. The developed countries also account for the bulk of FDI inflows. Their share was in fact slightly higher in the period after 1988 than before. Thus, well over three-quarters of FDI flows take place between the developed countries.

Table 4.3 shows the *net* flows (outflows minus inflows) of foreign direct investment by country for the period 1984–89.

Over the period 1984–89, the biggest net exporter of direct capital was Japan. At the other extreme, the United States had the largest net inflows of FDI. In fact, Japan's net FDI outflow was more or less matched by the United States' net inflow. This does not mean that the United States ceased to export direct capital abroad. On the contrary, she still ranks as the third largest capital exporter in gross terms. However, her large capital outflows were offset by capital inflows by nearly three times. This amounts to a remarkable turnaround in the U.S. capital account. In earlier periods, the United States was consistently the largest gross and net exporter of FDI to the rest of the world. The United Kingdom was the second largest capital exporter measured in net terms followed closely by Germany. Other major net exporters were Sweden, France and the Netherlands. In addition to the United States, the major net importers of FDI were Switzerland, Spain and Mexico.

Annual net flows of FDI are quite volatile, so a more meaningful way of looking at the geographical distribution of FDI is to take the stock of FDI held abroad. Table 4.4 shows the stock of direct investment abroad by both

Table 4.3 Net Flows of FDI by Country, 1984–1989, Annual Average ($ millions)

Country	*FDI outflows*	*FDI inflows*	*Net FDI flows*
United States	16,847	43,938	+27,091
United Kingdom	23,283	13,545	−9,738
Germany	9,599	1,833	−7,766
Netherlands	7,052	3,787	−3,265
Switzerland	4,165	8,506	+4,341
France	8,828	5,364	−3,464
Japan	20,793	81	−20,712
Canada	4,664	4,718	+54
Sweden	4,969	982	−3,987
Australia	3,338	4,306	+968
Belgium–Luxembourg	2,561	2,793	+232
Italy	2,775	2,560	−215
Spain	722	4,535	+3,813
Mexico	128	2,436	+2,308
China	581	2,282	+1,701
Singapore	286	2,239	+1,953
Hong Kong	1,833	1,422	−411
Brazil	184	1,416	−1.232

Source: UN (1996).

Table 4.4 The Stock of FDI by Host and Home Country, 1980–1995 ($ millions)

	Inward		Outward	
Country	*1980*	*1995**	*1980*	*1995**
United States	83,046 (17.2)	564,637 (21.2)	220,178 (42.9)	705,570 (25.8)
United Kingdom	63,014 (13.1)	244,141 (9.2)	80,434 (15.7)	319,009 (11.7)
Germany	36,630 (7.6)	134,002 (5.0)	43,127 (8.4)	235,003 (8.6)
Japan	3,270 (0.7)	17,831 (0.7)	18,833 (3.7)	305,545 (11.1)
France	22,617 (4.7)	162,423 (6.1)	23,604 (4.6)	200,002 (7.3)
Netherlands	19,167 (4.0)	102,598 (3.9)	42,116 (8.2)	158,613 (5.8)
Canada	54,163 (11.2)	116,788 (4.4)	22,572 (4.4)	110,388 (4.0)
Italy	8,892 (1.8)	64,696 (2.4)	7,319 (1.4)	86,672 (3.2)
Belgium–Luxembourg	7,306 (1.5)	84,605 (3.2)	6,037 (1.2)	57,768 (2.1)
Spain	5,141 (1.1)	128,859 (4.8)	1,226 (0.2)	34,271 (1.3)
Switzerland	8,506 (1.8)	43,075 (1.6)	21,491 (4.2)	108,253 (4.0)
Sweden	3,626 (0.8)	32,805 (1.2)	5,611 (1.1)	61,561 (2.3)
Australia	13,173 (2.7)	104,176 (3.9)	2,260 (0.4)	41,296 (1.5)
Brazil	17,480 (3.6)	49,530 (1.9)	652 (0.1)	6,460 (0.2)
Mexico	8,992 (1.9)	61,322 (2.3)	136 (0.0)	2,681 (0.0)

*Estimates.
Note: Figures in parentheses show percentages of total FDI.
Source: UN (1996)

host country (the inward FDI stock) and home country (the outward FDI stock).

In stock terms, despite declining net outflows of capital, the United States still accounts for roughly one-quarter of FDI held abroad. However, her share has fallen dramatically from 43% in 1980 to 26% today. By way of contrast, Japan's share of outward FDI has risen from only 4% in 1980 to 11% in 1995. The United Kingdom remained the second largest holder of outward FDI although her share also fell from 16 to 12%. Germany ranked as the fourth largest holder of outward FDI with a roughly constant share, followed by France and the Netherlands. The United States is also the world's largest recipient of FDI measured in stock terms. Moreover, due to rising inflows of FDI, her share measured in stock terms has risen. Germany, France, Spain and Canada are the next largest receivers of inward FDI.

The Rise of the Multinational Corporation

A simple way of defining an MNC is 'an enterprise that controls and manages production establishments in at least two countries' (Caves, 1982). Another definition is 'a corporation which owns (in whole or in part), controls and manages income-generating assets in more than one country' (Hood and Young, 1979). Yet, a third definition is 'an enterprise that engages in foreign direct investment (FDI) and owns or controls value-adding activities in more than one country' (Dunning, 1992). The essential characteristics of an MNC highlighted by these definitions is that (1) it is a company that *owns* productive assets in more than one country and (2) the parent company exercises managerial *control* over the affiliate company. Other definitions have stipulated that the overseas activities of the MNC must be at least as great as the domestic activities for the company to constitute a MNC, but this would seem unduly restrictive. As observed above, a 10% share of equity capital is commonly taken as the necessary minimum for a foreign company to be able to exercise control but the exact percentage is not important.

It should not be thought that the MNC is a post-Second World War phenomenon. MNCs did exist before 1939. Indeed, the Dutch and English trading companies of the 16th and 17th centuries might be regarded as the first examples of MNCs. Substantial amounts of FDI did take place in the late 19th and early 20th centuries, although it was less important than portfolio investment. An estimated one-half of all British foreign investment before 1914 was portfolio investment. Much of it was directed towards infrastructure (transportation, utilities and public works) needed to support primary-producing activities in the colonies of the British Empire. However, an estimated one-third of all British foreign investment took the form of the creation of free-standing quoted companies (i.e. direct investment) oriented mainly towards mining and utilities mostly in the British Empire and Latin America. A relatively small 10% of all foreign investment involved the establishment by British companies of overseas subsidiaries. These were the first British multinationals and included such famous names as Royal Dutch Shell, Consolidated Gold Field (today the Hanson Trust), Lever Brothers (today Unilever), British American Tobacco (BAT), Courtaulds, Dunlop to name just a few (see Cox, 1997, for a useful analysis of early forms of FDI). Further substantial direct investment took place in the inter-war period, although foreign investment in general was badly hit by the world economic crisis of that period. U.S. companies were the most active in establishing or acquiring new foreign subsidiaries mainly in Europe, Canada and South America. The period witnessed the emergence of U.S. MNCs such as Ford and General Motors and European MNCs such as Philips and I.G. Farben.

However, the major growth of the modern MNC only took place following the end of the Second World War. One reason was the revolutionary improvements which took place in methods of international travel and communication (e.g. the discovery of the jet aeroplane, new and cheaper ways of sending messages, a faster international postal system, etc.) all of which were essential if companies were to operate on a global scale. Before 1939, it was more difficult for managers to travel between parent company and foreign affiliate on a regular basis and information took much longer to transmit from one part of the world to another. A second reason was the change in the international political and economic climate. The ending of the War saw a determined effort by the victorious powers to create political and economic conditions favourable towards the maintenance of a stable peace. Economically, this was seen as best served by an open, rules-based multilateral world trading order supported by stable, yet adjustable, exchange rates and free convertibility of currencies. The creation of new international economic institutions such as the International Monetary Fund (IMF) and the World Bank and the drafting of a new General Agreement on Tariffs and Trade (GATT) lent considerable support to this process. Such an environment did much to raise business confidence and encourage firms to seek ways of expanding their operations overseas. At the regional level, the creation of the European Communities (EC) in 1958 and the European Free Trade Area (EFTA) in 1960 created a climate within Western Europe that was favourable to increased direct investment. At the same time, the success with which Europe recovered from the devastation caused by the War and was able to establish conditions of fast economic growth, full employment and relative price stability served to attract investment by foreign firms to the region.

In the post-war upsurge of multinational activity, U.S. companies played the leading role. The US emerged from the Second World War in a stronger position than any other country. The dollar shortage of the post-war period meant that many European countries were keen to attract U.S. investment, while the federal administration in the U.S. saw such investment as one means of alleviating the dollar shortage. On the supply side, U.S. firms needed larger markets for their manufactures to ensure adequate expansion. U.S. companies had gained a technological lead in a number of industries (such as electronics, telecommunications, automobiles, aerospace and synthetic materials). The domestic market for many of the new products, which U.S. firms had led the way in developing, was becoming increasingly saturated. Yet, U.S. firms, which sought to expand by exporting, often faced steep tariff and non-tariff barriers in their foreign markets plus the necessity of incurring heavy transport costs. Tough anti-trust laws in the United States also prevented companies from achieving faster growth through increasing their share of the domestic market. In addition, the oligopolistic character of many product markets meant that many U.S. companies were reluctant to risk upsetting rivals by an aggressive sales strategy at home. Instead, they preferred to expand abroad through the establishment of new subsidiaries that would produce and sell those products that had sold so well at home.

According to Vaupel and Curhan (1974), U.S. companies established new overseas subsidiaries at a rate of forty-five per annum between 1946 and 52, a rate roughly twice that of the inter-war period. This rate nearly doubled to ninty-four per annum between 1953 and 55, rose further to 146 per annum from 1956 to 1958 and doubled again to 300 per annum from 1959 to 1961 and 319 per annum from 1962 to 1964. Thereafter, the rate of expansion stabilised. The most important region to which U.S. MNCs were attracted was Western Europe. Western Europe was the logical market in which to sell U.S. products enjoying a high and rising per capita income and consumers with similar tastes to those in the United States. At the same time, the removal of tariffs on intra-European trade in the 1960s following the establishment of the EC and EFTA made the market a potentially large one in which to operate. The costs of transporting goods from the US and the fact that U.S. exports would face the EC's common external tariff plus other non-tariff barriers favoured servicing this market through the establishment of new European subsidiaries rather than by exporting. Indeed, the creation of the EC and EFTA meant that U.S. companies which failed to invest would find themselves at a competitive disadvantage vis-a-vis their European rivals. At the same time, European integration promised to give a new growth stimulus to the European market.

In the late 1960s and early 1970s, the rate of new investment by U.S. companies in Western Europe began to taper off and U.S. companies began to seek out new locations in other parts of the world. Latin America and the Middle/Far-East became important new locations for U.S. direct investment. One reason was that Western Europe was losing its advantage as a location for manufacturing production due to rising wage costs. Wages began to catch up with U.S. levels, while new social security legislation, minimum wage laws and employment protection measures imposed additional non-wage costs on all employers. U.S. MNCs also found themselves coming into frequent conflict with European trade unions representing workers who resented American styles of management. The fall in the value of the dollar in relation to the European currencies further reduced the attractiveness of acquiring productive assets in Western Europe. A further reason was that many U.S. products had lost their novelty value and 'come of age'. U.S. producers found themselves confronted with growing competition from producers in Europe and other parts of the world. The need was to seek out new, lower cost locations for producing the product. This favoured sites in developing countries which could, in turn, be used as a base for exporting back to the European or U.S. markets.

Beginning in the 1960s, a number of European companies began to challenge U.S. dominance in certain key markets. In the mid-1960s, there occurred a marked acceleration in the number of new overseas subsidiaries set up by European-based MNCs. While in the period from 1959 to 1964, the average number of new subsidiaries set up by continental European-based MNCs was about seventy-three per annum, by the late 1960s this had risen to 343 new subsidiaries per annum. The average number of new subsidiaries set up by U.K.-based MNCs rose from 111 per annum in 1959–61 to 243 per annum from 1968 to 1970 (Vaupel and Curhan, 1974). Initially, much of the FDI undertaken by European MNCs entailed the establishment of new subsidiaries in other European countries. In some respects, this was ironic given that the West European countries were in the process of dismantling tariff barriers on their trade with each other. Lower trade barriers reduce the need for a physical presence in the foreign market in order to expand foreign sales. However, the continued existence of most non-tariff barriers combined with differences in consumer preferences between countries meant that the European market remained highly fragmented. Very soon, however, many European MNCs began to seek out more distant locations. In particular, FDI by European firms in the United States expanded rapidly. Increasingly, many European MNCs discovered their ability to successfully challenge U.S. dominance in many branches of manufacturing in, as it were, the U.S. MNCs own 'back-garden'. In fact, U.K. MNCs had always been important investors in the US. What was new was that they were joined by a growing number of other European MNCs. At the same time, investment by U.S. MNCs in Western Europe began to taper off. By the late 1980s, European FDI in North America came to exceed North American investment in Europe by four times. Then, in 1989, European FDI outflows began to decline, suggesting perhaps that the European stock of FDI in Western Europe had reached some kind of equilibrium level in much the same way as did U.S. FDI in Western Europe (Thomson and Woolcock, 1993).

In the 1970s and to a greater extent the 1980s, the example set by the European companies was followed by Japan. In the past, Japanese companies had shown themselves much more reluctant to invest abroad preferring to service their foreign markets through exporting. Such overseas investment as they did undertake was more directed to the South-East Asian region mainly to overcome rising wage costs at home. One reason for the low level of Japanese FDI was the restrictions placed by the authorities on outward investment. In the late 1960s, however, these were gradually relaxed as the Japanese balance of payments moved into surplus (see Chapter 6). Initially, FDI took the form of the establishment of subsidiaries by Japanese manufacturing companies in North America and Western Europe, mainly as a means of circumventing the growing number of trade restrictions which these regions were imposing on Japanese exports. Substantial investments were made in the creation of new subsidiaries in both of these regions in an attempt to get round these restrictions. For example, Heitger and Stehn (1990) found that Japanese FDI in Europe was systematically related to the level of effective protection and the existence of a revealed comparative advantage on the part of Japanese firms. In the late 1980s and early 1990s, this trend was further encouraged by the rapid appreciation of the yen, which significantly reduced the profitability of producing and exporting from Japan. In the second half of the 1980s, however, investments in the tertiary sector (finance and services) came to account for the largest proportion of Japanese FDI. More recently, a growing proportion of Japanese FDI has gone to developing countries mainly in the East and South East Asian region. One reason for this was the need to counteract growing trade restrictions against Japanese-produced goods in western markets and to find lower cost locations for production. However, another reason was the increasing importance of the newly industrialising economies of East Asia as markets for Japanese goods and services. By the 1990s, Japan had become the world's leading source of FDI. Nevertheless, Japanese FDI still accounted for only 2.4% of GNP, compared with 4.4% in the US and 6.3% in Germany (Jun, Sader, Horguchi and Kwak, 1993). The collapse of the Japanese 'bubble economy' after 1990 has seen a dramatic fall in Japanese FDI.

Recently, there has been a significant growth of direct investment by companies in the newly industrialising countries. For the first time ever, South Korea (1990) and Taiwan (1991) have become net exporters of FDI (Chaponiniere, 1997). As with Japan, a key factor has been the lifting of exchange controls on capital outflows in these countries as the current account of the balance of payments swung into surplus in the second half of the 1980s. An increasing amount of FDI by these countries has been directed towards South East Asia and China. Largely, this has been in response to rising costs at home and the appreciation of local currencies. Like Japanese investment in the region, much of it has been designed to relocate the production of certain low value-added goods to countries where labour costs are lower. However, a number of companies in these countries have also been active in establishing subsidiaries in the western industrialised countries. As with Japanese FDI, this has been motivated by a proliferation of trade restrictions against the products of East Asian countries. In some cases, the subsidiaries established have been little more than 'screwdriver' plants concerned only with the assembly of a product using kits imported from the parent company. Thus, the names of Korean conglomerates such as Daewoo and Samsung have become well known to most North Americans and Europeans. The current financial crisis afflicting these economies, however, has resulted in a downturn of such investment.

The Regional Distribution of Multinational Investment Activity

Thus, the MNC is no longer the uniquely American phenomenon that it once was. One result is that the pattern of multinational investment activity is now much more geographically dispersed. The same is true of the regional spread of MNC activity. This is illustrated by Table 4.5.

The first column shows the origin by country of MNCs in the world by measuring the number of parent firms based in a country. Eighty-eight percent of all MNCs still originate in the developed countries and only 11% in developing countries. However, the fact that over 10% of all parent companies are based in developing

Table 4.5 The Geographical Pattern of MNC Activity by Home and Host Country, Mid-1990s

	Parent firms based in country		*Foreign affiliates located in country*	
Area	*No*	*%*	*No*	*%*
Developed economies	34,199	88.2	90,786	34.2
Australia	732	1.9	2,450	0.9
Austria	838	2.2	2,210	0.8
Belgium–Luxembourg	96	0.2	1,121	0.4
Canada	1,565	4.0	4,708	1.8
Denmark	800	2.1	1,289	0.5
France	2,216	5.7	7.097	2.7
Germany	7,003	18.1	11,396	4.3
Ireland	39	0.1	1,040	0.4
Italy	445	1.1	1,474	0.6
Japan	3,967	10.2	3,290	1.2
Netherlands	1,608	4.1	2,259	0.9
Norway	1,000	2.6	3,000	1.1
Portugal	1,165	3.0	7,602	2.9
Spain	236	0.6	6,232	2.3
Sweden	3,520	9.1	5,550	2.1
Switzerland	3,000	7.7	4,000	1.5
UK	1,443	3.7	3,376	1.3
USA	3,013	7.8	16,543	6.2
Developing countries	4,148	10.7	119,765	45.1
Brazil	797	2.1	9,698	3.7
China	379	1.0	45,000	16.9
Colombia	305	0.8	2,220	0.8
Hong Kong	500	1.3	4,137	1.6
India	187	0.5	926	0.3
Indonesia	313	0.8	3,472	1.3
Mexico	–	–	8,420	3.2
Philippines	–	–	14,802	5.6
South Korea	1,049	2.7	3,671	1.4
Singapore	–	–	10,709	4.0
Taiwan	–	–	5,733	2.2
Central and East European	400	1.0	55,000	20.7
World	38,747	100.0	265,551	100.0

Source: UN, 1996.

countries is significant and represents a large increase over the last decade. Of developing countries, South Korea and Brazil are the most important home countries. Of the developed countries, the United States now accounts for a smaller number of parent firms than either Germany, Japan or Sweden. Of course, these figures say nothing about the value of assets held by these companies or the value of their global sales.

The second column of the table illustrates the geographical dispersion of multinational investment activity by considering the countries in which foreign affiliates were located. It can be seen that 45% of all foreign affiliates were located in developing countries, 34% in developed countries and 21% in the Central and East European countries. Of the developing countries, China alone accounted for 17% of all foreign affiliates. However, the newly industrialising countries of East and South-East Asia also accounted for a large number of affiliates, as did Brazil in the Latin American region. Of the developed countries, the US and Canada together accounted for 8%, Germany for 4% and France, Spain, Portugal and Sweden each for over 2%. Of the Central and East European countries, the Czech Republic and Hungary had the largest number of foreign affiliates.

The Sectoral Distribution of Multinational Investment Activity

Table 4.6 sets out the sectoral distribution of both outward and inward FDI for five of the leading industrialised countries for the period from 1971 to the present.

Some obvious differences exist between countries. In terms of outward FDI, a relatively high proportion of U.K. investment is to be found in the primary sector. This undoubtedly reflects the importance of overseas investments by British oil companies. By way of contrast, Canada has a relatively high percentage of FDI in the manufacturing sector, while Japan has in services. A noteworthy trend, which was taking place in all five countries, was an increase in the proportion of outward FDI occurring in the service sector. However, this tendency has been greatest in Japan. With regard to inward FDI, the UK again has a relatively high proportion of FDI in the primary sector, while FDI in Canada and Japan has been orientated more towards manufacturing. Germany and the United States have a relatively high proportion of FDI in services. Once again, all five countries has witnessed a dramatic growth in the importance of the tertiary sector as a recipient of inward FDI, with Germany experiencing the largest proportionate increase.

The growing importance of FDI in the services sector is of particular interest. While, in the early part of the post-war period, FDI in manufacturing predominated, today, in many countries, services account for the largest proportion of FDI. Some writers have talked of the ascendancy of the service-sector multinational, a trend which they see as certain to continue in the next century (Clegg, 1996). As we shall see in Chapter 10, this is, in part, due to the nature of service provision. Many services have to be produced and consumed at the same time. Production and consumption cannot be separated as with goods because services cannot be stored. Therefore, if service firms are to provide services to buyers located in another country, they must establish a physical presence in the foreign country in order to do so. Although this will not always entail direct investment, it frequently does. However, other factors have also been at work. Many service firms tend to follow manufacturing MNCs because manufacturing firms are major buyers of their services. Thus, when manufacturing MNCs invest heavily in a particular region, service MNCs tend to follow suite. Another reason has been the gradual liberalisation of services trade in many parts of the world. Governments have seen that there are important advantages which accrue from deregulating the service sector and allowing more foreign service firms to enter the local market. A further cause of the growing importance of MNC activity in services has been a

Table 4.6 The Sectoral Distribution of FDI Abroad of Selected Developed Market Economies, 1971 to the present (percentage)

Country of origin	*Period*	*Primary sector*	*Secondary sector*	*Tertiary sector*	*Total*
A. Outward FDI					
Canada	1971	14.4	52.7	32.9	100.0
	1980	9.9	64.2	25.9	100.0
	1990	6.6	53.1	40.3	100.0
Germany	1971	4.8	79.8	15.6	100.0
	1980	4.4	47.6	48	100.0
	1990	2.3	39.1	58.6	100.0
Japan	1971	32.1	31.7	36.2	100.0
	1980	21.9	34.4	43.7	100.0
	1991	5.7	26.7	67.6	100.0
United Kingdom	1971	23.8	42.3	23.8	100.0
	1981	27.9	35.9	36.2	100.0
	1987	27	34.4	38.6	100.0
United States	1971	30.6	43.8	25.6	100.0
	1980	12.1	49	38.9	100.0
	1990	8.3	44.3	47.4	100.0
B. Inward FDI					
Canada	1975	9.3	66.2	24.5	100.0
	1980	7.5	67.5	25	100.0
	1990	4	63.3	32.7	100.0
Germany	1976	0.4	66.1	33.5	100.0
	1980	0.5	59.3	40.2	100.0
	1990	0.1	36.3	63.6	100.0
Japan	1975	–	81.6	18.4	100.0
	1980	–	77.7	22.3	100.0
	1990	–	63.9	36.1	100.0
United Kingdom	1974	28.2	45.6	26.2	100.0
	1981	34.3	40.6	25.1	100.0
	1987	29.1	36.2	34.7	100.0
United States	1975	22.5	41.2	36.4	100.0
	1980	4.4	51	44.6	100.0
	1990	3.5	46.8	49.7	100.0

Source: UNCTC, various issues.

tendency for many manufacturing MNCs to diversify into services, providing their own services through the establishment of their own service subsidiaries. We shall discuss these trends in greater detail in Chapter 10.

The Determinants of Foreign Direct Investment

What factors can explain the growth of FDI since the Second World War? What factors explain the emergence and subsequent expansion of the multinational enterprise? In answering this question, it is helpful to distinguish between three different types of FDI and, correspondingly, three types of multinational companies:

1. *Horizontal FDI and the horizontally integrated MNC.* Horizontal FDI occurs when a company locates the manufacture of the same product or group of products at more than one plant located in different countries. The giant multinational automobile manufacturers, such as General Motors, Ford, BMW and Nissan, are all examples of this.
2. *Vertical FDI and the vertically integrated MNC.* Vertical FDI occurs when a company locates different stages in the production and marketing of a single product or group of related products in different countries. Where the newly established subsidiary is producing at an earlier stage in the manufacture of a product, this is referred to as backwards vertical FDI. For example, a rubber manufacturer in Western Europe may invest in a rubber plantation in Malaysia. Where the newly established subsidiary is producing at a later stage of production or is concerned with the marketing and distribution of the finished good, this is referred to as forwards vertical FDI. An example would be a decision by an oil company involved in oil drilling and extraction to invest in an oil refinery or petro-chemical plant. In fact, oil companies provide very good examples of vertically integrated MNCs since they typically have investments at all stages in the process of mining, manufacturing and distributing oil. Some oil companies also hold investment further downstream in the production of petro-chemicals widely used as intermediate products by other branches of manufacturing.
3. *Conglomerate FDI and the diversified or conglomerate MNC.* The third type of FDI takes place when a company acquires a controlling interest in or amalgamates with another company located in a different country which produces an entirely unrelated product or group of products. In this way, a MNC is able to achieve product diversification. Modern examples of conglomerate FDI are the Hanson Trust of the UK, Mitsubishi of Japan or ITT of the United States.

The determinants of each type of FDI are likely to differ and, therefore, need to be considered separately. Box 4.1 provides a summary of the various theories explaining each type of FDI.

Box 4.1 Major Theories explaining different kinds of Foreign Direct Investment

1. Horizontal FDI – integrating with producers producing a similar range of goods at the same stage of production.

- The Market-Imperfections Approach – Hymer (1960), Kindleberger (1969)
- The Product Life Cycle Model – Vernon (1966, 1971)
- The Transactional Approach – Caves (1971, 1982), Johnson (1970)
- The Eclectic Theory – Dunning (1977)

Continued

2. Vertical FDI – integrating with producers at different stages in the production of a product or related group of products.

- The Internalisation Theory – Coase (1937), Buckley and Casson (1976), Casson (1986)

3. Conglomerate FDI – integrating with producers of unrelated goods or services.

- Diversification and risk-spreading – Grubel (1968)
- MNEs as a currency area phenomenon – Aliber (1970, 1971)

Horizontal Foreign Direct Investment

Much post-war FDI has been of the horizontal type. Most attempts to explain this kind of FDI have focused on the existence of *market imperfections* as the cause of FDI. Hymer (1960) and Kindleberger (1969) were among the first to emphasise the existence of imperfections in the markets for both goods and certain kinds of assets as the cause of horizontal expansion abroad by firms. They argued that, if markets were perfectly competitive, firms would not engage in overseas production. This is because foreign producers always face a cost disadvantage when competing with local firms in the foreign market. Local firms are better informed about local market conditions, laws and customs in the host country, local culture and language and are also able to secure better treatment from host country governments. In addition, they are not exposed to exchange rate risk to the same extent as foreign firms. Thus, a prerequisite for FDI to take place is that the foreign firm possesses some offsetting advantage, which is not shared with local firms. The existence of either natural barriers to imports in the foreign market (i.e. high transport costs) or artificially created barriers (i.e. tariffs or non-tariff barriers) means that foreign firms cannot profitably exploit this advantage merely by exporting the good to the foreign country. At the same time, because of imperfections in the market for such assets, it is not possible for the firm, simply, to sell that asset to firms in the foreign market, thereby avoiding the disadvantages of local production.

Such advantages are, generally, referred to as firm-specific or ownership-specific advantages. Vernon's *Product Life Cycle Model* discussed in Chapter 2 similarly emphasised the existence of such an advantage in the form of a new product as the motive for a firm investing abroad in the maturity stage of the cycle. Caves (1982) stressed two types of such advantage. First, the foreign firm may possess technological knowledge about how to produce a product or how to produce it more cheaply, possibly, but not necessarily, embodied in a patent. Second, the foreign firm may possess special marketing skills, which enable the firm to differentiate its product from that of its rivals, which may be embodied in a brand name or trademark. A characteristic of knowledge of this kind is that it can be more efficiently transferred from one country to another through the use of internalised as opposed to external markets. Caves (1982) emphasised the 'public good' nature of intangible assets such as knowledge. Once a piece of knowledge has been produced (e.g. about how to produce a particular product more cheaply), it costs next to nothing to put that knowledge to use in another place (e.g. another country). Since the marginal cost of supplying such knowledge is zero, the price that it would fetch if sold in a perfect market would be zero! If, however, the firm possessing such knowledge can internalise the market by selling it to a subsidiary in another country, it can obtain a positive return.

A further problem with knowledge is that it suffers from the problem of what Caves called 'information impactedness' and uncertainty. The seller of knowledge cannot reveal all that it contains before agreeing to a price; otherwise the buyer would be free to use the knowledge without paying for it. However, because the buyer cannot know the true value of what he is buying before agreeing to a price, he will tend to offer a price, which fails to reflect its true value. The problem is compounded by the fact that there is often great uncertainty about the usefulness and, hence, the value of a given body of knowledge, which makes it extremely difficult to price the knowledge being sold. Because most people are risk-averse, they will tend to offer a price which is less than the potential worth of the knowledge. Hence, firms that possess knowledge of this kind have a strong incentive to internalise the market for knowledge (i.e. to bypass the market altogether).

The MNC constitutes the means whereby transactions in such intangible, firm-specific assets can be internalised and the firm can, thereby, maximise the return from the ownership of such assets. This explanation for the existence of horizontally integrated FDI leads to the conclusion that horizontally integrated MNCs will be found most commonly in knowledge-intensive or research-intensive industries. These will be industries characterised by both high levels of R&D expenditure relative to total sales and a high ratio of qualified scientists and engineers (QSE) to total employment. Empirical evidence lends strong support to this hypothesis. The ratio of overseas production-to-world-wide sales of companies in high research-intensive industries is generally greater than for medium or low research-intensive industries (Dunning and Pearce, 1981). Knowledge-intensive industries, such as the pharmaceutical industry, are dominated by MNCs.

However, other factors may also give rise to horizontal FDI. Caves (1982) points to four other determinants of horizontal FDI. First, the existence of excess managerial capacity. Many intangible assets are 'discontinuous' or lumpy such that, at any given time, they may be underutilised. This may be the case with managerial capacity within the firm. FDI becomes a way of ensuring fuller utilisation of such capacity. Second, the existence of excess capacity in internally generated funds may give rise to horizontal FDI. A firm may be unable to use all its retained earnings profitably through expansion of its existing activities. Such funds command a low opportunity cost in comparison with externally secured funds. Hence they could more readily be invested in a marginal activity which would be unprofitable if the funds had to be raised externally. FDI becomes a way of ensuring fuller utilisation of such funds. Third, a further cause of horizontal FDI is the fact that many intangible assets possessed by firms cannot be separated from the firm that owns them. For example, the knowledge owned by a firm may be bound up with the expertise of the company's managers and employees. Attempts to sell the knowledge through the market would substantially reduce the value of the information. Finally, MNCs may enjoy economies of scale from operating a number of plants in several different countries. For example, the firm may be able to acquire raw materials more cheaply. Economies of transportation may also result. The multi-plant firm is less affected by localised fluctuations in demand. If demand in one country is depressed, a plant located in that country could switch some of its output to plants in other countries where demand is still buoyant. Lastly, the multi-plant firm may be able to achieve cost saving from greater product specialisation. Each plant may be able to specialise in the production of particular goods leading to longer production runs.

A weakness of the above explanation for horizontal FDI is that it provides an essentially static explanation of why firms expand horizontally. However, horizontal FDI may be better regarded as a strategy which firms employ at a particular stage in their development. In other words, it may be more useful to analyse the decision to produce abroad in a dynamic setting as part of the process whereby firms grow. On the other hand, it is not too difficult to modify the transactional approach of Caves to incorporate corporate growth. Firms grow initially through domestic expansion. As they develop a firm-specific advantage in the production of a particular good, their domestic sales expand. To begin with export sales are non-existent because of the information costs which expansion through exporting entails. However, a point is eventually reached where the profitability of further domestic expansion becomes quite low. Domestic sales can only be increased further by reducing the share of the market accounted for by rivals. This might risk upsetting rivals and provoking a price-cutting war. Hence, the firm begins to seek new outlets abroad for the product. This may take place initially through exports and only later through the establishment of a subsidiary in the foreign market. Initially, the firm will be attracted to markets with a similar culture and language and where information costs are, thus, lower. However, because the foreign firm possesses a firm-specific advantage, it can offset the increased costs of producing abroad against the cost/price advantage, which it enjoys from possessing a unique, firm-specific asset.

A further criticism of the *transactional approach* to explaining horizontal FDI discussed above is that it ignores locational factors. If firms prefer overseas production to exporting, this implies that there are some advantages from locating production abroad rather than at home. Indeed, if this were not so, firms would always prefer exporting to overseas production. Thus, although the possession by the foreign firm of a firm-specific advantage is a necessary condition for FDI to take place, it is not a sufficient condition. The locational advantages from producing abroad may simply be the avoidance of high transport costs. Alternatively, the foreign firm may face high tariffs in the foreign market or various kinds of non-tariffs barriers, which restrict entry or raise the costs of exporting. Further sources of locational advantage might be the existence of lower labour costs in the foreign country or of various kinds of tax incentives or government aid. If the foreign market is larger or faster growing, this too will favour producing abroad rather than at home. Incorporating locational advantages is useful for another reason: it can help explain why MNCs choose to invest in one foreign country as opposed to another. This is especially important these days where reduced transport costs and lower trade barriers have made it increasingly possible for MNCs to supply a particular market equally profitably from a number of different locations.

Taking these factors into account, Dunning (1977) has proposed an *eclectic framework* for summarising the various determinants of horizontal FDI. This identifies three conditions as necessary and sufficient for FDI to take place:

1. *Ownership-specific (O) advantages:* The MNC must possess some advantage, which may or may not be embodied in the form of an asset, which is exclusive or proprietary to the firm and which gives the firm a competitive advantage over the firms of other countries in which it invests.

2. *Location-specific (L) advantages:* The particular country in which the MNC invests must possess certain advantages in relation to both the MNC's home country and other alternative locations, for example, lower labour costs, more generous tax and other government incentives, a large and fast-growing market and so on.
3. *Internalisation (I) advantages:* There must be advantages from administering certain transactions internally (i.e. between different subsidiaries of the same MNC) rather than through external markets.

It is the simultaneous existence of these three sets of advantages – ownership-specific or O factors, location-specific or L factors and internalisation advantages or I factors – that explains horizontal FDI. The O advantages explain why firms engage in FDI in the first place. The L advantages explain why they prefer overseas production to exporting. Finally, the I advantages explain why overseas production is preferred to other methods of transferring assets internationally such as licensing. This has come to be known as the OLI paradigm or the eclectic theory of international production. It has the attraction that it brings together the full range of factors that contribute to the decision of the firm to establish an overseas subsidiary. It also provides a convenient framework for explaining FDI flows between different countries. On the other hand, it is clear that it is not itself a theory of FDI, only a taxonomy of the factors governing the FDI decision.

Vertical Foreign Direct Investment

Theoretical attempts at explaining why firms choose to integrate different stages of production under single ownership have tended to rely upon the *internalisation approach* first put forward by Buckley and Casson (1976). Building on the work of Coase (1937), Buckley and Casson identified a series of advantages that accrue to firms from conducting certain kinds of transactions internally rather than through the use of external markets. We have already discussed the specific problems involved in selling knowledge through the use of external markets. However, Buckley and Casson's internalisation theory sets out a broader range of factors which make external markets inefficient as a method of selling goods as well as assets. Against these advantages, there are also costs arising from internalisation. Where, however, benefits exceed costs, internalisation will be preferred. Although Buckley and Casson regard the internalisation theory as providing a general explanation for all kinds of FDI, the theory is most useful as an explanation for vertical FDI. Whether FDI occurs backwards to the raw material producer or forwards to the distribution stage, it substitutes internal markets for goods and assets in place of external markets. However, the kind of goods most affected by this process are intermediate goods or semi-finished goods rather than goods for final consumption.

Casson (1986) identifies the following types of market imperfection which give rise to the vertically-integrated MNC.

1. The Inability of Arms-Length Contracts to cope with Rigidities and Irreversibilities in the Production Process.

Casson lists four examples of these:

(a) High fixed costs confront an upstream producer, such that the competitive price for the intermediate product distributes inadequate rent to the upstream producer to enable him to cover his fixed costs. On the other hand, the downstream producer makes more than sufficient profits to be able to compensate the former for his losses and earn a satisfactory rent for himself. In the absence of vertical integration, however, there exists no mechanism for bringing this about, such that the upstream producer has no alternative but to withdraw from production altogether. Vertical integration, leading to an internalisation of the market for the intermediate good, provides a solution.

(b) Large non-recoverable costs are incurred by the producer of the intermediate product, such as the costs of investment in highly specific equipment, which has no alternative use and no scrap value. Having committed himself to such an investment, such a producer is vulnerable to threats by major customers not to buy the output derived from such equipment unless more favourable contract terms are renegotiated. Such uncertainty may deter upstream producers from incurring such non-recoverable costs. One solution is for upstream firms to merge with customer firms further downstream.

(c) The use of continuous-flow technology by a downstream producer places a premium on ensuring adequate supplies of essential inputs. An interruption in the supply of inputs will disrupt production with 'spill-over' effects for all stages of the production run. Holding large stocks is one solution but is likely to be very costly. Forward purchases of inputs (buying inputs today for delivery at some stage in the future) are another solution, but such contracts may be difficult to enforce. Therefore, the downstream producer may choose to integrate with an upstream supplier of such inputs to avoid disruptions.

(d) Where the intermediate products are perishable, storage of inputs is not possible. If no forward market exists, vertical integration may be the natural solution.

(e) The buyer of an intermediate product is confronted with uncertainty about the quality of the product. Sellers know more about the quality of the product than buyers such that buyers are suspicious about the quality of the product. Internalisation of the market for the intermediate product through vertical integration overcomes this problem by giving the buyer access to the seller's information.

2. The Tendency for Arm's Length Pricing to Distort Decisions Regarding Substitution in Production over Time and Space

First, let us take the case of *substitution over time*. This takes place when there is a need to speed up production at one stage of the production, which is difficult to bring about if the various stages are performed by independent producers. For example, a sudden increase in demand for downstream output may require that resources be switched away from upstream and into downstream production so as to increase the speed at which the intermediate product is transformed into a finished product. Where each stage of production is carried out by independent producers, it may be difficult to bring this about. Vertical integration makes possible a quicker redeployment of resources, bringing about greater flexibility of working capital.

Next consider *substitution over space*. This will occur where the production of an intermediate product is distributed over space and fluctuations occur in the supply or demand for the intermediate product. If the different stages of production are performed by independent producers who buy and sell products on an arms-length basis, large stocks of the intermediate product may be needed to smooth out such fluctuations. If, however, the stages are integrated within the same firm, economies may be made in the holding of stocks through the redirection of supplies to locations faced with shortages. However, where there exist good information linkages between locations, this will be achieved more quickly through arms-length transactions.

3. The Distortion of Intermediate Product Prices brought about by the Exercise of Monopoly Power

First, Casson cites the case of a monopolist who is an upstream producer and who charges a monopoly price for his intermediate product. As a result, he faces substitution against his product by downstream producers. If the downstream producer is also a monopolist, there will occur a further mark-up on costs when the final product is sold to the consumer. The two effects will cause a very substantial reduction in the demand for the intermediate product. However, if the monopolist integrates forwards with the downstream producer, the price charged for the intermediate product is a mere 'shadow' price equal to the marginal cost of upstream production, so avoiding any substitution against the intermediate product. Since upstream and downstream production are under common ownership, the distribution of profits between the two stages is a matter of indifference, the only concern being to maximise the joint profits of the two producers.

Second, vertical FDI may be a means whereby a dominant firm can create a barrier to entry for potential rivals at different stages of production. Thus, by refusing to supply a rival with an intermediate product or to buy an intermediate input from him, he forces the rival firm to make costly new investments either at the upstream or downstream stages, creating an entry barrier.

4. The Introduction of a New Division of Labour may create an Incentive for Vertical Integration

Much innovation involving both the development of new processes of production and new products gives rise to more advanced forms of division of labour. Casson has drawn attention to the way in which technological advances since the Second World War have led to the splitting up of the process of producing many manufactured goods into a much larger number of separate activities. This new division of labour has significantly multiplied the number of intermediate products that are traded whether through the market or within the firm. At the early stages of the introduction of this new technology, firms will prefer to rely on internalised markets. The main reason is the need for producers to synchronise their investments at different stages so as to get all the plants on stream at the same time. We discuss the nature of this new international division of labour in greater depth in the next chapter.

5. Government Intervention in Markets giving Rise to Incentives to Transfer Pricing

Transfer prices are the prices that MNCs charge on their intra-group sales, whether sales of intermediate goods from parent to affiliates or sales of finished goods from affiliates to parent. For a variety of reasons, MNCs may charge prices on such sales that significantly diverge from the arms-length price for equivalent transactions. One cause of such transfer-price manipulation is a difference in the levels of taxation between countries. For example, when taxes are higher in the parent country than the foreign country where the MNC's affiliate is based, global tax liability can be reduced by under-invoicing parent company sales of intermediate products to the affiliate company.

Possible reasons for transfer-price manipulation are discussed in greater detail below.

Against these possible *benefits* from vertical integration must be set certain *costs*. First, there are managerial diseconomies from the difficulty of co-ordinating the activities of the different stages of production, especially where these are separated by long distances. Second, there are technical diseconomies that arise where the optimum scale of production at each stage of production is different. In this case, the scale of operation for the enterprise as a whole has to be set at a level equal to the lowest common multiple of the optimum output at each stage. For example, if the minimum efficient scale of production is 100 units at stage 1, 200 units at stage 2 and 500 units at stage 3, the best outcome would be to have 10 plants at stage 1 each producing 100 units, five plants at stage 2 each producing 200 units and two plants at stage 3 each producing 500 units. However, if the market for the final product is less than 1000 units, some of the plants operating at each stage will have to operate at less than their optimum level. One solution is partial internalisation with a portion of the output of the intermediate product being sold on the external market. Finally, vertical FDI may create problems where subsidiaries are located in politically unstable countries or countries that are hostile towards foreign firms. In this case, it may be preferable to avoid the risk and buy the intermediate product on an arms-length basis from a local firm.

Conglomerate Foreign Direct Investment

The reason sometimes given for FDI of this type is the desire on the part of investors to minimise risk through diversification. It is argued that investors are risk-averse. For this reason they seek a portfolio of investments which minimises the variance of the return on an investment. They can achieve this by spreading their investments over a number of holdings rather than placing them all in one basket. The only requirement is that the return on each holding should be negatively correlated such that when one investment earns a bad return another earns a good return. It is argued that imperfections in the capital market make it costly for an individual investor to achieve such an 'efficient' portfolio. An alternative is for investors to invest their funds with an investment or unit trust, which will achieve the necessary portfolio diversification on their behalf. The trust will also have better information about different shares and their prospects than the individual investor who could only obtain such information at great expense. Nevertheless, there is still a cost for the trust in obtaining the information required to guarantee individual investors' optimum diversification. Because of these costs, trusts often spread investments over a relatively small number of fairly large shareholdings. However, by buying shares in an internationally diversified MNC, individual shareholders may be able to spread their investments more efficiently.

Internationally diversified MNCs provide shareholders with risk minimisation because (1) they produce a number of largely unrelated products and (2) they are located in a number of different countries. In other words, both product and geographical diversification is achieved. A slump in the demand for one product may be offset by buoyant demand for another or depressed demand in one geographical market may be offset by rising sales in another. Thus, the conglomerate or internationally diversified MNC may be viewed in the words of Alan Rugman as 'a potential surrogate vehicle for financial asset diversification' (Rugman, 1985). Moreover, conglomerate MNCs provide not only investors, but also risk-averse managers, with reduced risk. Salaried managers may attach as much importance to stable salaries and job security as to maximisation of earnings. It is sometimes argued that in the modern corporation true power resides with managers and not shareholders. In the desire to minimise risk through diversification, the interests of shareholders and investors may be the same.

A further explanation for conglomerate FDI has been suggested by Aliber (Aliber, 1970). Aliber regarded the internationally diversified MNC as largely a currency-area phenomenon. Investors who place their funds in assets denominated in different currencies are subject to the risk that the currency in which the assets are denominated will depreciate. One way of protecting a short-term investment against currency risk is by taking out forward cover. However, forward cover is not free and is usually available only for short-term investments. It follows that, if investors are to be persuaded to hold investments in weak or soft currencies which carry a high risk of depreciation, the interest paid must contain a premium to compensate them for the risk of currency depreciation. For investments in some countries where there are additional risks (e.g. the risk of the government suddenly imposing controls on the withdrawal of funds), the interest premium will be higher. However, Aliber has suggested that investors who buy shares in a company are myopic, acting as if all their investments were in a single currency area even when some of the assets of the company may be held outside the country and denominated therefore in a different currency. It follows that MNCs based in strong or hard currency countries will enjoy a financial advantage over other locally based firms in weak or soft currency countries. They will be able to obtain capital more cheaply which could cancel out any disadvantage that they might otherwise face in competing with local firms. (In effect, this is another form of ownership-specific advantage that was discussed above).

Specifically, Aliber applied his theory to U.S. direct investment abroad in the 1950s and early 1960s when the U.S. dollar was still a hard currency and when U.S. firms were beginning to expand abroad especially into Western Europe through acquisitions of companies in countries with relatively weak currencies. U.S. MNCs, the argument went, were able to raise capital at lower cost than their European rivals, which meant that the future earnings from the companies acquired could be capitalised at a higher rate than for European concerns. The argument, however, was no longer valid after the dollar weakened in the late 1960s and 1970s. In theory, it could explain some acquisitions abroad by MNCs in other strong currency countries in the 1970s and 1980s such as West Germany or Japan. This might have been the case where there was no other obvious motive for acquisition, such as the desire to take advantage of lower costs or gain easier access to foreign markets. However, as we shall see below, a great deal of FDI in recent decades has been two-way FDI with companies in different counties each investing in the markets of the other. Aliber's theory clearly explains only one-way FDI and that from a strong to a weak currency country. There are also good reasons for questioning Aliber's assumption that investors are myopic, acting as if their investment is held in a single currency when they know that the company in which they invest is a multinational one.

The Importance of MNCs in World Trade: Intra-Firm Trade

Such data as are available showing the importance of MNCs in world trade confirm the expectation that they account for a high proportion of the trade of advanced industrialised countries. Estimates published by the U.S. Department of Commerce show that nearly 100% of U.S. exports and 81% of U.S. imports are generated by MNCs, whether U.S.- or foreign-owned (UNCTC, 1983). If confined to U.S.-owned MNCs, the figures were 77 and 49% respectively. For the United Kingdom, an early estimate put the figure for manufacturing exports at 82%, including both U.K.-owned and foreign-owned enterprises (DTI, 1976). However, of more interest than the total amount of trade, which is handled by MNCs is the proportion of trade which constitutes so-called *intra-firm* or *in-house* trade. This may simply be defined as trade between an MNC and its affiliates in other countries. Also important is *intra-affiliate* trade, which is trade between two affiliates having the same parent company. Intra-firm and intra-affiliate trade can be distinguished from so-called *arms-length* trade which occurs when buyer and seller are unrelated in ownership. Intra-firm trade should not be confused with intra-industry trade, although, in some cases, intra-firm trade may also constitute intra-industry trade. Unfortunately, data concerning the nature and extent of intra-firm and intra-affiliate trade are available in a much less comprehensive form than for intra-industry trade. They only exist for countries where companies are required by law to reveal the extent of such trade taking place and, then, only for particular years.

The most complete and up-to-date data exist for the *United States* and arise out of the regular, five-yearly benchmark surveys carried out by the U.S. Department of Commerce and covering both foreign affiliates of U.S. companies and U.S. affiliates of foreign companies. The surveys cover roughly 30 separate manufacturing categories. *Affiliates* are defined as companies in which the parent holds at least 10% of the voting stock. If the parent owns 50% or more, the affiliate company is considered to be a *subsidiary* or *majority-owned foreign affiliate* (MOFA). Table 4.7 shows the importance of intra-firm trade in the trade of U.S. non-bank parents with their foreign affiliates and of non-bank U.S. affiliates with their foreign parents.

By 1989, 33.5% of U.S. exports were intra-firm exports, of which 24.5% were sales by U.S. MNCs to their foreign affiliates and 9% were sales by U.S. affiliates of foreign-owned MNCs to their parents. This compared with

Table 4.7 Intra-Firm Trade as a Proportion of Total U.S. Trade

Million U.S. Dollars	*1997*	*1982*	*1989*
U.S. intra-firm exports			
U.S. parents' sales to their foreign affiliates	32,397	46,559	89,151
As a percentage of total U.S. exports	26.3	21.5	24.5
U.S. affiliates sales to their foreign parents	11,691	25,024	32,796
As a percentage of total U.S. exports	9.5	11.6	9.0
U.S. intra-firm imports			
U.S. foreign affiliates' sales to their U.S. parents	32,639	41,598	75,984
As a percentage of total U.S. imports	20.3	16.3	15.4
Foreign parents' sales to their U.S. affiliates	30,878	51,915	127,970
As a percentage of total U.S. imports	19.2	20.4	26.

Source: OECD (1993).

35.8% in 1977 and 33.1% in 1982. For U.S. imports, intra-firm trade accounted for 41.4% of U.S. imports, of which 15.4% were imports by U.S. MNCs from their overseas affiliates and 26% were imports by U.S. affiliates of foreign-owned MNCs. This compared with 39.5% in 1977 and 36.7% in 1982. Thus, intra-firm trade was somewhat higher for U.S. imports than exports. Moreover, whereas the intra-firm import ratio has risen, the intra-firm export ratio has fallen when compared with 1977. The rise in the intra-firm import ratio appears to be entirely accounted for by U.S. affiliates' imports from their foreign parents. The main reason for this has been increased activity by firms from Japan and Korea in the US in the form mainly of wholesale trade in motor vehicles and equipment (OECD, 1993).

The decline in the share of intra-firm exports in total U.S. exports in the 1980s contrasts with earlier evidence suggesting a rising trend (Lall, 1978). One possible explanation is that much of the trend towards increased globalisation on the part of U.S. MNCs occurred in earlier decades (the 1960s and 1970s). By the 1980s, U.S. outward FDI assumed a different form in which less reliance was placed on trade with the U.S. parent. A further possible cause could have been a loss of competitiveness of U.S. companies vis-à-vis their foreign rivals.

Less comprehensive estimates are available for other countries. For the *United Kingdom*, a study by the Department of Trade and Industry found that, in 1976, 29% of manufacturing exports were intra-firm exports (14% by foreign-owned U.K. enterprises and 15% by U.K. firms with investments overseas). A more recent estimate shows the figure unchanged for 1984 (British Business, 1985). On the imports side, the intra-firm ratio was estimated for 1984 at a much higher 51%.

Various estimates exist for other countries. For *Sweden*, Helleiner (1981) estimated that, in 1975, 29% of exports and 25% of imports were intra-firm. More recent figures put the ratios for 1994 at 38 and 9%, respectively (UN, 1996). For *Japan*, drawing on data obtained by Japan's Ministry of International Trade and Industry (MITI), the OECD (1993) estimated that 33% of exports shipped by Japanese companies went to their foreign affiliates and 28% of imports shipped to Japanese companies came from their foreign affiliates. The UN (1996) quotes ratios for manufactured goods of 25% for exports and 14% for imports for 1993. For *France*, the UN (1996) quotes figures for 1993 of 34% for exports and 18% for imports respectively.

A further source of information concerning intra-firm trade in other countries was a survey of the world's 329 largest industrial enterprises carried out by Dunning and Pearce (1981). The results are summarised in Table 4.8.

This shows that, in 1977, an estimated 33% of parent company exports consisted of intra-firm sales. United States' MNCs had the highest ratio at 46% and Japanese MNCs the lowest ratio of 17%. The latter clearly reflects the low degree of multinationality of Japanese MNCs in 1977, a factor which has changed following the increase in Japanese FDI in the 1980s. Of the European countries, the ratio is high for Sweden and West Germany. Outside Europe, Canadian MNCs also appear to have high ratios.

There is some evidence to show that intra-firm trade is more important as a component of trade between industrialised countries (as with intra-industry trade). Helleiner and Lavergne (1980) found that, in 1977, 54% of U.S. imports from the industrialised OECD countries were 'related-party imports' (defined as imports by U.S. companies from firms in the foreign country in which they held 5% of equity capital

Table 4.8 Intra-Firm Trade in the Home Countries Exports of Large Industrial Corporations, 1977, by home country (percentage)

Home country	*Share of intra-firm trade in parent companies' total exports*
Canada	39.3
EEC	29.6
Europe (total)	29.7
France	32.2
West Germany	34.6
Japan	17.0
Other Western Europe	29.8
Sweden	36.1
United Kingdom	29.6
United States	45.5
Other countries	22.8
Total	32.8

Source: Dunning and Pearce (1981) in UNCTC (1983).

or more). However, only 28% of imports from developing countries and 8% from centrally planned economies were related-party imports. These figures are set out in Table 4.9.

One reason for this is that intra-firm trade is higher in trade in manufactured goods, which account for a higher proportion of trade with industrialised countries than less industrialised countries. As can be seen from the table, intra-firm trade is higher for manufactures than for semi-manufactures and for semi-manufactures than for raw materials if petroleum is excluded. Intra-firm trade is large in petroleum products reflecting the high degree of vertical integration existing in this sector. It follows that, as countries become more industrialised, the component of intra-firm trade in their total trade is likely to rise. In addition, the more friendly the stance adopted by a country towards MNCs, the higher is likely to be its intra-firm trade. Helleiner and Lavergne (1980) found that intra-firm trade was highest for trade with developing countries, which adopted a hospitable attitude towards MNCs.

Industry Variations

Variations do occur in the level of intra-firm trade across industries. Lall (1978) compared the level of intra-firm trade in total U.S. exports and imports for different industries using two ratios:

(1) the ratio of intra-firm exports-to-total MNC exports (the IFX ratio) and

Table 4.9 U.S. Related-Party Imports as Percentage of Total Imports by Product Group and Origin, 1977

	Primary					*Total*	
	Petroleum	*Primary excl. petroleum*	*Total primary*	*Semi-manufactures*	*Manu-factures*	*Total*	*Total excl. petroleum*
OECD	57.2	35.9	41.3	43.4	61.1	53.7	53.6
Centrally planned economies	0	3.2	2.8	8.9	8.1	7.7	7.8
Third World				59.6			
Total	59.4	23.5	47.3	37.6	53.6	48.4	45.2

Source: Helleiner and Lavergne (1980).

Table 4.10 Intra-Firm Export and Production Ratios of U.S. MNCs by Industry, 1970

Industry	IFX ratio	IPX ratio	Industry	IFX ratio	IPX ratio
Food products	34	5	*Non-electrical machinery*		
Grain mills	47	8	Farm machinery	44	15
Beverages	19	1	Industrial	27	12
Combinations	23	na	Office	75	17
Other	32	5	Computing	75	17
Paper	25	7	Other	40	20
Chemicals	36	7	*Electrical machinery*	23	8
Drugs	38	5	Household	25	5
Soap and cosmetics	54	3	Equipment	15	7
Industrial	15	9	Electronic	29	8
Plastics	88	12	Other	92	12
Combinations	100	na	*Transport Equipment*	41	17
Rubber	39	6	*Textiles, apparel*	40	6
Primary & fabricated materials	12	4	*Lumber, wood furnishings*	11	10
Primary	5	6	*Printing, publishing*	25	6
Fabricated (excl. aluminium, brass & copper)	24	4	*Stone, clay, grass*	32	6
Aluminium	9	2	*Instruments*	62	18
Other	50	6	*Other manufacturing*	23	3
			All manufacturing	35	10

na = no data available.
Source: Lall (1978).

(2) the ratio of intra-firm exports-to-the total production of majority-owned foreign affiliates (the IPX ratio).

His results are set out in Table 4.10.

Substantial variations exist between industries. He found in empirical testing that the variables which best explained these differences were as follows:

1. *The technological intensity of an industry as measured by R&D expenditure relative to sales turnover.* The greater the degree of technology intensity, the higher the level of intra-firm trade. Lall argued that this variable measured the degree of 'specificity' of the product or its uniqueness. In the case of intermediate products, a high degree of specificity might be expected to stimulate internalisation through vertical integration for the reasons discussed in the previous chapter.
2. *The divisibility of the production process*, as measured by the number of separate activities which it can be broken down into and which can be located in different countries. The more easily the production process can be split up into a large number of separate activities, the higher the level of intra-firm trade. This phenomenon is discussed more fully below.
3. *The degree to which an industry is internationally diversified*, as measured by the ratio of foreign-to-domestic investment. The more internationally diversified an industry, the higher the level of intra-firm trade.
4. *The need for after-sales service within an industry.* The greater the need for after-sales service, the stronger the incentive to channel

Table 4.11 Related-Party Imports as a Percentage of Total Imports by Category, 1977

Imports	*Percent*	*Imports*	*Percent*
Live animals	12	Mineral tar and chemicals from coal, petroleum and natural gas	34
Beverages and tobacco	20	Dyeing, tanning and colouring materials	70
Dairy products	13	Medical and pharmacuetical products	47
Fish and fish preparations	23	Essential oils and perfumes	27
Cereals and cereal preparations	12	Fertilisers, manufactured	23
Fruit and vegetables	40	Explosives and pyrotechnic products	9
Sugar, sugar preparations	3	Plastic materials	55
Coffee, tea, cocoa, spices	9	Chemical materials and products n.e.s	49
Feeding stuff for animals	16	Leather and leather manufactures	6
Miscellaneous foods	24	Rubber manufactures n.e.s.	73
Beverages	24	Wood and cork manufactures	15
Tobacco and manufactures	8	Paper, paperboard, etc.	21
Hides and skins	1	Textile yarn, fabrics, made-up articles	23
Oil seeds, nuts, kernels	19	Non-metallic mineral manufactures	16
Crude rubber (inc synthetic)	38	Iron and steel	62
Wood, lumber, cork	17	Non-ferrous metals	34
Pulp and waste paper	41	Manufactures of metals, n.e.s.	25
Textile fibres	17	Machinery other than electrical	60
Crude fertilisers and minerals	38	Electrical machinery, apparatus, appliances	63
Metaliferous ores and metal scrap	52	Transport equipment	84
Crude animal and vegetable materials	14	Sanitary and other fixtures	16
Coal, coke and briquettes	14	Furniture	26
Petroleum and petroleum products	57	Travel goods and handbags	13
Gas, natural and manufactured	55	Clothing	11
Animal oils and fats	15	Footwear	7
Fixed vegetable oils and fats	9	Professional and scientific instruments	51
Animal and veg.oils and fats, processed	5	Mescellaneous manufacturs	28
Chemical elements and compounds	43		

Source: Helleiner and Lavergne (1980).

exports through affiliates, especially in the case of high-technology products.

Helleiner and Lavergne (1980) examined the nature of intra-firm trade as a component of U.S. imports. Table 4.11 sets out their estimates of the share of related-party imports in total imports in different product groups measured at the two-digit level of aggregation.

An advantage of their study was that they distinguished between related-party imports of non-U.S. firms located in the U.S. and of U.S. firms and between imports from OECD and developing countries. Equally large variations in intra-firm trade clearly exist for U.S. imports as for exports. In econometric testing, the factors which best explained inter-industry differences in levels of intra-firm trade were as follows:

1. *The skill intensity of an industry*, as measured by the level of the average wage. For imports from developed countries but not for imports from developing countries, the higher the degree of skill intensity, the higher the level of intra-firm trade.
2. *The importance of barriers to entry of new competitors to an industry*, as measured by the size of firms in an industry. For imports from developed countries but again not for imports from developing countries, the higher the level of entry barriers to an industry, the greater the degree of intra-firm trade.
3. *The degree of technology- or research-intensity of an industry*, as measured by the level of R&D expenditure as a percentage of total sales. For imports from both developed and developing countries, the greater the degree of research-intensity, the higher the level of intra-firm trade. This variable worked particularly well in explaining industry differences for imports from developing countries and for changes in the level of intra-firm imports.

In a more recent study of industry differences in U.S. intra-firm exports and imports, Siddharthan and Kumar (1990) found that R&D intensity was the most important determinant of intra-firm exports and imports. Sales and administrative expenditures expressed as a percentage of turnover also had a positive and significant effect on the intra-firm export ratio. U.S. anti-pollution laws were also found to have encouraged U.S. firms to import pollution-intensive products on an intra-firm basis. In a later study, the OECD (1993) obtained similar results for U.S. trade. For intra-firm exports, the most important explanatory variables were the R&D intensity of an industry and the international orientation of firms in the industry (as measured by the ratio of sales to foreign affiliates divided by total sales of the U.S. parent). For intra-firm imports, their regression results found that R&D intensity, physical capital intensity and selling expenses intensity all had a positive effect on the level of intra-firm trade. However, contrary to Siddharthan and Kumar, the OECD study found that pollution intensity had a negative effect.

These results are broadly consistent with what theory says about the factors giving rise to vertical FDI that were discussed in the previous chapter. In particular, technology- or research-intensity stands out as being an important determinant of intra-firm-trade. As observed in the previous chapter, the incentive to internalise markets is especially great where the asset to be transferred across countries is knowledge. In a study of the intra-firm export share of the largest 300 U.S.-based MNCs, Buckley and Casson (1976) found that the industries that were the most research-intensive, had the highest intra-firm trade ratios. This point is further illustrated by Table 4.12 which shows the level of intra-firm exports for the world's largest 329 industrial corporations classified according to research-intensity.

If aerospace is omitted from the high research-intensive industries, it is apparent that the level of intra-firm trade is highest in this sector. If aerospace is included, however, the ratio is slightly higher in the medium research-intensive industries. This, however, is entirely accounted for by just two sectors, industrial and farm equipment and motor vehicles. Intra-firm trade ratios are significantly lower for all low research-intensive industries. The relationship between research intensity and the level of intra-firm trade is, of course, not a perfect one because of the range of other factors at work.

Transfer Pricing

One explanation for the increase in intra-firm trade in recent decades may be the opportunities

Table 4.12 The Share of Intra-Firm Exports in the Total Exports from their Home Countries of 329 Large Industrial Corporations by Industry, 1977

Sector	*Share*
High research-intensive industries	
Aerospace	1.8
Office equipment (including computers)	91.3
Petroleum	51.0
Measurement, scientific and photographic equipment	58.2
Electronics and electrical equipment	36.5
Chemicals and pharmaceuticals	35.0
Subtotal	34.5
Medium research-intensive industries	
Industrial and farm equipment	52.6
Shipbuilding, railroad and transportation equipment	0.1
Rubber	–
Motor vehicles (including components)	62.4
Metal manufacturing and products	12.8
Subtotal	36.9
Low research-intensive industries	
Building materials	8.7
Tobacco	0.5
Beverages	20.3
Food	9.2
Paper and wood products	9.5
Textiles, apparel, leather goods	12.8
Publishing and printing	5.4
Other manufacturing	5.9
Subtotal	9.5
All sectors	32.8

Source: Dunning and Pearce (1981); UNCTC (1983).

which intra-firm trade creates for transfer-price manipulation. Transfer prices are the prices used by MNCs for intra-firm transactions. The term *transfer pricing* or *transfer-price manipulation* is used when MNCs use prices on intra-firm transactions which diverge from those used in equivalent arms-length transactions. As is explained below, there are several reasons why MNCs may wish to manipulate transfer prices in this way. Such practices have also invited much criticism on the grounds that they undermine the sovereignty of national governments. The question as to whether or not transfer pricing takes place is also of interest for another reason. If a large growing proportion of world trade constitutes intra-firm trade, the use of transfer pricing will mean that the prices used in trade are not market-determined prices as is assumed in trade theory. This challenges one of the assumptions of orthodox trade theory. There may also be implications for the efficiency of certain economic policy weapons such as devaluation, since a lowering of the exchange rate may fail to effect any change in a country's export or import prices.

Although transfer pricing is generally applied to intra-firm trade in goods taking place between a parent company and its affiliates or between any two affiliates of the same MNC, transfer pricing in practice may extend to a wider range of transactions than these. First, there is the question of the relationship between the buying and selling company. How closely are they related in ownership? There is no problem where the affiliate is a wholly- or majority-owned subsidiary of the company in question. However, frequently, the MNC holds only a minority, non-controlling interest in the overseas company. Even if it owns no equity stake in the overseas company, it may exercise some element of control (e.g. a licensing agreement, management contract, subcontracting, etc.). In such cases the prices used in trade may not be manipulated in quite the same way as when the overseas company is wholly or largely owned MNC. However, prices may still not correspond to prices freely determined in an equivalent arms-length transaction.

Second, the concept of transfer pricing need not be confined to trade transactions. It may equally well apply to non-trade flows within the MNC. An MNC may divert funds from one unit to another through non-trade channels, such as the payment of fees to the parent company for the provision of services, the payment of royalties for licences covering patents or other forms of know-how or the payment of interest on loans from the parent company. Transfer pricing in non-trade transactions is often more difficult to identify because the payments involved are typically for resources which are highly specific to the firm and which, therefore, have no equivalent free-market, arms-length prices for comparison.

Motives for Transfer Pricing

Why might an MNC fix a different price on the sale of goods to an overseas affiliate than the free market, arms-length price for an equivalent transaction between two unrelated parties? There exist several possible motives for transfer pricing. Plasschaert (1979) has suggested the following.

1. Differences in Rates of Corporation Taxation between Countries

Whenever rates of corporation tax differ markedly between one country and another, an incentive exists for MNCs to manipulate transfer prices. By doing so, they can reduce their overall, global tax payments and thereby increase after-tax profits. Suppose that the rate of corporation tax is higher in Country A than in Country B. Then, it will pay a parent company based in Country A which sells goods to an affiliate in Country B to under-invoice the sale of such goods. In this way, some recorded profits can be shifted from Country A where tax is high to Country B where tax is low and the global tax liability of the MNC reduced. Conversely, if the rate of corporation tax were lower in Country A than Country B, it would gain by over-invoicing the sale of goods from the parent to the affiliate.

Since rates of corporation tax do differ between countries, it might be supposed that transfer pricing of this kind is quite common. If so, the effect will be to deprive the tax authorities in countries with high levels of profits of significant fiscal revenues. It is sometimes argued that transfer pricing of this kind undermines the ability of a poorer developing country to ensure that a larger share of the profits earned by foreign companies is retained by a policy of high taxation. Transfer price manipulation of this kind would, by raising the unit price of imports, also have an adverse effect on the terms of trade and balance of payments of the country in question. However, it does appear that nominal rates of corporation tax are typically lower in developing countries

(Plasschaert, 1985). In addition, developing countries tend to assess taxable profits less severely and offer more generous tax incentives in an effort to attract foreign capital. If effective rather than nominal rates of corporate tax are taken, tax rates are substantially lower in developing countries. However, there are a few cases of developing countries where above-average nominal rates are applied. It is also the case that many developing countries impose punitive withholding taxes on repatriated dividends, interest and royalties.

One factor which may reduce the incentive for MNCs to manipulate transfer prices to reduce their global tax liability, is the system operated by many industrialised countries for preventing the double taxation of profits. For example, in the United States, corporate taxes paid by an overseas affiliate to the host country on profits earned can be deducted from the tax payable in the United States when profits are remitted. Such taxes paid to host-country governments count as foreign tax credits against taxable profits in the United States. Withholding taxes paid on repatriated dividends, interest and royalties may also qualify for such tax credits. The aim of these arrangements is to ensure that profits earned overseas do not get taxed twice over and thus prevent any discrimination against foreign as opposed to domestic investment. In addition, the U.S. tax system contains a built-in incentive for MNCs to retain profits abroad. Any profits earned abroad but not repatriated are not subject to reassessment for tax in the US. This is known as the 'deferral rule'. At the same time, any MNC that reinvests profits in the local subsidiary rather than repatriating profits, avoids paying withholding tax. The effect of these arrangements is to reduce the gain to be reaped from transfer-price manipulation should overseas profit tax be higher than the rates applicable in the home country.

However, there are also the cases of so-called 'tax havens', countries where zero or extremely low rates of corporate tax exist. It appears that some MNCs have set up non-producing subsidiaries in such countries and used transfer pricing to siphon off profits to these companies. On the other hand, the ability of MNCs to avoid tax in this way is more limited than it may at first seem. Governments of most capital-exporting countries are now aware of these practices and have introduced legislation to prevent such abuse, although it may be more difficult for developing countries to do so. Moreover, from the point of view of the MNC, the incentive to switch funds in this way may not be so great. Eventually, profits recorded in the tax haven will need to be remitted to the parent company to pay dividends to shareholders at which point they will become liable to tax.

2. *Differences in the Levels of Tariffs between Countries*

Another inducement to manipulate transfer prices may arise from different import tariff levels. When an MNC is selling goods to an overseas affiliate and faces a high *ad valorem* tariff, the company can minimise the customs duty payable by under-pricing the merchandise. It is sometimes argued that MNCs engage in this type of practice when selling goods to affiliates based in developing countries. Many developing countries impose high tariffs on imported intermediate goods to promote import substitution. Customs duties are also an important revenue-raising device in poor developing countries that lack a large tax base. It is argued that such transfer pricing harms developing countries by undermining their attempts to protect infant industries and by depriving them of fiscal revenues. On the other hand, it is beneficial to their balance of payments and improves their terms of trade.

As a motive for transfer pricing, however, it may conflict with other objectives. Under-invoicing goods sold to an overseas affiliate will siphon off profits from the parent company abroad and increase the size of profits recorded in the foreign country. Where tax rates are lower in the host country, this may be desirable. However, where rates are higher in the host country, there is a clear conflict of aims. Furthermore, under-pricing sales to the overseas affiliate exposes the MNC to financial risk from a sudden devaluation or depreciation of the local currency or the imposition of tighter exchange controls on the outflow of capital by the host-country government. For these reasons, the MNC may not want to tie up too many profits in an overseas country especially one that is economically weak or politically unstable.

Much depends on the type of good imported. The tariff structure of both developed and developing countries tends to escalate. This means that the more advanced the stage of production, the higher the rate of import tariff applied. Thus, finished manufactures tend to be subject to higher tariffs than semi-finished manufactures or intermediate goods and semi-finished manufactures or intermediate goods than raw materials. Trade economists would say that the effective rate of protection is greater than the nominal rate. It is more likely that affiliates based in developing countries will import semi-finished rather than finished manufactures from the parent company, while the parent company will import finished rather than semi-finished manufactures from the overseas affiliate. In this case, the under-pricing of imports is more likely to take place when the affiliate supplies the parent company with the finished manufacture. It will therefore affect the exports not the imports of the developing country. In this case, developing countries will experience no loss of customs duties, although their balance of payments and terms of trade will suffer. On the other hand, one suspects that the customs authorities in developing countries will be able to identify any cases of blatant under-invoicing of this kind.

3. Exchange Risks

The existence of different currencies and the fact that exchange rates either fluctuate or are subject to frequent adjustments creates risks for all companies involved in trade. Hence all traders seek to reduce their exposure to losses caused by exchange rate changes. One way in which they seeks to do so is through alteration or variation of the *timing* of payments and receipts, known sometimes as 'leads' and 'lags'. 'Leads' occur when payments to be made in weak currencies expected to depreciate (i.e. cost more in foreign currency) are brought forward. 'Lags' refer to delays in payments in strong currencies thought likely to appreciate (i.e. cost less in foreign currency). Since they are designed to protect traders from the risk of currency depreciation/appreciation, they constitute a form of 'hedging'. Where they are undertaken to enable traders to take an exposed position in a particular currency thought likely to appreciate, they may also constitute a form of currency speculation.

Whatever the motive, they are, to varying degrees, a common practice among all companies engaged in trade, not just MNCs. However, MNCs are especially well placed to undertake such operations because a certain amount of their trade is intra-firm trade. By overpricing or under-pricing the sale of goods from one unit of the company to another, they can switch funds from weak to strong currencies. Consider the case of a U.K.-based MNC with an affiliate in the United States to whom finished goods are supplied for resale. Suppose that sterling is expected to depreciate (i.e. the dollar appreciate). If the price has been fixed in dollars, a sterling depreciation will raise the price that the parent company will get for the goods' in which case the parent company will be anxious to delay payment. This can in part be effected by under-invoicing sales to the affiliate for as long as sterling looks set to depreciate. Conversely, if sterling is expected to appreciate, the parent company will be anxious to bring forward payment. The sales can be over-invoiced for as long as sterling looks likely to rise.

4. Restriction on the Repatriation of Profits or Capital

Limitations on the repatriation of profits from other countries in which affiliates are located will create strong inducements for MNCs to engage in transfer-price manipulation. This will take the form of the overpricing of goods sold by the parent company to the affiliate and/or under-pricing of goods sold by the affiliate to the parent company. In this way, a disguised repatriation of profits by MNCs may be effected. Many developing countries seek to restrict the repatriation of profits by MNCs for both tax and balance of payments reasons. Such restrictions may take several different forms:

(i) Legal stipulations covering the maximum dividend payments out of profits to the shareholders of the parent company,
(ii) A system of multiple exchange rates under which foreign currency for the purpose of profit repatriation is only available at highly unfavourable exchange rates,
(iii) Severe and discriminatory taxation of profits that are remitted, often including payments of royalties on the use of know-how, management fees and the interest on any loans from the parent company.

5. Political and Social Pressures

A wide variety of different kinds of political and social pressure in either the home or host country may create an inducement for a MNC to manipulate transfer prices. Two such cases may be cited:

(i) Trade unions demand a larger share of the declared profits of the affiliates for their members in the form of higher wages, so the parent company may wish to disguise some of the profits made by the affiliate by overpricing goods sold to the affiliate.
(ii) The government of the host country threatens nationalisation on account of alleged excessive profits made by the MNC, so the parent company seeks to disguise profits by overpricing goods which it sells to the overseas affiliate.

However, in all of these situations, the MNC must tread carefully. Indiscreet and over-played manipulation of transfer prices will merely attract the attention of trade unions and/or the host-country government and increase the risk of industrial unrest or expropriation by the authorities.

6. Direct Threats to Profits

The profits of an MNC may be threatened in a variety of ways that give rise to transfer-price manipulation. Four different cases may be cited:

(i) The declaration of high profits by an MNC may cause the government of the host country to reduce or remove altogether any protection from imports that the MNC previously enjoyed. The level of the import tariff may be determined by reference to domestic costs of production plus some acceptable mark-up. If so, the MNC will have an incentive to overprice the cost of any goods imported from the overseas affiliate so as to secure a higher level of protection.

(ii) The declaration of high profits by an MNC may alternatively lead to the host-country government imposing price controls. Often these controls establish prices by reference to the domestic costs again with some acceptable mark-up for profits. This creates an incentive for the MNC to overprice the sale of semi-finished goods to the overseas affiliate. Such price controls are common in industries such as pharmaceuticals where MNCs enjoy patent protection and governments are fearful of excessive profits being made.

(iii) The declaration of high profits by the MNC may invite other MNCs or local firms to set up in competition so as to gain a share in the excess profits being earned. Transfer-price manipulation may constitute a device for both disguising such profits from envious onlookers and deterring entry to the industry by potential rivals.

(iv) The declaration of high profits by an MNC may cause the host-country government to impose higher taxes or to insist on greater local shareholder participation to ensure that more profits are retained locally. The MNC may see the latter as undermining its control as well as reducing the amount of profits going to the shareholders in the home country. Transfer-price manipulation may be used as a means of concealing such profits.

Constraints on Transfer Price Manipulation

Although there exist a variety of inducements for MNCs to engage in transfer pricing, these must be set against certain constraining factors. These are of two kinds.

1. Internal Limitations

The most important set of internal constraints on manipulation of transfer prices are as follows:

(i) Where a substantial proportion of shares are owned by local investors, it may prove more difficult to siphon profits abroad by the parent company overpricing its sales to the local subsidiary. Local shareholders will resist such a process because it reduces the amount of profit that goes to them. For this reason, local equity participation is one way in which a country can protect itself against transfer pricing by foreign companies. However, it will not work if local shareholders are indifferent or lack sufficient knowledge to notice that transfer prices are being manipulated in this way. Furthermore, there is the possibility that local shareholders may co-operate with the foreign partner if they see their interests as bound up with those of the parent company.

(ii) Where the local subsidiary is a joint venture between a foreign and a local company, the same constraints apply as with local equity participation. The local company will oppose any attempt to siphon profits abroad by the parent company overpricing sales to the subsidiary. On the other hand, the incentive to shift profits abroad in this way may be greater to ensure that the local partner gets a smaller share of the profits of the local enterprise.

(iii) Where it is thought desirable that the local subsidiary should enjoy a high degree of autonomy from the parent company, transfer pricing will not take place. Transfer pricing assumes a relatively centralised organisational structure in which the local subsidiary is seen as merely a branch of the same company and whose interests are therefore subordinate to those of the company as a whole. However, much modern management theory is opposed to over-centralisation because it stifles local effort and initiative. Where local managers are deprived of control, morale may suffer and a sense of commitment lost. This creates a preference for a more devolved structure involving the creation of autonomous 'profit centres' and the granting of freedom to local managers to maximise local profits. One way around this may be to operate two sets of accounts, one showing the real profits and the other the taxable profits. However, this leaves the problem that over-centralised control, makes for poor decision making. It makes for slower response to changed circumstances and requires a very large amount of information transmission. The parent company must be fed with large amounts of data, that have to be processed before decisions about prices and any changes in prices can be made. If, however, such a structure cannot be operated efficiently, scope for transfer pricing is likely to be small.

2. External Limitations

External constraints on transfer pricing arise from the intervention of governments, specifically the customs and tax authorities. Customs authorities will be concerned about loss of tariff revenue if MNCs' sales to local subsidiaries (or vice versa) are under-invoiced. The tax authorities in high-tax countries will be concerned about the loss of revenues, if profits are siphoned abroad through transfer-price manipulation, especially to tax havens. This can happen through overpricing or under-pricing exports and through non-trade channels, such as interest payments to the parent company and payments of royalties and fees for R&D. The great problem in the control of transfer pricing is that of identifying and determining its extent. The authorities require some comparable arm-length price against which to set the internal prices of the MNC. This will not be too difficult where the good or service is traded on the market involving a transaction between an independent buyer and seller. Where the internal price diverges significantly from this price, the authorities can require the MNC to make tax payments or pay customs duties taking the comparable uncontrolled price as the notional price.

However, many goods and services traded internally have no comparable uncontrolled price against which the internal price can be set. The good or service in question can be highly specific to the firm or there may exist no open market for such a good or service. In such cases, the authorities must use some other method to work out the equivalent arms-length price. At first, this may not seem too difficult. They should be able to collect information about costs and then all that is needed is to add some reasonable mark-up for profit. However, transfer prices often include some payments to the parent company for services such as R&D and other overheads, in which case there is a problem of how to apportion these among subsidiaries. Where transfer prices relate to the transfer of highly specific, intangible assets such as patents, technical expertise or management services, it is even more difficult to determine the appropriate comparable uncontrolled price. In brief, it is often difficult for the customs and tax authorities to control transfer pricing. Nevertheless, it remains the case that companies, which engage in overt transfer pricing risk attracting the attention of the authorities.

Empirical Evidence on Transfer Pricing

Empirical evidence on transfer pricing is still rather limited. Companies are unwilling to disclose information about their pricing policies except on a confidential basis and are unlikely to admit to transfer-pricing manipulation. In many cases, we do not know what prices are charged on intra-firm sales and, even when we do know these prices, we lack adequate information about equivalent arms-length prices for comparison. Even where we do have complete information, we have no way of knowing the extent to which MNCs have been constrained from transfer-price manipulation by the risk of being discovered. Despite these difficulties, some empirical work has been carried out. This would seem to suggest that transfer pricing does indeed take place, although it is difficult to know precisely how common and extensive it is. Below a selection of some of the most important such studies is surveyed.

Vaitsos (1974) made a comparison of the transfer prices declared by MNCs in Colombia with the prices of the same products sold on the open market. He found that intermediate goods imported by Colombian subsidiaries of MNCs were substantially overpriced – 40% in the case of rubber, 25% in the case of chemicals and 155% in the case of pharmaceuticals. Profit remittance was singled out as the main inducement with diversion of taxable profits to the tax haven of Panama as also important. In another study covering MNCs operating in Colombia, Lall (1973) found similar evidence for transfer pricing. Based on an examination of fourteen foreign firms operating in Colombia over the period 1966–1970, Lall found evidence of overpricing ranging between 30 and 300% in the case of pharmaceuticals and between 20–81% in the case of rubber and the electrical sector. Roumaliotis (1977) analysed the incidence and distribution of overpricing of imports to Greece. He found that, in one-half of eighty-four import cases covering the metallurgical, chemicals and pharmaceuticals sectors, substantial overpricing could be detected. Overpricing ranged from 5 to 230% with the highest percentages in chemicals (including pharmaceuticals). In another study covering the export of aluminium from a subsidiary in Greece to the parent company, Roumaliotis (1977) found that export prices were substantially lower than the comparable world price. Under-invoicing ranged from 1 to 19% according to the type of aluminium exported.

A study by Natke (1985) of import pricing in Brazil further supported the view that MNCs operating in developing countries typically overprice sales to their subsidiaries. Natke examined 141 manufacturing firms operating in Brazil, some of which were foreign and others domestically owned. The year covered was 1979 and the product coverage was some 127 product groups spread over 18 industries. He found that, in aggregate, MNCs paid higher prices for imports from their subsidiaries than those paid by Brazilian firms. However, there was great variety in the prices of such goods between foreign-owned and domestic companies suggesting that both over- and under-pricing of imports took place. In other words, although MNCs appear to manipulate transfer prices, they do not always do so in the same direction. Another study by Lecraw (1985) examined the import and export pricing practices of some 111 MNCs operating in 153 subsidiaries in six light manufacturing industries in five countries of the ASEAN region (Thailand, Malaysia, Singapore, Indonesia and the Philippines). For the year 1978, Lecraw found that MNCs engaged in widespread and systematic transfer pricing. Using multiple regression analysis, Lecraw tested to see which of the factors best explained these differences. These were found to be the following: a reduction of import duties, a reduction of profits taxation, movement of funds across national boundaries, reduction of risk and circumvention of government price and capital-profit remittance controls. There were, however, some interesting regional differences. Japanese MNCs operating in the ASEAN region were more inclined than U.S. or European MNCs to use transfer pricing in intra-firm trade. Lecraw explained this in terms of the purported tendency for Japanese MNCs to adopt more centralised systems of management control.

Benvignati (1985) investigated the transfer-pricing practices of leading U.S. manufacturing firms and found that non-market pricing was substantially more common for foreign than for domestic intra-firm transfers. An especially interesting finding of this study was that up to 85% of the variation in the use of market prices originated with firm-to-firm differences and no more than 7% with industry-to-industry differences. Using regression analysis, Benvignati found that the firm characteristics most strongly related to non-market pricing behaviour were advertising intensity, the volume of foreign transfers and the number of different countries where foreign firms operate. The latter two factors would suggest that government interferences, most notably in the tax policy area, create incentives for firms to under-price their intra-firm foreign transfers. However, large MNCs were found to be more strongly associated with market-based pricing, possibly because of their greater visibility to tax officials, the fact that they may suffer more from conflicting management objectives and the greater administrative costs incurred as a result of transfer pricing in such companies.

The Control of Transfer Pricing

The fact that transfer pricing does indeed appear to be quite common begs the question: does it matter? Is transfer pricing harmful and should it be controlled? If we do wish to control it, how can this be done? In assessing the effects of transfer pricing, it is important to distinguish between two considerations. Firstly, there are the effects of transfer pricing on economic *efficiency*. Are transfer prices economically efficient? Efficiency is generally interpreted in the sense of Pareto efficiency. A state of Pareto efficiency is said to exist when it is not possible to make one person better off without making someone else worse off. Resources are said to be optimally allocated between alternative activities whenever this condition is satisfied. It is possible to show that this condition is satisfied if producers each produce at a point where the market price equals private plus social marginal costs. Clearly, if market-based prices are set at a level where they do indeed equal private plus social marginal costs, transfer pricing will result in a movement away from a point of optimality and the effect on efficiency will be harmful. However, if market-based prices diverge from marginal cost, it is possible that transfer pricing could bring prices closer to a point of optimality in which case the effect on efficiency will be positive.

Now, as we saw in the last chapter, one of the reasons why firms seek to internalise markets is that external markets fail to allocate resources efficiently. For example, external markets may fail to ensure that firms, which possess firm-specific intangible assets such as knowledge, receive a price that adequately reflects the value of the knowledge that they have created. By creating an internal market for such knowledge, the MNC is able to ensure greater appropriability. In this case, the price at which such assets are transferred within the firm is likely to result in greater efficiency than market-based prices. Likewise, one reason for transfer pricing is the existence of certain kinds of market imperfections created by government intervention such as tariffs, taxes, controls on the repatriation of profits, etc. In some cases, these forms of intervention reduce efficiency by distorting the allocation of resources. For example, a tariff distorts efficiency by causing producers in the importing country to produce too much of the protected good and producers in the exporting country to produce too little. If, however, transfer pricing causes an MNC to under-price sales of the good to its foreign subsidiary, trade may take place at prices closer to the level which is desirable for efficiency. In other words, the effects of transfer pricing on economic efficiency are distinctly ambiguous. We cannot conclude that transfer pricing is *per se* harmful from an efficiency point of view.

A second consideration concerns the effects of transfer pricing on *equity*. Are transfer prices equitable? Equity can be interpreted either in the horizontal sense to mean equal treatment of identical people or the vertical sense of unequal treatment of unequal people. The latter implies some redistribution of income from richer to poorer countries. Clearly, if transfer pricing results in a redistribution of income from poorer to richer countries, it offends the principle of equity whichever interpretation is used. It is often argued that MNCs use transfer pricing to transfer funds out of developing countries for the reasons discussed above. As we have seen, there is no evidence to suggest, on average, that rates of profit tax are higher in developing than developed countries. It is, however, likely, that the level of ad valorem tariffs will be higher in developing countries, while developing countries probably do impose more restrictions on profit repatriation and prices than developed countries. It is also likely that MNCs will consider it more risky to tie up funds in subsidiaries located in developing countries subject to greater financial and political risk. The empirical evidence also appears to support the view that MNCs under-price sales to subsidiaries located in developing countries.

If transfer pricing is considered to be harmful, what can be done about it? Broadly speaking, there are two possibilities. Either government take unilateral action to eliminate the factors giving rise to transfer pricing or they co-operate together to agree to a set of rules which apply to MNCs either within a given region or on a multilateral basis. Clearly, governments could eradicate transfer pricing if they were to adopt measures that removed the incentive for MNCs to manipulate transfer prices. These might include the harmonisation rates of profit taxation, the reduction in the level of customs duties, the elimination of controls on the repatriation of profits or the elimination of controls on prices. Measures to eliminate financial risk from currency depreciation or asset expropriation might also prove effective. An alternative might be to require MNCs to provide more information about the prices charged on intra-firm purchases and sales so as to achieve greater transparency. The most direct way of tackling transfer pricing would be for the tax and customs authorities to determine what should be the prices used for a given intra-firm transaction. Taxes and duties would then be levied on this notional price rather than the actual price used by the company.

Clearly, however, this will constitute a major regulatory task for governments in countries where MNCs account for a substantial proportion of trade. This is the case for large industrialised countries but it may be a more manageable task for smaller developing countries where the number of firms involved in fewer. A further problem, as we have seen, concerns the absence in many cases of a comparable uncontrolled price in which case some formula must be adopted to determine the price. Another possibility is that the tax authorities tax MNCs using some notional allocation of profits rather than actual declared profits. This would necessitate taking the global profits of the company and allocating these between the parent company and overseas subsidiaries based on some criteria such as their share of global sales or assets. Last, the government of the host country may be able to counteract transfer pricing by insisting on local equity participation or requiring the foreign company to undertake a joint venture with local companies. As we saw above, the need to collaborate with local investors may make it difficult for MNCs to manipulate transfer prices.

The problem with countries adopting unilateral measures to control transfer pricing is that MNCs may be able to play off one country against another. Thus, governments may feel obliged to reduce the level of profits tax to the rate applying in the country with the lowest level of profits tax in order to eliminate the incentive for MNCs to under-price sales to their local subsidiaries. The same might apply to measures such as controls on prices or the repatriation of profits. A preferable solution might, therefore, be to reach an agreement either at a regional or global level to establish rules or codes of conduct by which MNCs are required to abide. Some attempt has been made to bring this about at a global level through the auspices of the OECD. In 1979, the OECD member states agreed on a set of recommendations for adjusting transfer prices for the purposes of determining taxable profits, using agreed methods for arriving at arms-length prices for intra-firm transfers of goods, services and assets and through co-operation between tax administrations in different member states (OECD, 1979). However, this applies to the western industrialised countries, which belong to the OECD and amounts only to a code to which member states have undertaken to adhere. Although much less action has been taken at the regional level, it is possible that closer regional integration between countries (e.g., the creation of the European Union (EU) and the North American Free Trade Area (NAFTA)), may in the future result in governments co-operating more at a regional level to ensure stricter control of transfer pricing.

Integrating Multinationals into Theories of Trade

A major weakness of conventional models of trade is that they assume that goods are produced by single country firms. This is, most certainly, the case with neo-classical trade theory. The Heckscher–Ohlin model of trade assumes that capital is largely immobile between countries. At the same time, the assumption that markets are perfectly competitive means that there is little or no rationale for firms engaging in direct investment abroad. Post-war theories of trade have come a little closer to incorporating FDI into trade theory. In particular, Vernon's *Product Life Cycle Theory* proposed a model in which direct investment constitutes a specific method of market entry when products reach the maturity stage in their development. In the standardisation stage, too, firms engage in FDI to take advantage of low labour costs in developing countries. More recently, trade theorists have constructed several models of trade in which MNC activity is an important element. Before examining some of these approaches, it is useful to consider whether or not MNC activity can, in any way, be introduced as an element in neo-classical models of trade.

International Production in the Neo-Classical Framework

Can the neo-classical model of trade be adapted to incorporate foreign direct investment? Somewhat surprisingly, the answer is yes, as has been demonstrated by Professor Max Corden (Corden, 1974). In his *Locational Model*, Corden, initially, retains all the assumptions of the neo-classical model except two. First, knowledge is incorporated as a third factor of production (along with labour and capital). Second, capital and knowledge are assumed to be perfectly mobile internationally while labour is assumed to be immobile between countries. (An alternative is to assume that there are two types of mobile capital, conventional capital and human capital, which embodies knowledge.) The fact that capital and knowledge are perfectly mobile internationally means that factor prices are equalised between countries. As capital flows from capital-abundant to capital-scarce countries, the marginal product of labour and therefore the wage rate is equalised in different countries. (Students of Economics should know that the marginal product of labour, that is, the amount of extra output created by the employment of one extra worker is determined by the amount of labour which is combined with a fixed amount of capital. So, if the stock of capital falls in capital-abundant countries and rises in capital-scarce countries, the marginal product of labour will rise in the former and fall in the latter until it is equalised in the two countries.)

Costs of production are therefore the same in all countries and MNCs will be indifferent as to where to locate their production. If, however, we relax other assumptions of the Heckscher–Ohlin model, we can see how the location decisions of the MNC are affected:

1. *The introduction of a second immobile factor*. If we assume that, instead of there being one immobile factor (labour), there are two immobile factors (say, skilled and unskilled labour or labour and land), then factor costs will no longer be equalised in all countries. Instead, countries well endowed with skilled labour will enjoy relatively cheap skilled labour and those well endowed with unskilled labour with relatively cheap unskilled labour. (The reason is that the Heckscher–Ohlin model is a two-factor model that breaks down if three factors are included. In this case, capital and knowledge still change the relative stock of capital and knowledge in different countries in the manner described above but because countries possess different amounts of skilled/unskilled labour, wage rates for the different kinds of labour cannot be equalised between countries.) In this case, MNCs will locate the production of goods that are intensive in skilled labour in the countries where skilled labour is cheap and the production of goods intensive in unskilled labour in countries where unskilled labour is cheap.
2. *The assumption of technology differences between countries*. If we assume that, for whatever reason (better infrastructure, more stable political conditions or immobility of certain types of knowledge), production efficiencies differ between countries, the result will be a flow of the two mobile factors (capital and knowledge) to these countries. This will give the countries in question a relative cost advantage in the industries which use relatively large amounts of the mobile factors, that is, capital-intensive or knowledge-intensive industries. MNCs will tend to locate the production of these goods in these countries.
3. *The introduction of transport costs*. High transport costs tend to discourage trade and encourage the location of production as close as possible to the market. Given high transport costs, MNCs will locate their production near to the largest markets. The exact location will depend on the particular tastes of consumers in different countries. However, differences in production costs due

to different factor endowments (see points 1 and 2) might act as an offsetting factor.

4. *The presence of government restrictions and taxation*. The existence of tariffs or other import restrictions will encourage MNCs to produce locally rather than service overseas markets through exports. Differences in levels of taxation will also influence location decisions.
5. *The introduction of increasing returns to scale*. If there are increasing returns to scale, this will encourage the MNC to locate all production of a good at a single location and supply markets in other countries through exports. Whereas the existence of high transport costs and tariff/non-tariff barriers to imports have trade-inhibiting effects, increasing returns may in part offset this. The tendency will be for production to be located where the domestic market is largest especially for goods that are costly to transport long distances. There is therefore an expectation that countries with large domestic markets will enjoy a comparative advantage in increasing-returns activities especially where transport costs are high relative to the unit value of the product.
6. *The introduction of dynamic factors*. If we assume that production efficiencies and factor endowments change over time, there will be implications for the location decisions of MNCs. For example, investment in education will increase a country's stock of human capital and improve its production function. Such changes will alter the comparative costs of producing a product in different locations and may cause a MNC to reallocate its resources. In a dynamic model, it might also be reasonable to assume, as do technology-based theories, that new knowledge is only diffused internationally with a time lag. In this case, the knowledge-producing country will enjoy a temporary comparative advantage in the production of the good.

Corden's contribution is helpful in showing how the neo-classical framework can be adapted to incorporate the existence of MNCs. FDI takes place as firms seek out the lowest cost location to produce goods. Far from undermining the predictions of the factor-proportions theory, such movements of direct capital serve to reinforce these. The existence of transport costs and government-imposed barriers to trade encourages firms to set up subsidiaries abroad as an alternative to exporting. In addition, the existence of increasing returns to scale creates an incentive for MNCs to centralise production in a small number of locations resulting in increased trade. Moreover, the model has a dynamic element that permits predictions to be made about the evolution of comparative advantage over time.

The Dunning Eclectic Approach

An alternative approach has been proposed by Dunning and Norman (1985), in which neo-classical theory is assumed to be capable of explaining some but not all forms of international economic involvement. Because different theoretical explanations are combined within a single integrated framework to explain different kinds of trade in both goods and assets, the approach may be described as an eclectic one. In the Dunning and Norman framework, international transactions can take the form of an exchange of *products* (both final products and intermediate products and services) or the transfer of *assets* (in the form of capital) or *asset rights* (technology). Where transactions take the form of products or assets belonging to different industries, *inter-industry trade/FDI* results. Where, however, they involve the products or assets of the same industry, the result

		Organization Transaction					
		SPOT MARKETS		CONTRACTS		HIERARCHIES	
		Perfect	Imperfect	Perfect	Imperfect	Perfect	Imperfect
INTER-INDUSTRY	ASSETS	A. Arms length transaction. No cross hauling. Portfolio investment.		B. Contract transactions. No cross hauling (e.g. of similar kinds of technology). Licensing, management contracts, etc.		C. Internalised transaction. FDI plus Joint ventures (General theories of FDI)	
	PRODUCTS	HOS Neo-factor trade	Neo-technology product cycle trade (e.g. Posner, Hufbauer, Vernon)	Subcontracting			Intra-firm trade
INTER-INTRA-INDUSTRY	ASSETS	D. Some cross-hauling of broadly similar assets/products		E. As above		F. Moving towards plant specialisation within Hierarchies ↓	Vertical and horizontal FDI
	PRODUCTS	Mixture of HOS trade (e.g. Linder, Falvey, Helpman)					Intra-firm trade (Helleiner and Lavergne, Lall)
INTRA-INDUSTRY	ASSETS	G. Cross hauling of identical or closely similar assets/products.		H. Cross hauling of identical or closely similar assets/products. Some control/influence exerted in contract. Cross licencing e.g. in chemical industry Cross sub-contracting in auto industry		I. Importance of economies of synergy and transaction cost minimising (See explanations of Caves, Coase, Buckley, Casson, etc) →Horizontal FDI MNE oligopolies Intra-firm trade	
	PRODUCTS	Trading Oligopolies (e.g. Brander, Brander-Spencer & Krugman) Trade under Monopolistic Competition (e.g. Lancaster-Helpman, Dixit-Stiglitz, Krugman)					

Figure 4.1 A typology of two-way international economic transactions (the Dunning–Norman matrix).

Source: Adapted from Dunning and Norman, 1985.

is *intra-industry trade/FDI*. Intra-industry FDI is the simultaneous export and import of FDI (i.e. outward and inward FDI) belonging to the same industry. This is discussed further in the next chapter. These transactions take place using a variety of mechanisms ranging from *spot markets* at one extreme to *hierarchies* (intra-firm or in-house transactions) at the other. In between, independent firms may enter into *contracts,* which combine elements of both extremes. These transactions may be conducted in markets which range from perfectly competitive to imperfectly competitive. Imperfectly competitive markets are characterised by a small number of buyers or sellers, product differentiation and barriers to entry and by government intervention.

Dunning and Norman proposed a matrix comprising nine cells each containing different combinations of these various forms of international economic involvement. Figure 4.1. gives a modified version of the Dunning/ Norman matrix.

Beginning at cell A, trade/capital flows is/ are of the inter-industry type and take place between independent buyers and sellers in spot markets. Such trade and investment is best explained by neo-classical factor proportions theory (where markets are perfectly competitive) and by technology-based theories of trade. Moving from cell A to cells B and C, while trade/capital flows is/are still of the inter-industry type, transactions may take place through means other than arms-length transactions in spot markets. Licensing, management contracts and sub-contracting are examples of non-equity forms of international economic involvement, which involve some element of contractual relationship between firms (Cell B). Internalised transactions involving both goods and capital are at the other extreme and result from the existence of imperfections in markets (Cell C). In the case of assets, these take the form of FDI or the creation of joint ventures with a foreign company. In the case of goods (and some assets), these result in intra-firm trade. General theories of FDI explain the reasons why firms internalise their transactions in this way.

Cells D–F involve hybrids of inter- and intra-industry trade/FDI. One particular form of this arises where MNCs establish plants overseas to process or assemble components and parts produced elsewhere or so-called 'cross-hauling' by MNCs. Since the factor intensities of each stage of production are different, such trade resembles Heckscher–Ohlin–Samuelson (HOS) inter-industry trade (Cell D). However, if components and parts are classified as belonging to the same industry, it may be treated as intra-industry trade (see Chapter 3). The same is true of FDI, which is undertaken to bring about greater plant specialisation (Cell F). This may be classified as inter- or intra-industry FDI depending on how broadly or narrowly the industry is defined. An outcome of increased plant specialisation is increased levels of intra-firm trade, where trade is internalised as a result of FDI. However, where a firm sub-contracts a producer in another country to perform one or more processes, the result is a form of trade intermediate between a spot and a hierarchial transaction (Cell E). Vertical intra-industry trade may be viewed as a hybrid of inter- and intra-industry trade, as factor intensities differ across the quality specturm. Therefore, theoretical explanations for vertical intra-industry trade also belong in Cell D.

Finally, Cells G to I cover the cases of where both trade and FDI is, unambiguously, of the intra-industry type. As this takes place at the other extreme, transactions take place in imperfectly competitive markets and result in both intra-industry and intra-firm trade in goods and intra-industry FDI. These can only be satisfactorily explained by trade theories and theories of FDI which incorporate imperfect competition. In the case of goods, intra-industry trade is most common in industries where markets are imperfectly competitive. As we saw in Chapter 3, the theories which can explain such trade assume either oligopoly (Brander-Spencer, Krugman) or monopolistic competition (Lancaster, Dixit and Stigilitz) (Cell G). Hierarchial intra-industry trade is a consequence of horizontal rationalisation in which MNCs establish plants that specialise in different models of the same product (Cell I).

While falling short of providing a theoretical model that can explain trade and FDI, Dunning and Norman's typology of international economic involvement provides a useful framework for thinking about trade and FDI at the same time. In particular, it demonstrates the relationship that exists between certain theories of trade (viz. those that predict intra-industry trade) and theories of FDI. It show how intra-industry trade and intra-industry FDI tend to arise out of the same characteristics of an industry. It also shows how forms of international economic involvement tend to evolve over time beginning with inter-industry trade in goods and one-way transfer of assets largely in the form of portfolio investment, proceeding through to intra-industry trade and one-way FDI and, finally, to intra-industry production and intra-firm trade.

Recent Attempts to Integrate Trade and Foreign Direct Investment

Other attempts to integrate theories of trade and FDI have employed a more formal, general equilibrium framework using the standard assumptions of new trade theory but allowing for the presence of both multi-product and multinational firms. Analysing the case of where multinational firms simply duplicate their production activities in another country, Markusen (1984) argued that a motive for FDI is the economies that accrue to such firms from multi-plant production. These arise from the fixed costs of providing certain central activities, mainly R&D, advertising, marketing and distribution to support varying levels of production in several locations. The result is that MNCs carry out production activities in more than one country but conduct their 'corporate' activities at home. At the same time, the existence of transport costs, tariff and non-tariff barriers to trade and geographical and distance costs encourages firms to produce in more than one location. On the other hand, the fact that unit costs fall with the volume of output at the plant level encourages geographical concentration of production.

Helpman and Krugman (1985) developed a similar model that focused more on vertically integrated MNCs. They drew a similar distinction between so-called 'headquarter activities' and actual production. The model assumed two sectors, one producing a finished differentiated good, the other a homogeneous good. Headquarters activities in the differentiated sector were assumed to be the most capital-intensive, the finished differentiated goods are assumed to be of intermediate capital intensity and the homogeneous goods sector was assumed to be labour-intensive. Increasing returns to scale were assumed but transport costs were ignored. These two factors caused the firm to tend towards geographical concentration of individual activities. However, what caused them to locate production activities in the differentiated goods sector in a different location from headquarters activities was the existence of substantially different factor prices which reflect differences in factor endowments. In this case, they tend to locate headquarters activities in the capital-abundant country and plant production in the labour-abundant country. Small differences in factor prices do not have this effect.

Instead, the capital-abundant country specialises in varieties of the differentiated good and the labour-abundant country in the homogeneous good. Trade will then bring about partial equalisation of factor prices. If, however, differences in factor endowments and therefore factor prices exceed a certain limit, the capital-abundant country specialises in the production of capital-intensive headquarters activities and imports both differentiated and homogeneous goods. In a subsequent follow-up paper, Helpman (1985) extended the model to include both horizontally and vertically integrated firms that have production facilities in more than one country in finished goods, intermediate goods and services.

Porter's Approach

One of the most interesting contributions to our understanding of the relationship between trade and international production has proposed shifting the focus of attention from *nations* to *firms*. In his book entitled *The Competitive Advantage of Nations* (1996), Porter argues that what determines the pattern of trade and specialisation is the competitiveness of the firms operating in a particular country. He begins with a critique of orthodox trade theory. Orthodox trade theory is unhelpful because it focuses too much attention on relative factor endowments and the relative factor cost of producing the same good in different countries. Too little attention is paid to the importance of technological change that can very rapidly overcome any problem of factor scarcity in a particular country. Not enough importance is attached to the role of economies of scale, differences in consumer preferences and product differentiation in trade. Also, and perhaps most important of all, the assumptions on which orthodox trade theory is based have been undermined by increased globalisation. Globalisation means that firms compete on a global and not a national scale. Moreover, in this process, they adopt global strategies that involve finding the lowest cost locations for producing different products and selling goods on a worldwide basis. Consequently, what firms possess in terms of factor endowments has become less important as a constraint on firms domiciled in a particular country. In particular, whether or not a country is a capital-scarce or capital-abundant country need not matter, since most firms are able to raise capital anywhere in the world.

Porter argues that, instead of looking at the comparative advantage that different countries possess, we should focus attention on the nature of the competitive advantage that firms within each country enjoy. In most cases, these are multinational corporations. Often, they are based in a few countries. The explanation for why particular countries possess a competitive advantage in particular industries or services is, therefore, to be found in the reasons why MNCs located in these countries have been successful where firms in other countries have not. Firms gain such an advantage through a process of competition, in which product differentiation, economies of scale and technological innovation are among the strategies employed. This process of competition is a dynamic one that not only changes the nature of the industries in which it is taking place, but also means that some firms fail where others succeed. This, in turn, means that countries may gain or lose a competitive advantage once enjoyed in a particular industry depending on how firms located in that country respond to these challenges.

Porter proposes a 'new paradigm' based on the determinants of national competitive advantage. He identifies four factors as determining the competitive advantage in a particular industry:

1. *Factor conditions* – the possession of the factors such as skilled labour and suitable infrastructure required to compete in a particular industry.
2. *Demand conditions* – home demand conditions (the composition of home demand, the size and rate of growth of home demand and the internationalisation of home demand) may favour the development of a particular industry or service.
3. *Related and supporting industries* – the presence or absence in the nation of supplier and related industries, providing these are internationally competitive.
4. *Firm strategy, structure and rivalry* – the ways in which firms are created, organised and managed within a country and the nature of the rivalry between them.

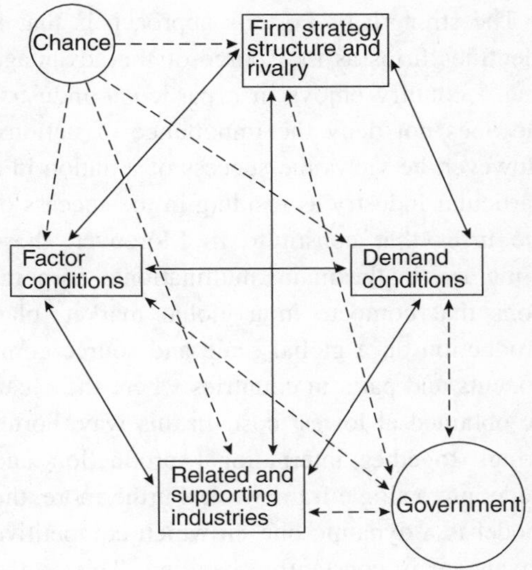

Figure 4.2 Michael Porter's diamond of national competitive advantage

In the advantage that a country gains in a particular industry, chance may also play an important role. Chance events (e.g. an invention, emergence of a strong local demand for a good, a political decision, the outbreak of war) may give firms in a particular country a head-start. They may also contribute towards competitive advantage shifting over time. A key factor, however, is the success with which a country takes advantage of chance events. A further important factor is the role of governments. By their policies, governments can contribute towards increased competitiveness in a particular sector or they can undermine it.

Porter refers to the four determinants of national competitive advantages as the 'diamond' of national success. Figure 4.2 illustrates the nature of Porter's diamond of national competitive advantage. However, success comes not merely from the possession of one or more of these factors. Rather, it is the manner in which they interact and reinforce each other. For example, the factors crucial to competitive success in a particular industry are, in part, created by the other determinants. A large and fast-growing market for a product results in factor creation through increased activity by firms in the industry. The growth of related and supporting industries creates or stimulates the creation of a pool of specialised factors (labour, science laboratories, training programmes) required by the industry and their upgrading. Finally, rivalry between domestic firms plays a crucial role in factor-creation by stimulating firms to invest in human capital and knowledge creation. These effects are especially pronounced when firms cluster in a particular region or locality. Other forms of interaction among the four factors can be identified. However, the nature of this interaction tends to change over time. Different factors assume greater importance at different stages in the development of an industry. They also have a different importance in different kinds of industries. Moreover, having gained an advantage in a particular industry, it is necessary that a country should sustain that advantage.

The strength of Porter's approach is that it identifies firms as the source of the advantage that a country enjoys in a particular industry. He does not deny the importance of nations. However, he views the success of a nation in a particular industry as residing in the success of the firms that constitute it. Moreover, these firms are, in the main, multinational corporations that compete in a global market, plan production on a global scale and source components and parts in countries where these can be obtained at lowest cost. In this way, Porter brings together international production and trade into a single framework. Furthermore, the model is a dynamic one, in which competitive advantage is constantly changing. This is the result mainly of the extent to which firms respond to changes in conditions in the global market place. What is lacking, however, is a formal theoretical model that integrates trade and FDI. This was not Porter's concern. His aim was to show how the study of trade needs to take much greater cognisance of the role that is played by multinational corporations domiciled in different countries.

Conclusion

In this chapter, the rise of the modern MNC has been described. MNC activity has been explained as the result of imperfections in the market for goods and assets that have created an incentive for firms to internalise markets by engaging in overseas production. In this respect, the rise of the MNC can be seen as arising out of similar factors to those that have resulted in the growth of intra-industry trade. However, the rise of the modern MNC has also spurned the growth of another type of trade, namely, intra-firm trade, taking place between different parts of the same company located in different countries. Intra-firm trade results wherever firms create internal markets for the goods and services that they wish to transfer across borders. In this chapter, we also saw that internalised markets create incentives for transfer-price manipulation, although internal and external constraints may place limits on the benefits from so doing.

The rise of the modern MNC has clearly affected the way in which countries trade with each other. Although conventional models of trade can be adapted to incorporate MNC activity, the results are not fully satisfactory, especially if many of the subtleties of international production are to be properly modelled. There is need for more work to be done in developing models in which trade and FDI are fully integrated. There is also need for policy makers to think differently about trade in a world in which firms typically operate in many different countries. It may be less meaningful for economists to talk in terms of comparative advantage than competitive advantage as Michael Porter has suggested. This is not to deny that comparative advantage exists and creates the basis for mutually beneficial exchange between any two countries. It is simply that what really determines patterns of trade and specialisation is the competitiveness of the firms within a particular country producing particular goods or services. A country's endowment of particular factors is less important than it once was, because MNCs can acquire these resources from wherever they wish. Rather, it is the success with which firms in a particular industry in a particular country compete with firms in other countries that determines whether or not a country becomes a net exporter or importer of the goods in question.

Notes for Further Reading

There exists a wealth of excellent texts on the multinational enterprise. Quite possibly, the most comprehensive text is the following:

Dunning, J. H. *The Multinational Enterprises and the Global Economy*, Reading: Addison, Wesley, 1992.

This has the advantage of having been written by one of the world's foremost authorities on the subject of direct investment. A further classic text on the theory of the multinational enterprise is:

Buckley, P. and Casson, M. *The Future of the Multinational Enterprise* (London: Macmillan, 1976).

Detailed statistical information about world stocks and flows of FDI is contained in the various *World Investment Reports* published by the United Nations Conference on Trade and Development (UNCTAD). The United Nations Centre on Transnational Companies (UNCTC) also publishes regular surveys entitled *Transnational Corporations in World Development*.

On the role played by multinationals in international trade, the interested reader should consult:

Casson, M. *et al.*, *Multinationals and World Trade – Vertical Integration and the Division of Labour in World Industries* (London: Allen and Unwin, 1986).

The best text on transfer pricing remains:

Plasschaert, S. *Transfer Pricing and Multinational Corporations: An Overview of Concepts, Mechanisms and Regulations* (Farnborough, Hants: Saxon House and New York: Praeger Publishers, 1979).

However, a more in-depth treatment of the subject is also contained in:

Rugman, A. M. and Eden, L. (eds), *Multinationals and Transfer Pricing* (Beckenham, Kent: Croom-Helm, 1985).

Students should also consult Michael Porter's classic volume for a study of the relationship between comparative and competitive advantage in trade:

Porter, M. *The Competitive Advantage of Nations* (London and Basingstoke: Macmillan, 1990).

Chapter 5

More Recent Forms of International Economic Involvement

CHAPTER OUTLINES: Introduction. Intra-Industry FDI – the measurement of intra-industry FDI, the causes of intra-industry FDI, the link between intra-industry FDI and intra-industry trade. Rationalised International Production – vertical disintegration and the new international division of labour, horizontal rationalisation, more complex patterns of integrated international production. Alternative Forms of International Business Involvement – joint ventures, licensing agreements, strategic alliances. Counter-trade – types of counter-trading, the importance of counter-trading, determinants of counter-trading, the effects of counter-trading. Conclusion.

Introduction

In the previous chapter, the growth of foreign direct investment and the emergence of the MNC since the Second World War were discussed. To begin with much of the FDI which occurred in the world took the form of one-way FDI, mainly by U.S. MNCs in Western Europe. Such FDI could be adequately explained by the wish of U.S. MNCs to more effectively exploit the technological and marketing advantages that they enjoyed in a number of branches of manufacturing. Although they could have done so through exporting, the need arose as many of their products reached maturity to seek out ways of servicing foreign markets at lower cost. The establishment of one or more subsidiaries abroad enabled them to cut transport costs, circumvent tariffs and non-tariff barriers and take advantage of lower production costs abroad. However, as we saw in the previous chapter, such one-way FDI rapidly gave way to two-way FDI as firms in other advanced industrialised countries (Western Europe and Japan) developed new ownership-specific advantages in particular branches of manufacturing, which they, too, sought to exploit by producing abroad. An interesting observation is that much of this two-way FDI takes place in the same branch of manufacturing. In other words, it constitutes what may be called *intra-industry FDI.* In this chapter, we discuss the nature and importance of intra-industry FDI and ask if any special theories are needed to account for this phenomenon.

When firms begin to expand abroad, they generally do so either by establishing distribution outlets for their products in the foreign market and/or by establishing a production plant that is a close replica of the plant in the home country that previously supplied the foreign market through exporting. Such local market-oriented FDI may generate substantial amounts of intra-firm trade in finished goods. Where, however, the finished good is produced abroad rather than at home, FDI acts as a substitute for trade. This type of FDI may, therefore, be described as *trade displacing*. Where, however, MNCs seek to integrate their activities in different countries in an effort to improve efficiency and lower costs, FDI may result in increased trade. This will take the form of intra-firm trade in intermediate goods and services. Such rationalisation may take several different forms. One involves breaking up the process of production into a series of different stages, each of which is located in different countries. Such vertical disintegration has become a feature of the production process in certain specific branches of manufacturing and is commonly referred to as the *new international division of labour (NIDL)*. A further possibility is that MNCs may rationalise their international production on a horizontal basis, with different plants specialising in producing different models of the same finished good. In this chapter, the nature of rationalised production and its effects on the pattern of trade is examined.

However, FDI is only one of the methods that firms may use in their attempts to achieve a global presence. In many cases, firms may be prevented by the host country government from establishing or acquiring a majority-owned subsidiary. One reason is that the host-country government wants to ensure that some of the benefit from the investment accrues to local firms. On the other hand, it may be prepared to admit a foreign company on a *joint venture* basis, in which case the equity capital is held jointly by the foreign firm and a local firm. Alternatively, the government of the host country may itself take an equity stake in the new company. Yet, a further possibility is that the foreign firm makes no direct investment in the foreign country, but licenses a local firm to produce the product on its behalf. Under the *licensing agreement*, the local firm agrees to pay the foreign firm a share of the resultant profits. Such non-equity forms of international economic involvement have become increasingly common in recent years, as ways in which foreign firms can exploit an advantage which they have gained without the risks of making an actual investment in the foreign market. From the point of view of the host country, they constitute a means of acquiring foreign technology without allowing foreign firms to acquire ownership and control of the local enterprise. Very often, however, firms enter into agreements with other firms, which are not motivated by the desire to gain access to any foreign market. Instead, they arise because both perceive that there are certain advantages to be gained from collaborating. For example, two firms may have particular strengths in different areas (one in production and another in marketing). By pooling their efforts, they may both be able to expand rapidly. However, they may choose to do so in ways that do not involve an actual merger of the two companies. Instead, they may enter into a *strategic alliance*, which involves co-operation only for a limited period of time over an agreed area of activities.

In this chapter, some of these newer forms of international economic involvement are discussed. In addition, the chapter examines a form of trading relationship between countries that has also become increasingly widespread in recent decades. This is so-called *barter trade* or *counter-trading*. Barter is the direct exchange of goods for other goods without the mediation of money. Barter remains quite rare, simply because barter is less efficient than money as a method financing international trade. However, it has become increasingly common for countries to part pay for goods imported from abroad by supplying other goods and services in return. One obvious reason is a lack of foreign currency to pay for all the imports required. Such counter-trading has become common in trade between developed and developing countries. We conclude this chapter by discussing the reasons for such trade and its effects.

Intra-Industry Foreign Direct Investment

Just as much trade between western industrialised countries over the past fifty years has taken the form of intra-industry trade (see Chapter 3), much of the FDI taking place in western industrialised economies has also been a two-way affair. Just as we have the phenomenon of intra-industry trade, so too we have intra-industry FDI. Intra-industry FDI may be defined as follows: 'two-way FDI by multinational enterprises based in different countries, in each other's home markets, to produce goods and services that are close substitutes in either consumption or production, and thus can be classified in the same industry' (Erdilek, 1985). As with the concept of intra-industry trade, there is a degree of ambiguity concerning the definition of an industry and, therefore, in distinguishing intra- from inter-FDI. Much, too, will depend on how broadly industries are defined.

The Measurement of Intra-Industry FDI

Intra-industry FDI can be measured using the same Grubel–Lloyd index which is used for the measurement of intra-industry trade (see Chapter 3). In this case, the index is measured as the proportion of a country's total stock of FDI (inward plus outward) for any industrial sector i which is matched or balanced (i.e. inward equals outward). The formula is:

$$\text{Intra-industry FDI for sector } i = \frac{(K_{xi} + K_{mi}) - |K_{xi} - K_{mi}|}{(K_{xi} + K_{mi})}$$

where K_{xi} is the country's outward capital stake in sector i and K_{mi} her inward capital stake. The closer the ratio is to one, the greater the importance of intra-industry FDI. As applied to FDI, the index is subject to the same problems as apply to the measurement of intra-industry trade. However, there are additional problems that arise from deficiencies in the data available for measuring FDI. As was shown above, measuring FDI in terms of the stock of assets held abroad says nothing about the actual amount of FDI taking place in any given year. There is also the problem of how the stock of assets abroad should be valued. A further problem is that most FDI data refer to FDI at a relatively aggregated level, more so than for trade. Aggregation bias is, therefore, likely to be stronger in the measurement of intra-industry FDI than intra-industry trade.

One of the first attempts to measure intra-industry FDI using the Grubel–Lloyd index was by Dunning (1982). Table 5.1 shows the results.

High levels of intra-industry FDI were found to exist in all five countries considered. Moreover, in all five, total intra-industry FDI had increased over the period from 1965 to 1975. Intra-industry was highest in West Germany (86%), the United Kingdom (78%) and the

Table 5.1 Intra-Industry Direct Capital Stake Ratios by Country and Industry, 1965, 1970 and 1975

	United States			*Japan*			*United Kingdom*			*Sweden*			*West Germany*		
	1965	*1970*	*1975*	*1965*	*1970*	*1975*	*1965*	*1970*	*1975*	*1965*	*1970*	*1975*	*1965*	*1970*	*1975*
More Technology Intensive															
Chemicals and allied products	0.77	0.75	0.79	0.14	0.28	0.51	0.91	0.99	0.99	0.66	0.53	0.57	0.86	0.77	0.79
Mechanical and instrument engineering	0.85	0.86	0.92	0.50	0.45	0.59	0.27	0.50	0.54	0.37	0.65	0.68	0.73	0.70	0.82
Electrical engineering	0.57	0.50	0.59	0.40	0.72	0.94	0.98	0.96	0.92	0.68	0.78	0.98	0.54	0.73	0.98
Transportation equipment	0.03	0.03	0.03	0.09	0.34	0.70	0.40	0.32	0.63	0.30	0.11	0.28	0.84	0.94	0.91
Total	0.65	0.65	0.71	0.27	0.42	0.63	0.65	0.77	0.81	0.53	0.63	0.70	0.76	0.78	0.85
Less Technology Intensive															
Food, drink and tobacco	0.74	0.71	0.75	0.48	0.59	0.44	0.50	0.62	0.64	0.12	0.19	0.10	0.57	0.64	0.73
Primary and fabricated metals	0.75	0.80	0.69	0.92	0.98	0.57	0.94	0.61	0.81	0.62	0.78	0.88	0.49	0.98	0.97
Textiles, leather, clothing and footwear	0.83	0.86	0.89	0.18	0.12	0.05	0.48	0.23	0.31	0.12	0.18	0.16	0.58	0.76	0.95
Paper, printing and publishing	0.99	0.93	0.99	0.21	0.15	0.21	0.49	0.62	0.90	0.68	0.42	0.53	0.96	0.86	0.78
Other manufacturing industries	0.79	0.98	0.98	0.78	0.75	0.78	0.89	0.75	0.94	0.54	0.36	0.76	0.86	0.67	0.66
Total	0.80	0.84	0.83	0.53	0.51	0.38	0.62	0.61	0.73	0.49	0.49	0.54	0.60	0.80	0.86
Overall total	0.71	0.72	0.76	0.39	0.46	0.53	0.64	0.70	0.78	0.52	0.59	0.65	0.71	0.79	0.86

Source: Dunning (1982).

United States (76%). It was slightly lower in Japan (53%) and Sweden (65%). However, Japan and Sweden experienced the fastest proportionate increase in intra-industry FDI over the period. There was no clear discernible pattern for intra-industry FDI across industrial sectors. For the United States the ratio was higher for the less-technology-intensive industries, whereas, for the UK and Sweden, the ratio was consistently higher for the more technology-intensive industries. However, with the single exception of West Germany, intra-industry FDI increased fastest in the more technology-intensive sectors.

Taking into account the aggregation problem discussed above, Norman and Dunning (1984) used the Aquino formula for measuring intra-industry trade (see Chapter 3) and applied this to the measurement of intra-industry FDI. Imbalance-adjusted intra-industry FDI ratios were estimated at a disaggregated level using data published by Vaupel and Curhan (1974) covering over 300 U.S. and non-U.S. MNCs which accounted for about 70% of all FDI in manufacturing. The date for U.S. MNCs was for January 1, 1968 and for the non-U.S. MNCs January 1, 1971. The average intra-industry FDI ratio for all countries across all product groups was found to be 58%. The level was highest for U.S. and U.K. MNCs (64% in both cases) and West German MNCs (61%). Japanese MNCs had the lowest ratio (46%) followed by France (56%).

Subsequently, Clegg (1990) has provided more recent estimates. These are summarised in Table 5.2. Intra-industry FDI is highest for Germany and the United Kingdom and lowest for the United States. In the United Kingdom, intra-industry FDI fell between 1974 and 1978 and then rose again between 1978 and 1981. In Germany, intra-industry FDI decreased from the very high level reached by 1980. In Germany and the UK, intra-industry FDI is higher in manufacturing than in industry taken as a whole. In the United States, the ratio for manufacturing is just below the average for industry as a whole. Outside the manufacturing sector, high levels of intra-industry FDI are also observable (banking, insurance and retail distribution in the United States, retail distribution in the UK and finance in Germany).

The Causes of Intra-Industry Foreign Direct Investment

In many respects, the fact that much FDI is a two-way affair between the advanced industrialised countries is not surprising. We know that FDI is not determined by differences in relative rates of return on investible funds in the same manner as portfolio investment. If that were the case, we would indeed expect to see one-way capital flows from capital-abundant to capital-scarce countries, as indeed was true of much foreign investment before 1914. However, the rationale for FDI is to be found in the possession by firms of certain unique, firm-specific advantages that they cannot efficiently exploit by means of exporting or licensing. Instead, because the foreign country enjoys certain location-specific advantages, foreign production is preferred to exporting. At the same time, as internal markets are preferred to external markets as a way of transferring intangible, firm-specific assets such as knowledge, foreign production is considered superior to licensing. Now, there is no reason at all why these considerations should lead to one-way FDI within the same industry except where all the firms of one country possess unique firm-specific advantages over all the firms of another country. For example, if Swiss pharmaceutical firms all enjoy certain firm-specific advantages over U.K. pharmacuetical firms, one might expect a one-way flow of FDI from Switzerland to U.K. in that industry.

Table 5.2 Estimates of Intra-Industry FDI for the United States, United Kingdom and Federal Republic of Germany, 1981 and 1985

Industry	United States 1980	United Kingdom 1974	United Kingdom 1978	United Kingdom 1981	Federal Republic of Germany 1980	Federal Republic of Germany 1985
Agriculture, forestry and fishing	85.8					
Mining	54.1				18.4	8.3[c]
Petroleum	35.1					
Manufacturing	54.1	87.7	80.1	86.0	97.1	83.2
Banking	61.1					
Finance	–			45.5[a]	89.1	88.6
Insurance	91.3					
Construction	67.4	75.3	35.4	41.7		
Wholesale distribution	68.2					
Retail distribution	96.3	67.7	62.4	80.2[b]	80.0	66.9
Transport and communications	58.3					
Property owning and managing	16.8				69.9	71.2
Other services	38.7					
Total non-manufacturing		63.0	57.2	55.7		
All Industries	55.7	78.9	72.6	74.5	91.9	74.8

Source: Clegg (1990).
[a] Financial excluding banking and insurance.
[b] Distributive trades, not just retailing.
[c] Mining and petroleum.
[d] Distributive trades, not just retailing.

It is more likely, however, that firms in different countries will each possess different firm-specific advantages and that they will wish to exploit these in other similar markets. If they do so by FDI, the result will be intra-industry FDI.

The pharmaceuticals industry provides a good illustration of the point as Rugman has demonstrated (Rugman, 1985). Relatively high levels of intra-industry FDI have been found for this sector. The industry is one characterised by relatively high levels of R&D spending. Firms must of necessity spend large amounts on R&D to survive. The number of new products appearing on the market at any given time is, accordingly, very great. At the same time, the market life of a product is typically quite short. This means that firms are faced with high risks and need to maximise the return on money spent on innovation as quickly as possible. Patents give firms temporary protection from competition, but such patents are not always respected by all countries and are sometimes easily circumvented. For all these reasons, firms have strong incentives to internalise markets in order to ensure full appropriability. They do so by setting up subsidiaries in a large number of different countries giving rise to the phenomenon of intra-industry FDI. For related reasons, high levels of intra-industry trade have also been found in the pharmaceuticals industry.

However, although intra-industry FDI is to be expected in industries where firms possess unique, firm-specific intangible assets and where an incentive exists for firms to internalise the markets for such assets, this is probably not the full explanation for why intra-industry FDI takes place. Intra-industry FDI also has its origins in the structure of the market in which firms compete. There are grounds for supposing that quite high levels of intra-industry FDI will result in industries that are oligopolies (i.e. industries in which sales are concentrated in the hands of a relatively small number of large sellers). As we saw in Chapter 3, a characteristic of such markets is uncertainty arising out of the high degree of interdependence existing among different producers. If one producer cuts his price, he cannot be sure whether his rivals will follow or leave their prices unchanged. If they follow suite, a price cut will have no effect on sales. For this reason, firms in oligopolistic markets often seek to reduce uncertainty by colluding together to fix a minimum price and restrict output. At the very least, they will avoid acting in ways which provoke their rivals (e.g. price cuts) and risk upsetting the equilibrium existing within the market unless they feel confident that they can gain by doing so. Firms will also be anxious not to allow their rivals to gain any cost or other advantage that could potentially threaten their own position in the market. Much FDI undertaken in oligopolistic markets may be motivated by the desire to reduce risks through preventing competitors from gaining any strategic advantage. For example, a backwards investment in the production of a key raw material may be designed to ensure that rivals do not cut off the supplies of the raw material in question through taking over the main supplier or entering into a vertical agreement with the supplier. Alternatively, a firm may set up a subsidiary in a foreign country to prevent a rival from gaining advantage through early entry and to ensure unimpeded access to the foreign market in the future.

One outcome of FDI that is motivated by the need to eliminate oligopolistic uncertainty, is a tendency towards the 'bunching' of FDI in a particular country or region. Bunching is the process whereby, when one firm in an oligopolistic industry sets up a subsidiary in a particular country, other rival sellers quickly follow suite. This may take the form of an investment by a firm in the production of some raw material that is vital for the production of a finished good. Other firms quickly follow suite for fear that their access to the raw material might as a consequence be restricted. Alternatively, one of the firms in an industry may set up a subsidiary in a foreign market in order to establish a foothold. Fearful of being pre-empted, rival sellers follow suite. Failure to do so may invite the first entrant to the market to exert pressure on the host government to impose import restrictions thereby depriving rivals of market access. Examples of bunching are not too difficult to find. In recent years, there has been a spate of FDI by leading automobile MNCs in the South East Asian region all anxious not to be left at a disadvantage as the Asian market expands. Knickerbocker (1973) found some early empirical support for this 'follow-the-leader' theory of FDI. He found that the bunching of FDI by U.S. MNCs was positively correlated with the degree of concentration, although the degree of bunching was also strongly correlated to factors other than concentration.

Along similar lines, through the 'exchange of threats' hypothesis, Hymer and Rowthorn (1970) and later Graham (1985) argued that intra-industry FDI arises of out inter-firm rivalry in oligopolistic markets. In oligopolistic industries, when threatened by a foreign company setting up subsidiaries in their own home market, the leading firms in the industry are likely to counter by setting up subsidiaries in the invader's market. The action is intended as a kind of shot across the bows to warn the aggressor that any attempt by him to compete energetically in the foreign market will be met by equivalent, retaliatory action in his own home market. Again, the underlying motive in such a sequence of cross-investments by firms belonging to the same industry is the desire to reduce risk, in this case risk created by the intrusion of a powerful rival in the home market of other sellers. Vernon (1985) emphasised the risk of lagging behind in technological innovation as a cause of FDI in oligopolistic industries. Oligopolists, he asserted, are afraid of falling behind their rivals. Most MNCs undertake the bulk of their R&D in their own home markets. As a result, local conditions exert a strong influence on the research effort. For example, many innovations by U.S. firms have involved labour-saving products or processes stimulated by the high cost of labour in the United States. This often leads oligopolists to invest in each other's markets for fear of being left behind in the technological race. Vernon cites the example of the superiority achieved by Japanese car producers in the production of small fuel-economy cars that U.S. car manufacturers have been unable to match. The stimulus was the high cost of petrol in the Japanese market. Faced with such risks, MNCs set up subsidiaries in the home markets of their rivals to keep abreast of changes taking place in other market environments and to avoid being outwitted by competitors in technological progress. Vernon suggests that such subsidiaries might be thought of as 'technological listening posts' created by MNCs within the territory of their international competitors.

The Link between Intra-Industry Foreign Direct Investment and Intra-Industry Trade

Is there any connection between the factors giving rise to intra-industry FDI and those giving rise to intra-industry trade? Dunning (1982) compared levels of intra-industry FDI with levels of intra-industry trade, differentiating among countries and industrial sectors and found that the ratios were broadly similar. The country with the lowest intra-industry FDI ratio, namely Japan, also had the lowest intra-industry trade ratio. Of the five countries considered, all except Japan experienced a rise in their intra-industry trade ratios at the same time as their intra-industry FDI ratios increased. However, intra-industry trade ratios were consistently higher than intra-industry FDI except in the case of West Germany. This, Dunning argued, was because patterns of direct investment tend to lag patterns of trade. Intra-industry FDI follows intra-industry trade with a time lag. Comparing different industries, Dunning found that, while intra-industry trade was always higher in the more technology-intensive industries, intra-industry FDI was generally but not always so. An important exception was the United States where intra-industry FDI was actually higher in the less technology-intensive industries (see Table 5.1). However, both intra-industry trade and FDI grew fastest in the more technology-intensive industries.

Dunning's findings lend superficial support to the hypothesis that intra-industry trade and FDI are interconnected. However, the number of countries considered is too small and the product groups used to measure intra-industry FDI too broad, although this probably does not affect comparisons over time. Rugman (1985) reworked Dunning's figures to test for any similarity between intra-industry trade and FDI in terms of industrial ranking. The results are shown in Table 5.3.

Table 5.3 Ranking of Industries by Percentage of Intra-Industry FDI

Intra-Industry FDI ranking	*Description*	*Intra-industry FDI percentage*	*Intra-industry trade percentage*	*Trade ranking*
1	Other manufacturing	77	74	3
2	Primary and fabricated metals	74	86	1
3	Chemicals and allied products	67	85	1
4	Paper, printing and publishing	67	39	8
5	Electrical engineering	63	72	4
6	Mechanical and instrument engineering	54	71	5
7	Food, drink and tobacco	48	39	9
8	Textiles, leather, clothing and footwear	44	53	7
9	Transportation equipment	33	62	6

Source : Rugman (1985).

For five of the nine industries, there is a deviation of only one in their ranking as between intra-industry FDI and intra-industry trade. For a further two industries, there is a deviation of only two. The only industries where there exists a major deviation are paper, printing and publishing and transportation equipment.

At a theoretical level, there are grounds for expecting some sort of statistical relationship to exist between the two phemonena. Both have their origins in the imperfection of markets. In the case of intra-industry trade, these imperfections take the form of product heterogeneity (product differentiation), entry barriers leading to market concentration and increasing returns to scale (see Chapter 3). In the case of intra-industry FDI, imperfections in the markets for both goods and assets create an incentive for firms to internalise markets. Seen in this way, intra-industry trade and intra-industry FDI are bedfellows. We should, therefore, expect high levels of intra-industry FDI to be found in precisely the same industries in which we find high levels of intra-industry trade. However, to some degree, FDI is a substitute for trade as we shall see in the next chapter. Overseas production is an alternative to exporting. This might lead us to a different conclusion concerning the relationship between intra-industry trade and intra-industry FDI, namely, that they are *unlikely* to be found together in the same industry. Where FDI is a substitute for FDI, this indeed is the likely outcome when the two are measured at the same time. It may, however, be the case that, at different points in time, both are still to be found in the same industry.

Agmon (1979) has given one possible reason, namely, that trade precedes direct investment as firms begin to expand internationally. Agmon has argued that, in oligoplistic industries, firms face a downward-sloping demand curve at home but a perfectly elastic demand when exporting abroad. Figure 2.15 in Chapter 2 can be used to illustrate the position of an oligopolist. As we saw in Chapter 2, a firm faced with this set of demand curves for its product will sell part of output on the home market charging a relatively high price and the rest abroad at a much lower price. If firms in other countries face a similar set of demand curves, they will behave in a similar fashion and the result will be intra-industry trade. However, Agmon argues that, eventually, trade will give way to FDI. At the outset, exporting is preferred because, unlike FDI, it does not give rise to any fixed costs and therefore entails lower risks if the product does not sell well. Through exports, the firm is able to gather information about the foreign market before making a decision about whether to engage in overseas production. Once uncertainty has been overcome, the decision will be made to set up a plant in the foreign market, thereby eliminating transport costs and getting round any tariff or non-tariff barriers that may exist. If all firms act in the same manner, intra-industry FDI will displace intra-industry trade.

This would lead to the occurrence of intra-industry FDI in the same industries in which high levels of intra-industry trade have been recorded but only after a time lag. This is consistent with the observations made by Dunning (1982) in his five-country study of intra-industry FDI and intra-industry trade. A further reason why we might expect to find intra-industry FDI and intra-industry trade occurring in the same industry is that FDI is not always a substitute for trade. As we shall see in the next section, certain kinds of FDI are 'trade-enhancing', that is, they increase trade between countries. One especially important case is where there exist potentially large cost savings from rationalising the production process on a global or regional basis to achieve greater plant specialisation. This may take the form of producing different models of a product at different plants or producing different components and parts at specialist plants. In both cases, large amounts of intra-industry trade are likely to result. At the same time, high levels of intra-industry FDI are likely to be recorded. Such rationalisation may be stimulated by the creation of regional free trade areas or customs unions that allow firms to move goods freely between countries within given regions. We turn now to a more detailed discussion of this case.

Rationalised International Production

Vertical Disintegration and the New International Division of Labour

One of the distinctive features of market-oriented FDI is that the foreign subsidiary is identical in appearance in most respects to that of the parent company. Such FDI takes the form of reproducing mere foreign 'clones' of the parent company. However, much post-war FDI has not been of this kind. Instead, the foreign subsidiary has been set up to perform an essentially different task to that of the parent company. One form of this is where an MNC sets up a subsidiary abroad to perform a specific stage in the vertical chain of production and distribution. Thus, an MNC may set up a distribution outlet in the foreign country to more effectively market its product abroad. Or it may set up a subsidiary to perform a particular part of the production process previously undertaken by the parent company. The latter is an example of what might be termed *vertical disintegration.* This is because it entails the breaking-up of the production process into a series of separate stages or processes and the relocation of some of these stages or processes to newly created, specialist plants in other countries. Instead of all the stages or processes involved in the production of the good being performed at single location, different stages or processes are now performed at different plants each situated in a different country.

One common form of this is where a product that is partly produced by the parent company in the home country, is exported to another country for assembly or further processing. This is known as *offshore assembly* or *offshore processing*. Another possibility is a separation of the production stages from the non-production or so-called 'headquarters activities' of the firm (i.e. research and development, managerial and financial services, etc.). In this case, the parent company performs mainly non-production tasks, the product being produced by plants located in other countries. The rationale for vertical disintegration is the fact that the factor proportions required at the various stages differ significantly. In so far as factor prices are also different reflecting relative factor endowments, firms can make cost savings by performing each of these stages according to where costs are lowest. However, such rationalisation is clearly only possible where the different stages are physically capable of being separated and performed long distances apart. Certain writers have come to refer to this process as the *new international division of labour (NIDL)* (see Frobel, Heinrichs and Kreye, 1980; Casson, 1986). The element of novelty lies in the fact that it involves a much finer division of labour than in the past.

One of the earliest forms of vertical disintegration was to be found in the *clothing and textile* industry. This took the form of fabric manufacturers in Western Europe sub-contracting the making-up stages to independent producers in low-wage countries. Textile and clothing production involves a number of stages, each of which can readily be separated and performed in a different location. The earlier fabric-making stages are relatively capital- and skill-intensive which favour location in the industrialised countries. However, the making-up stage, which involves sewing or knitting plus certain other finishing processes (e.g. dyeing) to make the finished garment, is more labour-intensive and, therefore, more efficiently performed in developing countries where labour is cheap. Beginning in the mid-1960s, West European textile producers spotted the opportunity to cut costs by sub-contracting independent producers in developing countries to produce a product according to pre-set designs using already-cut fabrics supplied to them. A survey of West German textile and garment companies found that, in 1977, for every 100 workers employed in Germany, there were more than ten foreign workers employed abroad. Over the period from 1966 to 1974–75, the foreign employment of the West German industry more than doubled while domestic employment decreased by roughly one-quarter (Frobel, Heinrichs and Kreye, 1980). Much of this so-called 'outward processing' was performed by producers in Mediterranean countries such as Greece, Malta and Tunisia, in certain South East Asian countries such as South Korea and certain East European countries, in particular Yugoslavia and Hungary.

Another industry in which vertical disintegration occurred was the *consumer electronics* industry. The production of most consumer electronics involved three stages: (1) the conception and development of new products, (2) the production of components, and (3) the testing of parts and components and their final assembly into finished goods. The first stage is highly research-intensive and is best located in advanced industrialised countries well endowed with supplies of highly skilled labour. The second stage is capital-intensive such that there are major economies of scale to be reaped from concentrated production and plant specialisation. Thus, the principal components tend to be produced at specialist plants located in developed countries. However, the final assembly and testing stages are more labour-intensive and are best situated where there exists an abundant supply of suitable labour available at low cost. As the cost of components has fallen so the importance of labour costs in total costs at the final assembly stage has increased. At the same time, greater automation has reduced the level of skill required of labour. These changes have made it increasingly worthwhile for manufactures to relocate assembly operations at suitable sites in low-wage economies in the developing world. In the consumer electronics industry, Japanese firms played a leading role in pioneering the development of offshore processing. Increasingly, the final assembly stages of production were relocated at sites in newly industrialising countries mainly in the East Asian region (Singapore, South Korea and Taiwan). The cost savings, which this made possible, increased the degree of competition posed by Japanese goods in the western industrialised countries and caused, first, U.S. firms and, then, West European manufacturers to follow suite. Companies like Philips and Thomson, somewhat belatedly, sought to match Japanese producers' costs by similarly shifting assembly operations to factories in the newly industrialising countries of East Asia.

A similar trend was apparent in *industrial electronics*. As competition has increased in the production of semi-conductors, U.S. manufacturers have sought to cut costs by shifting the final assembly stages of production to offshore sites in Mexico and other newly industrialising countries. The production of semi-conductors naturally divides into three stages – wafer fabrication, assembly and testing – creating the possibility for locating assembly operations a distance away from fabrication and testing without any loss of efficiency. At the same time, the type of labour required at the assembly stage is relatively low skilled such that manufacturing costs could be substantially reduced by performing these stages in newly industrialising countries where labour was cheap. One survey of the thirty-seven leading U.S., Japanese and West European companies (which in 1979 accounted for more than 90% of world semi-conductor production) found that the number of their ventures in developing countries rose from forty-six in 1974 to seventy-two in 1976 and eighty-seven in 1979. The number of ventures located in South East Asian countries rose from twenty-one in 1971 to forty-three in 1974 and sixty in 1979. The rest were located in Latin American countries such as Mexico (UNCTC 1983).

It appears that certain developments that have taken place over the post-war period have enhanced the NIDL. Casson (1986) has suggested the following explanations:

1. *Technology.* The period since the Second World War has witnessed major changes in the way in which products are designed which has in turn made it easier to subdivide the production process. This has affected both the design of new products and brought about a redesign of older, maturing products. Increasingly, products have been designed as assemblies of a large number of standardised components, each of which is capable of being produced separately. At the same time, the ease with which the subset of components can be varied has resulted in more versatile products capable of having several different uses. Large-scale production of components further makes possible fuller exploitation of available economies of scale. This has favoured concentrating component production in a few large, highly specialised plants each producing high volumes. The same changes have affected the design of components themselves. Components have been redesigned as multi-component goods giving rise to a hierarchy of components assembled at various stages before being used in the assembly of the final product. Japanese firms largely pioneered this change. In part, this contributed to the competitive

edge that they acquired in a number of branches of manufacturing.

2. *Improved transport systems.* Major improvements in methods of transport (in particular, the containerisation revolution in shipping) have made it cheaper to ship goods from one part of the world to another.
3. *Rural–urban migration in newly industrialising countries.* Migration of workers from the agricultural subsistence sector to the industrial sector in a number of developing countries has created a pool of relatively cheap labour. This has favoured the relocation of labour-intensive stages of production in newly industrialising countries. This has coincided with a rise in labour costs in the advanced industrialised countries. At the same time, improvements in education and standards of public health in a number of developing countries have enhanced the quality of the labour seeking employment. A greater willingness to accept high-productivity working practices may also have acted as an added attraction for MNCs.
4. *Lower co-ordination costs.* The splitting up of the production process into a large number of separate activities each undertaken by different subsidiaries in different parts of the world clearly calls for considerable co-ordination skills. Certain changes in recent decades have made such co-ordination easier. First, improved communications have resulted from technological advances in telecommunications and the increased convenience of air travel. Second, new management skills have been developed and applied through the spread of management education.
5. *Reduced trade barriers.* Barriers to trade have been lowered as a result of both regional and multilateral trade liberalisation through the GATT. Exports of manufactures from developing countries have further benefited from the granting of tariff preferences. The offshore assembly provisions introduced by many developed countries have acted as a further incentive for MNCs to shift final assembly/processing operations to offshore sites in newly industrialising countries. Under these arrangements, the importer of finished goods that have been assembled at an offshore location using components and parts supplied by a firm in the importing country, need pay a tariff only on the value-added abroad and not on the final selling price of the goods. For example, a compact disc player with a final selling price of \$1000 may have been manufactured in Taiwan using components and parts worth \$500. Suppose the components and parts had been supplied by the parent company in the United States. Further, assume that the *ad valorem* tariff applied by the US was 10%. Then, the duty that must be paid when the good is imported into the US would be only $\$500 \times 0.10 = \$50$ compared with $\$1000 \times 0.10 = \$100$ for other imports of the same product.
6. *The creation of new low-cost industrial sites in newly industrialising countries.* In a number of newly industrialising countries, special low-cost industrial sites have been created close to ports and other public transport systems, specifically designed to attract so-called *export platform investments.* These are companies established largely for the purpose of offshore assembly/processing and the sites are known as *export processing zones (EPZs).* They offer to foreign investors specially designed infrastructure at low cost (such as port facilities and subsidised electricity) and allow foreign firms to import components and parts without paying any import duty. Foreign companies may also enjoy exemption from certain taxes, the need to enforce

minimum wage laws and other forms of regulation applying to local firms.

7. *Higher incomes.* Rising incomes have led to increased demand for finished consumer goods and for intermediate goods required in their manufacture. A larger market makes possible an increase in the division of labour. Where technological change has made it possible to split up the production process into a series of distinct operations, the expansion of the market has created the incentive to do so.

Box 5.1 below summarises the main factors contributing to the growth of the NIDL.

Unlike market-oriented investment, FDI undertaken to bring about vertical disintegration is clearly trade-enhancing. It generates a considerable increase in the amount of trade taking place in intermediate goods and services. Moreover, most of this takes the form of intra-firm trade. If and when components and parts and finished products are classified as belonging to the same industry, this may also result in an increase in recorded intra-industry trade. Intra-firm trade should not, however, be confused with intra-industry trade.

Horizontal Rationalisation

A second type of rationalisation that has become more common in recent decades, is to be found in multi-product MNCs. Where an MNC produces a range of related products, it may

Box 5.1 Factors Contributing to the Growth of the New International Division of Labour

1. *Technological change* – changes in the design of products, more multi-component goods, possibility of separating assembly stages from component production and concentration of component production in specialist plants
2. *Improved transport systems* (e.g. containerisation) lower transport costs
3. *Rural–urban migration in newly-industrialised countries* creation of a pool of cheap unskilled labour in developing countries suitable for use in the more labour-intensive assembly stages of production
4. *Lower co-ordination costs* – due to improved management skills and lower costs of communication, due to growth of modern telecommunications and methods of air transport, easier to manage several different, separated operations located in different countries
5. *Lower trade barriers* – introduction of tariff preferences for exports of developing countries (e.g. Generalised System of Preferences) and introduction of offshore assembly provisions (OAPs) to tariff schedules of developed countries, lower trade costs
6. *New low-cost sites for simple, labour intensive operations in developing countries* (e.g. creation of Export Processing Zones (EPZs) in newly industrialising countries) increased export-platform investments in newly industrialising countries
7. *Higher incomes* – increased demand for finished consumer goods, greater scope for increased plant specialisation,

seek to rationalise its operations to achieve a higher degree of plant specialisation. This is likely to be especially beneficial for firms operating in the differentiated goods industries where unit costs fall sharply with the volume of output. The kind of economies of scale that are important in this case are cost reductions which result from the achievement of long production runs. In many branches of manufacturing, considerable cost savings can be reaped by keeping the production process for a particular good going for as long as possible. Where production has to be halted and the plant re-tooled to allow for the production of a new good, valuable working time is lost and costs thereby incurred. The more specialised the plant, therefore, the lower will unit costs be. It has been suggested that the introduction of new production methods such as computer-aided design (CAD) have increased flexibility in the manufacturing process, reducing the benefits from product specialisation (see Dicken, 1992 for a discussion of this point). However, it cannot be doubted that the advantages of achieving long production runs has played an important role in promoting horizontal rationalisation in some industries in the past.

Horizontal rationalisation takes the form of MNC concentrating the production of particular products at a single plant specially designed for the production of the good in question. For example, consider the case of a MNC in the so-called white-goods industry producing several differentiated products. Suppose that the range includes washing machines, tumble-dryers and dishwashers. Suppose the company currently seeks to sell its goods in three separate markets of equal size. It does so by producing all three goods at a single plant located centrally in each of the three markets. The volume of output in each market is constrained by the size of the market. If, however, the production of each product is concentrated in one plant that supplies the other two markets through exports, the volume of output can be trebled. The size of plant need not change, nor the number of plants under the same ownership. However, each plant becomes more specialised. Of course, the cost savings in production resulting from increased specialisation must be offset against the increased costs that are incurred in transporting the goods from the plant to the two export markets. Provided the net effect is favourable, the firm will undertake the requisite rationalisation.

One case of where such horizontal rationalisation has been common is that of the European Single Market. The costs of transporting goods between one Member State and another are relatively low and have been somewhat reduced by the establishment of the Single Market in 1993. No tariffs exist on trade between the Member States of the European Union, while many non-tariff barriers have also been eliminated. Harmonisation of technical regulations and standards has served further to unify the market. If Europe succeeds in establishing a single currency and thereby eliminating the risks arising from exchange rate changes, the integration of the market will be further advanced. In this case, MNCs with plants in several different parts of Europe, producing more than one product for local consumption, may find it beneficial to rationalise their operations in the manner described above. There is some evidence to show that a process of this kind has been taking place (see Cantwell, 1988). Similar benefits are likely to accrue to MNCs operating in other regions of the world where regional trade liberalisation has taken place (e.g. the North American Free Trade Area (NAFTA) or the ASEAN Free Trade Area (AFTA)). An offsetting factor may be non-uniformity of tastes. In this case, products will need to be adapted to cater for the different national preferences of consumers and the gain from plant specialisation may be less.

As with vertical disintegration, horizontal rationalisation is trade-enhancing. As the different overseas affiliates of the MNC become more specialised, the proportion of their output which is exported, increases. Since consumers want the opportunity to buy the full range of goods supplied by different affiliates, imports of other varieties of the same good increase at the same time. The type of trade that is generated by this kind of rationalisation is clearly intra-industry trade. If the exports of each affiliate are sold to the other affiliates before being distributed to the consumer, the result will also be increased intra-firm trade. Unlike vertical disintegration, however, the kind of intra-firm trade generated will be trade in finished and not intermediate goods. Moreover, the kind of finished goods traded are differentiated goods because the opportunities for reducing costs from such rationalisation are greatest in these products.

More Complex Patterns of Integrated International Production

In recent decades, more complex forms of rationalisation have taken place that cannot be conveniently classified as either vertical or horizontal. Rather, rationalisation may contain elements of both. The 1996 World Investment Report has defined a complex integrated-production strategy as one in which

> any value-added activity can be located, at least in principle, in any part of a TNC (transnational corporation) system, and integrated with other activities performed elsewhere to produce goods for national, regional or global markets (UN, 1996).

In other words, there may be geographical dispersion among units of the firm of different stages in the vertical chain of production (vertical rationalisation) and geographical dispersion among units of the firm of the production of different varieties or types of the same differentiated good (horizontal rationalisation). In short, the result is neither purely vertical nor purely horizontal linkages among different units of the firm, but multidirectional linkages and flows both within the firm and with unrelated firms.

The *automobile* industry provides one of the best illustrations of this kind of complex integration of production. In 1967, Ford Europe became the first automobile manufacturer to reorganise its entire European operations on a regional basis. Before 1967, its European production was split into three separate national operations, namely, the UK, West Germany and Belgium. After 1967, these operations were integrated with each plant performing a specialist task within the single operation. The new approach was applied first to the production of the Ford Fiesta. There were three final assembly plants located at Valencia in Spain, Dagenham in the UK and Saarlouis in Germany. These plants assembled body panels into a finished car using components and parts produced at nine other locations in different parts of Europe, each of which specialised in a few specific components. Some components were bought-in from other independent specialist suppliers. This integrated approach was later extended to the production of the Ford Escort. Subsequently, other car manufacturers adopted a similar strategy.

Outside Europe, other examples of rationalisation of production along regional lines by car manufacturers can be observed. Toyota of Japan has now established integrated manufacturing systems in all three of its main markets – North America, Europe and Asia. In Asia, Toyota operates a complex network for auto parts among countries belonging to ASEAN.

Its affiliate in Singapore co-ordinates intra-firm trade of parts and components within the region. Diesel engines are exported from the affiliate in Thailand, transmissions from the affiliate in the Philippines, steering gears from the affiliate in Malaysia and engines from the affiliate in Indonesia. These linkages are illustrated in Figure 5.1. In 1995, intra-firm trade among affiliates amounted to roughly 20% of exports of components and parts of the company's manufacturing affiliates world-wide. In the future, production will be further rationalised to make possible specialised production of particular models within the Asian region (UNCTAD, 1996).

Another industry in which integrated production on a regional basis is to be found is the *motor-cycle* industry. Honda of Japan operates a European network for the production of motorcycles. This is illustrated by Figure 5.2. Assembly takes place at three key affiliates located in Belgium, Italy and Spain, each specialising in the production of a different model (differentiated by size, engine power, engineering features and style). (The Belgium plant now produces just car parts.) Each supplied the other affiliates with their particular model and exported to other markets in the rest of Europe, the United States and Japan and some developing countries. Plants in the United States, Brazil and Japan also export to the European market. Initially, engines and key parts were supplied from Japan. However, some small and medium-size engines are now

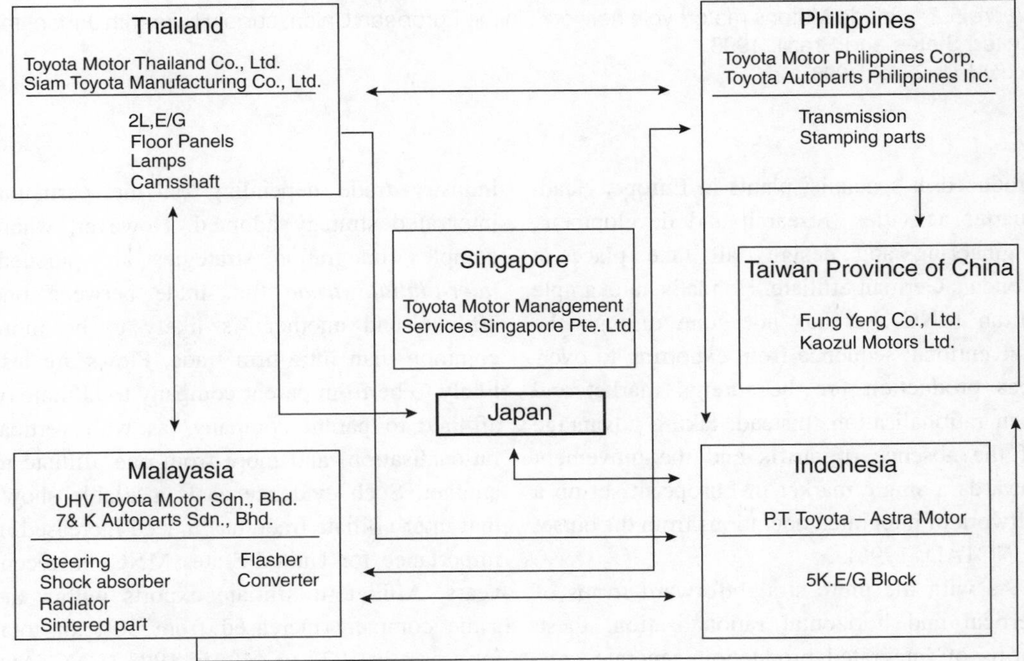

Figure 5.1 Toyota's Integrated Manufacting Operations in East Asia.
Source: UNCTAD, 1996.

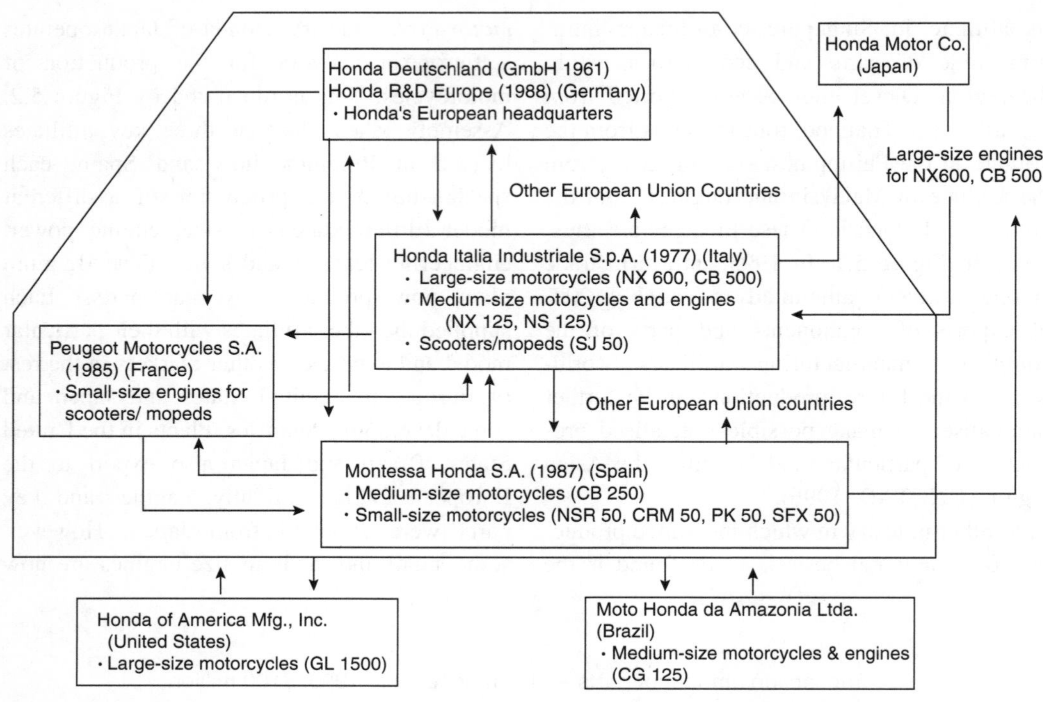

Figure 5.2 Honda Motor's motorcycle networks in the European Union, supply links with Japan, the United States and Brazil, 1996.
Source: UNCTAD, 1996.

produced at specialist plants in Europe. Headquarter activities (research and development, engineering and design) all take place at Honda's German affiliate. Honda is an example of an MNC that has not gone through the conventional sequence from exporting to overseas production for the foreign market and then rationalisation. Instead, taking advantage of the absence of tariffs and the movement towards a single market in Europe, it set up a network of integrated operations from the outset (UNCTAD, 1996).

As with the more straightforward forms of vertical and horizontal rationalisation, these forms of integrated production generate considerable trade among countries. This is likely to take the form of both intra-firm and intra-industry trade depending on the particular integrated strategy adopted. However, where complex integration strategies are pursued, *inter-affiliate trade* (i.e. trade between one affiliate and another) is likely to be more common than intra-firm trade. Flows are less likely to be from parent company to affiliate or affiliate to parent company (as with vertical rationalisation) and more from one affiliate to another. Such evidence as is available shows that inter-affiliate trade has indeed increased in importance for United States MNCs in recent years. Affiliate-to-affiliate exports within the same company increased from 30% of total intra-firm in 1977 to 44% in 1993 (UNCTAD, 1996). It was also higher for developed country affiliates suggesting greater integration within the MNC located in these regions, especially Europe. In 1993, 71% of intra-firm exports of U.S. MNCs were affiliate-to-affiliate exports in the European region.

Alternative Forms of International Business Involvement

One important development of the past quarter-to-half century has been the growth of forms of business involvement other than the setting-up or acquisition of a wholly owned overseas subsidiary. In this section, we examine some of these increasingly important, alternative methods which firms use to extend their influence internationally. A large number of possible relationships may exist among firms in different countries, of which the holding of a controlling interest or FDI is just one. Here, we focus on three of the most common types – joint ventures, licensing agreements and strategic alliances. A fourth type – international subcontracting – is discussed in a different context in the next chapter. Box 5.2 provides a summary of the main alternative forms of international business involvement, including exporting and direct investment discussed in earlier chapters.

Joint Ventures

One way in which firm may establish a presence in a foreign country other than by setting up or acquiring a wholly owned subsidiary is

Box 5.2 Alternative Forms of International Business Involvement

1. *Exporting* → selling directly to an independent wholesaler or retailer in the foreign country
   → selling through an independent agency

2. *Equity forms of involvement*

• *Direct investment abroad* → Creation of a sales or distribution outlet in the foreign country → Creation of a wholly- or partly-owned production subsidiary abroad
whether by setting up a new local subsidiary (greenfield venture) or through a merger with/acquisition of an existing company in the foreign country

• *Joint ventures* → with an existing local company or in partnership with a group of local investors
→ with the state authority or a local state enterprise in the foreign country
→ through a consortium of foreign firms without any local participation
with the foreign company holding anything between 10–50% of equity capital

3. *Non-equity forms of Involvement*

• *Licensing agreement* – allowing the foreign firm use of proprietary knowledge owned by the foreign firm with:
Either (a) a foreign company unrelated in ownership
or (b) a subsidiary of the company allowing it use of the assets of the parent company in return for payment of royalties to the licensor.

• *Management contract* – an agreement involving a company supplying a foreign company with management services in return for a payment of fees.

Continued

- *Subcontracting* – agreement with a foreign firm to carry out certain processes in the production of a good, using components and parts supplied by the contractor.
- *Turnkey contract* – agreement whereby the foreign firm designs, constructs and commissions a production facility right up to the stage of start-up for a local firm . This may include 'buy-back' provisions whereby the local firm pays for the know-how with the resultant output from the plant.
- *Strategic alliance* – agreement with a foreign firm to co-operate in some way (e.g. on a specific R&D project) without either company holding any equity stake in the other, although each may choose to acquire a minority stake in the other.

through a joint venture with another firm, either a locally based firm in the foreign country or another foreign company based in some third country. Each of the firms holds an equity stake in the new enterprise although not necessarily an equal one. The term, in fact, covers a variety of different types of arrangement. Three general categories may be identified:

1. A joint venture between a foreign- and a privately owned local firm or group of investors. This involves the setting up of a new company in which both the foreign multinational and the local firm or individual local investors hold an equity stake. The foreign multinational may own a majority or minority stake or the company may be co-owned with each partner having an equal equity stake in the company. Local shareholders may or may not be involved in the management of the company.
2. A joint venture between a foreign-owned firm and a local state enterprise or the local government. The equity capital is partly held by the foreign multinational and partly by a local state enterprise or by the host government. Again, the foreign multinational may have a majority or minority stake in the concern or an equal stake with the local state enterprise. Such arrangements are frequently found in the oil-processing industry.
3. A joint venture between a number of foreign-owned companies without any local participation. Each of the foreign firms holds an equity stake in the company. Such a company is often referred to as a consortium. They are particularly common in the raw material or extractive industries.

Joint ventures are not new. Examples could be found even before the Second World War. However, there is some evidence to suggest that their importance increased after the Second World War, especially as a mode of entry to developing countries. For example, Hladik (1985) found that, as a percentage of FDI by U.S. multinationals in less-developed countries (measured by total subsidiaries formed), joint ventures rose from 24% in 1951–55 to 45% in 1975. In the advanced countries, however, the share was roughly constant at 26%. For U.S. multinationals, roughly two-thirds of these joint ventures were found in manufacturing. Moreover, manufacturing has increased in importance at the expense of the extractive industries as the principal activity for joint ventures (Hladik, 1985). The majority of joint ventures by U.S. multinationals involved a partnership with local privately owned enterprises. However, a relatively high proportion of joint ventures in the extractive industries involved participation by a local state enterprise or the host government or a consortium of foreign companies. One reason for this may have been the size of investment required in the raw materials industry that could only be financed using the combined capital of a number of large companies.

Joint ventures tend to be undertaken where other modes of entry to the local market are barred. Exporting may be impeded by the occurrence of high transport costs and/or tariff or non-tariff barriers. At the same time, the establishment of a wholly owned subsidiary or purchase of a controlling interest in a local company may be precluded by the host government. Restrictions preventing foreign companies from direct investment by either of these methods are common in developing countries that want to attract foreign capital but wish to retain local control over the company established. By insisting on local equity participation in the company, they can ensure that more of the profits earned by the company filter back to the local economy. They may also be able to prevent transfer-price manipulation being used to siphon off profits to the parent company abroad (see Chapter 4). The greater control, which a joint venture permits, may result in other benefits. For example, through participation in a joint venture the host country may be able to insist that a greater proportion of inputs are bought locally rather than imported from abroad. A joint venture might also be the means of ensuring that the presence of the foreign company has a positive 'demonstration effect' on local companies. In short, joint ventures are a way in which the host country can 'unbundle' the package of resources that accrues from foreign investment. That is to say, the benefits accruing from the import of capital and the transfer of managerial skills and technology can be enjoyed without any loss of control of productive resources. Such a strategy may not be appropriate for the poorest, least-developed countries because they lack the capital to embark on a joint venture with a foreign firm. However, this is not a constraint for newly industrialising countries. Their concern is the need to obtain additional capital from abroad and import technology without loss of control.

Because joint ventures are frequently undertaken as a way of gaining entry to a foreign market, many joint ventures tend to be localised. That is to say, sales are largely for the home market rather than export. In fact, it is often more difficult for host country governments to insist on local control where the intended output is for export. MNCs will be less inclined to engage in a joint venture where production is for export because of the difficulty of controlling costs of production. For example, if the host government insists that certain inputs are purchased locally rather than imported from abroad, the result might be higher production costs and reduced competitiveness.

Another consideration might be the risk that the exports of the joint venture will compete in third markets with the exports of other subsidiaries of the foreign company. The MNC may be less able to prevent such an outcome if it is part of a joint venture as opposed to the establishment of a wholly owned subsidiary. A further reason why many joint ventures are localised is the low research intensity of most joint ventures. Typically, spending on R&D has been found to be quite low in most joint ventures. This suggests that the kind of technology that is transferred though a joint venture is mature and simple. MNCs are unlikely to undertake joint ventures where the technology transferred is advanced and exclusive because their ability to control the use of the technology is reduced. In addition, where the technology is firm-specific, the host country will be in a weaker bargaining position in insisting on local equity participation. However, there is some evidence to suggest that, in recent decades, joint ventures undertaken by U.S. MNCs have become less localised. Hladik found that, since 1975, about one-half of the joint ventures newly formed did plan some form of export activity (Hladik, 1985). In addition, over the same period, the importance of R&D in joint-venture activity by U.S. MNCs has been increasing.

Although MNCs will generally prefer the setting up of a wholly owned subsidiary to a joint venture – especially when output is designed primarily for export – a joint venture may still be preferred for other reasons. First, the amount of capital that must be raised is reduced as a result of collaboration with other firms or with the host government. Second, a joint venture may be better able to get around controls or restrictions imposed by the host government concerning, for example, borrowing from the local banks or selling to government enterprises. They may be better able to obtain access to local distribution channels or to secure the source of supply for an important raw material or intermediate good. Third, political risk is also reduced. The government of the host country is likely to view the company with less hostility if local firms and investors are participants. Joint ventures are often the most appropriate mode of entry to a foreign market for a small, less well-known, less experienced firm wanting to expand overseas. Such firms tend to lack the information, skills or capital to launch wholly owned subsidiaries. Firms with less to offer the host country in terms of scarce resources (e.g. technology or access to foreign markets) will also engage in more joint venture activity.

Licensing Agreements

A method of international business involvement, which involves no transfer of equity capital, is a licensing agreement. A licensing agreement is an agreement between the owner of some body of technological knowledge (e.g. a design for a new products, a new method of producing a good, a brand name or a trade mark or some other kind of industrial property) and a potential user. The technology is such that it cannot be easily imitated or obtained in any other form. The potential user is therefore prepared to pay a price for use of the technology. Payment may take the form of a lump sum or of a percentage of the profits from applying the technology, which is paid in the form of royalties or fees. A licensing agreement is a way in which an MNC in possession of some ownership-specific asset can earn profits on that asset without incurring the risks of overseas production. Whereas FDI internalises the market for such assets, licensing involves the creation of an external market in which the asset is sold by one firm to another usually on an arms-length basis.

The potential user may be an independent firm in no way related to the company selling the technology or it may be a wholly or partly owned subsidiary of the latter. Parent companies often supply their overseas subsidiaries with technology using a licensing agreement, by which the subsidiary must pay the parent company royalties or fees. In other cases, where the licensee is unrelated to the licensor, the licensor may wish to acquire an equity stake in the licensee. In this way, it may be able to gain greater control over the use of the technology sold. Thus, the sale of technology by means of a licensing agreement may be accompanied by a flow of capital to the recipient country. In general, however, licensing agreements do not involve an accompanying investment of capital. Hence, they constitute what is sometimes termed a non-equity form of international business involvement. To a greater extent than a joint venture, they represent an attempt to unbundle the FDI package. Specifically, they seek to separate the technology component from the investment of capital and transfer of managerial control. However, very often licensing agreements will involve accompanying management services and provision of technical information ancillary to the technology involved.

Usually, a licensing agreement will contain certain clauses designed to ensure that the proprietor retains some control over the use of the technology or, at least, that the costs of losing control are minimised. These will seek to ensure that the information acquired by the licensee is not passed on to another company, that the use of the technology is confined to a particular geographical territory (so that the licensor's sales in third markets is not affected) and that the product in question is produced in conformity with certain standards of quality. The need to ensure adequate quality standards is especially important where the licensee buys the use of the licensor's trademark. Other restrictions may also be stipulated. Such restrictions are often viewed as harmful by developing countries. One reason is that they may create a dependence of the licensee on the licensor. This is the case when the agreement requires the buyer of information to purchase components or further technology from the licensor. Agreements that prohibit the buyer from using the technology in third markets (because they might undermine sales of the licensor or its subsidiaries in these markets) clearly represent a restraint on competition that distorts the global allocation of resources. For these reasons, host country governments often intervene to outlaw agreements containing such restrictions.

From the point of view of the MNC licensing the technology the need is to retain some control over the use of the technology being sold or to minimise the cost of losing control. As we know, knowledge possesses many of the characteristics of a 'public good'. In particular, once the knowledge has been supplied by the creator to a user, it becomes difficult to prevent it from being dissipated. Others may be able to gain use of the knowledge without having to pay for it. If so, the value of the knowledge is depreciated and the innovator fails to get the full return from the amount spent on the generation of that knowledge. Thus, the main disadvantage of licensing is that the proprietor may be unable to ensure full appropriability. Even if clauses can be inserted into the agreement that restrict the use of the technology by the licensee, it may prove difficult to police the agreement to ensure that the restrictions are enforced. The licensee may disregard the restrictions as the penalty for doing so may not be very great. Enforcing adequate standards of quality, reliability and service to protect the reputation of the licensor, as when a trademark is sold, is notoriously difficult. Furthermore, as we have seen, host country governments may outlaw restrictive contracts. Hence, where control over the use of technology is important, MNCs will prefer FDI to licensing. This is likely to be the case where the technology in question is still relatively new and where, consequently, the risks of dissipation are relatively great. It follows that licensing is likely to be less common for products at the early stage of their life cycle.

By way of contrast, where the knowledge is relatively mature and likely, shortly, to become obsolete, the costs of losing control are less and licensing, therefore, is less risky. In this case, licensing may be the preferred way of exploiting the foreign market. For a highly diversified firm that lacks the resources to set up plants overseas to cover all its existing product lines, a licensing agreement may be especially attractive. Smaller firms may also find the licensing agreement attractive, as they often lack the resources or skills to engage in overseas production. Licensing may be a way in which a new entrant, who is not yet prepared to undertake inward investment, can gain initial access to the overseas market. Finally, it may be the case that the government of the host country prevents foreign companies from setting up or acquiring subsidiaries. Then, a licensing agreement will be the only way that the MNC can gain entry to the overseas market. For several decades after the Second World War, Japan imposed tough restrictions on inward FDI. Licensing agreements were often the only way, other than exporting, whereby U.S. and European MNCs could gain access to the Japanese market. (Moreover, imports were often subject to high tariffs or non-tariff barriers.)

Strategic Alliances

In recent decades, an increasingly common form of international collaboration has been through the creation of strategic or global alliances. In some respects, these are very similar to joint ventures except that the form of collaboration is less formal. Porter and Fuller (1986) have defined such alliances as '...long-term alliances between firms that link aspects of their business but fall short of a merger'. Dunning (1993) defines strategic business alliances as 'alliances deliberately designed to advance the sustainable competitive advantage of the participating firms'. Whereas a joint venture involves each company taking an equity stake in the newly created foreign subsidiary, a strategic alliance need not involve any transfer of capital, although it is not uncommon for the participating companies to buy minority equity stakes in each other. The essence of an alliance is that the firms involved sign a contract providing for some element of co-operation over a period of time. Often, it involves technological collaboration in which the firms agree to share the costs of developing a new product.

While the primary motivation for a joint venture in the past was to gain access to a foreign market, global alliances between firms are motivated by somewhat different considerations. Much depends on the form that the global alliance takes. Where technological collaboration is involved, the reason is usually the need to spread the costs of R&D and minimise the risk associated with product development. In high-technology industries, the costs of developing a new model or product are often considerable and beyond the resources available to any one firm. Moreover, because the market life of any new model or product is often comparatively short, there is a need to recover costs quickly. Technological collaboration is a way of overcoming these problems. Where the alliance takes the form of co-production, an important motive is the desire to minimise costs. If the firms participating in the alliance have strengths in different areas (research, production, marketing, etc.), synergy savings may result from collaboration. Joint sourcing of components and marketing of the end product may also yield a further source of cost reduction. The Airbus project in Western Europe is an example of an alliance involving four aerospace manufacturers designed to spread the costs of technological development.

The need to gain entry to a particular market, as with traditional joint ventures, may be a further motive. However, some global alliances are formed to reduce rather than increase competition. Each of the participants is anxious to prevent its rival from acquiring an increase in global market share at its own expense. In short, the alliance is a defensive reaction on the part of each participant to a perceived threat to their respective interests posed by the development of a new ownership-specific advantage by the other. A global alliance may be preferred to a joint venture precisely because they are less formal. The costs of setting up and administering the alliance are likely to be much less than for a joint venture. They are probably less risky since an alliance can be terminated at any time whereas a joint venture is more difficult to unravel. Moreover, most alliances provide for co-operation over a fixed period of time only.

In recent decades, there has been a significant increase in the number of global alliances taking place. Over the period 1980–89, there were 793 alliances formed in information technology, 306 in biotechnology, 183 in chemicals, 178 in new materials and 105 in automobiles (UNCTAD-DTCI, 1994). In all five industries except chemicals, the number of strategic alliances was higher in the period 1985–89 than the earlier period of 1980–84. The increase was especially great in the automobiles sector. This trend is probably a result of a variety of changes taking place in the global economy, often the same factors as have caused increases in other forms of international involvement. Markets have become more globalised, transport and communication costs have decreased and patterns of consumption in different countries have become more similar. Technological change has in many industries increased the scale of production at which unit costs can be minimised making it essential for producers to seek out large markets. At the same time, the rapid pace of technological innovation and the increased costs of conducting R&D in high-technology industries have increased the advantages to be gained from global co-operation. The increase in the number of global alliances may also be the result of increased competition as trade barriers have fallen. Firms seek alliances with rivals as a means of defending themselves from perceived threats to market share resulting from rivals acquiring new ownership-specific advantages.

Counter-Trade

One important development in trade in recent decades has been the increased role played by barter and so-called counter-trade. The strict meaning of the term 'barter' is the direct exchange of goods for goods without the mediation of money. A pure barter exchange remains a relatively rare occurrence in trade. More common, however, are forms of transaction which contain elements of barter but which still involve the use of money. The Economist Intelligence Unit (EIU) uses the term 'counter-trade' in a generic sense to refer to forms of trade which involve an element of reciprocity. In return for A buying from B, B buys from A. However, A's purchases from B may not be exactly matched by B's purchases from A, thus necessitating some use of money. It is also probable that the two transactions will be separated in time. Nevertheless, the two transactions are, to some degree, reciprocal and, therefore, constitute counter-trade. As the EIU puts it, 'the important point about counter-trade is that it aims to equalise or partially balance foreign exchange expenditures' (EIU, 1984).

Types of Counter-Trading

Counter-trade may take several different forms:

1. *Pure barter* involving the direct exchange of goods/services for other goods/services is unusual in international trade. Based on a sample of 230 completed counter-trade agreements over the period between 1984 and 1988, Marin (1991) found that only 26% involved pure barter. Usually, barter takes place on a government-to-government basis, with money entering the transaction only as a unit of account. The main problem with barter is that it involves a double-coincidence-of-wants. A must want what B has to sell and B must want what A has to sell. Furthermore, the two

transactions must have the same exchange value. These requirements make a barter transaction difficult to arrange at an international level and account for its relative unimportance.

2. *Counter-purchase* is probably the most common form of counter-trade. Marin (1991) found that 76.5% of all the transactions in the sample of counter-trade agreements that she considered were counter-purchases. A counter-purchase involves an exporter who secures a sales order undertaking to purchase in return certain goods and services from the importing country. The reciprocal purchase is a condition for the original sale. Sometimes this is called 'compensation trade'. It is most commonly found in trade between producers in western industrialised countries and state agencies or firms in the former Communist states of Central and Eastern Europe.

Usually, there will be two separate contracts. One will relate to the sale of goods/services by the western company for which it will be paid a specified amount of hard currency. The other will require the western company to spend some proportion of this revenue to buy goods from a shopping list provided by the importing country. The counter-purchase may vary in value between 10 and 100% of the original export order. The imports bought need not be related in any way to the goods/services exported. Usually, there will be a time period specified (normally three years) within which the counter-purchase must be made. Thus, in this form of counter-trading (unlike pure barter), exports only partly finance the purchase of imports. Rather, they simply help balance expenditures on imports at a later date. For this reason, a counter-purchase transaction is not undertaken because of a lack of convertible currency or inability to obtain credit. However, it has often been used by centrally planned economies as a device for controlling foreign trade and ensuring that exports balance imports.

3. *Buyback* is another type of counter-trade involving the supplier of capital plant or equipment (usually to a developing country) being paid with part of the resultant output. For example, a western company supplying a chemicals plant to a developing country may be paid with an entitlement to part of the resultant output of the plant. Buyback deals are most common where the product exported takes the form of process plant or mining equipment. Usually they are for longer periods of time (typically ten to fifteen years) than other forms of counter-trading. Marin (1991) found that, in her sample of counter-trade agreements, 12% were buybacks, with buybacks being slightly more common in transactions with developing countries than with centrally planned economies.

For both developing countries and centrally planned economies, however, buybacks have the attraction that they avoid the need for the importing country to pay for the capital goods in hard currency. For western companies, on the other hand, there is the problem that they have no control over the quality of the output from the plants constructed in the importing country. For this reason, western companies often insist on clauses being included in the contracts allowing them to exercise some quality control, after the delivery of the plant.

Similar in kind to buybacks are 'co-production agreements', in which western companies produce certain components used in the production of a particular good, while the developing country or centrally planned economy specialises in producing the less sophisticated parts. Reciprocal deliveries take place. Such agreements ensure, for the western company, access to the foreign market, while being able to take advantage of lower wages in the partner country. The local firm in the developing country or centrally planned economy, in return, gains access to western technology, while, at the same time, broadening its market. Developing countries may prefer this to allowing a western company to produce the entire product locally.

4. *Bilateral agreements and clearings* are a variety of agreements between two countries that involve some attempt, over a specified period of time (often five years), to roughly balance the exchange of goods and services. The agreement may rigidly define the products to be traded or involve little more than a loose and broad statement about best intentions. Usually, a clearing mechanism is established. This involves each country opening up a special account with the other country's central bank. Each country is paid for its exports by a credit entered into the special account. These credits may, then be used to obtain imports from the other country. A clearing currency that is to be used for settling any difference between credits and debits may be specified. Often, this will be the partner's own currency or a suitable foreign currency (e.g. the U.S. dollar). However, if credits equal debits, there may be no need for any use of foreign currency. In effect, 'book money' replaces foreign currency. This may be helpful to countries that lack adequate foreign currency reserves or whose currency is inconvertible and, therefore, not acceptable in settlement of debt. For these reasons, much use has been made of such agreements in East–West trade.

5. *Switch trading* is the most complex type of counter-trade. When two countries enter into a bilateral trading agreement, there may arise long-term payments imbalances. One country may accumulate large unused credit surpluses with the other country. Switch trading involves the resale of unused credits to third parties in exchange for convertible currencies. For example, suppose that A develops large unused credits as a result of bilateral trading with B. Under switch trading, A may use these credits to buy imports from some third country, C. C, in turn, can use the credits received to buy more goods from A. This is a relatively simple example. However, in practice, switch trading often involves more than three countries, making the arrangements highly complex. Discounts may also be used in the switch process. Certain banks and trading houses with a specialist knowledge of switch trading act as switch specialists, enabling holders of unused credits to sell credits for slightly less than their face value.

6. *Offset* is the last, but by no means least important, form of counter-trading. Indeed, its importance appears to be growing fast. It involves an agreement under which an exporter incorporates into his final product certain components and parts obtained from the foreign (importing) country. Offset is commonly used in the export of high-value goods such as civil or military aircraft or other types of military equipment. Typically, the exporter is a western aircraft or armaments firm selling hardware to a developing country. The exporter agrees to use certain components in the production of the good that has been made in the developing country. He may also agree to provide the developing country with technical assistance. In some cases, the western exporter may also agree to import other, entirely unrelated, products from the developing country, as part of the contract.

Of the six types of counter-trading listed above, counter-purchase appears the most common. A questionnaire carried out in the United States covering some 450 U.S. companies found that counter-purchase accounted for 55% of all counter-trade transactions, offsets for another 24%, buybacks 9%, switch trading 8% and pure barter only 4% (quoted in EIU, 1984).

The Importance of Counter-Trading

Counter-trade is not an entirely new phenomenon. Most countries have resorted to some form of barter at some stage in the past. The inter-war period, especially the years of the Great Depression, witnessed a spread of bilateral trading agreements among the countries of Europe. Bilateralism went hand in glove with the general proliferation of trading restrictions and exchange controls during this period. Nazi Germany attached a major importance to bilateral trading as part of its programme to cut unemployment. Barter trade remained widespread during and immediately after the ending of the Second World War. In the 1950s, however, most countries moved back to multilateral methods of trading and payment. This was encouraged by the setting up of bodies such as the IMF, GATT, OEEC (which later became the OECD), the European Payments Union and, later, the EEC and EFTA. Bilateralism was frowned upon as distorting the global pattern of trade and reducing global economic efficiency and, hence, economic welfare.

However, bilateral trading remained a common occurrence for some developing countries (especially those in Latin America) and the Communist bloc countries both with each other and with the rest of the world. There occurred some decline in the use of bilateral trading in Latin America, following the establishment of the Latin American Free Trade Association (LAFTA), but it never disappeared altogether. However, the Soviet Union, the CMEA countries of Eastern Europe and China continued to rely heavily on counter-trading for most of their trade with the West, with developing countries and with each other. This meant that most western companies that wished to trade with these countries, had to engage in counter-trading. The 1980s witnessed a resurgence of counter-trading, mainly involving developing and East European countries. The immediate cause appears to have been a decline in private lending to these countries, following the international debt crisis, as western creditors became fearful that loans would not be repaid. Counter-trading proved to be a way in which highly indebted countries, unable to finance imports in the normal way, could continue to obtain the imports that they needed. More recent evidence suggests that the importance of counter-trading has continued to grow. The collapse of Communism in Eastern Europe appears to have given a further fillip to counter-trading as a device for overcoming domestic liquidity difficulties and growing international indebtedness.

No one knows the precise extent of counter-trading. Estimates vary between 5 and 20% of world trade. The Economist Intelligence Unit guessed that the true range lay somewhere between 15 and 20% of world trade (EIU, 1984). The Group of Thirty, an international research group based in New York, estimated counter-trade at between 8 and 10% of world trade (The Economist, December 20, 1986). The United States International Trade Commission estimated counter-trade at some 5.6% of the exports of the United States' 500 largest companies with armaments sales accounting for 80% of the total (The Economist, December 20, 1986). Estimates by the OECD suggest a figure somewhere within the range of 10–20% of world trade (OECD, 1985–1991). For developing countries, counter-trading has a greater importance. In a study of barter trade in six developing countries, the OECD found that 'barter-like' trade varied from 7% of total exports in the case of Tunisia to 78% in the case of Egypt (OECD, 1979). In all six countries except Tunisia and Nepal (for which there were no data for the 1960s), the percentage had increased. As a component of total imports, barter-like trade ranged from 7% for Tunisia up to 53% for Egypt. In two countries – Egypt and India – this percentage increased compared with the 1960s, but fell slightly in three other countries – Sri Lanka, Ghana and Tunisia.

The Determinants of Counter-Trading

Why do countries engage in counter-trading? One way of answering this is to examine the motives of the different players involved. Broadly speaking, we may identify four different groups of players:

1. *The Eastern Bloc countries plus China.* Until recently, all of these countries were centrally planned economies, in which the State exercised a monopoly control of foreign trade. For such countries, counter-trade has obvious attractions. First, it enables them to control their balance of trade with the rest of the world, ensuring that, as far as possible, exports are matched by an equivalent amount of imports. Second, it enables the State to regulate the use of scarce foreign currency earnings. Foreign exporters are rarely prepared to accept payment in the form of inconvertible local currency. Foreign currency reserves are often inadequate to ensure payment in hard currency. In these circumstances, counter-trading may provide an escape route.

Counter-trading often takes the form of a counter-purchase agreement that ensures that purchases of foreign goods are offset by increased exports at some stage in the future. Buybacks are also common, as they enable these countries to acquire western technology by paying for it with goods produced by the plant supplied by western companies. In this case, the need for hard currency is avoided. A further advantage of counter-trading for these countries is that it obviates the need for these countries to seek out markets for their products in the West. Many of these countries suffer from a lack of access to markets abroad and lack experience in western marketing methods. Both buybacks and co-production agreements are useful in this respect. As the quality of Eastern Bloc products has improved, reliance on counter-trading has declined somewhat. Nevertheless, the proportion of counter-trading has been estimated at 25% of total East–West trade (DTI, 1985).

2. *The developing countries* have accounted for the major growth of counter-trading in recent decades. Economic reasons predominate:

(a) *Financial*: Lack of foreign exchange is a major reason for counter-trading, as with the Eastern Bloc countries. An OECD study found that, for a sample of six developing countries, this was the primary motive for counter-trading (OECD, 1979). Many developing countries find themselves unable to finance imports through conventional methods. Foreign currency reserves may have been used up. At the same time, they may be unable to obtain credit because they are considered by lenders to be bad risks. Counter-trade becomes a method of trade finance. This became a major problem for many developing countries in the 1980s as a result of the international debt crisis. Western banks became increasingly reluctant to lend more to countries with large, outstanding debts. At the same time, the export earnings of developing countries were depressed by falling commodity prices.

(b) *Commercial*: Counter-trade may also be a means whereby developing countries can secure increased export sales for their products. In the markets for many bulk commodities (e.g. minerals, coffee, cocoa, cotton, rubber), there is great struggle to secure a share of the market in the face of static and often declining demand. By forcing trading partners to accept exports of such commodities as payment for other goods or services, a developing country may be able to maintain sales.

(c) *Development:* Developing countries also use counter-trade both to obtain vital technology or capital goods needed for development and as a way of obtaining development assistance. In the first case, the developing country pays for the foreign technology or capital equipment with products, possibly on a buy-back basis. In the second case, the developing country agrees to purchase goods from a developed country as a condition for receiving development aid. There may be a requirement that the developed country source some of the components locally as under an offset agreement.

The greater part of the counter-trade of developing countries takes place in bulk commodities – agricultural products or raw materials. However, some counter-trade takes in non-traditional, value-added goods, including semi-processed and processed agricultural products, metals, textiles, handicrafts, petrochemicals and other industrial goods. Many developing countries face problems in marketing such goods and so conventional methods of trading are not appropriate. Counter-trading is a way of getting round this problem, since a western company, possessing greater marketing knowledge and expertise, in effect takes over the marketing function. However, there are many problems involved in counter-trading such products. One major difficulty is amassing sufficient value for the transaction, since these products are generally exported only in small quantities. Accordingly, such products appear to account for only a small proportion of counter-trade (EIU, 1984).

3. The *oil exporters* were frequent users of counter-trade in the wake of the oil crises of 1973–74 and 1979–80. They used counter-trade to purchase capital equipment and raw materials needed for development. Following the rise in oil prices, they enjoyed large oil revenues that they sought to use to accelerate their rate of economic development. At the same time, western oil companies were anxious to secure guaranteed, long-term supplies of oil to cover themselves against the risk of another oil shortage. They were willing to offer goods and services in exchange for oil on a counter-purchase basis. Nuclear power stations, military hardware and other goods were offered in exchange for oil. When, in the 1980s, the oil market weakened, counter-trade was used by oil-exporting countries as a way of ensuring high oil prices. Oil-importing countries agreed to buy oil at the previous year's price if the oil exporter accepted payment in the form of goods. Nevertheless, because the price of goods sold was often inflated, the oil-importing country still enjoyed an effective reduction in the oil price. For members of OPEC, counter-trade has often been an attractive method of selling oil, because it is a way in which they can sell more oil without cutting prices below the minimum level. In effect, they are selling oil at a discount, while maintaining the official cartel price.

4. The *western industrialised countries* engage in counter-trade to a lesser extent than other countries. One important exception to this concerns trade in military products, aircraft and high technology goods. Very often, these deals involve some element of offset, with the exporting company offering to offset part of the contract by purchases from the importing country as a means of clinching the deal. Often, western firms are forced to use counter-trade to secure sales to developing or state trading countries. Unwillingness to engage in counter-trade may result in the order being lost, especially when the company in question is not the leader in the market. This can create problems for western companies, as they are forced to find markets for the goods received in payment from the buyer. Because of the growing need to counter-trade as a condition for

exporting to certain countries, more and more western exporters have set up their own counter-trade departments to acquire knowledge and expertise in the marketing and distribution of goods received in payment for exports.

Although there exist many motives for countries engaging in counter-trade, some are more important than others. Contrary to what is often thought, the financial motive for countries engaging in counter-trade (a shortage of hard currency) is probably the least important. This is because most forms of counter-trade still require the importer to pay, in part, with money. Counter-trade helps reduce the need for hard currency, but does not eliminate it. A more likely motive is the need for developing countries to generate additional currency by exporting more goods to the developed world. Faced with increasing protectionism in western industrialised countries, counter-trade is seen as a way in which developing countries can boost their exports to western markets. On the other hand, there is the danger that, the more developing countries sell to western markets through counter-trade, the less they will be able to sell through conventional means. In this case, exports through counter-trade channels will merely displace sales through conventional means or drive down the price that they fetch. On the other hand, if the goods sold through counter-trade are sold to markets where no previous sales have been made, the outcome may still be favourable. Yet, a further possibility is that counter-trade contracts may place stipulations preventing the goods being re-sold to third markets, which would otherwise weaken the price in markets where the goods are being sold by conventional means. Marin (1991) found strong support for the view that counter-trade does help developing countries export more to western developed countries and to diversify their exports by selling more non-traditional products.

However, she questions whether this tells the whole story, as there are other less costly ways whereby developing countries could, more effectively, market their products. Instead, she sees the motive for counter-trade as residing in imperfections in markets, such that it becomes a more efficient way by which developing countries can expand their exports to the developed world. First, as was noted above in relation to oil-producing countries, counter-trade is one way in which a member of a cartel can expand sales without violating the agreement. It can do so by selling goods at the official price, while taking over-priced goods from the buyer as payment. The lack of transparency of a barter deal makes this type of transaction a convenient way in which firms can cheat. A second way in which counter-trading may be more efficient is that it may make it easier for a discriminating monopolist to charge different prices for the same product to consumers in different countries. Where the elasticity of demand for a product is greater in one market than another, price discrimination is a device whereby a monopolist can increase profits. A barter transaction enables the monopolist to obscure the fact that the price charged in one market is higher than in another. Marin found some empirical evidence to show that counter-trading was used in these ways to overcome market distortions.

However, a feature of much counter-trading is that it involves a long-term contract with little alteration of the price over the duration of the agreement. This suggests that counter-trading cannot be fully explained by the need to overcome market distortions. Marin argues that a further reason for its use is as a response to an incentive problem caused by incomplete contracting in situations where the buyer and seller are both required to make large, specific investments. Where both parties are bilateral monopolists, the gains from the sale of the good will depend on the relative bargaining strength of each party. This means that neither party can be sure at the time when the investment is made what the price will be. If, however, they enter into a long-term contract in which the division of future gains is determined in advance, uncertainty is reduced. Marin considers the case of a developing country, which is contemplating investing resources in an export industry. The developing country will need to protect itself against the risk of some random fluctuation in price or demand for the product. One way in which it can do so is by agreeing to a contract with a buyer in a developed country to buy the product at an agreed price at a certain date in the future. This will necessitate the firm in the developed country making an investment in marketing and distribution channels. Without this, the new product will confront reputational barriers to entry due to consumers lacking sufficient information about the quality of the good. However, this creates risks for the firm in the developed country. Once the investment in marketing has been made, the developing country has little incentive to meet the quality requirements for the counter-trade goods. Moreover, having made the investment, the firm in the developed country finds itself locked into a relationship that it is more costly to withdraw from than stay with. As a result, the firm in the developed country is unlikely to agree to the contract that the developing country is seeking.

On the other hand, if a contract can be reached which guarantees the firm in the developed country a fair share of the resultant profits, it may be induced to do so. This may be achieved by the firm in the developed country selling technology and machinery to the developing country, for which it is paid in kind with the goods produced with the equipment supplied. Because the firm in the developed country is paid with the resultant output, it has no incentive to supply low and outdated technology, which might otherwise be the case (due to the asymmetrical information problem discussed in Chapter 4). However, the contract does make the developing country dependent on the firm in the developed country for technology updating and after-sales service. This helps to counterbalance the vulnerability of the developed country firm to the developing country supplying only low quality goods. In short, counter-trading (more specifically, buy-back) arrangements of this kind serve to make both parties mutually dependent on each other in a way that overcomes the credibility problem that otherwise exists. Submitting her hypothesis to empirical testing, Marin found that counter-trading of this kind is more common, on the one hand, where transactions relate to exports of technology and machinery from developed to developing countries, and on the other hand, where counter-trade goods exported by developing to developed countries are differentiated in design and quality (where reputational entry barriers are most likely to exist).

More recently, Marin and Schnitzer (1997) have argued that a major reason for the growth of barter is that, in certain situations, it provides a superior credit enforcement mechanism to money. Where exports are paid for by the importer giving a promise to pay in money at an agreed date in the future, there is the problem of default. Where, instead, the exporter is paid with a promise on future goods, default is more difficult. Goods can more easily be earmarked as the property of the creditor and the debtor compelled to surrender these goods to the creditor. Where, however, the debtor defaults on a monetary payment, the only recourse is to threaten trade sanctions. Marin and Schnitzer argue that basic goods are more suited to being used as commodity money because they give rise to fewer asymmetric information problems. (Basic goods are standardised and are sold on organised commodity markets.) Consumer goods also have the advantage that they require an investment by the creditor in the marketing of the goods offered as payment. This creates a closer relationship between the creditor and the debtor that reduces the incentive of the debtor to offer low quality goods in payment and encourages the creditor to make the goods less anonymous by differentiating and designing the goods. Investment goods, however, are 'bad money' because the debtor has a greater incentive to supply low quality goods and the creditor has no incentive to invest in the relationship. Marin and Schnitzer provide empirical support for their hypothesis using actual barter contracts signed by OECD firms between 1984 and 1988.

The Effects of Counter-Trading

The increased use of counter-trading has been strongly condemned by organisations such as the World Trade Organisation, the International Monetary Fund and the OECD, who regard it as damaging to global economic efficiency. Counter-trading, it is argued, represents a retreat back to the bilateralism which characterised trading relationships in the period just before the outbreak of World War II. This was a period in which world trade fell and the major economies of the world experienced a prolonged and deep depression. In a similar manner, the growth of counter-trading today could serve to reduce the volume of world trade. The notion that every country should seek to balance its trade with each of its trading partners has no rationale in trade theory. Indeed, if each country were to pursue such a course, the volume of world trade would, necessarily, decline. A fall in the volume of world trade would, in turn, to lead lower output and smaller incomes in all countries of the world.

Is such a concern about the growth of counter-trading justified? Let us begin with the arguments against counter-trading. Seven arguments are commonly confronted:

1. *Counter-trading reduces world economic efficiency by distorting the global allocation of resources.* In a multilateral system of trade, countries buy goods from the cheapest possible source, allowing for differences in transport costs. In practice, the existence of tariffs and non-tariff barriers to trade distorts these relationships, favouring local production over imports. However, provided that the level of these barriers does not discriminate unduly against particular suppliers of these goods, production will take place where costs are lowest and the world's scarce resources will be put to the best possible use. Bilateralism (countries match exports to a particular country with an equivalent amount of imports from the same country) prevents this from happening. Some goods are bought from a particular source although an alternative lower cost supplier exists because of the need to pay for a consignment of goods exported to that country.
2. *Counter-trade reduces transparency.* Where goods are paid for with money, the prices and quantities sold are plain for all to see. This enables buyers to seek out the cheapest possible source. Under counter-trading, prices are expressed in quantities of the goods offered in exchange. It is difficult for the buyer to know if the goods are available at the lowest possible cost. Nor can the seller know whether the best possible deal has been secured. Changes in prices in response to changes in demand or cost conditions are also less apparent. Buyers and sellers are, therefore, unable to respond by altering their output or spending plans.
3. *Counter-trade may delay difficult decisions within developing countries.* Developing countries may use counter-trading to cope

with a problem of mediocre export performance. The problem may be a failure to supply goods of the right quality at the lowest possible price. Counter-trade may be a means whereby a developing country puts off introducing the changes needed to address these problems. For example, it may be the case that greater effort is needed to improve the marketing of the product. Counter-trading avoids the need to make this change by passing the marketing problem on to the counter-trader.

4. *Counter-trade creates additional costs that do not arise in conventional trade.* There are considerable transaction costs involved in drafting and executing a counter-trade agreement. Companies engaging in counter-trade may have to create special departments to handle the goods acquired through counter-trade. These functions may be better carried out by specialist institutions, in which case fees will have to be incurred. Legal costs associated with counter-trading can also be substantial. If these are passed on by the firm in the developed country to the exporter in the developing country, the developing country will get a lower price for its goods than otherwise.
5. *Counter-trade can also lead to the dumping of goods on world markets, causing market disruption and damage to local suppliers.* Dumping is easier to conceal where trade is conducted without the use of money. This may reduce the risk of the exporter being subject to an anti-dumping investigation in the importing country. Although consumers in the importing country acquire the goods more cheaply, local producers are harmed. Counter-trading is often used when a country has an unwanted surplus of a bulk commodity that it wishes to dispose of, but is anxious not to attract the attention of anti-dumping authorities.
6. *Counter-trading may penalise small- and medium-size companies in western industrialised countries that lack the resources to engage in counter-trading.* As we have seen, counter-trading is often a necessity for exporters wishing to gain access to the market of a developing or state-planned economy. Yet, counter-trading results in substantial costs that are likely to be prohibitive to all but the largest firms.
7. *Counter-trading may lead to increased protectionism.* If counter-trading causes the disruptive effects discussed above (e.g., the dumping of unwanted surpluses on foreign markets), it may lead to increased pressure for protection. This may take the form of higher tariffs, selective quotas, a voluntary export restraint or some other indirect means of limiting imports. At the very least, friction between developed and developing countries is likely to be increased.

On the other hand, counter-trading may bring some important benefits to developing countries, in particular, and to the global economy as a whole. The following are the main arguments put forward in favour of counter-trading:

1. *Counter-trading may cause some trade to happen which otherwise would not.* By offering to buy goods with payment in the form of an equivalent amount of other goods, a country may be able to expand its exports in a way which otherwise would have been more difficult. If this is the case, counter-trading will result in a higher, not lower, volume of world trade than otherwise. Defenders of counter-trading point to the fact that, in recent decades, counter-trading has risen faster than conventional trade. However, that does not mean that more trade is taking place, as some of the increase may have been at the expense of conventional trade (trade-diversion). Some conventional

trade may not have taken place because more goods were being sold through counter-trading means.

2. *Counter-trade enables developing countries to achieve a greater geographical diversification of their exports.* Through counter-trading, a developing country may be able to find new markets for its exports, thereby reducing its dependence on traditional markets. For example, if in the past, it was dependent on the former colonial power or another dominant, neighbouring country for the bulk of its exports, counter-trade may give it greater independence. It is sometimes argued that counter-trade has enabled developing countries to trade more with the formerly state-planned economies of Eastern Europe and with each other.
3. *Counter-trade may enable a developing country to boost its export sales of a particular commodity that it has proved difficult to market effectively abroad.* Once again, care must be taken to distinguish between trade-creation and trade-diversion. Increased sales achieved through counter-trading may lead to loss of sales through conventional means. Goods sold to another country under a counter-trading agreement may be re-exported to a third market, resulting in reduced sales by conventional means to the third country. Alternatively, increased sales through counter-trade may involve selling goods though conventional means at a reduced price. In a study of six developing countries, the OECD found that, in most cases, counter-trading led to trade-diversion. In a few cases, however, counter-trading provided genuine help in compensating for declining export sales to global markets (OECD, 1979).
4. *Counter-trade may enable a developing country to enjoy more stable export earnings.* A frequent concern of developing countries is the instability of their export earnings due to fluctuating commodity prices and their over-dependence on a few basic commodities for exports. Because the terms of a counter-trade agreement are fixed in advance, exports conducted through these means are less subject to volatility in world prices. However, the OECD in its study of six developing countries found little evidence that this was indeed the case (OECD, 1979). Barter trade appeared no more stable than trade conducted through conventional means.
5. *Counter-trade may enable a developing country to more effectively achieve balance of payments equilibrium.* Since counter-trading is reciprocal, it helps achieve a balanced expansion of exports and imports. Increased imports are less likely to lead to balance of payments difficulties. Given the shortage of foreign exchange which many of these countries face, this makes counter-trading an attractive option. State planned economies find counter-trading especially beneficial for this reason. Clearly, however, this is only true if all of a country's trade is conducted on this basis. Moreover, only if trade takes the form of pure barter can the need to provide hard currency be avoided.
6. *Counter-trade enables a developing country to achieve a more favourable terms of trade.* This might be the case if a developing country can secure a better price for its exports through counter-trading than by conventional means. This might be the case if the country is forced to cut the price when making a conventional sale to compensate for poor quality or a low degree of marketability. On the other hand, if the costs of counter-trading are borne by the exporter, counter-trade may result in a lower price even than that fetched through a conventional transaction.

7. *Counter-trade may enable a developing country to improve the commodity structure of its trade*. Through counter-trading, a country may be able to expand it's exports of non-traditional goods with higher value-added, mainly, processed and semi-processed goods. World demand for such goods, generally, grows faster than bulk commodities, so enabling developing countries to achieve faster export growth. Diversification of the commodity composition of their exports is important for many poor countries that wish to enjoy faster export growth. Yet, many poor countries lack the marketing knowledge or expertise to break into western markets for such goods. Counter-trade can help overcome this problem by utilising the expertise of firms already established in these markets.
8. *Counter-trading may be a means whereby developing countries can reduce their external debts*. As many developing countries have in recent decades experienced growing international indebtedness, counter-trading has provided a way of paying for goods needed without increasing the burden of monetary indebtedness. Earlier, we saw that barter frequently offers a superior credit enforcement mechanism to that of money, so that creditors in developed countries may also prefer payment in a commodity form. Increasingly, many international banks have come to accept payment in the form of goods rather than expanding their loans to debtor countries.
9. *Counter-trading may enable a developing country to get more development assistance.* Development assistance is often given to countries that buy capital goods or technology from the donor country. The developing country is offered a low-interest or interest-free loan (so-called 'soft credit') in exchange for agreeing to buy the goods. Such credit may take the form of a counter-trade agreement, in which all or part of the loan is repaid in the form of goods

Although counter-trading contains many undesirable features, the benefits that it brings to developing countries means that it is almost certainly here to stay. Far from disappearing, it is quite possible that, in the future, its importance may increase. Indeed, if as Marin (1991) has argued, counter-trade is a response to the presence of market imperfections, there is every reason to expect that both developed and developing countries will wish to make continued use of it. The fact, too, that the problems of developing country indebtedness show little sign of abating means that counter-trade will remain a popular means for financing a significant proportion of world trade. If so, trade economists will need to pay more careful attention to developing models capable of explaining this kind of trade. The comparative costs determinants of conventional trade are unlikely to be appropriate for explaining these types of trade flows. Patterns of counter-trade are better explained by analysing the role of contracts and institutions in trade.

Conclusion

In this chapter, some newer forms of international economic involvement have been discussed. The chapter began with the observation that, today, a major proportion of direct investment abroad carried out by developed market economies is two-way FDI taking place within the same industrial sector or so-called intra-industry FDI. A parallel with the growth of intra-industry trade was noted. This strongly suggests that firms use trade and FDI as different methods of competing in different markets at different points in time. The fact that they do so in each other's home market suggests that competitive advantage is rarely a one-way affair. It also suggests that trade and FDI are not alternatives, but frequently complement each other.

This was reinforced when the phenomenon of rationalised product FDI was introduced. If firms expand initially by establishing subsidiaries abroad that are replicas of the parent company, they rarely continue on this basis. After a while, the advantages of rationalising their global or regional operations in order to achieve greater efficiency become a major consideration. Such rationalisation may take the form of a vertical disintegration of the production process, in which case trade in intermediate goods and services is greatly increased. Alternatively, trade may take the form of horizontal rationalisation, with different plants specialising in particular models of the finished good. In this case, intra-industry trade is generated. Clearly, this kind of FDI is trade-enhancing and not trade-displacing, demonstrating the value of integrating trade and FDI in a single theoretical framework as was discussed at the end of the previous chapter.

However, neither trade nor FDI are the only ways in which firms get involved internationally. In this chapter, some of the wide variety of different ways in which firms may seek to enter a foreign market were examined. All of these entail some element of contractual relationship between firms. However, the purpose is not always one of gaining access to a foreign market. Firms may seek to collaborate internationally to enhance their competitiveness on global markets. The growth of counter-trade represents another form of contractual relationship between firms in different countries, although, in this case, the purpose is to conduct trade. It is interesting that many of the factors that have contributed to the growth of counter-trade in recent decades have their origins in imperfections within markets. As we saw in earlier chapters, market imperfections also explain the increased importance of intra-industry trade, intra-firm trade and intra-industry FDI.

Notes for Further Reading

Some of the reading suggested for the previous chapter should also be suitable for this one. On intra-industry FDI, a useful source is:

Erdilek, A., *Multinationals as Mutual Invaders: Intra-Industry Direct Foreign Investment* (Beckenham, Kent: Croom-Helm, 1985).

On rationalised international production, students should consult:

Casson, M. *et al.*, *Multinationals and World Trade: Vertical Integration and the Division of Labour in World Industries* (London: Allen & Unwin, 1986).

and

Dicken, P., *Global Shift: the Internationalisation of Economic Activity*, 2nd edn. (London: Paul Chapman, 1992).

A classic on the new international division of labour is:

Frobel, F., Heinrichs, J. and Kreye, O., *The New International Division of Labour* (Cambridge: Cambridge University Press, 1980).

A chapter by John Cantwell entitled 'The relationship between international trade and production' in:

Greenaway, D. and Winters, A. (eds.), *Surveys of International Trade* (Oxford: Basil Blackwell, 1994).

is also important to read.

On alternative forms of international business involvement, the reader will find the following text a useful source of information:

John, R. (ed.), *Global Business Strategy* (London: International Thomson Press, 1997).

There is a dearth of texts on the subject of counter-trading. However, the interested reader will find useful chapters on the subject in:

Buckley, P. and Clegg, J. (eds.), *Multinational Enterprises in Less Developed Countries* (London: Macmillan, 1990).

and

Page S., *How Developing Countries Trade* (London: Routledge, 1994).

The OECD has also published a variety of papers on the subject of counter-trading in developing countries that the interested reader should consult.

Chapter 6

Japan and the World Economy

CHAPTER OUTLINES: Introduction. Post-War Growth – the end of the Japanese miracle? Japan's Trading Imbalance with the Western Industrialised Countries – background to the problem, the structure of Japan's trade. Japan's Import Barriers: How Open is the Japanese market? The Macroeconomic Determinants of the Japanese Trade Surplus. Japan's Regulated Financial Markets. Conclusion.

Introduction

In Chapter 1, we saw that one of the most significant developments in world trade over the past half-century has been the sudden and rapid emergence of Japan as one of the leading industrialised nations of the world. In a relatively short space of time, Japan has grown from being a semi-industrialised nation with a low average income to become one of the world's largest exporters of manufactured goods and one of the most prosperous nations in the world. Although, in the 1990s, the 'Japanese miracle' experienced a dramatic setback, it remains the case that Japan's ascendancy has been one of the most important events of the post-war era. On reflection, the rise of Japan may be regarded as the first phase in a deeper and more extensive process that has resulted in a large number of developing countries achieving rapid industrialisation through export expansion. The next chapter discusses the growth of these 'other Japans'. In this chapter, we focus attention on Japan. As we shall see, although there are similarities between the experience of Japan and the 'newly industrialising economies', there are also some important differences.

The first part of this chapter discusses some of the reasons for Japan's post-war success and for the sudden, rude interruption to growth that she experienced in the 1990s. However, the primary concern of this chapter is with the problems that the rise of Japan has created for the western industrialised countries. As we shall see, a feature of Japan's post-war growth has been the success with which she has expanded her exports of manufactured goods to the western industrialised countries. At the same time, her imports of manufactured goods from them has not grown at an equivalent rate. This has led to friction between Japan and her western trading partners. Within the western industrialised countries, there have been growing demands for protection against Japanese goods. Disputes between Japan and her western trading partners have at times threatened the multilateral, rules-based system of world trade set up after the Second World War. The second part of this chapter examines the nature and causes of Japan's trading imbalance with the West. Micro- and macro-economic causes of the imbalance are discussed and proposals suggested for its resolution.

Post-War Growth

Japan began the post-war period as a semi-industrialised country that had been badly devastated by war. In 1947 one-half of the working population was employed in agriculture and forestry and only 16% in manufacturing. Her per capita GNP was a mere $188 lower than that of Brazil, Chile, Malaysia and several other developing countries. In her trade with the rest of the world, Japan specialised in relatively simple, labour-intensive, light manufactures, such as cotton textiles. The largest share of her exports went to other countries in Asia. In the early years of the post-war period, she suffered from a chronic balance of payments deficit as exports regularly failed to grow fast enough to pay for imports of food, raw materials and the energy needed for economic recovery and her post-war development. However, in the decades that followed, she succeeded in achieving a remarkable turn-around. Between 1953 and 1973, the economy grew at an annual average rate of 9.7% or roughly twice that of the western industrialised economies. (France, West Germany and Italy managed roughly 5% per annum over the same period, the USA under 4% and the UK only 2.6%.)

A profound structural transformation also took place. Over the period 1953 to 1973, output growth was fastest in the manufacturing sector, averaging 12.5% per annum. This was achieved by switching resources out of the agricultural subsistence sector. By 1979, only 10% of the working population were employed in agriculture compared with 24% in manufacturing and roughly one-half in services (Allen, 1981). Because services tend to be more labour-intensive, these figures understate the size of the manufacturing sector, which, by 1980, accounted for 42% of total production. The service sector contributed a further 54% and the primary sector 2%. By 1982, her GDP per capita had reached $8,974, higher than that of the United Kingdom and close to that of France ($9,962). By 1992, her per capita GDP stood at $26,913 compared with $20,034 in the United States.

In this process of expansion, an important role was played by exports, although they accounted for a relatively small share of the economy. Whereas in 1950 her exports accounted for only 1.3% of world exports, by 1981 the share had risen to 7.7%. Taking manufactures only, Japan's share of world trade rose from 7% in 1955 to over 18% in 1983, giving her a larger share of the world manufacturing exports than either the United States or West Germany. At the same time, the composition of her exports changed. Whereas, at the beginning of the post-war period, over 40% of her exports were textiles and clothing, by 1979, this share had fallen to 5%, while the share accounted for by machinery and transport equipment rose to 61% (Allen, 1981).

What factors account for this remarkable expansion? Why did the Japanese economy perform so much better than that of the western industrialised countries or, indeed, other countries that were at a similar stage of development at the start of the post-war period? Were there any special factors distinguishing the Japanese miracle from any other similar experience in history? How much of the Japanese growth could be attributed to Japanese ingenuity and inventiveness? Although it is not possible in a single chapter to answer all of these questions, it is possible to identify some of the factors contributing to Japan's success. The following are the most important explanations for her rapid growth over this period.

1. Fast Export Growth

There can be no doubt that export expansion was a major factor generating rapid economic growth during much of this period. This is illustrated by Table 6.1. Over the period from 1950 to 1980, Japanese exports consistently rose faster than the exports of other developed market economies (DMEs) except for West Germany whose exports grew somewhat faster in the first ten years. Over the period from 1950 to 1970, Japanese exports grew nearly twice as fast as those of DMEs as a whole. However, after 1970, although Japanese exports continued to rise faster than all other DMEs, the rate of growth was only marginally higher. Between 1984 and 1994, Japan's exports grew more slowly than those of West Germany or France, although still faster than the United States, United Kingdom or Canada.

However, although fast export growth was an important contributory cause of Japan's post-war success, some observers have questioned whether Japan's growth could be defined as export-led. If the contribution of the overseas sector to Japan's growth is compared with that of the domestic sector, it is apparent, as Table 6.2 illustrates, that private domestic demand (private consumption and fixed investment) played the more important role. Between 1961–70, net exports contributed only 0.2% to the 10.7% growth in real GNP. Only in the two recession periods, 1974–76 and 1979–81, was the contribution of the export sector equal to or greater than that of the private domestic sector. On these occasions, weak domestic demand was counterbalanced by buoyant export demand, enabling the economy to enjoy a tolerable rate of expansion at a time when most other developed market economies were in recession. On both these occasions, Japan along with the other advanced industrialised countries experienced a severe deterioration in her terms of trade due to the rise in world oil prices.

The reasons why the contribution of net exports was relatively modest for much of the post-war period were twofold. First, the size of the export sector was small in comparison with other countries. Throughout the 1950s and 1960s, exports accounted for only 11–12% of Japan's GNP compared with over 20% in the United Kingdom and West Germany and between 15–20% in countries such as France and Italy. (Only the United States had an export sector proportionately as small as that

Table 6.1 Annual Average Growth Rates of Exports of Developed Market Economies, 1950–1994 (percentage)

Country	*1950–60*	*1960–70*	*1970–80*	*1984–94*
Japan	15.9	17.5	20.8	12.2
United States	5.1	7.8	18.2	11.7
United Kingdom	4.8	6.3	19.1	10.8
Canada	5.3	11.8	14.9	7.6
West Germany	16.6	11.4	19.1	13.4
France	6.4	9.8	19.8	12.8
All DMEs	7.1	10.0	18.9	–

Sources : UNCTAD (1983) and WTO (1995).

Table 6.2 The Growth of Japan's Gross National Product and its Components (percentage)

Fiscal year	*Real GNP average, annual rates*	*Contributions by:* *Total*	*Private domestic demand*	*Government demand*	*Net exports*	*Annual percentage change in terms of trade*
1961–70	10.7	10.6	8.9	1.6	0.2	−1.0
1971–73	6.8	7.4	6.1	1.3	−0.6	−2.4
1974–76	2.8	0.9	0.3	0.6	1.9	−8.9
1977–78	5.2	5.6	3.6	1.9	−0.4	10.4
1979–81	4.4	2.5	2.2	0.3	2.0	−12.3
1982–84*	3.8	3.5	3.2	0.3	0.3	0.6

Source : Kagami (1983).
*Forecast.

of Japan.) Second, for much of the post-war period, rapid export growth was offset by equally rapid import growth, giving rise to severe balance of payments difficulties. As is explained below, Japan has always lacked sufficient indigenous sources of energy and other natural resources. In the first decade and half following the Second World War, as manufacturing industry began to grow fast, imports of raw materials also grew rapidly and the balance of payments on current account worsened. It was not until 1959 that Japan's exports reached their pre-war levels and not until 1963 that they regained their pre-war share of world trade. Only in 1964 did Japan succeed in achieving a surplus in her balance of trade. Even then, her large deficit on invisibles meant that her current account was frequently in deficit.

Nevertheless, export growth was an important contributory factor in Japan's post-war expansion. First, as we have seen, export growth helped pay for imports and, for the deficit on invisibles. Without rapid export growth, domestic economic growth would have been constrained. In short, Japan's export success enabled her to overcome the constraint on growth imposed in the early post-war period by her balance of payments deficit. With exports expanding fast, domestic demand could be allowed to increase before balance of payments difficulties compelled the authorities to curtail expansion. Second, the rapid growth of exports had a stimulatory effect on the rest of the economy, especially the manufacturing sector. It created a climate conducive to high levels of capital investment and enabled Japanese firms to reduce costs by exploiting both the static and dynamic economies of large-scale production.

2. *High Levels of Investment*

The Japanese economy was successful in achieving extremely high levels of fixed capital investment in relation to national income. Throughout the 1960s, capital investment averaged over 30% of GNP, compared with a ratio for other industrialised countries of between 17% in the United Kingdom and 25% in West Germany. Such high levels of investment enabled Japan to both widen its capital base by adding to its capital stock and deepen it by replacing outmoded plant and machinery with more up-to-date equipment. With a higher ratio of capital to labour, labour productivity grew rapidly. Between 1955 and 1970, output per worker rose at an average rate of 10% per annum compared with between 4 and 7% in Western Europe. So long as the growth in money wages was below the rise in productivity, Japanese manufacturers were able to cut costs and increase the competitiveness of Japanese goods in world markets. Fast export growth further stimulated capital investment bringing yet greater improvements in productivity and competitiveness. In short, Japan enjoyed a virtuous cycle of growth that was much envied by the western industrialised countries.

High levels of investment resulted from a number of factors. First, rapid export expansion meant strong overseas demand for Japanese goods. Japanese firms that invested in new capacity, could, therefore, be sure that capacity would be fully utilised. Second, the cost of capital remained relatively low. During the 1970s, the average real cost of capital was estimated at 1.56% in Japan compared with 2.44% in the United States. During the 1980s, it rose to 2.76% in Japan, but was still lower than in other industrialised countries (5.48% in the United States) (Bernheim and Shoven, 1986). Third, profits rose as increases in productivity outstripped the growth in wage-rates.

3. *High Levels of Savings*

No economy can achieve high levels of investment unless people are willing to deny some current consumption in order to enjoy more consumption in the future. By saving, households free resources for the production of capital goods as opposed to consumer goods. In a similar manner, companies undertake saving by retaining, rather than distributing, profits to shareholders. In Japan, throughout this period, both personal and corporate savings were extremely high by international standards. During the 1960s, personal savings were as much as 20% of distributed national income, well above those of other western industrialised economies. Subsequently, although levels of investment have fallen somewhat, the high savings propensity of Japanese households has been broadly maintained. Thus, from 1975 to 1983, the ratio of personal savings to disposable (i.e. after tax) income in Japan was 19.3% compared with 12.7% in West Germany and 8.3% in the United States. From 1984 to 1991, the ratio fell to 15% in Japan but was still higher than West Germany's 12.5% and the United States' 5.4% (Hamada, 1995). The large surplus funds of the household sector were channelled through the banking and financial sector and made available as relatively low-cost loans to the corporate sector. So long as the return to be earned on an extra sum of capital invested by companies exceeded the marginal cost of loans, firms were prepared to engage in additional investment.

Many factors appear to have contributed towards Japan's historically high propensity to save. First, rapid growth in personal incomes served to boost savings. A fast rate of income growth results in higher savings, because current levels of spending are more a function of *previous* than *present* income. However, institutional factors have probably played the main role. The absence of a modern welfare state has meant that families needed to put more income aside as a reserve against sickness, unemployment and old-age. The inadequacy of the state education system has required households to save more to meet the costs of children's education. The Japanese wages system, whereby employees receive a high proportion of their annual earnings in the form of biannual bonuses, may also have contributed to the high levels of savings. Greater fluctuations in take-home pay, means that workers must save more of their income in good years to provide for lower incomes in bad years. The high cost of residential land may also have increased household savings by pushing up the cost of home ownership and discouraging most households from borrowing to buy their own home. High levels of borrowing for the purpose of home-ownership have been a major cause of 'negative saving' in western industrialised countries. Finally, for many years, the Japanese tax system encouraged savings by exempting interest on savings from tax.

4. *A High Rate of Technological Innovation*

Technological change plays a major role in the process of economic growth in any country. No country can continue to grow fast for very long merely by adding more inputs of capital and labour to the production process. It is also necessary to increase the efficiency with which these inputs are used in the process of production. Technological change may take the form of an improvement in the quality of capital stock and the skill of the labour force, the introduction of new and better methods of production or improved methods of organising and managing the process of production. Attempts to estimate the contribution of technological change to economic growth in Japan found that, over the period 1953–1971, productivity gains contributed 4.82% towards the growth rate of 8.81% that Japan experienced. Only 1.85% was contributed by increased inputs of labour and 2.1% by increased inputs of capital (Denison and Chung, 1976). In other words, regarded from the supply side, technological progress made the biggest contribution to economic growth. In this process, the major role was played by knowledge as applied to technology, better business organisation and improvements in management practice (Sato, 1998).

Technological change may be generated indigenously by applying new ideas originating inside the country or by introducing new technology developed in other countries and applying it to the production process. To begin with, Japan relied largely on the latter. Technology was imported from other western industrialised countries, mainly by Japanese companies entering into licensing agreements with western companies. Other catching-up countries have relied more on attracting inward FDI. However, Japan strictly controlled the volume of inward investment, usually allowing western companies entry only through the establishment of a joint venture with a local firm. A further source of technology transfer occurred when Japanese scientists and engineers, who had spent time working in the West, returned home to work and brought with them knowledge acquired.

This has sometimes led westerners to criticise Japanese firms for 'copying' western ideas, rather than developing any new ideas of their own. Certainly, this was true of some of the products (consumer electronics in particular) in which Japanese companies later excelled. The modern video-cassette recorder serves as a good example. VCRs were first commercially launched in the USA by an American company, Ampex, but were suitable for professional use only. However, Sony of Japan bought the technology from Ampex and succeeded in developing a commercial product having a much wider application. The secret was to introduce a new technique that made it possible to cram a lot of viewing material on to a single small tape. Sales of the new product took off and grew rapidly. As the volume of production increased, unit costs fell making possible lower prices which households in high-income countries could afford. However, Japan's success was never simply due to imitation. Although many of the ideas used so successfully by Japanese companies originated in the West, western companies never achieved the breakthrough that their Japanese competitors managed. The secret of Japan's success appears to have been her skill in turning ideas developed in the West into mass-market products which households in high-income countries could afford. This is aptly illustrated by the example of VCRs. However, the same approach was repeated in a similar fashion in the production of a wide range of other goods (video cameras, semi-conductors, advanced colour televisions, computer displays and computer-controlled machines) for which Japan has since become famous.

Many reasons have been put forward to explain this success story. Clearly, high levels of investment in education and training have been more important. Another factor has been the importance that Japan has attached in schools and universities to engineering and scientific knowledge. In most years, Japan trains ten times as many engineers as Britain! Japanese companies have also attached more importance to research and development (R&D) than western companies. On average, more people are employed in R&D in Japanese industry than in other western industrialised countries. The level of R&D spending as a proportion of GNP does not appear much higher in Japan than in other western industrialised countries and the ratio of R&D spending to total sales is no greater than for western companies. However, such spending has been applied to greater effect.

5. An Abundant Supply of Labour

Countries can grow faster by improving the allocation of their resources, shifting resources out of activities where they are relatively unproductive and into others where they can be used more efficiently. In the early stages of growth, this can be achieved by transferring resources from the agricultural subsistence sector where productivity is generally low and into the manufacturing sector where it is much higher. At the beginning of the post-war period, Japan had a relatively large subsistence sector and was, therefore, able to enjoy rapid growth in this way. At the same time, the existence of a ready pool of labour ensured that wages in the manufacturing sector did not grow too fast and profits were kept high. In addition, because of past investment in education, the quality of the labour transferred into the new manufacturing sector was high.

Eventually, however, this source of growth dried up. Once the pool of under-employed labour from agriculture had been used up, it was not long before labour shortages began to develop causing wages to rise fast. However, because, by this time, Japan was no longer reliant on labour-intensive goods for her export success, the sharp rise in wage-rates did not impose as severe a penalty on Japan as might otherwise have been the case. Beginning in the late 1950s and early 1960s, Japan had begun to shift resources out of labour-intensive manufactures and into capital-intensive, heavy goods such as cars, shipbuilding and steel. Wage costs were less critical to success in these sectors than those on which Japan had depended for export success in the past.

6. A High Degree of Adaptability

It is often argued that a key factor in Japan's success was the high degree of structural adaptability of her economy. In order to enjoy continuous success, any economy needs to be able to adapt to changes in world demand and supply conditions. In Japan's post-war history, there have been a number of occasions where structural changes were required if Japan was to continue to grow fast. The first occurred in the late 1950s and early 1960s when world demand patterns turned against the kind of labour-intensive manufactured products such as textiles in which Japan had specialised in the past. Instead, growth appeared to favour the more capital-intensive, heavy goods industries. Beginning in 1955, the Japanese government sought to encourage increased investment in industries such as iron and steel, the heavy and chemical industries and power generation.

A second occasion was the rise in world oil prices in the mid-1970s and early 1980s. Higher oil prices were especially damaging to Japan because of her lack of any indigenous energy reserves and reliance on oil imports from the Middle East. The higher cost of oil necessitated a shift away from energy-intensive industries such as chemicals. The industries with the best prospects for fast growth were the knowledge-intensive industries such as electronics, telecommunications and information technology. As before, the government took a leading role in encouraging firms to invest in these sectors that offered the best prospects for future growth. The speed with which resources were shifted out of the energy-intensive industries meant that Japan suffered less from the second oil crisis than other developed market economies. At the same time, the emphasis placed on building up a strong competitive advantage in knowledge-intensive products meant that she was able to maintain a respectable rate of export growth at a time when world trade was growing more slowly.

7. The Role of the Government

It is sometimes argued that the greater adaptability of the Japanese economy was due to the role played by government in Japan's industrial development. In particular, attention is drawn to the role played by the Ministry of International Trade and Industry (MITI) in Japan's post-war development. Japan is often cited as a model of how government intervention can play a critical role in industrial growth. However, the kind of planning pursued in Japan differed markedly from that of a centralised, state-planned economy. Production remained in the hands of private enterprise and no attempt was made to direct industry. The role played by MITI was largely one of identifying priorities for production and investment and setting targets for each industry. These were set out in five-yearly plans for the economy. The aim was to discuss these targets with industrialists and, where appropriate to use a mixture of guidance, exhortation and coaxing to ensure that the targets were achieved.

At the beginning of the post-war period, the government made great use of financial aid (mainly in the form of low-interest loans), depreciation allowances for strategic industries, tariffs and non-tariff barriers for 'infant industries', preferential allocation of foreign exchange to priority industries and administrative guidance. The latter was a system whereby governments gave informal advice, information and instructions to businessmen to bring about changes in firms' production and investment strategies. A characteristic feature of Japan has been the close links that have always existed between industry and the state bureaucracy. These links have helped foster the implementation of state plans for industrial development.

However, it remains unclear to what extent intervention improved the performance of the Japanese economy. The Japanese have always claimed that their model of capitalism works better than its western counterpart. For several decades, the performance of the Japanese economy appeared to lend support to this. More recently, however, as growth has given way to crisis and stagnation, doubts have crept in. What is the evidence? Most observers agree that, in some industries, if not all, government intervention played a valuable role. The targeting by the MITI of key industries such as shipbuilding, steel and computers for priority treatment appeared to assist their subsequent growth. Co-operation between companies in R&D, encouraged by the authorities, may also have helped reduce duplication in investment. Import protection may have temporarily helped the development of new industries by keeping the domestic market for Japanese producers. In other cases, however, intervention has done little more than accelerate trends that would have happened anyhow through market forces. The conclusion of recent empirical work is that the main help provided by the government was in ensuring a favourable institutional and market environment within which business could function (see El-Agraa, 1997). In other words, it was the role played by the government in facilitating the operation of market forces, rather than as an alternative, that was crucial.

8. Social Harmony

For much of the post-war period, Japan was a relatively harmonious society unaffected by the industrial unrest and social instability that characterised the western industrialised countries. Some observers have attributed this to the lifetime employment system that existed in Japan and which helped workers to feel more secure. Under this system, Japanese workers enjoyed a virtual job for life. Once taken on by a company, they would be likely to stay with that company for their entire working lives. However, the counterpart of employment stability was earnings instability. As noted above, a proportionately much larger element of the take-home pay of Japanese workers consists of bonus payments that are dependent on the profitability of the firm. This means that earnings fluctuate much more in accordance with the overall state of the economy. In recession years, earnings fall but employment remains high. Japanese workers have been content to accept this situation because in return, they have job security. This, in turn, may have facilitated structural change. Workers might change jobs within the company in which they were employed, but there was no need for a period of unemployment while they changed jobs. As a result, resistance to change was weaker. On the other hand, in recent years, the Japanese lifetime employment system has been viewed as a source of weakness of the Japanese economy. Faced with declining demand for their products Japanese companies have been unable to shed labour and so have faced rising unit costs.

9. Non-Economic Factors

An important role in the process of economic growth is played by non-economic factors, including culture, religion and political systems. Clearly, factors such as these which contribute to growth are not amenable to measurement. Generally they are treated as a residual, that is, the part of growth which cannot be attributed to other quantifiable factors. Some observers have argued that the Japanese belief in Confucianism assisted growth. They argue that, because Confucianism emphasises authoritarian values (respect for elders and superiors) and the superiority of group achievements over individual success, it has created an environment favourable to economic success. Authoritarian values, it is argued, have made for greater discipline on the shop floor (fewer strikes, less industrial unrest) while group loyalty has meant a greater commitment of employees to the companies to which they belong. Japanese workers have also displayed a greater willingness to forego wage increases because loyalty to the company has over-ridden the desire for personal gain.

Box 6.1 shows the results of a quantitative study carried out to measure the contribution of different factors to Japan's post-war growth.

The End of the Japanese Miracle?

In the 1990s, Japanese growth came to an abrupt and dramatic end. What, at first, appeared to be a relatively minor slowing down of the economy, following a period of frenzied growth, has turned into a slump of a more serious magnitude. For a period lasting seven years, the Japanese economy has experienced virtual stagnation and even periods of negative growth. This has led many observers to conclude that the Japanese miracle has now ended. What, in

Box 6.1 Accounting for Japan's Post-War Growth

In neo-classical models of economic growth, economic growth is a function of three factors – increased inputs of labour (L), increased inputs of capital (K) and technical progress plus any residual factors (A). In 1976, two authors, Denison and Chung estimated the contribution of each of these factors to Japan's growth over the period 1953–71 and compared this with growth in the United States over the period 1948–69. The results are shown below:

	Japan 1953–71 Average growth-rate = 8.81%	United States 1948–69 Average growth-rate = 4.00%
Contribution of:		
Labour	1.85	1.103
Employment	1.14	1.17
Hours	0.21	−0.21
Sex, age composition	0.14	−0.10
Education	0.34	0.41
Unallocated	0.02	0.03
Capital	2.10	0.79
Inventories	0.73	0.12
Nonres. struc & equip.	1.07	0.36
Dwelling	0.30	0.28
International asset	0.00	0.03
Technological progress and residuals	4.86	1.91
Knowledge	1.97	1.19
Improved res. alloc.	0.95	0.30
Scale economies	1.94	0.42

Source: Denison and Chung (1976).

Thus, inputs of labour contributed 1.85% to Japan's growth and accounted for about 21% of her growth, less than in the US. Inputs of capital contributed 2.10% and accounted for 23.8% of her growth, slightly more than in the US. Finally, technological progress accounted for well over one-half of Japan's post-war growth or 4.86%. This compares with only 1.19% in the US. Thus, technological progress appears to have played the major role in Japan's growth in the first two decades after the war, with efficiency gains resulting from improvements in knowledge and fuller exploitation of economies of scale being the most important factors.

the past, were regarded as the peculiar strengths of the Japanese economy have come to be regarded as inherent weaknesses. Instead of Japan being regarded as the pioneer of the new, Asian model of capitalist development, she has come to be seen, increasingly, as the pariah of the developed world. What has gone wrong? Are we to conclude that the Japanese miracle is over?

In fact, long before the current crisis, economic growth had begun to slow down in Japan. As in the western industrialised world, Japan was badly hit by the oil crises of 1973–74 and, again, 1979–81. However, as was noted above, she succeeded in riding these crises more successfully than the western industrialised countries, largely due to expanding export demand. In the second half of the 1980s, however, export-led expansion came to an end. The main reason was a rapid appreciation of the Japanese yen that dramatically cut the profitability of Japanese exports. However, in the latter half of the 1980s, growth was sustained by buoyant domestic demand. Indeed, in the second half of the 1980s, Japan enjoyed her most enduring upswing of the entire post-war period! The boom was fuelled by increased consumption spending by households and large increases in capital spending by firms. This, in turn, was stimulated by a lax monetary policy that resulted in declining interest rates. Falling interest rates encouraged unwise speculation by individuals and, especially, by banks and other financial institutions in shares, securities and real estate.

The stock and property markets both boomed. Prices of financial assets and property rocketed. In all booms based on speculation, prices rise mainly because investors expect them to. For a while, these expectations prove to be self-fulfilling. However, the moment investors begin to doubt the ability of the market to ensure further increases, panic sets in. Investors begin selling, anxious to cash in their capital gain and to avoid being caught holding assets whose prices have begun falling. In the early months of 1990, share prices on the Japanese stock market ceased rising and began falling at a rapid rate. The collapse of the stock market was followed in late 1991 by a similar crash in property prices. Individuals who had invested heavily in shares or property saw the value of their assets plummet. They responded by reducing their spending on goods and services, leaving producers with mounting stocks of unsold goods. The problem was made worse by the fact that many companies, optimistic that the boom would continue for some time to come, had over-invested in increased capacity. Now, they found themselves with too much capacity. In an effort to get rid of unwanted stocks of finished goods, prices were cut. Falling prices meant declining profits. However, because many workers enjoyed lifetime employment guarantees, costs could not be immediately reduced by sacking workers. Instead, these workers experienced a sharp drop in earnings. The effect was to further reduce private consumption spending.

Unlike on previous occasions, the decline in domestic demand was not offset by increased export demand. This option was no longer available to Japan, due to the appreciation of the yen. However, the severity of the crisis was made worse by a crisis within the Japanese financial system. Much of the brunt of the stock and property market collapse was borne by Japanese banks and financial institutions, many of whom had made loans to companies and individuals against the security of assets acquired. Now, these loans could not be repaid. Several leading banks and other financial institutions found themselves in difficulty. The Japanese authorities faced a choice. On the one hand, they could allow these institutions to go bankrupt, possibly compensating depositors for all or part of their funds which they were unable to recover. However, this carried the risk that the crisis would spread to other institutions, as the confidence of depositors was undermined. Otherwise healthy financial institutions might, then, find themselves in similar difficulty and be forced to close down. On the other hand, they could intervene, bailing out bankrupt institutions, by providing both short-term liquidity and injecting capital so as to enable them to write off their bad loans. However, if this were seen by financial institutions as an assurance that the authorities would always rescue a bank unable to repay depositors, the effect would be to reduce the risk element in lending. This would, in turn, encourage such institutions to continue making bad loans with poor future prospects. This is the problem of so-called 'moral hazard'.

This latter problem mattered because the financial crisis was, in part, the result of unwise lending by banks and other financial institutions. In many cases, banks had increased their lending beyond what was prudent. Moreover, insufficient care had been given to determining the ability of borrowers (many of them companies) to repay their loans. Much lending was based on the assumption that asset prices would continue rising, while insufficient attention had been paid to what might happen if prices were to collapse. In part, too, the crisis was a responsibility of the supervisory authorities who had failed to provide an effective system for monitoring and regulating the activities of the banking sector. The crisis within the banking system caused banks to take a tougher attitude towards companies wishing to borrow money. Many companies found themselves unable to obtain new loans needed to pay debts, forcing them to make cost savings by more drastic means. For the first time since the Second World War, many Japanese workers faced the prospect of unemployment, with no welfare state to support them. The monetary authorities sought to provide more liquidity by cutting short-term interest rates. By 1998, these had reached an all-time low of 0.5%. However, given that the general price level within the economy was falling, this amounted to a somewhat higher real short-term interest rate. Moreover, there was now no further scope for cutting nominal short-term rates. This meant that, as the rate of price deflation accelerated, real interest rates, in effect, rose!

In 1992, Japan's GDP growth rate fell to 1.5% compared with 4.1% in the previous year. This was followed by two years of virtually zero growth. In 1993, GDP rose by 0.5% and, in 1994, by 0.6%. In 1995, the growth rate edged up to just over 1% and, then, in 1996, it rose to 4%. For a short while, it looked as if the crisis might be over. However, in 1997, the growth rate fell back again to under 1%. Forecasts for 1998 predict negative growth, with GDP falling by 2.6%. One factor was the crisis in East Asia, now a major market for Japanese exports. The crisis, affecting a number of important countries in the region (Thailand, Indonesia, South Korea), led to a sharp drop in output and falling incomes in these countries. This, in turn, hit demand for Japanese exports. However, the bigger problem is the reluctance of Japanese households to spend. This is despite the fact that prices of goods and services are falling. Consumer confidence has been badly shaken. Not only have many Japanese households experienced an adverse wealth effect due to the collapse of asset prices, but many workers are no longer assured of continuing employment. Monetary policy can do little to alleviate this situation, as nominal short-term rates are unable to fall any further. Instead, reliance must be placed on fiscal policy to get the economy going again. It remains to be seen whether the government can deliver a fiscal package strong enough to persuade households to increase their spending.

However, what is clear is that Japan can no longer rely upon the kind of economic growth that she enjoyed in the past. The rise of the yen has meant that Japanese exports can no longer play the lead role in Japan's growth as happened in previous decades. Instead, reliance must be placed on ensuring adequate domestic demand, if future growth is to be restored. In this respect, one can say that Japan has 'come of age'. The economic miracle of the post-war period is, surely, well and truly over. Japan can still enjoy growth rates at least equal to that of the western industrialised countries, especially if the lessons of the current crisis are correctly drawn. However, it seems unlikely that the exceptional growth rates that she enjoyed in the past can be restored.

Japan's Trading Imbalance with the Western Industrialised Countries

For much of the past forty years, relationships between Japan and her western trading partners have been fractious. At the root, the main problem has been what the West perceives to have been Japan's 'excessive' trade surplus. There have been two aspects to this. First, Japanese exports, mainly of manufactured goods, have risen at a phenomenal rate over the post-war period (see Table 6.1). Much of this has been targeted at the markets of the western industrialised countries. This has meant that certain particular branches of manufacturing within the western industrialised countries have been subject to more intense competition from abroad. The western industrialised countries have had to choose between imposing import restrictions on Japanese goods or allowing their manufacturing firms to face more competition and, where appropriate, assisting them to adjust. Second, at the same time as Japan's exports to the West have risen, her imports from the West have increased at a much slower rate. To westerners, this is seen as *de facto* evidence that the Japanese domestic market is closed to foreign goods. The West has accused Japan of trading unfairly, combining an 'aggressive' exporting strategy with a relatively 'protectionist' import policy. As the surplus grew, the impatience of the western industrialised countries increased. At first, criticism was levelled at Japan's exporting policy, not least, the excessive cheapness of Japanese goods in the West compared with the prices charged for the same goods in Japan. More recently, attention has switched to the closed nature of Japan's domestic market and the barriers, which, the West maintains, have been erected by Japan in a deliberate attempt to shut out foreign goods. Pressure on Japan to introduce measures to open up her domestic market have increased, usually with the implicit threat that a failure to do so will result in retaliatory measures being taken against Japan's exports. Is the West's criticism of Japan a justified one? Does Japan trade unfairly? In order to answer this, it is necessary to examine the nature of Japan's trading imbalance.

Background to the Problem

First, we need to put the problem into its historical perspective. The problem of Japan's trade surplus dates, approximately, from the late 1960s onwards. As we saw earlier, for the first two decades after the Second World War, the Japan's trade was in deficit and the Japanese economy was balance-of-payments-constrained. Growth often had to be curtailed because of the threat to foreign currency reserves posed by a mounting trade deficit. Moreover, in the early part of the post-war period, roughly one-half of Japan's exports went to other regions of Asia. North America and Europe were less important. Furthermore, 40% of exports comprised textile and clothing products and so threatened only one sector of manufacturing in the western industrialised countries. During the late 1950s and early 1960s, both the geographical and the commodity composition of Japanese exports changed. North America and Europe became more important as markets for Japanese goods and Asia less. Textiles and clothing declined in importance, while machinery and transport equipment, metals and metal manufacture and chemicals all grew. In short, Japan shifted from a reliance on labour-intensive, light manufactures towards specialisation in capital-intensive, heavy goods.

Of particular importance was the growing proportion of Japan's exports going to the United States. By 1970, 31% of Japan's exports went to the United States compared with 23% in 1955. This made the United States Japan's most important market. This rapid expansion of exports to the United States was not matched by an equivalent rise in Japan's imports from the United States. The result was a rise in her trade surplus with the US that reached \$3.6 billion in 1971. This more than fully accounted for the record trade deficit recorded by the United States for that year. Perhaps not surprisingly, public opinion in the US regarded Japan as the primary cause of the deterioration in the U.S. trading position. An obvious reason for this surplus was the relative cheapness of the yen relative to the U.S. dollar. At this time, most countries were operating the Bretton Woods system of exchange rates set up after the Second World War. (Box 6.2. provides a summary of key events in the development of the post-war international monetary system.) Under this regime, countries were required to keep fluctuations within 1% either side of their par values expressed in terms of U.S. dollars. Although these par values could be adjusted upwards or downwards in the event of a persistent disequilibrium in a country's balance of payments, in practice, parities were rarely changed and,

Box 6.2 The Evolution of the Post-War International Monetary System

The post-war international monetary system was set up at the Bretton Woods Conference of 1944 and was known as the Bretton Woods system. Its main features were:

- All currencies to be eventually freely convertible
- All currencies to have fixed central (par) values in terms of the U.S. dollar
- Currencies to fluctuate by no more than plus or minus 1% of their central values
- Central rates to be adjusted in the event of a 'fundamental disequilibrium' in a country's balance of payments
- Gold to have a fixed price in terms of the U.S. dollar of \$35 an ounce
- IMF created to lend foreign currency to countries experiencing balance of payments diffuculties
- Scarce currencies to be rationed if drawings from the IMF became excessive.

Continued

This system worked moderately well for the first two decades following the ending of World War II. However, it began to experience difficulties in the 1960s for several reasons:

- It was too rigid: exchange-rates were not changed sufficiently to reflect changes in the competitiveness of different countries
- Speculators enjoyed a one-way bet whenever currencies became under- or over-valued
- Reserve currency countries (US and UK) could not easily devalue their currencies if faced with a balance of payments deficit
- Gold had a fixed price in terms of the U.S. dollar which encouraged holders of gold to hoard gold
- Adequate world liquidity could only be ensured by reserve currency countries running current account deficits, that is, exporting capital to the rest of the world.
- Reserve currency countries enjoyed 'seigniorage rights' allowing them to pay for balance of payments deficits by printing more money.

In 1971, in response to continuing speculative pressure, President Nixon temporarily suspended the convertibility of dollars into gold and imposed a 10% tariff surcharge on imports. Because of the uncertainty that these measures created, several countries temporarily floated their currencies. Fixed exchange rates were restored under the Smithsonian Agreement of December 1971, but with wider bands (plus or minus 2.25%).

However, the new parities did not last long and, in the years that followed, most countries switched to a floating exchange rate system. In December 1973, the U.S. dollar was floated. In April 1976, the IMF's articles were amended to legalise floating exchange rates. Although the member states of the European Community sought to maintain stable exchange rates among themselves, most other countries allowed the exchange rate to find its own level and did not intervene in the foreign exchange market.

However, in September 1985, it was recognised that, as a result of speculative pressure, several currencies had become badly misaligned. Meeting at the Plaza Hotel in New York, the G7 agreed to engage in co-ordinated intervention to reduce the value of the U.S. dollar and increase the value of the Japanese yen. Two years later, meeting at the Louvre in Paris, it was agreed that the dollar had fallen far enough. Instead, intervention was aimed at maintaining the value of the dollar within agreed reference levels.

However, when share prices fell dramatically on the U.S. stock market in October 1987, the dollar fell and no attempt was made to prevent this. The U.S. authorities chose not to raise short-term interest rates for fear that this would put an undue squeeze on domestic liquidity. There was a brief attempt to re-establish a reference range for currencies in December, but with greater freedom to allow fluctuations outside the prescribed margins. In practice, the monetary authorities were not prepared to subordinate domestic monetary policy to the task of keeping currencies within the agreed limits. Instead, currencies were left free to find their own levels in response to market forces.

then, only after long intervals. The par value for the yen had remained unchanged from the time that the system was set up. Yet, it was clear that the parity deemed appropriate in the immediate aftermath of the War was no longer the right one, given the increase in the competitiveness of Japanese goods that had happened since. Rapid productivity growth combined with modest increases in wage rates had reduced unit labour costs in Japan relative to the United States, resulting in a substantial fall in the real value of the yen against the U.S. dollar.

As the U.S. trade deficit increased, the U.S. dollar came under speculative attack as investors anticipated a devaluation of the U.S. dollar. Along with the German mark, the Japanese yet looked a prime candidate for a sizeable revaluation. In fact, because the U.S. dollar was the representative or 'pivot' currency under the Bretton Woods system, it could only be devalued by other countries re-valuing their currencies against the U.S. dollar. Countries with strong currencies were, however, reluctant to re-value which would have reduced the profitability of their export industries. Moreover, they regarded the U.S. deficit as the result of a failure of the US to curb over-expansion of demand at home and escessive expenditures abroad. In August, 1971, in an effort to force the hand of surplus countries such as Japan, President Nixon introduced a temporary 10% tariff surcharge on all imports and suspended convertibility of dollars into gold. (Under the Bretton Woods Agreement of 1944, the United States undertook to sell gold to holders of dollars at the official price of $35 per ounce of gold, thereby ensuring that dollars were fully convertible into gold at a fixed price. Since all other currencies adopted fixed par values for their currencies against the dollar, this ensured that all currencies had a value, which was fixed against gold. This was seen as necessary to create confidence in the post-war world monetary system. However, the U.S. balance of payments deficits of the late 1950s and early 1960s led to a build-up of dollar liabilities outside the US. As these came to exceed U.S. gold reserves, speculators sought to switch dollars into gold in the expectation that the official gold price would soon be raised.) Most countries responded to the Nixon measures by temporarily floating their currencies.

Figure 6.1 Yen–dollar market exchange-rate

As was to be expected, the Japanese yen appreciated strongly against the U.S. dollar. In December 1971, under the *Smithsonian Agreement*, however, fixed exchange rates were temporarily restored. The dollar was substantially devalued in terms of all other currencies including the yen. (The Agreement also established new wider bands of fluctuation for currencies amounting to ±2.25% instead of ±1% under the Bretton Woods Agreement.) As it turned out, the attempt to restore fixed exchange rates did not last long. Further outbreaks of currency speculation led most countries to re-introduce floating exchange rates. In February 1973 the U.S. dollar was floated, bringing to a decisive end the post-war system of fixed exchange rates. The new freedom which floating rates brought did result in a substantial nominal appreciation of the yen against the U.S. dollar. Figure 6.1 charts the course of the yen–dollar rate over the period since 1970. From Y360 to the dollar in 1970, the yen rose to Y210 in 1978. However, this did not result in a significant correction of the Japanese surplus as might have been expected. Table 6.3 shows the development of the Japanese trade balance over the period after 1972.

Although there was a fall in the surplus between 1972–1974, this was entirely due to the rise in world oil prices that increased Japan's import bill measured in dollar terms. If

Table 6.3 Japan's Balance of Payments, 1972–1994 ($ billion)

Year	*Trade balance*	*Services and transfers (net)*	*Current balance*	*Long-term capital*	*Overall balance*
1972	+8.94	−2.3	+6.64	−4.35	+2.85
1973	+3.64	−3.76	−0.13	−3.35	−6.35
1974	+1.35	−6.07	−4.72	+5.98	+1.25
1975	+4.94	−5.61	−0.68	+0.53	−0.59
1976	+9.8	−6.11	+3.71	−0.05	+3.80
1977	+17.16	−6.25	+10.91	−4.96	+6.48
1978	+24.30	−7.76	+16.54	−6.7	+9.96
1979	+1.74	−10.48	−8.74	−6.82	+13.14
1980	+2.13	−12.88	−10.75	+18.88	+5.03
1981	+19.96	−15.19	+4.77	−1.56	+3.64
1982	+18.08	−11.23	+6.85	−16.2	−4.7
1983	+31.46	−10.66	+20.8	−21.32	+1.55
1984	+44.26	−9.26	+35.0	−36.57	+2.12
1985	+55.99	−6.82	+49.17	−53.53	−0.58
1986	+92.82	−6.99	+85.83	−73.42	−14.84
1987	+96.42	−9.4	+87.02	−45.37	+37.94
1988	+95.00	−15.39	+79.61	−66.22	+16.52
1989	+76.89	−19.9	+56.99	−47.93	−12.76
1990	+63.58	−27.71	+35.87	−43.60	−7.20
1991	+103.00	−27.8	+72.9	+37.10	+76.4
1992	+132.30	−30.1	+117.6	−28.5	+71.6
1993	+141.50	−14.8	+131.4	−78.3	+38.4
1994	+145.9	−10.1	+129.1	−82.0	+20.4

Sources : IMF Financial Statistics.

services and transfers are included, the current balance moved briefly into deficit in 1973. However, this was short-lived. By 1978, the surplus had risen to $16.54 billion. Although Japanese exporters found exporting to the US somewhat less profitable because of the depreciation of the dollar, this was not the case when exporting to Western Europe. Thus, efforts were stepped up in selling goods to West European markets where Japanese exports remained relatively cheap. Whereas in 1967, Europe took only 16% of Japan's exports, by 1979, the share had risen to 19%. Between 1970 and 1980 Japan's exports to the European Community increased ten times. However, EC exports to Japan increased only five times. By 1980, Japan had a trade surplus with the EC of $11.1 billion. The problem was acutely depicted by the imbalance of trade in motor cars. In 1981 Japan imported from the EC only one car for every nine which she exported (Wilkinson, 1983).

The onslaught of the second oil crisis did result in another decline in the Japanese surplus. Indeed, as after the first oil crisis, the current balance swung into deficit. In 1980, Japan recorded a current account deficit of $10.75 billion. However, this did not last long. When oil prices subsequently started to fall, Japan benefited and the deficit turned into a healthy surplus once again. At the same time, Japanese exporters enjoyed a significant increase in their competitiveness on account of a fall in the value of the yen. Between 1978 and 1985, the yen depreciated from Y210 to 250 yen to the dollar. (The depreciation in the real exchange rate was greater since unit labour costs in Japan fell relative to those in the US.) The fall in the yen made Japanese goods cheaper in western markets and western goods more expensive in Japan. Hence, the trade surplus rose reaching a record $55.99 billion in 1985. The reason for the depreciation of the yen is apparent from an examination of the capital account of the balance of payments in Table 6.3. A negative sign indicates that Japan was experiencing a large net outflow of long-term capital. Since much of this capital was invested in the United States, the effect was to increase the supply of yen and increase the demand for dollars on the foreign exchange markets, driving the yen down in value against the U.S. dollar. This point is discussed further below.

It meant that exchange rates were moving in the opposite direction to that required to achieve current account equilibrium. This is a case of what economists call 'exchange-rate perversity'. In September 1985, the leaders of the top five trading nations of the world, the so-called 'Group of Five' or G5 (the United States, United Kingdom, West Germany, France and Japan), meeting in September 1985 at the Plaza Hotel in New York for their annual economic summit, agreed to a policy of co-ordinated intervention on the foreign exchange markets to bring about a re-alignment of rates. The aim was to engage in a joint selling of dollars and buying of yen, sufficient to force the dollar down and the yen up. The *Plaza Accord* signalled the end of the policy of 'benign neglect' that had operated since the abandonment of fixed exchange rates in the early 1970s. In the next two years, the dollar depreciated sharply against the yen. By the time of the meeting of the G5 at the Louvre in Paris in February 1987, the yen had risen to Y144 to the dollar. It was agreed that sufficient adjustment had, by then, taken place. Hence, as part of the *Louvre Accord,* it was agreed that the aim of subsequent intervention should be to stabilise the yen–dollar rate at its new level.

However, despite the fact that the yen had appreciated against the U.S. dollar, the Japanese trade surplus continued to rise. By 1987 it had reached a new high of over $96 billion, of which roughly three-quarters was accounted for by Japan's trade with the United States. One reason for this is the so-called '*J*-curve' effect familiar to students of international economics. An appreciation should reduce the *volume* of Japanese exports and increase the *volume* of Japanese imports, since the prices of Japanese goods have risen in foreign currency terms and the prices of imports to Japan have fallen in yen terms. However, if the demand for Japanese exports is price-elastic, the *value* of goods exported abroad measured in dollar terms will increase following appreciation, serving to increase the size of the surplus. Since demand is always more inelastic in the short run, the current account surplus often tends to rise following an appreciation of the currency before it falls. This is accentuated by the fact that the demand for imports is also more price inelastic in the short run. (The value of imports measured in foreign currency terms, however, will tend to rise following appreciation.) Other factors, too, may explain why the surplus did not, at first, fall as the yen rose in value. To begin with, an appreciation of the exchange rate lowers the costs of raw materials imported from abroad, in part offsetting the fall in the price which exporters receive on every unit exported abroad. Also, Japanese companies responded to the higher yen by moving up-market into higher quality, higher value-added goods where non-price factors such as quality are more important.

Eventually, however, the dearer yen did lead to a decline in Japan's trade surplus. By 1990, this had fallen to $64 billion. The boom in the Japanese economy experienced between 1986–91 also helped reduce the surplus by increasing demand for imports. Consumers began to buy more foreign goods. At the same time, manufacturing industry needed to import more raw materials from abroad. However, when, in 1991, the Japanese economy moved into recession, this worked in the opposite direction. Import demand fell and the surplus increased once again. By 1994, it had reached a record $145.9 billion. The problem was aggravated by the fact that the yen, having risen strongly for several years, then began to weaken once again. In 1995, the yen hit an all time high of Y80 to the dollar and there was even talk of a further rise to Y50. Instead, over the course of the next three years, it depreciated steadily reaching Y121 in November 1998. By September 1998, the trade surplus stood at $119.3 billion.

The Structure of Japan's Trade

A detailed analysis of Japan's trade with the rest of the world reveals a number of distinct features. Table 6.4 shows the *commodity composition* of Japan's exports and imports. Whereas Japan's exports are made up almost entirely (97.6%) of *manufactures*, more than one-half her imports comprise *food, raw materials* and *fuels*. This is due to Japan's notorious deficiency in natural resources and indigenous energy reserves. Over 90% of her energy requirements have to be met by imports. Demand for vital natural resources such as iron, copper, lead, zinc, etc. has to be largely satisfied through trade. To pay for these imports, Japan must export mainly manufactured goods. Until the late 1970s, about 75% of Japan's imports consisted of primary products. Since then, the proportion of her imports constituting manufactures has risen significantly. Nevertheless, it remains below that of the western industrialised countries. On the export side, a comparatively small number of manufacturing product groups account for a high proportion of exports. Thus, *office and telecommunications equipment* accounts for 24% of total exports, and *automotive products* for 21%.

One way in which economists can measure the degree of specialisation of a country in particular product groups is to compile an index of so-called 'revealed comparative advantage'

Table 6.4 The Commodity Composition of Japan's Exports and Imports, 1994 (percentage)

	Exports	*Imports*
Agricultural products	1.0	24.7
Mining products	1.4	24.1
fuels	–	17.5
Iron and steel	3.8	1.5
Chemicals	6.0	7.2
Other semi-manufactures	4.5	4.9
Power generating machinery	1.4	0.8
Other non-electrical machinery	12.9	2.6
Office and telecommunications equipment	23.9	8.3
Electrical machinery and apparatus	6.7	2.3
Automotive products	20.8	3.1
Other transport equipment	6.2	1.9
Textiles	6.8	5.2
Clothing	0.1	5.6
Other consumer goods	7.5	9.1
Total	100.0	100.0

Source : GATT (1995).

Table 6.5 Patterns of Export and Import Specialisation in Japan, the United States and Germany, 1994 (percentage)

	Japan	*United States*	*Germany*
Agricultural products	0.08	1.10	0.59
Mining products	0.13	0.36	0.32
Iron and steel	1.28	0.26	1.11
Chemicals	0.63	1.10	1.45
Other semi-manufactures	0.57	0.70	1.05
Office and telecommunications equipment	2.07	1.34	0.51
Automotive products	2.17	1.01	1.73
Other machinery and transport equipment	1.53	1.36	1.50
Textiles	0.55	0.41	0.96
Clothing	0.03	0.32	0.46
Other consumer goods	0.82	1.07	0.97
Standard deviation	0.7652	0.4213	0.4641

Source : Based on GATT (1995).

(RCA). This measures the share of a product group (e.g. automotive products) in a country's total exports divided by the share of the product group in world exports. In Table 6.5, this is calculated for Japan and for two other advanced industrialised economies, the United States and Germany. A value greater than one indicates that a country has a higher share of world exports for that particular product group than for total exports. The higher the value, the greater the degree of specialisation. In the final row, the standard deviation has been estimated to show the spread of these values between the extremes of low and high specialisation. A high standard deviation indicates a high degree of specialisation in a relatively small number of product groups. It is apparent from Table 6.5 that Japan has a very high degree of export specialisation in two sectors – namely, automotive products, office and telecommunications equipment. Moreover, the index of specialisation for these two sectors is higher than for the sectors in which the other two countries do well. For example, the United States' highest value is 1.36 for 'other machinery and transport equipment', while Germany's highest value is 1.73 for automotive products. The standard deviation for Japan is also much higher than for the United States or Germany.

Next let us consider the *geographical composition* of Japan's trade. Table 6.6 shows the geographical destination of her exports and source of her imports. Just over 40% of both imports and exports are with the rest of the Asian region. Over the post-war period, the share of Japan's exports going to Asia fell as other markets in the western industrialised countries became more important. However, in the last thirty years, the Asian region has again become more important. Japan's main trading partner is still the United States, which accounts for 30% of Japanese exports and 23% of imports. The share of her exports going to the United States has risen steadily over the post-war period from roughly 20% in 1954. Since a much smaller proportion of Japan's imports come from the United States, Japan enjoys a large surplus on her trade with the US. Indeed, the surplus with the US accounts for nearly one-half of the entire Japanese surplus! This shows that the problem of the Japanese trade surplus is in part a bilateral one.

Finally, Europe takes 17.1% of Japanese exports, the bulk going to the European Union. In the earlier part of the post-war period, the share of Japanese exports going to Europe rose,

Table 6.6 The Geographical Composition of Japan's Trade and Her Trade Balance with Different Regions, 1994 (percentage)

	Exports	*Imports*	*Trade balance (Billion $)*
North America	31.5	26.3	+52.35
United States	30.0	23.0	+55.42
Latin America	3.1	3.3	+3.37
Western Europe	16.6	15.7	+22.55
European Union	14.6	12.9	+22.11
Central/Eastern Europe/f.USSR	0.5	1.5	−2.17
Africa	1.2	1.5	+0.83
Middle East	2.5	10.1	−17.75
Asia	42.6	41.6	+54.69
China	4.7	10.0	−8.79
South Korea	6.1	4.9	+10.83
Chinese Taipei	6.0	3.9	+13.10
Hong Kong	6.5	0.8	+23.57
Total	100.0	100.0	+120.86

Source : GATT (1995).

but, in the last fifteen years, this has fallen slightly. The most striking difference between imports and exports is the much greater importance of the Middle East in Japan's imports, with whom Japan runs a significant trade deficit. Japan's imports from other natural resource producing countries such as Australia and Canada are also relatively high. To pay for her deficit with these countries, Japan has to earn a surplus on her trade with the United States and Western Europe.

A particular feature of Japan's trade, to which attention was drawn in Chapter 3, was the relatively low importance of intra-industry trade in total trade. For 1990, the average level of intra-industry trade for Japan was found to be 58% compared with 83% for the United States, 73% for Germany, 79% for the United Kingdom, 77% for France and 66% for Italy (Noland, 1995). This is consistent with the observation made above that Japan has a relatively high degree of specialisation in a relatively small number of manufacturing industries. These exports are then exchanged for either primary commodities (food, raw materials or fuels) or the products of different manufacturing industries. This is inter-industry specialisation. By way of contrast, the trade of the other advanced industrialised countries is characterised more by an exchange of manufactures for manufactures that in many cases belong to the same industry. This is intra-industry specialisation. As we shall see in Chapter 8, intra-industry specialisation invariably gives rise to fewer adjustment problems than inter-industry specialisation and, therefore, leads to less friction among countries than when inter-industry specialisation is the norm. The fact, therefore, that Japan's specialisation in her trade with the West has tended towards inter- rather than intra-industry specialisation may account for some of the frictions that have arisen between herself and her western trading partners.

How can we account for the much lower level of intra-industry specialisation in Japan? Part of the answer must lie in the fact that Japan imports large amounts of natural resources that have to be paid for by exporting manufactures. However, even within the manufacturing sector, Japan has tended to specialise in a comparatively small number of sectors. This may be the lagged result of the relatively low stage of economic development from which she began the post-war period. We saw in Chapter 3 that countries at a lower stage of development have lower levels of intra-industry trade. Where households have low average incomes, consumers demand less variety. Hence, producers tend to specialise more in standardised as opposed to differentiated goods. Since intra-industry trade is more common in differentiated goods than standardised goods industries, her trade is more inter- than intra-industry. If it is true that the Japanese domestic market has been relatively closed to foreign manufactures, this may also explain Japan's relatively low intra-industry trade. Another factor may also have been the relative cheapness of the Japanese yen for much of the post-war period. A cheap yen may have encouraged Japanese exporters to concentrate on standardised, low value-added goods that sell largely on the basis of price. These goods tend to be produced by industries in which inter- rather than intra-industry specialisation prevails.

Clearly, however, many of these conditions are changing. Today Japan has a per capita income that is among the highest in the world, although the high propensity of Japanese households to save means that consumption per head is low. Higher average incomes should mean greater demand for variety in which case more of Japan's trade will assume the form of intra-industry trade. At the same time, in response to western pressure (see below), the Japanese domestic market is becoming more open to imported manufactures, although the share remains lower than for the western industrialised economies. Finally, the era of the cheap yen is over. One consequence of the appreciation of the yen since the mid-1980s has been a tendency for Japanese exporters to move up-market into higher quality, higher value-added goods. Since these are produced by industries in which intra-industry specialisation is high, the importance of intra-industry trade in Japan's total trade can be expected to increase. On the other hand, should the yen weaken further, this tendency could be reversed. As was noted earlier, in recent years, due largely to the recession and the low level of real short-term interest rates, the yen has weakened significantly.

Finally, we turn to Japan's trade in *services*. These are recorded in the invisibles part of the Current Account of the Balance of Payments. As can be seen in Table 6.3, Japan has consistently run a large deficit on invisibles and, hence, must earn a surplus on her merchandise (visibles) trade to achieve overall Current Account balance. Traditionally, Japan's deficit on invisibles has been due to four factors. First, the need to make payments of royalties and fees to overseas companies for foreign technology acquired under licensing agreements. Second, the need to pay investment income to foreign companies operating in Japan, mainly under joint ventures. This exceeded any income received by Japanese MNCs with subsidiaries overseas. Third, a deficit from tourism and travel as more Japanese took holidays abroad than foreigners in Japan. Fourth, a deficit on transport and shipping. As was noted earlier, Japan was a 'catching-up' country for much of the post-war period. Any 'catching-up' country tends to import capital and technology from abroad and so runs a deficit on invisibles. However, once a country has caught up, payments of royalties and fees and investment income to foreign companies begin to decline. Indeed, the country in question may eventually become a net recipient of income from abroad, as its own companies establish subsidiaries abroad. In Japan, the investment income account moved into surplus in 1980. As Japan increasingly became a net investor of long-term capital abroad (see Table 6.3), earnings from assets held abroad came to exceed payments made on assets held in Japan. At the same time, payments of royalties and fees for imported western technology began to fall, as Japan became less dependent on imported technology. Indeed, as Japanese companies became major innovators in their own right, earnings from 'know-how' sold abroad increased. Nevertheless, as can be seen in Table 6.3, Japan continues to run a deficit on invisibles, due mainly to the deficit on tourism and on transport and shipping.

Japan's Import Barriers: How Open is the Japanese Market?

In recent years in particular, western criticism has focused on the relatively low proportion of total domestic consumption of manufactured goods in Japan that is accounted for by imports. In 1990, the share of imports in domestic consumption was 5.9% in Japan compared with 15.3% in the United States, 15.4% in Germany, 17.7% in the UK, 13.7% in France and 12.6% in Italy (Noland, 1995). Moreover, whereas in most other industrialised countries the share of imports in domestic consumption has risen over the post-war period, in Japan it has hardly changed and never exceeded 6%. One explanation for this may be the fact that Japan is a capital-abundant, yet resource-scarce, country and, therefore, must of necessity export manufactures in exchange for natural resources. An alternative explanation is that, as is often claimed in the West, the Japanese market remains relatively closed to foreign goods. What is the evidence?

Certainly, with regard to tariffs, there are hardly any grounds for arguing that the Japanese domestic market is a protected one. Japan's average import tariff is among the lowest in the world. Before the Uruguay Round, Japan's trade-weighted average tariff for industrial goods was 3.9%, lower than that of the US (4.6%) or the European Union (5.7%). Once the reductions agreed in the Uruguay Round have been implemented, Japan's tariff average will fall to 1.7%. Of course, a low average tariff may still disguise high tariffs on particular goods. Nor has it always been true that Japanese tariffs were low. When, in 1955, Japan acceded to the GATT, her high levels of tariff protection were one of the reasons why some countries were unwilling to extend to her full GATT rights. However, in the decades that followed, Japan progressively lowered her tariffs on industrial goods, although protection has remained high in agriculture.

Are foreign products excluded by a relatively high level of non-tariff protection? Non-tariff barriers (NTBs) include a wide range of different kinds of measures, including import quotas, customs valuation procedures, technical regulations and standards, lengthy testing procedures for products, discriminatory government procurement policies and direct or indirect subsidies to domestic producers (see Chapter 8 for a discussion of non-tariff protectionism). Attempts to quantify the importance of NTBs show these to be no higher in the case of Japan than in other advanced industrialised countries. For example, Laird and Yeats (1990) estimated that, using a relatively broad definition of NTBs, 36.9% of Japanese imports were covered by one kind of NTB or another and 43.5% were affected (see Chapter 8). Although a much lower proportion of U.S. imports (16%) and EC imports (29.8%) were covered by NTBs, a higher proportion (45 and 54.1% respectively) were affected. The more subtle and non-quantifiable, informal or 'hidden' barriers that restrict imports may be more of a problem. Especially important in this regard are the bureaucratic controls that restrict access for foreign products to the Japanese market. It is a frequent complaint of western exporters that exports are held up by excessive 'red tape' for example, lengthy testing procedures, complex customs formalities, long delays at points of entry, etc. It is argued that, because Japan relies relatively more on bureaucratic regulation, it is easier for well-organised producer groups to exert pressure to keep out foreign products. Certainly, there now exists some case study evidence to show that bureaucratic intervention has been an important factor in limiting foreign imports (see Balassa and Noland, 1988).

The precise nature of the impediment to foreign entry may tend to be specific to particular industries. For example, in the Computer Industry, discriminatory public procurement has been identified as a problem. It is argued that government bodies frequently favour Japanese firms over domestic firms when purchasing equipment or awarding contracts. In the automobile industry, excessively strict and discriminatory technical regulations and standards were seen as creating a barrier to foreign goods. In a recent dispute concerning photographic film, Kodak of the United States complained that penetration of the Japanese market was impossible because of anti-competitive practices by its main rival, Fujitsu. Specifically, Fujitsu imposed conditions on distributors that prevented distributors from selling Kodak film. In this case, the barrier that existed arose because of the failure of the public authorities to act against the anti-competitive practices of a local firm. For much of the post-war period, Japan lacked an anti-trust policy such as existed in the United States and other western industrialised countries. It was frequently argued that Japanese firms could impose restrictions that made it difficult for foreign firms to gain entry. In response to western pressure, Japan has now introduced its own Fair Competition Law. However, western firms still complain that restrictions on competition exist because the Law is only weakly enforced.

A characteristic of the Japanese market which inhibits competition is the so-called *keirestu* system linking companies together in complex networks or corporate webs. It is argued that firms that belong to the same group, act out of loyalty to other members of the group, in effect discriminating against foreign firms that are regarded as outsiders. Three different kinds of *keiretsu* exist in Japan:

1. *Production keiretsu.* Each is made up of one core firm plus its subsidiaries with a centralised system of decision making. The main aim of a production *keiretsu* is to establish efficient relations between parent company and suppliers. Through such arrangements, Japan pioneered her now famous 'just-in-time' system of production that enabled producers to reduce the amount of working capital tied up in inventories of components, while ensuring reliable delivery of components combined with quality control. It is argued that such arrangements discriminate against outsiders, although those discriminated against may equally well include Japanese firms that do not belong to the *keiretsu*.
2. *Financial keiretsu.* These link together a number of companies through a system of cross-stockholdings dominated by a main bank that provides capital to the members of the group. Cross-stockholdings have been estimated by the Nomura Research Institute (NRI) to account for roughly 29% of the total stock market in Japan (Dawkins, 1994). Japan claims that these arrangements make for stable customised relationships between lenders and borrowers allowing banks to minimise the costs of monitoring the performance of borrowers and borrowers to obtain capital easily and more cheaply (Yoshitomi, 1990). Furthermore, they are thought to promote more 'long-termism' in corporate strategies for investment and R&D expenditure. On the other hand, foreigners complain that these arrangements protect Japanese companies from hostile take-over bids by foreign firms.
3. *Distribution keiretsu.* Under these arrangements, producers of mass consumer goods establish a distribution network for their goods by integrating wholesalers and retailers in a single vertical chain often using anti-competitive practices that would be illegal in most western industrialised countries. Japanese argue that these arrangements bring efficiency gains by preventing other distributors from 'free-riding' on a manufacturer's nation-wide advertising (Yoshitomi, 1990). On other hand, they also lead to price-fixing arrangements whereby oligopolistic manufacturers are able to enforce high minimum prices by preventing entry by new producers.

Westerners argue that the dominance of the *keiretsus* renders the Japanese market less contestable than in western industrialised countries. Not only does this create a structural barrier for western firms exporting to Japan, it may also give rise to unfair competition when Japanese firms export to western markets. Specifically, if Japanese firms are able to operate a cartel in the Japanese market, they can use the high profits made on domestic sales to sell the same goods at a much lower price abroad. At the same time, non-tariff barriers restrict imports preventing the re-export of these goods back to Japan. This is the practice of 'dumping', which we discuss in more detail in Chapter 8. The fact that Japanese companies have often being the target of dumping complaints by firms in the western industrialised countries appears to support this argument. Japan has argued that the Japanese market is no less contestable than in the West. Such empirical evidence as exists does not show prices in Japan for the same product to be any higher than abroad. A survey covering 122 products was conducted in October 1989 jointly by the U.S. Department of Commerce and the MITI in Japan. This found that 29 products out of 50 of Japanese origin sold at higher prices in the US than in Japan while 21 sold at lower prices (Yoshitomi, 1990). Some economists also argue that the methods used in western anti-dumping policy for measuring the margin of dumping, exaggerate the true amount of dumping taking place (Hindley, 1988).

With regard to imports, a particular concern of western firms is the entry-deterring effect of the *keiretsu* system. It is argued that the long-term relationship which exists between core firms and their component suppliers make entry by foreign firms more difficult. Equally, the control exercised by Japanese companies over the distribution system may give rise to an effective entry barrier. The problem is made worse by the Japanese retail system with the preponderance of a large number of very small retailers. Small retail stores employing less than five people are estimated to account for 57% of all retail stores in Japan compared with 3% in the United States and 5% in the United Kingdom (Wagstyl, 1989). The main reason for this is the protection which small shopkeepers have enjoyed under the Japanese *Large-Scale Retail Store Law*. Under this Law, retailers who wished to open shops bigger than 500 square meters had to get the approval of local residents and shopkeepers beforehand. If the shop was to be larger than 1,500 square meters, they had to get the permission of MITI. The existence of many small shops is thought to give greater power to manufacturers to enforce high prices and exclude the products of other sellers, particularly foreign ones. Large retail stores have more shelf space to stock foreign goods.

On the other hand, examples can be found of western firms that have been very successful in penetrating the Japanese market. Coca Cola has managed to win 60% of the market for soft drinks in Japan by setting up its own distribution system. Schick, the safety razor manufacturer, used a distribution agreement with Hattori Seiko, the watch and calculator manufacturer, to secure 70% of the market. In the automobile industry, while U.S. companies have found it difficult to make headway, BMW of Germany succeeded by setting up its own dealer network in place of reliance on local agents (Wagstyl, 1989). However, some empirical support for the argument that *keiretsus* render entry for foreign firms more difficult is provided by studies carried out of the buying behaviour of Japanese companies. For example, Lawrence (1991) compared the buying patterns of *keiretsu* with those of non-*keiretsu* Japanese companies and found that *keiretsus* were less likely to buy foreign goods. However, there is some evidence that the *keiretsu* system is beginning to change in response to increased global competition (Dawkins, 1994). The deep recession of recent years is forcing Japanese companies to seek new ways of being more efficient. This is resulting in a greater openness to doing business with foreign partners, a reduction in the importance of cross-shareholdings following the collapse of the equity market and a broadening of purchasing patterns with more buying of components and parts outside the group. In the future, a key issue will be the willingness of the Japanese authorities to enact and enforce tougher laws to prosecute Japanese firms for anti-competitive practices.

In an attempt to secure a lowering of Japan's structural barriers, the United States began in

1989 a series of bilateral talks with Japan that came to be known as the *Structural Impediments Initiative* (SII). A motive behind the talks was undoubtedly the desire of the U.S. administration to avert a threat by U.S. Congress of retaliation against Japan unless Japan took steps to open up her domestic market to U.S. goods. Three years earlier the US negotiated an agreement with Japan governing semi-conductors, in which Japan undertook to increase the U.S. share of Japan's domestic market and in which both countries agreed not to sell microchips below a stipulated price both in the US and third markets. The SII resulted in an agreement in which Japan agreed to take action in a number of sectors with a view to increasing the share of foreign manufactures in her domestic market. Among the large number of actions agreed were measures to ensure a tougher approach towards anti-competitive practices by Japanese firms.

In 1993, following the election of Bill Clinton to the U.S. Presidency, the SII talks were replaced with a new set of so-called *Framework Negotiations*. Unlike the SII, these involved an attempt by the US to commit Japan to specific numerical targets for expanding the share of imports in sectors where it was felt that import penetration was especially low. This was inspired by the apparent success of the Semi-Conductor Agreement (SCTA) in raising the share of imports to 20% of the Japanese market. The SCTA was unique in being the first time that two countries had signed an agreement in which an importing country agreed to import more of a particular product from an exporting country. Bhagwati (1988) introduced the term 'voluntary import expansion' (VIE) to describe this kind of managed trade and to contrast it with the more common phenomenon of a 'voluntary export restraint' (VER). (See Chapter 8 for a discussion of VER.) Sectors in which the US sought to secure such agreements included public procurement of telecommunications, medical technology, insurance and the market for cars and car parts. In October 1994, after a series of tense negotiations, in which the US threatened retaliation against Japanese exports if its demands were not met, agreements covering most of the sectors in question were concluded. However, the US was forced to abandon its earlier insistence on so-called 'numerical targets' and settle for more general commitments to import expansion. A dispute concerning automobiles and automotive parts, however, dragged on until June 1995, when an agreement was reached that narrowly averted a threat of retaliatory tariffs by the US against Japanese goods.

If the Japanese home market is protected, are the western industrialised countries justified in pressing Japan to open up her market? Perhaps, but it is by no means certain that liberalisation would result in the western industrialised countries exporting more manufactures to Japan. The reason is that Japan's comparative advantage lies in manufacturing and her import protection is actually strongest towards agriculture. By way of contrast, the US has a strong comparative advantage in agriculture and her import protection is relatively more biased towards manufacturing. Saxonhouse (1986) has shown that, for these reasons, any lowering of Japanese tariffs and non-tariff barriers would paradoxically benefit U.S. agriculture and not manufacturing. If both countries were to establish free trade with each other, each country would expand its exports of the products in which it enjoys a comparative advantage. This would favour U.S. agricultural exports and Japanese manufactured exports. However, if services are included, the outcome is different because Japan applies relatively greater protection to her services sector than the US. In this case, trade liberalisation would favour U.S. services. Nevertheless, manufacturing exports would still fall and not increase. Saxonhouse argues that the Japanese current account surplus is essentially a *macroeconomic* not a *microeconomic* phenomenon. That is to say, it is the expression of an imbalance between 'aggregates' in the national economy of the two countries, not the result of restrictions placed on the import of particular products. It is to this issue which we must now turn.

The Macroeconomic Determinants of the Japanese Trade Surplus

To understand the macroeconomic determinants of a country's Current Account Balance of Payments, it is necessary to rehearse some simple macroeconomic relationships. In any economy, the level of national output (Gross National Product or GNP) can be measured either (a) by the amount spent on buying the goods and services produced (gross national expenditure or GNE) or (b) by the income which factors of production have derived from producing goods and services (gross national income or GNI). From this, two important accounting relationships can be established. The first is that national output (Y) must be equal to the level of national expenditure (E). The latter comprises consumption spending (C), investment spending (I), government spending (G) and exports (X) minus imports (M). Therefore, we can write:

$$Y = C + I + G + X - M \qquad (1)$$

The second is that national output (Y) must also be equal to the amount of income consumed by households (C), the amount of income saved by households (S) and the amount of income paid in taxes (T). This gives the following expression:

$$Y = C + S + T \qquad (2)$$

Putting (1) and (2) together, we obtain the following:

$$I + G + X - M = S + T \qquad (3)$$

We can rewrite this as follows:

$$X - M = (S - I) - (G - T) \qquad (4)$$

In other words, the Current Account of a country's Balance of Payments (exports of goods and services less imports) is determined by two relationships. The first (S–I) is the *Savings–Investment Balance* or the difference between the savings of households and the investment spending of companies. The second (G–T) is the *Budget Balance* or the difference between government spending and taxes. This measures how much the government must borrow or repay in any year. If both of these are equal to zero or if the Savings–Investment Balance is exactly offset by the Budget Balance in the opposite direction, the Current Account will exactly balance. If, however, either the Savings–Investment Balance is negative – so that household savings are insufficient to finance the amount which firms need to borrow for investment purposes – or the Budget Balance is negative – meaning the government must borrow to cover its spending needs – the Current Account will be in deficit. Alternatively, if the Savings–Investment balance is positive – so that households are saving more than companies need to borrow – or the Budget Balance is positive – the government is running a budget surplus which it can use to repay past debt – the Current Account will be in surplus. Thus, we can see that the Current Account is, in this sense, a residual that can only be changed by affecting either the balance of Savings–Investment in the economy or the Budget Balance.

Table 6.7 shows the level of these balances in both Japan and the United States for two

Box 6.3 Balance of Payments Adjustment under Flexible and Fixed Exchange Rates

Flexible exchange rates. Under flexible exchange rates, adjustment to a disequilibrium in the balance of payments should happen through upwards or downwards changes in a currency's external value. This is because a currency's external value is determined by the amount of the local currency foreigners wish to buy (to pay for goods or assets sold by the home country) and the amount of local currency residents want to sell (to pay for goods or assets sold by foreign countries). A deficit in the balance of payments means that the supply of the local currency exceeds the demand for it on the foreign exchange market. Therefore, its value will decline until demand again equals supply.

However, a depreciation of the local currency raises the cost of imports and lowers the price of exports in foreign currency. If imports cost more, the demand for foreign goods will fall; if exports are cheaper in foreign currency terms, demand for exports will rise. This will continue until the deficit disappears. This, however, assumes that the demand for foreign goods is elastic, otherwise the import bill will rise following depreciation. In the short run, demand is generally more inelastic, so imports may increase. In this case, the balance of payments will get worse before it gets better (the so-called *J* curve effect).

In practice, exchange rates are influenced by capital account, not just current account, transactions. This creates the possibility that exchange rates will move in a perverse direction, as happened to the Japanese yen between 1981 and 1985. Large capital outflows from Japan outweighed the effects of the current account surplus and the yen fell in value. The reverse was true of the U.S. dollar.

Fixed exchange rates. Under fixed exchange rates, if the supply of local currency exceeds the demand on the foreign exchange markets, the authorities intervene by buying the excess supply and providing foreign exchange in return. If this continues for any length of time, the authorities will run out of reserves. One option is to increase the demand for local currency by raising short-term interest rates. However, this is no solution to a long-run equilibrium caused by loss of competitiveness.

If countries are faced with a fundamental disequilibrium in their balance of payments that persists (i.e. it is not cyclically determined), the only solution is to lower the prices of locally produced goods relative to foreign goods. This can be done by reducing the aggregate demand for goods and services in the economy by monetary and/or fiscal means (exchange reduction policies). This will mean some loss of output and employment in the short run depending on the degree to which domestic costs and prices fall in response to a fall in demand. The alternative is a devaluation, which raises the cost of foreign goods relative to domestically produced goods, encouraging foreigners to buy more of the goods of the home country and domestic residents to buy fewer foreign goods (expenditure-switching).

However, devaluation brings only a short-run advantage, as higher import prices will eventually feed through into domestic prices as the cost of raw materials and intermediate inputs rises and as wages chase prices. On the other hand, if producers use the interval to switch more resources into exporting and less into domestic cosumption, devaluation may bringing lasting gains. Much will depend on whether or not the authorities in the devaluing country support the devaluation by measures to curb domestic consumption and free resources for exporting.

Table 6.7 U.S. and Japanese Sectoral Financial Balances, 1981–1985 and 1988–1992 (as percentages of GNP)

	Public	*Non-financial enterprises*	*Personal*	*Overseas*
United States				
1981	−2.2	−2.1	4.7	−0.3
1982	−4.7	−0.3	5.2	0.0
1983	−5.1	0.7	3.5	1.0
1984	−4.2	−1.6	3.7	2.4
1985	−5.0	−0.3	2.5	2.9
1988	−3.9	−0.5	2.6	0.3
1989	−3.5	−0.5	4.1	0.2
1990	−3.3	−0.3	4.0	0.2
1991	−4.6	0.5	4.0	0.0
1992	−6.1	0.8	4.2	0.1
Japan				
1981	−7.3	−3.0	11.0	−0.4
1982	−6.9	−3.8	10.8	−0.7
1983	−6.8	−3.7	10.4	−1.8
1984	−5.8	−2.1	9.3	−2.8
1985	−4.1	−2.4	9.4	−3.6
1988	0.6	−4.5	7.4	−2.7
1989	0.6	−6.7	9.1	−2.0
1990	0.8	−9.0	9.9	−3.2
1991	0.7	−6.9	8.4	−2.2
1992	−1.6	−6.0	9.9	−3.2

Sources: Masera (1986) and Hamada (1995).

periods, 1981–85 and 1988–92. The table shows the *flow of funds* between different sectors of the economy. A positive figure means the sector in question enjoys a financial surplus (income exceeds spending) that it lends to the other sectors. A negative figure means that the sector is running a financial deficit (spending exceeds income) that it finances by borrowing from the other sectors. All flows must balance out within the economy of a country, that is, the net lending of surplus sectors must equal the net borrowing of deficit sectors. In all cases, financial surpluses and deficits are expressed as a percentage of GNP in order to show their quantitative significance.

The position of the *public sector* is shown by the column headed 'public' In the case of Japan, the public sector was in deficit in the first half of the 1980s (i.e. government spending exceeded taxes) but swung into surplus (i.e. taxes exceeded government spending) between 1988–91 before moving back into deficit in 1992. By way of contrast, the United States ran a large budget deficit throughout both periods. Although some limited success was achieved in reducing the deficit as a percentage of GNP between 1988–90, by 1991 the deficit was, once again, on the increase. The column headed 'non-financial enterprises' shows the borrowing needs of the *corporate sector* excluding financial institutions. (Financial institutions are intermediaries channelling the funds of surplus sectors to deficit sectors and, therefore, do not count as a separate sector.) In the case of Japan, this was much higher in the boom years of the late 1980s when firms undertook high levels of investment spending, but began to fall with the recession of the 1990s. The higher level of corporate borrowing reflects the much greater dependence of Japanese firms on funds borrowed from financial institutions to finance their investment spending. The column headed 'personal' shows the savings of the *household sector*. Here there is a noticeable difference between the two countries. The savings of Japanese households account for a much higher proportion of GNP than in the United States. Although savings as a percentage of GNP in Japan were slightly lower by the end of the period than at the start, the percentage was still more than twice that of the US.

The final column shows the contribution made by the *overseas sector* to the country's flow of funds. A plus figure in this column means that the country is borrowing funds from abroad, that is, inflows of capital exceed outflows. A negative figure means that a country is lending funds abroad, that is, outflows of capital exceed inflows. In any country, the Balance of Payments is made up of (a) the Current Account that records the difference between current income and spending, and (b) the Capital Account that records the difference between inflows and outflows of capital, including any net borrowing/lending by the monetary authorities and any increase/decrease in official reserves. In an accounting sense, credits and debits must equal each other since no country can spend money abroad which it has not obtained from abroad. It follows that, if a country has a deficit on Current Account, this must be offset by a surplus on Capital Account. Likewise, if it has a surplus on Current Account, this must be offset by a deficit on Capital Account. Now, a surplus on Capital Account means that the overseas sector is a net borrower of funds from abroad which shows up as a positive figure in the table. Likewise, a deficit on Capital Account means that a country is a net lender of funds to other countries that shows up as a minus item in the table. For almost the entire period, the United States was a net borrower of funds from abroad (i.e. a debtor nation). This means that she was running a broadly equivalent deficit on Current Account. Conversely, throughout the entire period, Japan was a net lender of funds to the rest of the world (i.e. a creditor nation) This means that she was running a broadly equivalent surplus on Current Account.

Since, for each country, in any given year, minuses must cancel out pluses the figure in the final column (for the overseas sector) may be regarded as the outcome of the financial decisions of the three other sectors, shown in the preceding columns. In the case of Japan, her Capital Account deficit, which should offset her Current Account surplus, may be regarded as the result of two factors: (a) the very high level of household savings and (b) the relatively low level of public sector borrowing. In all years, the surplus funds of the household sector far exceeded what the public and corporate sectors together wished to borrow. Unable to find enough profitable outlets in Japan, these funds were channelled abroad through the overseas sector. This large capital outflow required that Japan run an exactly offsetting surplus on the Current Account. In the case of the United States, her Capital Account surplus, which was matched by an equivalent Current Account deficit, was due to different factors. These were (a) a very high public-sector deficit, due to government spending exceeding income from taxation and (b) a relatively low level of personal savings, due to households spending a high share of their incomes. The huge inflow of funds from abroad enabled the US to meet the borrowing needs of the public sector. However, it also meant that the US, of necessity, ran a large Current Account deficit.

Viewed in this way, the payments imbalance between the two countries is merely a reflection of different macro-economic relationships within the two countries. It is also obvious that, in itself, the existence of such an imbalance need not matter. If one country chooses to spend more of its income on investment than can be afforded out of current savings, it must borrow the additional funds from abroad. This necessitates running a Current Account deficit. Likewise, if another country wishes to save more than it spends on investment, it must lend funds to the rest of the world and, therefore, run a Current Account surplus. Neither country should be concerned. Although the net borrower will accumulate debt that will have to be repaid, provided that the funds borrowed from abroad are productively employed, it will be able to do so out of the additional income generated by an expansion of the capital stock. More of a concern, however, is justified if the funds borrowed from abroad are used to finance increased consumption spending. In this case, the country is 'living on capital'. Eventually this will result in a reduction in real incomes as and when foreign creditors must be repaid. If a country wishes to avoid such a situation, it must act to reduce current consumption. In the case of the United States, its Current Account deficit was the result of an excessive budget deficit which was due to a failure to reduce spending and a reluctance to increase taxes.

It is important to understand the mechanism whereby a Capital Account surplus (or deficit) is converted into an equivalent Current Account deficit (or surplus). Where a country's exchange rate is free to find its own level in the foreign exchange market (i.e. it is floating), this happens through changes in the exchange rate. Take the case of Japan where funds flow out of the country because household savings exceed what companies and the public sector together wish to borrow. A net outflow of capital from Japan will increase the supply of yen on the foreign exchange market relative to the demand for yen. Consequently, the yen will depreciate. As it does so, imports will become more expensive and exports cheaper. Assuming normal elasticities (i.e. no elasticity pessimism), this will cause Japan's Current Account to move into surplus. The process will continue until the Current Account surplus exactly equals the Capital Account deficit. Next, consider the case of the United States where funds are flowing into the country because the borrowing needs of the public sector exceed the surplus of the personal sector. These flows of capital increase the demand for dollars relative to their supply on the foreign exchange market. As a consequence, the dollar appreciates. Again, assuming normal elasticities, this will cause the U.S. Current Account to swing into deficit. Again, the process continues until the Current Account deficit exactly equals the Capital Account surplus.

Of course, changes in the exchange rate are also result from changes in a country's Current Account transactions. Thus, a country that experiences an increased demand for its exports of goods and services will, all other things being equal, find that its exchange rate appreciates. Likewise, a country that experiences an increase in the demand for its imports of goods and services, will find that its exchange rate depreciates. However, very often movements of capital into and out of the country exert a stronger influence on the exchange rate than changes on the Current Account. At times, this has been true for the yen–dollar rate. Consider Figure 6.1. This shows the trend in the nominal exchange rate over the period since 1971. Before 1978, the yen rose in value against the

U.S. dollar, reflecting the fact that Japan was in Current Account surplus and the U.S. in Current Account deficit. However, after 1978, the yen began to fall in value, despite the existence of a large current account surplus. The reason is now self-evident. Because savings exceeded investment in Japan, funds flowed out of Japan driving the yen downwards. As the yen depreciated against the U.S. dollar, her Current Account surplus increased. Likewise, the appreciation of the U.S. dollar caused the U.S. Current Account to move further into the red. This was to the chagrin of the US, who blamed her mounting Current Account deficit on the over-cheap Japanese yen.

This, however, missed the point. The yen was cheap because capital funds flowed from Japan to the US. The US could justifiably blame the Japanese for saving too much, but Japan could, equally fairly, accuse the US of failing to correct its budget deficit! However, the cheapness of the yen in terms of the dollar was the consequence and not the cause of the Current Account imbalance between the two countries. If the US was concerned to reduce its Current Account deficit with Japan, it was clear that the solution was to reduce its budget deficit, either by raising taxes or reducing government spending. In addition, any measures that encouraged U.S. households to spend less of their income and save more would lead to a bigger financial surplus in the US and reduce its dependence on capital borrowed from abroad. At the same time, Japan's Current Account surplus could be reduced by the authorities encouraging households to spend a larger proportion of their incomes and save less. An increase in government spending or reduction in taxes would also help absorb some of the financial surplus of the personal sector.

Although there was some recognition that domestic economic policy changes were needed if payment imbalances between the two countries were to be tackled, the mistaken belief that adjustment could be achieved by altering the exchange rate prevailed. Hence, in September 1995, the Plaza Accord committed the public authorities in each of the G5 countries to engage in co-ordinated intervention to force the U.S. dollar down and the Japanese yen up. It is clear from Figure 6.1 that some success was achieved in halting the decline of the yen. Most likely, however, this reflected changes in 'economic fundamentals' rather than the results of intervention on the foreign exchange market. In the US, some success was achieved in reducing the size of the budget deficit. At the same time, in Japan, personal savings as a share of GNP fell (see Table 6.7). In the absence of these changes, however, it is doubtful whether co-ordinated exchange-rate intervention would have succeeded.

The fall in the value of the U.S. dollar in terms of the yen may have contributed towards some reduction in Japan's Current Account surplus after 1987. Adjustments in the Current Account tend to lag changes in the exchange rate because of the *J*-curve effect discussed earlier. However, of much greater importance in bringing about a decline in Japan's Current Account surplus was the upswing in the Japanese economy, in which rising personal consumption played a major role. In 1998, the ratio of personal savings to GNP in Japan fell to 7.4%. At the same time, increasing demands were placed on the surplus funds of the household sector to meet the investment demand of the corporate sector (see Table 6.7). After 1988, personal savings as a percentage of Japan's GNP began rising once again. At the same time, following the ending of the economic upswing in 1991, corporate borrowing as a percentage of GNP fell. In the US, the Federal administration achieved some success in curbing public sector borrowing. However, after 1990, the public sector deficit rose as a percentage of GNP, reaching a record high of 6.1% in 1992 (See Table 6.7). The combined result of these changes was to cause Japan's Current Account surplus to rise once again. In 1994, a $129.1 billion surplus was recorded.

Japan's Regulated Financial Markets

An important role in the macroeconomic adjustment mechanism described above was played by long-term interest rates. Long-term interest rates are a reward payable to owners of surplus funds to persuade them to part with their wealth for a period of time. At the same time, they are the cost which borrowers (companies and households) must incur if they wish to acquire income-generating assets. In a closed economy, where interest rates are left free to find their own level rather than being regulated by the public authorities, they will settle at a level where savings equal investment. However, where owners of surplus funds are free to lend these funds to borrowers in other countries, this need not be so. If long-term interest rates are higher in other countries, surplus funds may flow abroad to where they can earn more. In a perfect capital market, this would cause long-term rates at home to rise and long-term rates abroad to fall until they are equal. In practice, this never happens. The existence of exchange rate risk is one reason. Investors may require a higher rate in countries where there is a risk of the currency depreciating. Political risk is another factor: investors may fear the sudden imposition of capital controls in the foreign country and demand a risk premium.

A further reason, however, is that capital markets are not perfect. Governments impose all sorts of restrictions on financial institutions for a variety of reasons. These include controls on the interest rates that may be charged for loans or paid to lenders. So differences in long-term rates between different countries may persist. Table 6.8 shows differences in both short-term and long-term interest rates between Japan and various other countries of the world for the period between 1984 and 1996.

It is very clear that, over the period from 1984 to 1996, the yield obtainable by Japanese investors on both long-term bonds and equities was consistently below that prevailing in the United States, Germany or the United Kingdom. Short-term interest rates are more directly determined by the stance of monetary policy in different countries and investors' expectations regarding future currency movements. Nevertheless, up to 1990, Japan's short-term interest rates were also well below those prevailing in either the United States or the United Kingdom. Between 1991 and 1992, Japan's short-term rates rose above those in the United States, although this was reversed in 1993. However, our concern is less with Japan's short-term interest rates and more the long-term yield to holders of bonds and equities.

One consequence of this difference in long-term interest rates was that Japanese savings were invested abroad rather than at home. In other words, the exodus of long-term capital from Japan to the US and other western industrialised countries was due not only to Japan's savings–investment imbalance. It also resulted from the fact that the return which holders of financial assets held abroad vastly exceeded that which could be obtained if the same funds were loaned to borrowers in Japan. Why was this so? The answer is to be found in the highly regulated nature of Japan's financial markets compared with those of the West. There appear to have been two aspects to this. First, the authorities exercised strict control over interest rates, such that rates were not free to find their own levels as on western financial markets. Second, laws placed strict limits on the kinds of lending activities which financial institutions could engage in and the types of assets that

Table 6.8 Relative Short-term and Long-term Interest Rates and Equity Market Yields in Four OECD Countries, 1984–1996

Year	*United States*	*Japan*	*Germany*	*United Kingdom*
A. Short-term interest rates, %				
1984	10.22	6.48	5.99	10.03
1985	8.00	6.62	5.45	12.32
1986	6.49	5.12	4.63	11.02
1987	6.82	4.15	4.03	9.77
1988	7.65	4.42	4.33	10.41
1989	8.99	5.31	7.12	13.96
1990	8.06	7.62	8.49	14.82
1991	5.87	7.21	9.25	11.58
1992	3.75	4.28	9.52	9.74
1993	3.22	2.83	7.28	5.99
1994	4.67	2.12	5.36	5.57
1995	5.93	1.12	4.53	6.77
1996	5.41	0.48	3.31	6.11
B. Long-term interest rates, %				
1984	12.43	6.80	7.96	11.33
1985	10.62	6.34	7.09	11.03
1986	7.68	4.94	6.19	9.97
1987	8.38	4.21	6.33	9.52
1988	8.84	4.27	6.58	9.69
1989	8.49	5.11	7.02	10.30
1990	8.55	7.27	8.63	11.65
1991	7.86	6.40	8.42	10.08
1992	7.00	5.24	7.80	9.09
1993	5.86	4.18	6.47	7.40
1994	7.08	4.20	6.86	8.01
1995	6.57	3.39	6.82	8.16
1996	6.43	3.03	6.21	7.79
C. Equity market yield, %				
1984	n.a.	n.a.	n.a.	n.a.
1985	n.a.	n.a.	n.a.	n.a.
1986	3.43	0.84	1.79	4.35
1987	3.12	0.55	2.21	3.60
1988	3.61	0.54	2.81	4.48
1989	3.43	0.48	2.22	4.36
1990	3.60	0.65	2.11	5.07
1991	3.21	0.75	2.38	4.97
1992	2.95	1.00	2.45	4.91
1993	2.78	0.87	2.11	4.01
1994	2.86	0.78	1.77	3.94
1995	2.61	0.86	2.00	4.15
1996	2.15	0.75	1.81	4.08

Notes:
A. The short-term interest rate is the period average of 90-day commercial paper in the United States, 3-month certificates of deposit in Japan, 3-month LIBOR in Germany and 3-month LIBOR in the United Kingdom.
B. The long-term interest rate is the period average yields on long-term benchmark government bonds.
C. The equity market yield is the period average of the gross dividend yield on the relevant FT-A world index.
Source: Financial Times, November 25, 1991 and March 11, 1997.

they could hold. One effect was the separation of financial institutions into different compartments (the provision of long-term credit, short-term finance, investment management, securities trading, etc.).

Controls on interest rates existed for much of the post-war period. These placed limits on the interest rate financial institutions could pay in order to attract funds, thus preventing competition for funds. This meant that borrowing was relatively cheap for companies, but holders of surplus funds got a poor return on funds invested. Low interest rates did little to discourage Japanese households from engaging in a high level of saving. (This is not surprising since households will need to save more when interest rates are low to generate a given amount of investment income.) However, they did encourage some holders of surplus funds to instead buy overseas financial assets where the return was higher. This increased the supply of yen on the foreign exchange markets and so helped to keep it cheap. It also meant that there was little incentive for overseas holders of yen to invest their liquid funds in yen-denominated assets. Better to buy dollar or DM assets instead. Thus, the demand for yen was lower than it would otherwise have been, again contributing to its relative cheapness.

One aspect of this process of interest rate control was the arrangements that existed for financing any government borrowing in Japan. Strict controls on interest rates helped keep down the costs of government borrowing. For several decades, the government was able to meet all of its borrowing needs by issuing bonds at a rate below the market rate. Unlike in other countries, any increase in government borrowing did not result in higher interest rates. Under the special arrangements that existed between the central authorities and the banks, the bond issue was substantially underwritten by the city banks. If the authorities needed to borrow more than they anticipated, the banks would buy up any bonds that could not otherwise be sold. However, these arrangements became unworkable when government borrowing reached very high levels. This first happened following the oil crisis of 1973–74. Then, the borrowing needs of the government could only be fully met by persuading non-bank investors to buy bonds. For this to work, it became necessary to foster the development of a large secondary bond market with rates determined by market forces. (A secondary bond market is a market in which holders of bonds can sell their bonds if they so wish before they reach maturity.) This made it more difficult to hold down other interest rates. For example, unless banks are free to raise rates paid on deposits, a rise in bond rates will cause banks to lose funds forcing them to curtail their lending. As a consequence, the authorities were compelled to relax some of the controls existing on interest rates.

Second, fewer financial instruments have been available both for Japanese holders of investment funds and for foreign investors wishing to hold yen-denominated assets. For example, up until the mid-1980s, the only type of government bond available was a seven-year coupon bond. Before 1979, there was no certificate of deposits market of the kind that exists in other financial markets. (A certificate of deposit (CD) is a piece of paper issued by a bank in return for a deposit of a certain amount usually for a period of three months which earns the holder a fixed rate of interest. CDs are an important means whereby banks can obtain more funds if they wish to expand their lending and constitute a useful income-earning liquid asset for institutions with spare funds to invest.) One of the consequences has been to reduce international demand for yen-denominated assets. For example, until the mid-1980s, there was no bankers' acceptance market. Such a market facilitates the use of commercial bills by enabling the issuers of such bills to get their bills 'accepted' by a reputable financial institution. (Importers of merchandise generally pay for goods received by issuing commercial bills or bills of exchange which promise to pay the holder the money due in three months time. Holders of these bills can then discount (sell) these bills to a bank or other financial institution for less than their face value if they want payment before the date stated on the bill. In return for a commission, a specialist institution will 'accept' a bill presented to it by signing their name on the bill and thereby undertaking to pay the sum due on the date of maturity if the issuer should fail to do so.) The absence of such a market has meant that yen-denominated bills could not be traded. The effect was to limit the use of the yen in trading settlements. For example, in 1982, only 37% of Japan's exports were denominated in yen and only 2% of imports, whereas 80% or more of Germany's exports were priced in D-Marks and 40% of imports (*The Economist*, November 19, 1983).

Again, until recently, the volume of Euro–yen lending was tightly controlled, while Japanese residents were restricted in issuing Euro–yen bonds. Euro yens are yen deposited with banks in Europe that are then re-loaned to borrowers inside or outside Japan. The restrictions preventing banks from lending yen to non-residents has limited the volume of such deposits held outside Japan. At the same time, if Japanese residents are prevented from issuing Euro–yen bonds, this limits the demand for yen-denominated assets outside Japan. By way of contrast, an active Euro–dollar market has existed since the 1950s. This began when American banks sought to borrow additional dollar deposits from banks in Western Europe because of the ceiling imposed by the U.S. authorities on interest rates under so-called Regulation Q which prevented them from attracting more dollars domestically. In the late 1980s, only 5.5% of eurocurrency deposits were yen-denominated, only 8% of external bond issues were in yen and only 5.5% of external bank loans were in yen (Tavlas and Ozeki, 1991). This absence of a large Euro–yen market further reduces the demand for yen on foreign currency markets and contributes to its cheapness.

Third, although progress has been made towards the removal of restrictions on foreign investment in Japan, capital inflows are still subject to certain restrictions. This has further reduced the demand for yen and contributed to its under-valuation. In particular, foreign banks and other financial institutions wishing to establish themselves in Japan have often faced restrictions. Until the mid-1980s, foreign banks were not free to buy and sell Japanese government bonds. Admission of foreign securities firms to the Japanese stock market has been strictly limited, although the situation is now changing.

In April 1998, Japan embarked on a major programme of financial deregulation designed to bring Japanese financial markets into line with those of other advanced industrialised countries. The changes will begin with the abolition of all remaining exchange controls, thus allowing Japanese individual and corporate investors greater freedom to buy financial services outside Japan. Although this affects both inflows and outflows of capital, it could potentially lead to a surge of outward investment that could aggravate the problem of an undervalued yen. On the other hand, if deregulation leads to a more competitive financial services sector in Japan, this could be reversed. As with the British 'Big Bang' introduced in 1986, the Japanese measures provide for the abolition of brokerage commissions for securities trading. A fifty-year ban on the creation of financial holding companies will also be ended which could lead to a restructuring of the financial services sector. The reforms will also give greater freedom to different categories of financial business to compete with each other by offering a wider range of financial services. Banks, securities companies and insurance companies will be able to start up investment trusts (so-called mutual funds) for the first time. Firms will also enjoy greater freedom to enter the securities business, although they will face stricter capital adequacy requirements. Non-bank financial institutions will enjoy freedom to issue corporate bonds, making it easier for them to raise additional funds to expand lending. Finally, banks, securities companies and insurance companies will eventually be granted freedom to enter each other's business through the setting up subsidiaries, so fostering greater competition.

Conclusion

The rise of Japan over the course of the post-war era from the status of a war-devastated, semi-industrialised economy to that of one of the world's leading producers and exporters of manufactured goods has been one of the most significant developments of the past half-century. As we shall see in the next chapter, Japan has served as a prototype for a group of other developing countries anxious to imitate the Japanese experience. From a global perspective, however, Japan's sudden ascent has created problems for the western industrialised world. This is most poignantly demonstrated by the large and persistent surplus that Japan has enjoyed in her trade with these countries. For the counterpart of Japan's surplus has been the mounting deficits which certain of her major trading partners have experienced. This has resulted in a state of more or less permanent friction between Japan and her major trading partners in the West, often resulting in the imposition of trade restrictions on Japanese goods.

Although the West has regarded Japan's trade surplus as evidence that Japan trades unfairly, this chapter has shown that Japan's formal import barriers are not the cause. The Japanese domestic market is relatively unprotected if measured by the height of her tariffs and the frequency with which non-tariff barriers are used. An important exception remains agriculture but, in this regard, Japan is not alone among the advanced industrialised countries. A greater problem are the so-called informal or hidden barriers. One factor that may have made access to the Japanese market more difficult for western exporters, has been the traditionally close relationship which exists between Japanese firms as a result of the existence of the *keiretsu* system of industrial organisation. At the same time, the lack of a strong competition authority equivalent to that which exists in other western industrialised countries and able to combat anti-competitive practices by dominant firms may have made it more difficult for western companies to gain access. Also because Japanese industry has in the past been subject to much more government regulation than is common in western industrialised countries, western exporters may confront excessive bureaucracy when exporting to Japan. On the other hand, one of the major reasons for the low share of foreign manufactures in domestic consumption may simply be that Japanese households prefer domestically produced to foreign-made products.

However, as this chapter has argued, the main explanation for Japan's Current Account surplus is a macroeconomic one. In Japan, the volume of personal savings has regularly exceeded the borrowing needs of either the corporate or public sectors. This has resulted in a large outflow of long-term capital in search of higher returns than those obtainable in Japan's highly regulated financial markets. By way of contrast, in the United States, Japan's largest trading partner, the level of personal savings has been inadequate to finance the large and mounting deficits of the public sector, necessitating borrowing from abroad. As funds have flowed from Japan to the United States, the dollar has risen and the yen fallen, making Japanese goods cheap in the US and U.S. goods expensive in Japan. The problem cannot be resolved by forcing the dollar down or the yen up without addressing the 'economic fundamentals' that underlie the problem. On the U.S. side, this requires action to curtail the budget deficit, while Japan could do more to stimulate private consumption. It is, however, by no means obvious why a Current Account surplus, which is the result of an imbalance between private savings and investment, need matter. If Japanese households wish to save more than firms are seeking to invest, it makes sense for Japan to export her surplus savings to the rest of the world where investment needs exceed what people are prepared to save.

What is clear, however, is that the relationship between Japan and her western trading partners is changing fast and is likely to do so even more in the immediately foreseeable future. There is every reason for expecting Japan's high savings ratio to fall further in the future. One reason for this is that her population is ageing fast. The ratio of the retired population to working age population is rising as the birth rate declines and life expectancy increases. Old people tend to dissave during their retirement while young people save in order to provide for the future (Horioka, 1983). At the same time, improved pensions and social security benefits are likely to result in a lower propensity to save among those still working. Greater availability of house mortgages is also likely lead to more people borrowing to buy their own home. The reduction in the Japanese savings surplus will lead to reduced capital outflows, although this could potentially be offset if investment spending falls by a similar amount. The latest recession of the Japanese economy has badly damaged both the profitability of Japanese industry and the confidence of investors. It has also caused households to increase their propensity to save because of uncertainty about future income.

The other big change that has taken place over the past decade has been a gradual appreciation of the Japanese yen. Japan can no longer be accused of deliberately undervaluing the yen. As the yen has appreciated, two important changes have occurred. The first is that more Japanese companies have shifted production abroad both to take advantage of lower costs and to prevent profits being squeezed by the rising yen. The second is that Japanese companies have increasingly moved up-market into higher value-added goods so as to increase the profit earned per unit sold abroad. Also, high value-added goods often sell less on price and more on factors such as quality. They are, therefore, less affected by a rise in the exchange rate. The first of these changes will likely reduce the volume of Japanese exports leading to a reduced trade surplus.

The second need not do so and could even lead to an increase in the value of Japan's exports. A higher exchange rate does not always lead to a decline in a country's trade balance. Indeed, to the extent that a higher exchange rate lowers costs to exporting companies, it may even cause an increase in the size of the surplus. However, the composition of Japanese exports will change and this may lead to Japan undertaking more intra-industry specialisation. As we saw in Chapter 3, levels of intra-industry trade are generally higher in more sophisticated, higher quality goods. If Japan's intra-industry trade ratio should rise, this will result in her trade becoming more balanced with a greater proportion of her imports consisting of finished manufactures. This should make for fewer frictions with her trading partners.

Japan's institutions are also changing, partly, in response to pressure from the West and, partly, as a consequence of the economic crisis. The *keiretsu* system is undergoing a fundamental change. More importance is now attached to combating anti-competitive practices by dominant firms. Measures are being taken to eliminate unnecessary bureaucratic interference in the economy and to de-regulate. The tax system is being reformed. Financial markets are being opened up to more foreign competition. In short, Japan is slowly becoming more like her western counterparts. These considerations probably justify cautious optimism regarding the prospects for less fractious economic relationships between Japan and the West in the next few decades. On the other hand, the problems that have resulted from Japan's rapid and sudden emergence on the world trading scene, may be repeated as other newly industrialising countries follow in her wake. In the next chapter, the impact of the rise of the so-called 'other Japans' is discussed.

Notes for Further Reading

The exists a wide range of excellent texts on Japan's post-war economic development such as:

Argy, V. *The Japanese Economy* (London: Macmillan, 1996).

Franks, P. *Japanese Economic Development, Theory and Practice* (London: Nissan Institute/Routledge Japanese Studies, 1999).

Ito, T. *The Japanese Economy* (Cambridge, MA: MIT Press, 1992).

Sato, K. *The Japanese Economy* (1998).

For an analysis of Japan's role in the world economy, the interested reader should consult:

Balassa, B. and Nolan, M. *Japan in the World Economy* (Washington DC: Institute for International Economics, 1988).

El-Agraa, A. M. *Japan's Trade Frictions: Realities or Misconceptions?* (London: Macmillan, 1988).

The March, 1995 issue of *World Economy* (Vol. 18, No. 2) contains papers from a very useful Mini-Symposium on Japan's Trade Policy.

For a useful discussion of the changing nature of Japanese trade policy, a useful source is:

Yumiko, M. *Japan's Trade Policy: Action or Reaction?* Routledge Studies in the Growth Economics of Asia 4 (London: Routledge, 1996).

For a detailed case study analysis of government intervention in industry in Japan, the reader should consult:

Tyson, L. D'A. *Who's Bashing Whom? Trade Conflict in High-Technology Industries* (Washington DC: Institute for International Economics, November, 1992).

Chapter 7

The Emergence of the Newly Industrialising Countries

CHAPTER OUTLINES: Introduction. Who are the NICs? Reasons for the Rapid Emergence of the NICs – internal economic success, the external environment. The Effects of the Rise of the NICs on the Advanced Industrialised Countries – the problem of adjustment, adjustment policy, the effects on wage inequality in the advanced industrialised countries. Conclusion.

Introduction

This chapter examines Japan's successors – the group of so-called 'newly industrialising' countries (NICs) or economies (NIEs) that have followed in the wake of Japan. Although this term has been used to refer, in particular, to the 'tiger economies' of East Asia – namely, Hong Kong, South Korea, Singapore and Taiwan – it is applicable to a broader group of countries. NICs or NIEs are countries that have been successful, in a way that other developing countries have not, in breaking through into rapid economic growth. Like Japan, their growth performance has been closely related to their success in exporting manufactures to the rest of the world. Such countries have experienced not only a big increase in their per capita income, but also a radical transformation of their economy. In particular, the importance of agriculture within the economy has declined and that of manufacturing industry increased. An important feature of the industrialisation process of all these countries has been the adoption of outward-looking, export-oriented trade policies. However, despite these similarities, all are very different in other respects. Some have placed reliance upon state regulation and direction of the economy, while others have attached greater importance to market forces. They also differ greatly in their political systems, culture and religion.

Their growth has had a profound effect on the world economy. In particular, these countries have provided a potent source of new, import competition for the advanced industrialised countries in certain important sectors of manufacturing. To begin with, they specialised in relatively simple, labour-intensive manufactures, although some NICs were also successful in expanding exports of capital-intensive goods. Often, these were the industries which were experiencing secular decline in the advanced industrialised countries. Because they were often concentrated in particular regions and sometimes employed relatively large numbers of ethnic and women workers, the threat to employment posed by the NICs has caused severe social strains on the advanced industrialised countries. The NICs were often blamed for declining employment levels in these industries and pressure has mounted for import restrictions to be placed on their exports. More recently, the NICs have begun to broaden the range of industries in which they specialise and to move up-market into more skill-intensive, higher value-added products. However, this has not always lessened the problems posed for the western industrialised countries by the rise of these economies. It has simply meant that the competitive challenge is now being experienced over a broader range of sectors.

This chapter begins by defining the NICs and seeking to identify their salient characteristics. This is followed by an examination of the importance of NIC exports in the imports of the advanced industrialised economies. Next, the reasons for their rapid and sudden economic growth are discussed. The part played by internal economic policies has clearly been an important factor, although economists are not agreed on whether export expansion was the main cause of their fast economic growth. A favourable external environment may also have been an important factor contributing to their success. The remainder of the chapter is concerned with the effects of the emergence of these countries on the western industrialised countries. The main effect of increased import competition from the NICs has been on employment in the western industrialised countries. However, it is argued that this is due largely to the difficulties experienced by the western industrialised economies in transferring resources from declining to expanding sectors. The chapter considers what measures could be pursued by these countries to promote more rapid adjustment. Finally, the chapter concludes with a discussion of the effects of the NICs on wage inequality within the western industrialised countries.

Who are the NICs?

There is no official definition or list of newly industrialising countries, but the term has come to be loosely applied to a relatively small group of developing countries that have, in recent decades, become major exporters of manufactured goods. The term NIC appears to have been used first by the OECD in its now famous 1979 Report entitled *The Impact of the Newly-Industrialising Countries* (OECD, 1979). In this report, the OECD listed three criteria which distinguish an NIC from other developing countries:

1. Fast growth in both the absolute level of industrial employment and the share of industrial in total employment.
2. A rising share of the world exports of manufactures.
3. Fast growth in real per capita GDP such that the country was successful in narrowing the gap with the advanced industrialised countries (OECD, 1979).

Using these criteria, the OECD identified ten countries, by way of illustration, as fulfilling these conditions: Spain, Portugal, Greece and Yugoslavia in Europe; Brazil and Mexico in Latin America; Hong Kong, South Korea, Singapore and Taiwan in South East Asia. The list was not intended to be a complete one. The report acknowledged that there were other developing countries with a large industrial base which satisfied some of the criteria and could have been included (e.g. India or Argentina). Over the period 1963–79, all ten countries were found to have experienced an increase in the share of industry in total employment. Their combined share of world manufacturing exports rose from 2.6% in 1963 to 8.9% in 1979. All ten countries saw their real per capita GDP rise relative to that of the advanced industrialised countries over the period in question.

In a subsequent report (OECD, 1988), the OECD focussed on a narrower sample of four Asian economies (South Korea, Taiwan, Singapore and Hong Kong) and two Latin American countries (Brazil and Mexico). (The three south European NICs – Spain, Portugal and Greece – could be regarded as having graduated to the league of the industrialised countries.) These countries were found to have grown at an average annual rate of 8.4% between 1964 and 1973 slowing to 5.3% between 1973 and 1983, compared with 4.8 and 2.1%, respectively, for all developed market economies. As a consequence, their share of the total GDP of all market economies rose from 3.5% in 1964 to 6.2% in 1983. The output of the manufacturing sector (manufacturing value-added) of these economies grew at an even faster rate of 10.9% per annum between 1964 and 1973 and 5.3% per annum between 1973 and 1984, compared with rates of 5.5 and 1.6% for all developed market economies. Finally, these countries raised their share of world exports of manufactures from 1.9% in 1965 to 8.7% in 1983.

Subsequently, the term 'newly exporting countries' (NEC) was introduced to refer to a second tier of developing countries that were enjoying rapid growth of manufacturing exports and which looked poised to repeat the experience of the 'first-generation' NICs. This second group included a number of relatively large manufacturing exporters such as Malaysia, Thailand, the Philippines and Indonesia in East Asia; Chile, Colombia, Peru and Uruguay in South America; Morocco, Tunisia, Malta and Cyprus in the Mediterranean region. Of these, the four ASEAN countries (Malaysia, Thailand, the Philippines and Indonesia) are often widely regarded as now qualifying for inclusion in the list of NICs. Following the adoption of its now-famous 'open-door' policy, China should also be regarded as a recent latecomer to the ranks of NECs.

Table 7.1 shows more recent trends in the rate of growth and other measures of structural transformation for a select group of twenty-seven countries which fit the OECD definition of an NIC. All twenty-seven countries satisfy some, but not necessarily all, of the criteria used by the OECD. Of these, exactly one-half fulfilled three of the four criteria used in the table, that is, an above-average growth rate, above-average export volume growth, a rising share of manufacturing output in GDP and a rising share of manufactures in total exports. These were Chile, Ecuador, China, Hong Kong, India, Indonesia, South Korea, Malaysia, Mauritius, Singapore, Tunisia, Thailand, Turkey and Pakistan. A few countries included in the original OECD list, such as Brazil, Mexico, Portugal and Greece, experienced somewhat more sluggish growth in the period after 1980.

Chowdhury and Islam (1993) criticise the OECD definition for ignoring the *qualitative* dimension to the development process. Economic development, the argument goes, is not just about economic growth. Development involves a change in the conditions of the population. For this to happen, growth must be sustained and lead to a reduction in poverty and inequality and a continuous improvement in people's standard of living. They use the following fourfold criteria:

1. A savings ratio equal to 15% (empirical evidence supports the view that, when the

Table 7.1 Economic Growth and Structural Transformation in Newly Industrialising Countries

Country	*Average annual growth % 1980–90*	*Average annual growth % 1990–95*	*Average annual export volume growth 1989–90*	*Average annual export volume growth 1990–95*	*Share of manufacturing value-added in GDP 1980*	*Share of manufacturing value added in GDP 1995*	*Share of manufacturing in total exports 1980*	*Share of manufactures in total exports 1993*
Argentina	−0.3	5.7	3.1	−0.8	20	20	23	32
Brazil	2.7	2.7	6.1	6.6	33	24	39	60
Chile	4.1	7.3	5.7	10.5	21	–	10	19
Colombia	3.7	4.6	9.7	4.8	23	18	20	40
Costa Rica	3.0	5.1	4.9	10.1	19	19	34	33
Ecuador	2.0	3.4	3.0	8.9	18	21	3	7
Honduras	2.7	3.5	1.3	10.7	15	18	13	13
China	10.2	12.8	11.4	14.3	41	38	48	81
Hong Kong	6.9	5.6	15.4	15.3	24	9	93	96
India	5.8	4.6	6.3	7.0	18	19	59	75
Indonesia	6.1	7.6	5.3	21.3	13	24	3	53
Jamaica	2.0	2.9	1.2	1.3	17	18	63	65
Korean Rep.	9.4	7.2	13.7	10.4	29	27	90	91
Malaysia	5.2	8.7	11.5	17.8	21	33	20	65
Mauritius	6.2	4.9	8.6	2.0	15	23	28	67
Mexico	1.0	1.1	12.2	14.7	22	19	12	75
Philippines	1.0	2.3	2.9	10.2	26	23	37	77
Peru	−0.2	5.3	−1.9	11.0	20	24	18	17
Portugal	2.9	0.8	12.2	0.5	–	–	72	78
Greece	1.4	1.1	5.1	11.9	30	21	47	48
Singapore	6.4	8.7	12.2	16.2	29	27	51	80
South Africa	1.3	0.6	0.9	2.8	23	24	40	74
Tunisia	3.3	3.9	6.2	7.7	12	19	27	72
Thailand	7.6	8.4	14.3	21.6	22	29	28	73
Turkey	5.3	3.2	12.0	8.8	14	21	27	72
Uruguay	0.4	4.0	2.9	−3.1	26	18	38	43
Pakistan	6.3	4.6	9.5	8.8	16	17	48	85
Israel	3.5	6.4	5.9	10.0	–	–	82	91
World	3.1	2.0	4.7	6.0	23	21	–	–

Source: World Bank, World Development Report (1997).

savings ratio has reached this level, a 'take-off' point is reached).

2. A real GDP per capita equal to US$ 1,000.
3. A share of manufacturing in GDP and employment equal to 20%.
4. The United Nations' Human Development Index (which measures relative deprivation combining purchasing power, life expectancy and literacy) equal to 0.75.

Using these criteria, Chowdhury and Islam have identified twenty-one NICs and a further ten potential NICs. In East Asia, these include not only the 'four dragons', but also Thailand and Malaysia with China, Indonesia and the Philippines listed as potentials. In West Asia, India and Pakistan are listed as potentials. In South America, the list includes Colombia, Ecuador, Peru, Chile, Brazil, Uruguay, Argentina and Venezuela. In Central America, NICs include Cost Rica, Mexico and Jamaica. African NICs include Mauritius and South Africa, with Morocco, Nigeria, Zambia and Zimbabwe as potentials. In Europe, Turkey and Portugal are listed. Finally, in the Middle East, Israel counts as a potential.

Lorenz (1989) has suggested that, if we regard Japan as the first post-war NIC, four generations of NICs can be identified. Following Japan, there occurs the rise of a second-generation of NICs considered in the original 1979 OECD study. Lorenz identifies a third generation of NECs as emerging from 1980 onwards. The fourth generation are the most recent entrants to the league of 'fast growers', that is, from 1990 onwards. Table 7.2 distinguishes between each of these generations.

Although all of these countries differ greatly, a common characteristic of their economic development has been the pursuit by all of them of an outward-looking, export-oriented economic strategy. To varying degrees, all of these countries have sought to grow by expanding their exports of manufactured goods. Such a strategy may be contrasted with an inward-looking, import-substitution policy of the kind that was fashionable in many less developed countries in the earlier years of the post-war period. An inward-looking policy is more concerned with protecting nascent industry from foreign competition by erecting high import barriers and encouraging local production of goods that are substitutes for imports. Later in this chapter, we compare the relative merits and demerits of these two approaches. Economists are divided on how central export expansion was to the success of these economies. At one extreme are those who consider the adoption of export-oriented trade strategies as being the key to the success of these countries. According to this school of thought, the success of countries that have achieved take-off in this way provides a model for other developing countries. At the other extreme are those who deny any linkage between export expansion and economic growth, arguing that the success of these economies should be attributed to other factors.

These arguments are discussed further below. At this stage, it is sufficient to note that all NICs enjoyed fast export growth and this was accompanied by rapid domestic growth. Most began by concentrating on the export of a small number of relatively simple, labour-intensive goods. This was consistent with the fact that they enjoyed relatively large amounts of unskilled labour and could, therefore, produce these goods at lower cost than the developed countries. The three most important product groups were textiles and clothing, leather and footwear products and a wide range of other miscellaneous manufactures (e.g. children's toys, sports goods, wood and cork manufactures). A few of these countries also specialised in more capital-intensive, heavy goods such as iron and steel production, shipbuilding

Table 7.2 The Four Generations of Newly Industrialising Countries

1st Generation (Post-war)	*2nd Generation (The NICs from 1965 onwards)*	*3rd Generation (The NECs from 1980 onwards)*	*4th Generation (New entrants since 1990)*
Japan (joined the OECD in 1964)	Far East/Gang of Four:	The ASEAN countries:	Potential new NECs:
	Hong Kong Singapore Taiwan South Korea	Malaysia Thailand Philippines Indonesia	Costa Rica Ecuador Honduras Peru South Africa
	Latin America: Brazil Mexico (Argentina)	Other second-tier countries: Chile Colombia China India Mauritius Pakistan Turkey Tunisia	
	South Europe: Greece Spain Portugal (Israel)		
	Eastern Europe: Poland Hungary Romania Bulgaria		

and chemicals. These tended to be the larger NICs (e.g. Brazil, Argentina) which enjoyed a sufficiently large home market to enable these industries to produce at a level of average costs equal to producers in the western industrialised countries.

Later, however, most of the first generation of NICs began to lose their comparative advantage in labour-intensive manufactures as unskilled labour became scarcer and wage rates began to rise. In response, they moved up-market into more skill-intensive and even knowledge-intensive sectors such as telecommunications, consumer electronics, office machinery and electrical machinery. Many of them did so by attracting large inflows of capital and technology from MNCs in the western industrialised countries initially in the form of export processing or offshore assembly plants. In some cases, reliance was also placed on sub-contracting. Table 7.3 shows the share of OECD imports of manufactures from NICs accounted for by different product groups. In 1964, textiles and clothing together accounted for roughly one-half of all NIC exports to the OECD countries. Miscellaneous manufactures accounted for a further 16%. However, by 1985, the share accounted for by textiles and clothing had fallen to 23% and of miscellaneous manufactures to 10%. A major share of NIC exports

Table 7.3 The Share of OECD Imports of Manufactures from NICs by Product Group, 1964–1985, Percentage share

Product group	*1964*	*1973*	*1985*
Cork and wood manufactures	5.57	6.78	1.19
Textiles	17.61	10.65	3.92
Non-metallic mineral manufcts.	3.82	2.36	2.06
Iron and steel	2.19	2.20	3.55
Manufactures of metal, n.e.s.	1.62	2.09	3.78
Power-generating machinery and equipment	0.54	1.11	3.19
General industrial machinery	0.17	0.38	2.07
Office machines and automatic data processing equip.	0.03	2.12	5.89
Telecommunications and sound recording apparatus	2.19	10.41	9.81
Electrical machiney and apparatus	1.29	9.27	10.73
Road vehicles	0.12	1.30	3.46
Travel goods	1.73	1.57	2.05
Articles of apparel and clothing accessories	32.30	26.90	18.55
Footwear	3.51	4.42	6.71
Photographic apparatus, optical goods, watches	0.60	1.22	2.16
Miscellaneous manufacturing articles, n.e.s.	15.48	10.66	9.95

Source: OECD (1988).

now comprises more technology-intensive goods such as telecommunications and sound recording apparatus, office machinery and data processing equipment and electrical machinery and apparatus.

Table 7.4 further illustrates the change that has taken place in the composition of NIC exports by separating the technology intensity level of different exports. Whereas, in 1964, 81% of NIC exports were low technology, by 1985, this percentage had fallen to 53%. In 1964, only 2% of NIC exports were high technology, but by 1985, this percentage had risen to 25%.

As the first generation NICs lost their comparative advantage in labour-intensive manufactures, they created room for the emergence of a second generation of NICs/NECs to emerge as exporters of these goods. A similar process is now happening as second generation NICs move into more sophisticated sectors, vacating the market in labour-intensive goods for a new third or fourth generation. This process is sometimes referred to as the 'flying geese' hypothesis because it resembles a V-formation. According to this view, Japan

Table 7.4 The Changing Composition of NIC Exports to the OECD: Manufactures by Technology Level, Percentage share

	Technology level			
Year	*High*	*Medium*	*Low*	*Total*
1964	2.2	15.9	81.6	100.0
1973	17.6	13.9	68.4	100.0
1978	20.0	16.3	63.5	100.0
1979	20.7	17.4	61.7	100.0
1980	21.5	18.5	59.8	100.0
1981	22.0	18.0	59.5	100.0
1982	22.1	18.9	58.9	100.0
1983	24.1	19.1	56.7	100.0
1984	25.3	20.2	54.4	100.0
1985	25.0	21.6	53.2	100.0

Source: OECD (1988).

was the first country to pioneer a comparative advantage in labour-intensive manufactures and make inroads into western markets. As Japan grew, she abandoned labour-intensive manufactures for more sophisticated skill-intensive manufactures, creating room for the rise of the first NICs. As these second generation NICs followed in the wake of Japan they in turn vacated the labour-intensive end of the market for a third and fourth generation. It is clear, however, that there is nothing automatic about this process. The fact that some developing countries succeed while others fail suggests that additional factors must be present for a country to successfully transform itself into an NIC.

Reasons for the Rapid Emergence of the NICs

What factors can account for the sudden and very rapid rise of the NICs beginning in the late 1960s and extending through to a second and third generation in the 1980s and 1990s? Probably, the explanation is to be found in what the OECD (1988) has termed the 'double dynamic' of, on the one hand, internal economic success and, on the other, changes within the world trading system and in the strategies of western multinationals in response to these changes. In what follows, each of these factors is discussed.

Internal Economic Success

There has been much discussion in recent decades as to the reasons why the NICs have succeeded where other developing countries have failed and whether these countries – the East Asian NICs in particular – provide a model for other developing countries. One explanation for the success of these economies is their adoption of outward-looking, export-oriented trade policies in place of the failed policies of import substitution that were in vogue in the early years of the post-war period. As noted above, a characteristic of all these countries is that, to varying degrees, they adopted outward-looking trade policies that promoted exports rather than encouraging import substitution. In some of the East Asian NICs – notably, Hong Kong and Singapore – outward-looking strategies were pursued from the beginning. In others, however, a conscious decision was made to liberalise their trade and adopt measures specifically designed to encourage exports. The adoption of such measures enabled these economies to embark on a path of rapid and sustained economic growth.

Inward-looking, import substitution policies were the fashion in developing countries in the first decade and a half after the end of the Second World War. It was argued that such countries would fall further behind the advanced industrialised countries if they relied upon trade. One reason was the assertion that over time the international terms of trade moved in favour of the advanced industrialised countries. It was argued that, because less developed countries export mainly primary commodities and import manufactures, their terms of trade tend to deteriorate in the long run, because the prices of primary commodities tend to fall relative to the prices of manufactured goods. It was also argued that, because less developed countries rely on a small number of primary commodities for exports earnings, their export earnings are more unstable than those of developed countries. This is because primary commodity prices fluctuate by more than manufactured goods prices. Furthermore, to the extent that developing countries succeed in establishing manufacturing industries, their goods face import barriers if and when they are exported to the developed countries. Instead, it was argued less developed countries should reduce their dependence on trade by encouraging the development of manufacturing industries which would produce goods that otherwise would have to be imported. As far as possible, only essential items should be imported from abroad, thereby conserving the country's scarce foreign currency earnings.

To successfully establish new industries, it was argued that developing countries should give protection to their 'infant industries' by imposing high tariffs on imports, operating strict import licensing and through the use of import quotas. Exchange controls were also deemed necessary to ration scarce foreign currency and, in the manner of a wartime economy, ensure that foreign currency was used only for the purchase of essentials. Such policies were often accompanied by the maintenance of an overvalued exchange rate (usually by pegging the currency to the U.S. dollar or pound sterling) to keep down the cost of imported food and raw materials. In many countries, reliance was also placed on state control of key industries and centralised planning on the grounds that market mechanisms are inappropriate for allocating resources in developing countries. Structural rigidities, imperfect information and externalities, the argument went, all render markets inadequate as mechanisms for ensuring that resources are allocated in an optimal manner. Usually, a two-stage strategy was favoured. In the first stage, the aim was to establish local consumer goods industries, initially to produce non-durable consumer goods such as food and beverages but later extending to certain durable consumer goods such as automobiles also. In the second stage, the emphasis switched to the development of local capital goods industries (e.g. industrial machinery) and intermediate goods industries (e.g. chemicals, iron and steel) to supply the consumer goods sector.

In practice, few import substitution policies ever worked well. The reasons are several fold:

1. Although the aim of the policy was to conserve scarce foreign currency for the import of essentials only, most import-substitution strategies ran into balance of payments difficulties. The reason was that the new industries created behind high tariff walls needed to import more raw materials, intermediate goods and capital goods as they were established and began to grow. The problem was particularly acute in the first phase, where the emphasis was on building up local consumer goods industries. The demand for capital goods (machinery, equipment, etc.) and raw materials/intermediate goods rises fast as the new industries are established. Invariably, the second stage was never reached. At the same time, the use of high import barriers raised costs to exporters that reduced their competitiveness and, hence, export earnings.
2. Import substitution strategies led to an increased dependence on the advanced industrialised countries for capital and technology. Most less-developed countries suffered from a low level of domestic savings and inadequate or non-existent capital markets. This meant that the programme of industrialisation had to be financed by importing capital from abroad. Where the technology to produce these goods was not available locally, this had to be imported from abroad whether through direct investment or under licensing agreements. Large-scale inflows of foreign capital increased the overseas indebtedness of these countries, necessitating large outflows in later years to service overseas borrowings and repay loans be coming due for redemption.
3. A policy of protecting newly established local industries from foreign competition by high tariffs and non-tariff barriers raised

the prices of manufactures relative to the price of non-manufactured goods in the local economy. This implied discrimination against the agricultural sector which did not enjoy the same level of protection. An overvalued exchange rate also served to depress domestic farm prices by flooding the local market with cheap food supplied from abroad. The consequent fall in agricultural output created shortages at home and led to increased imports of food from abroad. This added to the balance of payments difficulties caused by increased imports of raw materials and other manufactures. At the same time, the long-term development of farming was impeded.

4. The policy of protecting local producers from foreign competition led to the creation of local monopolies. Very often, a single dominant producer controlled the entire local market, with the power to restrict supply and drive up price. At the same time, he had little or no incentive to increase efficiency and cut costs. Instead, the main concern was to bribe local officials to ensure the continuation of the local monopoly. High and rising prices added to inflationary pressures within the local economy. These were further aggravated by the adoption of expansionary fiscal and monetary policies designed to create a buoyant market for the new industries.

Because of these disadvantages of an inward-looking, import-substitution policy, many developing countries began, in the late 1960s, to switch to outward-looking, export-oriented strategies. (Box 7.1 compares the two types of policy.) In 1974, *South Korea* embarked on a

Box 7.1 Inward-Looking Import Substitution versus Outward-Looking Export-Oriented Policies

An Inward-looking Import-substitution Strategy	An Outward-looking Export-oriented Strategy
• High import tariffs on manufactured goods	• Reduction in import tariffs on manufactured goods
• Import embargoes	• Elimination of some import quotas
• Import quotas	• Direct export subsidies
• Import licensing	• Low-cost credit for exporters
• Import deposit schemes	• Preferential access to credit for exporters
• Local content programmes	• Tax exemptions/rebates for exporters
• Restrictions on outflow of capital	• Creation of special export processing zones (EPZs)
• Multiple exchange rates	• Relaxation of controls on capital outflows
• Overvalued exchange rate	• Reduce restrictions on inward investment
• Expansionary fiscal/monetary policy	• Low exchange rate through exchange rate depreciation
• Price controls	• Tight monetary/fiscal policy to hold down inflation

policy of export-led industrialisation. Special financial and fiscal incentives were introduced for exporters and customs duties on imports of capital goods were lowered. A single exchange rate was introduced and the Korean won devalued. *Taiwan* was one of the first developing countries to make the transition. In 1958, she introduced similar measures to stimulate exports. Again, a single exchange rate replaced multiple exchange rates and the rate was kept down. Tariffs and other import controls were lowered and low interest loans were introduced for exporters. *Thailand* switched to export promotion more recently. Only in 1981 did policy shift in the direction of export promotion. Export taxes were reduced, the baht devalued and tariffs lowered. Subsidised export credits were introduced and an attitude of greater openness towards foreign investment was adopted. In South America, the change occurred somewhat later. In *Mexico*, the shift towards export promotion did not take place until the mid-1980s. Import restrictions were gradually lowered and the Mexican peso devalued. This was combined with a more open policy towards foreign investment. *Brazil*, faced with declining foreign currency earnings in the late 1970s and early 1980s, also abandoned import substitution in favour of export promotion. The local currency was devalued, although much less was done than in other NICs to liberalise trade.

The essence of an outward-looking, export-oriented strategy is that the emphasis of policy is placed primarily on boosting export earnings, rather than protecting local industries from imports. Indeed, because tariffs and other import barriers raise costs to exporters, they are lowered on certain goods, such as capital and intermediate goods, as a means of increasing competitiveness. At the same time, the exchange rate is lowered whether through pegging the exchange rate at a lower level or allowing it to find its own level on the foreign exchange market. Depreciation makes exports more competitive on world markets, while raising the costs of imports. If it is successful in cutting imports and raising exports, it provides the solution to a deteriorating balance of payments position. In addition, most governments make use of a wide range of financial and fiscal incentives to assist the export sector, including low-cost credit, direct export subsidies, input subsidies and more favourable tax treatment. A more friendly attitude towards inward FDI is a further ingredient of such a policy, the aim being to attract export-platform investments. The introduction of relatively tight monetary and fiscal policies sometimes accompanies such measures, the aim being to curb excess demand and hold down domestic costs and prices.

An additional feature of many of the export promotion policies pursued by NICs has been the creation of special *export-processing zones* (EPZs). These are areas within the local economy specifically designed to attract export-platform investments by foreign firms. (See Chapter 5 for a discussion of this type of investment.) Foreign MNCs, which set up subsidiaries in an EPZ, enjoy special privileges not available to other firms. In particular, they are allowed to import raw materials and other semi-finished goods for further processing without restriction or the need to pay any tariff. They are often granted exemption from certain taxes, minimum wage laws and other regulations and have access to cheap, subsidised infrastructure (e.g. port facilities, electricity supply, etc.). According to the UNCTC (1983), in 1980, there were 53 such EPZs in developing countries employing nearly one million people. Seventy-two percent of the total employment was located in seven NICs (South Korea, Singapore, Mexico, Hong Kong, Malaysia, the Philippines and Brazil). EPZs were most common in electrical machinery, electronic goods, textiles and clothing.

The main advantages of an outward-looking, export-oriented strategy are as follows:

1. It shifts the bias of economic policy towards, precisely, those industries in which developing countries enjoy a comparative cost advantage. To begin with, these are likely to be relatively simple, labour-intensive manufactures. By way of contrast, an import substitution policy tends to favour the development of capital-intensive industries. However, over time, as wage costs rise as a consequence of economic development, comparative advantage will move away from the labour-intensive industries and towards the more skill- or technology-intensive sectors. An export-oriented strategy facilitates this shift by favouring those industries in which the country enjoys the most export success.
2. Particularly for countries with a small domestic market, an export promotion policy is more likely to provide firms with the large, dynamic market needed to fully exploit available economies of scale. For small countries, the domestic market is likely to be too limiting, especially for the capital-intensive industries that an import substitution strategy seeks to develop, as these are industries in which unit costs fall rapidly with the scale of production.
3. Fast export growth is also likely to feed through into the local economy creating expanding demand in other capital or intermediate goods industries that supply inputs to the export firms and other ancillar industries which provide services for firms in the export sector. The possibility exists of generating a virtuous cycle of expansion in which export growth feeds through into capital investment, which in turn, raises output and incomes and expands demand for locally produced goods and services.
4. By exposing formerly protected industries to increased competition, trade liberalisation lowers costs and prices in these sectors, with beneficial effects on other parts of the economy, and makes it easier for the authorities to control inflation.
5. The effect on the distribution of income within the country is likely to be more favourable under an export promotion policy. One reason is that the policy shifts the bias away from capital-intensive industries and towards labour-intensive industries (at first unskilled and then skilled labour-intensive). It therefore, boosts the price of labour relative to the price of capital. As owners of capital are richer than unskilled labourers, the result is a more egalitarian distribution of income. Increased import competition also eliminates the rents of local monopolists, previously sheltered from competition by high import barriers.

The World Bank (1987) has produced evidence to show a that relationship exists between the adoption of outward-looking trade policies and economic performance in developing countries. The World Bank examined the policies of some forty-one developing countries over two consecutive periods, 1963–73 and 1973–85, to see if countries pursuing outward-looking strategies performed any better than those pursuing inward-oriented policies. Countries were put into one of four categories – strongly outward-oriented, moderately outward-oriented, moderately inward-oriented and strongly inward-oriented – according to the policies pursued during each of the two periods. A *strongly outward-oriented policy* was defined as one in which there was little or no policy bias towards the domestic market. This means that, if import barriers existed creating such a bias, these were roughly matched by export incentives creating a bias in the opposite direction. It also required that the exchange rate be set at an economically appropriate level, that is, that the currency was not overvalued. A *moderately outward-oriented policy* was one in which there was only a slight bias towards the domestic market (which would be the case if export incentives did not offset the bias created towards domestic industries by import barriers and/or the exchange rate was slightly overvalued). A *moderately inward-oriented policy* was defined as one in which there was an unmistakable bias towards production for the domestic market due to high and variable levels of import protection and/or a permanently overvalued exchange rate. Finally, a *strongly inward-oriented policy* was one in which a very pronounced discrimination existed towards production for the domestic market, characterised by very high tariffs, quantitative trade barriers as the norm rather than the exception and a grossly overvalued exchange rate. Table 7.5 shows the results.

In both periods, the three most outwardly oriented countries – Singapore, South Korea and Hong Kong – grew faster than any of the other forty-one countries. (Cameroon enjoyed a slightly faster rate than South Korea in the second period.) In the first period, the outwardly oriented countries grew on average faster than the inwardly oriented ones. However, there were a few cases where inwardly oriented countries performed better (Yugoslavia, Mexico, Nigeria, Tunisia, Kenya, Turkey and the Dominican Republic). In the second period, the growth rate in the moderately inward-oriented countries was slightly faster than the moderately outward. A perfect correlation is, of course, improbable because trade policy is likely to have been only one of the factors affecting growth in different countries. Nevertheless, the evidence tends to favour the view that economic growth in developing countries is enhanced by the adoption of an outward-looking export policy.

Alas, the existence of a strong correlation between economic growth and the adoption of an outward-looking export strategy does not prove that one caused the other! The direction of causation could have been in the opposite direction: economic growth may have led to export expansion. A weakness of the trade expansion hypothesis is that it assumes that there are no supply constraints on export growth. However, export expansion is only possible if the capacity to export more is created in the first place. This presupposes that exporting firms have undertaken previous investment. Yet a third possibility is that both domestic growth and export expansion are the results of some third factor. Rodrick (1994, 1998) has argued that the World Bank attaches too much importance to export orientation as the cause of faster growth in these economies. He has argued that a more careful examination of what took place in these countries shows that increased exports played only a small role in the expansion that they enjoyed. Instead, the main cause of faster growth was a massive increase in the volume of capital investment far in excess of what can be attributed to export growth. Certainly, high levels of investment in physical capital were an important factor in the growth of the East Asian NICs. For example, in 1990, gross investment in the East Asian NICs averaged 37% of GDP compared with 26% in developing countries as a whole (World Bank, 1993). This, in turn, was made possible by a big increase in the proportion of GDP that was saved. In the 1960s, East Asian NICs typically saved roughly 16% of GDP. By the early 1990s, the ratio of savings to GDP was raised to more than 36%. High levels of investment in human capital (especially in primary and secondary education) appear also to have played an

Table 7.5 The Outward-Looking Way to Faster Growth: Real GNP per Person, Annual Average Growth (percentage)

Outward-oriented		*Inward-oriented*	
Strongly	*Moderately*	*Moderately*	*Strongly*
1965–73			
Singapore 9.0	Brazil 5.5	Yugoslavia 4.9	Turkey 3.5
South Korea 7.1	Israel 5.4	Mexico 4.3	Dominican Republic 3.4
Hong Kong 6.0	Thailand 4.9	Nigeria 4.2	Burundi 3.2
	Indonesia 4.6	Tunisia 4.0	Argentina 3.1
	Costa Rica 3.9	Kenya 3.9	Pakistan 3.1
	Malaysia 3.8	Philippines 2.2	Tanzania 2.7
	Ivory Coast 3.5	Bolivia 2.0	Sri Lanka 2.3
	Colombia 3.3	Honduras 1.9	Ethiopia 1.9
	Guatemala 2.7	El Salvador 1.4	Chile 1.7
		Madagascar 1.1	Peru 1.5
		Nicaragua 1.1	Uruguay 1.5
			Zambia 1.2
			India 1.1
			Ghana 0.4
	Cameroon −0.1	Senegal −0.6	Bangladesh −1.4
			Sudan −1.9
1973–85			
Singapore 6.5	Malaysia 4.1	Cameroon 5.6	Bangladesh 2.0
Hong Kong 6.3	Thailand 3.8	Indonesia 4.0	India 2.0
South Korea 5.4	Tunisia 2.9	Sri Lanka 3.3	Burundi 1.2
	Brazil 1.5	Pakistan 3.1	Dominican Republic 0.5
	Turkey 1.4	Yugoslavia 2.7	
	Israel 0.4	Colombia 1.8	
	Uruguay 0.4	Mexico 1.3	
	Chile 0.1	Philippines 1.1	
		Kenya 0.3	
		Honduras −0.1	Ethiopia −0.4
		Senegal −0.8	Sudan −0.4
		Costa Rica −1.0	Peru −1.1
		Guatemala −1.0	Tanzania −1.6
		Ivory Coast −1.2	Argentina −2.0
		El Salvador −3.5	Zambia −2.3
		Nicaragua −3.9	Nigeria −2.5
			Bolivia −3.1
			Ghana −3.2
			Madagascar −3.4

Source: World Bank (1987).

important role in raising the productivity of the workforce.

Rodrick (1994) argues that the role played by the government was an important factor in the success of these economies. Not only did governments provide a favourable environment for an investment boom, they directly stimulated investment through a series of strategic interventions including the use of investment subsidies, administrative guidance and public enterprise. At the same time, the existence of favourable initial conditions, in particular a skilled labour force, was important. The relatively equal distribution of income in these countries compared with other developing countries (due largely to historical factors) also helped. High levels of investment in primary and secondary education promoted greater income equality. This, in turn, meant the absence of powerful industrial or landed interest groups exerting pressure on governments for special treatment. Instead, the public bureaucracy was left relatively free to concentrate on the pursuit of economic aims. In countries where these conditions were absent, government intervention was generally less successful.

Certainly, in several of the East Asian NICs, governments did intervene extensively. In its report on *The East Asian Miracle*, the World Bank (1993) argued that some of these forms of intervention were beneficial. In particular, export promotion policies and the use of directed credit to boost export industries played a positive role in promoting growth. In Japan and South Korea, governments used 'contests' between firms to allocate resources. Companies were judged on their success as exporters and rewarded with subsidised credit, foreign exchange or public funds. However, the success of these 'contests' as a means of allocating resources depended heavily on the existence of a high quality and relatively honest state bureaucracy. This ensured that intervention was not used to bestow favours on particular producers in return for bribes and that the performance of companies receiving selective support was monitored. However, some of the more ambitious interventions by governments in these countries were much less successful. Some attempts by certain countries to promote particular sectors of industry (South Korea in chemicals and Japan in computer chips) were largely failures. The World Bank found that, in South Korea and Taiwan, the sectors which were not promoted performed as well as those that were. In other words, in these countries, success was more in spite of than because of government intervention.

Rodrick (1998) has argued that a major explanation for the success of these economies is to be found in the effectiveness of the macroeconomic policies which they pursued in the face of external disturbances. The reason why the East Asian NICs performed better than other developing countries was that they adjusted quicker and more decisively to the oil shocks of the 1970s. The rise in world oil prices inflicted a severe terms of trade loss on most of these countries. However, the economies which did best were those which took appropriate action by devaluing their exchange rate to counter their worsening payments imbalance, tightening fiscal and monetary policy to control inflation and introducing microeconomic measures to raise energy efficiency. Countries that took these measures, experienced an initial downturn but were subsequently able to resume normal economic growth. Other developing countries, that failed to adopt these measures, ended up in difficulty. Their balance of payments deficit widened, government borrowing escalated and inflation took off. The result was that, in the long run their economies under-performed relative to others. Rodrick has found a strong correlation between the speed with which macroeconomic adjustment took place and the extent to which these countries were free of social conflicts and/or were better able to manage social conflicts that arose. Social conflict was measured by reference to factors such as the degree of income inequality, ethnic and linguistic fragmentation and social distrust and conflict management by the existence of democratic political institutions, the quality of government institutions and the amount spent by the public sector on social insurance. This suggests that the 'missing factor' in explaining the success of the East Asian NICs may have been the absence of deep social conflicts of the kind found in other developing countries as well as their ability to manage potential social conflict more effectively.

More recently, Professor Paul Krugman has challenged the 'conventional wisdom' by arguing that there was, nothing exceptional about the performance of the East Asian NICs (Krugman, 1996). Krugman bases his argument on work carried out by Alwyn Young, who looked at GDP growth in some 118 countries over the period from 1970 to 1985 (Young, 1992). Young split GDP growth into three elements – increases in capital and labour inputs and increases in total factor productivity (TFP) – and found that growth of TFP was no higher in East Asia than in the advanced industrialised countries. However, Krugman's riposte has not gone unchallenged. Young's study has been criticised for treating TFP as a residual (i.e. any growth which cannot be attributed to increased inputs of capital and labour). It has been argued that some of the growth attributed to capital accumulation should have been counted as an improvement in efficiency. Other studies have obtained higher estimates of TFP (UBS, 1996 and IMF, 1996). Anyhow, the high level of investment achieved by these economies should itself be viewed as a significant achievement.

The External Environment

The second factor in the sudden emergence of the NICs has been the changes that have taken place in the global pattern of comparative advantage and international division of labour. In the early years of the post-war period, North America and Europe enjoyed a comparative advantage in the production of most manufactured goods. The reasons were, of course, historical. These countries had been the first to industrialise in the preceding century or half-century. They enjoyed a relative abundance of capital and a well-educated and skilled labour force. In those industries subject to rapid technological change, they had a head start. The much higher levels of income in these countries also meant a much greater demand for consumer goods. In increasing returns activities, this meant that the established industries of these countries enjoyed a cost advantage from being able to produce on a larger scale.

However, in the course of the post-war period, these countries found their traditional cost advantage in certain branches of manufacturing disappear. These were the low technology, labour-intensive industries, such as clothing, textiles, footwear and leather goods, as well as certain of the more capital-intensive capital and intermediate goods industries such as shipbuilding and steel. To some extent, this was inevitable as countries in other regions of the world industrialised and began to catch up with the already industrialised countries in the richer half of the world. Partly, too, it was due to rising wage costs in the advanced industrialised countries, as workers began to demand a bigger share in the rewards from faster growth. Their power to extract higher wages and better working conditions increased through their organisation into trade unions. In the more labour-intensive branches of manufacturing, this left producers in the western industrialised economies at a distinct cost disadvantage when competing with producers in developing countries where the capital and skills existed to do so.

Partly, too, it reflected the out-workings of the product life cycle discussed in earlier chapters of this book. Certain new products discovered in the advanced industrialised countries had come of age and begun to enter their standardisation phase. In these industries, competition became intense, leading to a search by the established producers in the advanced industrialised countries for new, lower cost locations to produce these goods. As we know, one result of this process was that producers began building factories in certain low-wage economies in the developing world and exporting products back to the home country. Developing countries, which possessed large amounts of relatively cheap, moderately skilled labour and which could provide a stable environment for investors from the advanced industrialised countries, were able to attract large amounts of investment of this kind. As a result, they were able to develop a comparative advantage in industries in which the advanced industrialised countries had once been the leaders.

However, as was observed in Chapter 5, western MNCs rarely transferred their entire production of a particular good to a new location in the developing world. Rather, their approach was to transfer those stages in the production process that require relatively large proportions of labour relative to capital, to countries where labour was cheap. In some industries, they preferred to sub-contract producers to perform these stages using components and parts supplied from the home country. In electronics, for example, MNCs in all the western industrialised countries have found it profitable to export components and parts to newly established plants in NICs for final assembly and then to re-import the finished product for sale. In the textiles industry, western producers have often preferred to sub-contract producers in the NICs to make up a finished garment using a fabric produced in the home country. As we saw in Chapter 5, such so-called 'offshore' or 'outward processing' has resulted in a fragmentation of the production process and brought into being a new international division of labour. However, this has played an important role in enabling the NICs to achieve accelerated growth through export expansion.

Trade policies in the advanced industrialised countries have assisted this process. Thus, many of the advanced industrialised countries have built into their tariff schedules special *offshore assembly provisions* (OAPs). The essence of these measures is that, where an imported product has been assembled abroad using components and parts supplied by a firm located in the importing country, the tariff is applied only to the value-added abroad and not the final price. For example, suppose a British producer of video cassette recorders exports kits worth £250 each to Malaysia for assembly and packaging. Suppose the finished product is worth £500 and is imported back to Britain for sale on the home market. Suppose further that the tariff on imported VCRs is 10%. If the VCR has been wholly produced abroad, it would have attracted a tariff of £500 × 0.10 = £50. However, because the product was made using components and parts produced in the UK, a tariff of only £250 × 0.10 = £25 is levied. The evidence shows that imports of products subject to offshore processing have grown faster than total imports of the product in question in all countries where these provisions apply. For example, Lall (1980) estimated that, between 1970 and 1976, developing country exports of manufactures to the United States which were subject to OAPs grew by 530% while exports of all manufactures by developing countries to the United States grew by only 305%. Also, over the period from 1966 to 1972, U.S. imports of OAP manufactures from developing countries grew at an annual rate of 60% compared with 12% for imports of non-OAP manufactures. The corresponding figures for West Germany were 36 and 11% and for the Netherlands 39 and 2%.

Finally, exports from NICs benefited from the *tariff preferences* granted in the 1970s by the developed countries on imports of manufactures from developing countries. In 1971, the GATT countries agreed to a waiver from Article I of the General Agreement – which requires all signatories to treat imports from fellow signatories the same (i.e. not to discriminate) – allowing developed countries to introduce special preferences on imports of processed goods from developing countries. Such 'positive discrimination' in favour of imports of manufactures from developing countries had been first advocated by the United Nations Conference on Trade and Development (UNCTAD) in 1964 as part of a programme for creating a 'new international economic order'. The scheme known as the *Generalised System of Preference* (GSP) came into effect in the European Community and Japan in 1971, Canada in 1974 and the United States in 1976. In most cases, these arrangements allowed developing countries tariff-free access for their manufactures to the markets of the advanced industrialised countries although subject to various qualifications. The U.S. scheme excluded certain developing countries and certain so-called 'sensitive products'. The EC scheme was more comprehensive in its coverage but put stricter limits on the amount of an individual product that could be imported under the scheme. All schemes applied strict 'rules of origin' which required that products be substantially produced within the beneficiary country to qualify. In addition, the EC had its own system of preferences for the African, Caribbean and Pacific (ACP) countries that were signatories of the Lomé Convention of 1975.

There seems little doubt that these schemes have had a positive effect on developing country exports of manufactures. However, a disproportionate share of the benefits appears to have accrued to a relatively small group of developing countries. Langhammer and Sapir (1987) estimated that three countries – Taiwan, South Korea and Hong Kong – accounted for about two-thirds of the trade effect of the GSP, taking imports to all OECD countries into account. Some ten developing countries shared 90% of the gain. They put the trade effect at $4.6 billion for 1983 or roughly 3.2% of MFN dutiable imports. Clearly the GSP was an important factor in the expansion of the NICs even if its effect on growth in the developing world as a whole was disappointing.

The Effects of the Rise of the NICs on the Advanced Industrialised Countries

What has been the impact of the rise of the NICs on the advanced industrialised countries of Western Europe and North America? We begin with an examination of the statistical evidence. How important are imports from NICs in the total trade of the western industrialised countries (i.e. the members of the OECD)? Much depends on how broadly the NICs are defined. Using a narrow definition of NICs (the four East Asian NICs plus Brazil and Mexico), the OECD found that their share of OECD manufacturing imports rose from 1.6% in 1964 to 9.5% in 1985 (OECD, 1988). If, instead, attention is focused on the dynamic Asian economies (defined as China, Chinese Taipei, Hong Kong, South Korea, Malaysia, Singapore and Thailand), their share of OECD imports of *machinery and transport equipment* rose from 0.2% in 1964 to 5.8% in 1985 and 11.5% in 1993 (OECD, 1995). For *other manufactured goods*, the share rose from 2.8% in 1964 to 11.2% in 1985 and 14.1% in 1993. In 1993, an estimated 18% of OECD imports of machinery and transport equipment and 30.1% of imports of other manufactures came from countries other than the members of the OECD. Thus, imports from NICs have grown significantly as a proportion of total OECD imports. Although they are less important than imports from other advanced industrialised countries, they nevertheless account for a major share of total trade.

A method commonly used by economists to measure the degree of competition posed by imports from a particular source is to calculate the level of so-called *import penetration*. This is given by the ratio of imports-to-apparent consumption, the latter being defined as domestic production (Q), less exports (X) plus imports (M) ($AC = Q - X + M$). Estimates of import penetration provided by the OECD show the trend over the period from 1970 to 1985 (Table 7.6). In 1970, overall level of import penetration for OECD imports from NICs was quite low. In all OECD countries, NIC imports accounted for less than 1% of apparent consumption of manufactured goods. By 1985, this had risen to well over 1% in most countries, especially Australia and the United States. Nevertheless, the degree of import penetration remained relatively modest overall. If, instead, attention is focussed on particular product groups in which the NICs have competed most fiercely, it is clear that the level of import penetration is significantly higher and has risen rapidly. In the traditional sectors in which NICs have competed strongly, namely, textiles, clothing, leather and footwear, high levels of import penetration were evident, particularly for Sweden, Australia and the United States. In the more skill-intensive sectors also, the degree of import penetration rose sharply. In electrical machines and appliances, the import penetration ratio in 1985 was high in the United States, Australia and Canada. In radio, TV and communications equipment, very high import penetration ratios were to be found in Australia and Canada and, to a lesser extent, the United States.

Figures for the second half of the 1980s show that the level of import penetration has

Table 7.6 Import Penetration Ratios for OECD Imports from NICs, 1970–1985 (percentage)

	Total Manufacturing		*Textiles, clothing, leather and footwear*		*Electrical machines and appliances*		*Radio, TV and communication equipment*	
Country	*1970*	*1985*	*1970*	*1985*	*1970*	*1985*	*1970*	*1985*
Australia	0.49	3.09	2.50	11.55	0.12	4.98	0.11	16.23
Canada	0.43	1.98	2.08	9.99	0.08	2.23	0.90	11.82
France	0.15	0.79	0.11	2.08	0.01	0.73	0.06	2.39
Germany	0.38	1.40	1.33	7.96	0.04	1.32	0.38	5.36
Italy	0.27	0.91	0.34	1.18	0.07	0.52	0.40	3.91
Japan	0.30	0.85	1.17	3.82	0.10	0.73	0.19	0.68
Sweden	0.65	1.80	4.03	18.72	0.02	1.09	0.20	5.31
United Kingdom	0.41	1.42	2.10	7.74	0.14	1.15	0.37	4.11
United States	0.49	2.41	1.53	11.16	0.44	5.93	1.55	7.54

Source: OECD (1988).

Table 7.7 Import Penetration Ratios for OECD Countries from 1985 to 1991 (percentage)

	EU		*USA/Canada*		*Japan*		*Total*	
	1985–86	*1990–91*	*1985–86*	*1990–91*	*1985–86*	*1990–91*	*1985–86*	*1990–91*
Textiles	2.30	2.34	2.22	2.54	1.23	1.62	2.03	2.24
Clothing	10.99	11.36	20.62	20.82	8.36	11.03	15.55	15.15
Wood products, paper and printing	0.94	0.54	1.01	1.13	0.49	0.77	0.89	0.96
Chemicals	0.60	0.56	0.67	0.72	0.76	0.81	0.67	0.68
Transport equipment	0.53	0.65	0.77	1.84	0.03	0.12	0.57	0.99
Machinery and other manufactured goods	2.77	3.49	5.86	0.35	0.84	1.64	3.82	4.65
Total Manufactures	1.48	1.65	2.66	3.57	0.92	1.35	1.92	2.20

Source: UNCTAD (1994).

increased further. Table 7.7 shows the level of import penetration for a wider range of manufacturing imports from developing countries which are major exporters of manufactures. By 1991, it was still the case that the overall level of import penetration remained relatively low, although it was higher for the United States/ Canada than for Japan or the EU. However, high levels of import penetration were apparent in particular sectors. Clothing had the highest recorded import penetration ratio, although the trend was a downward one. A high and rising level of import penetration was apparent in machinery and other manufactured goods. The fastest increase in the level of import penetration was apparent in transport equipment.

Given the relatively low share of total consumption in the advanced industrialised countries accounted for by imports from NICs, it might seem that the anxiety expressed by these countries regarding the growth of imports from the NICs is unwarranted. However, it is clear that, in certain specific sectors, the challenge is a real one. Are the advanced industrialised countries, therefore, justified in attributing some loss of employment in these industries to low-cost imports from NICs? Clearly, an increase in imports will cause some decrease in employment in the sectors affected. This might be called the 'employment displacement effect' of expanded trade with NICs. However, to reach any conclusion regarding the overall employment effect, it is necessary to examine *total* trade between the NICs and the advanced industrialised countries. As the NICs have grown, exports from the advanced industrialised countries have also expanded. This has served to increase employment in the export sector, just as increased imports have decreased employment in the import substitute sector. This is the 'employment creation' effect. There is no reason why employment creation should not match the employment displacement effect if there is a balanced expansion of trade between the two groups. It may be the case that, because NICs have in the past enjoyed a comparative advantage in labour-intensive goods, increased imports from NICs destroy more jobs than are created by increased exports to the NICs. This, however, needs to be demonstrated. It is also possible that the type of employment created in the export sector is more skilled than the labour displaced by the growth of imports from NICs. In this case, workers will face difficulties in moving out of the declining sector and into the expanding sector of the economy. However, this is a problem of re-allocating labour within the economy, not of a decline in the number of jobs available.

The problem of 'adjustment' is considered in greater depth below. However, before doing so, it is necessary to examine the impact of the rise of the NICs on the balance of payments of the western industrialised economies. Using a narrow definition of the NICs (the four East Asian NICs – Hong Kong, Taiwan, Singapore and South Korea – plus Brazil and Mexico), the OECD showed that, before 1980, OECD exports of manufactures to NICs consistently exceeded OECD imports of manufactures (OECD, 1988). After 1980, however, OECD exports fell while imports increased, such that the trade balance moved in favour of the NICs. However, they found this to be entirely due to a deterioration of the U.S. trade balance caused by the appreciation of the U.S. dollar. U.S. imports rose strongly, while certain NICs reduced their imports because of mounting international indebtedness. Because the United States dominates OECD trade with the NICs, swings in the U.S. balance have a major impact on the overall balance of the OECD countries.

Table 7.8 shows the balance of trade in manufactured goods between the OECD countries and the Asian NICs only. The Asian NICs are defined more broadly than in the OECD study reflecting the subsequent emergence of other NICs in the region. The table reveals how the trade balance moved in favour of the NICs in 1984, whereas, in earlier years, it favoured the OECD countries. Although the West European countries ran a small deficit in their trade with the Asian NICs, the main cause of the turnaround was the U.S. deficit. Unlike other OECD countries, the US was in deficit in her trade with the Asian NICs in the earlier years also. The OECD deficit persisted in 1993, although the export–import ratio was higher than in 1984. Once again, the main cause of the deficit was U.S. trade. The declining U.S. export–import ratio shows that the main cause of this was rising U.S. imports from the Asian NICs. By way of contrast, Japan ran a large surplus on her trade with these countries, although the surplus was falling in relative terms. The EU ran a small deficit on her trade with these countries, although Germany's deficit with the NICs disappeared.

If, therefore, attention is focussed on trade between the OECD countries and the Asian NICs alone, it is clear that trade in manufactures has expanded in a fairly balanced way with OECD exports growing at a rate only slightly slower than that of OECD imports. This would suggest that as much employment was created as was displaced as a result of increased trade. However, if the employment content of NIC exports was greater than the employment content of OECD exports, the net effect may have been negative. In the case of the United States, however, the growth of U.S. imports from Asian NICs was clearly much greater than the growth of U.S. exports to these countries. In this case, increased trade with the NICs probably has resulted in net employment displacement. Given, too, that the U.S. import penetration ratio for imports of manufactures from NICs was higher than in other advanced industrialised countries, it is, perhaps, not

Table 7.8 Exports and Imports of Manufactured Goods by OECD Countries to Asian NICs, 1964–1993 (millions of U.S. dollars)

		1964	*1974*	*1984*	*1993*
United States	Exports	369.11	3,629.8	15,715.67	55,409.11
	Imports	397.08	6,011.87	26,991.31	115,954.36
	Balance	−27.97	−2,382.07	−11,275.64	−60,545.25
	Export–Import Ratio	0.9296	0.6038	0.5822	0.4786
Japan	Exports	1,011.23	9,543.17	35,716.43	111,992.56
	Imports	143.99	2,651.32	7,791.36	37,450.33
	Balance	867.24	6,891.85	27,925.07	74,542.23
	Export–Import Ratio	7.0229	3.5994	4.5841	2.9904
Germany	Exports	204.02	2,169.95	4,346.65	18,073.17
	Imports	81.79	1,182.99	4,726.82	17,728.68
	Balance	122.23	986.96	−380.17	344.49
	Export–Import Ratio	2.4944	1.8343	0.9196	1.0194
European Union	Exports	951.56	5,027.59	14,777.72	51,085.06
	Imports	507.97	4,181.23	15,571.56	57,212.89
	Balance	443.59	846.36	−793.84	−6,127.83
	Export–Import Ratio	1.8733	1.2024	0.9490	0.8929
OECD	Exports	2,493.76	20,502.73	69,790.85	248,276.96
	Imports	1,184.25	14,297.39	73,775.4	255,459.4
	Balance	1,309.37	6,205.34	−3,984.55	−7,182.44
	Export–Import Ratio	2.1058	1.4340	0.9460	0.9719

Source: Derived from OECD (1995).
Notes: The Asian NICs consist of China, Taiwan, Hong Kong, Malaysia, South Korea, Singapore and Thailand. The European Union consists of Austria, Belgium, Denmark, Finland, France, Germany, Greece, Ireland, Italy, Luxembourg, The Netherlands, Portugal, Sweden and the United Kingdom.

surprising that concern about the rise of the NICs has been greatest in the United States.

The Problem of Adjustment

Does this mean that the rise of the NICs has created no problems for the western industrialised countries? Problems have arisen because of the need to re-allocate labour from those sectors that have declined due in part to increased import competition from NICs to those that have expanded as the western industrialised countries have been able to export more to NICs. This problem is a major one for the western industrialised countries. It is, therefore, important to examine the process whereby adjustment takes place in a market-based economy. The best way of showing this is to construct a relatively simple two-sector model in which there are two countries, each with an export sector and an import-competing sector. There are just two factors of production, labour and capital. At the same time, to make the model realistic, it is assumed that only labour moves between the two sectors. The other factor, capital, is assumed to be specific to the sector in which it is employed and, therefore, not capable of being used in any other sector. Such a model is called a *specific factors model* and was first developed by Samuelson (1971) and Jones (1971). (See Neary, 1985, for a thorough discussion of the model.)

Figure 7.1 illustrates the model. On the horizontal axis the number of workers employed in the two sectors, x and y, is measured. A movement from O_x to the right means that more workers are employed in sector x and a movement from O_y to the left means that more workers are employed in sector y. The vertical axis measures the wage rate, w. L_x is the demand curve for labour in sector x showing that, the lower the wage rate, the more workers employers will take on. L_y is the demand curve for labour in sector y, which is drawn as sloping upwards from left to right because the origin, O_y, is at the bottom right of the figure and an increase in the demand for labour in this sector is measured by a movement to the left of O_y. If the labour market is a perfect one, the wage rate will settle at point a with O_xf workers employed in sector x and O_yf workers employed in sector y. The labour market clears and all workers who are willing and able to work are able to find work. At any other wage rate, there would be either an excess supply of labour or excess demand and the labour market would not be in equilibrium.

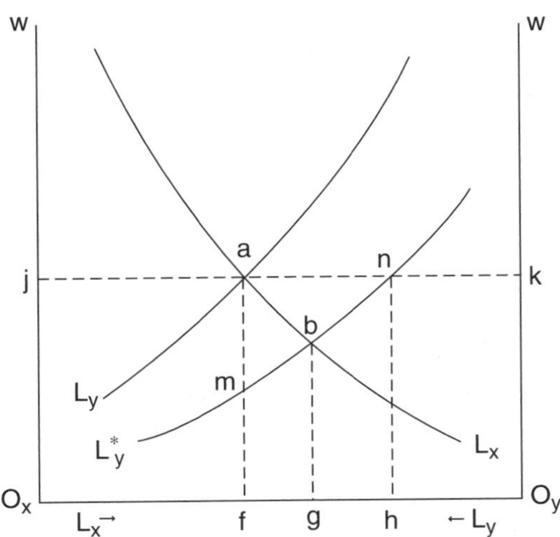

Figure 7.1 Adjustment to trade expansion in a specific-factor model

Now let us suppose that a new, low cost producer of the product of sector y emerges in some other part of the world and begins to export his product to the country shown in Figure 7.1. The immediate effect is to cause a fall in the price of the product produced by sector y. This will cause producers to reduce their output and, hence, their demand for labour, shown by a shift in the demand curve for labour from L_y to L_y^*. At the wage rate, O_yk, the demand for labour is now only O_yh. Unemployment equal to $an = fh$ now exists. The excess supply of labour causes the wage rate to fall until a new equilibrium is established at b. The fall in the wage rate is sufficient to persuade employers in sector x to employ more workers (*fg* workers shift out of sector y and into sector x) and employers in sector y to cut employment by less than they would have done (employment falls to O_yg not O_yh). Adjustment takes place smoothly with no unemployment of workers who are able and willing to work at the equilibrium wage rate.

Why, then, should increased competition from NICs cause an adjustment problem for the western industrialised countries? The reason is that the adjustment mechanism described above works only in the long term. In the short term, there exist major impediments that prevent the adjustment mechanism from working in the manner described above. There are two particular types of impediment:

1. *Segmentation of the labour market*. The labour market is not a homogeneous market in which employers can hire only one sort of labour and in which all workers are paid the same wage rate. Rather, it is more meaningful to think of the labour market as being made up of a series of segments or sub-markets in which different kinds of labour offer their services and between which workers are not free to move. The main cause of such segmentation is that workers possess different skills. A coal miner is not free to offer his services as a heart surgeon because the skills required of a heart surgeon are possessed by only a few and can only be acquired after a long period of medical training. It may be that the kind of labour required by the export-competing sector (x) is more skilled than that required by the import-competing sector (y). Given sufficient time, workers in sector y may be able to retrain and get jobs in the expanding sector x. In the short run, however, this is not possible.

Another reason why workers fail to move between sectors in response to differences in wage rates is a reluctance on the part of workers to move to different parts of the country if the export-competing sector is located in a different region to the declining one. If the workers whose jobs have gone as a result of import competition cannot be re-employed in sector x, the wage rate in sector y will have to fall much further. Instead of a new equilibrium being established at b, the equilibrium wage rate will settle at m, where employers are prepared to employ all the workers who want jobs. The labour market clears and no unemployment results but only by depressing wages for all workers employed in the declining sector. As a result, a sizeable wage differential is created between the two sectors of *am*.

2. *Downward stickiness of wage rates*. A second type of impediment arises because wage rates are not free to fall. In some countries, this is because government legislation fixes a minimum wage rate below which wages cannot fall. In addition, in countries where trade unions exert strong bargaining power, reductions in real wage rates may be successfully prevented from taking place. If, for either of these reasons, the wage rate is not free to fall below O_yk, the result will be a fall in employment to O_yh, leaving $fh = an$ workers unemployed. It is probable that the existence of such a high level of unemployment will, in the long run, cause a fall in the wage rate thereby pricing some workers back into work. However, it may take some time for this to happen, resulting in high levels of unemployment in the declining sector for a while to come.

Both of these impediments amount to imperfections in the workings of the labour market. They create major problems for countries whenever adjustment needs to take place rapidly due to a sudden expansion of imports. As we have seen, this has been the case for western industrialised countries as a result of the rise of the NICs. Given sufficient time, the labour market in the western industrialised countries would, no doubt, achieve the required adjustment. In the long run, workers have time to retrain and equip themselves with the new skills required in the expanding sector. Time probably also weakens the reluctance of workers to dig up roots and find work in another part of the country. In addition, as we have seen, the ability of trade unions to resist a reduction in the wage rate in the import-competing sector is likely to weaken with time. This is because of the existence of a pool of unemployed labour on which employers can draw and the fear of those workers still in employment that they might join the pool if they push too hard on wages. These days, in most countries, wage rates are negotiated annually or biannually which means that the price of labour is 'sticky' in the short run. Given time, however, wage rates will be renegotiated to reflect more closely the balance of demand and supply in the labour market. Finally, some re-allocation of the workforce between expanding and declining sectors will take place automatically as new workers enter the labour force and old workers leave. As older workers in the declining sector retire, their jobs are not re-filled. At the same time, some of the new jobs that are created in the expanding sector, can be filled by younger workers who are entering the labour force from school or college for the first time.

The failure of the labour market to bring about a sufficiently rapid adjustment creates costs both for the individuals concerned (private costs) and for society at large (social costs). The losses to individual households have three elements. First, there is the income foregone by those workers who are made redundant but unable to find another job. To some extent, all workers made redundant in the import-competing sector will experience some temporary or 'transitional' unemployment. Although they will be eligible for state benefits and may also receive a lump-sum redundancy payment, which compensates them partly for loss of income, they will still suffer some income loss. Unemployment benefit is always less than the income earned from work and may be reduced the longer the worker is out of work. Other workers may be unemployed for a longer period of time because they lack the right skills or because the costs of moving to an area where jobs are available are prohibitive. Second, shareholders will experience a decline in their wealth caused by the drop in the value of assets used in the declining industry. Third, those workers, who are still employed in the declining sector, will experience a fall in their wages. If adjustment took place instantaneously, workers in the declining sector would experience only a temporary fall in their wage rate relative to the wage rate earned in other sectors of the economy. However, because various barriers impede mobility of labour between different sectors, wage rates are depressed in the declining sector. Part of this loss of income reflects adecline in the value of the skills possessed by workers, skills that cannot be re-employed elsewhere. These skills are embodiments of human capital that belongs to the workers. Thus, the decline in the value of human capital may be regarded as a wealth loss analogous to that experienced by the owners of physical capital invested in the sector.

The existence of private costs of adjustment is important because it leads workers and capitalists in industries subject to import competition to pressurise governments for protection against lower cost goods from abroad. The greater the potential loss, the more the pressure that will be brought to bear. One solution is for governments to provide the individuals who experience an income loss with adjustment assistance, in the form of a sum of money, which, wholly or partly, compensates them for the loss of income during the period of adjustment. This has the advantage that it weakens the resistance of workers and industrialists to the expansion of trade and reduces the pressure for import protection. However, of equal importance are the costs to the economy as a whole. These are given by the costs to the government of unemployment benefits and redundancy payments and the lost output to the country because a part of the labour force is idle. The faster the speed with which adjustment can be effected, the lower the social cost. The greater the social costs of adjustment, the smaller the net gain to countries from increased trade. It is possible that these social costs could be sufficient to wipe out any welfare gain accruing from increased trade. It follows that any measures that governments can take to promote more rapid adjustment will reduce social costs and maximise the net welfare gain from trade.

One of the problems that has been experienced by all of the western industrialised countries over the past half-century has been that adjustment has become more difficult to bring about. This has taken place at the same time as increased competition from the NICs has demanded a more rapid pace of change. Several factors have made the labour market of the western industrialised countries less flexible. These are summarised below:

1. Trade union restrictive practices. Three kinds of trade union practice have been especially important causes of labour-market inflexibility:

(a) *Monopoly pricing of labour:* Where a trade union is able to exert control over the supply of labour, it may act like a monopolist withholding supply and forcing up the price. If, in this way, the price of labour is kept higher than the competitive rate, firms will substitute capital for labour and some workers will be priced out of employment.

(b) *Fixed wage relativities:* In some countries, wage rates are fixed at a nation-wide level with the same wage rate being set for workers employed in different industries and possibly in different regions of the country. In this case, wages are not free to fluctuate so as to reflect differences in either the demand for or the supply of labour in different parts of the country. In this case, wrong signals will be sent to workers and employers, resulting in a misallocation of labour among sectors and regions and reflected in high levels of structural and regional unemployment.

(c) *Resistance to the introduction of new technology:* From time to time, trade unions may block the introduction of new technology or impose conditions on its use. This may leave companies less able to withstand competition from low-cost imports from abroad.

2. Minimum wage legislation. We have already seen how minimum wage laws may, if they fix minimum wage rates too high, prevent wages from adjusting downwards and, thereby, price certain workers out of employment. Minimum wage laws are usually introduced to protect low-paid, generally unskilled workers from exploitation by unscrupulous employers. However, those industries in the western industrialised countries which have typically been most adversely affected by competition from NICs have often been ones which employ a disproportionately large number of unskilled workers at relatively low wage rates (e.g. clothing, footwear, children's toys, etc.). Downward stickiness of wage rates due to minimum wages legislation can be a source of adjustment difficulty in these industries. It may be better to protect low-paid workers through the state benefits–tax system rather than enforcing minimum wage rates that lead to higher unemployment of unskilled workers.

3. Employment protection legislation. Certain kinds of legislation introduced by governments in western industrialised countries to protect workers against unfair or arbitrary dismissal may impose costs on employers that result in unemployment. They raise the non-wage element entering into the total costs of employing workers which means that the wages element must fall by much more in order to clear the labour market when the demand for labour falls than would otherwise be the case. Furthermore, by raising the costs of employing additional workers, they may encourage employers to substitute capital for labour wherever possible resulting in the creation of fewer new jobs. Governments in some western industrialised countries may need to ask whether such legislation has not gone too far in its efforts at protecting those in work at the expense of those currently out of work.

4. High levels of social security benefit and high marginal rates of income tax. In all western industrialised countries, the last half-century has witnessed the rise of the welfare state and an increase in levels of personal taxation to meet the costs of increased spending on the welfare state. One consequence of higher benefits is that some low-paid workers find themselves worse off in work than out of work. The problem is made worse by high marginal rates of income tax (the amount of tax paid on an extra £ of income earned) which reduce the net take-home pay of low-paid workers. For many low-paid workers, the combined effects of the loss of benefits and the need to pay tax on any income earned means that they are better off remaining unemployed.

5. Imperfections in capital markets. Capital markets play an important role in the adjustment process by making loanable funds available to companies in the expanding sectors of the economy that need to take advantage of new export opportunities, at the same time as capital is withdrawn or written off in the declining, import-competing sector. Changes in the rate of return on different kinds of investment signal to investors the need to put their funds into those companies producing the goods for which demand is rising fastest. However, various kinds of interference by governments often distort this process. Governments may grant subsidies to ailing firms or declining industries in order to safeguard jobs, especially in depressed regions. This may encourage over-investment in sectors with only poor prospects, while denying funds to other sectors with much better prospects. In some countries, tax systems unintentionally discriminate against small- and medium-sized firms, which are often the more adaptable wealth creators in the economy. In other countries, interest rates are subject to controls designed to hold down the cost of capital to borrowers or to prevent competition among lending institutions for deposits from driving up rates. Such controls may mean that companies in the more dynamic, profitable sectors of the economy face difficulties in obtaining the funds needed to finance expansion and the creation of new jobs. High rates of inflation can also have damaging effects on both the overall level of investment in the economy while distorting the allocation of funds. This is because high inflation leads to higher long-term interest rates, making it more difficult for investors to compare the real rate of return on funds invested in different sectors of the economy.

6. Monopoly and other anti-competitive distortions in product markets. Imperfections in the markets for goods also impede the adjustment process. In order for funds to be invested in the sectors with the best prospects for expansion, the rate of return on capital in those sectors must exceed that which can be earned by investing in other parts of the economy. Where, however, markets are distorted by the assertion of monopoly power or where firms in the industry collude to rig the price, the rate of return is kept artificially high. Funds are attracted into these sectors at the expense of other more dynamic sectors. The trend towards oligopoly in many product markets may also lead to another problem, namely, that prices become more 'sticky' or less responsive to changes in demand and supply. If so, prices may fail to change sufficiently to inform investors of the need to re-allocate funds between different sectors of the economy.

7. Impediments to the mobility of labour. Finally, during the last half-century impediments to labour mobility have increased. As many jobs have become more specialised and the skills required more specific to a particular sector, the need for workers to retrain as and when their existing jobs disappear has increased. Technological change has contributed to making workers' skills more specific to particular sectors or activities. At the same time, although workers may be more willing to move to a different part of the country to find work than was true in the past, changes within many western industrialised countries may have made this more difficult. Large differences in the costs of housing in different regions, the costs of buying and selling and the costs of moving all deter workers from doing so. When house prices fall home owners have difficulty in selling their homes or selling at a price which covers the costs of funds borrowed. As increasing affluence leads to more workers buying their own homes, these impediments to geographical mobility will increase.

Adjustment Policy

What can governments in western industrialised countries do to promote adjustment in response to increased import competition from NICs? A distinction may be drawn between two types of adjustment policy. The first type is concerned with removing those impediments that hinder the workings of factor (in particular, the labour) markets and product markets. Box 7.2 illustrates the type of measures governments can introduce to increase the flexibility of labour and product markets.

The second type of adjustment policy involves measures to augment the workings of the market and so speed up the process of adjustment. As we have seen, the adjustment problem is essentially a short-term one. Given sufficient time, adjustment will take place. Any measures, therefore which can help the adjustment process to work more quickly can serve to reduce the costs of adjustment. Examples of market-augmenting measures are grants or tax relief to assist firms with the scrapping of capital or the closure of plants in declining industries, grants paid to firms to meet the costs of redundancies, grants towards the retraining of workers whose skills have become redundant and so forth. All such measures help accelerate the process of change.

Adjustment policies of both kinds are now a common feature of industrial policy in most advanced industrialised countries. However, damage may be done if governments introduce the wrong kinds of adjustment policy. Adjustment policies are beneficial if they help adjustment to take place more rapidly and, thereby, reduce the costs of adjustment. However, policies which are essentially defensive measures delay or prevent adjustment from taking place. For example, blanket subsidies which are granted to ailing firms in import-competing sectors and which are not attached to any specific adjustment measures serve only to delay adjustment. The effect is to add to the adjustment pressures facing producers in other countries. Where, however, the grant is conditional upon a producer making cuts in capacity or reducing the size of the workforce, the subsidy is market-augmenting. More problematic are measures of adjustment assistance that compensate either workers or capital owners for some of the adjustment costs caused by increased imports. To the extent that such measures buy off resistance to the expansion of trade, they may be viewed as facilitating

Box 7.2 Measures to make Labour and Product Markets more Flexible

Examples of measures to increase labour market flexibility include the following:

- Industrial relations reforms to curb the excessive powers of trade unions, such as fixing the wage rate by threatening to withdraw labour supply and so preventing the wage rate from falling to a market-clearing level.
- Measures to encourage more local wage rate bargaining and to discourage centralised negotiation of wage rates.
- The abolition of national minimum wage laws which prevent employers from recruiting additional workers at wage rates below the legal minimum, or the lowering of minimum wage rates closer to market-clearing levels.
- Measures to reduce the non-wage costs of employing workers (e.g. social security contributions, employment protection legislation) which require wage rates to fall by more than otherwise when the demand for labour falls.
- Tax and social security reforms designed to lower the high, punitive marginal rates of taxation operative at very low levels of income.
- Measures to deregulate financial markets and free interest rates to move upwards and downwards in response to market conditions.
- Tougher competition and anti-trust legislation to reduce barriers to entry and make product prices more responsive to changes in market conditions.
- Measures to increase the occupational mobility of labour through increased investment in education and vocational training, support for retraining programmes, and so forth.
- Measures designed to increase the geographical mobility of labour, such as a reform of housing policies, assistance with the costs of moving and so forth.

adjustment. On the other hand, in certain circumstances they act as a deterrent to adjustment and serve only to delay the transfer of resources out of declining sectors.

Where governments adopt measures which delay adjustment, the effect is to increase the pressure to adjust in other countries. This will create greater resistance to trade in these countries and may provoke governments in these countries into introducing similar defensive measures. The pressures to adjust will, then, pass to third countries. In short, global adjustment becomes more difficult to bring about where governments adopt the wrong sort of adjustment measures. The need is to encourage what the OECD has called *positive adjustment policies* (OECD, 1978). These may be loosely defined as any measure that improves the capacity of an economy to adjust in response to pressures generated by the expansion of trade. The OECD has proposed the following criteria for ensuring that adjustment policy plays a positive role:

1. *Minimal reliance on purely compensatory, damage-limitation measures.* Although compensating workers or capital owners for loss of income caused by increased import

competition may prove a useful means of counteracting pressure for protectionism, purely compensatory policies should be kept to a minimum.

2. *A reduction in the number of sector-specific adjustment measures.* The OECD has argued for a shift away from sector-specific adjustment policies – designed to help a particular firm or industry which is in difficulty – and towards more general, non-sectoral measures (e.g. measures to improve the functioning of the labour market, improved access for industry to capital markets). Sector-specific measures favour one sector of the economy over the rest. By giving special help to declining industries, they may cause discrimination against expanding ones.
3. *Time limits on the duration of adjustment assistance and gradual reductions in the level of assistance over time.* If aid is to be given to a particular industry faced with adjustment difficulties, a definite time limit should be fixed from the outset and the level of assistance progressively reduced. Unless this is done, the assistance given to the industry will serve to shut resources into the industry rather than encouraging their withdrawal. Ideally, too, the aid should give encouragement to the most efficient producers within the industry rather than the least efficient as too often is the case.
4. *Greater reliance to be placed on the tax system rather than subsidies to correct inequities caused by adjustment and to achieve any desired redistribution of income.* If it is felt desirable to compensate income earners in the declining sector for loss of income incurred as a result of adjustment, it is more efficient to do so through the granting of tax relief. For example, firms in declining industries faced with falling profits might be allowed tax relief for accelerated depreciation of redundant capital. Workers might also could be allowed to offset part of the costs of retraining against taxable income.
5. *The use of a greater proportion of public funds on measures which promote economic growth.* The OECD recommends that a larger amount of public assistance given to industry should be devoted to the support of long-term research and development, reducing the so-called 'costs' of economic growth (e.g. pollution, exhaustion of indigenous energy sources, etc.) and providing small- and medium-sized firms with greater access to venture capital. Adjustment is easier the faster the rate at which the economy is growing overall. If few new jobs are being created, workers will be reluctant to give up their existing ones and will demand greater protection against imports.

However, reliance on exhortation to encourage positive adjustment is unlikely to achieve results. Governments may make verbal commitments to behave virtuously while in practice do the very opposite. Budgetary pressures have played an important role in recent years in causing some western industrialised countries to cut the amount of purely defensive assistance given to industries in decline. However, there is always a danger that such expenditure reductions may also cut genuine forms of adjustment assistance. There may be a need to go beyond the largely voluntary approach adopted by the OECD that goes no further than securing the agreement of member states to a set of guidelines that are non-enforceable. A step in this direction was taken with the drafting of a new Subsidies Code in the Uruguay Round of multilateral trade negotiations which is now binding on all countries that belong to the World Trade Organisation (WTO) (see Chapter 8). This identified certain kinds of so-called 'actionable subsidies' which, if they 'nullify or impair' the rights of other members and cause or threaten injury to the domestic producers of another country, may become the subject of a complaint to the WTO. It remains to be seen how effective this code will prove in deterring countries from measures that are damaging to the process of global adjustment, which the emergence of new pockets of import competition necessitates.

The Effects on Wage Inequality in the Advanced Industrialised Countries

A related concern has been the effect of increased import competition from the NICs on wage inequality in the advanced industrialised countries. In both the United States and the United Kingdom, the ratio of earnings of high-skilled relative to low-skilled workers has widened significantly over recent decades. This has occurred at precisely the same time as imports from NICs have increased as a proportion of total imports. The OECD has calculated that wage inequality increased in twelve of the seventeen industrialised countries it examined. This trend has been most apparent in the United States. During the 1980s, male college graduates earned on average 30% more than those who had completed high school only. Moreover, the real wages of young men with fewer than twelve years of schooling fell by 20% (quoted in *The Economist*, October 1, 1994). Is this growing wage inequality the consequence of increased imports of low-cost labour-intensive manufactures from NICs?

At the theoretical level, there are grounds for expecting increased trade between the NICs and advanced industrialised countries to result in a decline in the relative wages of unskilled workers. The factor–price equalisation theorem states that, where trade takes place among countries with different factor endowments, the income of a country's scarce factor of production will fall relative to that of the country's abundant factor. Thus, if NICs are well endowed with unskilled labour and the advanced industrialised countries with skilled labour, increased trade might be expected to lead to a fall in the wages of unskilled workers in the advanced industrialised countries relative to those of skilled workers. The Stolper–Samuelson theorem goes a step further and proves that, under certain conditions, trade might even lead to a fall in the *real* income of unskilled workers. This is not an argument for import restrictions. The country as a whole is still better off as a result of trade. The solution is to find some way of skilled workers compensating unskilled workers who have suffered a loss due to trade. This could be achieved through the tax-benefits system. However, where unskilled workers are not compensated, import restrictions will be seen as a way of restoring their incomes.

Does the empirical evidence show that imports from NICs have been the cause of wage inequality? An early attempt to test this hypothesis appeared to show that trade was not the cause of the declining wages of unskilled workers in the United States. Lawrence and Slaughter (1993) argued that, if trade were the cause of wage inequality in the US, there should occur a fall in the ratio of skilled-to-unskilled labour in all sectors of industry. The reasoning behind this is as follows. As trade expands, the result is a shift in the composition of output from sectors that use much unskilled labour to sectors that use more skilled labour. This causes the demand for skilled labour to rise relative to that of unskilled labour and the wage rate of skilled workers to rise relative to that of unskilled workers. As a result, firms in all sectors of the economy reduce the amount of skilled workers they employ relative to unskilled. Relative wages will need to change sufficiently to ensure that the switch from skilled to unskilled workers in all sectors of the economy exactly offsets the rise in the demand for skilled to unskilled caused by the change in the sectoral mix. At the end of the day, the employment of both types of labour will be the same as before the process started. Their research showed that exactly the opposite had happened: the ratio of skilled-to-unskilled labour had risen across all manufacturing sectors. They concluded that trade was not the cause of growing wage inequality. Rather, the demand for skilled workers has risen relative to the demand for unskilled workers for some other reason, the most likely candidate being technological change. This is not a surprising result, they argue, as the bulk of U.S. trade is still conducted with other advanced industrialised countries whose workers have similar skills.

A rather different conclusion was reached by Adrian Wood in a major study of the effects of trade between developed and developing countries on employment and wage inequality (Wood, 1994). An attraction of his study is that it examined the effects of trade on both employment and wage differentials in fourteen developed countries. Wood estimated that 20% of the decline in demand for unskilled labour in developed countries over the period 1960–90 was due to trade. Three-quarters of the decline was concentrated in the last decade of the period. He found evidence for a strong correlation between the increase in manufacturing imports from developing countries and both employment rates and wage differentials in developed countries. In America and Britain, where there is greater flexibility in labour markets, the effect was greater on wage inequality. In continental Europe where wages are more rigid, the impact was largely on employment levels. An important aspect of Wood's analysis is that it takes into account the secondary effects that increased imports have on the demand for unskilled labour induced by greater competition. Faced with more intense competition from low-cost imports, employers respond by introducing more labour-saving methods of production in an effort to cut costs. By way of contrast the direct effect of trade on the demand for unskilled labour was found to be quite low – less than one quarter of the 20% reduction in demand recorded for the period.

Subsequent empirical work (e.g. Sachs and Schatz, 1994) appears to demonstrate that trade has had some effect on the demand for unskilled labour in advanced industrialised countries, although possibly less than the Wood study concludes. Where labour markets are flexible, the impact is largely on the wage rates of unskilled workers. In other countries, imports have led to lower employment levels. The fact that imports account for a low proportion of the imports of OECD countries does not mean that the effect of such imports on the demand for unskilled workers is insignificant. This is because the NICs tend to compete most strongly in sectors that employ relatively large amounts of unskilled labour. However, what remains unresolved is the importance of trade relative to factors such as technology in depressing the demand for unskilled labour in developed countries. Clearly some of the fall in demand was due to trade. A further complication is that some technological change may itself have been a response to increased import competition from abroad.

Conclusion

The emergence of a group of developing countries as major exporters of manufactured goods has been one of the most important changes in the world trading system over the past half-century. Major changes in the world trade environment have combined with more successful development strategies in the developing world to bring about this change. With regard to the latter, the adoption of outward-looking, export-oriented trade policies has been an important factor, although disagreements exist about how important was the contribution of export expansion to economic growth in these countries. The countries that have pursued these policies with the greatest success, have been the East Asian NICs. However, the recent financial and economic crisis within the region has worn some of the gloss off the 'Asian model'. It remains to be seen whether this crisis will prove to be a minor interruption in a process of sustained expansion or whether it defines the end of the 'Asian miracle'.

The fact that much of the expansion enjoyed by the NICs has been export-led has had major implications for the western industrialised countries. They have found that a growing proportion of their markets for manufactured goods has been filled by imports from developing countries. The much lower level of costs in these countries has made it often difficult for producers in the developed world to respond to the new competition. Frequently, this has led to demands for import protection. Mostly, this has been based on unsound arguments about the effects that such imports have on employment levels and the wages of low-skilled workers. Insufficient account is taken of the fact that the growth of the NICs has also enabled the western industrialised countries to export more manufactures.

With regard to the effects of NIC exports on employment levels in the western industrialised countries, the major problem is an adjustment one. Increased trade with NICs has meant a loss of jobs in certain traditional industries which employ relatively large amounts of low-skilled labour. However, the opportunity to export more to these countries has created more high-skilled jobs in the newer branches of manufacturing. The need is to transfer labour from the declining to the expanding sectors. However, it would be mistaken to deny the magnitude of these problems for the western industrialised countries. Adjustment is often difficult to achieve in the short run. Increased trade with NICs means that some groups in the advanced industrialised countries lose out. The culprit often appears to be low-cost producers in developing countries. Demands for import protection are understandable. The task for policy makers is to devise solutions that provide a genuine response to the grievances expressed by those losing out, while ensuring that the benefits which trade brings to the world as a whole are not forfeited.

Notes for Further Reading

An essential source for further reading on the subject of the newly industrialising countries are the two pioneer studies carried out by the OECD:

OECD. *The Impact of the Newly-Industrialising Countries on Production and Trade in Manufactures* (Paris: OECD, 1979).

OECD. *The Newly-Industrialising Countries: Challenges and Opportunity for OECD Countries* (Paris: OECD, 1988).

An excellent specialist text on the role played by different trade policies in developing countries is:

Greenaway, D. and Milner, C. *Trade and Industrial Policy in Developing Countries* (London: Macmillan, 1993).

For an in-depth study of the impact of different trade policies on economic development, the reader should also read:

World Bank. *World Development Report 1987* (Washington DC: World Bank and Oxford: Oxford University Press, 1987).

On the problem of adjustment, an invaluable source is:

Banks, G. and Tumlir, J. *Economic Policy and the Adjustment Problem*, Thames Essays No. 45, (London: Gower for the Trade Policy Research Centre, 1986).

An excellent source on the theory of adjustment is a chapter entitled 'Theory and Policy of Adjustment in an Open Economy' by J. Neary in:

Greenaway, D. (ed). *Current Issues in International Trade,* 2nd ed. (London: Macmillan, 1996).

For a study of the growth of the East Asian newly industrialising economies, an essential source is:

World Bank. *The East Asian Miracle, Economic Growth and Public Policy* (Oxford: published for the World Bank by Oxford University Press).

This also contains a very useful discussion of the role played by industrial policy in the growth of the East Asian 'tigers'.

Chapter 8

Free Trade Versus Protectionism

CHAPTER OUTLINES: Introduction. The Gains from Free Trade – the gains from inter-industry specialisation, the gains from intra-industry specialisation, adjustment costs. Tariff Protectionism. Non-Tariff Protectionism – import quotas, voluntary export restraints, anti-dumping and countervailing duties, subsidies, other types of non-tariff protectionism. Arguments for Protection. Strategic Trade Policy and the New Trade Theory – criticisms of strategic trade policy. The Political Economy of Protection. Conclusion.

Introduction

In Chapter 1, we saw that one of the reasons for the growth of world trade over the past half century has been the reduction in the level of trade barriers. This made it possible for world trade to grow at a faster rate than world output. This, in turn, has resulted in an increase in the degree of interdependence existing between countries. Although increased economic interdependence makes it more difficult for countries to pursue an independent economic policy, it does make countries more prosperous. This is because countries tend to specialise more either in particular industries in which they enjoy a cost advantage or in particular products within those industries. The former constitutes inter-industry specialisation and the latter intra-industry specialisation. Both forms of specialisation bring welfare gains to countries. However, the nature of the gain differs according to the type of specialisation that results. In this chapter, some of the benefits which accrue to countries from freer trade and increased specialisation are examined.

However, governments are rarely prepared to allow complete free trade. Most countries give some protection to domestic producers by imposing tariffs or other forms of non-tariff restriction. In this chapter, the effects of different types of import protection are examined. The chapter concludes by discussing whether or not there exist any sound economic arguments for government intervention in trade whether in the form of restrictions on imports or measures to boost exports. It is argued that, although there exist a few good reasons for governments intervening in trade, global economic welfare will be maximised if governments pursue a policy of free trade. The chapter begins with an outline of the case for free trade, distinguishing between inter- and intra-industry specialisation. This is followed by an analysis of the effects of different types of protectionism – 'old-style' tariff protection and 'new-style' non-tariff protection.

The remainder of the chapter discusses whether or not there exist any sound arguments for government intervention in trade. Finally, the chapter assesses the merits and demerits of the new trade theory in its advocacy of intervention in high technology, oligopolistic industries.

The Gains from Free Trade

How does free trade benefit countries? It does so by enabling countries to specialise in producing those goods at which they are best. In earlier chapters, it was seen that such specialisation can take the form of either inter-industry or intra-industry specialisation. Whereas much of the specialisation, which took place in the half century preceding the First World War, assumed the form of inter-industry specialisation, the kind of specialisation which has been most common in the half century following the ending of the Second World War has been of the intra-industry type. As the gains from freer trade differ somewhat according to the type of specialisation that results, it is necessary to consider the two cases separately.

The Gains from Inter-Industry Specialisation

Inter-industry specialisation is the specialisation of a country in the full range of products belonging to an industry. This is the kind of specialisation considered in the classical and neo-classical models of trade discussed in Chapter 2. These models show that when two countries engage in unimpeded trade with each other, each will specialise in the goods in which it has a comparative cost advantage. As a consequence, each country is able to obtain a greater bundle of the two goods exchanged than it was able to produce under autarky (i.e. in the absence of trade). The welfare gain takes the form of a movement from a consumption point located on the country's transformation curve to a point beyond (see Figures 2.2 and 2.8).

Conceptually, this gain has two elements. First, there is a *production gain* resulting from the fact that the country can now use its scarce resources (land, labour and capital) more efficiently, that is, they are optimally allocated. Specialisation enables the country to employ its resources in those industries in which it is relatively more efficient. Second, there is a *consumption gain* resulting from the fact that consumers are able to buy more of the imported product at a lower price. (In Figures 2.2 and 2.8, this is given by the change in relative prices.) Figure 8.1 illustrates the nature of these two effects.

Before trade, relative prices are represented by PP and the country is producing and consuming at point E. However, after trade, relative prices are represented by P*P*. This

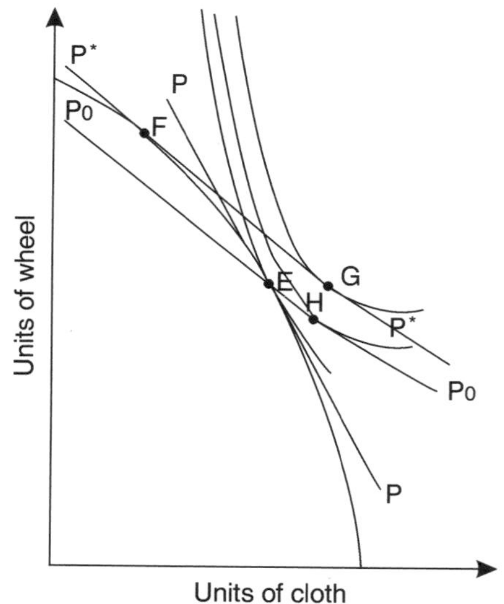

Figure 8.1 The gains from trade under inter-industry specialisation

causes the country to move up its transformation curve to point F, where it produces more wheat and less cloth than before. However, because it can exchange some of its wheat for cloth through trade, it can consume at point G, a point beyond its transformation curve. To separate the consumption from the production gain, a line, P_0P_0, is drawn through E but parallel to P^*P^*. The point of tangency between P_0P_0 and an indifference curve is located at H. Now, the movement from E to H constitutes the consumption gain, resulting from an increase in the price of wheat in terms of cloth. The movement from H to G is the production gain, resulting from the country's scarce resources being used more efficiently.

Such gains are the *static* gains from inter-industry specialisation. They are once-and-for-all improvements in economic welfare which accrue to the countries involved. However, in addition to these static gains, trade leads to another set of gains which go on accruing for several years after trade barriers have been removed and trade commenced. These are commonly referred to as the *dynamic* gains. Five sources of such long-term gain from the expansion of trade may be identified:

1. *Gains from economies of scale.* Increased trade will enable producers in a country's export sector to increase their volume of output and, hence, the scale of their production. This may result in lower costs per unit of output due to both an increase in the size of plant (static economies) and 'learning-by-doing' effects (dynamic economies). In industries where unit costs fall with the volume of output (e.g. the car industry), the domestic market may be too small to enable firms to achieve an optimum scale of production – the so-called 'minimum efficient scale' (MES). By expanding the size of the market confronting the firm, exports may provide an escape route from this constraint. In some industries (e.g. semi-conductor production), unit costs fall also with the *cumulative* volume of output. The more experienced firms become at producing a product, the more efficient they become. Also where products have short market lives, firms may find it difficult to expand output fast enough to achieve minimum average cost. Again, by increasing the size of the market confronting the firm, exports will provide an escape route.
2. *Efficiency gains resulting from increased competition.* In industries where unit costs fall sharply with output, the size of the domestic market may leave room for only a small number of competitors. New entrants will be deterred by the existence of large fixed costs of production and the need to produce on a large scale in order to spread these costs. Where a small number of large firms dominate the market for a product, competition may be restricted. This will lead to a further source of economic inefficiency, commonly referred to as 'X-inefficiency'. Because firms face little or no competition, they will fail to pursue a cost-minimising strategy. Trade liberalisation exposes domestic producers who, previously, were sheltered from foreign competition, to increased competition and so eliminates waste due to managerial slack.
3. *Stimulus to capital investment.* The increased export opportunities which result from trade liberalisation will stimulate firms to undertake more investment in plant and machinery in order to expand their capacity to meet increased demand (capital-widening). In addition, the exposure to increased competition from abroad will stimulate firms to invest in modernising their existing plant and machinery so that more output can be derived from the same amount of capital

(capital-deepening). The higher level of fixed investment within the economy will lead to increased economic growth. It is, of course, possible that firms in the import-substitution sector, if they expect demand for their product to fall, may reduce investment. However, because gross fixed investment can never be negative, the net effect must be a positive one.

4. *An increase in the rate of technological innovation.* A wider and faster growing market for firms in the export sector, plus an environment of more competition at home, will stimulate greater innovation both in the form of new, lower-cost methods of production and new products. A more rapid rate of technological advancement is one of the main sources of faster growth in any economy.
5. *Output expansion from reduced inflation.* Both by directly lowering prices and by exposing domestic monopolies and oligopolists to more competition, trade serves to reduce inflation. Although the relationship between the rate of inflation and economic growth is ambiguous, there is some support for the view that lower inflation results in faster long-run growth. One reason is that a low rate of inflation is likely to result in a lower long-run rate of interest. This means that the cost of raising capital to finance investment is lower and, hence, firms are likely to invest more.

Although inter-industry specialisation will yield definite welfare gains for the countries in question, it will also give rise to certain distribution effects. Chapter 2 introduced Professor Paul Samuelson's important extension of the Heckscher–Ohlin theory, namely, the Factor Price Equalisation theorem. The relevance of this theorem was discussed further in Chapter 7 in the context of trade between NICs and the western industrialised countries. According to the theorem, inter-industry specialisation will tend to bring about an equalisation not only of goods but also of factor prices when two countries with different factor endowments enter into trade. This will mean that the price of the country's scarce factor will fall and the price of its abundant factor will rise, which means that owners of the scarce factor will lose out relative to owners of the abundant factor. In a different paper, Stopler and Samuelson (1941) demonstrated that the owners of the scarce factor could even lose in absolute terms if the price which they received for their services fell by more than the price of consumer goods that satisfy their wants. This does not constitute an argument against lowering trade barriers as the owners of the abundant factor can still compensate the owners of the scarce factor and be better off. In practice, however, this may not happen.

The Gains from Intra-Industry Specialisation

Intra-industry specialisation tends to occur in industries characterised by the existence of imperfect competition. In Chapter 3, several models of trade under imperfect competition were discussed. In most cases, intra-industry specialisation involved countries exchanging different varieties of the same good. In these cases, the gains from trade come more from an increase in the number of varieties of a good from which consumers can choose, rather than a reduction in the prices of these goods or more efficient use of resources. (In some models of intra-industry trade, prices also fall, but this is not true in all cases.) In other words, the static welfare gains are different where free trade leads to intra-industry specialisation. For various reasons, intra-industry specialisation is also likely to result in bigger dynamic gains than inter-industry specialisation. One reason is that intra-industry specialisation is more common in industries where average costs fall with the volume of output. Trade enables producers to get further down their average cost curve, in which case further gains accrue to the importing country either in the form of lower prices (if cost reductions are passed on to consumers) or increased profits (if they are not). Another reason is that intra-industry trade exposes producers to greater competition, compelling firms to cut costs and lower prices. Yet, a further reason is that intra-industry specialisation enables producers in research-intensive industries to recover fixed R&D costs more quickly. As a result, firms will be more willing to engage in R&D, leading to a more rapid rate of product innovation.

Greenaway (1982) has proposed a theoretical framework for analysing these gains which builds on the Lancaster model of horizontal differentiation discussed in Chapter 3. The reader will recall that, in this model, different varieties of the same good all possess the same 'core attributes' but, in each case, these are combined in a different way. We saw that one way of showing this is to imagine that there are just two main attributes, x and y, which all varieties of the product possess. Each variety can be positioned on a horizontal line according to the proportions of each attribute that it possesses. This is called the *variety specification* and is illustrated in Figure 8.2.

In Figure 8.2, consumer preferences are uniformly distributed between S and T. However, because of the existence of heavy fixed costs, it is profitable for producers to produce only one variety, V_1. It follows that some consumers will not be able to buy the variety which they would like. Consumers whose preference is for a variety other than V_1 will, therefore, enjoy less satisfaction from buying V_1 than consumers for whom this is their preferred variety. One way of measuring the welfare gain enjoyed by consumers from the purchase of a unit of any product is to calculate their *consumer surplus*. This is the difference between the satisfaction, which they derive from the consumption of a unit of the product and the price, which they pay for it. Clearly, no consumer will buy a product that generates less satisfaction than the price, which must be paid to purchase it. However, all consumers will derive differing degrees of satisfaction from the consumption of

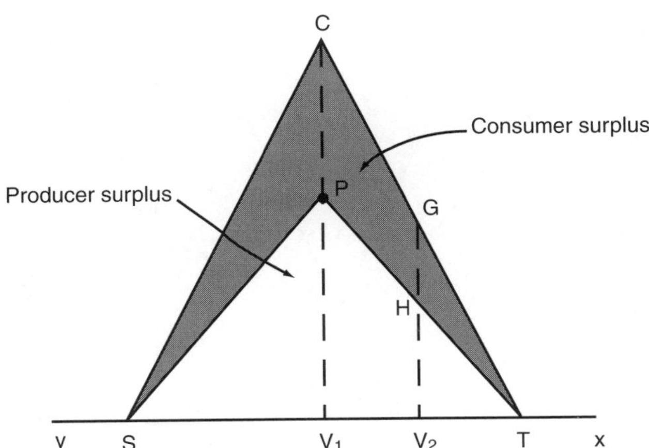

Figure 8.2 The gains from trade under intra-industry specialisation: before specialisation

a good. Since they pay the same price, it follows that most consumers will enjoy some consumer surplus. The more satisfaction they enjoy, the bigger the consumer surplus.

For consumers whose preferred variety is indeed the one that is available, V_1, consumer surplus is the vertical distance PC. However, consumers, whose preferred variety is somewhere between V_1 and T or V_1 and S, derive less consumer surplus. Consumers, who are located at the two extremes, S and T, derive no consumer surplus from purchasing V_1. In other words, they pay a price for the good, which exactly equals the satisfaction which they derive from it. The total consumers' surplus, which all consumers derive from the purchase of V_1, is shown by the shaded area SCTP.

However, to derive a welfare gain to the country as a whole from V_1, we must measure the surplus which domestic producers obtain from supplying this particular variety or *producer surplus. Producer surplus* is simply the difference between the price which a producer receives for a particular unit of V_1 and the cost of producing it. For simplicity, let us assume constant average costs. Then, the more units which a producer sells of V_1, the greater his producer surplus. Consumers who are located at V_1 will, presumably, buy many units of the product because this is their preferred variety. Hence, their purchases will generate a lot of surplus for producers. This is given by the vertical distance V_1P. However, consumers located to the left or right of V_1 will buy fewer units of the good and so generate less producer surplus. Consumers located outside the range ST will buy no units of the good and so generate zero producer surplus. Thus, we can show total producer surplus by the area SPT. If, now, we add producers' surplus to consumers' surplus, we obtain the triangle SCT. This measures the total welfare derived by consumers and producers from the production of V_1.

Now what happens when trade takes place? Suppose that Country 1 enters into trade with Country 2 whose consumers have different preferences. Consumers in Country 1 prefer V_1 and consumer in Country 2 prefer V_2. The situation is illustrated in Figure 8.3. However, because of heavy fixed costs, producers in each

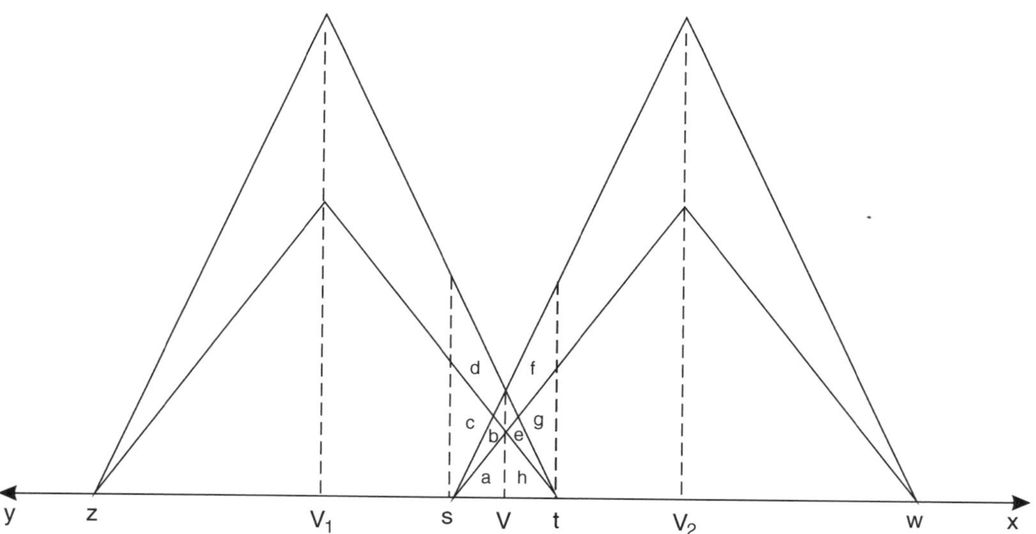

Figure 8.3 The gains from trade under intra-industry specialisation: after specialisation

country initially find that it is only profitable to produce just one variety, V_1 in Country 1 and V_2 in Country 2. If the two countries now trade, the result is intra-industry specialisation. Country exports V_1 to Country 2 and Country 2 exports V_2 to Country 1. This enables consumers in both countries to obtain a variety closer to their preferred one. Specifically, consumers in Country 1 whose preferences lie in the range Vt can now buy V_2, while consumers in Country 2 whose preferences lie in the range Sv can now buy V_1. It is obvious that economic welfare in both countries will now be higher. First, consider consumers in Country 2 whose preferred variety lies in the range Sv and who will switch from buying V_2 to buying V_1. Their consumer surplus will rise by $(d-b)$, the difference between the consumer surplus now enjoyed on V_1 and the consumer surplus previously enjoyed on V_2. In addition, producers in Country 1 gain increased producer surplus equal to areas $(a+b+c)$. From this must be deducted the loss of producers' surplus experienced by producers in Country 2 equal to area a. So the total gain derived from consumers in Country 2 switching to variety V_1 supplied by producers in Country 1 is:

$$(d-b)+[(a+b+c)-a]=(d+c)$$

Secondly, consider consumers in Country 1 whose preferred variety lies in the range *vt* who switch from buying V_1 to V_2. Once again, the consumers enjoy increased consumer surplus equal to $(f-e)$. In addition, producers in Country 2 enjoy increased producers' surplus equal to area $(h+e+g)$. However, producers in Country 1 lose producer surplus equal to area h. So the total gain resulting from consumers in Country 1 switching to buying V_2 instead of V_1 is:

$$(f-e)+[(h+e+g)-h]=(f+g)$$

The total gains from increased intra-industry trade may be summarised as follows:

	Gains to Country 1	Gains to Country 2
Consumer surplus	$(f-e)$	$(d-b)$
Producer surplus	$(b+c)$	$(g+e)$

In this particular model, the gains are distributed proportionately between the two countries. If, however, different assumptions were made, the gains might be less equally shared. The total size of the gains will depend on the extent to which consumer preferences in the two countries overlap. The greater the area of overlap, the greater the potential gain.

A further important source of welfare gain from intra-industry specialisation arises from the increased incentive which producers have to*innovate. Innovation may take one of two forms. First, producers may introduce new varieties of existing products (variety innovation). Second, they may add new products to the range of existing ones currently available (product innovation). Consider first the case of *variety innovation.* In the absence of trade, it may be profitable for a producer to produce only one variety of a product as in the example above. However, now that the possibility exists to sell other varieties not only to consumers at home, but also in the foreign market it may become profitable to produce more than one variety. Clearly, this will be a variety somewhere between the type they are currently producing and the type produced in the foreign country (e.g. V_1 and V_2 in Figure 8.3). In addition, by expanding the number of varieties which he produces, the producer can create barriers for potential new entrants to the home market. Any new entrant then has to produce more than one variety of the good to gain a reasonable share of the market. If he cannot do so, he may not be able to sell a sufficient amount to cover the costs of entry. However, existing producers must beware of introducing too many new varieties since each new variety will reduce the market for existing ones. Where, however, variety innovation does take place, consumers enjoy a welfare gain from being able to buy a variety closer to their preferred one in the manner set out above.

Next, consider the case of *product innovation*. Lower trade barriers may stimulate firms to engage in more product innovation for much the same reasons. Product innovation may be a way of both defending and expanding market share in the face of increased competition from abroad. At the same time, the risks associated with innovation are reduced. The discovery of a new product typically requires expenditure of large amounts on R&D often over quite long periods of time and with no certainty that the product will prove a success. In the pharmaceuticals industry, for example, products have to undergo lengthy testing procedures before the product can be legally produced and sold. Once the product has been brought to market, the time period in which firms can recuperate their costs is usually quite short. Most new products often have quite short market lives, as rival producers soon develop other products which are superior. This means that firms must seek to earn as much as they can from the sale of the product as quickly as possible. Meyer (1978) has argued that intra-industry specialisation creates an important escape route for firms in such industries. Each firm can concentrate on a limited range of products which it can sell in an enlarged market for the highest price which the market will bear. In this way, fixed R&D costs can be spread over a much larger volume of output and recuperated more rapidly.

A further difference between intra- and inter-industry specialisation concerns the effects on the distribution of income. Whereas inter-industry specialisation may adversely affect certain income-earners in the importing country, no such effects are likely to result from intra-industry specialisation. As we have seen, factor intensities are quite similar within industries, that is, products belonging to the same industry require broadly similar factor proportions in the process of production. It follows that intra-industry specialisation will have little, if any effect on relative factor prices. Krugman (1981) has provided a formal proof of this. In his model, there are two countries which each possess identical factor endowments. Trade takes the form of intra-industry trade in which each country exchanges different varieties of the same product. Because factor intensities are the same, no change in factor prices results. All income groups, therefore, share in the gains from trade. One important conclusion that follows is that domestic resistance to lowering trade barriers in industries where intra-industry specialisation is the outcome is likely to be less. Since the owners of a country's scarce factor suffer no absolute or relative decline in the return for their factor services, they are less likely to oppose the opening up of trade.

Adjustment Costs

From these gains from trade, it may be appropriate to deduct the adjustment costs discussed in the previous chapter. Free trade requires a movement of resources out of the declining, import-competing sector and into the expanding, export sector. If this happened instantaneously, there would be zero adjustment cost. In practice, however, this is never the case. Clearly, what counts here are the social and not the private costs of adjustment. The income and wealth losses experienced by workers and capitalists in the import-competing sector can, in theory, be compensated by the income and wealth gains of workers and capitalists in the export sector. However, the social costs of adjustment represent a real welfare loss to the country as a whole. They must, therefore, be subtracted from the welfare gain from trade to derive the net benefit for each country. There is, however, the difficult question as to whether all the costs of adjustment constitute genuine losses to the importing country. As Banks and Tumlir (1986) have argued only those costs that are unavoidable should be included in the calculation of social costs. As we saw in the previous chapter, the costs of adjustment arise in part because of imperfections in factor markets, such as impediments to labour mobility and the absence of wage-rate flexibility. Some of these costs could be avoided if governments adopted measures to facilitate labour mobility and increase wage-rate flexibility.

However, as we saw in the previous chapter, the existence of adjustment costs is an important factor creating opposition within countries to free trade. These are likely to be greater where free trade leads to inter-industry rather than intra-industry specialisation. This is because inter-industry specialisation requires resources to shift out of one sector and into another, whereas intra-industry specialisation requires only a shift of resources *within* the sector. Resources are likely to find it easier to move within than between sectors. One reason is that the type of skills required of workers differ less within a given sector than between different sectors. Another reason is a greater likelihood that firms within a particular sector of the economy are located in the same geographical region, thus lessening the need for workers to move to a different area. Furthermore to some extent, intra-industry specialisation can take place within the same firm. That is to say firms reduce the range of products that they produce. In this case, workers need not change employment, although the tasks that they perform in their employment may still alter. These considerations suggest that countries will find it easier to lower trade barriers between themselves where freer trade leads to intra- as opposed to inter-industry specialisation. As we saw in Chapter 6, much of the trade, which has taken place between Japan and the western industrialised countries, has resulted in inter-industry specialisation. This may explain why it has been subject to considerable friction. Much the same has been true of trade between the western industrialised countries and the NICs. By way of contrast, trade between the western industrialised countries has resulted in increased intra-industry specialisation. As a result, trade liberalisation between these countries has generally been easier to bring about.

Box 8.1 summarises the different effects of trade expansion under inter- and intra-industry specialisation.

Tariff Protectionism

Despite the fact that free trade increases global economic welfare, most governments interfere in trade. Usually, the main reason for doing so is to grant protection to a particular industry threatened by foreign competition. Protection may take the form of imposing tariffs on imports or the creation of various kinds of non-tariff barriers. Trade may also be distorted by government measures that favour domestic producers over foreign producers (e.g. granting a subsidy to a domestic producer). In the next two sections of this chapter, the effects of these kinds of government interference in trade are examined. We begin with tariffs because they are perhaps the most obvious form of government-imposed barrier to trade.

Tariffs may take the form of a specific duty payable on each unit imported or an *ad valorem* tariff expressed as a percentage of the unit

Box 8.1 The Effects of Increased Trade: Inter- and Intra-Industry Specialisation Compared

The Effects of Inter-Industry Specialisation

- Static effects – lower prices and improved resource allocation
- Dynamic effects –

  Economies of large plant size
  Increased price competition
  Increased capital investment
  Increased rate of technological change
  Higher output due to higher real incomes
- Industry trade balances widen – may lead to resistance to lowering trade barriers in import-competing sectors
- Adjustment costs –

  Need for inter-sectoral re-allocation of factors
  Need for relative factor prices to change (where factor intensities differ between export and import-competing sectors)
- Distributional effects – price of country's scarce factor may fall relative to price of country's abundant factor

The Effects of Intra-Industry Specialisation

- Static Effects –

  More varieties of each type of good become available (love for variety)
  Consumers able to get a variety closer to their preferred type
  Some reduction in prices due to increased competition
- Dynamic Effects –

  Scale economies due to more plant specialisation (long production runs)
  Learning by doing effects (dynamic scale economies)
  Faster rate of product innovation in research-intensive industries
- Industry trade balances narrow – less resistance to trade liberalisation
- Adjustment Costs –

  No need for inter-sectoral re-allocation of factors (only intra-sectoral)
  Less need for relative factor prices to change
  Possibility of some structural unemployment due to wrong skills mix
- Distribution effects unlikely to be very great as relative factor prices less likely to change

value of goods imported. Tariffs generally raise the price of imports although not always by the full amount of the tariff. Thus, under certain circumstances, the incidence of the tariff may be borne both by the consumer in the importing country and the foreign supplier. The reason for imposing tariffs may not always be protectionist. In poorer countries which lack an

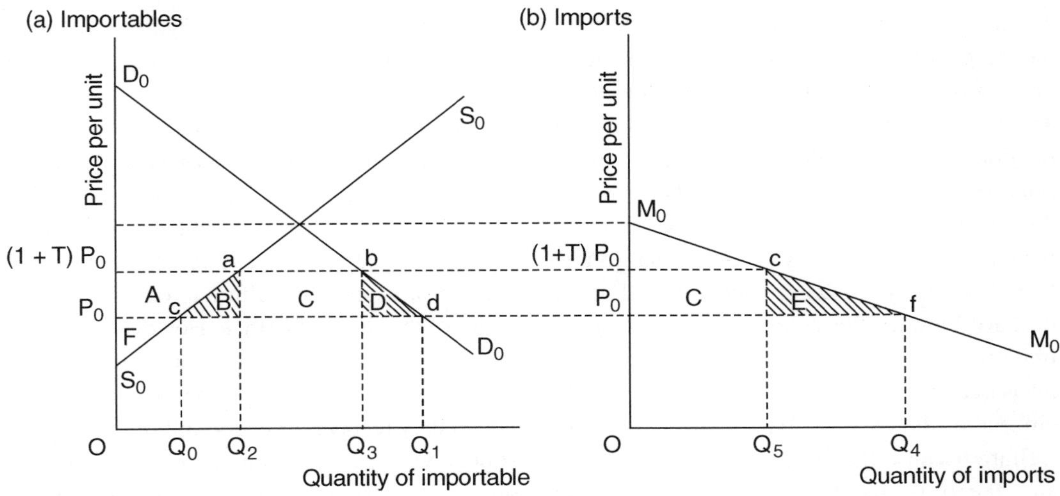

Figure 8.4 The small-country partial equilibrium model of the effects of a tariff

adequate base for raising sufficient revenues from the taxation of incomes, reliance is often placed on customs duties along with other forms of commodity taxation for the finance of public expenditure. In most cases, however, tariffs reduce the economic welfare not only of exporting countries, whose access to foreign markets is thereby restricted, but also of the importing country imposing the duty.

Figure 8.4 illustrates the effects on a small importing nation of the imposition of a tariff. The left-hand side of the diagram shows the demand and supply for a product in the importing country. Suppose the world price is OP_0. Suppose also that the importing country is a small trading nation which is unable to influence the world price of the product in question. Then, it can buy all that it wants from the rest of the world at the world price P_0, but nothing at all at a price of less than OP_0. D_0D_0 is the demand curve for the product and S_0S_0 the domestic supply curve in the importing country. Let us further assume that the product is a homogeneous product such that there is no difference between the product supplied by the foreign producer and that by the domestic producer. This ensures that the product will sell at one price only. In the absence of any tariff and disregarding any transport costs, consumers would pay the price P_0. (If domestic producers charge more than P_0, they will be unable to sell any of the product.) Domestic consumption would equal OQ_1, domestic production OQ_0 and imports Q_0Q_1. Q_0Q_1 is also equal to OQ_4 in the right-hand side of the diagram. Now, suppose the authorities impose a tariff, T. The effect is to raise the price of imports in the importing country to $(1+T)P_0$. (Note that the world price is unaffected because the importing country is a small trading nation.) Domestic producers also raise their prices by the amount of the tariff because, if they do not, consumers will switch all their purchases from foreign to domestic suppliers. This will force domestic producers to raise their prices to choke off the excess demand. As a result of the increase in price, domestic consumption will fall to OQ_3, domestic production will rise to OQ_2 and imports will fall to Q_2Q_3. Q_2Q_3 is equal to OQ_5 in the right-hand side of the diagram.

The tariff has five different effects. First, the rise in the price of the product reduces consumption – the *consumption effect*. Second, the increased price leads to increased domestic production of the good – the *protection effect*. Third, the fall in consumption plus the increase in domestic production results in reduced imports – the *balance of trade effect*. Fourth the tariff generates increased fiscal revenues for the importing country. This is equal to area C and is known as the *revenue effect*. Finally, the tariff lowers the economic welfare of the importing country – the *welfare effect*. This is measured by the loss of real income of the citizens of the country. Tariffs lower economic welfare because they raise prices to consumers and, therefore, reduce their real income. This loss to consumers is measured using the concept of *consumers' surplus*.

Previously, we saw that an individual's consumer surplus is the difference between the utility or satisfaction which he/she derives from the consumption of a unit of a product and the amount they pay for it. Consumer satisfaction from a product tends to diminish with the number of units bought. Thus, the last unit, which is bought, brings less satisfaction than the first unit bought. This is why an individual consumer's demand curve normally slopes downwards from left to right. Now, a rational consumer will continue buying more units until he reaches the point where the satisfaction derived from the last unit bought (marginal utility) equals the price. It follows that, because the consumer normally pays the same price for all units purchased (not a higher price for the first unit than for the last), he/she will enjoy consumer surplus on all units bought except the last unit. Thus, consumer surplus is measured by the area under the consumer's demand curve but above the market price. Aggregate consumer surplus is the sum of the consumer surplus of all consumers of the product. This, too, is measured by the area under the market demand curve but above the market price. In Figure 8.4, under free trade and with the price at OP_0, this is the area P_0D_0d.

The effect of imposing a tariff is to reduce the amount of consumers' surplus. An increase in the market price of TP_0 reduces the area representing consumers' surplus by the sum of (A + B + C + D). This measures the loss of real income or economic welfare to consumers as a result of the rise in the price. However, the tariff makes domestic producers of the imported product better off. This is because the price, which they receive for every unit of the product supplied has risen, although part of this gain is absorbed by the costs of producing the increase in domestic output. If unit costs increase with output, it will cost more to produce the extra output than the existing level of output. The gain to producers is the difference between the increase in price obtained for each unit sold and the higher costs which must be incurred in producing the extra output.

This gain to producers is measured by total *producers' surplus*. All producers confront a rising marginal cost curve. That is to say, the cost of producing the last unit is greater than the cost of producing the first unit. This is why each producer's supply curve slopes upwards from left to right. However, they get the same price for each unit sold. Thus, they enjoy producer surplus on all except the last unit sold. If we aggregate the supply curves of all producers, total producers' surplus is equal to the area above the supply curve but below the market price. Under free trade, this is area F in Figure 8.4. Now, the effect of imposing a tariff is to increase the market price by TP_0 and, hence, to increase the amount of producers' surplus by area A.

Finally, the imposition of the tariff increases fiscal revenues to the government of the importing country. The revenue generated by the tariff is given by the quantity of imports multiplied by the tariff per unit imported (assuming the tariff is a specific duty). This is shown by area C. If the gain to domestic producers (area A) and the increase in fiscal revenues to the government (area C) are deducted from the loss to consumers, the 'net' loss of economic welfare or the 'deadweight' loss is obtained. This is equal to the areas (B + D), the two triangles below the supply and demand curves respectively. These, in turn, are equal to area E in the diagram on the right-hand side. These are often referred to as the 'Marshallian triangles' after the neo-classical economist, Alfred Marshall. They are measured by multiplying the change in the volume of imports following the imposition of the tariff by one-half the rate of tariff:

$$\text{Net Welfare Loss} = \Delta M.0.5\,T$$

The more inelastic the demand for and supply of imports (i.e. the steeper the slope of the demand and supply curves), the smaller the drop in imports following the imposition of the tariff and the lower the welfare loss.

The analysis is somewhat different if we assume the importing nation to be a large country. In this case, the amount which it imports from the rest of the world affects the world price. The more it imports from the rest of the world, the higher the world price. This case is illustrated by Figure 8.5. In this diagram, the world supply curve is superimposed on the domestic supply curve to give a combined, domestic-plus-world supply curve, S_0S_T. (Note that S_0S_T is flatter than S_0S_0 because world supply is more elastic than domestic supply, but not perfectly elastic as in the case of the small country.) Under free trade, equilibrium exists where combined, domestic-plus-world supply equals demand, that is, the price $0P_0$. At this price, domestic consumption equals OQ_1, domestic production equals OQ_0 and imports equal Q_0Q_1. Once again, an equal tariff is imposed, causing the price to rise. The effect is to shift the world supply curve (and therefore the combined domestic-plus-world supply curve) upwards to $S_0S_T^*$ by the amount of the tariff. The vertical distance between $S_0S_T^*$ and S_0S_T measures the amount of the tariff per unit. A new equilibrium price, $(1 + T)P_1$, is established. Consumption falls to OQ_3, domestic production increases to OQ_2 and imports fall to Q_2Q_3. The effects are identical to those of the small importing nation with one important exception. The world price of the product falls to OP_1. This means that the importing country is getting the product from the rest of the world at a lower price than before. In short, her terms of trade have improved. True, consumers are paying more for the product, but the price has risen *by less than* the full amount of the tariff. Whereas the price to the consumer has risen by TP_0, the tariff per unit is TP_1. In other words, a part of the tariff is paid for by the foreign exporter, the rest being paid for by the consumer in the importing country. By way of contrast, in the case of a small importing nation, the whole of the incidence of the tariff falls on consumers.

This terms-of-trade gain to the importing nation must be offset against the welfare loss. In the large country model, the tariff imposes the same deadweight loss, given by areas (B + D), as in the small country model. However, this must now be set against the 'gain' to the importing country resulting from the improvement in the terms of trade. This is given by the fall in the world price, P_0P_1, multiplied by the volume of imports Q_2Q_3. In Figure 8.5, this is given by area E. The welfare loss from the imposition of the tariff is, therefore, areas (B + D) 'less' area E. Clearly, if area E exceeds areas (B + D), the tariff will 'raise' not lower the economic welfare of the importing nation. In other words, a large importing nation, which

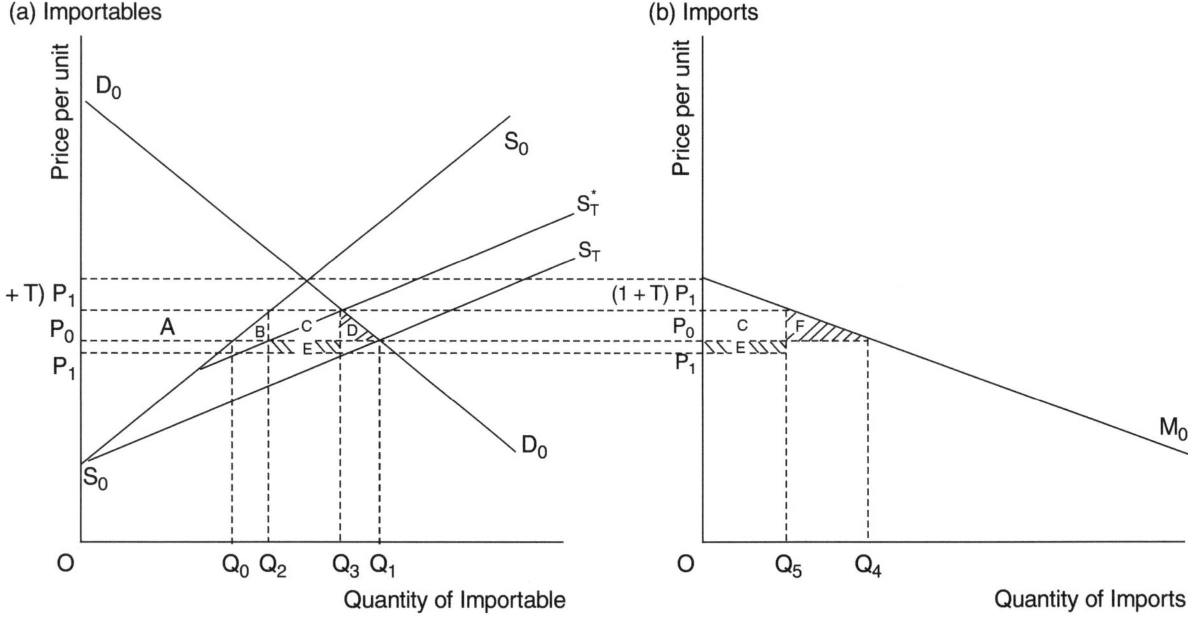

Figure 8.5 The large-country partial equilibrium model of the effects of a tariff

has the power to influence the world price of an imported product, may so improve its terms of trade by imposing a tariff that the net effect on its economic welfare is positive. This constitutes what is often referred to as *the terms of trade argument* for a tariff. However, the importing country's gain is the rest of the world's loss. In other words, *global* economic welfare is not increased but, is merely redistributed between the importing nation and the rest of the world. Moreover, the tariff rate must be carefully calculated so as to maximise the difference between area E and areas (B+D). That is to say, the tariff must maximise the terms of trade again relative to the static welfare loss. The tariff rate, which achieves this, is called the 'optimum tariff'. Mathematically, it is given by the formula $t = 1/e$ where e stands for the elasticity of supply of imports (i.e. the change in the supply of imports from the rest of the world resulting from a change in the price of imports). In practice, few governments have sufficient information to calculate the optimum tariff. Exactly how the supply of imports will change in response to the imposition of a tariff can only be guessed at. Furthermore, they cannot be sure that the rest of the world will not retaliate by imposing a similar tariff on products, which the importing nation exports to the rest of the world. By imposing a tariff, they risk provoking a 'tit-for-tat' tariff war, which will serve only to reduce the total volume of world trade and could leave both countries worse off than before. Thus, the optimum tariff has little practical value for trade policy. However, it may provide a rationale for why large countries or trading blocs, which enjoy monopsony (buying) power, often do impose tariffs on goods coming from the rest of the world despite the fact that such tariffs impose an efficiency loss.

How important are tariffs as a barrier to trade? In the immediate aftermath of the Second World War, the average tariff on industrial goods has been estimated at approximately 40%. By the time the latest round of multilateral tariff reductions (the Uruguay Round) are fully implemented, this will have fallen to just under 3%. Tariffs are somewhat higher in developing than in developed countries. The trade-weighted average, post-Uruguay Round tariff on industrial goods for developing countries will be 12.3% compared with 3.9% for developed countries. Among the so-called 'Quad' countries (Canada, EU, Japan and the USA), the average ranges from 1% in Japan to 4.8% in Canada. It is also the case that the majority of tariffs are 'bound', which means that countries have agreed not to raise their tariffs above a certain level. This gives certainty to exporters that access to foreign markets will not be suddenly restricted by a tariff increase. As a result of the Uruguay Round, 97% of all tariffs of developed countries on industrial goods are now bound and 65% for developing countries. Thus, tariffs are no longer a major impediment to trade and the level of tariffs has fallen significantly over the past half century. Nevertheless, a low average tariff may still disguise high tariffs on particular products. For example, most developed countries apply higher tariffs on 'sensitive' products such as clothing and textiles. Moreover, a bound tariff is only meaningful if a tariff is bound at or below its current rate. Otherwise, an importing country may be able to increase the degree of protection by raising its tariff without breaking any agreements.

Non-Tariff Protectionism

As tariffs have fallen, countries have found other, often more subtle, ways of protecting domestic producers from foreign competition. The spread of non-tariff protectionism in recent decades is sometimes referred to as the 'new protectionism'. In fact, many of the non-tariff barriers which exist are not new and have been used as methods of restricting imports from the very beginning of overseas trade. However, as tariffs have been lowered, the extent to which these restrictions impede trade has become more apparent. Moreover, as pressure builds up on governments to come to the aid of a beleaguered domestic producer of a product, non-tariff barriers (NTBs) are often preferred to tariffs as a response. However, certain kinds of NTBs are relatively new and have arisen as result of particular developments in the rules and procedures for regulating world trade. Other kinds of NTBs have emerged for reasons other than protectionist ones. They are a reflection of the increased role of governments in the western industrialised countries since the Second World War in pursuit of a wide variety of economic and social objectives. As governments have become more involved in the running of the economy and the regulation of markets, new kinds of barriers to trade have arisen largely as a side effect. For example, the efforts of governments to protect consumers from unhealthy or unsafe products frequently give rise to trade barriers which are not intended to favour domestic over foreign producers. Concern for the environment may similarly have a protectionist outcome even though the motivation for the measure may be non-economic.

Because of the sheer range of different kinds of NTBs, it is difficult to gauge their importance. The available evidence seems to show that a considerable growth in the extent of such protectionism has taken place over the last twenty to thirty years. Page (1981) estimated that, by 1980, as much as 48% of world trade was *controlled* or *managed*, loosely meaning subject to some kind of non-tariff intervention. This compared with 40% in 1974. Page distinguished between three kinds of intervention:

1. *International agreements*, such as international cartels (e.g. OPEC, international commodity agreements, etc.) and market-sharing agreements (as exist in textiles, steel and shipbuilding)
2. *National controls*, such as import quotas, anti-dumping duties, certificates of origin and other administrative controls, price controls, voluntary export restraints and government-imposed restrictions on the purchase of imports.
3. *Other national controls* whose major effect has been on trade but where the main motive is domestic rather than any desire to restrict imports, such as safety, health or technical product standards, domestic subsidies, customs clearance procedures, patent laws or licences and price controls.

Page found that, while the share of trade which was managed was higher for non-manufactures than manufactures, it had risen fastest in the case of manufactures. Between 1974 and 1981, the share of trade in manufactures that was managed rose from 12.9 to 23.6%. The percentage was highest on trade between the western industrialised countries and developing countries. In 1979, as much as 30% of trade in manufactured goods between industrialised and developing countries was managed, compared with 11% for trade between industrialised economies. Thus, not only has there been a growth in the importance of non-tariff barriers, especially in relation to manufactured goods, but much of this has been targeted at developing countries that are major exporters of manufactures, that is, the newly industrialising countries.

A more recent estimate of the extent of non-tariff protectionism has been provided by Laird and Yeats (1990). They calculated two ratios: (a) a coverage ratio, which is the value of imports covered by NTBs, and (b) a frequency ratio which measures the percentage of tariff lines affected by NTBs. Their definition of NTBs covered national controls only but distinguished between 'hard-core' NTBs and other kinds of NTBs. Hard-core NTBs are either ones where the primary intention is to restrict imports or where there is a different primary motive for the measure but where a restriction of imports is, nevertheless, a secondary intention. Their results showed that, by 1986, roughly 27.2% of all imports were covered and 48% affected by hard-core NTBs. Moreover, between 1966 and 1986, the share of imports affected by hard-core NTBs rose from 29.5 to 48%. These figures demonstrate the extent to which non-tariff protectionism has increased in recent decades.

Although non-tariff protectionism may take a wide range of different forms, certain types of NTBs have become more important in recent years than others. A useful distinction to make is between quantitative restrictions, which place limits on the amount of a product that may be imported or exported, and those which operate, like a tariff, by raising the cost of imports. Table 8.1 summarises the most important types of NTBs under each of these headings. In the section that follows, some of the most important forms of non-tariff protection, especially those that have become important in recent years are discussed.

Import Quotas

An import quota is a quantitatively operating form of NTB which involves governments putting a physical limit on the volume of a particular product which may be imported during a particular period of time. They may be 'global' if they are applied to all imports of a particular product regardless of source. Alternatively, many quotas are 'bilateral' being confined to imports coming from a specific source. They operate by governments issuing importers with licences permitting them to import a specified quantity of the product. Licences may be issued administratively or auctioned to the highest bidder. If the latter is the case, a further possibility is that the quotas are tradable between importers. Figure 8.6 illustrates the effects of a non-discriminatory, (global) import quota applied by an importing country to a particular product and allocated on a *pro rata* basis.

Table 8.1 Main Types of Non-Tariff Barriers to Trade

	Quantitatively operating	*Operating on price/cost*
Direct measures	Import quotas Import licensing Embargoes Voluntary export restraints Discriminatory public procurement	Variable import levies Advance deposit requirements Anti-dumping duties Countervailing duties Domestic subsidies
Indirect measures		Packaging and labelling requirements Health and safety regulations Customs clearance procedures Customs classification procedures Customs valuation procedures

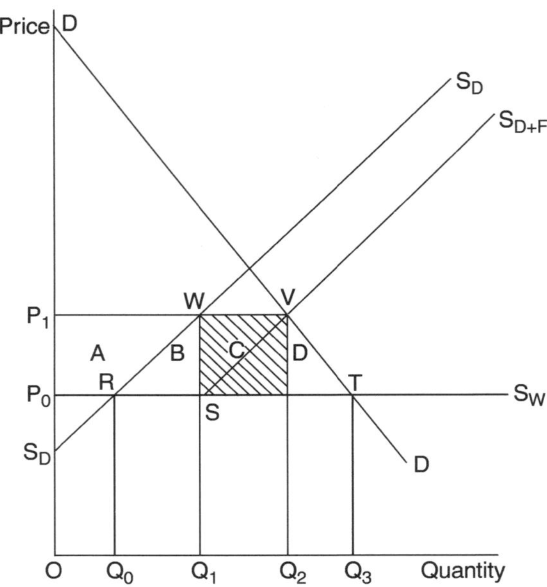

Figure 8.6 The effect of the imposition of an import quota

DD is the domestic demand curve for the product and S_DS_D the domestic supply curve. OP_0 is the world price of the product. Under free trade, domestic producers will supply the quantity OQ_0, consumers will buy the quantity OQ_3 and imports will amount to Q_0Q_3 (= RT). Next, a quota equal to WV is imposed. Then, total (domestic plus foreign) supply is represented by the supply curve S_{D+F}. Demand equals supply at the price OP_1. Price has risen from OP_0 to OP_1. Consumption falls by Q_2Q_3 to OQ_2. Domestic supply rises by Q_0Q_1 to OQ_1. Imports are, of course, equal to the quota $WV = Q_1Q_2$. Comparing the effects of a quota with those of a tariff, it is clear that the effects are much the same. In both cases, prices rise. As with a tariff, consumers suffer a welfare loss equal to areas A+B+C+D. Area A constitutes increased producers' surplus and is therefore not a loss to the importing nation. In the case of a tariff, area C represents revenue to the government of the importing nation. However, this is not the case for a quota except in the case where quotas are auctioned. If quotas were auctioned, the government would be able to sell them for the price P_0P_1, thereby generating revenues equal to area C. If, however, quotas are allocated according to some other criteria, the main beneficiary will be the middleman, who will buy imports at the price OP_0 and sell them at the price OP_1. Therefore, the shaded area C will constitute economic rent for middlemen and, as such, not a loss to the importing nation. This leaves areas B+D as the net welfare loss or deadweight loss from the quota. This is exactly the same as for a tariff.

From the point of view of the importing country, quotas may be more attractive than tariffs as a device for restricting imports. With a tariff, the effect of a given tariff on the volume of imports is uncertain; it depends on the domestic elasticities of demand for and supply of the product. If the aim is to restrict imports to a specific amount, this may be better achieved by imposing a quota. On the other hand, a quota raises no revenue for the public authorities unless quotas are auctioned to the highest bidder. Quotas may also be more damaging to economic efficiency than tariffs. The reason is that, whereas, with tariffs, resources are allocated through the price mechanism, under quotas resources are allocated administratively by the state. Under tariffs, any importer can import as much of the good as he likes provided he is prepared to pay the tariff-inclusive price. Under quotas, if it is left to government officials to allocate licences to importers and, thereby, to determine how much of the good each importer is allowed to import, they may do so on a first-come-first-served basis or they may allocate licences based on past performance (e.g. the share of the market in previous years). Alternatively, quotas could be auctioned to the highest bidder. The latter alternative would achieve the same effect as a tariff. Administrative allocation, on the other hand, is likely to result in an inefficient allocation of resources. It may also result in bribery of state officials by importers wishing to acquire licences in excess of their allocation.

Quotas also tend to freeze the pattern of production in the importing country. Where the quota-restrained product is a raw material or intermediate good, which is used as a input by other industries, efficient producers may be unable to expand their output at the expense of inefficient producers because they cannot obtain sufficient essential inputs from abroad. Another problem with quotas is that they tend to result in an increase in the degree of protection accorded to an industry over time. If the market for the final good is an expanding one, then, unless import quotas are increased in line with the growth of the domestic market, all of the extra demand will be met by higher cost domestic production. This is illustrated in Figure 8.7. A rise in domestic demand causes the demand curve to shift from DD to D^*D^*. In the absence of any increase in the quota of WV = XY, all of the increase in demand has to be satisfied by higher cost domestic production rather than lower cost imports. Consequently, price rises to OP_2. In the case of a tariff, a rise in demand is fully met by an increase in imports (WZ) and price does not rise at all.

From a global perspective, quotas also cause another kind of distortion. Invariably, quotas

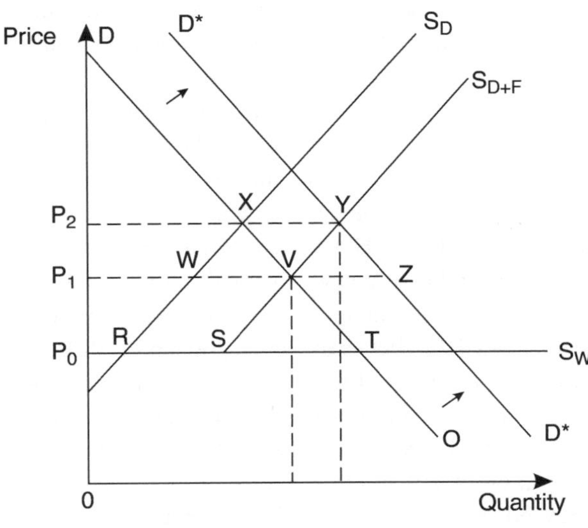

Figure 8.7 Fixed import quotas in an expanding domestic market

are discriminatory, that is, they are imposed on imports from a particular source. Very often, the source is the world's lowest cost suppliers of the product. Therefore, not only do they reduce the volume of trade, but they also divert trade (and hence production) from a low- to a high-cost source. Global resource allocation is thereby harmed. It is, therefore, perhaps not surprising that international law generally takes a tougher stance towards quotas than tariffs. For example, the General Agreement on Tariffs and Trade (GATT) makes it clear that, if countries need to protect a domestic industry from foreign competition, they should do so by tariffs and not quotas (see Chapter 9). In practice, however, quotas has remained a common form of protection. Partly, this is because of ambiguity in the rules governing the use of quotas under international law. Partly, it is because some important exceptions to the general ban on quantitative restrictions under the GATT have always been allowed. Furthermore, not all countries in the world are GATT signatories or members of the World Trade Organisation (WTO) which enforces GATT rules. This means that, for example, developed market economies of the world have been largely free to impose quotas on imports from state-planned economies.

Voluntary Export Restraints

Bearing a close resemblance to import quotas are voluntary export restraints (VERs). However, unlike quotas, VERs are a relatively new form of barrier to trade. (The earliest example of a VER was an agreement in 1937 between American and Japanese exporters to limit Japanese textile exports to the United States.) The past three decades, in particular, have witnessed a major proliferation of this kind of trade restriction. VERs are bilateral agreements negotiated between an exporting and an importing country under which the exporting country agrees to limit its exports of a particular product to the importing country to a fixed amount or share of the market. Unlike with import quotas, the restraining is done by the exporting not the importing country. Usually, the government of the exporting country will issue licences to exporters that allow the exporter to supply only a certain amount of the product to the importing country during a particular year. Moreover, VERs are negotiated agreements, not unilaterally imposed measures as with quotas. However, negotiations are often accompanied by the implicit threat of unilateral action by the importing country should the exporting country not agree to limit its exports.

Although most VERs are discriminatory (i.e. they are applied to imports of a product from a particular source), it is analytically easier to examine the effects of a non-discriminatory VER (i.e. one targeted at all suppliers of the product). Figure 8.8 illustrates such a case. D_0D_0 is the demand curve for the product in the importing country and S_DS_D the domestic supply curve. S_WS_W is the combined domestic plus foreign supply curve which is more elastic than the domestic supply curve. OP_0 is the equilibrium price under free trade with domestic consumption equal to OQ_4, domestic production equal to OQ_1 and imports equal to Q_1Q_4. The importing country wishes to reduce the level of imports to Q_2Q_3. To do this, it enters into a VER with foreign suppliers. (One can imagine either that it enters into a VER with all foreign suppliers simultaneously or that the only foreign producer is the one with whom it negotiates a VER.) The effect of the VER is identical to that of an import quota – the equilibrium price rises to OP_1, domestic consumption falls to OQ_3, domestic production rises to OQ_2 and imports fall to Q_2Q_3. However, although the market price in the importing country has risen to OP_1, the foreign supply

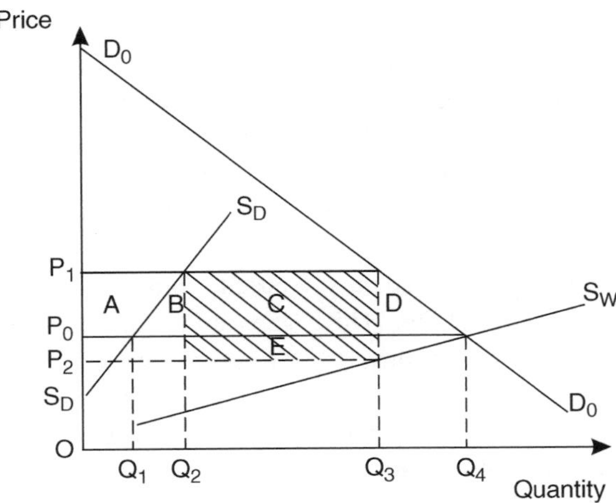

Figure 8.8 The effects of a voluntary export restraint

price has fallen to OP_2. The logic behind this is that a non-discriminatory VER applied to all suppliers will create excess capacity in the world industry resulting in lower short-run marginal costs. Thus, foreign suppliers can enjoy a mark-up on the price of P_0P_1 on every unit sold compared with the free-trade situation. However, since costs per unit have also fallen, the mark-up as a result of the VER is actually larger, being equal to P_2P_1.

At first impression, the effects of the VER are identical to that of a tariff and import quota. In both cases, the domestic price rises. Domestic production increases, consumption falls and the volume of imports decrease. Because the price has gone up, consumers also suffer a welfare loss. In Figure 8.8, this loss is given by area A+B+C+D (the same as with a tariff or quota). As with the tariff and quota, area A is a redistribution of income from consumers to domestic producers. However, area C is different in the case of a VER. Whereas, for a tariff, this constitutes increased fiscal revenues to the public authorities and, in the case of a quota, increased rent to importers, in the case of the VER, this goes in rent to the exporting country. In fact, exporters enjoy rents equal to the shaded areas C+E. To see this, observe that the mark-up on each unit sold is P_2P_1. The volume of units now sold is Q_2Q_3 (compared with Q_1Q_4 before). Therefore, the total gain to exporters is C+E. Area E represents the increase in profits accruing to foreign exporters because costs per unit fall following the implementation of the VER. This leaves area C as the redistribution of income from consumers in the importing country to exporters in the foreign country. It is, therefore, a loss to the importing country. This makes the total welfare loss from the VER to the importing country to be areas B+C+D.

Clearly, this is much greater than for either a tariff or import quota. How did this happen? The reason for this is that a VER worsens the terms of trade of the importing country by raising the cost of imports to the importing nation. This does not happen with either a tariff or quota. The price paid by the domestic consumer goes up, but not the cost of the imports to the importing nation. With a VER, both increase. The fact that foreign exporters enjoy a mark-up on every unit sold is one reason why exporting countries are willing to agree to restrain their exports. Although they are not able to export as much in quantity as before, they enjoy a significant mark-up on the price obtained for every unit sold. What is less obvious is why the importing country should prefer a VER to a tariff or quota as a device for restricting imports. As with a quota, a VER will achieve the desired reduction in the volume of imports. However, it will not improve the balance of trade of the importing country unless the demand for imports is elastic. This is because, although the volume of imports falls, the price per unit increases. Only if the volume of imports falls by proportionately more than the price increases will the value of imports be lower. On the other hand, the purpose may be to stimulate domestic production or increase the profits of domestic producers. A VER will achieve both of these effects but only at a cost to the country as a whole.

One attempt to estimate the importance of VERs found that, by 1987, roughly 10% of world trade was covered by VERs and about 12% of non-fuel trade (Kostecki, 1987). The most prolific users of VERs have been the EC and the USA, accounting for over 70% of all arrangements. In recent decades, they have negotiated a whole series of VERs either with Japan or newly industrialising countries to secure protection for domestic producers in those industries most affected by increased import competition. In general, these have been the so-called 'sensitive' goods industries, in which Japan and the NICs have been most competitive in recent decades. Often, these are industries which, in the western industrialised countries, are declining or experiencing major structural change, such that employment is stagnant or falling. They are often concentrated in particular regions in which little alternative employment exists for displaced workers. In some cases but not all, they are also industries which employ large numbers of ethnic or migrant workers and have a large female labour force.

Beginning in the late 1960s, the *steel industry* began to experience difficulties due, partly, to over-investment and over-capacity at home and, partly, to increased competition from abroad. The first VER concerning steel products was negotiated in 1968 between both the US and Japan and the US and the EC. The agreement lasted until 1974 when imports fell below the ceiling and the agreement was scrapped. However, in 1977, faced with an increased flow of low-cost imports from the rest of the world, the United States introduced the so-called 'trigger price mechanism' whereby no imports could be sold in the US below a stated reference price based on estimates of costs of production in Japan. At the same time, beginning in the late 1970s, the US entered into a tacit agreement with Japan limiting Japanese exports to the US. At approximately the same time the EC entered into a number of VERs with major suppliers designed to curtail imports of steel. These were introduced as part of a package of crisis measures known as the Davignon Plan for tackling the problems of overproduction and excess capacity by enforcing minimum prices for basic steel products and closing down unwanted, inefficient plants. At the same time, the crisis in the EC meant that much steel, which could not be sold in Europe was exported at knock-down prices to the US. U.S. producers complained to the authorities that European steel was being 'dumped' on the U.S. market and called for the imposition of anti-dumping duties. Instead, in 1982, the EC signed a VER with the US. This was followed by a series of VERs between the US and most other major foreign suppliers.

The *automobile industry* has been another sector in which VERs have been extensively used. As with steel, the automobile industry in the western industrialised countries has been adversely affected by over-investment and increased competition from abroad. The rise of Japan as a major automobile manufacturer has become the main source of the challenge facing western car producers. The first VER involving motor cars was signed between the UK and Japan in 1977 and froze Japan's share of the U.K. market at 11%. At about the same time, France negotiated a similar agreement with Japan. In May 1981, the US negotiated a VER with the Japanese government which effectively reduced U.S. imports from Japan by 140 000 units (about 7.5%) from their 1980 level. As with textiles, this came into being under threat of statutory quotas. Following the US–Japan agreement, West Germany negotiated an agreement with Japan designed to limit the rate of increase of Japanese exports to 10% a year. The Netherlands and Belgium also negotiated agreements with Japan, which froze the Japanese share of the market at the 1980 level. Some of these agreements subsequently expired but several others were renewed. With the decision to establish a 'single market' in which goods could no longer be checked as they crossed national borders, it became impossible for the EC to operate national VERs. In the absence of any border controls, quotas in 'controlled markets' would be undermined as Japanese cars were imported through 'uncontrolled markets'. Therefore, in June 1991, the various national VERs then in place were replaced with a new Community-wide VER negotiated with Japan which, in effect, froze Japan's share of the EC market. The EC has declared its intention to fully liberalise the European car market by the end of the decade. See Box 8.2.

Box 8.2 The 1991 EU–Japan Voluntary Export Restraint governing Imports of Japanese Automobiles

During the 1970s, a number of West European countries found themselves faced with an intensification of competition in their car industries caused by a rapid growth of car imports from Japan. As a consequence, several countries either introduced import quotas or negotiated voluntary export restraints with Japan. The United Kingdom first negotiated a VER with Japan in 1977, fixing the share of Japanese imports at 11% of the U.K. market. France, likewise, negotiated a VER of 3%, while Italy, Spain and Portugal imposed import quotas that limited the number of cars Japan could supply in any given year. By way of contrast, in the rest of the EC, where no controls applied, the Japanese share of the market stood at 24% in 1990.

The existence of these restrictions on imports of Japanese cars to certain member states meant that free trade within the EC was not possible. Those member states with controlled markets had to apply restrictions on imports of cars coming from member states with uncontrolled markets, otherwise Japanese exporters could re-route their supplies of cars to controlled markets via uncontrolled markets. (A special provision in the European Treaties, Article 115, allowed the European Commission to authorise such restrictions in special circumstances). When however, in 1987, the EC launched its 'single market' programme, it became apparent that these national restrictions would have to disappear. With the abolition of all commerciai frontiers at the end of 1992, it would no longer be possible to monitor cross-border flows. This meant that either the EC (now the EU) would have to end all restrictions on imports of Japanese cars (although the Common External Tariff, of course, would still apply) or establish a common EU-wide system of quotas. It was decided to opt for the second alternative and a new EU-wide VER governing cars was negotiated with Japan.

Continued

A so-called 'consensus' was negotiated with Japan in July 1991, whereby Japan would monitor the growth of her exports of cars to the EU as a whole on the assumption that its, exports would reach no more than 1.23 million units in 1999 in a total EU market forecast at 15.1 million units, that is about 8% of the combined EU market. In addition, until January 1, 1993, Japan would also monitor her exports to the five more restricted markets. The agreement provided for complete liberalisation of the European car market by the end of 1999, whereupon all quantitative restrictions on Japanese imports would be terminated. An important issue concerned whether the restrictions should include Japanese cars produced within the EC (as argued by the French and Italians but opposed by the British). The European Commission later made it clear that the agreement was based on the assumption that, by 1999, annual sales of European-built Japanese vehicles in the EC would total 1.2 million. This would give Japanese producers a global figure of 2.43 million as the number of cars that could be sold in the EU in 1999 or just over 16% of forecast demand. In 1991, imports of Japanese cars amounted to 1.4 million or 10.1% of the EU market, while cars produced by Japanese transplants amounted to 180 000 or 1.3% of the EU market. Thus, the agreement provided for some increase in the overall market share from just over 11 to 16%, although the share of imported Japanese cars was assumed to fall from 10 to 8%.

The agreement provided for a twice yearly consultation between the EU and Japan to examine current export trends and forecasts for the following years. A further area of ambiguity concerned whether or not Japanese exports would be adjusted downwards if the demand for cars proved lower than the forecast used in the negotiations. This resulted in a disagreement between the two countries in the early years of the agreement when EU demand did fall below forecasts. Japan argued that there was no provision within the agreement for her exports to be adjusted downwards in the event of such a decline in demand.

The replacement of national quotas/VERs with an EU-wide VER clearly provided for a fall in the share of Japanese imports in the EU market. However, this was offset by the fact that Japanese producers could raise their market share by increased production within the EU. In addition, Japanese producers could enjoy increased sales in the previously restricted markets of the EU. In fact, in the first four years of the agreement, the share of Japanese cars (both imports and those produced from European transplants) in total EU car registrations appeared to fall from just under 12 to just over 10.5% (Grimwade, 1998). The reason appears to have been the decline in competitiveness of Japanese cars caused by the appreciation of the yen. A similar decline in the Japanese share occurred in other uncontrolled non-EU markets over the same period. Thus, in the early years of the agreement, the EU–Japan VER probably did not result in any undue restriction on the volume of cars imported from Japan. However, this was due more to fortuitous circumstances than the outcome of any deliberate planning by policy makers.

A third sector in which the use of VERs has been widespread has been *consumer electronics*. The crux of the problem has been the emergence of more intense competition from the East Asian region, first from Japan and, more recently, the newly industrialising countries. Low labour costs have been an important cause of the greater competitiveness of products coming from the region. Producers in Western Europe and North America have responded by pressing their governments for import restrictions. In 1977, imports of television sets to the UK from Taiwan, South Korea and Singapore were subject to a VER. In 1979, the US negotiated a VER with Japan restricting imports of television sets which was later widened to include Taiwan and South Korea. In 1983, the EC negotiated a VER with Japan covering imported video cassette recorders (VCRs).

Finally, the *footwear industry* has been another sector where increased competition from NICs has led to a proliferation of VERs. In recent decades, restrictions on imports of shoes have been introduced by most western industrialised countries. Although in some cases, these have been in the form of import quotas, VERs have also been used. For example, in 1977, the United States negotiated an orderly marketing arrangement (OMA) (much the same as a VER) with Taiwan limiting imports of shoes. The same year a similar agreement was signed with Korea. In the EC, both France and Italy signed similar VERs with Taiwan and South Korea governing various kinds of imported footwear. In 1990, in preparation for the launching of the 'single market', this was replaced by a community-wide VER. More recently, the EU has introduced measures to eliminate most remaining restrictions on footwear imports.

Anti-Dumping and Countervailing Duties

One of the commonest forms of non-tariff intervention in trade in recent decades in the western industrialised countries has been the imposition of anti-dumping or countervailing duties on imports. Article VI of the GATT (see next chapter) allows countries to impose anti-dumping duties on a product which is sold abroad at less than its 'normal value', if the importing country can demonstrate that such imports have caused 'material injury' to its domestic producers. It was intended that, in most cases, normal value would be taken as the domestic price of the product in the exporting country. However, if no domestic price exists, normal value may be derived either by taking the costs of production in the exporting country and adding a 'reasonable' mark-up for profits and selling costs or by taking the 'highest comparable price for the like product for export to any third country'. If dumping results in material injury to domestic producers, the importing country is allowed to impose anti-dumping duties providing that these do not exceed the 'margin of dumping', which is determined by the difference between the export price and normal value. The comparison must be made 'at the same level of trade' which is normally the ex-factory level and, as far as possible, in respect of sales occurring at the same time. This means that any costs incurred after the product leaves the factory (i.e. transport costs, distribution costs, import duties, etc.) are deducted from the price. Normal value is calculated by taking a weighted average of all domestic sales over a period of time. A comparison is then made between the estimated normal value and each export sale to obtain the estimated margin of dumping. In a similar manner, Article VI allows countries to impose countervailing duties on products that have been subsidised by the exporting country. Once again, there is a requirement that the rate of duty must not exceed the element of subsidy.

Most advanced industrialised countries – and increasingly several developing countries also – have anti-dumping laws that provide for the imposition of anti-dumping measures if and when dumping takes place. These laws allow domestic producers who are harmed by dumping to lodge a complaint with the anti-dumping authorities who will then carry out an investigation into the complaint. Provisional anti-dumping duties may be imposed for a period of up to four months (six months in exceptional cases) pending the completion of the investigation. These are be replaced with definitive duties if the investigation establishes that dumping has indeed taken place and that it has been the cause of material injury to domestic producers. Prior to the Uruguay Round, no time limit was placed on the duration of such measures. However, the new Anti-Dumping Code which took effect on January 1, 1995 has set a time limit of no more than five years, although this may be exceeded if it can be demonstrated that the expiry of the duty will lead to dumping or injury to domestic producers. Most anti-dumping laws also allow the anti-dumping authorities to settle an antidumping investigation by securing price undertakings from the exporters concerned. This means that no duties are imposed but, instead, the exporters accused of dumping are required to raise their prices by a sufficient amount as to eliminate the injury caused to domestic producers.

The main justification for anti-dumping and countervailing measures is that dumping and subsidisation represent forms of 'unfair trade'. Thus, the imposition of anti-dumping or countervailing measures is not protectionism but a legitimate means whereby countries can protect themselves from harmful trading practices adopted by other countries. It is argued that dumping is a means whereby a dominant producer in a foreign country whose domestic market is protected by import barriers can exert market power to drive out rivals in the foreign market. By charging a high price at home, the foreign supplier can use the profits from domestic sales to subsidise sales abroad, possibly at below costs of production, and force producers in the foreign market to cut their prices or go out of business. Japan has been a popular target of dumping complaints in western industrialised countries and of subsequent anti-dumping measures. The argument is that the Japanese domestic market is protected by impenetrable 'hidden barriers' and that Japanese firms collude to drive up the price on domestic sales. In a similar manner, it is argued that exports from state-planned economies are frequently heavily subsidised. Such subsidies enable state-owned firms in these countries to export products at substantially lower prices than exist in the foreign market and, in some cases, at prices that fail to cover costs. The monopoly enjoyed by the state over foreign trade ensures that subsidised exports are not imported back into the country, which would otherwise undermine the benefits reaped from subsidising exports.

However, the problem with anti-dumping (and to some extent with countervailing) is the opportunities that it creates for abuse. Instead of being a legitimate form of defence against unfair trading practices in other countries, it may become a convenient device whereby domestic producers can gain protection from foreign competition which might not be possible by any other means. Governments may be willing to grant such protection because anti-dumping measures do not involve reneging on any international obligations such as might happen if tariffs are raised or quotas imposed. Since the practice of unfair trading is condemned by GATT, trading partners cannot reasonably complain against anti-dumping measures which are supported by a demonstration that dumping has occurred and is injuring domestic producers. However, the complex procedures involved in the calculation of the dumping margin may make it relatively easy to prove that dumping is taking place or to exaggerate the actual margin of dumping so as to secure the imposition of excessive anti-dumping duties. It may also be too easy to demonstrate that dumping is causing material injury to domestic producers when, in fact, the main cause of the difficulties experienced by domestic producers lies elsewhere. Moreover, the mere threat of an anti-dumping investigation may be sufficient to deter exporters from entering a foreign market or in forcing them to raise their export prices. In other words, dumping may not actually be happening, but, rather than risk provoking a complaint leading to a costly anti-dumping investigation, exporters prefer to curtail sales or raise prices.

Because of these concerns regarding the potential protectionist impact of anti-dumping, the members of the WTO operate an Anti-Dumping Code, to which anti-dumping laws in all WTO members must conform. Any country can make a complaint to the WTO if another member's anti-dumping laws do not conform with the Code or any measures are imposed which are not compatible with the Code. This Code was, significantly, improved during the Uruguay Round. However, anti-dumping remains an important form of non-tariff intervention in trade. Along with safeguard measures, it constitutes one form of what is commonly referred to as 'contingent protection'. This is protection which is conditional upon the demonstration that domestic producers are being harmed by imports from abroad. Unlike tariffs, both these forms of non-tariff intervention have the attraction for the importing country that they do no require any legislation that must be approved by national parliaments. They can, therefore, be implemented relatively quickly without the need to secure the prior support of the legislature. Moreover, unlike tariffs or quotas, they do not require compensating trading partners even though the trading rights of partners may have been impaired. These considerations help explain the popularity of these instruments of trade policy in recent years. Although the EU has not been the worst or even the most frequent user of anti-dumping, Box 8.3 provides

Box 8.3 Recent Examples of Anti-Dumping Actions by the European Union

January 1990. Council of Ministers imposed definitive duties ranging from 8.5 to 32% on imports of *compact disc players* from Japan and South Korea. Provisional duties had been imposed in July, 1989

March 1990. European Commission opened an anti-dumping investigation into South Korean exports of widely used *memory chips* (so-called Dynamic Random Access Memory (DRAM) chips). The previous year, the EC secured a voluntary agreement with Japanese manufacturers to establish minimum prices.

July 1990. European Commission imposed provisional anti-dumping duties of 24.6% on Chinese imports of *woven silk material* for use in making typewriter ribbons, following a complaint by a German company, the sole manufacturer of the product in the EC.

August 1980. European Commission opened an investigation into dumping of Japanese *hydraulic excavators*. Definitive duties on excavators had been imposed in 1985, but were due to expire under the EC's sunset provisions. However, in February 1991, the duties were lifted.

November 1990. European Commission imposed provisional anti-dumping duties on imports of *audio cassettes* from Japan, South Korea and Hong Kong. Duties ranged from 2.4 up to 22.3%. Japanese producers threatened to stop investing in the EU if these were imposed. These were later confirmed by the Council of Ministers in May 1991.

Continued

May 1991. EC imposed provisional anti-dumping duties on imports of *disposable cigarette lighters* from Japan, China, South Korea and Thailand, following a complaint by the EC's main producers. The duties ranged from 5.8 to 35.7%.

October 1992. The European Commission imposed provisional anti-dumping duties on imports of Japanese *thermal fax paper.*

November 1992. European Commission imposed anti-dumping duties on *seamless steel tube* imports from Croatia , CSFR, Hungary and Poland. The highest duty of 30.4% was imposed on the CSFR.

March 1993, EC agreed to minimum prices from *DRAM chips* from three South Korean manufacturers after threatening anti-dumping duties. A similar agreement already existed with Japanese manufacturers. However, anti-dumping duties of 24.7% were imposed on other South Korean manufacturers.

January 1994. European Commission opened an investigation into dumping of *excavators* by South Korea, following a complaint by European manufacturers.

May 1994. Anti-dumping proceedings were opened against imports of *Portland cement* from Poland, Slovakia and the Czech Republic at the instigation of German producers. Provisional duties were imposed in November and definitive duties ranging from 10.8 to 21.7% confirmed by the Council of Ministers in May 1995.

May 1994. EU imposed definitive anti-dumping duties of as much as 96.8% on imports of *broadcasting cameras* made by five Japanese electronics companies, following complaints by BTS and Thomson.

January 1995. European Commission opened an investigation into dumping of *sports shoes* (running spikes, ski boots and other sports shoes) from China, Indonesia and Thailand, after a complaint of dumping by European manufacturers.

January 1995. European Commission imposed provisional anti-dumping duties on imports of *soda ash* from the US, after Solvay of Belgium complained of dumping. Duties ranged from 5.4 to 14.3% and enraged European glass producers.

July 1995. European Commission launched an investigation into dumping of *iron and non-alloy steel beam* exports by Hungarian and Czech steel producers, following complaints by Eurofer, the European steel federation.

September 1995. European Commission decided to re-impose anti-dumping duties on imported Japanese *photocopiers.* Duties were first imposed in 1987.

October 1995. European Commission imposed provisional anti-dumping duties on *microwave ovens* imported from China, South Korea, Thailand and Malaysia. Rates of duty ranged from 4.8 to 32.8%.

January 1997. European Commission imposed provisional anti-dumping duties on imports of *cotton fabrics* from India, Pakistan, Indonesia, China, Egypt and Turkey. These duties, however, were dropped, following a decision of the Council of Ministers which failed to agree.

February 1997. European Commission imposed anti-dumping duties of up to 39% on imports of *handbags* from China, following a complaint by European leather manufacturers. Duties, however, were not imposed on Chinese travel luggage or sports bags.

Continued

February 1997. European Commission opened an investigation into a dumping complaint by European manufacturers against Japan and SE Asian exporters of *personal fax machines.* In September, anti-dumping duties of as much as 89% were proposed on imports.

March 1997, European Commission announced the re-introduction of minimum price undertakings on imports of *DRAM chips* from Japan and South Korea, after evidence finding that manufacturers were selling below cost.

April 1997. Council of Ministers agreed to definitive anti-dumping duties of 13.7% on imports of Norwegian *salmon.* However, in subsequent negotiations with the Commission, it was agreed, instead, to accept undertakings from Norway not to sell below agreed minimum prices and to limit growth of imports.

October 1997. European Commission opened investigation into alleged dumping of *in-car laser-optical reading systems* from Japan, South Korea, Malaysia, China and Taiwan.

March 1998. The European Commission re-opened the case concerning *cotton* dumping with a recommendation to impose anti-dumping duties on unbleached cotton cloth from six countries mostly in Asia. Provisional duties of between 15.7 and 32.5% were imposed after a narrow vote of the Commission. However, the proposal for definitive duties were rejected by the Council of Ministers in September.

November 1998. EU steel makers lodged a complaint against dumping of *steel products* by eight Asian, African and East European countries.

a selection of anti-dumping cases initiated by the EU over the past ten years.

Subsidies

The growth of government involvement in the economy in all western industrialised countries over the post-war era has meant that subsidies now play a more important role in world trade than ever before. GATT has always condemned the use of *export* subsidies as these involve an obvious form of distortion to trade. Moreover, as was observed above, any GATT signatory is empowered, where an export subsidy has been paid, to impose a countervailing duty equal to the element of the subsidy. In practice, many forms of export subsidy do exist, most commonly in the sphere of agricultural trade. Throughout the period since the Second World War, agricultural trade has not been subject to the same discipline as trade in manufactured goods and many practices, which are not allowed in respect of manufactures, are tolerated in the case of agriculture. It has been argued by the developed countries in particular that agriculture is different from other sectors and, therefore, must be treated differently. In most advanced industrialised countries, agriculture is subsidised, partly, to reduce dependency on imports from abroad and, partly, to preserve the countryside and rural way of living. Few countries are prepared to abandon these subsidies, although the Uruguay Round secured an agreement to reduce the scale of subsidy going to agriculture.

Indirect forms of export subsidy are also common in non-agricultural forms of trade. For example, many countries seek to boost their exports by subsidising loans made by banks to importers in foreign markets. Some success has been achieved by the western industrialised countries in agreeing to limits on the amount of interest-rate subsidy, which is permissible, to prevent the costs from escalating. Developing countries also are treated differently in respect of export subsidies. Subsidies to boost exports are allowed as a way of offsetting the disadvantages which these countries face when trading with the rest of the world, and as a way of assisting the development process in these countries.

However, until the Uruguay Round, there were no GATT rules relating to a *domestic* subsidy. Whereas an export subsidy is paid only on the portion of the output of a product, which is exported, a domestic subsidy is paid on the entire output of the industry regardless of whether or not the product is exported or sold domestically. Domestic subsidies, therefore, are not as overt a form of interference with trade as an export subsidy. Indeed, they are usually paid to a firm or industry for reasons unrelated to any wish to boost exports or reduce imports. For example, many countries give grants to firms, which invest in depressed regions, in an attempt to attract new investment to areas of high unemployment or slow growth. Subsidies are also frequently paid to firms experiencing financial difficulties in order to avert closures. Nevertheless, many domestic subsidies do impact on trade. If part of the output is exported, then the effect of the subsidy may be to give producers in the country granting the subsidy an unfair advantage over producers in other countries that do not receive equivalent subsidies. Alternatively, if domestic sales of the product are partly satisfied by imports, the subsidy gives an unfair advantage to domestic producers relative to importers. The effect is much the same as that of an import tariff, except that consumers enjoy paying a lower rather than a higher price.

Other Types of Non-Tariff Protectionism

Other common forms of non-tariff intervention have been the following:

1. Technical Regulations and Standards

Technical regulations are laws that government passes concerning a particular product which producers must adhere to before a product can be lawfully marketed inside the country. An example might be a law which requires all motor cars to be fitted with catalytic converters. These may be used to prevent the product of another country from being sold in the country. Technical standards have no legal force but may have much the same effect in denying the products of another country market access. Although these may be introduced for social reasons (e.g. protection of the ozone layer), they may distort trade by imposing costs on foreign producers. In other cases, they may be used by domestic producers as a device for gaining protection from foreign competition. This has happened in the consumer electronics industry where producers have lobbied governments to secure the adoption of their own technical standard for a product so as to exclude products from other countries which do not conform with the domestic standard. For example, in the battle for the market for high-definition television (HDTV), producers in different countries have developed products which each conform to a different technical format. By pressurising their own governments to officially adopt the format pioneered by local producers, foreign rivals can be excluded from the domestic market.

2. Health and Safety Standards

Although these are usually intended to protect consumers from products which are a threat to public health and safety, they can be used for protection. In recent years, this has become an important issue for trade in food products. Under pressure from consumer lobbies, governments are becoming more sensitive to the danger to health which may be created by new products. Two important cases have recently gained publicity. One was the decision of the European Union to ban hormone-treated meat imported mainly from the US on the grounds that it presented possible risks to public health. This became the subject of a U.S. complaint to the WTO which came out in favour of the US. Another case has concerned genetically modified crops. The US is a major producer of such goods and has complained that exports of such products to the EU were being subjected to long delays in gaining approval because of worries about the risk to consumer health. In part, the problem is caused by technological advances that have increased the number of new food products becoming available, which have to secure approval in other countries before they can be imported. In part, it is a reflection of increased concern on the part of consumers of the possible dangers to public health posed by such products. Scientists may differ in their assessment of the risk posed to public health by such goods. Although the reasons for such barriers to trade may not be protection, there is always the possibility that domestic producers will use such arguments to gain protection for their own industry.

3. Customs Formalities

Administrative procedures may be used to restrict access to foreign products. For example, in a famous incident in the 1980s, the French government issued an instruction that all imports must pass through the port of Poitiers. Japan has sometimes been accused of creating a customs barrier by insisting that all customs documentation should be written in Japanese. In the 1960s, the United States was criticised for basing tariffs on the American selling price for chemical products, which was higher than the actual value of the equivalent product imported from abroad. Costs may also be imposed on importers by creating administrative delays in the completion of customs formalities.

4. Discriminatory Public Procurement Policies

Governments may favour national firms in the award of public works contracts (e.g. the building of a new power station) or the purchase of equipment (e.g. the purchase of military hardware by the Ministry of Defence). They may make it difficult for firms to tender for a contract by restrictive advertising of invitations to tender. Even when foreign suppliers submit a tender at lower cost than national firms, the contract may be awarded to the national supplier for protection reasons. Government agencies account for between 10–20% of all purchases of goods and services in most advanced industrialised countries. Therefore, such policies potentially affect a large sector of the economy.

Arguments for Protection

Most forms of protection are harmful because they reduce the economic welfare of the importing and exporting country. Yet, governments make widespread use of such measures. It is necessary, therefore, to consider whether there exist any sound arguments in favour of protection? In this section, the various economic and non-economic arguments commonly put forward for protection are discussed.

1. The Optimum Tariff Argument

Earlier in this chapter, we saw that a country which is a large importing nation and which enjoys monopsony power, may be able to impose an 'optimum tariff' which leaves it better off. From the viewpoint of the importing nation, this case clearly constitutes an exception to the rule that a tariff lowers the economic welfare of the importing country. Of course, the tariff will still damage the exporting country. The tariff does not raise global economic welfare; it merely re-distributes it from the exporting to the importing country! For this reason, an optimum tariff risks provoking retaliation by the exporting country. If the exporting country retaliates by imposing an equivalent tariff on the exports of the country, which initiated the action, the latter may derive no gain from the measure. Of course, this will only work if the foreign country enjoys monopsony power in the market for goods for which the first country is a major exporter. If the first country is a big nation and the second country a small one, this may not be the case. The desire to acquire such bargaining power may create an important motive for countries forming themselves into a customs union (see next chapter).

A further problem with this argument for a tariff is the difficulty of determining what constitutes an optimum tariff. Earlier, we saw that this is given by the formula: $t = 1/e_s$ where e_s is the elasticity of supply of imports. Thus, if e_s is, say, unity, a tariff of 1% would maximise the welfare of the importing country. In practice, however, governments do not have this information at their disposal. They may be able to make an intelligent guess at what the optimum tariff might be. However, the risk is that a tariff will be imposed which lowers economic welfare. Too high a tariff risks reducing the volume of imports (and, so, reducing the gain from an improved terms of trade) and increasing the static efficiency loss. Too low a rate of tariff will ensure a minimal efficiency loss, but there will be little gain from the improvement in the terms of trade. In short, it is after impossible for governments to know what the optimum tariff rate is.

2. *Competitive Distortions*

It is often argued that the case for free trade assumes that markets are perfectly competitive. Because markets are perfectly competitive, resources are optimally allocated. Then, it is not too difficult to show that government interference in trade will cause a departure from this position of optimality, resulting in a decrease in economic welfare. In other words, the case for free trade rests on 'first-best' assumptions. However, the world in which we live is a 'second-best' one in which markets are not perfectly competitive. Therefore, the argument goes, it cannot be assumed that government interference in trade will reduce economic welfare. It is entirely possible that it could take us closer to, rather than further away from, the point of optimal allocation of resources.

Where there exist distortions within the economy such that resources are not allocated in an optimal manner, a case exists for government intervention. However, this need not take the form of an interference with trade. A major source of such distortions is the existence of so-called 'externalities' in the production of different goods. In the case of some goods the social marginal cost may exceed the private marginal cost. Pollution, for example, may impose costs on the community which are not born by domestic producers. In this case, firms will produce more of the good in question than is desirable from an efficiency point of view. In other industries, marginal social revenues may exceed marginal private revenues. Where the production of a particular good brings benefits to other producers that are not reflected in their cost or revenue functions, this will be the case. Then, in the absence of government intervention, too few resources will be devoted to the production of the good in question. It is clear, however, that what is required to correct these distortions is a domestic tax in the first case and a domestic subsidy in the latter. Where social marginal costs exceed private marginal costs, a tax would be sufficient to force producers to reduce production of the good. Where social marginal revenues exceed private marginal revenues, a subsidy will stimulate increased production. In other words, the existence of second-best assumptions does not create a sound argument for abandoning free trade. Rather, it is a reason for government action to correct the distortion, but in a way that does not create further efficiency losses by discriminating against imports.

3. The Infant Industry Argument

One of the oldest and most well-known arguments for import protection is to assist the growth of a new industry in a country at the early stages of its economic development. Such industries, it is argued, are, of necessity, small to begin with. Consequently, they cannot produce at the same level of average cost as the established industries of the developed world. If there is free trade, no investor would be prepared to provide the necessary capital as the expected return would be too low and even negative. Although, in the long run, as the industry grows to a size comparable with that of established producers in the developed world, the return might become more attractive, investors are unwilling to wait. They need adequate positive, short-term returns to be persuaded to make the necessary initial investment.

For the argument to be valid, a number of conditions must be satisfied. First, there must exist economies of large-scale production that can only be enjoyed when output has expanded to a certain level. Second, it must be demonstrated that private investors lack sufficient information to make an optimal decision about whether to invest or not. For, if the industry is not viable in the long run, no case can be made out for short-term protection. On the other hand, if it is viable in the long run, it is not clear why, if private investors have the necessary information at their disposal, they will not carry out the necessary investment. Clearly, this would only be the case if investors attached a much greater value to short-term as opposed to long-term returns. Third, a further possibility is that there exist substantial externalities, such that the social return from investing in the industry significantly exceeds the private return. This may be the case in a developing country where the establishment of a new industry brings important 'spill-over' benefits to producers in other parts of the economy.

Although a valid case can be made out for import protection to aid an infant industry in a developing country, there are practical problems in doing so. First, the government must judge which industries are worthy of such protection. These should be industries where it can be demonstrated that a high long-run return on capital is assured. The danger is that governments in poorer countries will take an excessively optimistic view about the long-run prospects for a particular industry and back industries that have no sound future. The problem will become even more serious if government decisions are taken in the absence of adequate information about future prospects for the industry. Second, even if a case can be made for protecting an industry, it is necessary that the level of protection should be gradually lowered as the industry grows and eventually disappears altogether. In practice, this may be difficult to do because producers will lobby governments to retain tariffs long after they are needed. Finally, it must be shown that a tariff is the best way of giving temporary protection to the new industry. At a theoretical level, it can be shown that granting a subsidy to the industry is better than imposing a tariff. Consider Figure 8.9. In the case of a tariff, the price of the

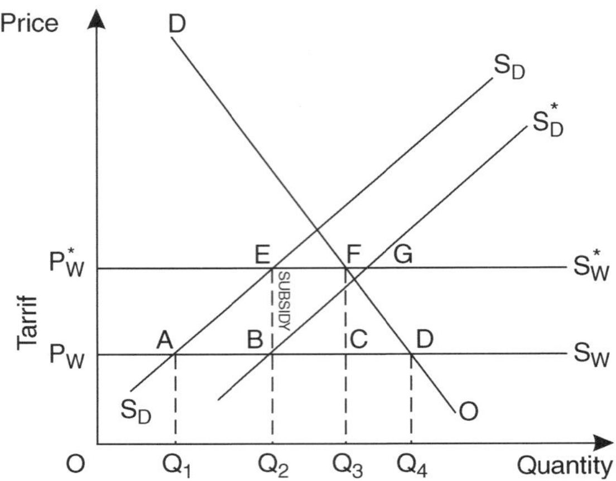

Figure 8.9 The effects of a domestic subsidy compared with the effects of a tariff

product is raised from OP_W to OP_W^*. However, a subsidy of an equivalent amount raises domestic production by the same as with a tariff (Q_1Q_2) but leaves the price paid by the consumer unchanged. As a result, the tariff results in a net welfare loss to the importing country equivalent to the triangles AEB and CFD, but the welfare loss from the subsidy is only AEB.

4. The Domestic Employment Argument

A popular argument for import restrictions is the need to boost domestic employment in a particular sector of the economy. In simple partial equilibrium terms, it is true that, in so far as the restrictions succeed in boosting domestic output, employment in the protected sector will be higher as a result. However, the measures will only succeed if there exist high levels of unemployment within the economy. If this is not the case, the effect of the import restrictions will be to draw workers away from other sectors of the economy and into the protected sector. Total employment will not have changed, but more will now be employed in the protected sector and less in other sectors of the economy. If the measures are retained for any length of time, the effect will simply be to raise production in the protected sector of the economy at the expense of other sectors. Since the protected sector may be presumed to be less efficient than the other sectors, resources will be shut into relatively inefficient, slow growing sectors of the economy. This will damage the country's long-run international competitiveness and rate of economic growth. If the measures are intended to be temporary to allow time for the industry to adjust, it is essential that the degree of protection is progressively reduced to create an incentive for domestic producers to make the required efficiency changes.

If, on the other hand there exist substantial resources of unemployed labour that can be drawn upon, total employment may be increased by the use of import restrictions. However, there is still a cost to the economy as a whole if only because prices are higher than otherwise. The government needs to carry out a cost–benefit analysis to determine whether import controls are the most efficient way of reducing unemployment. Moreover, there is a presumption that the country's trading partners abroad do not retaliate by imposing equivalent restrictions on imports from the country initiating the measures. If they do, the effect may be merely to shift unemployment from the import-substitution to the export sector. Even if partner countries do not retaliate, the fall in the demand for their exports is likely to result in a long-run depreciation of their currency. Depreciation will make their exports cheaper and imports more expensive. In this case, the country that imposed import controls will find its exports decline leading to a decline in employment in the export sector. This was the scenario that occurred in the 1930s when, faced with mounting unemployment at home, one country after another tried to boost employment by imposing restrictions on imports from the rest of the world. The end result was a reduced volume of world trade and higher unemployment in all countries.

5. The Balance of Payments Argument

Rather than impose selective import controls, a country may impose across-the-board restrictions or general import controls in order to effect an improvement in its balance of payments. Such measures are sometimes proposed as a solution to the problem of a persistent balance of payments disequilibrium. In theory there is no rationale for such measures if a country operates a floating exchange rate. Any long-run disequilibrium in the balance of payments should result in an eventual depreciation of the currency, boosting exports and reducing imports. However, a problem of this kind can arise under a system of fixed exchange rates. This would arise if the exchange rate is pegged at too high a level, with the result that the country's exports are uncompetitive internationally and it imports too much. A particular problem can arise if the domestic economy grows too fast. In this case, it may soon run into balance of payments difficulties and macroeconomic measures will be required to halt the expansion before unemployment has fallen to a desired level. Such an economy could be described as being 'balance of payments constrained'.

Clearly, however, if a country is experiencing these kinds of problems, its currency must be over-valued. In this case the obvious solution is a devaluation. Under certain circumstances, this alternative may be ruled out, as when a country needs to establish credibility by pegging its currency to a country that has a low inflation rate. In this case, generalised import controls could constitute an alternative method of tackling the disequilibrium. Nevertheless, it will be an extremely costly way of doing so. First, it will impose costs on the other sectors of the economy including the export sector both, by raising the costs of raw materials and intermediate goods which must be imported from abroad and by bidding workers and other resources away from these sectors. Second, it will generate considerable inflationary pressures within the domestic economy both, by raising costs and creating excess demand, unless considerable spare capacity already exists in the economy. Clearly, if the wish is to maintain an overvalued currency for other reasons, the cost of doing so must be confronted. Balance of payments equilibrium can only be ensured if domestic costs and prices grow at a slower rate than in other trading partners. Only in that way can exports be made more competitive and import discouraged. Import controls achieve entirely the opposite result, causing costs and prices to rise even faster than before. In this case, they create major problems for a country in the long run if and when the controls are ended.

6. The Unfair Competition Argument

A country may put restrictions on imports of a product which it considers to be competing unfairly with goods produced domestically. Clearly, this does not refer to a situation where the foreign supplier is supplying these goods at a lower price, as this may be due, simply, to its ability to produce these goods more cheaply. To impose controls merely because the foreign producer can produce these at lower cost would be to deny the very basis for trade. It is sometimes argued in developed countries that developing countries enjoy an unfair advantage because they can produce manufactured goods at lower cost because labour is cheap. Often attention is drawn to labour conditions in some developing countries – the absence of strong trade unions, the denial of the right to strike or the use of child labour or other forms of labour unacceptable in developed countries – to justify such controls. This, however, is a moral and not an economic argument for protection, as it necessitates a value judgement about the acceptability or otherwise of these practices.

A more precise use of the term 'unfair competition' is in relation to the practice of dumping discussed earlier in this Chapter. Dumping, we saw, is defined as a situation where an exporter supplies goods at a lower price in the foreign country than the price that is charged for these same goods domestically. It arises where the foreign producer enjoys a degree of monopoly power and where the domestic market is protected by high import barriers. Dumping is sometimes considered to be harmful to the importing country because domestic producers are forced to cut their prices as a consequence. Domestic output and employment are likely to be lower and long-run investment may be discouraged. On the other hand, consumers in the importing country gain because they are able to obtain the foreign product more cheaply.

A more serious outcome may occur if the foreign producer engages in so-called 'predatory pricing', which is selling the product abroad at a price that is below costs in a deliberate attempt to drive competitors out of the market. Having done so the price may then be raised to monopoly levels at the expense of consumers. Clearly, however, this is a special case. The foreign producer must enjoy superior financial resources to be sure of success. Otherwise the strategy would be too risky. The losses incurred during the period of predation may never be recuperated and the predator would end up worse off than before. Even if competitors in the foreign market could be driven out by a period of sustained below-cost pricing, unless substantial entry barriers exist new firms will enter the industry when the price is raised in the long run. Even if local firms find it difficult to re-enter the industry, there may be nothing to stop other foreign rivals from doing so. A more rationale strategy would be for the dominant producer to buy-up or merge with local firms and create a monopoly in the foreign market.

Similar to the case of dumping is a situation where the government in the exporting country subsidises exports. This gives the foreign producer the right to sell the goods abroad at a price which is lower than that charged at home and, possibly, below cost. As with dumping, importing countries may wish to protect themselves against such unfair competition by imposing restrictions on the imported product. Such practices are common in state trading countries where the use of subsidies is considerably more widespread. As with dumping, the effect of subsidised exports is to damage the industry in the importing country, forcing producers to reduce their prices, thereby cutting profitability, lowering output and employment and discouraging investment. On the other hand, consumers gain from lower prices. If the imported product is an intermediate good used in the production of other goods, producers in other sectors of the economy may enjoy lower costs and, hence, higher profits.

7. Non-Economic Arguments for Protection

Many of the arguments used by governments for protection are not economic ones. Examples are the following:

a. *National pride:* Governments give protection to an industry because it is regarded as a symbol of national pride. For example, in the 1960s, the British and French governments subsidised the development of Concorde, despite the enormous costs of the project, because the technological achievement was considered worthwhile in itself.
b. *Distribution of income:* Governments may give protection to a particular sector of the economy in order to assist a group of income-earners who might otherwise be disadvantaged. An obvious example of this is agriculture where governments in most developed countries pay generous subsidies. If farmers were not assisted, it is argued, their incomes would fall behind those of other sectors of the economy.
c. *National defence:* Governments subsidise particular industries considered vital to national security. For example, government protection of shipbuilding or aircraft production has often been justified on these grounds. Modern high-technology industries such as semi-conductors are also considered in western industrialised countries as essential to national defence.
d. *Environmental laws:* governments impose restrictions on goods which have been produced by methods which breach international environment agreements as a way of enforcing compliance with these agreements. For example, some countries have banned the import of furs from countries that use cruel methods of bear hunting.

In general, economists can comment on the desirability or otherwise of these measures, as they depend on value judgements. However, they can point to the costs of such measures and ask the question whether import restrictions are the best method of achieving the objectives sought.

Box 8.4 summarises the arguments for protection.

Strategic Trade Policy and the New Trade Theory

Recently, a new debate has begun concerning the merits or otherwise of government intervention in international trade with the emergence of the so-called 'new trade theory'. A number of models of trade have been developed which show that, contrary to what has been 'received wisdom' for a century more, there are certain circumstances in which government in trade can be beneficial. Hitherto, most economists regarded the optimum tariff argument as the only theoretically sound argument for government intervention in trade. Even this was regarded as having a relatively limited application and subject to a large number of constraints. The new trade theorists, however, have argued that government intervention in trade may be more beneficial than economists have often assumed. The case is applicable to industries in which the normal assumptions of perfect competition do not apply and where the market is dominated by a comparatively small number of large firms. These are industries in which there exist substantial entry barriers that prevent new firms from competing away any excess profits that the existing firms may enjoy. A particular form of entry barrier is the existence of high fixed or start-up costs, such that average cost falls sharply with the volume of output. New firms entering the industry face much higher average costs than established firms, which renders entry unprofitable.

Box 8.4 Theoretical Arguments for Protection

1. *Optimum Tariff Argument* – applicable only to a large importing nation with monoposonistic power, assumes importing country possesses sufficient information to impose an optimum tariff and assumes no foreign retaliation.
2. *Competitive Distortions* – tariffs are always inferior to domestic taxes/subsidies for correcting distortions caused by the occurrence of externalities.
3. *Infant Industry Argument* – applicable only to developing countries in industries subject to falling average costs and where private investors lack perfect information. However, a subsidy is superior to a tariff as a way of assisting such industries. If a tariff is applied, protection must be progressively removed as the industry grows.
4. *Domestic Employment Argument* – may raise domestic employment in the short run, assuming no foreign retaliation, but in the long run will result in a loss of international competitiveness.
5. *Balance of Payments Argument* – can provide emergency help, but devaluation is a preferable solution.
6. *Unfair Competition Argument* – strictly only valid in the case of predatory dumping, but may be used where exporter is paid an 'unfair' subsidy by its own government.
7. *Non-economic arguments* – no economic rationale and there may be more efficient ways of achieving the desired outcome.

New trade theorists have developed two types of model which show government intervention in trade as being beneficial in sectors characterised by imperfect competition. Let us consider each of these in turn.

1. Export Subsidies under Imperfect Competition

In Chapter 3, we discussed a particular model of trade in which two countries, each having just one producer of a homogeneous good, entered into trade. The model made certain assumptions about firm behaviour, namely, that each firm took the output of its rival as given and fixed its output at whatever was the most profitable level given the level of output of the other firm. Such behaviour is known as Cournot behaviour. It has the advantage that it by-passes the problem that, in oligopolistic markets, firms need to take into account how rivals will react to their decisions about output (or price). The model, known as the Brander–Krugman model after its authors, predicted that the kind of trade that would result would be of the intra-industry type. Because the introduction of transport costs results in each producer selling its product abroad at a price which is less than the price that it charges at home, it is also known as the reciprocal dumping model.

Using a similar model, Brander and Spencer (1985) have demonstrated that, under special circumstances, government intervention can shift monopoly profits from the foreign to the domestic producer. An important difference is that the Brander–Spencer model assumes that there is no domestic consumption of the product. Each firm is competing only for sales in the rest of the world. Consider Figure 8.10. As in the Brander–Krugman model, Cournot

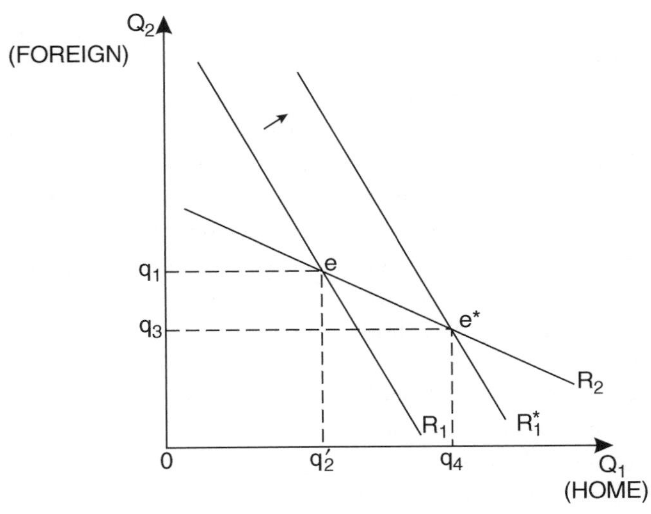

Figure 8.10 Cournot competition with export subsidies

equilibrium occurs where the two reaction curves intersect at e, where neither producer has any incentive to change their output. Because the market is imperfectly competitive for each firm, price will exceed marginal cost. However, neither firm will seek to increase its output because, if they do so, they will drive down the price. On the other hand, if they could, somehow, persuade the other firm to reduce its output, the other could increase its output without forcing as large a reduction in the price. In that case, some of the profits that were previously earned by the foreign producer, would now accrue to the home producer. This is known as 'profit-shifting' or 'rent-snatching'. It is analogous to the case of an optimum tariff, where by imposing a tariff on the trading partner, a large country with monopsony power can gain at the expense of its partner. The problem is how to persuade the foreign firm to cut its output. A unilateral decision by the home producer to increase its output is likely to, simply, provoke a price war. If the foreign producer does reduce his output, he loses at the expense of the home producer. On the other hand, if he leaves output unchanged and cuts price, he can hope that the home producer will change his mind when he sees that the decision to increase output has served merely to inflict damage on himself!

Suppose, however, that the government of the home country intervenes by granting an export subsidy to the home producer. The reduction in marginal costs will cause the home producer's reaction curve to move from R_1 to R_1^*. This changes the terms of the game. Now, the home producer can maintain its higher output, even if the foreign producer makes no change. The foreign producer knows that, if he fails to cut his output, price will fall and he will suffer more than the home producer. The foreign producer must, therefore, respond by lowering his output so as to ensure that the price is not forced down. In the end, a new Cournot (Nash) equilibrium is established at e*. As a result, the profits of the home producer have increased at the expense of the foreign producer. It can be shown that the rise in the profits of the home producer exceeds the amount of the subsidy, so that the home country enjoys a net increase in economic welfare. Although foreign producers suffer an equivalent reduction in their profits, consumers in the rest of the world gain because supplies of the good have increased and the price is lower. Taking all these effects into account, global economic welfare has also increased!

The effect of the subsidy was to give credibility to the decision of home producers to expand output. In the absence of the subsidy, the foreign producer would realise that the decision of the home producer could not be sustained without the foreign producer cutting his output. The resultant fall in price would result in lower profits. Hence, the foreign producer would have no incentive to cut his output. If, however, the decision of the home producer to increase output is supported by a subsidy granted by the government of the home country, the foreign producer will know that the home producer will suffer less than he will from any reduction in the price. He will, therefore, cut his output. Of course, there is the possibility that the foreign government could retaliate by granting an equivalent subsidy to its own producer. Clearly, if this happens, no profit shifting will take place. Both countries will end up losers. In this case, they would be better off co-operating. If they do so, it can be shown that the optimal policy is for both countries to impose a tax on exports to the third country. This would shift both countries' reaction curves inwards, resulting in reduced output but a higher price.

The model can be generalised to situations where the good is also consumed domestically. A *production* subsidy will have the same effect. One difference is that some of the effects on economic welfare will benefit consumers at home, not just in the rest of the world. There is also the possibility that the foreign country may gain if the benefit to consumers from lower prices outweighs the loss to producers! However, if the subsidy takes the form of an *export* subsidy, the situation is more complicated. The export subsidy may reduce domestic consumers' welfare because some output will be diverted from the domestic to the foreign market. The loss to domestic consumers could conceivably offset any gain to domestic producers such that the economic welfare of the home country falls. In the foreign country, consumers would gain and this could offset any loss to producers such that economic welfare rises.

2. *Import Protection as Export Promotion (The Krugman Model)*

Krugman (1984) has proposed a second model which shows how in industries, where average costs fall with output, the imposition of a tariff can turn a protected industry into an exporter, yielding positive welfare gains for the country in question. In some respects, the model is similar to the infant industry argument for protection discussed above. However, the Krugman model differs from this in several important respects. The global market for the product is an oligopolistic market with just two firms, one domestic and the other foreign. The products of the two firms are close, but not necessarily, perfect substitutes. Each producer sells in both the foreign and domestic market. However, the two markets are segmented such that a good sold in one market cannot be re-sold for the same price in the other. A further difference is that the kind of economies of scale assumed in the model, are dynamic economies associated with 'learning by doing' – the improvement in a firm's skills as their experience increases.

Figure 8.11 illustrates this case. The diagram shows the reaction curves for each producer in the two markets. Cournot equilibrium occurs at point e in both markets where the two reaction

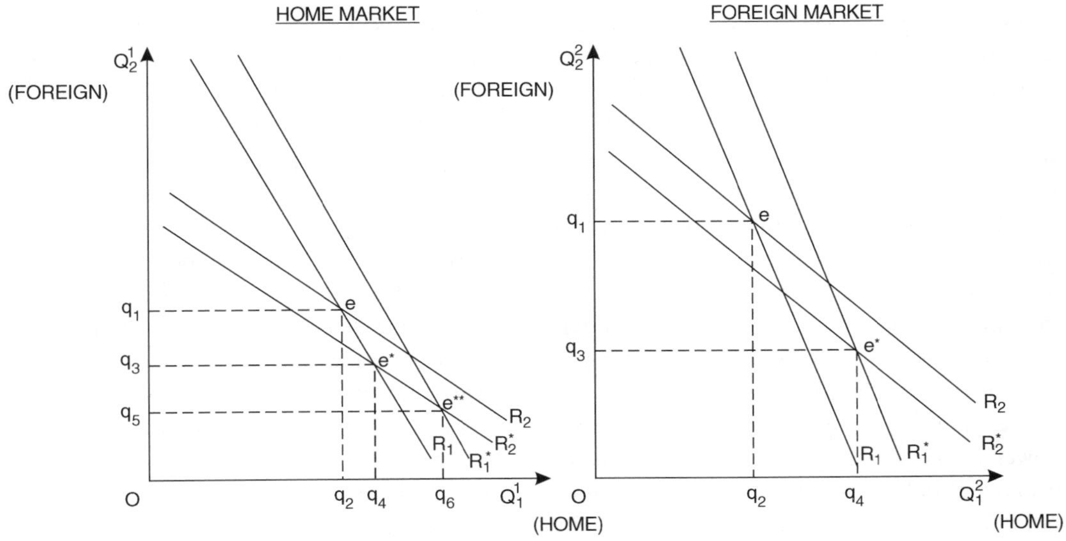

Figure 8.11 A model of import protection as export promotion

curves intersect. Now, suppose the home country government imposes an *import tariff*. This causes the foreign producer's reaction curve to shift downwards from R_2 to R_2^*. A new equilibrium is established in the home market at point e* at which the foreign producer supplies less and the home producer more than before. However, because the home producer is producing more in the home country, his average and marginal costs fall, while those of the foreign producer rise. This causes the home producer's reaction curve in the home market to shift upwards from R_1 to R_1^*. As a result, there occurs a further movement of the equilibrium point to e**. The home producer is now supplying q_6 and the foreign producer q_5. However, this is not the end of the matter. Because the home producer's average and marginal costs have fallen and those of the foreign producer rise, their reaction curves in the foreign market also shift. R_1 shifts upwards and R_2 downwards, establishing a new equilibrium at e*. The home producer in the home country has not only increased its share of the home market but also has made major gains in the export market. To summarise, because of the imposition of the import tariff, the foreign producer was persuaded to reduce his output supplied to the home country. As a result, the home producer was able to move more quickly down his average and marginal cost curve by exploiting dynamic economies of scale through learning-by-doing. At the same time, this enabled him to expand his output to the foreign market, again forcing the foreign producer to reduce his supplies to the foreign market. A tariff, which initially provided import protection for the home producer, has served also to promote the home producer's exports to the foreign market.

The model aptly depicts the kind of intervention which has taken place in many East Asian economies, in which high import barriers have been used to bring about an expansion of domestic production, which, in turn, has given producers cost advantages in selling increased volumes of output as export abroad. It can be applied most readily to high-technology industries (e.g. industrial electronics, computers, aircraft production) where dynamic economies of scale caused by learning-by-doing are especially important. The welfare effects of such measures, however, are unclear. Although the protected industry gains from being able to earn higher profits, its expansion will probably occur at the expense of other sectors. Resources are drawn out of other unprotected sectors and into the sheltered sector. These other exporters will, therefore, have to contract, resulting in some loss of profit. Also, prices will be higher in the home country because the monopoly power of the home producer is raised. So the economic welfare of the home country could fall. Global economic welfare will certainly fall because production is more concentrated. This, therefore, constitutes a more ambiguous argument for government intervention in trade.

Criticisms of Strategic Trade Policy

To what extent do these models demonstrate the desirability of government intervention in trade in strategic industries? Several criticisms have been made of these arguments:

1. *The arguments contained in these models are very sensitive to the assumptions on which the models rest.* In particular, the model assumes that firms behave in a Cournot fashion. That is to say, they fix output at whatever is the most profitable level, assuming that other firms will not react by changing their output. It can be shown that, if these assumptions are dropped, a different result is obtained. Specifically, if we assume that, instead of choosing output levels and letting prices adjust accordingly, firms set the prices of their products and then satisfy the demand which emerges (so-called Bertrand competition), the optimal trade strategy becomes an export tax not a subsidy (see Eaton and Grossman, 1986)! It is argued that, because economists have little or no idea whether firms behave in a Cournot or Bertrand way, they cannot be sure about the type of competition which is taking place in oligopolistic markets and, therefore, what kind of intervention is desirable. A further assumption on which the model rests is that firms engage in zero conjectural variation, that is, each firm takes its rivals' behaviour as given and immutable. However, it is entirely possible that firms take a different view and expect rivals to react to any changes in their price/output policy. In this case, the arguments contained in the model break down.
2. *A further problem concerns the assumptions about the number of domestic firms.* It can be shown that, if there is more than one domestic firm in each of the two countries, the optimal strategy is an export tax not a subsidy (see Grossman, 1988). If there is more than one domestic firm, firms will tend to invest too much in capacity, offer too much of their product for export and charge too low a price. An export tax would induce these firms to reduce their output and behave less aggressively towards each other. The export tax would improve the country's terms of trade in a similar manner to an optimal tariff. Once, however, the number of firms falls to one, the situation changes and an export subsidy becomes the appropriate measure.
3. *The argument for strategic intervention rests on the existence of above-normal profits and excess returns in a given industry.* If such situations exist, however, they are not likely to persist indefinitely. Large long-run excess profits will induce new firms to enter the industry. As entry takes place, long-run excess profits disappear. Thus, the benefits from export promotion are likely to be only

temporary. If subsidies induce new firms from the exporting country to enter the industry, the result might be higher average costs. This might also result in excessive competition in the home country, which drives down the price of the export good and worsens the terms of trade of the exporting country (see Horstman and Markusen, 1986).

4. *A further difficulty may be one of identifying situations where excess profits are being earned.* What appears to be a high rate of profit may just be a return on some earlier, risky investment. In this case, most of the profit is normal profit, a payment to investors to cover for the risks of investment undertaken. Any decision by governments to subsidise such industries will not serve to shift any profits from foreign producers (since there is no excess profit to be shifted!) but will simply result in more R&D resources being invested in the industry. This will take place at the expense of other sectors of the economy.
5. *A major problem concerns how governments are to choose the industries that should be targeted for such support.* The decision to target one particular industry has implications for other non-targeted industries that compete with the targeted industry for a common pool of resources (scientists, engineers, skilled workers). The expansion of one sector would occur at the expense of others. An alternative would be to adopt a policy of general pre-empting, that is, to give a general subsidy to all oligopolistic industries which compete for a common pool of resources in this way. However, in this event, the main effect would be an increase in the real wages of scientists, not a shift of profits to domestic producers (see Dixit and Grossman, 1986). If, instead, a policy of selective pre-empting is pursued, the question is how to choose the sectors to support. The criteria are complex and governments will face great difficulties in practically applying theoretical criteria. In practice, there is a danger that governments will be driven by special interests in their choice of which industries to subsidise.
6. *A big problem concerns the threat of foreign retaliation.* If subsidies are met with counter-subsidies, the relative positions of exporters will be left unchanged and all exporters will suffer from an excessive build-up of capacity in the industries in question. Non-intervention is clearly better than intervention, which is met with retaliation. The problem is that, for any one country, the worse possible strategy is not to intervene; it can always do better by imposing a subsidy. This is a classical example of the problem of so-called 'prisoner's dilemma'. The best solution is an agreement between the two countries that neither will intervene. However, the problem with such agreements is that both countries must have the assurance that the other country will not cheat. One way of enforcing any agreement might be to codify it through the WTO, such that any breach of the agreement invites the prospect of sanctions being imposed on the culprit. The effectiveness of such agreements, however, will depend on the speed with which any dispute brought to the WTO can be dealt with and the severity of the penalty imposed on countries that break the agreement.

The Political Economy of Protection

One of the problems with the theory of commercial policy expounded in this Chapter is that it fails to provide a rationale for why, in practice, governments impose import restrictions and grant protection to their domestic industries. If national economic welfare is lowered by such measures, it is unclear why governments should adopt such measures. One possible explanation is that governments respond to particular vested interests within the country which stand to lose from free trade despite the fact that the economic welfare of the country as a whole is thereby lowered. In recent decades, various writers have proposed a 'political economy model' of protection, which explains the political as well as economic factors that shape a country's commercial policy. One such model, first developed by Frey (1984, 1985), depicts the level of protection as being determined in a political marketplace in which those demanding protection for a particular industry interact with the public authorities as the suppliers of protection.

Frey and Weck-Hannemann (1996) argue that, at any given time, there exists a demand for protection from producers and workers in industries that compete with imports because higher tariffs mean higher economic rents for these groups. To gain protection, these groups must lobby the government for protection. As this will entail costs, the groups in question must weigh the benefits that they gain from any resultant protection they are granted, against the lobbying costs which must be incurred to obtain protection. The higher the tariff secured, the greater the benefit to producers and workers in the protected sector. On the other hand, the higher the tariff sought, the more that must be expended in lobbying the authorities to obtain such protection. This can be illustrated by a diagram in Figure 8.12. The benefits which protection brings may be assumed to be an increasing function of the degree of protection, as is illustrated by the line OC. The curve becomes flatter because it is assumed that the *marginal* benefits from any increase in the tariff level decline beyond a certain point. Indeed, it may be that at some point such as B, they fall to zero. The costs of lobbying are also an increasing function of the degree of protection,

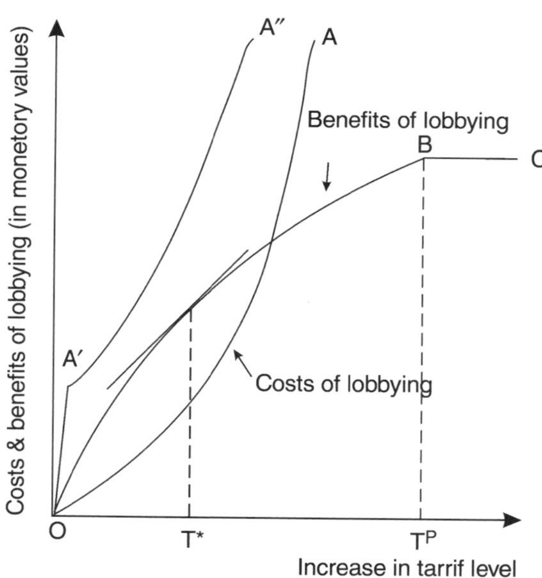

Figure 8.12 A political economy model of protection
Source: Frey and Weck-Hennemann (1996)

as illustrated by OA. Because it becomes increasingly difficult for producers and workers to secure tariff increases beyond a certain level, the OA curve is drawn as becoming steeper. Producers and workers in the sector seeking protection will lobby for the tariff rate at which the marginal costs of lobbying equal the marginal benefits. In Figure 8.12, this is the tariff rate denoted by T^*, where the gradient of the two curves is identical. In seeking protection, however, these groups will confront opposition from other groups within the country. These will comprise exporters who naturally favour open markets, domestic producers for whom the protected product is an essential input and consumers who stand to pay higher prices. It is conceivable that, for some producers and workers in import-competing sectors, it is not worthwhile lobbying the authorities for protection at all because the initial costs of lobbying are too high. OA′ might be the initial lobbying costs that must be incurred, after which lobbying costs rise at a more gradual rate. Clearly, if OA′ are the costs of lobbying, there is no level of tariff which would yield rents sufficient to cover the costs of lobbying.

Protection is supplied by the state, which comprises of elected politicians and appointed bureaucrats. Politicians are guided by their particular ideological preferences, subject to the constraint of having to secure re-election. One consequence of this is that politicians who feel less secure about being re-elected may seek to obtain extra votes by granting protection to particular vested interests. A further consequence is that politicians are more likely to grant protection to particular voters, the closer the date when they must submit themselves for re-election. Public bureaucrats, on the other hand, have no need to seek re-election. Instead, they seek to maximise their own individual utility function in much the same way as managers of a firm. Major elements in this utility function will be factors such as prestige, power and influence in the particular sectors of the economy within which they function. For example, civil servants working in the Agriculture Ministry will place much importance on maintaining influence among farmers' groups. This may incline them towards granting protection in response to lobbying from the groups within the sector who stand to gain from protection.

Frey and Weck-Hannemann suggest that three factors will determine the level of protection in any particular sector of the economy:

1. *The greater the size and strength of the pro-tariff groups, the higher the level of protection.* Pro-tariff groups comprise domestic producers in the sector, trade unions acting on behalf of the workforce and firms producing complementary products or supplying inputs to firms in the sector receiving protection. They are usually able to exert strong political influence because they can show visibly and directly the precise effects of imports on domestic production and employment.
2. *The greater the size and strength of anti-tariff groups, the lower the level of protection.* These include firms in the export sector, which will favour liberalisation as a device for gaining better access to foreign markets and need to obtain inputs at the lowest possible cost, and consumers. Exporters may lack strength because of the difficulty of demonstrating the indirect damage which protection leads to and because the damage is felt more in the long term. Because consumers are also workers, their attitude may be a more ambivalent one. Although protection leads to higher prices, it will also raise nominal incomes for those workers employed in the protected industry and supporting industries. Moreover, the effects

of increased protection are often difficult to demonstrate, especially in an inflationary environment when the overall price level is rising.

3. *The extent to which pro- and anti-tariff groups are able to organise themselves, politically, for the purposes of lobbying the authorities will effect the degree of protection that results.* For pro-tariff groups, the major problem is that some beneficiaries from protection may seek to 'free ride', that is, to contribute nothing to the costs of lobbying in the knowledge that they will benefit from any protection that is granted in response to the lobbying of other producers. This may make it difficult for producers demanding protection to organise and finance effective lobbying. On the other hand, anti-tariff groups may also find it difficult to wage a campaign against protection because the effects of protection (in contrast to the benefits) are very widely diffused.

Frey and Weck-Hannemann subjected their model of protection to empirical testing to see how well it explained inter-industry differences in the level of protection. Their results appear to lend strong support to the predictions of the model. This suggests that political institutions and processes play a crucial role in shaping the commercial policy of countries. If economists are to understand why protection is granted to particular industries and why considerable differences exist in the level of protection accorded to different sectors, it is clearly essential that account is taken of these factors. A political economy approach can also be extremely useful in explaining the growing use of non-tariff measures as a method of granting protection to a particular sector in response to lobbying pressure. For example, a number of economists have used a political economy approach to explain the growing use of anti-dumping as a form of protection (see, e.g. Finger, Hall and Nelson 1982; Tharakan 1991, 1995). The increased use of anti-dumping appears not to be the result of any increase in the number of cases of dumping taking place. Rather, it become a relatively easy way in which domestic producers can secure protection. Anti-tariff groups generally lack strength and are poorly organised when it comes to resisting pressures applied by producers for anti-dumping measures. In particular, consumers and users of goods subject to anti-dumping measures often lack sufficient information about the effects of these measures on prices. Anti-dumping is also one way in which politicians can secure votes from vested interest groups and public bureaucrats can maximise their utility functions by increasing their influence among producers in the sector of the economy with which they relate.

Conclusion

In this chapter, the benefits to be reaped for all countries from maintaining open markets have been demonstrated. Free trade results in welfare gains for all countries individually and for the world as a whole. The nature of the gains differs depending on whether increased trade leads to inter- or intra-industry specialisation. However, in practice, governments use a wide variety of methods to restrict imports or boost exports. In the past, tariffs were the main instrument used to grant protection to domestic producers. Over the past half century, however, tariffs on industrial products have fallen. Instead, new forms of non-tariff protection have emerged. In some cases, the effects of these newer forms of protection have been even more damaging than old-style tariff protectionism. Very few sound economic arguments exist for protection in any form, except, perhaps, as temporary measures to cope with short-term adjustment problems. In recent years, however, trade theorists have challenged the received wisdom by showing that, where the traditional assumptions of perfect competition do not hold, government intervention in trade may be beneficial. On the other hand, the models proposed are highly sensitive to the assumptions made about the market and about how firms behave. They are also applicable only to industries where average costs fall with output and existing firms earn excess profits in the long run. The practical usefulness of these models as a guide for countries in formulating their trade policies is open to question. However, if the case for government intervention in trade is a weak one, this begs the question why governments do, indeed, intervene extensively in trade whether by restricting imports or artificially subsidising exports. To answer this, we need to examine the political as well as the economic processes that help shape the commercial policy of countries, which, in modern times, takes place in an international context. The use of a political economy model to explain levels of protection, such as has been used by a number of economists in recent years, constitutes a positive step in this direction.

Notes for Further Reading

The best presentation of the standard gains from free trade that distinguishes between inter- and intra-industry specialisation is to be found in:

Greenaway, D. and Milner, C. *The Economics of Intra-Industry Trade* (Oxford and New York: Basil Blackwell, 1986).

This also contains a very useful chapter on adjustment cost and adjustment policy. Conventional texts on international trade often fail to separate the gains from trade under each type of specialisation.

For a thorough and rigorous examination of the major arguments for protection, students should use a conventional text such as:

Krugman, P. and Obstfeld, M. *International Economics: Theory and Policy*, 5th edn. (Addison-Wesley, 2000).

This also provides an excellent survey of the different forms of tariff and non-tariff protection. On protectionism, however, the interested reader should also read:

Bhagwati, J. *Protectionism* (Cambridge, MA, MIT Press, 1988).

It compresses into a small book a lot of excellent material on this subject. This covers both tariff and non-tariff forms of protectionism.

Another valuable text that contains several useful chapters on the subject matter covered in this chapter is:

Greenaway, D. (ed.). *Current Issues in International Trade*, 2nd edn. (London, Macmillan, 1996).

One of the chapters provides an excellent summary of political economy models of protection.

On strategic trade policy and the new trade theory, the reader will find the following a most helpful volume:

Krugman, P. (ed.). *Strategic Trade Policy and the New International Economics* (Cambridge, MA, MIT Press, 1988).

Chapter 9

Multilateralism Versus Regionalism

CHAPTER OUTLINES: Introduction. Multilateral Trade Liberalisation – the GATT rounds, the World Trade Organisation (WTO), a millennium round? Regional Trade Liberalisation – the theory of regional economic integration, the new regionalism, does the growth of the new regionalism matter? Conclusion.

Introduction

If protectionism reduces global economic welfare by restricting trade and reducing economic efficiency, it follows that trade liberalisation– the process of reducing or eliminating man-made barriers to trade – can bring efficiency gains and make the world as a whole better off. Countries could reap these gains themselves simply by getting rid of their import restrictions. In practice, however, governments are rarely prepared to do so. Instead, they prefer to keep the lowering or removal of import barriers as a bargaining counter which can be used to secure improved access for their exports in the markets of their trading partners. Hence, the negotiation of trading agreements with other countries has, historically, been the main way in which the global liberalisation of world trade has taken place. Each country offers some reductions in its own tariffs or non-tariff barriers in exchange for other equivalent concessions from its partners. The negotiated approach to trade liberalisation also has the advantage that it enables the government of each country to play off the export sector, which favours liberalisation, against the import substitution sector, which is more inclined to protection and opposes any lowering of import barriers.

Countries may negotiate trading agreements on a bilateral basis with any of their trading partners, which they choose. Bilateral negotiations, however, suffer from several disadvantages. It takes much longer to achieve freer trade if each country bargains one-by-one with all its trading partners. Moreover, countries are unlikely to concede much in a bilateral negotiation because they do not want to lose a bargaining counter in any subsequent negotiations with other partners. This will be especially true in negotiations with countries that are not principal suppliers. Much more can be achieved where countries negotiate within a multilateral forum. The signing of the General Agreement on Tariffs and Trade (GATT) in 1947 by some twenty-three leading trading nations created such a forum. A key provision of the GATT was for contracting parties to meet on a regular basis to engage in multilateral negotiations which resulted in each country making mutually beneficial, balanced reductions in its import barriers. In the decades that followed, GATT organised a series of so-called 'rounds' in which trade was progressively liberalised. Moreover, the number of countries signing the GATT grew, such that, by the time of the Uruguay Round of 1986–93, there were 117 contracting parties. On January 1, 1995, GATT was subsumed into the newly established World Trade Organisation (WTO), which now performs the role previously undertaken by GATT.

An important principle of GATT is that all countries are to treat each other equally. This does not preclude bilateral trading agreements with particular trading partners. However, it does mean that any concessions made to another country in a bilateral agreement must be extended automatically to all other GATT contracting parties. This, however, has not prevented countries from entering into regional trading agreements with other countries which grant *preferential* treatment to the products of member countries. In fact, GATT rules have always allowed countries to create free trade areas or customs unions with other countries that provide for internal free trade but normal protection against imports from the rest of the world. Regional trading agreements, however, of this kind constitute an essentially different way of liberalising world trade to the *multilateralist* approach of GATT or WTO. Whereas reductions in import barriers which are negotiated through the WTO are extended automatically to all countries belonging to the WTO, reductions in trade barriers negotiated as part of a regional trading agreement apply only to the countries participating in the agreement. Regional trading agreements have been commonplace throughout the past fifty years. However, in recent years, the number of such agreements has increased enormously. There has been much debate as to whether this new *regionalism* reinforces or conflicts with the process of multilateral liberalisation being pursued by the WTO.

This chapter discusses both these forms of trade liberalisation. The first half of the chapter discusses the role played by the GATT in bringing about multilateral liberalisation of world trade over the post-war period. The second half of the chapter examines the effects of the large number of regional trading arrangements that have emerged in recent decades. Several questions are asked. Why the increasing fascination with regional trading arrangements? Does this reflect a disenchantment with multilateral liberalisation through the WTO? More seriously, do regional trading arrangements constitute a stepping stone towards free trade or could their formation lead to a drift towards protectionism?

Multilateral Trade Liberalisation

As was observed at the beginning of the chapter, if countries wish to enjoy the welfare gains available from expanded trade, one way in which they can do so is by entering into trading agreements with each other. Such trading agreements involve both countries agreeing to make reciprocal reductions in their tariffs and other trade barriers in a way which is mutually beneficial to both. Bilateral trading agreements of this kind were not uncommon in the past. Where they were implemented, they did go some way towards bringing about lower trade barriers. However, the bilateral approach has a number of disadvantages as a method of bringing about freer trade:

1. Since most countries have many trading partners, a large number of such agreements are needed to achieve significant results.

2. They can result in discrimination, if the reductions in trade barriers agreed between any two countries are not as a matter of course extended to all other trading partners. Discrimination tends to distort the global allocation of resources and adversely affects smaller trading nations with less bargaining power.
3. Bilateral negotiations are unlikely to result in a major cut in tariffs or other trade barriers because countries are reluctant to 'throw away' bargaining counters in any subsequent negotiations with other trading partners. Thus, if Country A makes a big tariff reduction on imports of widgets as part of a trading agreement with Country B, it will have less to offer Country C with whom it might wish to sign another trading agreement, especially if Country C is A's main supplier of widgets. This is known as the 'principal supplier constraint'.

Multilateral negotiations in which each country negotiates with each other all at the same time do not suffer from these drawbacks. They, therefore, make possible a quicker path towards free trade.

Following the ending of the Second World War, the United States was keen to bring about freer trade as a way of facilitating rapid economic recovery and promoting political stability in the post-war world. In particular, the allies were concerned with preventing a return to the depressed economic conditions of the 1930s. It was against this background that the General Agreement on Tariffs and Trade (GATT) came into being. The U.S. recognised that the quickest and most effective way of bringing about freer trade was through multilateral trade negotiations. GATT was an international treaty that required the signatories to commit themselves to regular, multilateral negotiations with the aim of bringing about freer trade. The idea was that, in these periodic 'rounds' of negotiation, countries would offer each other 'concessions'. These concessions would take the form of some improvement in access to the markets of the other countries. An important requirement was that all countries were expected to act 'reciprocally' and not to 'free ride', that is, each was expected to offer something and not just enjoy the benefits of concessions made by the others. Concessions could take the form of some undertaking to treat the exports of another country in particular way; for example, not to discriminate against them. Alternatively, the concessions could assume a more tangible form, such as an agreement to cut a tariff on a particular product by a certain amount or to 'bind' a tariff at a particular level. The latter meant that the tariff could not be raised above the bound rate except by offering trading partners compensation in the form of another equivalent concession.

A central pillar of the GATT system was the principle of non-discrimination or the Most-Favoured Nation (MFN) rule. This meant that all GATT signatories undertook to treat each other equally in matters of trade. In particular, they agreed to apply the same rate of tariff on imports of a particular product coming from GATT contracting parties. It also meant that, if one country agreed to cut its tariff on imports of a product coming from another GATT contracting party, this concession had to be extended automatically to all other contracting parties. In other words, any concessions agreed by any country in the course of a GATT round applied as a matter of course to imports coming from all other GATT parties. This principle of 'unconditional' MFN had been an important feature of U.S. trade policy since 1923. At that time, it did not lead to freer trade because the US was unwilling to cut its tariff. However, following the passage of the U.S. Reciprocal Trade Agreements Act of 1934, it was used to bring about substantial reductions in the U.S. tariff. After the Second World War, the US was keen to make this a central element of international trade policy. Thus, not only did GATT result in multilateral negotiation of lower tariffs, the non-discrimination rule ensured that the results of these negotiations were multilaterally applied.

In fact, the GATT contained several loopholes that allowed discrimination between GATT contracting parties. Many countries that still operated certain kinds of preferential tariff arrangement were allowed to continue doing so. Thus, the United Kingdom was allowed to retain her preferences on imports coming from her colonies and ex-colonies. In addition, Article XXIV of the General Agreement allowed countries to set up free trade areas or customs unions providing that these resulted in the total elimination of tariffs on 'substantially all trade' with each other. A free trade area involves internal free trade (i.e. no tariffs on trade among the members of the area), while a customs union goes a stage further in creating a common or harmonised external tariff applying to imports from the rest of the world. Customs unions and free trade areas are discussed in more detail below. Finally, in 1968, the GATT countries agreed to grant a 'waiver' allowing the advanced industrialised countries to introduce preferences for imports of manufactures from developing countries. This scheme known as the Generalised System of Preferences (GSP) was introduced in response to complaints from developing countries that GATT did little to help the poorer countries of the world.

Although GATT was concerned with bringing about *freer* trade, it did not seek to bring about *free* trade. Countries were allowed to impose import restrictions in certain circumstances. However, these were subjected to a set of clearly defined rules and procedures. Thus, it was stated that these should generally take the form of tariffs and not quantitative restraints (QRs) on imports. Important exceptions to this ban on QRs have included agricultural goods (where quotas on imports were allowed to support domestic supply restrictions), quotas to correct a balance of payments disequilibrium providing these were temporary, quotas imposed by developing countries to assist their economic development and, finally, quotas imposed on imports of textiles and clothing under the Short and Long Term Cotton Textile Arrangements (1961–62) and Multi-Fibre Arrangement (1975). Article XIX, the Safeguards Clause, also allowed countries to temporarily withdraw concessions made in negotiations if and when a sudden increase in imports of a particular product caused 'serious injury' to domestic producers. However, a requirement was that, where possible, other parties should be consulted and offered compensation in the form of other equivalent concessions. Article VI also allowed countries to impose duties on imports that had been 'dumped' or subsidised by the authorities of the exporting country. A requirement was that imports of the product should have resulted in 'material injury' to domestic producers. Also, the rate of anti-dumping duty should not exceed the margin of dumping or element of subsidy in the case of a countervailing duty.

An important area of ambiguity has concerned the rights of countries to give emergency protection to an industry subject to a sudden surge of imports from abroad. Article XIX of the GATT allowed countries to introduce temporary import safeguards where a sudden increase in imports of a particular product caused serious injury to domestic producers. Article XIX did not make it clear whether these should take the form of a tariff or a quota. In practice, governments have often preferred quotas. One reason is that quotas are more certain and possibly work more quickly. Moreover, they can be applied only to imports coming from the exporting country causing the disruption rather than being applied to imports from all trading partners. Although GATT signatories are not supposed to discriminate against each other (the Most-Favoured Nation rule), in practice, bilateral quotas under Article XIX have always been allowed. Although the measures are supposed to be temporary, prior to the Uruguay Round, no time limit was put on the duration of such measures. Nor was there any requirement that the restrictions be progressively removed as the damage was removed. Under the Uruguay Round, a new Safeguards Agreement has established a time limit of four years with the possibility under certain circumstances of an extension for a further four years. Also, there is a stricter requirement that the measures could be gradually relaxed as the problem abated.

GATT rules also specifically allowed the use of import quotas in certain specific circumstances. One important area has been agricultural trade. Quotas are allowed where the importing country is seeking to restrict domestic supply of a product (so as to support the market price) or to remove a temporary surplus of the domestic product (which threatens to undermine the market price). Quotas are widespread in agriculture. Most governments seek to control the volume of imports in an effort to support the price which farmers get for their produce on the domestic market. The European Union has, in the past, used variable import levies, which achieve much the same effect. These were set at the difference between the price of a consignment of imports entering the EU from the rest of the world and the EU's own threshold price (in turn derived from the artificially determined target price). If the world price should fall, the levy would be increased. Under the Uruguay Round Agreement, the EU along with other WTO members undertook to convert these existing NTBs on agricultural goods into tariffs. Because quotas are so widely used to grant protection to domestic farmers, liberalisation of world agricultural trade requires action to remove quotas rather than cut tariffs.

Article XII of the GATT also permitted the use of quotas for the purpose of safeguarding a country's balance of payments. However, any restrictions imposed for balance of payments reasons were to be progressively relaxed as the country's balance of payments improved. In practice, many countries, invoking Article XII, have preferred tariff surcharges to quotas as a device when faced with such difficulties. So, these are not very common among developed countries. However, developing countries that frequently encounter balance of payments problems have made considerable use of this provision to impose import quotas. In addition, Article XVIII of the GATT gives special dispensation to developing countries to impose quantitative restrictions on imports for general developmental reasons. For example, in order to encourage the establishment of an infant industry. Consequently, the use of quotas is common in the developing world.

Finally, a major departure from the GATT rules on quotas was allowed in the case of *textile and clothing products*. Quotas have always been widely used by developed countries to protect their textile and clothing industries from low-cost imports from countries where labour is in abundant supply. These quotas continued in existence after the Second World War despite the fact that many of these countries were GATT signatories. In view of this widespread failure to implement GATT rules, it was decided to make the textile and clothing trade a special exception. In 1961, a Short Term Arrangement for Cotton Textiles (STA) was signed by the major developed and developing countries who imported and exported cotton textiles to permit the imposition of quotas on cotton fabrics and clothes as a temporary measures. Meanwhile, a special GATT working party was set up to investigate the problem of textile protectionism. The report found that there was a problem of 'market disruption' for developed countries caused by import surges from low-wage countries and, therefore, quotas should be allowed as a temporary measure subject to strict conditions. In 1962, the Long Term Cotton Textile Arrangement (LTA) took the place of the STA. It required all importing countries to drop their existing restrictions on imports of cotton textiles but allowed new ones only if and when they faced market disruption from actual or planned imports. These could take the form of import quotas, but the quotas could not be less than actual trade before the disruption with a built-in growth factor of 5% a year.

In 1973, the Multi-Fibre Arrangement (MFA) replaced the LTA and extended the arrangements to cover non-cotton textiles including man-made or synthetic fibres such as polyester and acrylic. The 1974 MFA was for three years only but was replaced by a MFA2 in 1978. Each subsequent MFA similarly lasted for three years and was followed by a new agreement. Each agreement involved some modification of the previous one. Most developing countries have long resented this treatment by the developed countries of one of their major manufacturing export products and have pushed for the MFA to be phased out. In turn, the developed countries have always argued that the MFA was a temporary measure to allow time for their own industries to adjust to increased competition from the developing countries. In the Uruguay Round, the developed countries eventually agreed that the MFA should be phased out over a ten year period commencing January 1, 1995.

One reason why importing countries often prefer VERs (see Chapter 8) to quotas or tariffs is their administrative convenience. Where tariffs have been bound through the GATT, the option of raising a tariff may not be available. At the very least, it will be necessary to demonstrate that imports are causing serious injury to domestic producers. Even then, GATT rules require that any tariff increase should be non-discriminatory. Moreover, any trading partner who is damaged by a tariff increase is entitled, under GATT rules, to claim compensation. This means that the importing country must offer its trading partners adversely affected by the tariff some other benefits (e.g. lower tariffs on other goods) of equivalent effect. If suitable compensation cannot be offered, they are entitled to retaliate by withdrawing benefits from the country raising the tariff (e.g. by raising tariffs on goods for which the offending country is a major exporter). This could be costly to the country wishing to protect its domestic industry. It may, therefore, prefer to by-pass the GATT and settle the matter bilaterally with the exporting country whose exports are the main cause of the damage. In this case, there is no need to offend other trading partners or offer compensation to them. In effect, the exporting country signing the VER gets a form of 'built-in' compensation. Should it be unwilling to agree, the threat to impose higher tariffs or quotas can always be enacted.

Before the Uruguay Round, it was unclear whether VERs were covered by GATT rules. Unlike tariffs and quotas, they are not measures *imposed* by one country on another. Rather, they amounted to an agreement between two countries. The trading rights of another country were, therefore, not being infringed. Hence, GATT rules did not apply. On the other hand, they were clearly a discriminatory trading measure and, therefore, offended against the spirit of the GATT if not the letter. However, the legality of VERs could only be tested if other countries were prepared to make a complaint against their use by another trading partner. Clearly, any country wishing to make a complaint is unlikely to have signed an agreement in the first place! Third countries only serve to gain so they will not complain either. So, for several decades, VERs were tolerated as a form of 'extra-legal' restriction on trade or so-called 'grey-area' measure. However, as part of a package of measures to reform the use of safeguard measures, the Uruguay Round secured an agreement from WTO members to phase out all existing VERs and other 'grey-area' measures over a four-year period commencing January 1, 1995. This does not preclude converting these restrictions into the form of tariffs or quotas providing these conform with WTO rules. Each country was allowed to exclude one VER agreement from the phase-out up until December 31, 1999.

GATT also provided a mechanism whereby one country could make a complaint against another country that it was denied its rights under the GATT. If one contracting party considered that the actions of another contracting party 'nullified or impaired' its rights under the GATT, it was required to first seek a resolution of the problem through bilateral negotiations with the country concerned. If no solution was found, the aggrieved party could take the matter to the GATT Council, which would set up a panel of experts to investigate the complaint and make a recommendation. A consensus of the Council was required for a panel report to be adopted, which meant that any one contracting party could block the findings of the report. Once adopted, the party that was found to be at fault was required to implement the recommendations of the panel. If it failed to do so, the contracting parties could authorise suspension of concessions or obligations granted to the offending country. In practice, this hardly ever happened. It meant that the GATT frequently lacked teeth when it came to resolving disputes between contracting parties and enforcing GATT rules. The new World Trade Organisation, which was set up on January 1, 1995, was given a new disputes settlement machinery that provided for swifter and more effective sanctions against other members that failed to abide by the collective decisions of the WTO. Box 9.1 summarises the key provisions of the GATT.

Box 9.1 Key Provisions of the General Agreement on Tariffs and Trade (GATT)

Article 1.1 (The Most Favoured Nation Clause) states that 'any advantage, favour, privilege or immunity granted by any contracting party to any product originating in or destined for any other country shall be accorded immediately and unconditionally to the like product originating in or destined for the territories of all other contracting parties'.

Article XXIV (Customs Unions and Free Trade Areas) makes clear that an important exception to the principle of non-discrimination applies in the case of customs unions and free trade areas, providing that the level of external tariffs are '...not on the whole higher or more restrictive' than the 'general incidence' of such tariffs in the member states before the formation of the union.

Continued

Article XI (General Elimination of Quantitative Restrictions) states that any restriction other than an import duty is not permissible on imports from other contracting parties, although other articles of the Agreement allow for such restrictions in special cases (e.g., import restrictions necessary to enforce standards or regulations for goods in a country).

Article VI (Antidumping and Countervailing Duties) states that dumping (the export of goods to another country 'at less than the normal value of the products') is to be condemned 'if it causes or threatens material injury to an established industry or ...materially retards the establishment of a domestic industry' in another contracting party. Contracting parties may impose antidumping levies on such imports providing that the duty does not exceed the 'margin of dumping'.

Article XII (Restrictions to Safeguard the Balance of Payments) allows countries to impose import restrictions to safeguard their balance of payments, although these must be 'progressively relaxed' as conditions improve.

Article XIX (Emergency Action on Imports of Particular Products) allows any contracting party to impose emergency restrictions where the imports of a particular product increase due to 'unforeseen developments' such as 'to cause or threaten serious injury to domestic producers'. However, the restrictions must be only at the level required and for the time necessary 'to prevent or remedy' the injury.

Article XVIII (Economic Development) states that a country may impose trade restrictions so as to promote economic development.

Article XXVIII (Modification of Schedules) requires contracting parties to enter into periodic negotiations 'on a reciprocal and mutually advantageous basis' regarding reductions in the level of tariffs and other restrictions on trade.

Article XXV (Joint Action) provides for contracting parties to act jointly on the basis of one vote per contracting party and applying the rule of a simple majority, although in practise the principle of consensus operated. The article also allows the contracting parties at any time to grant a country a general 'waiver' from any aspect of its GATT obligation where a two-thirds majority of votes cast is achieved.

Article XXVII (Withholding or Withdrawal of Concessions) permits any contracting party to withhold from any new contracting party concessions granted to other contracting parties.

Article XXII (Consultation) requires contracting parties to grant to other countries the right to bilateral consultation whenever a dispute concerning GATT obligations arises.

Article XXIII (Nullification and Impairment) sets out the procedure for settling disputes whenever one contracting party considers its rights have been nullified or impaired as a result of the actions of another contracting party or the failure of another contracting party to carry out its obligations under the Agreement. These allow the aggrieved party to bring the matter to the GATT, for the GATT to carry out the necessary investigation and to make recommendations or a ruling as appropriate. These could include the suspension by the aggrieved party of equivalent obligations or concessions to the offending country.

A new Part IV was added to the GATT in 1966 that dealt with the area of trade and development, releasing developing countries from certain GATT obligations and recognising the principle that developing countries should be entitled to special and differential treatment.

The GATT Rounds

Since 1947 when the GATT was first signed (initially by only 23 countries) and the present day, there have been a total of eight GATT rounds. Each 'round' followed the decision of U.S. Congress to grant the President a tariff-cutting authority. The reason for this is that, without such an authority from Congress, the President could not enter into meaningful negotiations. Although he could offer to cut the U.S. tariff on particular products by an agreed amount, he would need to go back to Congress to secure their approval. Because their approval was not assured, it was improbable that other countries would be prepared to offer the US very much in the way of concessions. Where, however, the President had a specific authority, no such constraint existed. Although he would still need to secure ratification by Congress of any package of measures negotiated, Congress could not alter any particular aspects of the package provided it did not exceed the authority granted. Thus, other countries could make concessions to the US in the sure knowledge that the entire agreement would either be accepted or rejected in its entirety without any alterations being made to particular details. In addition, because the US was the biggest trading nation in the world, multilateral negotiations had little meaning without U.S. involvement.

Table 9.1 sets out the main details of each of the eight rounds. To begin with, the U.S. Congress was prepared to grant the President considerable authority to make tariff cuts. Consequently, much was achieved in the early rounds both in lowering the average level of industrial tariffs and the binding of tariffs. This contributed much to the expansion of world trade in the first two decades after the Second World War. In particular, the US was keen to make big reductions in her own tariffs in order to gain the accession of as many countries as possible to the GATT. In the *1st Round* at Geneva in 1947, the U.S. President was negotiating under a tariff-cutting authority which empowered him to cut tariffs by up to 50% of the rates in force on January 1, 1945. As a result, tariffs were cut by an average of just over one-third and affected just one-half of all dutiable imports. The next three rounds were mainly concerned with the accession of new contracting parties (Italy in 1949, West Germany in 1951 and Japan in 1956). The *fifth Dillon Round* was mainly concerned with

Table 9.1 The Trade Negotiating Rounds of the GATT, 1947–1994

Round	*Date*	*No. of countries*	*Value of trade covered (US $ billion)*	*Average tariff cut (%)*	*Average tariffs, afterwards (%)*
Geneva	1947	23	10	35	n.a.
Annecy	1949	33	n.a.		n.a.
Torquay	1950	34	n.a.		n.a.
Geneva	1956	22	2.5		n.a.
Dillon	1960–61	45	4.9		n.a.
Kennedy	1962–67	48	40	35	8.7
Tokyo	1973–79	99	155	34	4.7
Uruguay	1986–93	117	464	38	2.9

Source: Updated from Jackson (1992).

dealing with the problems created by the formation of the European Community in 1958.

By this time, Congress had become somewhat less keen on further reductions in U.S. tariffs. The feeling in the US was that it was the turn now of other countries to make the bigger concessions. However, the formation of the European Community in 1958 posed a challenge for the US. At the time, the Community consisted of only six countries (France, West Germany, Italy, Belgium, the Netherlands and Luxembourg). However, there was a possibility that the UK might join. As a result, the US became concerned that she might be at a major disadvantage when competing in the fast-growing West European market. The only solution was to offer the EC another round of multilateral tariff negotiations in the hope that the US could secure a major reduction in the EC's Common External Tariff (CET) (see below). As a result, in 1962, the Congress granted the U.S. President a new and very substantial authority to cut U.S. tariffs by a further 50% on existing levels, already much lower than in 1947. The EC was keen to respond. The result was the *Sixth Kennedy Round*, named after the U.S. President, which led to the largest reductions in tariffs on industrial goods since 1947. The United States made tariffs cuts of an average of 44% on 64% of dutiable imports. Other industrialised countries made roughly equivalent concessions on an estimated 70% of dutiable imports.

Once fully implemented, the effects of these first six rounds were to bring the average level of tariffs down from roughly 40% in 1945 to 8.7%. This amounted to a substantial element of trade liberalisation and did much to boost world trade. However, there were a number of important omissions. First, tariff reductions had largely been confined to industrial products. Very little had been done to free trade in agricultural products, especially temperate zone products where the advanced industrialised countries were anxious to protect their own farmers. The creation of the EC had, in fact, resulted in a considerable increase in agricultural protectionism in Western Europe with the adoption of the Common Agricultural Policy (CAP). Under the CAP, West European farmers received very high guaranteed prices for their produce enforced by a system of intervention buying. At the same time, these high internal prices were protected from external competition by a complex system of variable import levies, which ensured that no produce could enter the EC below the EC's own 'threshold price'. European farmers were also paid generous subsidies on their exports to ensure that exporting was no less profitable than selling on the domestic market. Second, tariff reductions on industrial goods mainly applied to products that were traded between the advanced industrialised countries. Tariffs remained high on manufactures in which developing countries enjoyed some cost advantage (e.g. textiles and clothing, footwear, steel, etc). One reason for this was that tariff reductions in these products tended to result in inter- rather than intra-industry specialisation. As was explained in the previous chapter, intra-industry specialisation brings potentially larger welfare gains and involves fewer adjustment problems than inter-industry specialisation. This may explain why the advanced industrialised countries were less willing to cut tariffs on imports of manufactures from the developing world. Third, the focus of these earlier rounds was on *tariff* liberalisation. However, as the previous chapter demonstrated, lower tariffs may not mean freer trade if tariffs are merely replaced with non-tariff barriers.

The seventh *Tokyo Round* was the first Round to seriously address the problem of non-tariff protectionism. Further cuts in tariffs of an average of roughly one-third were agreed. At the same time, the Round succeeded in securing agreement on a series of codes for tackling the problem of NTBs. Negotiations to reduce NTBs tend to more complex than those concerned with tariff cutting. To begin with, the incidence of NTBs is more difficult to measure than that of a tariff, so that countries cannot know what they are 'giving away' if they remove a particular type of NTB, nor what they are gaining if other countries reciprocate. However, there is also the problem that many kinds of NTBs arise out of laws which governments have passed, whether with a protectionist intent or otherwise. For example, laws passed by governments to protect the public from unsafe goods or goods which are damaging to public health or the environment. Certain kinds of NTBs (e.g. VERs) have their origins in deficiencies within GATT rules (e.g. the Safeguards Clause) and therefore require for their remedy revision of these rules.

The codes approach adopted by the Tokyo Round provided a mechanism for overcoming some of these problems. These amounted to special 'side agreements' to the main GATT Agreement, to which countries could choose to adhere or not, unlike the rest of GATT to which all contracting parties were bound. Codes were negotiated covering the following areas:

1. *Technical regulations* – a code was agreed to prevent governments from devising new technical standards which favour home over foreign products.
2. *Customs valuation* – a code was agreed to lessen the flexibility of customs inspectors to assign arbitrarily high values to imported goods subject to tariff duties. However, developing countries dissented, wanting measures included to prevent MNCs from under-pricing exports for customs purposes.
3. *Government procurement* – a code requiring governments to treat domestic and foreign producers equally in government purchases.
4. *Subsidies and countervailing duties* – a code prohibiting direct export subsidies on non-primary products and containing guidelines for the use of domestic subsidies and a code for the use of countervailing duties were agreed.
5. *Anti-dumping* – a code was agreed to regulate the use of anti-dumping policy concerned with the calculation of the dumping margin, the injury test and the rights of exporters subject to such measures.
6. *Civil aviation* – a special code was agreed for this sector aimed at reducing both tariff and non-tariff barriers and regulating the use of subsidies.

The Round also addressed the issue of how to reform the *Safeguards Clause* of the GATT but was unable to reach agreement. The stumbling block was the issue of selectivity. Specifically, the EC insisted that Article XIX should be reformed to allow for the use of selective safeguards, that is, emergency measures which applied only to imports coming from the country causing or threatening injury to domestic producers. As we have already observed, the requirement that measures should be non-discriminatory meant that the use of Article XIX risked provoking retaliation from other trading partners. Consequently, countries often preferred to negotiate VERs with the exporting country in question giving rise to a surfeit of extra-legal measures having the same effect as selective controls. The United States and the developing countries, however, were strongly opposed to these proposals. The developing countries, in particular, feared that anything which made Article XIX easier to invoke would lead to an increase in the level of protectionism applied by the developed countries to their products.

The last round was the *Uruguay Round* that was completed in December, 1993, after seven years of negotiations, the final agreement being formally signed at Marrakech in Morocco in April, 1994. Like the Tokyo Round, this round was not solely concerned with tariff reductions, although considerable progress was made in bringing about a further substantial reduction in industrial tariffs. *Tariffs* were reduced by a further 38% bringing the average trade-weighted tariff in developed countries to just under 4%. In addition, tariff bindings were extended to roughly 97% of all tariffs in developed countries and 65% in developing countries. However, the significance of the Uruguay Round lay more in the success achieved in tackling certain outstanding issues left over from previous rounds and in extending GATT discipline to certain new areas never previously addressed. With regard to the former, the major concerns were agriculture, textiles and rules revision. With regard to the latter, three 'new issues' were included for the first time on the agenda of the round – services, trade-related intellectual property rights (TRIPs) and trade-related investment measures (TRIMs).

All previous GATT rounds had failed to make hardly any progress extending liberalisation to trade in *agricultural products*. The problem was the reluctance of the advanced industrialised countries to abandon the high levels of protection accorded to their agricultural sector. Such protectionism largely took a non-tariff form, including quantitative restrictions on imports, variable import levies set at the difference between the world price and the domestic price support level and subsidies paid to domestic producers to stimulate domestic production. Such policies were justified on various grounds, namely, the special problems encountered by the farming sector in advanced industrialised countries and the need to reduce dependence on imports and increase self-sufficiency. However, by the 1980s, it was apparent that such policies had become extremely costly even to the western industrialised countries themselves. They had resulted in massive overproduction of temperate zone food products, which had to be either stockpiled or disposed of at subsidised prices. The effect of the latter was to further depress the world price necessitating the payment of ever larger subsidies to exporters, creating a colossal burden on taxpayers at a time when budgetary restraint was needed. At the same time, countries that were major net exporters of agricultural products were not prepared to make concessions in other areas until the advanced industrialised countries (mainly Europe and Japan) were prepared to make meaningful progress in reducing farm subsidies.

The United States and the so-called Cairns Group (some fourteen independent agricultural exporting nations including Australia, New Zealand, Canada, Brazil and Argentina) were keen to see the elimination of all trade-distorting subsidies on agricultural goods. However, it became apparent that the European Community, other West European countries and Japan were unprepared to go as far in this direction as the U.S. & Cairns Group. Instead, what emerged was a 'package' of liberalisation measures which had three main elements:

1. *Market access*: it was agreed to convert all non-tariff measures imposed on agricultural goods into tariffs (so-called 'tariffication') and then to reduce tariffs by an average of 36% over six years in the case of developed countries and 24% over ten years in the case of developing countries.
2. *Domestic support*: it was agreed that the level of domestic support given by governments to their farmers should be expressed in terms of an 'aggregate measurement of support' (AMS) and the level of AMS should be reduced by 20% over a six-year period in the case of developed countries

and by 13.3% over ten years in the case of developing countries.

3. *Export subsidies*: it was agreed that developed countries should reduce the *value* of their export subsidies to a level 36% below the 1986–90 base year period and the *volume* of subsidised exports by 21% over the six-year implementation period.

At the same time, it was agreed that after five years from January 1, 1995, a second round of negotiations would take place, in the light of how well or otherwise the Agreement had worked.

As we have seen, *textiles and clothing products* were largely exempt from normal GATT discipline. Since the Short- and Long-term Cotton Textile Arrangements (STA and LTA) of 1961 and 1962, respectively, and the Multi-Fibre Arrangement (MFA) of 1973, the developed countries have been allowed to negotiate or impose bilateral quotas on imports of any product which was deemed to be causing 'market disruption'. At the time, these arrangements were regarded as temporarily exempting a single sector from the provisions of the General Agreement. Moreover, the aim was to ensure that quotas did not result in a greater degree of restriction than was necessary to safeguard domestic producers and that quotas would be progressively increased over time. As it turned out, temporary protection proved extremely difficult to get rid of. Developing countries, many of which depended on textiles for a significant component of their export earnings, regarded these restrictions as damaging and had pressed hard for textiles to be brought back under the discipline of the General Agreement that applied to other sectors. As part of the Uruguay Round's Final Act, it was agreed that the MFA should be phased out over a ten-year period. The idea was that products subject to the MFA would be reintegrated into the GATT in four stages commencing January 1, 1995 and ending on January 1, 2005. A weakness of the agreement, however, was that the developed countries were left free to choose which products were to be included at each of the four stages. This left open the possibility that they could leave the most sensitive products to the final stage, such that significant liberalisation would not be achieved until the end of the ten-year phasing-in period.

As we observed above, the Tokyo Round failed to secure any agreement on how to reform the *Safeguard Clause*. There were other GATT rules, too, that were in urgent need of revision such as anti-dumping, the use of subsidies and the formation of regional trading arrangements. With regard to the Safeguard Clause, agreement was reached on certain changes to Article XIX. These steered a careful balance between the concerns of the developing countries that the clause was too lax and the demands of certain developed countries for selective safeguards to be allowed. The agreement made it clear that voluntary export restraints and other grey-area measures were incompatible with GATT rules and were to be phased out within four years (although the EC was allowed to retain its VER with Japan covering cars until the end of 1999). The use of safeguards was made subject to new disciplines. A time limit of four years, which could be extended for a further four years, was to be placed on such measures, while all such measures were to be progressively liberalised. On the issue of selectivity, it was agreed that measures should be applied 'irrespective of source'. However, the door was left open for selective measures by applying stricter quotas on imports of the product from countries where, in the previous period, imports had increased 'in disproportionate percentage in relation to the total increase of imports of the product concerned'.

Anti-dumping rules were also made subject to a revised code, which sought to satisfy the conflicting demands of, on the one hand, anti-dumping users such as the United States and the EC and, on the other hand, anti-dumping victims such as Japan and the newly industrialising countries. In essence, the former wanted greater freedom to act against dumping, while the latter wanted stricter rules to prevent misuse of the anti-dumping provisions of the GATT. In response to demands from the United States in particular, GATT rules governing the use of *subsidies* were strengthened. The approach was to build on the Tokyo Round Subsidies Code and to place limits on the use of certain kinds of 'actionable' domestic subsidies, not just the more obvious kind of distortion created by export subsidies, which had long been prohibited under the General Agreement. Actionable subsidies were, broadly, any subsidy which nullifed or impaired the trading rights of other members. Certain changes were also made to the rules relating to *regional trading arrangements*. These will be explained at a later stage of the chapter.

However, perhaps the most important aspect of the Uruguay Round was the fact that, for the first time, it addressed three kinds of issues, which in the past had not been regarded as a GATT concern. The first was the increasingly important subject of *trade in services*. Trade in services is examined in depth in the next chapter. However, suffice it to say at this stage if GATT was to bring about freer trade in the world, it was no longer possible for it to be confined to trade in goods. A growing proportion of world trade now comprised trade in services. Some services are traded across borders in much the same way as goods. However, many kinds of services cannot be traded in this way and require the service-provider to locate in the country in which he / she wishes to sell services. This implies a movement of capital and / or personnel not just goods. Other kinds of services require the service-buyer to travel to where the service is being provided (e.g. tourism). Trade in these kinds of services is impeded less by border controls of the kind which impede trade in goods and more by government laws and regulations which discriminate against service-providers coming from other countries. A different approach is therefore required to the liberalisation of trade in services than of goods. The approach adopted in the Uruguay Round was to secure agreement on a new General Agreement on Trade in Services (GATS), which applies a set of rules, similar to those applying to trade in goods, to the services sector. These include rules such as MFN, although temporary exemptions are allowed in specified cases. At the same time, countries were required to make as many specific commitments – covering particular service sectors – as they were able, providing for guaranteed market access, the principle of national treatment for foreign service-providers and a commitment to further liberalisation in the future. (Chapter 10 provides a more detailed outline of the GATS agreement.)

The two other new issues covered were *trade-related intellectual property rights* (TRIPs) and *trade-related investment measures* (TRIMs). A new agreement on TRIPs required all countries to introduce laws and systems of enforcement governing forms of intellectual property such as patents, copyright, trademarks, etc. within a period of one year or five years in the case of developing countries. Least developed countries were allowed a period of eleven years. Under the agreement, any infringement of the rules (e.g. the failure of a country to respect the patent laws of another country) could lead to a complaint to the World Trade Organisation (WTO) with the possibility of retaliatory measures if the infringement persists. (Chapter 10 provides a more detailed review of the TRIPs agreement.) TRIMs refer to measures which countries may introduce on foreign companies operating in their territory that result in a distortion of trade. Local-content rules, which require the foreign company to buy a certain proportion of its components and parts from a local supplier are an example. Although GATT has not in the past considered matters pertaining to FDI as something with which it should be concerned, it is clear that these measures have trade implications. The new agreement, therefore, states that countries should not apply any TRIMs that undermine any obligations that they have entered into under the GATT. As with TRIPs, any country that feels that a particular measure has reduced its rights under the GATT can make a complaint to the WTO and secure redress.

The World Trade Organisation (WTO)

The Uruguay Round also brought another significant development in international trade policy. This was the creation of the World Trade Organisation (WTO) to act as the new institutional mechanism for applying GATT rules, upholding GATT rights and enforcing GATT disciplines. One of the weaknesses of the GATT was that it was not an organisation to which countries belonged. Rather, it was a treaty which countries signed. This meant that its effectiveness as an instrument for enforcing international trading rules was undermined. By its very nature, it could only operate on the basis of consensus. All the contracting parties had to agree to its decisions and to apply these. Persuasion rather than force was required to act against any contracting party which failed to do so. Moreover, being a treaty, it lacked flexibility. New rules could not simply be grafted onto the Agreement in response to new challenges. Instead, new issues had to be tackled by negotiating separate agreements to which some, but not necessarily all countries, might wish to be bound. It was also the case that GATT had only ever had a provisional application. In 1947, it was intended that a permanent International Trade Organisation would eventually be established equivalent in nature to the International Monetary Fund on the monetary front. However, this never happened. A charter for the creation of such a body was drafted but never ratified. The reason was the unwillingness of U.S. Congress to cede sovereignity over trade policy to an international organisation.

The WTO came into being on January 1, 1995. It incorporates the Agreement on Trade in Goods (GATT), but including all amendments, additions to, understandings and interpretations that the contracting parties have made since 1947. However, it also incorporates the new Agreement on Services (GATS), the TRIPs Agreement, a new Trade Policy Review Mechanism for monitoring the trade policies of the member states on a regular basis and a new mechanism for settling trade disputes. WTO members are required to abide by all these agreements and cannot pick and choose. The dispute settlements mechanism constitutes a considerable improvement on the arrangements under the old GATT. In some respects, the approach is similar. Member states are expected to, first, seek to settle their disputes by bilateral means. Where, however, they cannot do so, they may bring the matter before the WTO. The WTO will set up a special panel of experts to investigate the dispute and make recommendations. However, there are some major changes. To begin with, there is a strict timetable for the setting up of a panel, the writing up of the report and its adoption. Once a report has been issued, the Dispute Settlements Body has sixty days in which to adopt the report. A weakness of the old system was that, because there were no deadlines, disputes could drag on for a very long time.

Another change concerns the procedure for implementing a panel report once adopted. As before, a single country can block a report from being adopted, but only for a while. It may do so by notifying the Disputes Settlement Body that it wishes to appeal, in which case the report will go before a special Appellate Body which must reach a decision within sixty days. If the Appellate Body upholds the recommendations of the report, a consensus *against* adopting the report is required for the report not be adopted. If the Appellate Body fails to uphold the recommendations, then the report may not be adopted. In effect, the requirement for consensus has now shifted from being a consensus in favour to being a consensus against. This makes it virtually impossible for a country to prevent a panel report with which it disagrees from being adopted if other members are in agreement with it. Moreover, if it fails to adopt the recommendations within twenty days, it could face retaliation in the form of a withdrawal of equivalent concessions. A further difference is that such retaliation may include cross-retaliation with concessions relating to one aspect of WTO rules (e.g. trade in goods) being withdrawn due to an infringement of some other aspect (e.g. TRIPs). This was not possible under GATT and increases the penalty that could face a recalcitrant country.

The creation of the WTO has, therefore, gone some way to improving the means by which international trading rules are applied. At the time of writing, the WTO has been in existence for more than four years. It is still too early to assess whether or not these changes are leading to stricter adherence to trading rules. However, countries do appear to have greater confidence that, if they make a complaint, the problem will be resolved in their favour, if indeed their rights have been genuinely infringed. The number of complaints to the WTO has been much greater than under the GATT, which suggests that countries do expect quicker and more effective findings in their favour. Table 9.2 shows which countries have been the most active users of the disputes settlement system. The figures show that the United States has been the most frequent complainant, followed closely by the EC. On the other hand, developing countries have collectively been the main target of complaints. There is also some evidence to suggest that countries are taking more seriously the decisions reached by the WTO including the threat of retaliation if they fail to remedy the infringement.

Table 9.2 Countries involved in WTO Disputes Cited 1995–1999*

			With developing countries	
Disputes involving	*As complainant*	*As respondent*	*US/EC/Japan as complainant*	*US/EC/Japan as respondent*
United States	60	38	22	14
EC	47	28	21	11
Japan	7	12	3	0
Developing countries	44	61		

*As on October 18, 1999.
Source: WTO (1999).

The WTO has shown, on a number of occasions, that it is not afraid to make tough decisions, even when this brings it into conflict with large and powerful member states. Two recent examples were the disputes involving the United States and the European Union relating to bananas and beef. Box 9.2 describes these disputes in more detail. In both cases, the WTO ruled against the European Union, ordering it to make changes to its import regime. When the EU failed to do so by the deadline set, the WTO authorised the United States to apply sanctions against EU exports to the US. Only on one previous occasion under the old GATT had sanctions of this kind been authorised. At the time of writing, a third dispute relating to U.S. tax policy threatens to escalate in a similar manner. In this case, the EU is the complainant, arguing that U.S. tax policy allows U.S. companies to avoid paying corporation tax on the profits derived from exporting. The EU maintains that this is a type of informal export subsidy that breaches the WTO's subsidy code. The WTO has ruled in favour of the EU in this case and the US has only a short time to pass the necessary legislation through Congress to bring tax policy into line with WTO obligations.

However, the increased powers that the WTO appears to enjoy, have led to increased hostility

Box 9.2 The Bananas and Beef Disputes between the United States and the European Union

Bananas Dispute

- This dispute centred on the EU's system of preferences granted to a number of relatively poor banana exporters in the Caribbean, mainly former colonies of the EU and all of whom were signatories of the EU's Lomé Convention. Banana growers in other Latin American states (the so-called dollar banana producers) complained that these preferences discriminated against them. Although the United States does not exports any bananas herself, a number of U.S. multinationals (e.g. Chiquita) were large producers of bananas in the Latin American region they successfully lobbied the U.S. administration to lodge a complaint with the WTO.

- The EU's import regime was the subject of two complaints under the old GATT, both of which ruled that the EU regime was illegal. However, the EU was able to ignore the findings of the panel. In 1997, a WTO panel also found against the arrangement and, under the new rules, the EU was unable to block the adoption of the panel report. The EU made amendments to its import regime, but in a way that was not acceptable to the US.

- Impatient with what was seen as foot-dragging by the EU, the US threatened to impose sanctions by March, 1999 unless the EU complied with the WTO ruling. The U.S. was accused of threatening unilateral action against the EU without first seeking WTO authorisation to do so.

- In April, 1999, however, WTO authorisation was granted for the US to impose sanctions amounting to $191 million on EU imports to cover the losses incurred as a result of the failure of the EU to comply with the WTO ruling (the US had claimed losses amounting to $520 million so the scale of retaliation was less than the US had wished for). The US announced that 100% tariffs would be imposed on nine European products, aimed mainly at France and the UK, who were seen as the countries most influential in maintaining the EU's banana regime.

Continued

Hormone-Treated Meat Dispute

- This dispute centred on a ban imposed by the EU in 1987 on imports of beef that had been produced using artificial hormones that were regarded as a possible cause of cancer. In January, 1996, the United States, the world's major producer of hormone-treated beef, lodged a complaint with the WTO under the WTO's new Sanitary and Phyto-sanitary (SPS) Agreement signed as part of the Uruguay Round. This stated that any restrictions imposed on imports on health or safety grounds had to be justified scientifically. However, most scientific studies of the effects of using hormones in the production of beef found there to be no discernible danger to human health. However, the EU was concerned about falling consumption of beef due to a loss of consumer confidence about food safety, due in large measure to the BSE (mad-cow) crisis.

- In 1997, the WTO ruled against the EU on the grounds that no proper scientific risk assessment had been carried out. One problem concerned the vagueness of the SPS agreement that failed to specify both how such an assessment should be carried out and what degree of risk was necessary to justify trade restrictions. The EU appealed against the WTO ruling. However, in February, 1998, a report by the Appellate Body upheld the original WTO ruling, although it did state that any risk assessment need not be confined to strictly quantifiable risks and could include concerns about controls on the administration of hormones.

- In October, 1998, the US warned that it would consider trade sanctions unless the EU complied with the findings of the WTO. The EU claimed that it needed longer to complete its own risk assessment. In February, 1999, however, the EU was warned that it had until May 13 to lift its ban. When the EU failed to do so, the WTO authorised the US and Canada to impose sanctions of up to $124 million on EU agricultural products. The US listed a range of European products that would be subject to increased tariffs that were sufficient to freeze them out of the U.S. market.

towards the WTO in many countries. This reached a climax at the WTO's Ministerial Conference held at Seattle in the United States in November 1999, when widespread protests by a variety of different, mainly single-issue, groups succeeded in holding up the negotiations. In addition to concerns about the ability of the WTO to override decisions made by the governments of sovereign nation states, the protesters were expressing concern about the manner in which WTO rulings were reached. Specifically, it was argued that the WTO was undemocratic because panelists were accountable to no one and secretive because panel investigations took place behind closed doors. Protesters also complained that, in making their decisions, WTO panels were not required to take representations from interested third parties. Underlying the concerns of the protesters were widespread fears about the consequences of increased globalisation, which many saw as resulting from the efforts of the WTO to lower barriers to trade. Green groups expressed concern about the implications of trade liberalisation for the environment, and complained about the biased nature of rulings concerning restrictions imposed to enforce international environmental agreements. Trade unionists complained that lower trade barriers compelled advanced industrialised countries to import goods from poorer countries where basic labour rights were non-existent and where goods were produced by ethically unacceptable means. Much of this reflected a misunderstanding about the role of the WTO, whose task is largely one of enforcing rules agreed by member state governments. In fact, by ensuring that trade takes place according to rules agreed among countries, the WTO protects small, poorer nations which might otherwise be the victims of measures imposed by the large and more powerful. Nevertheless, it is clear that one of the challenges facing the WTO in the new century will be to explain how and why it makes the decisions it does. This will necessitate making its procedures more transparent and easier for outsiders to understand.

A Millennium Round?

The purpose of the Seattle Ministerial of the WTO was to discuss whether or not WTO member should embark on a ninth round of multilateral trade negotiations. As it turned out, the members were unable to reach agreement on what should be included on the agenda of any new round. It is quite probable, however, that by the time this book is published, agreement will have been reached to proceed towards a new round. At first, it may seem strange why the members of the WTO should be contemplating yet another round of multilateral negotiations so shortly after the completion of a previous round and before many of the agreements of that round have been fully implemented. One of the reasons is that some form of negotiation was required under the terms of the agreement of the Uruguay Round in relation to certain areas where only limited progress was made in the Uruguay Round. Two such areas were agriculture and services. In both of these areas, the Uruguay Round Final Act required further negotiations to take place in the year 2000 to extend liberalisation beyond that achievable in the Uruguay Round. In addition, there were a number of issues where it was felt negotiations were needed to deal with matters not properly addressed in the Uruguay Round. These included issues such as labour rights, trade and the environment, trade and competition policy and trade and investment.

Much of the debate at Seattle concerned with whether to adopt a narrow or broad agenda. Advocates of the narrow agenda (the United States) argued that the inclusion of too wide a range of issues would make the round excessively complex and prevent progress being made on those matters for which fresh negotiations were explicitly required under the terms of the Uruguay Round Agreement. Others including the European Union favoured a broad agenda, on the grounds that, only by negotiating about a wide range of issues, could the necessary trade-offs be achieved to make agreement possible. Developing countries were not at all certain that any negotiations were needed, given that developed countries had still failed to implement many of the commitments made in the Uruguay Round (e.g. on textiles and the MFA). Although it remains unclear what will constitute the substance of a ninth round (if indeed, there is one), it seems likely that it will cover some, if not all, of the following:

- *Agriculture*. Under the terms of the Agricultural Agreement reached in the Uruguay Round, negotiations must be re-opened by the end of the century with a view to achieving further liberalisation. Agricultural exporting countries will be seeking further progress in improving market access for agricultural products (through lower tariffs and increases in tariff quotas), tighter controls on what types of domestic subsidies to farmers are permissible and the elimination of all export subsidies. Countries such as the European Union and Japan have argued strongly for agriculture to be treated differently to other sectors and for some subsidisation of farming to continue.

- *Services.* As with agriculture, there is a mandate for new negotiations to start on liberalising trade in services by the start of 2000. The aim will be to improve on the package of liberalisation measures agreed in the Uruguay Round (see next chapter).
- *Trade-related intellectual property Rights (TRIPs).* This agreement is due for review in 2000. There will be pressure to make certain changes to this agreement and pressure from developing countries to postpone the full implementation of the agreement that has caused difficulties for some.
- *Trade-related investment measures (TRIMs).* This agreement is also due for review in 2000. Since 1997, discussion has been taking place within the WTO about the relationship between trade and investment. This has led to pressures from some countries for foreign investment rules to be included in the WTO, although this will be strongly resisted by many developed and developing countries.
- *Textiles and clothing.* The agreement for phasing out the Multi-Fibre Arrangement (MFA) is due for review in 2001. Developing countries have argued that developed countries are failing to honour the spirit, if not the letter, of this agreement and that very little quota liberalisation has actually taken place.
- *Information technology products.* In 1996, twenty nine WTO members negotiated a new Information Technology Agreement (ITA) that provides for the complete elimination of tariffs and other duties on a wide range of IT products by January 1, 2000. Now, the WTO wants to expand the product coverage and may be to expand the agreement to cover non-tariff barriers.
- *Trade facilitation.* This concerns the so-called 'red tape' that exists when goods cross borders. The aim of any agreement would be to simplify procedures and reduce administrative barriers to trade.
- *Trade and competition policy.* In recent years, increasing concerns have been expressed about the effects of anti-competitive practices by firms on the efforts to liberalise trade. Although many countries have national laws for tackling such practices, not all countries do and some of these laws are inconsistent. The aim of negotiations would be to agree a multilateral framework to support the implementation of national competition policies. However, this will be strongly resisted by some countries who regard this as unnecessary.
- *Transparency in government procurement.* The aim of negotiations would be to make the procedures for awarding public sector contracts / purchasing deals more open so that it becomes more difficult for governments to favour national bidders / buyers.
- *Trade and labour standards.* The US and certain other developed countries want provisions added to existing agreements to allow developed countries to impose restrictions on goods produced by countries using 'unacceptable' labour standards. This was strongly resisted by the developing countries at the Seattle meeting as an unwarranted interference in their domestic affairs and as a backdoor form of protectionism.
- *Dispute settlement.* Certain changes may be needed to the WTO's system for settling disputes to meet concerns expressed both by members states and outsiders. Likely issues to be discussed will concern the procedures for implementing panel decisions, the need to achieve greater transparency and access to the dispute settlement system and measures to make it easier for developing countries to make use of the system.
- *Electronic commerce.* The growth of electronic commerce has posed new challenges for

WTO members and there is a need for new rules to govern this increasingly important sector of world trade.

- *Members and accession.* There exists a growing list of countries that wish to apply for membership of the WTO. Of these, the most important in terms of size is the People's Republic of China. WTO members must all be in agreement before a new member can be admitted. This means that acceptable terms of entry must be agreed with any countries wishing to accede.

Some of these issues are more contentious than the others and so risk being jettisoned from the agenda. On the other hand, there are other issues (e.g. anti-dumping) that some countries (e.g. Japan) want included and that may subsequently find their way on to the agenda. Clearly, if all of these matters are the subject of negotiations, any ninth round will prove as complex, if not more so, than the round that preceded it. For this reason, it may be better to adopt a more piecemeal approach, with negotiations on several different issues proceeding separately although at the same time.

Regional Trade Liberalisation

The other way in which countries can achieve freer trade is through regional trading agreements. These can take several different forms. A simple form of arrangement is the case of a *preferential trading agreement* (PTA) in which one country agrees to apply lower tariffs on goods from another country. In the case of a *free trade agreement* (FTA), the member states go a step further and agree to abolish their tariffs on all trade between themselves (i.e. to give the partner a 100% tariff preference). A third possibility is to form a *customs union* (CU), in which, in addition to the elimination of tariffs on all trade between the member states, a common external tariff (CET) is also adopted. This gets around one of the problems created by FTAs, namely, the possibility that non-member states might 'deflect' their trade through the member-state with the lowest external tariff. For example, if A has a 10% tariff and B a 20% tariff and they form an FTA, a third country, C, will choose to export to B through A rather than directly to B. B will lose tariff revenues to A and its high tariff will be undermined. This necessitates introducing strict rules of origin to ensure that only goods substantially produced within A or B are allowed to pass freely into the partner country without a tariff being imposed. However, origin rules are often difficult to agree and to enforce. Instead, by harmonising their tariffs at, say, 15%, a CU between A and B avoids the risks of any problem of trade deflection occurring. The fourth possibility is that countries could set up a *common market*, in which they abolish restrictions not only on trade in goods, but also services, persons and capital. Clearly, this goes significantly further than the other three arrangements.

The Theory of Regional Economic Integration

What are the effects of regional trading arrangements of this kind? At first sight, it may appear that they represent a step towards free trade. However, as was first demonstrated by Jacob Viner in 1950 (Viner, 1950), this need not be so. This is because any kind of regional trading arrangement will have a mixture of two opposite kinds of effects. First, the removal of tariffs on trade between the member states will result in *trade creation*. That is to say, some lower cost imports of certain products will displace higher cost domestic production of the good. This represents a step towards free trade resulting in an improved allocation of global resources (goods are now being produced where

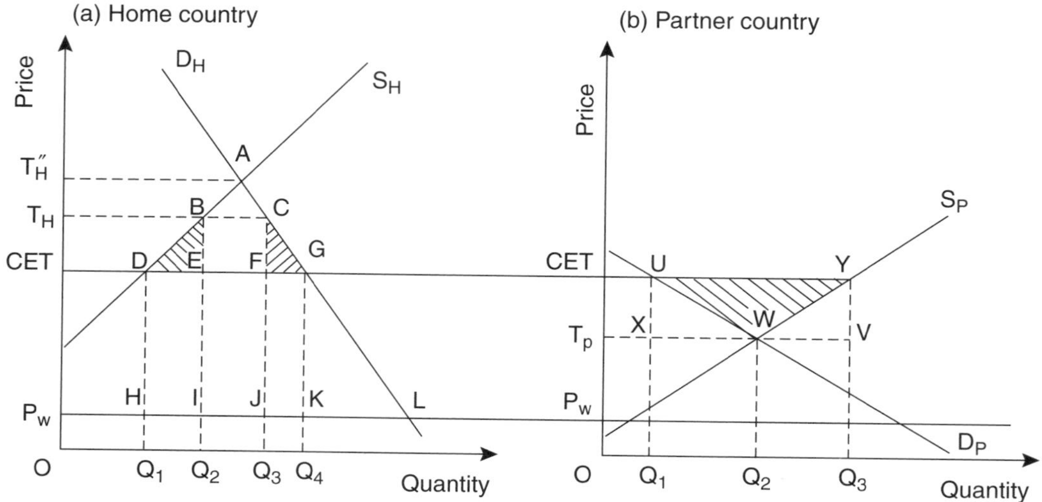

Figure 9.1 The effects of a customs union on the home and partner countries

they are cheapest). Second, the discrimination that results against goods coming from non-member states, will result in *tradediversion.* That is to say, some low-cost imports from countries outside the arrangement will be displaced by higher cost imports from inside. This represents a movement towards protectionism with global resources being allocated less efficiently than before. Now, everything depends on which of these two effects is strongest. If TC exceeds TD, the customs union / free trade area will be welfare enhancing, that is, it will improve global economic welfare. If, however, TD exceeds TC, the reverse will be true.

We may illustrate these two effects with the aid of Figure 9.1 which uses the same kind of partial equilibrium framework as was used in the previous chapter to analyse the effects of tariffs. The world (free-trade) price is assumed to be OP_w. Before the formation of a customs union, both countries are assumed to apply a non-discriminatory tariff on imports, of P_wT_H in the case of Country H and P_wT_P in the case of Country P. As a result, Country H imports the quantity BC all of which comes from the rest of the world and Country P is self-sufficient with consumption equal to domestic production at W. Next, Country H and P form a customs union and establish a common external tariff equal to P_wCET. In Country H, the price falls, consumption increases from C to G and production falls from B to D. Imports increase to DG. Trade creation equal to DE plus FG results. However, imports now come from the partner country instead of the rest of the world. Trade diversion equal to EF has, therefore, resulted. Trade creation yields a welfare gain to the home country of DBE plus CGF (as with any tariff reduction). However, trade diversion generates a welfare loss equal to EFJI (given by the difference between the free trade price and the volume of imports diverted). The net welfare gain / loss is given by the difference between these two amounts. In Country P, the price rises, consumption falls to U and production increases to Y. The country becomes a net exporter of the product with exports equal to UY, all of which go to the partner country. Producers gain extra producer surplus equal to T_pCETYW. However, consumers suffer a loss of consumers' surplus equal to T_pCETUW. This leaves the shaded area UYW as the net gain.

Certain factors will make a FTA/CU more likely to be net trade-creating than net trade-diverting:

1. The larger the area covered, the less the scope for trade diversion and the greater the opportunities for trade creation.
2. The lower the level of the CET in the case of a customs union in comparison with the level of tariffs existing before, the less the trade diversion.
3. The greater the degree of complementarity of the countries (as measured by differences in the range of industries enjoying protection), the greater the likelihood of trade diversion.
4. The greater the degree of competitiveness of the countries (i.e. similar industries enjoying high levels of protection), while being potentially complementary (i.e. with different levels of unit costs in the same industries in the two countries), the greater the likelihood of trade creation.
5. The higher the level of tariffs in potential export markets outside the union with respect to products in which the members have a comparative advantage under free trade, the less the risk of trade diversion.

It follows that CU / FTAs among certain groups of countries are more likely to be welfare-enhancing than others. In particular, CUs/FTAs involving countries at a similar stage of economic development are more likely to be beneficial, as their economies will be competitive rather than complementary.

In addition to these resource allocation effects, a CU/FTA may result in at least two other sources of *static* gain for the countries involved. The first is the possibility that the formation of the CU/FTA may result in a favourable shift in the terms of trade. If the formation of the union leads to trade diversion, the result may be a fall in the world price of some of the products imported from the rest of the world. This is equivalent to the case of a large importing nation that can increase its economic welfare by imposing an optimum tariff. The second is the possibility that, in industries subject to decreasing average costs, an efficiency gain may result from an enlargement of the market. This assumes that the domestic market for the product was too small such that firms were previously unable to produce at their optimal level. It further assumes that the country was faced with high tariffs in the rest of the world and, therefore, could not overcome the constraints of the domestic market by expanding exports. If unit costs fall with output, either consumers will gain from lower prices or domestic producers will enjoy higher profits. Either way the exporting country enjoys an additional net gain in welfare.

One of the problems with the Vinerian theory of customs unions is that it fails to provide an economic rationale for customs unions. Even if the formation of a CU/FTA results in net trade creation, countries can always increase economic welfare by more by reducing tariffs on a non-discriminatory basis, as Cooper and Massell (1965) demonstrated. The logic behind this is straightforward: a non-discriminatory cut in tariffs will lead to trade creation but without any trade diversion. If, therefore, the motive for forming a CU/FTA is to increase economic welfare, CU / FTAs are always *second best*. The *first best* solution is for each country to reduce tariffs on a non-discriminatory basis, whether unilaterally or as part of negotiated trading agreement. One explanation for why a country may seek a CU / FTA suggested by Wonnacott and Wonnacott (1981) is that it wishes to expand its exports but is constrained from doing so by high tariffs in third countries. By negotiating a CU/FTA, a country will be able to gain improved access for its exports to the partner country by offering to eliminate its tariff on imports from the partner country as a bargaining counter. If the partner country is keen to gain improved access for its exports of products belonging to different industries, it will be prepared to eliminate its own import tariff in return.

An alternative rationale for the formation of customs unions was proposed by Johnson (1965), namely, that customs unions were the best way in which developing countries could achieve the goal of industrialisation. Johnson argued that, in developing countries, manufacturing industry possessed many of the qualities of a 'public good'. That is to say, the benefits derived from an increase in manufacturing output could not be measured by the *private* returns to capitalists who invested in such production. Because the *social* return exceeded the private return, an argument could be made for developing countries imposing an import tariff to encourage import substitution. In the case of a country that is a net exporter of such goods, however, the same argument would justify an export subsidy coupled with a tariff to prevent re-importation. Because GATT rules prohibited export subsidies, the alternative was to negotiate preferential tariff reductions with a partner country. If both countries made reciprocal reductions in their tariffs on trade with each other, both could expand their exports of those manufactures in which they enjoyed a comparative advantage. Such reasoning appears to have inspired a number of the attempts of developing countries to achieve more rapid industrialisation through the formation of CUs and FTAs. One obvious drawback with the argument is that it assumes that the two countries have complementary and not competing interests. If both countries enjoy a comparative cost advantage in the same industries, neither will wish to cut tariffs on those products and each country will be unable to achieve its objectives through such an arrangement. Indeed, this is the precise reason why many of the attempts at regional economic integration among developing countries during the 1960s and 1970s were unsuccessful. Moreover, the argument can only apply to developing countries for whom increased manufacturing output may bring gains over and above the private returns to investors. In developed countries, there is nothing 'special' about manufacturing output that would justify such a policy.

More recently, in their search for a rationale for regional integration, economists have emphasised the *dynamic gains* that accrue from the formation of CU/FTAs. The formation of a CU/FTA may, in addition to the once-and-for-all increase in real income resulting from improved resource allocation, bring about a permanent improvement in the *rate* of economic growth. In other words, output will go on increasing for several more years after the formation of the union or area. There are four reasons for this. First, the larger market will enable firms to expand their *scale* of production, thereby producing at a permanently lower average cost. Second, the removal of barriers to trade will expose firms to greater competition. This may result in permanently lower prices and eliminate so-called 'X-inefficiency' caused by managerial slack. (Managers are compelled by competition to pursue cost-minimising strategies.) Third, dynamic export growth will encourage firms to spend more on investment resulting in a rise in the country's rate of fixed investment. A higher rate of investment will lead to a higher rate of economic growth. Fourth, the rate of technological innovation will increase both because firms in high technology industries face more competition (and must innovate to survive) and because the larger market reduces the risk of investment in (R&D).

Although these gains are more difficult to measure than the static gains, attempts to do so have found them to be substantial. Early attempts to measure the effects of economic integration in Western Europe found that trade creation did exceed trade diversion, but amounted to less than 1% to the GDP of the member states. If, however, the dynamic effects are included, the welfare gain appears much larger. Thus, Owen (1983) estimated that, if dynamic effects are taken into account, the GDP of the original six EC member states was, approximately, 3–6% higher by 1980 than it would otherwise have been. Focusing on the macroeconomic effects of the EC on internal economic growth, Marques-Mendes (1986) estimated that, by 1972, the GDP of the EC was 2.2% higher than it would have been without integration and, by 1981, 5.9% higher. It is, however, true that the dynamic effects may equally well be enjoyed by multilateral tariff reductions. If, on the other hand, other countries are reluctant to lower their tariffs, it may be difficult to achieve these gains though multilateral negotiation. A regional trading agreement, which offers partner countries equivalent gains, may be the only means available of doing so.

The New Regionalism

GATT rules have always made CUs/FTAs an exception to the non-discrimination rule. Article XXIV makes it clear that these are allowed subject to certain conditions:

1. *They must result in the elimination of tariffs and other restrictions on 'substantially all the trade' between the partner countries.* It is not sufficient that tariffs are merely reduced, or even that they are eliminated, if this does not embrace 'substantially all trade'. The only preferences, therefore, that are acceptable are 100% preferences. It is, however, unclear how much trade constitutes 'substantial'. It is not a requirement that this should be brought about immediately after an agreement is signed. However, any agreement must set a timetable for the creation of a CU/FTA over 'a reasonable length of time'.
2. *The level of external restriction (the common external tariff in the case of a customs union) must not exceed the average level of tariffs that existed before the CU was created.* The original Article XXIV referred to the unweighted average, but an amendment introduced in the Uruguay Round now refers to a weighted average. The purpose of this provision is to ensure that the elimination of internal tariffs is not accompanied by a raising of the level of external tariffs. In other words, the aim is to minimise the degree of trade diversion that might result. Because this requirement may be circumvented by member states using other methods to restrict imports from third countries, the amended version of Article XXIV now extends the provision to other forms of restrictions, while recognising that the impact of these measures may be difficult to quantify.
3. *If the formation of a CU/FTA should result in a trade loss for another GATT/WTO country, Article XXIV entitles that country to compensation.* Such a loss may arise if a third country now faces a higher tariff in one or more of the member states as a result of the external tariffs of the member states being harmonised. For example, if a high- and low-tariff country form a customs union, the low-tariff country may have to raise tariffs on imports from third countries following the formation of the union. In

this case, third countries are entitled to trade (not financial) compensation in the form of other equivalent concessions. This may be dealt with by the customs union cutting its common external tariff in a way that exactly compensates the third countries experiencing the loss.

The original Article XXIV provided for the reporting and monitoring of CU / FTAs by the GATT. In theory, if a contracting party failed to comply with any of these rules, it could be required to dismantle or amend any agreement entered into. In practice, this never happened. Rules were frequently flouted without any action being taken to discipline the countries involved. Over the period 1948–1990, the GATT received notification of some seventy regional trading agreements. None of these was ever declared incompatible with the GATT, yet only four were deemed to be compatible! In many respects, the problem began with the formation of the European Communities in 1958 when the GATT decided against making any ruling on the compatibility or otherwise of the proposed arrangement. The reasons were political. The United States supported the formation of the EC as a means of strengthening Western Europe in the face of the security threat from the East. At the same time, the US was anxious not to do anything that might cause the EC countries to leave the GATT.

However, apart from the formation of the EC in 1958 and EFTA in 1960, most of the attempts at regional integration in the first two and a half decades after World War II involved developing countries. Many of these were unsuccessful. Moreover, their effect on world trade was minimal. They did not, therefore, constitute a serious challenge to the non-discriminatory system of world trade existing under the GATT. However, in the late-1980s and 1990s, the situation changed dramatically. The world witnessed a proliferation of regional trading arrangements that embraced developed and not just developing countries. Especially important in this respect was the conversion of the United States, previously the custodian of multilateralism, to the regionalist cause. In 1985, the United States signed a free trade agreement with Israel. Clearly, this was not even a regional free trade agreement, although the effects on world trade were minimal not least because Israel already enjoyed preferential access to the U.S. market under the Generalised System of Preferences (GSP).

Then, in October, 1987, the US signed a free trade agreement with its neighbour, Canada, that provided for the elimination of all tariffs and quantitative restrictions over a ten-year period commencing on January 1, 1989. Tariffs were already fairly low between the two countries so that the trade effects were minimal. However, the agreement also provided for the elimination of many non-tariff barriers, ended many restrictions on direct investment between the two countries and sought to liberalise trade in services. Then, in March, 1990, the United States' southern neighbour, Mexico, pressed for a free trade agreement. Clearly, preferential access to the U.S. market was an important motive, being seen as an important way of attracting new inward investment to Mexico. However, a further consideration was the desire of the Salinas administration to 'lock-in' the economic reforms introduced in an attempt to liberalise the economy. The US was anxious to encourage this process. However, rather than sign a separate free trade agreement with Mexico, it proposed the creation of a new *North American Free Trade Area* (NAFTA) comprising the US, Canada and Mexico, but modelled on the free trade agreement already existing between the US and Canada. Although NAFTA met with considerable domestic resistance in the United States because of fears that the

US would lose jobs to Mexico, NAFTA was approved by Congress in 1993.

Although concerns were expressed that the US was abandoning multilateralism for regionalism, the US argued that the two were complementary and not alternatives. It was clear, however, that the U.S. regional trading agreements programme was motivated by disappointment within the US with what could be achieved through the GATT. Increasingly, the United States was of the view that more could be achieved by negotiating bilateral agreements with willing partners than seeking global agreement among all GATT countries. At the same time, the US saw regional trading agreements as a useful way of pushing its major global trading partners into multilateral negotiations.

An important consideration, undoubtedly, was the deepening of the process of European economic integration that was taking place. See Box 9.3. In 1985, the European Community signed the Single European Act which provided for the creation of a *Single European*

Box 9.3 Key Milestones in European Integration

1948. Creation of the Organisation for European Economic Co-operation (OEEC): set up to control the economic recovery programme of Western Europe after the Second World War.

1949. Creation of the Council of Europe to achieve certain very broad cultural and political objectives at a European level.

1952. Creation of the European Coal and Steel Community (ECSC) following the signing of the Treaty of Paris (France, West Germany, Italy, Belgium, the Netherlands and Luxembourg).

1954. Formation of the West European Union (WEU) providing for a limited amount of intergovernmental political co-operation.

1958. The creation of the European Economic Community (EEC) and the European Atomic Energy Authority (Euratom), following the signing of the Treaty of Rome (France, West Germany, Italy, Belgium, the Netherlands and Luxembourg.

1960. The creation of the European Free Trade Area (EFTA) following the signing of the Stockholm Convention (UK, Austria, Switzerland, Norway, Sweden, Denmark and Portugal).

1967. The creation of the European Community as a result of the Merger Treaty that combined the three communities – EEC, ECSC and Euratom – into a single entity.

1973. First enlargement of the EC through the accession of the UK, Republic of Ireland and Denmark.

1979. The creation of the European Monetary System (EMS) to stabilise exchange rates among members of the EC.

1981. Greece was admitted as a full member of the EC.

1985. The Single European Act was passed providing for the creation of a Single European Market (SEM) by the end of 1992.

Continued

1986. Spain and Portugal were admitted to the EC.

1991. Maastricht Treaty signed providing for the transformation of the EC into an economic and political union, including the eventual adoption of a common currency.

1992. The Single European Market came into being with the abolition of all frontiers among members of the EC.

1993. Creation of the European Economic Area (EEA) between members of the EC and EFTA.

1995. Sweden, Austria and Finland accede to full membership of the EU.

1997. The Amsterdam Treaty was signed providing for various institutional changes to the EU to make for easier and more democratic decision making.

1999. Realisation of full economic and monetary union and launching of the Euro with eleven countries (France, Germany, Italy, Belgium, Netherlands, Luxembourg, Spain, Portugal, Austria, Finland and Eire). Creation of the European Central Bank.

Market (SEM) characterised by free trade in goods and services and free movement of labour and capital by the end of 1992. The aim was the elimination of all internal frontiers and the establishment of a new '*acquis communautaire*' to which all laws in Europe would eventually be aligned. This threatened to leave producers in third countries at a significantly greater cost disadvantage when competing in the European market. This would have been increased if, at the same time as internal barriers were lowered, the EC had resorted to greater external protection. The fear of exclusion was increased by the decision of the EC to expand its membership from ten to twelve countries, thereby widening the area of discrimination. Furthermore, under an agreement to be signed with the members of the European Free Trade Area, many of the benefits of the Single Market were to be made available to producers in EFTA countries also. Subsequently, a number of these countries applied for full membership of the EU. (In 1991, following the Maastricht Treaty, the EC became the EU.) On January 1, 1995, three EFTA countries – Sweden, Finland and Austria – became EU members.

The possibility of the polarisation of the world into three regional trading blocs was increased by parallel developments in the Asia–Pacific region. In 1983, Australia and New Zealand signed a new *Australia and New Zealand Closer Economic Relations and Trade Agreement* (ANZCERTA), which replaced the previous New Zealand–Australia Free Trade Agreement (NAFTA) set up in 1965. ANZCERTA provided for the elimination of all tariffs by January 1, 1988 and all quantitative restrictions by July 1, 1995. On January 1, 1993, the six members of the Association of South East Asian Nations (ASEAN) embarked on a programme for an *ASEAN Free Trade Area* (AFTA) involving the complete elimination of tariffs over a fifteen-year period. A further step towards closer integration in the Pacific followed the formation of the *Asia–Pacific Economic Co-operation* (APEC) forum in 1989. This comprised fifteen countries – Australia and New Zealand, the six ASEAN countries, the United States and Canada (but not Mexico), Japan, South Korea, China, Hong Kong and Taiwan. In November 1994, the APEC countries, meeting at Jakarta, entered into a commitment to free trade by the year 2020. Although no detailed schedule of tariff reductions or list of products to be included was agreed, it was decided that any tariff reductions that were made would be automatically extended on a non-discriminatory basis to other GATT countries also.

In recent years, there have been a host of regional trading arrangements in other regions of the world also. A complex network of overlapping agreements has been created by counztries in the Latin American region. Arguably, the most important development was the

Table 9.3 Regional Trading Agreements Notified to the GATT/WTO and in Force at the End of 1995

A. Under Article 24

EEC and EURATOM	1957	EFTA–Israel FTA	1992
EFTA	1960	Czeck Republic and Slovak Republic Customs Union	1992
Central American Common Market (CACM)	1960	Lithuania–Switzerland FTA	1992
Arab Common Market	1960	EFTA–Poland Agreement	1992
EC–Turkey Agreement	1963	EFTA–Romania Agreement	1992
EC–Certain non-European countries and territories	1970	NAFTA	1992
EC–Malta Association	1970	CEFTA	1992
EC–Switzerland/Liechstentein Agreements	1972	Estonia–Switzerland FTA	1992
EC–Iceland Agreements	1972	Latvia–Switzerland FTA	1992
EC–Cyprus Agreements	1972	Faroe Islands–Iceland FTA	1992
EC–Norway Agreements	1973	Faroe Islands–Norway FTA	1992
CARICOM	1973	Faroe Islands–Switzerland FTA	1992
EEC–Israel Agreement	1975	EEC–Bulgaria Interim Agreement	1993
EEC–Algeria Agreement	1976	EFTA–Bulgaria FTA	1993
EEC–Morocco Agreement	1976	EFTA–Hungary FTA	1993
EEC–Tunisia Agreement	1976	EC–Czeck Republic Europe Agreement	1993
Australia–Papua Guinea Agreement	1976	EC–Slovak Republic Europe Agreement	1993
EEC–Egypt Agreement	1977	Slovak Republic–Slovenia FTA	1993
EEC–Jordan Agreement	1977	EEC–Romania Interim Agreement	1993
EEC–Lebanon Agreement	1977	EC–Estonia Agreement	1994
EEC–Syria Agreement	1977	EC–Latvia Agreement	1994
ANZCERTA	1983	EEC–Slovenia Cooperation Agreement	1993
Israel-US FTA	1985	Hungary–Slovenia FTA	1994
CUS FTA	1988	EC–Lithuania Agreement	1994
EC-Faroe Islands	1991	Czeck Republic–Romania FTA	1994
EFTA–Turkey Agreement	1991	Slovak Republic–Romania FTA	1994
EC–Hungary Interim Agreement	1991	Czeck Republic–Slovenia FTA	1994
EC–Poland Interim Agreement	1991	EFTA–Slovenia FTA	1995
EFTA–Czeck and Slovak Federal Republic Agreement	1992	EFTA–Estonia FTA	1995
Estonia–Norway Agreement	1992	EFTA–Latvia	1995
Latvia–Norway Agreement	1992	EFTA–Lithuania	1995
Lithuania–Norway Agreement	1992		

B. Under the Enabling Clause

The Tripartite Agreement (Egypt, India and Yugoslavia)	1967	GSTP	1981
Protocoal relating to trade negotiations among developing countries	1971	Laos-Thailand Trade Agreement	1988
Bangkok Agreement	1975	MERCOSÜR	1991
ASEAN Preferential Trading Arrangements	1977	Preferential Tariffs among Members of the Economic Cooperation Organisation	1992
South Pacific Regional Trade Cooperation Agreement	1992	Andean Pact	1987
Latin American Integration Association (LAIA)	1980	South Asian Preferential Trade Arrangement	1993
Gulf Cooperation Council	1980	Common Market to Eastern and Southern Africa	1993

Note : The Enabling Clause was negotiated as part of the Tokyo Round in 1979 and allows developing countries to do whatever they like in the area of trading preferences extended towards other developing countries through regional trading agreements. In other words, they are not subject to the disciplines of Article XIV.

Mercosür Trading Agreement of August 1994, which provided for the creation of a customs union among Brazil, Argentina, Uruguay and Paraguay with effect from January 1, 1995. In October 1996, Chile became an associate member of *Mercosür* and Bolivia in December 1996. The spread of regionalism is illustrated by the fact, of the seventy agreements notified to the GATT and in force at the end of 1995, forty-five had come into being since 1990. Table 9.3 lists regional trading agreements currently in force that have been officially notified to the GATT.

Does the growth of the New Regionalism matter?

The theory of regional integration has demonstrated that there is nothing inherently harmful or damaging about free trade areas or customs union. So long as they result in net trade creation, the effect on global economic welfare is positive. The provisions of Article XXIV go some way in ensuring that this will be the case. In particular, while not precluding the possibility that a CU/FTA could result in net trade diversion, the requirement that the average level of external tariffs after the formation of the CU/FTA should be no higher than the level before increases the likelihood that net trade creation will be the outcome. Moreover, such evidence as is available would suggest that, to date, most regional trading blocs formed among *developed countries* have resulted in net trade creation. Early attempts at regional integration among *developing countries* were less successful and may have resulted in net trade diversion. Even then, however, the effect on global economic welfare was marginal.

In certain ways, regional trading blocs may actually speed up the process of global trade liberalisation. Liberalising world trade through multilateral trade negotiations suffers from a number of problems. The first is the so-called 'free rider' problem. Because the GATT/WTO is based on the principle of unconditional MFN, any country will always be tempted to offer as little as possible in concessions, knowing that it will automatically receive whatever reductions in barriers other countries negotiate among themselves. Recognising this problem, the General Agreement makes it clear that countries are expected to act reciprocally, that is, to offer concessions to other countries and not just to benefit from concessions which other countries make. However, even when countries are prepared to act reciprocally, they may still be constrained from making big concessions if they sense that other countries are seeking, in some measure, to 'free ride'. This gives rise to what Wonnacott and Lutz (1989) have called the 'convoy problem', namely, that the least willing participant dictates the pace of negotiations. Regionalism may provide one way around this problem. Those countries that are keen to make big reductions in their trade barriers, can do so without the need to extend these to all trading partners. The effect may even be a salutary one if, as a result, the more reluctant countries are galvanised into making concessions. This may be the case if they are afraid of being placed at a significant preferential disadvantage in the markets of the countries cutting tariffs fastest.

A second problem with multilateral agreements is that they can take a long time to negotiate both because of the number of countries involved and the complexity of the agenda. There are more countries that have to agree to any package of measures negotiated and a more complex web of trade-offs may be needed. Each round of GATT has got bigger and more complex. As a consequence, negotiations have tended to drag on for longer. For example, the Tokyo Round took six years to complete and the Uruguay Round seven years. On the other hand, the range of issues covered in regional negotiations is often broader and sometimes more complex than in multilateral negotiations. Few regional agreements are concerned merely with lowering tariffs on trade in goods. Most also seek to tackle non-tariff barriers and may extend to other issues such as investment, services, free movement of labour and competition policy. In this respect, regional trading agreements may involve more complex negotiations. One problem is that of so-called 'sequencing'. When a country already has a regional agreement with another country, the negotiation of a new agreement with a second country potentially reduces the value of the preferences enjoyed by the first. As a result, it may be necessary to renegotiate the first agreement to offer the partner adversely affected some improved benefits as compensation. For example, if the United States and Japan were to negotiate a free trade agreement, it would affect the concessions that the US has granted Canada and Mexico under NAFTA. Canadian and Mexican exporters would now have to share their preferences in the U.S. market with Japanese exporters. Canada and Mexico may, therefore, demand some re-negotiation of their agreement with the US.

Although regional trading agreements can constitute stepping stones towards free trade, there are a number of ways in which their proliferation may undermine the attempt to achieve free trade. First, there is a danger that the time spent on negotiating regional trading agreements will divert the energy and resources of governments away from the need to achieve further global trade liberalisation. In this case, regionalism will undermine and not reinforce multilateralism. Thus, in the Uruguay Round negotiations, the pre-occupation of the US with the negotiations to establish NAFTA temporarily acted as a distraction. Once NAFTA had been agreed and ratified by U.S. Congress, more rapid progress in the GATT negotiations became possible. Second, there is a danger that the proliferation of a large number of regional trading blocs will increase trading tensions between countries. As we have seen, each new agreement entered into by one country with another undermines the value of any preferences offered in previous agreements to other partner countries. In addition, to the extent that regional trading arrangements result in trade diversion, the potential is created for offending trading partners and provoking retaliation. Other technical problems may arise where regional tariff reductions are phased at different times, inconsistent rulings are made by dispute settlement procedures set up under different agreements and where different rules of origin are applied in different trading areas. Third, to the extent that regionalism polarises world trade into a small number of powerful trading blocs, smaller countries which are excluded are likely to suffer. One of the merits of the unconditional MFN principle is that it protects smaller countries from the big and powerful.

Finally, there is the danger that regionalism might lead to increased protectionism. As trade barriers are reduced internally, steeper barriers may be erected against imports from the rest of the world. One reason for this is that, for an individual country, the costs of imposing restrictions on imports from a supplier from the rest of the world are lowered if that country is part of a regional trading bloc. This is because restrictions need only be imposed on extra-area imports thus reducing the number of trading partners it risks upsetting. Another reason is that large trading blocs have an incentive to assert monopsonistic power by imposing optimum tariffs in an attempt to shift the terms of trade in their favour.

A further reason may be that the internal decision making process of trading blocs is more likely to result in protectionism against imports from the rest of the world than that of an individual country. Winters (1993) gives several reasons for how this happens within the EU. First, the need for the European Commission to gain the support of individual member states if it is to be effective forces it to 'broker compromises' with national governments. This, he argues, encourages a drift towards generalised protection in EU trade policy. It also creates greater opportunities for Community-wide lobbies (e.g. farmers, steel producers, etc.) to bring pressure to bear, not only on the Commission, but also member state governments. Another reason is the so-called 'restaurant bill' problem. This is relevant to the determination of agricultural prices in the EU. If a party of people go out for a meal together and everyone is required to contribute equally to the cost of the bill, each person will have whatever item on the menu brings them the most satisfaction with little regard for the cost. In the EU, the costs of the CAP are borne collectively by consumers and taxpayers. However, the benefits accrue to producers in the different member states according to how much they produce. This means that, in the annual agricultural price negotiations, each member state government will seek to obtain high prices for those commodities for which they have a high share of production. In other words, the system works to push prices up rather than down. In a similar way, there is a bias towards increased protectionism in the determination of EU industrial policy. The fear of being left on the outside in the event of a protectionist measure being adopted causes member states to press for protection for those products of most concern to themselves. The result is that even liberal members of the EU who are opposed to protectionist measures fail to fight vigorously to prevent their adoption. Third, a bias towards protectionism arises from the efforts of the Commission to gain control over trade policy. In order to do so, the Commission is compelled to adopt and to propagate a policy close to that of the most protectionist member state. One example of this concerns EU policy towards imported Japanese cars following the abolition of internal borders. Before 1992, a number of member states applied national restrictions on imports of Japanese cars. With the arrival of the Single Market, it was necessary to replace these with a Community-wide policy. The Commission negotiated a voluntary export restraint agreement with Japan that limits the rise in cars exported by Japan to the entire EU until the end of the century when full liberalisation will be achieved. In order to secure the agreement of the member states for national controls to be replaced by Community-wide restrictions, the Commission had to negotiate a level of restraint which was acceptable to the most protectionist member state (Winters, 1993).

In an attempt to address the issue of whether the spread of regional trading arrangements is a desirable or harmful development, economists have attempted to construct dynamic models that analyse the effects of the world being organised into a declining number of trading blocks. Krugman (1991) developed a model in which the world consisted of a large number of small provinces, each of which specialised in the production of a single, distinct product. The products of each province entered symmetrically into world demand, with a constant elasticity of substitution between any two such products. The world was assumed to be organised into a certain number of trading blocs of equal size with internal free trade, but a common external tariff on imports from the rest of the world. Each bloc acted non-co-operatively and set its external tariff at whatever level maximised its economic welfare. Regionalism was analysed as a movement towards a smaller number of blocs. Two effects resulted. The fact that a larger share of world trade, now, took place within the blocs (where no tariffs applied) led to trade creation. On the other hand, because each bloc had greater market power than before, it had an incentive to levy a higher tariff on imports from the other blocs, resulting in trade diversion. The effect of a trend towards regionalism on global economic welfare is, therefore, ambiguous. Clearly, the best outcome would be if all countries joined a single trading bloc, in which case only trade creation would result. Failing this, however, a large number of small, trading blocs is to be preferred, because, in this case, each bloc has less monopsony power than before and, hence, the incentive to charge a high external tariff is reduced.

As Krugman (1993) has argued, there are two major problems with this model. The first is that it assumes that each of the blocs sets tariffs in a non-co-operative manner, such that the external tariff of each bloc increases as the number of blocs decrease. However, suppose that tariffs are set through negotiation rather than in a non-co-operative manner. Consolidation into a smaller number of blocs may make negotiated agreements to lower tariffs more likely because the number of players involved is fewer. The second is that it ignores the extent to which countries that are part of the same bloc, are 'natural' trading partners. If they are, indeed, natural trading partners (because transportation and communication costs between the countries are low), the risk that consolidation of the world into a smaller number of blocs will reduce global economic welfare is reduced. Krugman's conclusion is that, while more careful modelling is required to take account of these factors, the answer to whether or not regionalism is good or bad must be ambiguous. A related issue concerns why so many such blocs are being formed. The answer to this may be found, Krugman argues, in the advantages that regional negotiations have over multilateral negotiations as a method of trade liberalisation. The number of participants in regional negotiations is fewer, which reduces the risk of 'free riding' and makes agreements easier to reach.

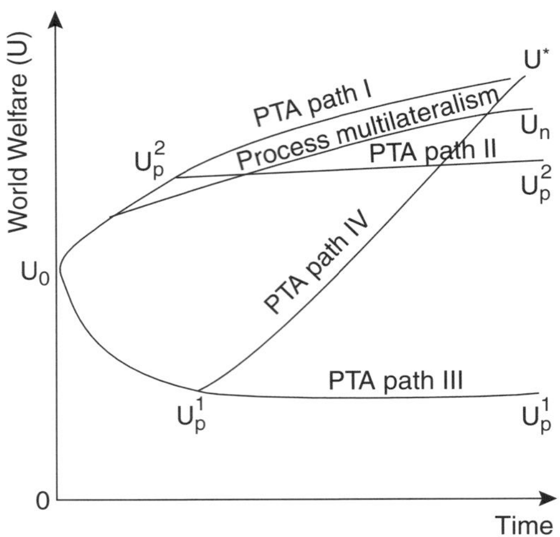

Figure 9.2 Bhagwati's dynamic time path framework for comparing regionalism with multilateralism

Also, adherence to an agreement is easier to monitor when it has a regional as opposed to multilateral application. There is also a greater likelihood that the countries involved will have institutional similarities that enhance a sense of trust that each country will keep to the agreement. Multilateral agreements confront the familiar problem of 'prisoner's dilemma'. National economic welfare can always be maximised by different blocs agreeing to negotiate mutually beneficial reductions in tariffs that is, setting tariffs in a co-operative manner. However, for each bloc to pursue a co-operative outcome, there must be the assurance that the other blocs will adhere to the agreement and not cheat. This may be more difficult to achieve under a multilateral agreement than an agreement reached at a regional level among countries that share similar goals.

Bhagwati (1998) examines the issue of whether regional trading blocs take us closer or further way from free trade using a 'dynamic time-path' framework. Multilateral trade negotiations and regional trading negotiations may be viewed as two distinct and separate ways of achieving global free trade. Then, five distinct time-paths can be identified. These are illustrated in Figure 9.2. World economic welfare is measured on the vertical axis and time on the horizontal axis. The goal is assumed to be global free trade by a certain point of time. If achieved, global economic welfare is maximised at U*. Preferential trading areas (PTAs) may increase or decrease global economic welfare, depending on whether they are net trade-creating or net trade-diverting. At the same time, PTAs may be stagnant in terms of membership or their membership may expand. If their membership expands, a situation would ultimately be reached where their membership would include all countries of the world and the result would be global free trade. This latter possibility is represented by time paths I or IV, depending on whether the initial effect of the formation of the PTA is net trade-creating (time path I) or net trade-diverting (time path IV). The case where a PTA is stagnant or results in a negligible expansion of membership is represented by time paths II and III, again depending on whether the PTA is net trade-creating (time path II) or net trade-diverting (time path III). Finally, the case of a negotiated movement in the direction of free trade is represented by the curve labelled 'process-multilateralism'. It is assumed that process-multilateralism fails to result in complete free trade because of the free-rider problem discussed above. It follows that, under certain circumstances, PTAs may be preferable to negotiating free trade through the WTO. This would still be the case if the PTA was initially net trade-diverting, provided that membership of the PTA expands continuously. One way of ensuring this would be to require all PTAs to have an open-ended membership, so that any country in the world would have the right to join a PTA at any time. On the other hand, countries may be reluctant to form a PTA if this were the case, as entry of other countries at a later stage would undermine the degree of preference that each enjoys in the market of the other in a way that cannot be foreseen in advance.

One problem with the Bhagwati model is that it assumes that the two processes, of preferential trade liberalisation and negotiated multilateral liberalisation are separate, such that one does not influence the other. However, this may be argued either way. There is some evidence that, in the past, the formation of preferential trading areas by a small group of countries (e.g. the European Economic Community in the late 1950s) has acted as a spur to other countries to negotiate further tariff reductions through the GATT (e.g. the formation of the EEC led to the Kennedy Round in the 1960s). On the other hand, pre-occupation with negotiating regional free trade may cause countries to divert their attention away from multilateral negotiations, as happened in the late 1980s when the Uruguay Round negotiations were delayed because the U.S. was busy negotiating the NAFTA. Baldwin (1997) has argued for a 'domino theory' of regionalism. He argues that, over the past fifty years, each new regional trading bloc has caused a multiplier effect in which bilateral import barriers have fallen in a domino-like fashion. The argument is as follows. The formation of a preferential trading area causes both trade and investment diversion, which leads, in turn, to a 'pressure for inclusion' within the non-participating countries. The bigger the trading bloc, the greater the pressure to secure entry. Moreover, the more countries that join, the greater the pressure on outsiders to avoid being excluded. Where membership is open, the membership of each bloc will increase rapidly. Where, however, membership is barred, the excluded countries may prefer to negotiate preferential trading arrangements of their own.

An important aspect of the domino theory is the incorporation of a political economy dimension, in which national trade policies are endogenously determined. At any given time, different groups within a country will adopt different attitudes towards membership of a particular regional trade grouping, some in favour and others against. If an existing bloc should decide to deepen its integration or a group of countries decide to create a new preferential trading area, exporters in the excluded country will face a new discrimination which lowers their profits. Hence, they will engage in pro-integration political activity. If, previously, the government was indifferent about whether to seek membership of the regional grouping, the result of this activity may be to tilt the balance in favour of doing so. If the country chooses to join, the bloc becomes larger and the costs of non-membership increase, leading to increased lobbying for membership in other excluded countries. The result is a second round of pro-integration political activity that may lead to yet another phase of enlargement. An added reason given by Baldwin for why the pressure for inclusion among exporters in excluded countries will increase following the establishment of a new regional trade grouping concerns the behaviour of special interest groups. Special interest groups tend to fight harder to avoid losses from increased discrimination due to the creation of a new regional trade grouping than to secure any gains from multilateral liberalisation. One reason is that, in order to gain entry to a particular market, firms must incur certain non-recoverable costs (in product development, training, brand name advertising or production capacity). If, as a result of the formation of a regional grouping, they face reduced profits or even losses (which they cannot, in the short run, eliminate by closing down), they will lobby hard for membership of the new grouping. By way of contrast, multilateral liberalisation, which leads to improved access to a foreign market, is less beneficial. This is because there is a greater likelihood that any long-run excess profits that are made will serve simply to attract new competitors.

Sapir (1997) has provided an interesting econometric test of the domino theory, using a gravity model of trade. He sought to test the hypothesis that increased integration within the EC has impacted negatively on non-members and, thereby, prompted their application for EC membership. He concentrated on the members of EFTA over the period 1960–1992, all of whom depended on the West European market for roughly two-thirds of their exports. He found that, in the period up to 1985, intra-EFTA trade (trade among the members of EFTA) fared well because EFTA countries enjoyed preferences in EFTA markets that were comparable with those enjoyed by EC countries in each other's markets. However, following the launching of the Single Market programme, intra-EFTA trade became less intensive than trade within the original five EC member states (France, Germany, Italy, Belgium-Luxembourg and the Netherlands). Sapir argues that the evidence lends support to the widely held view that the Single Market programme resulted in investment diversion in the economies of EFTA. The fact that, a number of EFTA countries (Austria, Switzerland, Finland, Sweden and Norway) applied in 1989 to join the EC, may be seen, in the light of this evidence, as support for the domino theory.

An important aspect of the domino theory is that, contrary to more traditional arguments about regionalism, regionalism does not occur because regional trading arrangements are easier to negotiate than multilateral agreements. Baldwin argues that there is little evidence to show that they are politically easier, as the ground covered in regional agreements is often more complex. Rather, countries typically pursue the two paths in parallel, as did the United States in the early 1990s, when the negotiations to create NAFTA took place alongside the Uruguay Round negotiations. Rather, the main force behind regionalism in the domino theory is the desire of outsiders not to be excluded from new regional groupings. If the domino theory is correct, there is every reason to expect the membership of regional trade groupings to grow over time, setting in motion the favourable dynamic time-path discussed above. If, of course, members try to bar entry to new applicants, this will not be the case. In this event, however, the likelihood is that exporters will press for multilateral liberalisation as a way of reducing, if not eliminating, discrimination in the regional grouping. Moreover, as Baldwin argues, regionalism strengthens the hand of proponents of free trade (exporters) within the countries involved, while weakening the position of the opponents (import competitors). Exporters expand as barriers are eliminated within the regional trade grouping, while importers are forced to scale back their operations or shut down altogether. In this way, regionalism will lead towards free trade, rather than act as an impediment.

Conclusion

In this chapter, we have seen that an important aspect of a country's trade policy is to use its tariff as a device for negotiating freer trade with trading partners. In part, this is important because exporters require larger markets in which to sell. In part, too, it is because national economic welfare can be raised by lowering tariffs and other barriers to imports. Although this latter objective could be achieved by the country acting unilaterally without waiting for its partners to reciprocate, a negotiated agreement, in which the benefits from improved access for exports helps offset possible pain resulting from increased import competition, is important for internal reasons. Where the government can offer some producers better markets for their exports, alongside lower prices for consumers, it becomes easier to resist pressure from import-competing industries to retain existing tariffs and non-tariff barriers.

Multilateralism and regionalism are two different ways of bringing this about. Over the past half century, the main forum for achieving multilateral liberalisation has been the GATT, which in 1995 was brought within the ambit of the newly created World Trade Organisation. Under the GATT, substantial progress has been made in bringing about freer trade in industrial products, particularly where trade takes place among the advanced industrialised countries. GATT was somewhat less successful in containing the growth of non-tariff forms of protection that in some cases, resulted from ambiguity in the rules governing the use of contingent protection such as safeguards and anti-dumping. GATT also suffered from having no organisational existence and enjoying only a provisional basis. It was these considerations that led to the decision to create the WTO in 1995 and to equip the WTO with a more effective mechanism for resolving disputes between members.

Disillusionment with the ability of GATT to meet the interests of some countries may have contributed to the growth of regionalism in the second half of the 1980s and 1990s. Because regional trading arrangements involve discrimination against countries that are not members of the grouping, they potentially conflict with the aims of GATT. At the theoretical level, the main concern is whether preferential trading areas lead to net trade creation or trade diversion. However, there is a further issue involved. This concerns whether regional trading arrangements impede the attempts of the GATT/WTO to bring about global free trade or assist it. Arguments exist on both sides. No firm conclusion can be reached in either direction. What is clear, however, is that regionalism has become a popular option for many countries in recent years. A task for the WTO is to ensure that the large number of new discriminatory arrangements of this kind that have sprung up in recent years, are made compatible with the goal of global free trade.

Notes for Further Reading

For a text on international trade policy, the reader should consult the following:

Grimwade N. *International Trade Policy: A Contemporary Analysis*, (London: Routledge, 1996).

A more detailed text written from a legal perspective is:

Trebilock M. and Howse R., *The Regulation of International Trade: Political Economy and Legal Order*, 2nd edn. (London: Routledge, 1995).

For an assessment of the Uruguay Round, the interested reader should consult:

Schott J.J., *The Uruguay Round: An Assessment* (Washington DC: Institute for International Economics, 1994).

For an assessment of the issues likely to dominate a new round of multilateral trade negotiations, the reader should consult:

World Economy, Vol. 22, No. 9, December, 1999, *Bonus Issue: Towards the Millennium Round: A View from Europe*.

For a text on regionalism, the reader should use:

El-Agraa Ali M. *et al.*, *Economic Integration Worldwide* (Basingstoke and London: Macmillan, 1997).

Anderson Kym and Blackhurst Richard (eds.), *Regional Integration and the Global Trading System* (Hemel Hempstead: Harvester Wheatsheaff, 1993).

Chapter 10

Trade in Services

CHAPTER OUTLINES: Introduction. The Importance of Services in the Domestic Economy – defining services, size of the services sector. Importance of Services in International Trade – defining trade in services, measuring trade in services, reasons for the growth of trade in services, geographical distribution of trade in services. Determinants of Trade in Services. Liberalising Trade in Services. The Uruguay Round Negotiations. Trade-Related Intellectual Property Rights. Conclusion.

Introduction

In Chapter 1, we saw that a significant proportion of world trade consists of trade in services as opposed to goods. The post-war era has witnessed a major growth of service activity within the advanced industrialised countries of the world. Well over one-half of the Gross Domestic Product of most developed market economies is now contributed by what is loosely termed the 'service sector'. This represents a major transformation in the structure of economic activity within these countries. The relative decline of manufacturing and the rise of services has been variously described as a process of *de-industrialisation* or, perhaps less emotively, as *post-industrialisation*.

Although many services are non-tradable, service trade accounts for a large and probably growing proportion of world trade. The World Trade Organisation has estimated that 19.8% of world exports and 20.4% of world imports are accounted for by commercial services (WTO, 1996). Exports of services constitute an important source of export earnings for a number of developed countries and quite a few developing countries also. For these reasons, any book concerned with the changing pattern of world trade must concern itself with trade in services and not just with trade in goods.

Although it is not always possible to distinguish a good from a service, there is value to be gained from discussing trade in services separately from trade in goods. To begin with, for a variety of reasons that will be explored in this chapter, the manner in which many services are traded differs from trade in goods. The determinants of trade in services may also differ from trade in goods. Then, too, the factors that impede trade in services are generally different. Trade in services tends to be reduced by the regulatory laws of countries that deny foreign service-providers access on the same terms as domestic service providers.

Border controls such as tariffs and non-tariff barriers are less important because many services cannot be traded across borders in the same way as goods.

This chapter begins with a discussion of how goods may be distinguished from services and the factors that account for the rise of the 'service economy' within the advanced industrialised countries over the last half-century. This is followed by a discussion of the growth of trade in services that is linked with a growing tendency in recent decades towards an internationalisation of service activity. In the service sector especially, trade complements rather than substitutes for FDI. Moreover, much of trade and FDI in services takes the form of intra- as opposed to inter-industry exchange. Next, there follows a discussion of the problems involved in measuring the true extent of services trade. The best available data on trade flows are examined and an attempt made to analyse the most important geographical and sectoral trends in service trade. The next section of the chapter discusses trade liberalisation in the services sector including the new General Agreement on Trade in Services (GATS) negotiated in the Uruguay Round and now incorporated in the rules of the World Trade Organisation (WTO). Finally, the chapter concludes with a brief discussion of the subject of trade-related intellectual property rights, as a particular form of services trade that was also the subject of negotiations in the Uruguay Round and gave rise to a second WTO agreement.

The Importance of Services in the Domestic Economy

Defining Services

What are services and how do they differ from goods? Most writers who have grappled with this issue have emphasised at least four characteristics of services that distinguish them from goods – *intangibility, invisibility, transience* and *non-storability*. Unfortunately, not all activities that we generally regard as services, possess each one of these features although many do. Although many services are intangible, not all are. A meal served in a restaurant, although treated as a service, is no less tangible than a ready-made meal bought in a supermarket. Although the results of many service activities may be invisible, some are very plain to see. For example, the results of a visit to the hairdresser should be visible if it is worth the expense! Although many service activities may not last very long (e.g. a check-up at a dentist), many do (e.g. a flight from London to Brisbane). Although, because they are transient, many services cannot be stored in the same way as a product, this is not true of all services. For example, loading software onto a personal computer enables the user to store a particular programme and to use it repeatedly on a number of occasions. The modern fax machine and electronic mail have made it possible to store information for long periods of time and make repeated use of the service provided.

One attempt to get closer to the real difference between a good and a service has emphasised the *outcome* of a service activity. T.P. Hill has defined a service as:

> a change in the condition of a person, or of a good belonging to an economic unit, brought about by the activity of another economic unit with the former's consent (Hill, 1977).

By way of contrast, he defines a good as:

> a physical object which is appropriable and therefore transferable between units.

Thus, a service activity is one which effects change either in a person's condition (such as a haircut, a visit to the dentist, a medical check-up, a visit to the theatre or attendance at a musical concert) or in the state of a product (such as the storing of goods in a warehouse, the distribution of goods by a retailer or wholesaler, the transportation of goods by air, sea or rail, providing insurance to protect producers of goods against loss or the financing of the production or purchase of goods by a bank). This approach to defining services has been criticised as placing too much emphasis on the effects from the performance of a service activity. After all, do all service activities effect change? A student may attend a course on Economics with no discernible effect on his or her condition! At the same time, the consumption of many goods (e.g., eating food or drinking alcohol or smoking cigarettes) also changes the condition of the consumer.

A better approach might, therefore, be to focus on the *process* itself, as Nicolaides (1989) has suggested. He defines a service as:

> an agreement or undertaking by the service-provider to perform now or in the future a series of tasks over a specified period of time towards a particular objective.

Whereas a service is a process, a good is an object. When consumers enter into a transaction which involves the exchange of money for a physical object such as a washing machine, television set or groceries from the local supermarket, what takes place is, unquestionably, the purchase of a good. However, if instead, consumers exchange money in return for the performance of a process, such as the washing of their laundry, the hiring of a television or paying for access to certain television channels or the buying of a meal at a restaurant, a sale of a service takes place. The buyer is paying the provider to carry out on their behalf a series of activities rather than to supply them with a physical object, although the use of a physical object for a period of time (as with hiring a television set) may be part of the service provision. Nicolaides has argued that the difference lies in the nature of the transaction that takes place between economic agents. Specifically, whether the transaction entails the acquisition of a physical object (as in the case of a good) or a contract requiring one of the economic agents to perform a series of tasks on its behalf (in the case of a service).

The problems involved in distinguishing goods from services create problems when measuring the true extent of service activity within national economies. How should the value added by different suppliers be assigned? Do they belong to the services or the goods sector? It is not too difficult to decide where to classify the activities of law companies, accountancy firms, retailers, airlines or banks. All would agree that these are essentially service-providers. However, many goods producers also engage in service activities, the sales from which are subsumed in overall sales such that no distinction may be drawn between the two activities. This will result in the underestimation of the actual amount of service activity taking place within the economy. One aspect of this concerns the practice of some large firms performing certain kinds of services in-house rather than buying-in the particular service from outside firms. For example, large companies may employ their own lawyers, accountants or computer programmers rather than purchasing these services from outside firms. To the extent that this happens, the true extent of the service economy will be underestimated. Conversely, should a tendency develop for firms to contract out service activities that were previously performed in-house (e.g. catering services, cleaning services, child care, health care, etc), the growth of the service economy will be exaggerated.

The Size of the Services Sector

How important is the service sector in the economies of different countries? Much depends on the method of measurement used. One approach is to measure the contribution of services to total output or GDP. In the United Kingdom, this rose from 53% in 1970 to 67% in 1995. An alternative method is to measure the share of services in total employment. Table 10.1 shows the importance of services in the total employment of the United Kingdom and the changes in employment which have taken place in recent years.

In 1997, the service sector accounted for over three-quarters of total employment, whereas manufacturing employed only 18% of the labour force. Moreover, over the period from 1980 to 1997, employment in services rose by 1.2% a year, whereas employment in manufacturing fell by 2.7% a year. In terms of total employment, the biggest group of service activities was those supplied by government (education, hospitals, health care and welfare services). However, the fastest growth occurred in business services and finance, where employment grew at a rate of 2.9% a year.

A similar trend was apparent in other advanced industrialised countries. Table 10.2 shows the share of services in both employment and GDP of six industrialised countries over the period since 1960. On average, services accounted for about two-thirds of GDP and employment. In terms of both GDP and employment, the United States had the largest service sector, followed closely by France. By way of contrast, Japan had a somewhat smaller service sector than the other five countries. In all six countries, the share of the services sector in both GDP and employment has increased over the period since 1960.

This growth in the size of the service economy within the advanced industrialised economies has led many writers to talk of a new phase of *post-industrialisation*. The possibility has been raised that, if a further shrinking of the manufacturing goods sector should take place within these countries, their economic structure might be transformed into one largely based on service provision. However, for a variety of reasons, it may be too soon to make such a prognosis. First, a large proportion of service activity is directly related to the production of goods; for example, transport, wholesale distribution, retail distribution and financial services. Second, as we observed earlier, the growth in the importance of many producer services is due to a tendency for firms to

Table 10.1 The Importance of Different Service Industries in Total Employment, 1980–1997

	Annual percentage change 1980–97	*Percentage share*		
		1980	*1990*	*1997*
Manufacturing sector	−2.7	28.1	20.6	18.0
All services, of which:	1.2	61.6	71.4	76.0
Distribution, hotels & catering	1.0	19.4	21.5	23.0
Business services and finance	2.9	10.8	15.4	17.6
Transport, storage & communications	−0.6	6.5	6.1	5.9
Government and other services	1.0	24.9	28.4	29.5

Source: Adapted from Julius and Butler (1998).

Table 10.2 The Share of Services in Employment and GDP, 1960–1993 (percentage)

	Share of GDP	*Share of Employment*
United Kingdom		
1960	53.8	47.6
1974	60.1	55.1
1984	62.6	65.1
1996	61.3	68.3
United States		
1960	57.9	56.2
1974	62.9	63.4
1984	65.7	68.2
1996	72.9	73.7
Japan		
1960	42.7	41.3
1974	49.7	50.1
1984	55.5	56.3
1996	64.3	58.9
Germany		
1960	41.0	39.1
1974	51.2	46.3
1984	57.7	54.1
1993	64.6	56.7*
France		
1960	50.4	39.9
1974	56.6	49.9
1984	65.3	59.3
1996	67.3	70.2
Italy		
1960	46.4	33.5
1974	52.1	43.2
1984	59.8	53.6
1996	64.3	63.4

Source: OECD, various issues.
* 1991

contract out specialist activities previously performed in-house. This is a process that Bhagwati (1984) has termed *splintering* and which is thought to account for much of the reported increase in service activity. Since it amounts to no more than a reclassification of an activity which was performed just as much before as after, it constitutes a largely spurious increase in the extent of service activity taking place. Third, our discussion of the difference between a service and a good raises doubts about the meaningfulness of any attempt to draw a clear line of demarcation between the two sectors.

On the other hand, it may be equally possible that official statistics under-record the growing importance of services. One reason for this is the growth of the so-called *hidden economy*. Many services may be performed by self-employed workers but not declared in order to escape paying tax. Higher rates of personal taxation have encouraged this trend. It is also likely that the reduction in the length of the working week and the accompanying growth in the amount of leisure time available to households has caused more people to perform services for themselves (e.g. house repairs, decorating, gardening, servicing the car, etc.) rather than pay others to do so. Equally, the tendency towards splintering in certain branches of manufacturing has been offset partly by a counter tendency for large firms to perform certain service activities (e.g. accountancy, legal advise, computer programming) from within the firm. As some large manufacturing firms have sought to diversify the range of their activities by acquiring service firms, the service economy may appear smaller than is actually the case.

One of the fastest growing spheres of service activity has been the growth in the importance of what might be called *information-intensive* services, such as computer programming, telecommunications, satellite broadcasting, the Internet, etc. The main reason for this has been the giant leap that has taken place in technological knowledge in sectors such as data processing and telecommunications. Closely connected with these changes has been the growth in the importance of financial services (banking, insurance, securities trading, etc.). As the growth of these kinds of services has, in part, resulted from technological change in the goods sector of the economy, it may be argued that this is hardly a symptom of de-industrialisation. Rather, it may be more useful to talk in terms of a *softening* process taking place in the industrial structure of advanced industrialised countries. This may be described as a tendency for the software element within all economic activities to grow relative to the hardware content. Nevertheless, the result is still a real increase in the importance of service jobs within the economy.

Another reason often given for the growth of the services sector is the high income-elasticity of demand for certain kinds of consumer services. As per capita incomes rise, household demand for services grows proportionately more than their demand for goods. For example, as people enjoy higher incomes and more leisure time, the demand grows rapidly for services that fill leisure time, such as entertainment, hotels and catering, travel, sports facilities, cable TV, etc. In addition, rising per capita incomes may give rise to an increased demand for goods that have high service inputs. For example, many consumer-durable goods (e.g. motor cars) which can be afforded only with a certain level of income require extensive after-sales service. Other goods whose demand is also a function of rising incomes require for their use the purchase of additional software (e.g. personal computers, televisions, telephones, etc.). It is, therefore, perhaps surprising to find that consumer services have not been among the fastest growing area of service employment. For example, in the UK, consumer expenditure on services appears to have grown no faster than expenditure on goods (Bank of England, 1985). One reason for this may have been a tendency for the prices of services to rise faster than the prices of goods causing households to buy fewer services relative to goods. Another explanation is a tendency for wants, that were previously satisfied by unmeasured services performed within households (e.g. washing the laundry, doing the washing-up, sweeping the floor, cleaning the car, cooking the food, etc.), to be satisfied by buying goods that do the work instead (e.g. washing machines, spin dryers, dishwashers, vacuum cleaners, microwaves, etc.) (Bank of England, 1985).

One of the most surprising results of cross-country comparisons is the absence of any systematic relationship between the share of services in total output or employment and a country's level of per capita income. In 1978, services in developing countries accounted for 45.2% of GDP compared with 55.3% in developed market economies. Between 1960–80, the share of the services sector in GDP in developing countries rose from 42.9 to 45.2% (UNIDO, 1988). Only in the high-income developing countries did the share fall as one would expect in countries undergoing industrialisation. One explanation for this may be a tendency for many white-collar workers employed in services in developing countries to earn considerably higher wages than manual workers. It is often the case that the contribution of the services sector to GDP is measured by the factor cost, that is, the earnings of factors used in their production. This may, therefore, inflate the importance of service activity within the economy as a whole. A further explanation may be the large numbers of workers in developing countries employed in so-called 'porterage, petty trade and personal services' to be found in developing countries. This is the result of both the high rate of population growth occurring in these countries and the large flows of migrant workers from the countryside to the towns and big cities (Ballance and Sinclair, 1983).

The Importance of Services in International Trade

Defining Trade in Services

One of the differences between the service and goods sectors is that a much smaller proportion of service output tends to be traded. This is because many (but not all) services must be produced and consumed at the same time. In the case of these kinds of services, for trade to take place either the service provider must move to where the buyer is located or the buyer must move to the country where the service provider is located. In the past, the notion of trade in respect of services has often been restricted to those kinds of services that it is possible to transfer across borders in much the same way as goods. Essentially, these are what different writers have called *separated services* (Sampson and Snape, 1985), *disembodied services* (Bhagwati, 1984) or *long-distance services* (Bhagwati, 1984). They have been so called because the service element has been separated from its original production or 'disembodied' and, instead, is contained within a good for separate sale. Obvious examples are books, scientific documents, legal documents, computer software, films, etc. A further category of services can be transferred across borders because of the emergence of new technologies. Examples are television programmes broadcast by satellite, other satellite messages, telephone or fax messages, transactions through the Internet, etc. More problematic are transport services such as civil aviation or shipping. These may be performed without any physical movement of the service provider (who remains based in the home country) or the service user (who embarks on the airline or shipping line of a foreign company without the need to move to the foreign country). For example, British Airways does not need to be established in Australia to provide a flight for Australians from Brisbane to London, although British Airways must have the right to land a jet in Brisbane and allow passengers to board for the service to be purchased.

However, as Stern and Hoekman (1987) convincingly argue, it is unduly restrictive to confine trade in services to such categories. Rather, trade in services can be deemed to take place whenever 'domestic factors receive income from non-residents in exchange for their services' (Stern and Hoekman, 1987). This broadens the definition of services to include so-called *non-separated services* or *factor services*. These are services where production and consumption take place at the same time but where either the service provider moves to where the service buyer is located or where the service buyer moves to where the service provider is located. Thus, when service buyers travel to a foreign country to buy service from service providers in the foreign country (as with tourism), factor-owners in the foreign country receive income from non-residents. Alternatively, when service providers move to a foreign country to sell services in those countries to service buyers located there, factor-owners receive an income, albeit one earned abroad, from non-residents.

Stern and Hoekman have categorised the first category as trade in *provider-located* services, as the buyer moves to where the producer is located. Apart from the obvious example of tourism, other illustrations of this kind are education (overseas students doing courses in universities or schools outside their home country) and medical treatment (foreigners receiving medical treatment at a hospital in a country other than their own). The second category Stern and Hoekman call trade in *demander-located* services as the service provider must move to where the buyer is located.

This kind of trade requires a prior movement of factors of production to the foreign country. Either capital must be invested in setting up of an overseas subsidiary to supply services in the foreign country or workers and other personnel of the firm must move to the foreign country on a permanent or temporary basis. In some cases, both are required. Obvious examples of demander-located services which require direct investment abroad by service providers are financial services such as banking and insurance (although these can be sold without a physical presence), distribution services (retailing or wholesaling) or telecommunications. Certain kinds of demander-located services may be supplied without the need for such an investment but will require a temporary or permanent movement of personnel. Examples are advertising, accountancy services, management consultancy, construction services or engineering. Where direct investment abroad is required, it is clear that a close relationship exists between trade in these kinds of service and FDI.

Figure 10.1 summarises the above typology of international service activity.

Measuring Trade in Services

Any measure of the level of trade in services requires that all these different modes of service delivery be included. Most attempts at measuring the volume of world trade in services fail to include all of these and, therefore, probably under-estimate the true magnitude of trade in services. The main source of information on the extent of a country's trade in services is contained in the Balance

	Service provider does not move	Service provider moves
Service buyer does not move	Separated or disembodied services e.g. computer software, books, transport	Demander-located services (FDI/Migration or temporary movement of personnel) e.g. banking, insurance, retailing, construction, consultancy
Service buyer moves	Provider-located services (temporary movement of people) e.g. tourism, education or medical treatment	

Figure 10.1 Typology of international service activity

of Payments statistics. The invisible receipts recorded in the balance of payments provide a measure of the value of services exported by the country, while invisible payments measure the value of services imported. Countries that belong to the International Monetary Fund (IMF) are required to collect and report these amounts according to a common system of classification. The results are published in the IMF Balance of Payments Yearbook. Invisibles have three main elements:

1. *Net income from services* measures the value of net exports of certain kinds of services grouped under six headings – namely, shipping, other transportation, passenger services, travel, other private services and other government services. Other private services comprise the incomes of temporary workers, income from royalties and other intellectual property and residual services. Residual services covers a vast range of private services including some of the fastest growing areas such as banking, insurance, telecommunications, construction, software and data processing.
2. *Net investment income on property held abroad* is the difference between gross income on property held abroad (a mixture of interest, profits and dividends derived from overseas investments) and payments of the same kind made to foreigners holding investments in the reporting country.
3. *Transfers* consist of both private transfers (including the remittances of migrant workers) and official transfers (payments abroad made by governments to cover the costs of maintaining embassies or the maintenance of armed forces abroad).

However, as Stern and Hoekman (1986) have shown, balance of payments data are inadequate for providing a true measure of the extent of trade in services for several reasons. First, a large but unknown proportion of trade in services goes unrecorded. Although this may also be true of some trade in goods, the problem is greater in the case of services because so many services are intangible. A particular problem is created by the fact that a lot of intra-firm trade in services is never counted. Second, some trade in separated services gets subsumed under the heading of trade in goods. Some of the value contained in many goods that enter into trade arises from a service activity (e.g. transport, insurance, legal and financial services). However, since there is no way of distinguishing this from the value created by non-service activity, all trade is treated as merchandise trade. In the United States, the Office of Technology Assessment (OTA) estimated that U.S. balance of payments data under-recorded the extent of trade in services by between 45 and 100% (Stern and Hoekman, 1986). Third, some trade in provider-located services is not included in balance of payments data. Although tourism is so recorded, earnings from education and medical services purchased by non-residents are often not reported. Fourth, trade in demander-located services involves foreign direct investment. It is the flow of income accruing to service firms from their overseas investments that measures the value of trade in such services. However, balance of payments data do not distinguish between goods-related and service-related investment. Moreover, because some of the earnings of overseas subsidiaries are re-invested and not repatriated to the parent company, the net income from abroad of service firms would still fail to fully measure income from these activities. Furthermore, such flows of income, if they were known, could probably be affected by transfer price manipulation and therefore be inaccurate.

Drawing on the Balance of Payments statistics provided by the IMF, the World Trade

Organisation (WTO) now provides the best source of information regarding world trade in services. The WTO measures world trade in 'commercial services' comprised of the following:

1. *Transportation services* – sea, air and other forms of transport concerned with the carriage of both goods and people.
2. *Travel* – defined as 'goods and services acquired by personal travellers, for health, education or other purposes'.
3. *Other private services*, which breaks down further into:
   - Communication services (telecommunications, postal and courier services)
   - Construction services
   - Insurance services (freight, other insurance, agents commissions)
   - Financial services
   - Computer and information services (including news agency services)
   - Royalties and licenser fees connected with trade in intellectual property rights such as patents, copyright, trademarks, industrial design, franchises
   - Other business services, including operational leasing, legal services, accounting, management consultancy, advertising, market research, engineering, etc.
   - Personal culture and recreational services, including audio-visual services.

Up until 1995, commercial services had included labour income but this is now treated separately. In 1994, transportation services accounted for roughly 30% of world exports of services, travel services for another 30% and 'other private services' for 40% (WTO, 1995). Data published by the WTO show that between 1984 and 1994 world trade in commercial services increased from $402 billion to $1099 billion or by $697 billion. This represents an increase of 173% or 17.3% per annum. In comparison, world merchandise exports grew by 11.6% per annum over the same period. However, the WTO warns that the recorded figures almost certainly understate the importance of services trade.

Reasons for the Growth of Trade in Services

It is, of course, true that some of the growth of services trade mirrors the growth of the service economy *within* the advanced industrialised countries of the world. This, however, can only provide a partial explanation, given that many services supplied domestically are not widely traded internationally. Accompanying the growth of service activities within the industrialised countries of the world, another process has been at work that has promoted the growth of cross-country *trade* in services. In many service industries, service provision has become increasingly internationalised. In the case of separated, non-factor services, this has taken the form of increased cross-border trade of a kind that is not so different from increased trade in goods. Perhaps the most important causal factor at work in this process has been the major technological changes taking place in data processing and communications discussed above. These advances have made possible the transmission of a much greater volume of information at a more rapid pace and at lower cost than was possible before. This has had an especially big impact on those service industries (e.g. banking and financial services such as securities trading) which rely heavily on the trans-border transmissions of data. These are precisely the kinds of services where trade has grown most rapidly. At the same time, cheaper and better world-wide communication has made it easier for service firms to interact with remote buyers often reducing the need for physical movement.

Technological change has had another effect on the services sector. It has increased the element of fixed costs in service provision which, in turn, has meant that many services can be provided more cheaply if supplied on a global rather than domestic scale. For example, the costs of technology development or the provision of training infrastructure may give advantages to global service firms over those that are purely domestically orientated. The growth of global banking is in part the result of the considerable cost savings available to banks from operating on a world-wide basis. On the demand side, Porter (1990) argues that service needs in different countries have become more alike. This has fostered the growth of the global service firm which is able to provide the same service in several different countries, modified a little to take account of national differences. The internationalisation of the fast-food industry reflects the fact that the demand for the service offered by companies such as MacDonalds or Kentucky Fried Chicken is the same across the world. Service buyers have also become more mobile and therefore, better informed and so able to seek out the best services available internationally. At the same time, marked differences exist in the cost, quality and range of services available in different countries so that, when barriers to trade are lowered, considerable scope exists for increased trade and specialisation.

In part, too, the growth of services is a consequence of the growth of merchandise trade and the internationalisation of production. An important group of service activities – mainly, transport and distribution – are concerned with bringing goods produced in one part of the world to buyers in another part. The demand for these services has increased rapidly as world merchandise trade has grown. At the same time, the trend in recent decades towards integrated production within the multinational company has not only promoted increased trade in intermediate goods, but also stimulated a demand for supporting services. The growth of air travel is, partly, the cause and, partly, the consequence of the growth of the global service firm. The increased complexity of co-ordinating the production process has created an increased demand for other types of services, for example, management consultancy, computer programming, etc. Multinational companies are also more aware of differences in the costs and quality of services provided in different parts of the world and better able to search out the best deal. This, too, makes it incumbent on firms supplying certain kinds of services to business to strive for a global presence.

The Geographical Distribution of Trade in Services

Table 10.3 shows the importance of services in the trade of different countries and the rate of expansion of service exports over the period 1984–94. The importance of services exports in the total trade of different countries is measured by the ratio of services exports to merchandise exports expressed as a percentage. Among the advanced industrialised countries, the United States, France, the United Kingdom, Italy, the Netherlands and Belgium–Luxembourg all have high levels of service trade relative to goods trade. Other countries with heavy dependence on services for export earnings include Austria, Spain, Norway and Switzerland. However, it is noteworthy that several newly industrialising countries such as Hong Kong, Singapore and Mexico all have relatively high service export ratios. In terms of the rate of growth of service exports, the fastest growth occurred in the South East Asian economies. Hong Kong, Taiwan, China, South Korea and Singapore all enjoyed rapid growth in service exports. The United States, Austria,

Table 10.3 The Importance of Services Trade and Its Rate of Expansion in Different Countries

Country	*Value of merchandise exports 1994 ($ billion)*	*Value of services exports 1994 ($ billion}*	*Ratio of exports-to-merchandise exports (%)*	*Rate of growth of services exports 1984–94 (%) per annum*
United States	512.5	178.2	34.77	21.11
Germany	424.0	63.1	14.88	14.50
Japan	397.0	57.2	14.41	17.63
France	234.8	91.8	39.10	16.82
United Kingdom	205.0	57.5	28.05	11.58
Italy	189.5	59.4	31.35	23.59
Canada	165.4	17.6	10.64	11.49
Netherlands	155.1	39.6	25.53	17.58
Hong Kong	151.5	32.5	21.45	35.77
Belgium–Luxembourg	140.1	40.6	28.98	26.70
China	121.1	12.5	10.31	32.59*
Singapore	96.8	25.7	26.55	19.75*
Korea, Rep. of	96.0	18.8	19.58	21.83
Chinese Taipei	92.9	13.5	14.53	40.80
Spain	73.1	35.0	47.88	18.11
Switzerland	70.3	20.3	28.88	17.83
Sweden	61.3	13.4	21.60	11.55
Mexico	60.8	14.4	23.68	15.50
Norway	34.7	13.0	37.46	8.55
Austria	47.6	29.3	61.55	22.54

Source: Drawn from GATT (1995).

Belgium–Luxembourg and Italy also experienced above-average rates of growth.

Table 10.4 shows the share of different countries in world trade in services. Table 10.4 shows the value of world exports and imports for three categories of services – transportation, travel and other commercial services – accounted for by the top fifteen countries. These account for over two-thirds of world trade in all three categories. For *transportation services* (mainly shipping, civil aviation and road haulage), the world's largest net exporters were the United States ($2.5 billion), the Netherlands ($3.4 billion), Hong Kong, Belgium–Luxembourg ($2.1 billion) and Norway ($2.0 billion). For *travel services*, the world's largest net exporters were the United States ($24.2 billion), France ($10.9 billion), Italy ($11.5 billion), Spain, Austria ($3.6 billion), Switzerland ($1.9 billion), China, Singapore, Mexico, Australia and Thailand. Finally, for *other commercial services*, the world's largest net exporters were the United States ($26.5 billion), France ($9 billion), the United Kingdom ($17 billion), Belgium–Luxembourg ($2.9 billion), the Netherlands ($2.1 billion), Austria ($2.7 billion), Switzerland, Singapore ($5.3 billion) and Hong Kong ($20 billion). Among the developed countries, the major net exporters of services were the United States, followed by the United Kingdom (other commercial services), France (travel and other commercial services), the Netherlands (transport and other commercial services), Belgium–Luxembourg (transport and

Table 10.4 The Share of Various Countries in World Exports and Imports of Commercial Services, 1994

Exports	*Value in billion $*	*% Share of world exports*	Imports	*Value in billion $*	*% Share of world imports*
A. Transportation Services					
United States	43.6	16.1	United States	41.1	12.7
Japan	20.3	7.5	Japan	31.7	9.8
France	17.2	6.4	Germany	22.1	6.8
Netherlands	17.2	6.4	Italy	18.6	5.8
Germany	17.1	6.3	France	18.0	5.6
United Kingdom	15.3	5.6	United Kingdom	16.2	5.0
Italy	12.8	4.7	Netherlands	13.8	4.3
Hong Kong	11.9	4.4	Korea, Rep. of	7.9	2.4
Belgium–Luxembourg	8.4	3.1	China	7.6	2.4
Korea, Rep. of	8.1	3.0	Chinese Taipei	6.4	2.0
Norway	7.5	2.8	Belgium–Luxembourg	6.3	1.9
Denmark	6.1	2.3	Thailand	5.9	1.8
Spain	5.0	1.9	Denmark	5.8	1.8
Russian Fed.	4.7	1.7	Australia	5.7	1.8
Australia	4.5	1.7	Norway	5.5	1.7
Above 15	199.7	73.7	Above 15	212.6	65.8
B. Travel Services					
United States	68.7	20.5	United States	44.5	13.9
France	24.8	7.4	Germany	41.9	13
Italy	23.9	7.1	Japan	30.7	9.6
Spain	21.6	6.4	United Kingdom	22.3	6.9
United Kingdom	15.2	4.5	France	13.9	4.3
Austria	13.1	3.9	Italy	12.4	3.9
Germany	11.1	3.3	Canada	10	3.1
Hong Kong	8.3	2.5	Austria	9.5	2.9
Switzerland	8.3	2.5	Netherlands	9.4	2.7
China	7.3	2.2	Hong Kong	8.7	2.7
Singapore	7.2	2.1	Belgium–Luxembourg	7.8	2.4
Canada	7.1	2.1	Chinese Taipei	7.6	2.4
Mexico	6.4	1.9	Russian Fed.	7.1	2.2
Australia	6.1	1.8	Switzerland	6.4	2
Thailand	5.8	1.7	Mexico	5.3	1.7
Above 15	234.9	70	Above 15	237.5	73.9
C. Other Commercial Services					
United States	66.0	15.3	Japan	43.1	10.7
France	47.0	10.9	United States	39.5	9.8
Japan	33.0	7.7	France	38.0	9.4

(*Continued*)

Table 10.4 (Continued)

Exports	*Value in billion $*	*% Share of world exports*	*Imports*	*Value in billion $*	*% Share of world imports*
United Kingdom	29.7	6.9	Germany	35.7	8.9
Germany	26.7	6.2	Italy	27.0	6.7
Belgium–Luxembourg	22.7	5.3	Belgium Luxembourg	19.8	4.9
Italy	22.5	5.2	Netherlands	17.6	4.4
Netherlands	19.7	4.6	United Kingdom	12.7	3.2
Austria	12.9	3.0	Canada	12.6	3.1
Switzerland	12.3	2.9	Austria	10.2	2.5
Singapore	11.6	2.7	Spain	9.1	2.3
Hong Kong	11.2	2.6	Korea, Rep. of	7.8	1.9
Canada	8.8	2.0	Chinese Taipei	7.1	1.7
Korea, Rep. of	7.4	1.7	Sweden	5.7	1.4
Spain	7.1	1.6	Singapore	5.3	1.3
Above 15	338.6	78.7	Above 15	291.2	72.2

Source: WTO (1996).

other commercial services), Italy (travel) and Austria (travel and other commercial services). Other West European countries had strength in particular services such as Norway in shipping and Spain and Switzerland in travel. Of the developed market economies, Japan and Germany were net importers for all three categories of services.

Several newly industrialising countries are also net exporters of particular services. These include Hong Kong (transport and other commercial services), South Korea (transportation services), China (travel services), Singapore (travel and other commercial services), Mexico (travel services) and Thailand (travel services). Several of these countries have experienced the fastest rates of growth in service exports in the world in recent years. In *transportation services*, for example, the Republic of Korea doubled her share of world trade between 1985 and 1994, while Hong Kong's share also rose dramatically. In *travel services*, China experienced a faster growth in exports than any other country, more than doubling her share between 1985 and 1994. In *other commercial services*, all the East Asian countries performed well. Singapore nearly doubled her share of world exports of commercial services between 1985 and 1994, while Hong Kong also experienced a large increase. In the four years from 1990 to 1994, Korea's exports of commercial services grew at a faster rate than in any other country.

Clearly, trade in services is important for many newly industrialising, as well as industrialised, countries. Service exports account for a large proportion of the export earnings of a number of developing countries. Moreover, many of these countries are important net exporters of services to the rest of the world. However, it is the case that, in their trade in services with developing countries, the developed countries have traditionally enjoyed a net surplus. One explanation for this is that exports of services tend to be either capital-intensive (e.g. shipping) or knowledge-intensive (e.g. financial services). That favours developed countries that are richly endowed with these resources. Empirical studies also show that countries well endowed with physical and human capital enjoy a comparative advantage in service trade (Sapir and Lutz, 1981). However, as was observed in previous chapters, some NICs have abundant supplies of these resources. The NICs of East Asia have, as a consequence of several decades of saving and investment, become rich in the knowledge and skills required for success in a growing range of service industries. Other developing countries, however, will continue to be large net importers of services from the industrialised world.

The Determinants of Trade in Services

How readily can the tools of conventional trade theory be applied to the analysis of trade in services? In orthodox trade theory, countries will specialise in those products in which they enjoy a comparative cost advantage and exchange these for goods in which other countries have a comparative advantage. This enables both countries to enjoy a larger bundle of the two goods than is available in the absence of trade. Is this also true of services? Hindley and Smith (1994) have argued that there is no fundamental difference between trade in goods and trade in services. The theory of comparative advantage can be equally applied to both sectors.

Deardorff (1985), however, has shown that there are some differences between trade in services and in goods that may create difficulties when applying the principle of comparative advantage to trade in services:

1. Many services are supplied in order to make possible trade in goods (e.g. transport), that is, they complement trade in goods. This means that, in the absence of trade, these services would not be supplied at all, which makes it impossible to compare post-trade with pre-trade prices to measure the gains from trade in the same manner as with goods. This does not render the principle of comparative advantage invalid but it does make it impossible to measure the gain from trade in the same way as for goods. Moreover, since the pre-trade prices of services is non-existent, it is not possible to predict the pattern of trade, that is, which country will export services and which goods.
2. As was observed above, certain kinds of services require the movement of factors (capital and labour) for trade to take place. These are the so-called factor or non-separated services. Such trade involves trade in factor services rather than in goods. However, the result is the same. Countries specialise in those factor services in which they have a comparative cost advantage. Thus, if a country has a relative abundance of skilled labour and certain kinds of service activity are intensive in skilled labour, that country can be expected to export factor services that are skilled labour-intensive.
3. Some factor services are supplied without physical movement. For example, a management consultant may be able to advise a company located in another country by telephone, fax message or messages passed by electronic mail and, therefore, need not maintain a physical presence in the foreign country. However, the determinants of specialisation are the same as where the service provider moves to the foreign country. A country well endowed with 'management' (a special type of skilled labour) will enjoy a comparative advantage in the export of 'management services' such as consultancy.

Despite these difficulties, the principle of comparative advantage can be applied to trade in services. However, a characteristic of many service industries is that they operate under conditions of increasing returns to scale and are sold under imperfect competition. This complicates applying orthodox models of trade to the service sector. Because the provisions of certain kinds of services require heavy fixed costs, unit costs typically fall with output. The growing importance of information technology in many service industries has meant that these services have become more capital-intensive (e.g. banking and financial services). At the same time, the replication of the same service across space permits sizeable savings in unit costs, resulting in economies of scope. In addition, externalities play an important role in some forms of service provision. For example, the creation of a telephone network in a particular area brings increased revenues not only to the company establishing the network but potentially to other companies which make use of the network to make connections for their own customers. Cases of natural monopoly can also be found in some services such as telecommunications or transport (railways). In other cases, the market structure is highly oligopolistic with the market dominated by a small number of large service providers (e.g. banking or transport services). Also, the service supplied by a particular service industry is rarely if ever homogeneous. On the contrary, by the very nature of a service, there exist important differences between the service provided by one firm and another. Invariably, this takes the form of real or perceived quality differences that allow the consumer to choose among alternative suppliers. Competition often takes the form, not only of classical price competition, but attempts by service firms to differentiate their service from that of their rivals.

The fact that the market for many services is imperfectly competitive and that service firms face decreasing average costs means that a high level of intra-industry trade is to be expected in the services sector. In the case of demander-located factor services, however, this will take the form of intra-industry FDI. Intra-industry trade is very difficult to measure for the services sector because disaggregated data for either bilateral or multilateral trade flows are often not available. Data for intra-industry FDI for demander-located factor services are even more difficult to obtain at the required level of aggregation. We, therefore, do not know the exact importance of such trade. Clearly, however, to the extent that trade in services does take the form of intra-industry trade, conventional models of trade will be of limited use in explaining trade flows among countries. In recent years, a number of models of trade have been developed by theorists that include a service sector, while introducing assumptions of imperfect competition. In some cases, services are treated as complementary to goods (e.g. Kierzkowski, 1986; Markusen, 1989; Francois, 1990). In others, they are treated as a trade channel separate from that of goods (e.g. Jones and Ruane, 1990; Melvin, 1989). Sapir (1994) gives a useful survey of these models. On the whole, these models succeed in showing that models similar to those used to explain trade in goods, can be employed to explain trade in services, albeit modified to take account of the distinctive aspects of trade in services. They also show that, as in the goods sector, freer trade results in increased global economic welfare.

What about the determinants of specialisation in services? Are patterns of specialisation in services determined by the same factors as for goods? Neo-classical trade theory states that the basis for a country specialising in a particular activity is to be found in the factor proportions required to produce those goods and the relative factor endowments of different countries participating in trade. Various studies have been carried out to test for this relationship for services. One study carried out to test the applicability of the factor-proportions theory to trade in services found support for the view that factor endowments are an important determinant of trade in services (Sapir and Lutz, 1981). This used multiple regression analysis to explain cross-country differences in trade in several service industries and included both developed and developing countries. The results showed that countries that were abundant in physical capital had a comparative advantage in transportation services, while those that were abundant in human capital had a comparative advantage in insurance and other private services. Trade in other services was found to be largely related to the possession of technological know-how but this, in turn, was linked to the availability of human capital. However, comparative advantage was found to exist within a dynamic setting, in which the source of advantage shifted over time with changes in relative factor endowments. In another study, Langhammer (1986) similarly found that the pattern of trade in a broad group of services among a select group of developed countries and developing countries was related to relative factor endowments.

Applying the notion of competitive advantage to services (see Chapter 4), Porter (1990) emphasised the importance of a wide range of factors that give the service firms of particular countries an advantage when competing internationally. Factor conditions are important in some service activities. For example, factor conditions are clearly important in provider-located services such as tourism, education or health services. However, this is clearly not so in the case of demander-located services, as much of the personnel employed come from the country where the service is bought. On the other hand, geographical location, clearly, is an important factor in some service industries, as is illustrated by London's strength in financial services. The possession of a supply of highly skilled professional and technical workers appears also to play an important role in service competition. For example, the United States' strength in service industries such as accounting, management consulting and advertising is due, partly, to the large pool of graduates with MBAs, which, in turn, reflects investment in business training. However, Porter argues that demand conditions are the single most important determinant of national competitive advantage in services. The success that particular countries have enjoyed in certain service industries can, in large measure, be ascribed to so-called 'early mover' advantages. The existence of a strong local demand for a particular type of service enables firms in that country to gain a head-start on firms in other countries. One obvious example is the fast-food industry, which originated in the United States and in which U.S. firms occupy the leading positions in the world. A linkage exists between competitive strength in certain branches of manufacturing and in related service activities. Thus, the strong position which Italian firms occupy in design services may, in part, be due to Italy's world leadership in fashion, furnishing and design-intensive products. In financial services, the success of U.S. firms such as American Express bears some relation to the fact that U.S. consumers travel a great deal. Other factors in Porter's 'diamond' of competitive advantage, (see Chapter 4) namely, the strategy, structure and rivalry of firms within a particular country and the existence of related and supporting industries, also affect the global strength of particular countries in certain services industries.

Liberalising Trade in Services

Trade barriers in the services sector result mainly from the desire of governments to exercise a high degree of regulatory control over service provision. Thus, government regulation is far more widespread in the service than the goods sector. Nicolaides (1989) has suggested three reasons why government regulation of service provision can be justified on efficiency grounds:

1. The fact that the information available to buyers is often imperfect or incomplete. Because of the intangible nature of services and the fact that a service may only be purchased at the same time as it is provided, buyers cannot assess the quality of a service in advance of consumption. Services are an example of what economists call an 'experience good', as opposed to a 'search good' where quality can be assessed before consumption takes place. This gives rise to a problem of asymmetric information between service providers and buyers. The service provider has more information about the service than the buyer. This would seem to be particularly true of professional services like accountancy, medicine and law. The existence of asymmetric information creates a problem of 'moral hazard', namely, that the service provider can make higher profits by reducing the quality of the service provided below the perceived quality. As a result, government regulation may be needed to protect the consumer from low-quality services.

2. Regulation is also needed to deal with the *adverse selection problem* that also results from the existence of asymmetric information. Where service buyers lack sufficient information to distinguish between high-quality and low-quality service providers, high-quality service providers will suffer. This is a case of the honest being tainted by the practices of the dishonest. For example, garages that provide good quality car servicing may suffer because of the existence of disreputable garages that fail to do so. Self-regulation may be the solution. For example, associations of service providers may enter into contracts with consumers guaranteeing that certain minimum standards will be maintained by members of the association. Although self-regulation will serve to increase consumer confidence, there is the risk that some service providers will 'free ride' on the reputation of the others. For this reason, government regulation may also be needed (e.g. a system of licensing and monitoring of service providers).

3. Services sometimes suffer from a problem of *systemic failure*. This can be seen in the banking sector where the failure of one bank may have adverse effects on the entire banking system if the confidence of depositors is undermined. Regulation is needed to prevent unsound or imprudent banks from inflicting damage on competent ones. Again, self-regulation may be sufficient, for example, in ensuring that banks act prudently. However, to strengthen the confidence of investors, it may be necessary to give this legal backing. A requirement that banks contribute towards some deposit insurance scheme to protect depositors from a deposit-taking institution being forced to close its doors might be an additional way of reducing the risk of systemic failure.

Whenever governments regulate any economic activity, a potential barrier to trade exists. This is all the more so where rules differ among countries. On grounds of economic efficiency, such regulations may be desirable although the regulatory measure may not be 'efficient' if it is not sufficiently targetted at the specific market imperfection in question and/or has other adverse side effects. The problem with many forms of regulation in the service sector is they give rise to a number of undesirable distortions.

This is the case whenever regulation discriminates against a particular supplier country. The discrimination may be intentional or incidental. For example, if government-imposed rules for a particular services sector are more lenient in one country than another, service firms in the stricter country may be at a competitive disadvantage when selling services to a country with more lenient requirements. The potential may also exist for competition being distorted whenever regulatory policies leave a large measure of discretion to regulatory authorities in applying the rules to different firms. Nicolaides (1989) argues that this is more likely to be the case where a country depends on self-regulation of a particular service activity as opposed to government-imposed rules. What is far from assured, is that the end result of all service sector regulation will be increased efficiency. Very often, efficiency arguments conceal protectionist motives, that is, the desire to favour national service providers over those of other countries.

Trade liberalisation in the services sector is largely about removing forms of discrimination existing in the regulatory policy adopted by governments for individual service industries. Unlike liberalising merchandise trade, it is not primarily about removing border controls. However, just as with free trade in goods, liberalising trade in services can bring benefits for service exporters and importers alike. Service exporters enjoy improved access to foreign markets for their services, while service importers are able to purchase services at lower prices. Greater competition in domestic markets for services should also result in lower prices and better quality service provision. Countries can enjoy these benefits by unilaterally removing or lowering barriers to free trade in services. However, as with trade liberalisation in the goods sector, this may be difficult to achieve due to domestic resistance from local service firms fearful of more competition. It may be easier to overcome such resistance if, at the same time, concessions can be won from trading partners that grant improved access for service exports. In other words, a negotiated approach involving reciprocal liberalisation may be more realistic. This may be achieved within the context of a regional trading agreement (as with the European Single Market) or through multilateral negotiations (under the auspices of the GATT/WTO).

However, the method of bringing about freer trade in services must of necessity differ from that employed in the case of goods. Because of the complex and diverse forms in which trade in services is restricted, it is more difficult for countries to reach agreements on a balanced reduction in trade barriers. First, the effects of lowering any particular barrier in services are more difficult to quantify than in the case of goods. Second, very often there is more than one barrier impeding access. Moreover, as Nicolaides (1989) has shown, many barriers arise as a result of legitimate regulatory intervention by governments necessary to correct a particular form of market failure. In this case, the solution is not to remove the restriction, but to ensure that the particular form of regulatory measure does not create undesirable trade distortions by, for example, discriminating against foreign service providers. A further consideration is that, whenever regulatory policies differ among countries, trade barriers inevitably emerge in order to prevent the effectiveness of policy in the more strictly regulated country from being undermined by the less strictly regulated one. For example, in the banking sector, one country may impose stricter capital and liquidity requirements than another. To ensure that foreign banks do not undermine the effectiveness of these measures, restrictions have to be placed on their freedom to set up branches in the country with stricter requirements. These considerations may favour a dual approach. On the one hand, there may be particular service sectors where countries choose to negotiate a reciprocal lowering of existing barriers to ensure improved market access. On the other hand, a rules-based approach is also necessary in which countries agree to adhere by certain principles designed to ensure fairness and efficiency in the global allocation of resources.

As we saw in Chapter 9, GATT/WTO rules applying to trade in goods are based on the principle of unconditional *Most-Favoured Nation* (MFN) treatment which each member country is required to extend to every other. A key issue, both in academic debate and in services negotiations within GATT/WTO, has been whether or not this principle should be applied to trade in services. This would mean that each country would undertake to treat service providers of other countries equally and not to discriminate against services coming from a particular country. Grey (1990) has urged caution in applying this principle to trade in services in the same way as goods. To begin with, as we have seen in earlier chapters, there have been so many exceptions to the unconditional MFN rule as applied to goods that one must doubt whether it can practically be applied to services. He concludes: 'With regard to the concept of *unconditional MFN treatment*, there would appear to be little scope for the application of such a clause, given the emerging concern for a measure of *reciprocity,* particularly as regards services delivered by establishments'. On the other hand, he adds, it would be a serious mistake to set this key policy concept aside. Reciprocity makes non-discriminatory treatment conditional upon the other country treating service providers of the country imposing the restrictions in an equivalent way. 'I will treat your service firms in the same way as you treat mine'.

It is worth pointing out that this approach has a precedent within the GATT. It was adopted as the basis for the GATT Codes on Subsidies and Countervailing Duties and Government Procurement in the Tokyo Round. A country was only required to extend the benefits contained in the two codes to those countries adhering to the agreement and could withdraw benefits from any country that ceased doing so. It has come to be adopted as a key principle by a number of countries with respect to their service sectors. For example, the European Union has an important clause in its 1989 Second Banking Directive which threatens to withdraw certain benefits to foreign banks operating in the Single Market (e.g. suspension or delays in authorisation) that come from a country which denies national treatment to EU banks. Reciprocity is also widely practised in the civil aviation industry. For example, one country may reduce or withdraw landing rights from the carrier of another country that is deemed to be discriminating against the airline of the former in its route allocations. This was illustrated by the recent conflict between the US and Japan which began when Japan refused to allow United Airlines to extend its New York–Tokyo flights to Sydney (so-called 'beyond rights') which the US alleged violated the 1952 bilateral aviation agreement between the two countries. The US responded with threats to withdraw equivalent rights from Japanese airlines. Since countries with a fairly open policy towards their service industries (e.g. the US) are unlikely to be willing to grant guarantees of access to foreign service firms without a reciprocity proviso, unconditional MFN may be difficult to apply to services.

A second principle in any rules-based approach to the liberalisation of service trade is the *principle of national treatment*. This is the principle of treating foreign service providers in the same way as national firms. It therefore addresses a different aspect of non-discrimination. It has been suggested that this is preferable to a stipulation that countries treat all foreign, service firms equally (see Nicolaides, 1989) in view of the difficulties of applying unconditional MFN in a world where regulatory systems differ so much. The principle allows each country to continue to operate whatever regulatory system it deems appropriate subject only to the requirement that national and foreign firms are treated alike. The principle has, in the past, been extensively used in negotiating international agreements in particular service industries. For example, it is written into the so-called Chicago Convention of 1944 that established the International Civil Aviation Organisation (ICAO) regulating aviation. Countries are to afford national treatment to foreign airlines with respect to the use of airports and other facilities although it does not cover route sharing. The principle of national treatment is also established by the OECD in its Decision on National Treatment (OECD, 1978) which requires OECD countries to treat multinational companies equally with domestically owned companies once they have been established. This applies to service industries as well as manufacturing but does not specifically cover rights of establishment. The GATT itself under Article III also requires signatories to provide national treatment to products imported from other member states 'with regard to matters affecting the internal taxation and regulation of trade in goods'. This applies to goods and so cannot be applied to non-traded services, although it could be applied to 'separated services'. In many service industries, however, it seems unlikely that all countries would be prepared to agree to this principle. For example, would countries be prepared to allow foreign airlines equal rights with domestic carriers to operate domestic routes? The same may be true of shipping where many countries restrict shipping within their own territorial waters to vessels owned by domestic shipping companies.

The Uruguay Round Negotiations

The original proposal to include services in the Uruguay Round negotiations came from the United States supported by Canada, Japan and the European Community. According to McCulloch (1993), there were three groups within the US pressing for services to be included. First, there were those U.S.-based companies in the financial services sector (most notably, American Express) which were keen to secure improved access to markets abroad. Second, U.S. public officials and business people were becoming concerned about the U.S. trade deficit in manufactures, some of whom argued that U.S. comparative advantage had shifted towards services. Third, there were trade policy experts wishing to see trade liberalisation extended to services. Initially, the proposal was strongly opposed by a number of developing countries led by India and Brazil (the so-called Group of Ten). Their opposition was based on a number of considerations. First, there was a concern that free trade in services would result in a number of their service sectors (e.g. banking) falling under foreign control. Second, it was argued that many service sectors were already covered by other international agreements (e.g. shipping by the UNCTAD Liner Conference, aviation by IATA, etc.). Third, there was a fear that they would get caught in a damaging trade-off between services and manufactures with developed countries making any lowering of trade barriers on goods conditional upon a liberalisation package that included services. These countries argued that further progress was still necessary in bringing down trade barriers affecting goods before services should be included. One aspect of this was a proposal from the developed countries to offer 'roll backs' of voluntary export restraints and 'standstills' on new protection on goods of interest to developing countries as concessions. Developing countries argued that these should not be concessions but merely an acceptance of existing obligations and should not be linked to the issue of liberalisation of service trade which was a new issue.

Because of the opposition expressed by the Group of Ten to the inclusion of services, progress in negotiating freer trade in services was initially quite slow. In the end, a way of moving forward was found involving a separation of negotiations relating to goods from those pertaining to services. This so-called 'dual-track' or 'twin-track' approach (first proposed by Brazil) helped assuage the fears of developing countries of a trade-off between goods and services. When the Uruguay Round was launched in September 1986, it was agreed to create a special Group of Negotiations on Services (GNS) separate from that covering goods, although it would report to the Trade Negotiations Committee (TNC) in charge of the negotiations as a whole. When the Round was concluded at the end of 1993, the Final Act included an entirely new agreement on trade in services, which, for the first time ever, extended GATT rules and disciplines to trade in services. At the same time, the foundation was laid for making further progress in the future in opening up service markets to freer trade.

The new agreement, entitled the General Agreement on Services (GATS) established a new set of rules to govern trade in services equivalent to that existing for goods. Box 10.1 provides an outline of the GATS Agreement. As can be seen, the Agreement is divided into three parts. The first two parts set out certain general obligations and disciplines that all countries are required to enforce. These include important principles such as the MFN rule and the principle of national treatment that are important obligations in the GATT Agreement. However, there are a number of other obligations such as the principles of transparency and provisions for emergency protection designed to ensure that, as far as possible, foreign service providers are not prejudiced. With regard to the MFN rule, an important provision allows countries to exclude sectors from this obligation for a period of ten years with a review after five years. The third part of the Agreement

Box 10.1 The General Agreement on Trade in Services (GATS)

The GATS is divided into three parts:

1. *Part I and II list a set of general obligations and disciplines* which apply to any measures taken by member states which affect trade in services (except services supplied in the exercise of governmental authority). Trade in services is defined so as to cover all modes of supply. That is to say, it covers cross-border transactions (which do not require the movement of providers or consumers), services which require the movement of consumers to the country where the service is being provided, services which require the commercial presence of the service provider in the territory of another member state and services which require the temporary movement of natural persons (service suppliers or persons employed by a service supplier).

Continued

The major obligation contained in this part of the agreement is the unconditional MFN rule set out in Article II. This is defined as 'treatment no less favourable than that it accords to like services and service suppliers of any other country'. However, member states may request *temporary* exemption of a particular sector from the non-discrimination provisions of Article II. Such exemptions should not exceed a period of ten years and would be reviewed after five years.

Other general obligations include:

(a) *Transparency* (Article III): requiring each country to 'publish promptly and, except in emergency situations, at the latest by the time of their entry into force, all relevant measures of general application, which pertain to or affect the operation of this Agreement'. In addition, member states are required to establish within two years 'enquiry points' that can provide upon request information to other countries regarding measures in force.

(b) *Economic Integration* (Article V): allowing countries to enter into regional agreements involving liberalisation of service trade. The conditions are that any such agreement should have 'substantial coverage' (in terms of sectors, volume of trade affected and modes of supply) and should provide for 'the absence or elimination of substantially all discrimination...between or among the parties'. However, developing countries would be allowed greater flexibility with regard to these conditions to take account of their level of development. The same requirements for notification of such agreements to the Council for Trade in Services are stipulated as for all regional trading arrangements including provisions for periodic review.

(c) *Domestic Regulation* (Article VI): recognises a country's right to regulate but requires that 'all measures of general application affecting trade in services are administered in a reasonable, objective and impartial manner' in sectors where countries have made specific commitments. It states that 'measures relating to qualification requirements and procedures, technical standards and licensing requirements' should not 'constitute unnecessary barriers to trade in services' and provides for the future establishment and development by the Council of Trade in Services of disciplines necessary to ensure that these requirements are met.

(d) *Recognition* (Article VII): provides for member states mutually recognising through harmonisation or otherwise 'the education or experience obtained, requirements met, or licenses or certifications granted in a particular country'.

(e) *Monopolies* and Exclusive Service Suppliers (Article VIII): requires countries to ensure that monopoly service suppliers do no act in a discriminatory manner inconsistent with Article II and specific commitments made and do not abuse their monopoly power when providing a service to another country.

(f) *Business Practices* (Article IX): contains a recognition that 'certain business practices of service suppliers' can restrict competition and, if necessary, countries should seek to eliminate such practices.

(g) *Emergency Safeguards* (Article X): simply states that there shall be multilateral negotiations on the question of emergency safeguards based on the principle of non-discrimination' within three years of the Agreement entering into force.

Continued

(h) *Payments and Transfers* (Article XI): states that countries 'shall not apply restrictions on international transfers and payments for current transactions relating to its specific commitments'.

(i) *Balance of Payments Safeguards* (Article XII): allows countries to apply restrictions to trade in services in the event of a serious Balance of Payments crisis providing that the measures do not exceed those needed to deal with the crisis and providing that they do not discriminate among members. The measures must also be temporary and be phased out progressively as the situation allows.

(j) *Exceptions* (Article XIV): these are to include any measures necessary to protect public morals, maintain public order, to protect public health, to prevent fraud, protect individual privacy or ensure public safety.

(k) *Subsidies* (Article XV): recognises that subsidies may distort trade in services and provides for future negotiation of the 'necessary multilateral disciplines'.

2. *Part III* contains a list of *Specific Commitments* that countries have agreed to apply only to those service sectors and sub-sectors listed in their schedules. Article XVI sets out a country's obligations in respect of *market access*. It lists measures that a country may not adopt in sectors where market access commitments are undertaken. These include limits on the number of service suppliers, limits on the total value of service transactions, limits on the number of service operations, limits on the number of natural persons to be employed necessary for the supply of a particular service, measures that force a service supplier to supply a service through a particular legal means and limits on the percentage share of a foreign investment that may be accounted for by foreign shareholders.

Article XVII requires countries to guarantee *national treatment* for foreign service suppliers in those sectors listed in their schedules. This is defined as 'treatment no less favourable than that it accords to its own like services and service suppliers'. However, this need not mean identical treatment to that which it accords to domestic service suppliers as, in some cases, this could mean less favourable treatment for foreign service suppliers.

Article XX of Part IV makes it clear that schedules of specific commitments must specify the '(a) terms, limitations and conditions of market access; (b) conditions and qualifications of national treatment; (c) undertakings relating to additional commitments; (d) where appropriate the time-frame for implementation of such commitments; (e) date of entry into force of such commitments'.

Article XIX requires all members of the GATS to enter into successive rounds of negotiations no later than five years after the agreement comes into force to achieve a 'progressively higher level of liberalisation'. However, it specifically recognises that greater flexibility should be allowed for developing countries in the opening up of their services sectors in accordance with their 'development situation'.

3. Attached to the framework agreement, there are a number of annexes for sectors that are to be subject to special provisions. First, there is an annex of exemptions from Article II, that is, the MFN requirement. Second, there is an annex on movement of natural persons supplying services or employed by a service supplier. Third, there are sector-specific annexes for financial services, telecommunications, air transport services, basic telecommunications and maritime transport services.

contains the specific sectoral commitments made by member states in the course of the negotiations. This lists the sectors that each country has chosen to include and the commitments in respect of market access that each is prepared to make in the sectors listed. In each of the sectors included, countries must specify the extent of market access that it to be allowed (e.g. what proportion of the shares of a domestic service company may be owned by a foreign company) and any limits to be placed on national treatment (e.g. rights enjoyed by local firms that are not available to foreign firms). These commitments are then 'bound' in the same manner as a tariff under the GATT that means that any reduction in these commitments allows a country to lodge a complaint with the WTO and to seek compensation.

This three-tiered structure for the GATS conforms with what was proposed by leading experts on the subject in the early stages of the negotiations. Many countries would not have agreed to a set of general obligations to be applied to all service activities in an indefinite and unclear way. This would have been like asking countries to sign a blank cheque since the information did not exist for determining the precise effect of each obligation on all service activities. For example, few countries would have been prepared to agree to the principle of national treatment being applied to all service sectors. The preferred approach was therefore to experiment with these rules in a small number of service sectors to begin with and, in the light of that experience, seek to spread similar rules to other sectors as and when countries were ready to do so. Furthermore, it is clear that many of the rules that are desirable for most trade in services may not be workable in particular service sectors. Hence, these sectors had to be treated separately.

The main achievement of the GATS was to bring trade in services, for the first time, within the rules-based framework of the GATT/WTO. In terms of actual liberalisation measures, a start was made. All the major industrialised countries made substantial offers covering a wide range of service industries. Hoekman (1993) estimated that, by early 1993, the EU and the United States had made offers covering, respectively, two-thirds and one-half of listed service sectors. On the other hand, many of the offers took the form of commitments to maintain the status quo, rather than to eliminate any particular restriction or distortion. If sectoral coverage is calculated so as to take account of the degree of restrictiveness implied and the relative importance of different services sectors in a country's GDP as well as global GDP, this picture is confirmed (Hoekman, 1995). Hoekman estimated the proportion of sectors, in which commitments implied no restriction at all on either market access or national treatment, had a weighted average ratio of 28% for high-income countries and only 6.4% for other members. Nevertheless, the fact that existing practices were effectively bound by their incorporation in country schedules represented some progress. At least, the degree of restriction could not be arbitrarily increased as before.

Following the signing of the GATS, further negotiations took place covering three sectors – financial services, telecommunications and maritime transport services – where it had not been possible to reach agreement. Subsequently, separate agreements were negotiated for two of these sectors, financial services and telecommunications. The agreement on financial services that was concluded in December, 1997 was especially important given the extent of trade affected. Under the GATS agreement, a new round of trade negotiations must take place in the year 2000. These negotiations will constitute part of the so-called 'built-in' agenda for any new Millennium Round.

Trade-Related Intellectual Property Rights

A further aspect of trade in services that has also assumed importance in the recent multilateral trading negotiations concerns so-called intellectual property rights (IPRs). IPRs may be defined as assets that are created by the discovery of new information and that have commercial or artistic usefulness (Maskus, 1991). Just as goods can be traded across borders so can IPRs. In this way, countries are able to obtain technology available in other countries. The most important forms of IPRs are the following:

1. *Patents.* In many countries, there exist patent laws designed to protect an innovator of a new industrial product or process of manufacture from imitation. Clearly, if producers are free to imitate new products or processes discovered by another firm, little incentive exists for producers to invest in innovation. Patent laws are designed to give to innovators the sole right to produce a new product or use a new process for a specified period of time. Practice varies among countries, but in the UK and most of Europe the normal duration of a patent is 20 years from the date when the patent is filed. In the US, patents are normally granted for 17 years from the date when the grant is issued. Since it usually take 2–3 years to grant a patent, the period is more or less equivalent to that in Europe. Patents for the same product or process can be registered in more than one country. Alternatively, patents may also be sold or licensed to another producer in return for payments of royalties giving the owner of the patent a share in future profits.
2. *Copyright.* In a similar manner to patents, copyright law protects authors, musical recording artists, software writers and others against the copying of their ideas contained in the form of a book, musical recordings, computer software, paintings, etc. Generally, copyright protection runs for the author's life plus 50 years or, where there is no author, 50 years from the date of publication. Differences nevertheless exist among countries over the products that should be covered by copyright law. For example, in the recent past, there has been a dispute about whether or not the law should be applied to computer software. Enforcement practice may also differ among countries. Products which breach copyright law may be allowed to circulate more freely in some countries than in others because the former lack the means with which to outlaw illegal products.
3. *Trademarks.* In most countries, there are laws that protect the trade marks of producers from unauthorised use. The procedure is for a company to register its trade mark in each country in which it intends to make sales. Again, countries disagree on how widely to define a trademark. Should it be confined to the company logo on the product or should it embrace the distinctive physical appearance of the product? American law is much tougher in this respect than U.K. law. Should it be applied to exclude goods which are different but which use the same mark? Much depends on the objectives which trade mark law seeks to attain. The primary objective may be to protect the buyer from confusion over the true source of the good. Alternatively, trademark law may be seeking to protect the trademark owner from goods which undermine the value of the trademark in which he/she has invested money.
4. *Trade secrets* are recognised in some countries and given legal protection. A trade secret is any information belonging to a company which it does not wish to be made known to any other company. In some countries, any

good which has been manufactured and sold using illegally obtained trade secrets may be prevented from entering the market of the country extending such protection.

5. *Geographical indications*. The are place names (or words associated with a place) that are used to identify products. Well known examples are Champagne, Tequila or Roquefort. These names have become associated with a particular quality, reputation or other characteristic of the product coming from those places. For this reason, producers of these products are anxious to protect their product from cheap imitations that will undermine the quality or reputation of the original item.

The major exporters of TPRs are, not surprisingly, the advanced industrialised countries, with the United States as the main supplier to the rest of the world. In 1985, the US enjoyed a net balance on trade in technology (defined as net receipts of royalties and licence fees for the use of technological information) of $8.5 billion. The only other major net exporter was the UK with a surplus of $0.2 billion (Maskus, 1991). All other countries were net importers of technology although Japan's balance was moving towards surplus. However, a great deal of trade in intellectual property rights take places within rather than between firms. As a result, measures of direct trade in intellectual property under-estimate the true extent of such trade.

Trade-related intellectual property rights became an important issue in the Uruguay Round. The United States and other developed countries wanted an agreement providing for protection of IPRs included in the arrangements for creating a new World Trade Organisation. To begin with, this was opposed by developing countries which stood to lose revenues to the developed countries if such an agreement was reached. Developing countries argued that IPRs were already adequately covered by other international bodies, such as the World Intellectual Property Organisation (WIPO) an affiliate of the United Nations. However, a weakness of the WIPO was that a large number of countries remained outside the various international agreements that WIPO sought to enforce for protecting IPRs. In particular, many developing countries refused to recognise the concept of intellectual property rights. Furthermore, WIPO lacked any mechanism for forcing countries to adhere to agreed rules. The idea of a WTO agreement governing IPRs was that member states would be able to lodge a complaint against any country that failed to enforce IPRs and seek redress in the normal way.

Despite their reluctance to do so, the developing countries agreed to negotiate a new TRIPs agreement that would become part of the WTO. The alternative was to face retaliatory trade measures against their products by the advanced industrialised countries. The agreement which emerged after lengthy negotiations went most of the way towards meeting the demands of the developed countries. The details of the agreement are set out in Box 10.2. In essence, the agreement required all WTO member states to introduce, if they did not already exist, laws granting protection of IPRs belonging to producers resident in other WTO member states and systems for enforcing these laws in their territory. Most of the main forms of IPRs were included. Developed countries were allowed a one-year period and developing countries a five-year period from January 1, 1995, to implement these measures. The poorest least developed countries were granted an eleven-year transitional period. Once this period was completed, any WTO member who considered that the IPRs of its own producers were being infringed by another WTO member state could seek redress through the WTO. If

Box 10.2 The Trade-Related Intellectual Property Rights (TRIPs) Agreement

- *Part 1* sets *out general provisions and basic principles*. These require signatories to pass the necessary national laws so as to bring into effect the provisions of the agreement. These laws must conform with the normal WTO requirements of *national treatment* (Article III) and *most-favoured-nation treatment* (Article IV). However, there are provisions for exemptions from both requirements. For example, with regard to MFN treatment, there are so-called 'grand-fathering rights' for agreements entered into before the Uruguay Round was completed.
- *Part 2* is concerned with standards concerning the availability, scope and use of intellectual property rights. In this section, it is made clear that the agreement will cover seven categories of intellectual property:

  1. Copyright will be protected for at least 50 years and would include computer programmes and data compilation. Authors of computer programmes and cinematographic works will largely have exclusive rental rights, as will performers and producers of sound recordings and broadcasts.
  2. Trademarks (defined as 'any sign or any combination of signs, capable of distinguishing the goods or services of one undertaking from those of another') would be protected for at least seven years.
  3. Geographical indications are defined as 'indicators which identify a good as originating in the territory of a Member, or a region or locality in that region, where a given quality, reputation or other characteristic of the good is essentially attributable to its geographic origin'. This is important for wine growers who need to prevent fraudulent attribution of geographical origin.
  4. Industrial designs would be protected for at least ten years.
  5. Patents covering new products or processes would enjoy protection from the filing date for a period of twenty years regardless of the place of invention, the field of technology and whether products are imported or locally produced. The most important permitted exclusions were so-called 'patents on life' defined as 'plants and animals other than micro-organisms and essentially biological processes for the production of plants or animals, other than non-biological and microbiological processes'. These provisions created considerable controversy in the negotiations. The United States wanted greater international patent protection for life forms but this was bitterly opposed by other groups which regarded such patents as unethical. It remains unclear how far this exclusion will succeed in preventing patents on life forms from being taken out and enforced. However, there is a stipulation that these specific provisions should be reviewed four years after the agreement comes into force. Strict limits are also placed on compulsory licensing of patented products by governments. Governments may only license production of a patented good without the patent holder's consent if the patent holder refuses use of the patent on 'reasonable commercial terms and conditions' and subject to the patent holder being paid 'adequate remuneration' (Article XXXI).

Continued

6. Lay-out designs (topographies) of integrated circuits. Semi-conductor lay-out designs will be protected for ten years. Both the US and Japan have specific laws covering this area while the UK uses its copyright laws for this purpose.
7. Protection of undisclosed information. For the first time ever, trade secrets are protected from unauthorised disclosure.

- *Part 3* deals with the issue of enforcement of intellectual property rights requiring countries to put in place effective enforcement procedures to deal with the infringement of IP rights.
- *Part 4* deals with the acquisition and maintenance of intellectual property rights, that is, registration of rights, etc.
- *Part 5* deals with dispute prevention and settlement. This includes a requirement that national laws and regulations governing the protection of IPs satisfy the usual GATT requirement for transparency (Article 63). There is a provision for the notification of all such laws and regulations with and their review by a new Council for Trade-Related Aspects of Intellectual Property Rights. It also makes clear that disputes concerning IP rights will be subject to the integrated dispute settlement machinery of the World Trade Organisation (WTO). The significance of this would be the scope that it creates for 'cross sanctions' that is, retaliation on goods trade for breaches of the intellectual property agreement.
- *Part 6* deals with the transitional arrangements. Whereas developed countries are required to apply the provisions of the agreement within a year, developing countries (and economies in transition from central planning to market-based) are allowed a transitional period of five years (Article 65). Least-developed countries are not required to apply the provisions (except for the National Treatment and MFN provisions) for eleven years (Article 66). Moreover, where a developing country has to apply protection to an area of technology not currently subject to IP protection, it can delay applying patent protection for another five years over and above the five-year transitional period allowed. This was of particular significance for pharmaceutical companies in developed and developing countries since many developing countries have not in the past extended IP protection to drugs companies in the developed countries. Clearly, any drug coming on the market in the next ten years will not be affected by the provisions. However, developing countries are required to permit the filing of patents for pharmaceuticals and agricultural chemical products from the time of the agreement and to treat them in ten years time as if legislation had been in effect from the point when they came on the market (Article 70:8). Most drugs require at least ten years safety testing before they can be marketed so these provisions ensure that products invented now will receive protection. If they are marketed earlier, the patent holder would be given exclusive marketing rights in the interim (Article 70:9).
- *Part 7* of the agreement sets out the institutional provisions including the creation of a new Council for Trade-Related Aspects of Intellectual Property Rights to supervise the agreement.

necesssary, this could lead to the offending country granting compensation to the complainant. Alternatively, the offending country could face retaliation that could affect any of its exports to the offending country.

The TRIPs agreement is due for review at the start of the new century and will, therefore, be an item on the agenda for any Millennium Round. There are aspects of the protection of so-called geographical indications that require further negotiation to meet the demands of some member states. The question of intellectual property protection for bio-technological inventions and plant varieties that was left unresolved in the Uruguay Round, will be a second item. A further concern will be the need to review the extent to which member states have complied with the agreement. Developing countries, in particular, have had difficulty in doing so and will be requesting for more time in which to fulfill their obligations.

Conclusion

The rise of the service economy has been one of the most distinctive features of the structural transformation experienced by the advanced industrialised economies during the past half century. In terms of both employment and output, the services sector now dwarfs manufacturing in these countries. Hitherto, trade in services has been much less important than trade in merchandise. This was because of the characteristic of services, as requiring production and consumption to occur simultaneously. Only in so-called 'separated services' could trade take place across borders in much the same manner as with goods. Major technological changes, however, have made it possible for many kinds of services to be supplied in one part of the world, yet consumed in another. This has spawned the growth of international trade in services, such that now as much as one-fifth of world trade comprises trade in services. Other processes have been at work which have assisted this growth. The desire of service firms to exploit the economies of, both, scale and scope that were available encouraged many to internationalise their activities. The removal of restrictions on direct investment abroad has enabled and further facilitated the international expansion of many service firms. Easier and cheaper air travel has made both service providers and buyers more mobile. At the same time, the growth of merchandise trade has created an increased demand for a range of ancillary services essential for trade to take place.

This growth of trade in services has implications for trade theory. Although many conventional trade theories can be used as much to explain trade in services as goods, trade in services often takes place in markets where perfect competition is non-existent and where governments intervene heavily. Many of the newer trade theories, with their assumptions of increasing returns and product heterogeneity, seem more relevant to this kind of trade. Moreover, given that many services are delivered internationally through FDI, it becomes increasingly unrealistic to regard FDI as an alternative to trade and to compartmentalise these two forms of exploiting overseas markets. However, the growth of trade in services also has some important policy implications. Where a large and growing proportion of the exports of many countries take the form of services, the liberalisation of world trade must seek to tackle impediments to free trade in services and not just goods. In particular, countries that are major net exporters of services cannot be expected to show a willingness to further reduce barriers on goods trade if they are not offered equivalent benefits in services.

It was the recognition of this changed situation that resulted in services being included in the Uruguay Round for the first time in multilateral negotiations. The result was a new General Agreement on Services (GATS) to parallel the GATT for goods. Both agreements are now the property of the WTO and are binding on all members of the WTO. However, while GATS represents an important step towards applying rules and disciplines to trade in services, much ground has still to be covered in opening up domestic markets to foreign competition. Thus far, many countries have shown a marked reluctance to expose their domestic service sectors to the full blast of foreign competition. This is perhaps not surprising given the political sensitivity of the sectors in question. Liberalisation is further complicated by the fact that barriers to trade in services invariably take a different form to trade in goods. Mostly, they result from different regulatory practices in different countries. Liberalisation, therefore, necessitates each country making specific commitments to alter some national laws. The consequences of any such commitments are often difficult to measure, so that countries can never be sure that the concessions that they make are matched by equivalent benefits as a result of similar commitments by other trading partners. Trade in services will remain a major item on the agenda of multilateral trade negotiations in the next century. Pressures will increase from the western industrialised countries for faster progress. To the extent that these negotiations are successful, trade in services can be expected to become more important as a component of world trade in the future.

Notes for Further Reading

Few conventional textbooks on Trade include a separate chapter on Service Trade, as this is assumed to be governed by the same principles as trade in goods. However, one exception to this is:

Greenaway D. and Winters A., *Surveys in International Trade* (Oxford: Basil Blackwell, 1994).

which contains an excellent chapter (Chapter 10) by A. Sapir and C. Winters on service trade. Another useful reference is:

Porter M. *The Competitive Advantage of Nations* (London: Macmillan, 1990).

This also contains an excellent chapter on the internationalisation of service activity with some useful case studies.

On the liberalisation of trade in services, the following are essential reading:

Nicolaides P. *Liberalising Services Trade, Chatham House Papers*, (London: RIIA/Routledge, 1989).

although the book pre-dates the signing of the GATS Agreement. An additional source is:

Trebilock M.T. and Howse R., *The Regulation of International Trade*, 2nd edn. (London and New York: Routledge, 1995).

which has excellent chapters on trade in services and TRIPs.

A more recent source on trade liberalisation dealing exclusively with financial services is:

Key S.J., *Financial Services in the Uruguay Round and the WTO*, Occasional Paper 54 (Washington DC; Group of Thirty).

For statistical information on trade in services, see the WTO's *Annual Report*.

For information on the service sector in the U.K. economy, the reader should consult:

Julius DeA. and Butler J., *Inflation and Growth in a Service Economy* (Bank of England Quarterly Bulletin, November, 1998).

References

Adler, J. H. (ed.) (1967). *Capital Movements and Economic Development*. London: Macmillan.

Adler, M. (1970). Specialisation in the European Coal and Steel Community. *Journal of Common Market Studies 8*.

Agmon, T. (1979). Direct investment and intra-industry trade, substitutes or complements? In H. Giersch (ed.). *On the economics of intra-industry trade*. Tübingen: J.C.B. Mohr.

Aliber, R. Z. (1970). A theory of direct foreign investment. In C. P. Kindieberger (ed.). *The international corporation*. Cambridge, MA: MIT Press.

Allen, G. C. (1981). *The Japanese economy*. London: Weidenfeld and Nicolson.

Andersen, K. and Blackhurst, R. (eds.) (1993). *Regional economic integration and the global trading system*. Hemel Hemsptead, Herts: Harvester Wheatsheaff.

Andersen, K. and Norheim, H. (1993). In Andersen, K. and Blackhurst, R. *Regional economic integration and the global trading system*. Hemel Hemsptead, Herts: Harvester Wheatsheaff.

Aquino, A. (1978). Intra-industry trade and inter-industry specialisation as concurrent sources of international trade in manufactures. *Weltwirtschaftliches Archiv 14*(2).

Argy, V. (1996). *The Japanese economy*. London: Macmillan.

Balassa, B. (1974). Trade-creation and trade-diversion in the European Common Market. *Manchester School*, June, No. 2.

Balassa, B. (ed.) (1975). *European economic integration*. Amsterdam: North Holland.

Balassa, B. (1979). Intra-industry trade and integration of developing countries in world trade. In H. Giersch (ed.) *On the economics of intra-industry trade*. Tübingen: J.C.B. Mohr.

Balassa, B. (1981). *The newly-industrialising countries in the world economy*. Oxford: Pergamon Press.

Balassa, B. (1986). Determinants of intra-industry specialisation in United States trade. *Oxford Economic Papers*, No. 38.

Balassa, B. and Bauwens, L. (1987). Intra-industry specialisation in a multi-country and multi-industry framework. *Economic Journal 97*.

Balassa, N. and Noland, M. (1988). *Japan in the world economy*. Washington DC: Institute for International Economics.

Baldwin, R. (1971). Determinants of the commodity structure of US trade. *American Economic Review 61*.

Baldwin, R. (1997). The cause of regionalism. *World Economy 20*(7).

Ballance, A. and Sinclair, S. (1983). *Collapse and survival: Industry strategies in a changing world*. London: Allen & Unwin.

Bank of England (1985). Services in the UK economy. *Bank of England Quarterly Bulletin*, September.

Banks, G. (1983). Economics and polities of countertrade. *World Economy*, June.

Banks, G. and Tumlir, J. (1986). *Economic policy and the adjustment problem*. Thames Essay, No. 45, Trade Policy Research Centre.

Batchelor, R. A., Major, R. L. and Morgan, A. (1980). *Industrialisation and the basis for trade*. Cambridge: Cambridge University Press.

Bergstrand, J. H. (1983). Measurement and determinants of intra-industry international trade. In P. K. M. Tharakan (ed.) *Intra-industry trade*, Amsterdam: North Holland.

Bhagwati, J. (1964). The pure theory of international trade: A survey. *Economic Journal 74.*

Bhagwati, J. (ed.) (1982). *Import competition and response.* Chicago: University of Chicago Press.

Bowen, H., Leamer, E. and Sveikauskaus, L. (1987). Multicountry, multifactor tests of the factor abundance theory. *American Economic Review 77.*

Bhagwati, J. (1984). Splintering and disembodiment of services and developing nations. *World Economy 7.*

Bhagwati, J. (1988). *Protectionism.* Cambridge, MA. and London: MIT Press.

Bhagwati, J. *et al.* (eds.) (1971). *Trade, balance of payments and growth: Essays in honour of C. P. Kindleberger.* Amsterdam: North-Holland.

Bhagwati, J., Greenaway, D. and Panagriya, A. (1998). Trading preferentially: Theory and policy. *Economic Journal 108.*

Brander, J. (1981). Intra-industry trade in identical commodities. *Journal of International Economics 11.*

Brander, J. and Krugman, P. (1983). A reciprocal dumping model of international trade. *Journal of International Economics 13*: 313–21.

Brander, J. and Spencer, B. (1985). Export subsidies and market share rivalry. *Journal of International Economics 18.*

Buckley, P. J. and Casson, M. (1976). *The future of the multinational enterprise.* London: Macmillan.

Buckley, P. J. and Clegg, J. (1990). *Multinational enterprises in less developed countries.* London: Macmillan.

Cable, V. (1981). *Protectionism and industrial decline.* London: ODI / Hodder & Stoughton.

Cantwell, J. (1988a). *The reorganisation of European industries after integration: Selected evidence on the role of multinational enterprise activities*, University of Reading Department of Economics Discussion Papers in International Investment and Business Studies, No. 115.

Cantwell, J. (1988b). *The growing internationalisation of industry: A comparison of the changing structure of company activity in the major industrialised countries*, University of Reading Department of Economics Discussion Papers in International Investment and Business Studies, No. 116.

Casson, M. (1986). *Multinationals and world trade.* London: Allen & Unwin.

Caves, R. E. (1971). International corporations: the industrial economics of foreign investment. *Economica*, 1938.

Caves, R. E. (1981). Intra-industry trade and market structure in the industrial countries. *Oxford Economic Papers*, July.

Caves, R. E. (1982). *Multinational enterprise and economic analysis.* Cambridge: Cambridge University Press.

Chaponniere, J. R. (1997). The NIEs go international: The NIEs' regional pattern of investment and trade, in de Bettignies H.-C. *Trade and investment in the Asia-Pacific region.* London and Boston: International Thomson Press.

Chenery, H. and Keesing, S. (1981). The changing composition of developing country exports of manufactures. In S. Grassman and E. Lundberg (eds.) *The world economic order: Past and prospects*, London: Macmillan.

Chowdhury, A. and Islam, I. (1993). *The newly industrialising economies of East Asia.* London and New York: Routledge.

Clegg, J. (1990). Intra-industry foreign direct investment: A study of recent evidence. Chap. 7. In A. Webster and J. H. Dunning (eds.) *Structural Change in the world economic.* London and New York: Routledge.

Clegg, J. (1996). The development of multinational enterprises. Chap. 7. In P. W. Daniels and W. F. Lever (eds.) *The global economy in transition*, Harlow, Essex: Addison, Wesley, Longman, Ltd.

Cline, W. R. (ed.) (1983). *Trade policy in the 1980s*, Cambridge, MA: Institute for International Economics and MIT Press.

Coase, R. H. (1937). The nature of the firm. *Economica 4.*

Cohen, S. (1978). Coping with the new protectionism. *National Westminster Bank Review*, November.

Cooper, C. A. and Massell, B. F. (1965). A new look at customs union theory. *Economic Journal 75.*

Corden, W. M. (1974). The theory of international trade: In J. H. Dunning (ed.) *International investment: Selected readings*, Harmondsworth: Penguin.

Corden, W. M. (1974). *Trade policy and economic welfare.* Oxford: Clarendon Press.

Corden, W. M. (1985). *Protection, growth and trade*, Oxford: Blackwell.

Cournot, A. (1838). *Researches into the mathematical principles of the theory of wealth*, translated by N. T. Bacon, New York: Macmillan, 1897.

Cox, H. (1997). The evolution of international business enterprise. In R. John, G. Ietto-Gillies,

H. Cox and N. Grimwade (eds.) *Global business straligy*, London and Bacon, International Thomson Press.

Culem, C. and Lundberg, L. (1986). The product pattern of intra-industry trade: Stability among countries and over time. *Weltwirtschaftliches Archiv 122*.

D'Andrea Tyson, L. (1992). *Who's bashing whom? Trade conflict in high technology industries.* Washington DC: Institute for International Economics.

Daniels, P. W. and Lever, W. F. (eds.) (1996). *The global economy in transition,* Harlow, Essex: Addison Wesley Longman Ltd.

Dawkins, W. (1994). Loosening of the corporate web, *Financial Times*, 20 November, 1994.

Deardorff, A. (1985). Comparative advantage and international trade and investment in services. In R. Stern (ed.) *Trade and investment in services: Canada/US perspective*. Toronto: Ontario Economic Council.

De Bettingnies, H.-C. (ed.) (1997). *Trade and investment in the Asia–Pacific region.* London and Boston: International Thomson Press.

Department of Trade and Industry (1979). *Analysis of foreign enterprises in the United Kingdom: Census of production 1975*. Trade and Industry, 27 July.

Department of Trade and Industry (1985). *Countertrade: Some guidance for exporters* (July), London: DTI.

Dicken. P., *Global shift: The internationalisation of economic activity,* 2nd ed., London: Paul Chapman.

Diebold, W. Jr. and Stalson, H. (1983). Negotiating issues in international services transactions. In W. R. Cline (ed.). *Trade policy in the 1980s*, Cambridge, MA: Institute for International Economics and MIT Press.

Dixit, A. K. and Grossman, G. (1986). Targeted export promotion with several oligopolistic industries, *Journal of International Economics 21*.

Dixit, A. K. and Norman, V. (1980). *The theory of international trade*, Cambridge: Cambridge University Press.

Dixit, A. K. and Stiglitz, J. (1977). Monopolistic competition and optimum product diversity, *American Economic Review 67*.

Dunning, J. H. (ed.) (1974a). *International investment: Selected readings*, Harmondsworth: Penguin.

Dunning, J. H. (ed.) (1974b). *Economic analysis and the multinational enterprise*. London: Allen & Unwin.

Dunning, J. H. (1977). Trade, location and economic activity of the multinational enterprise: A search for an eclectic approach. In B. Ohlin (ed.) *The international allocation of economic activity,* London: Macmillan.

Dunning, J. H. (1982). A note on intra-industry foreign direct investment. Rome: Banca Nazionale del Lavoro, March.

Dunning, J. H. (1992). *The multinational enterprise and the global economy,* Reading: Addison-Wesley.

Dunning, J. H. (1993). *The globalisation of business: The challenge of the 1990s,* London: Routledge.

Dunning, J. H. and Norman, G. (1985). Intra-industry production as a form of international economic involvement. In A. Erdilek (ed.) *Multinationals as mutual invaders*, Beckenham: Croom Helm.

Dunning, J. H. and Pearce, I. F. (1981). *The world's largest enterprises*, Aldershot: Gower.

Eaton, J. and Grossman, G. (1986). Optimal trade and industrial policy under oligopoly. *Quarterly Journal of Economics 101*.

Economist Intelligence Unit (1984). *North–south countertrade*, Special Report, No. 174.

El-Agraa, A. M. (1988). *Japan's trade frictions: Realities or misconceptions?* London: Macmillan

El-Agraa, A. M. (1997). UK competitiveness and Japanese industrial policy. *Economic Journal 107*(444).

El-Agraa, A. M. (1997). *Economic integration worldwide,* Basingstoke and London: Macmillan.

Ellis, M. (1983). An alternative interpretation and empirical test of the Linder hypothesis. *Quarterly Journal of Business and Economics 22*.

Ellsworth, P. T. (1954). The structure of American foreign trade: A new view examined. *Review of Economics and Statistics 36*.

Erdilek, A. (ed.) (1985). *Multinationals as mutual invaders: Intra-industry foreign direct investment.* Beckenham: Croom Helm.

Erzan, R. and Laird, S. (1984). *Intra-industry trade of developing countries and some policy issues*, Institute for International Economic Studies, University of Stockholm, Seminar Paper No. 289, August.

Falvey, R. E. (1981). Commercial policy and intra-industry trade. *Journal of International Economics 2*.

Falvey, R. E. and Kierkowski, H. (1984). *Product quality, intra-industry trade and imperfect competition*, Discussion Paper, Graduate Institute of International Studies, Geneva.

Finger, J. M., Hall, H. K. and Nelson, D. R. (1982). The political economy of administered protection, *American Economic Review 72*.

François, J. F. (1990a). Producer services, scale and the division of labour, *Oxford Economic Papers 42*.

François, J. F. (1990b). Trade in producer services and returns due to specialisation and the monopolistic competition, *Canadian Journal of Economics*.

Franko, L. G. and Stephenson, S. (1982). The micro picture: Corporate and sectoral developments. In L. Turner and N. McMullen (eds.) *The newly industrialising countries: Trade and adjustment*, London: Allen & Unwin.

Franks, P. *Japanese economic development. Theory and practice*, London: Nissan Institute/Routledge Japanese Studies.

Frey, B. (1984). *International political economics*, Oxford: Martin Roberston.

Frey, B. (1985). The political economy of protection. Chap. 9. In D. Greenaway (ed.) Current issues in international trade: Trade and policy. London: Macmillan.

Frey, B. and Weck-Hannemann. (1996). The political economy of protection. Chap. 8. In Greenaway, D.

Fröbel, F., Heinrichs, J. and Kreye, O. (1980). *The new international division of labour*, Cambridge: Cambridge University Press.

General Agreement on Tariffs and Trade (GATT) (1983). *International trade*, Geneva: GATT.

General Agreement on Tariffs and Trade (GATT) (1986). *International trade*, Geneva: GATT.

General Agreement on Tariffs and Trade (GATT) (1993). *International trade,* Geneva: GATT.

Giersch, H. (ed.) (1979). *On the economics of intra-industry trade*, Tübingen: J.C.B. Mohr.

Giersch, H. (1986). Perspectives on the world economy. *Weltwirtschaftliches Archiv 121*.

Glejser, H. (1983). Intra-industry trade and inter-industry trade specialisation: Trends and cycles in the EEC. In P. K. M. Tharakan (ed.) *Intra-industry trade*, Amsterdam: North Holland.

Glejser, H., Goosens, K. and Vanden Eede, M. (1979). Inter-industry and intra-industry specialisation do occur in world trade, *Economic Letters 3*.

Glejser, H., Goosens, K. and Vanden Eede, M. (1982). Inter-industry versus intra-industry specialisation in exports and imports (1959–1970–1973). *Journal of International Economics 12*.

Globerman, S. and Dean, J. W. (1990). Recent trends in intra-industry trade and their implications for future trade liberalisation, *Weltwirtschaftliches Archiv*, Band 126, Heft 1.

Godley, W. and May, R. M. (1977). The macroeconomic implications of devaluation and import restriction, *Cambridge Economic Policy Review 3*.

Graham, L. M. (1985). Intra-industry structure, firm rivalry and performance. In A. Erdilek (ed.) *Multinationals as mutual invaders*, Beckenham: Croom Helm.

Grassman, S. and Lundberg, E. (eds.) (1981). *The world economic order: Past and prospects*, London: Macmillan.

Gray, H. P. (1979). Intra-industry trade: The effects of different levels of data aggregation. In H. Giersch (ed.) *On the economics of intra-industry trade*, Tübingen: J.C.B. Mohr.

Gray, H. P. (1990). The role of services in global structural change. Chap. 5, In A. Webster and J. H. Dunning (1990).

Greenaway, D. (1982). Identifying the gains from pure intra-industry exchange. *Journal of Economic Studies 9*(3).

Gray, H. P. (1983a). *International trade policy: From tariffs to the new protectionism*, London: Macmillan.

Gray, H. P. (1983b). Patterns of intra-industry trade in the UK. In P. M. K. Tharakan (ed.). *Intra-industry trade*, Amsterdam: North Holland.

Gray, H. P. (ed.) (1985). *Current issues in international trade: Theory and policy*, London: Macmillan.

Gray, H. P. (ed.) (1988). *Economic development and international trade,* London: Macmillan.

Gray, H. P. (ed.) (1986). *Current issues in international trade*, 2nd ed., London: Macmillan.

Greenaway, D. and Hine, R. (1991). Intra-industry specialisation, trade expansion and adjustment in the European economic space. *Journal of Common Market Studies XXIX*(6).

Greenaway, D. and Milner, C. R. (1983). On the measurement of intra-industry trade. *The Economic Journal 93*.

Greenaway, D. and Milner, C. R. (1986). *The economics of intra-industry trade*, Oxford: Blackwell.

Greenaway, D. and Winters, A. (1994). *Surveys of international trade*, Oxford: Basil Blackwell.

Greenaway, D., Hine, R. and Milner, C. (1995). Vertical and horizontal intra-industry Trade: A cross industry analysis for the United Kingdom. *Economic Journal 105*(433).

Greytak, D. and Tuchinda, U. (1990). The composition of consumption and trade intensities: An alternative test of the Linder hypothesis, *Weltwirtschaftliches Archiv* Band 126, Heft 1.

Grimwade, N. (1996). *International trade policy: A contemporary analysis*, London: Routledge.

Grimwade, N. (1998). The external impact of the EU's internal market programme. *European Business Journal 10*(2).

Grossman, G. (1988). Strategic export promotion: A critique. Chap. 3. In P. Krugman (ed.). Strategic trade policy and the new international economics, Cambridge, MA and London: MIT Press.

Grubel, H. G. (1987). Traded services are embodied in materials or people. *World Economy*, September.

Grubel, H. G. and Lloyd, P. J. (1975). *Intra-industry trade: The theory and measurement of international trade in differentiated products.* London: Macmillan.

Hamada, K. (1995). Behind the US–Japan trade conflict. *World Economy 18*(2).

Hamilton, C. (1985). Economic aspects of voluntary export restraints. In D. Greenaway (ed.). *Current Issues in International Trade*, London: Macmillan.

Haberler, G. (1937). *The theory of international trade*, London: Macmillan.

Havrylyshyn, O. (1964). *The direction of developing country trade: Empirical evidence of differences between South–South and North–South trade.* World Bank Conference series, Washington DC: World Bank.

Havrylyshyn, O. and Civan, E. (1983). Intra-industry trade and the stage of development. In P. M. K. Tharakan (ed.). *Intra-Industry Trade*, Amsterdam: North Holland.

Heckscher, E. (1919). The effect of foreign trade on the distribution of income. *Ekonomisk Tidskrift 21.*

Heitger, B. and Stehn, J. (1990). Japanese direct investments in the EC – Response to the internal market 1993? *Journal of Common Market Studies XXIX*, September.

Helleiner, G. K. (1981). *Intra-firm trade and the developing countries.* London: Macmillan.

Helleiner, G. K. (1979). Transnational corporations and trade structure: The role of intra-firm trade. In H. Giersch (ed.). *On the economics of intra-industry trade*, Tübingen: J.C.B. Mohr.

Helleiner, G. K. and Lavergne, R. (1980). Intra-firm trade and industrial experts to the United States. *Oxford Bulletin of Economics and Statistics*, November.

Helpman, E. (1981). International trade in the presence of product differentiation, economies of scale and monopolistic competition. *Journal of International Economics 11.*

Helpman, E. (1984). A simple theory of international trade with multinational corporations. *Journal of Political Economy 92.*

Helpman, E. (1985). Multinational corporations and trade structure. *Review of Economic Studies 52.*

Helpman, E. and Razin, A. (eds.) (1991). *International trade and trade policy.* Cambridge, MA: MIT Press.

Hill, T. P. (1977). On goods and services. *Review of Income and Wealth*, Series 23, No. 4, December.

Hindley, B. (1988). Dumping and the Far East trade of the European Community. *World Economy 11*(4).

Hindley, B. and Smith, A. (1984). Comparative advantage and trade in services. *World Economy 7.*

Hladik, J. (1985). *International joint ventures.* Lexington, MA: Lexington Books.

Hoekman, B. (1993). *Developing countries and the Uruguay Round negotiation on services.* CEPR Discussion Paper No 822, London: Centre for Economic Policy Research.

Hoekman, B. (1995). *Tentative first steps: An assessment of the Uruguay Round agreement on services.* CEPR Discussion paper no. 1150, London: Centre for Economic Policy Research.

Hoftyzer, J. (1984). A further analysis of the linder trade thesis. *Quarterly Review of Economics and Business 24.*

Holtferich, C.-L. (ed.) (1989). *Interactions in the world economy.* Brighton: Harvester Wheatsheaff.

Hood, N. and Young, S. (1979). *Economics of the multinational enterprise.* London: Longman.

Horioka, C. Y. (1986). Why is Japan's private savings rate so high? *Finance and Development*, December.

Horstmann, I. and Markusen, J. (1986). Up the average cost curve: Inefficient entry and the new protectionism. *Journal of International Economics 20.*

Houthakker, H. S. (1957). An international comparison of household expenditure patterns, commemorating the centenary of Engel's law. *Econometrica 25*.

Hufbauer, G. C. (1966). *Synthetic materials and the theory of international trade*, London: Duckworth.

Hufbauer, G. C. (1970). The impact of national characteristics and technology on the commodity composition of trade in manufactured goods. In R. Vernon (ed.). *The technology factor in international trade*. New York: Columbia University Press.

Hymer, S. (1960). *The international operations of national firms: A study of direct investment.* Ph.D. thesis, MIT, published 1976, Cambridge MA: MIT Press.

Hymer, S. and Rowthorn, R. (1970). Multinational corporations and international oligopoly: The non-American challenge. In C. P. Kindleberger (ed.). *The international corporation.* Cambridge, MA: MIT Press.

International Monetary Fund (IMF) (1998). *World economic outlook 1989–99.* Washington DC: International Monetary Fund.

Ito, T. (1992). *The Japanese economy*, Cambridge, MA: MIT Press.

Jacquemine, A. (ed.) (1984). *European industry: Public policy and corporate strategy.* Oxford: Clarendon Press.

John, R., Ietto-Gillies, G., Cox, H. and Grimwade, N. (1997). *Global business strategy.* London and Boston: International Thomson Press.

Johnson, H. G. (1965). An economic theory of protectionism, tariff bargaining and the formation of customs unions. *Journal of Political Economy 73*.

Johnson, H. G. (1970). Efficiency and welfare implications of the international corporation. In C. P. Kindleberger (ed.). *The international corporation*. Cambridge, MA: MIT Press.

Jones, R. (1956). Factor endowment and the Heckscher–Ohlin model. *Review of Economic Studies 24*.

Jones, R. (1971). A three-factor model in theory, trade and history. In J. Bhagwati, *et al.* (eds.), Trade, balance of payments and growth: Essays in honour of C. P. Kindleberger. Amsterdam: North Holland.

Jones, R. and Ruane, F. (1990). Appraising the options for international trade in services. *Oxford Economic Papers 42*.

Julius, D. and Butler, J. (1998). Inflation and growth in a service economy. *Bank of England Quarterly Bulletin*, November.

Jun, K. W., Sader, F., Horaguchi, H. and Kwak, H. (1993). *Japanese foreign direct investment: Recent trends, determinants and prospects.* World Bank Policy Research Working Paper 1213, Washington DC: World Bank.

Kagami, N. (1983). Maturing of the Japanese economy in the 1980s. *National Westminster Bank Review*, November.

Keesing, D. (1967). The impact of research and development on United States trade. *Journal of Political Economy 75*.

Kenen, P. B. (1965). Nature, capital and trade. *Journal of Political Economy 73*.

Key, S. (1997). *Financial services in the Uruguay Round and the WTO.* Occasional Paper 54, Washington DC: Group of Thirty.

Kierzkowski, H. (1984). *Monopolistic competition and international trade.* Oxford: Clarendon Press.

Kierzkowski, H. (1985). Models of international trade in differentiated goods. In D. Greenaway (ed.). *Current issues in international trade.* London: Macmillan.

Kierzkowski, H. (1986). *Modelling international transportation services*, Washington DC: IMF Research Paper, DM/86/35.

Kindleberger, C. P. (1968). *International economics,* 4th ed. Homewood, IL: Richard D. Irwin, Inc.

Kindleberger, C. P. (1969). *American business abroad.* New Haven, CT: Yale University Press.

Kindleberger, C. P. (ed.) (1970). *The International Corporation.* Cambridge, MA: MIT Press.

Kindleberger, C. P. (1982). *The world economic slowdown since the 1970s.* Seminar Paper No. 229, Institute for International Economic Studies, Stockholm University, November.

Kitson, M. and Michie, J. (1995). Trade and growth: A historical perspective. Chap. 1. In J. Mitchie and J. Grieve Smith (eds.), Managing the global economy. Oxford: Oxford University Press.

Knickerbocker, F. T. (1973). *Oligopolistic reaction and the multinational enterprise.* Boston: Harvard University Press.

Kohlhagen, S. B. (1977). Income distribution and representatve demand in international trade flows: An empirical test of Linder's hypothesis. *Southern Economic Journal 44*.

Kojima, K. (1978). *Direct foreign investment: A Japanese model of multinational business operations.* Beckenham: Croom Helm.

Kostecki, M. (1987). Export restraint arrangements and trade liberalisation. *World Economy 10*(4).

Kravis, I. B. (1956). Availability and other influences on the commodity composition of trade. *Journal of Political Economy 64.*

Kreinin, M. (1979). *Effect of European integration on trade flows in manufactures.* Seminar Paper No. 125, Institute for International Economic Studies, Stockholm University, August.

Krugman, P. (1979). Increasing returns, monopolistic competition and international trade. *Journal of International Economics 9.*

Krugman, P. (1980). Scale economies, product differentiation and the pattern of trade. *American Economic Review 70.*

Krugman, P. (1981). Intra-industry specialisation and the gains from trade. *Journal of Political Economy 89.*

Krugman, P. (1982). Trade in differentiated products and political economy of trade liberalisation. In J. Bhagwati (ed.). *Import competetion and response.* Chicago: University of Chicago Press.

Krugman, P. (1984). Import protection as export promotion: International competition in the presence of oligopoly and economies of scale. Chap. 11. In H. Kierzkowski (ed.). *Monopolistic competition and international trade.* Oxford: Clarendon Press.

Krugman, P. (ed.) (1988). *Strategic trade policy and the new international economics*, Cambridge, MA and London: MIT Press.

Krugman, P. (1991). Is bilateralism bad? In E. Helpman and A. Razin (eds.), *International trade and trade policy.* Cambridge, MA: MIT Press.

Krugman, P. (1993). Regionalism versus multilateralism: Analytical notes. In de Melo and Panagariya (1993).

Krugman, P. (1996). *Pop internationalism*, Cambridge, MA and London: MIT Press.

Krugman, P. and Obstfeld, M. (2000). *International economics: Theory and policy*, 5th ed. Reading, MA: Addison Wesley, Longman.

Laird, S. and Yeats. A, (1990). Trends in non-tariff barriers of developed countries, 1966–86. *Weltwirtschaftliches Archiv*, Band 126 Heft 2.

Lall, S. (1973). Transfer pricing by multinational manufacturing firms. *Oxford Bulletin of Economics and Statistics*, August.

Lall, S. (1978). The pattern of intra-firm exports by United States multinationals. *Oxford Bulletin of Economics and Statistics,* August.

Lall, S. (ed.) (1980). *The multinational corporation*, London: Macmillan.

Lall, S. (1981). *Developing countries in the international economy*, London: Macmillan.

Lancaster, K. (1966). A new approach to consumer theory. *Journal of Political Economy 74.*

Lancaster, K. (1980). Intra-industry trade under perfect monopolistic competition. *Journal of International Economics 10.*

Langhammer, R. and Sapir, A. (1987). *Economic impact of generalised tariff preferences.* Thames Essays No 49, London: Gower for the Trade Policy Research Centre.

Lassudrie-Duchene, B. and Muchieli, J. L. (1979). Les échanges comparés dans le commerce international. *Revue Economique*, May.

Lawrence, R. (1991). Efficient or exclusionist? The import behaviour of Japanese corporate groups. *Brookings Papers on Economic Activity 1.*

Lawrence, R. and Slaughter, M. (1993). International trade and American wages in the 1980s: Giant sucking sound or small hiccup? *Brookings Papers on Economic Activity 2.*

Leamer, E. E. (1980). The Leontieff Paradox reconsidered. *Journal of Political Economy 88.*

Lecraw, D. (1985). Some evidence on transfer pricing by MNCs. In A. Rugman and L. Eden (eds.), *Multinationals and transfer pricing*, Beckenham: Croom Helm.

Leontieff, W. (1954). Domestic production and foreign trade: The American capital position re-examined. *Economia Internazionale 7.*

Leontieff, W. (1956). Factor proportions and the structure of American trade: Further theoretical and empirical analysis. *Review of Economics and Statistics 38.*

Leontieff, W. (1964). International factor cost and factor use. *American Economic Review 54.*

Lewis, A. (1981). Growth of world trade. In S. Grassman and E. Lundberg (eds.), *The world economic order.* London: Macmillan.

Linder, S. B. (1961). *An essay on trade and transformation*, New York: John Wiley.

Lloyds Bank (1985). *Japan 1985.* Lloyds Bank Group Economic Report.

Lorenz, D. (1986). New situations facing NICs in East Asia. *Inter-economics*, November–December.

Lorenz, D. (1989a). Trade in manufactures, newly Industrialising economies (NIEs) and regional development in the world economy. *Journal of the Institute of Developing Economies XXVIII*(3).

Lorenz, D. (1989b). Newly industrialising countries in the world economy: NICs, SICs, NECs, EPZs or TEs? In C.-L. Holtferich (eds.), *Interactions in the world economy.* Brighton: Harvester Wheatsheaf.

MacDougall, G. D. A. (1951). British and American Exports: A study suggested by the theory of comparative costs. *Economic Journal 61*(62).

Maddison, A. (1991). *Dynamic forces in capitalist development.* Oxford and New York: Oxford University Press.

Marin, A. (1991). Typing in international trade: Evidence on countertrade. *World Economy 13*(3).

Marin, A. and Schnitzer, M. (1997). *The economic institutions of international barter.* Centre for Economic Policy Research Discussion Paper No. 1658.

Markusen, J. R. (1984). Multinationals, multi-plant economies, and the gains from trade. *Journal of International Economics 16.*

Markusen, J. R. (1989). Trade in producer services and in other specialised intermediate inputs. *American Economic Review 79.*

Marques-Mendes, A. J. (1986). The contribution of the European Community to economic growth. *Journal of Common Market Studies XXIV*(4).

Masera, R. (1986). Europe's economic problems in an international perspective. *Banca Nazionale del Lavoro, Quarterly Review 159*, December.

Maskus, K., Normative concerns in the international protection of intellectual property rights. *World Economy 13*(3).

McAleese, D. (1977). Do tariffs matter? *Oxford Economic Papers*, March.

McAleese, D. (1979). Intra-industry trade, level of development and market size. In H. Giersch (ed.) *On the economics of intra-industry trade*, Tübingen: J.C.B. Mohr.

McCulloch, R. (1993). Services and the Uruguay Round. *World Economy 13*(3).

de Melo and Pangariya, A. (eds.) (1993). *New Dimensions in Regional Integration*, London: Centre for Economic Policy Research (CEPR).

Melvin, J. R. (1989). Trade in producer services: A Heckscher–Ohlin approach. *Journal of Political Economy 97.*

Meyer, F. V. (1978). *International trade policy.* Beckenham: Croom Helm.

Michie, J. and Grieve Smith, J. (eds). *Managing the global economy*, Oxford: Oxford University Press.

Mikinagi, Y. (1996). *Japan's trade policy: Action or reaction?* Routledge Studies in the Growth Economics of Asia 4, London: Routledge.

Moore, L. B. (1985). *Growth and structure of international trade since World War II*, Brighton: Wheatsheaf Books.

Moroney, J. R. (1967). The strong factor-intensity hypothesis: A multi-sectoral test. *Journal of Political Economy 75.*

Murray, R. (ed.) (1981). *Multinationals beyond the market: Intra-firm trade and the control of transfer pricing.* New York: John Wiley.

Natke, P. (1985). A comparison of import pricing by foreign and domestic firms in Brazil. In A. Rugman and L. Eden (eds.), *Multinationals and transfer pricing*. Beckenham: Croom Helm.

Neary, P. (1985). Theory and policy of adjustment in an open economy. In D. Greenaway (ed.). *Current issues in international trade*, London: Macmillan.

Nicolaides, P. (1989). *Liberalising services trade: strategies for success.* Chatham House Papers, London: Royal Institute for International Affairs and Routledge.

Noland, M. (1995). US–Japan trade friction and its dilemmas for US policy. *World Economy 18*(2).

Norman, G. and Dunning, J. H. (1984). Intra-industry foreign direct investment: Its rationale and trade effects. A paper presented to the International Economics Study Group, 9th Annual Conference, September.

Ohlin, B. (1933). *Inter-regional and international trade.* Cambridge, MA: Harvard University Press.

Ohlin, B. (ed.) (1977). *The international allocation of economic activity.* London: Macmillan.

Organisation for Economic Cooperation and Development (OECD) (1979a). *The impact of the newly industrialising countries.* Paris: OECD.

Organisation for Economic Cooperation and Development (OECD) (1979b). *The impact of barter in developing countries.* Paris: OECD.

Organisation for Economic Cooperation and Development (OECD) (1979c). *Transfer pricing and the multinational enterprises.* Paris: OECD.

Organisation for Economic Cooperation and Development (OECD) (1981a). *The impact of the newly industrialising countries: An update.* Paris: OECD.

Organisation for Economic Cooperation and Development (OECD) (1981b). *East–west trade: Recent developments in countertrade.* Paris: OECD.

Organisation for Economic Cooperation and Development (OECD) (1985a). *Annual economic surveys: Japan.* Paris: OECD.

Organisation for Economic Cooperation and Development (OECD) (1985b). *Countertrade: Developing country practices.* Paris: OECD.

Organisation for Economic Cooperation and Development (OECD) (1988). *The newly industrialising countries: Challenges and opportunities for OECD countries.* Paris: OECD.

Organisation for Economic Cooperation (OECD) (1992). *Services – Statistics on international transactions 1970–89.* Paris: OECD.

Organisation for Economic Cooperation and Development (OECD) (1993). *Trade policy issues, 1 Intra-firm trade.* Paris: OECD.

Organisation for Economic Cooperation (OECD) (1995). *Foreign trade statistical bulletin.* Paris: OECD.

Owen, N. (1983). *Economies of scale, competitiveness and trade patterns within the European Community.* Oxford: Oxford University Press.

Ozawa, (1979). *Multinationalism, Japanese style.* Princeton, NJ: Princeton University Press.

Page, S. (1981). The revival of protectionism and the consequences for Europe. *Journal of Common Market Studies*, September.

Page, S. (1994). *How developing countries trade.* London: Routledge.

Panic, M. and Joyce, P. L. (1980). UK manufacturing industry, international integration and trade performance. *Bank of England Quarterly Bulletin*, March.

Pearce, J. and Sutton, J. (1986). *Protectionism and industrial policy in Europe*. London: Routledge.

Plasschaert, S. R. F. (1979). *Transfer pricing and multinational corporations: An overview of concepts, mechanisms and regulations*. New York: Praeger.

Plasschaert, S. R. F. (1985). Transfer pricing problems in developing countries. In A. Rugman and L. Eden (eds.), *Multinationals and transfer pricing*, Beckenham: Croom Helm.

Porter, M. E. (ed.) (1986). *Competition in global industries*. Boston: Harvard University Press.

Porter, M. E. (1990), *The competitive advantage of nations.* London: Macmillan.

Porter, M. E. and Fuller, M. (1986). Coalitions and global strategy. In Porter M. E. (ed.). *Competition in global industry.* Boston: Harvard University Press.

Posner, M. (1961). International trade and technical change. *Oxford Economic Papers 13.*

Ricardo, D. (1817). *Principles of political economy,*

Robinson, R. (1956). Factor proportions and comparative advantage: Part 1. *Quarterly Journal of Economics 70.*

Rodrick, D. (1994). *King Kong meets Godzilla: The World Bank and the East Asian miracle*. Centre for Economic Policy Research (CEPR) Discussion Paper No. 944, April.

Rodrick, D. (1998). Globalisation, social conflict and economic growth. *World Economy 21*(2).

Roumaliotis, P. (1977). Underinvoicing aluminium from Greece. In R. Murray (ed.). *Multinationals beyond the market*. New York: John Wiley.

Rugman, A. (1985). Determinants of intra-industry direct foreign investment. In A. Erdilek (ed.). *Multinationals as mutual invaders*. Beckenham: Croom Helm.

Rugman, A. and Eden, L. (eds.) (1985). *Multinationals and transfer pricing*. Beckenham: Croom Helm.

Sampson, G. and Snape, R. (1985). Identifying the issue in trade in services. *World Economy 8.*

Samuelson, P. (1948). International trade and the equalisation of factor prices. *Economic Journal 59.*

Samuelson, P. (1971). Ohlin was right. *Swedish Journal of Economics LXXIII.*

Sapir, A. (1985). North–South issues in trade in services. *World Economy 8.*

Sapir, A. (1994). Services trade. Chap. 10. In D. Greenaway and A. L. Winters (eds.). Services of international trade. Oxford: Basil Blackwell.

Sapir, A. (1997). *Domino effects in West European trade, 1960–1992*, CEPR Discussion Paper, London: Centre for Economic Policy Research.

Sapir, A. and Lutz, E. (1981). *Trade in services: Economic determinants and development-related issues.* World Bank Staff Working Paper No. 410.

Sapsford, D. (1988). The debate over trends in the terms of Trade. Chap. 7. In D. Greenaway (ed.).

Sato, K, (1995). Economic growth, roreign trade, and trade policy in Japan. *World Economy 18*(2).

Sato, K. (1998) *The Japanese Economy.*

Saxonhouse, G. (1983). The micro- and macroeconomics of foreign sales to Japan. In W. R.

Cline (ed.). *Trade policy in the 1980s*, Cambridge, MA: Institute for International Economics and MIT Press.

Saxonhouse, G. (1986). Japan's intractable trade surpluses in a new era. *World Economy*, September.

Schott, J. J. (1994). *The Uruguay Round: An assessment*. Washington DC: Institute for International Economics.

Schumacher, D. (1983). Intra-industry trade between the FDR of Germany and developing countries. In P. K. M. Tharakan (ed.). *Intra-industry trade*. Amsterdam: North Holland.

Siddharthan, N. S. and Kumar, M. (1990). The determinants of inter-industry variations in the proportion of intra-firm trade: The behaviour of US multinationals. *Weltwirtschaftliches Archiv 126*.

Smith, A. (1776). *An inquiry into the nature and causes of the wealth of nations*. Reprinted by Methuen, London, 1961.

Stein, L. (1985). *Trade and structural change*. Beckenham: Croom Helm.

Stern, R. (1962). British and American productivity and comparative costs in international trade. *Oxford Economic Papers 14*.

Stern, R. (ed.). *Trade and Investment in Services: Canada/US perspectives*, Toronto: Ontario Economic Council.

Stern, R. and Hoekman, B. (1987). Negotiation on services. *World Economy 10*(1), March.

Stern, R. and Maskus, K. E. (1981). Determinants of the structure of US foreign trade, 1958–76. *Journal of International Economics 11*.

Stewart, M. (1983). *Controlling the economic future*, Brighton: Wheatsheaf Books.

Stolper, W. F. and Samuelson, P. (1941). Protection and real wages. *Review of Economic Studies 9*.

Stopford, J. M. (1982). *The world director of multinational enterprises, 1982–83*. London: Macmillan.

Stopford, J. M. and Dunning, J. H. (1983). *Multinationals: Company performance and global trends*. London: Macmillan.

Tavlas, G. S. and Ozechi, Y. (1991). The internationalisation of the yen, *Finance and Development*, June.

Tharakan, P. K. M. (ed.) (1983). *Intra-industry trade*. Amsterdam: North Holland.

Tharakan, P. K. M. (ed.) (1984). Intra-industry trade between the industrial countries and the developing world. *European Economic Review 26*.

Tharakan, P. K. M. (ed.) (1991). The political economy of anti-dumping undertakings in the European Communities. *European Economic Review 35*.

Tharakan, P. K. M. (ed.) (1995). Political economy and contingent protection. *Economic Journal 105*(433)

Thomas, B. (1967). The historical records of international capital movements to 1913. In J. H. Adler (ed.). *Capital movements and economic development*. London: Macmillan.

Thomsen, S. and Woolcock, S. (1993). *Direct investment and European integration: Competition among firms and governments*. Chatham House Papers, London: RIIA and Pinter.

Trebilock, M. and Howse, R. (1999). *The regulation of international trade: Political economy and legal order*, 2nd edn., London: Routledge.

Tschoegl, E. A. (1985), Modem barter. *Lloyds Bank Review*, October.

Tugendhat, C. (1971). *The multinationals*. Harmondsworth: Pelican.

Turner, L. and McMullen, N. (1986). *The newly industrialising countries: Trade and adjustment*. London: Allen & Unwin.

United Nations Centre on Transnational Corporations (UNCTC) (1983). *Transnational corporations in world development*, Third Survey, New York: United Nations.

United Nations Conference on Trade and Development (UNCTAD) (1980). *A case study approach to trade-related structural adjustment*. September, Secretariat Report.

United Nations Conference on Trade and Development (UNCTAD) (1983). *Handbook of international trade*. Geneva: UNCTAD.

United Nations Conference on Trade and Development (UNCTAD) (1996). *World investment report*.

United Nations Industrial Development Organisation (UNIDO) (1982). *Handbook of industrial statistics*. New York: United Nations.

Vaitsos, C. (1974). *Intercountry income distribution and transnational enterprises*. Oxford: Clarendon Press.

Valvanis-Vail, S. (1954). Leontieff's scarce factor paradox. *Journal of Political Economy 62*.

Vanek, J. (1959). The natural resource content of foreign trade, 1870–1955, and the relative abundance of natural resources in the United States. *Review of Economics and Statistics 41*.

Vanek, J. (1963). *The natural resource content of United States foreign trade, 1870–1955.* Cambridge, MA: MIT Press.

Vaupel, J. W. and Curhan, J. (1974). *The world's multinational enterprises: A sourcebook of tables.* Cambridge, MA: Harvard Business School.

Venables, A. (1984). Multiple equilibria in the theory of international trade with monopolistically competitive industries. *Journal of International Economics 16*

Vernon, R. (1966). International investment and international trade in the product cycle. *Quarterly Journal of Economics 80*, May.

Vernon, R. (1970). *The technology factor in international trade.* New York: Columbia University Press.

Vernon, R. (1974). The location of economic activity. In J. H. Dunning (ed.). *Economic analysis and Multinational interprise.* London: Allen & Unwin.

Vernon, R. (ed.) (1981). *Economics of international business*, 3rd ed. London: Prentice-Hall.

Vernon, R. (1985). *Exploring the global economy.* Cambridge, MA: Harvard University and University Press of America.

Viner, J. (1923). *Dumping: A problem in international trade.* Chicago: Chicago University Press.

Viner, J. (1950). *The customs union issue.* Carnegie Endowment for National Peace.

Webster, A. and Dunning, J. H. (eds.) (1990). *Structural change in the world economy.* London and New York: Routledge.

White, G. (1984). Intra-industry adjustment: European industrial policies. In A. Jacquemine (ed.) *European industry: Public policy and corporate strategy.* Oxford: Clarendon Press.

Wilkinson, E. (1983). *Japan versus Europe*. Harmondsworth: Pelican.

Winters, L. A. (1991). *International economics*, 4th edn., London: Harper Collins Academic.

Winters, L. A. (1994). *The EC and world protectionism: Dimensions of the political economy.* Centre for Economic Policy Research (CEPR) Discussion Paper No. 897, London: Centre for Economic Policy Research.

Wood, A. (1994). *North–South trade, employment and inequality*, Oxford: Clarendon Press.

Wolf, M. (1983). Managed trade in practice: Implications of the textile arrangements. In W. R. Cline (ed.). *Trade policy in the 1980s.* Cambridge, MA: Institute of International Economics and MIT Press.

Wonnacott, P. and Lutz, M. (1989). Is there a case for free trade areas? In J. J. Schott (eds.). *The Uruguay Round: An assessment.* Washington, DC: Institute for International economies.

Wonnacott, R. J. and Wonnacott, P. (1981). Is unilateral tariff reduction preferable to a customs union? The curious case of the missing foreign tariffs – or beware of the large country assumption. *American Economic Review 71.*

World Bank (1984). *World development report.* Washington, DC: World Bank.

World Bank (1985). *World development report.* Washington, DC: World Bank.

World Bank (1987). *World development Report.* Washington, D.C: World Bank.

World Bank (1993). *The East Asian miracle: Economic growth and public policy.* Washington DC and Oxford: published for the World Bank by Oxford University Press.

World Trade Organisation (WTO) (1995). *Trends and statistics.* Geneva: World Trade Organisation.

World Trade Organisation (WTO) (1996). *Annual report 1996.* Geneva; World Trade Organisation.

World Trade Organisation (WTO) (1999). http://heva.wto-ministerial.org/english/about_e/19/dis2_e.htm

Young, A. (1928). Learning by doing and the dynamic effects of international trade. *Quarterly Journal of Economics 106.*

Young, A. (1994). *The tyranny of numbers: Confronting the statistical realities of the East Asian growth experience.* National Bureau of Economic Research (NBER) Working Paper No 4680, March.

Yoshitomi, M. (1990). *Keiretsu*: An insider's guide to Japan's conglomerates. *Economic Insights*, September/October.

Yumiko, M. (1996). *Japan's trade policy: Action or reaction*? Routledge Studies in the Growth Economics of Asia, London: Routledge.

Glossary

Absolute Advantage

This refers to a situation where one country is able to produce one or more goods at a lower cost than other countries. Wherever this exists, it pays that country to specialise in those goods at which it is best.

Adjustment

This is the process whereby resources shift out of one industry or sector into another industry or sector in response to either changes in the pattern of demand or changes in relative costs of production or changes in international comparative advantage.

Adjustment Costs

These are the costs both to the country as a whole and to individuals (workers and investors) that result from the failure of adjustment to take place automatically and instantaneously as a result of an expansion of trade. As adjustment will eventually take place, adjustment costs are essentially short-run costs.

Adjustment Policy

This refers to the various measures governments use to re-allocate resources among different sectors in response to changes in relative prices, including those resulting from a growth of import competition. Such policies may seek to speed up the process of adjustment taking place through the market or they may seek to prevent adjustment by directly influencing relative prices.

Barter Trade

This refers to any trade which involves some element of reciprocity between countries; that is, in return for A buying from B, B buys from A. Another name for such trade is countertrade. Pure barter involves the direct exchange of goods for goods without the mediation of money.

Bilateralism

This is the name given to a situation in which any two countries consciously seek to balance their trade with one another rather than seeking to balance their overall trade with the world as a whole. Such a trade policy is a common feature of trade in state planned economies.

Common Market

This is an area characterised by four commercial freedoms – namely, free trade in goods, free trade in services, free movement of labour and free movement of capital. The Single European Market is an example of a common market.

Comparative Advantage

This refers to a situation where a country is relatively more efficient at producing at least one product, although it may still be unable to match the absolute level of costs in other countries. However, specialisation will still be worthwhile, since this will enable it to use its resources more efficiently than if it tried to produce all the goods that consumers want.

Competitive Advantage

This is a term used to refer to the strength that a particular country may enjoy in a particular industry or group of industries due to the success of firms located in that country. Although this may be reflected in the ability of these firms to produce at lower cost than their rivals in other countries, it may also result from non-price factors, such as the ability to innovate or to differentiate their goods from those of other firms or to produce goods of a certain quality.

Concentration

Market or industrial concentration refers to a situation where a small number of large sellers account for a large proportion of the total sales of a product.

Conglomerates

This is the name given to companies which produce a wide range of different and largely unrelated products. Such highly diversified companies have often become conglomerates by buying up other companies involved in different activities.

Countertrade

Countertrade is another name for barter trade in which some element of reciprocity exists between the two countries engaged in trade. Thus, one country agrees to buy *x* amount of a certain product from another country if the latter buys *y* amount of exports from the first country.

Cross-hauling

This is the practice whereby a multinational company may shift certain stages of the production of its product to low-cost sites in other (possibly neighbouring) countries. Components and parts are shipped out to the subsidiary for processing before the finished good is re-imported back to the parent company for sale on the domestic market or for export.

Customs Unions

Customs unions are formed by two or more countries agreeing to abolish tariffs on trade among themselves and establish a common external tariff on imports coming from the rest of the world.

De-industrialisation

This is a term generally used to describe the absolute and relative decline of manufacturing industry and the growth of the services sector which has taken place in many developed market economies in recent decades.

Diversification

This is a term used to refer to the practice of an investor spreading his/her investments over a wide range of different financial assets in order to minimise the risk from any one investment becoming non-performing. However, the term is also used to refer to the practice of firms minimising the risk from a downturn in the demand for a product by producing several different unrelated products. It may further be applied to a firm spreading its sales of a product across several different geographical markets to minimise the risk of a downturn in one particular market.

Dumping

This is defined by the GATT as a situation when the products of one country are sold to another country at a price which is less than the price at which they are sold in the exporting country. The exporting firm may be subsidised by the government of its own country or may temporarily incur losses in an attempt to gain a foothold in the foreign market.

Expenditure-changing Policies

This is the name given to macroeconomic policy measures introduced by a government to correct a balance-of-payments disequilibrium by changing the level of domestic expenditure. In the case of a deficit country, the government will act to reduce domestic expenditure; in the case of a surplus country, it will act to increase domestic expenditure.

Export-platform Investment

This is the name given to foreign investment by a multinational company which involves the establishment of a factory in a foreign country for the sole purpose of exporting finished goods. The finished good is usually processed or assembled in the foreign country using components and parts imported from the parent company or one of its other foreign subsidiaries.

Export-Processing Zones

This refers to special regions within a particular country where foreign companies can invest and pay low taxes, pay zero or very low tariffs, and enjoy exemption from minimum-wage laws and other kinds of legislation which are applied to domestic firms. Cheap or subsidised infrastructure such as low-cost port facilities and cheap power supplies are also provided. Such regions are designed to attract export-platform investments.

Export Promotion Policies

This covers a wide range of policy measures that governments might adopt to boost exports, including direct subsidies, tax incentives, low-cost credit, credit guarantees and measures to reduce the costs of inputs for export firms. Maintenance of a low exchange rate and reductions in tariffs on raw materials, intermediate goods and capital goods used by exporting firms may also classified as export promotion measures.

External Economies of Scale

This refers to the process whereby an individual firm's average cost curve shifts downwards, as a result of the expansion of the industry to which he belongs. These types of scale economies should be distinguished from internal economies of scale that involve a movement down a firm's long-run average cost curve, as the scale of production is increased.

Factor Intensities/Proportions

These refer to the proportions in which different factors of production – land, unskilled and skilled labour, human capital and physical capital, natural resources, technology – are combined in the production of a particular product or group of products.

Factor Price Equalisation

This refers to the process whereby trade, based on differences in factor endowments, may lead to a tendency towards factor prices (the price of labour or capital) being equalised in different countries. For example, as a result of trade, labour will become cheaper in a capital-abundant country and more expensive in a labour-abundant country.

Foreign Direct Investment

This refers to foreign investment by a multinational company involving either the establishment of a wholly owned foreign subsidiary or the acquisition of a controlling interest usually taken to be a minimum 10% of equity capital – in a foreign company.

Free Trade Areas

A free trade area is created by two or more countries agreeing to abolish tariffs on their trade with each other. However, unlike a customs union, no common external tariff is applied to goods coming from the rest of the world and each member of the area is free to apply whatever tariff its wishes to such imports.

Generalised System of Preferences

The name given to the system of trading preferences – that involved the granting of preferential treatment to the exports of developing countries – introduced by most western industrialised countries after 1971. Those exports of developing countries which are subject to GSP may enter the market of developed countries at low or zero tariff.

Globalised Production

This is a term most commonly used to refer to a situation where a multinational company plans the production of a product on a global basis, with different stages or processes being formed at different establishments each located in a different country.

Horizontal Differentiation

This refers to a situation where the products belonging to an industry possess the same core attributes, but these are mixed in different ways, giving rise to differences in style, appearance and marginal performance capabilities as between one product and the other.

Horizontal Foreign Direct Investment

The name given to foreign investment by a multinational company that involves either the setting up of a new overseas subsidiary or the acquisition of a controlling interest in a foreign company that produces the same or a similar range of goods.

Horizontal Intra-Industry Trade

This refers to intra-industry trade in goods that are horizontally differentiated.

Human Capital

This is the term used by economists to refer to the capital embodied in the workforce in the form of skills and know-how that have been acquired through education and training. This is distinct from physical capital in the form of plant, machinery and equipment.

Import Substitution Policies

Any government measure that seeks to reduce imports by encouraging more domestic production of goods that are substitutes for imports constitutes an import substitution measure. These include increased import tariffs, import quotas or other quantitative restrictions on imports, restrictions on the availability of foreign currency to buy non-essential goods from abroad and the granting of subsidies to domestic firms.

Import Quotas

These place a quantitative restriction on the amount of a particular good that may be imported during a given period of time. They are administered by the public authorities through the issue of licences to firms wishing to import the product during the time when imports are subject to control.

Interdependence

This is a term used by economists to refer to the extent to which countries are affected by cyclical fluctuations in the level of economic activity in other countries.

Indifference Curves

This is an analytical tool used in trade theory to represent different combinations of any two products that yield consumers the same amount of satisfaction. Through trade, however, countries are able to move onto higher indifference curves and thereby increase their economic welfare.

Inter-industry Trade

This is the name given to trade between countries that involves the exchange of products that belong to different industries. For example, one country exports cloth to another country in exchange for steel.

Inter-regional Trade

This refers to the proportion of a country's total trade (exports plus imports) that takes place with countries that belong to a different region of the world.

Internalisation

This is the name given to the process whereby, through the multinational expansion of companies, certain transactions – whether in goods or asset rights – are administered internally rather than through the use of external markets.

Intra-firm Trade

This is the name given to trade between a multinational company and its overseas affiliate or associate companies in another country. Sometimes, such trade is called in-house or intra-group trade.

Intra-industry Foreign Direct Investment

This is the name given to two-way direct investment between any two countries that takes place within the same industry. Thus when United States chemical manufacturers invest in Western Europe and West European chemical manufacturers invest in the United States, such direct investment is called intra-industry direct investment abroad.

Intra-industry Trade

This is the name given to trade between countries which involves the exchange of products that belong to the same industry. For example, Germany exports Volkswagens to Italy and Italy exports Fiats to Germany.

Intra-regional Trade

This refers to the proportion of a country's trade (exports plus imports) that takes place with countries that belong to the same region of the world.

Invisibles

This is the term given to a wide variety of intangible items which appear in the current account of a country's balance of payments. They include receipts from, less payments to, other countries for trade in services (e.g. tourism, banking and insurance, transport, etc.); interest, profits, and dividends earned on overseas investments (less payments abroad); and transfers. Invisibles are distinct from visibles, which are trade in tangible goods.

Joint Ventures

This is the name given to an enterprise which involves a partnership between one or more foreign companies and a locally based firm that may be privately or state owned.

Keiretsus

This is the name given to special groupings or families of firms in Japan, in which close ties of loyalty exist among the members of the group. Members may be bound together through a complex system of cross-shareholdings or through dependence on the same bank for capital. Yet, a further possibility is that firms may be bound together in contractual relationship of buying or selling.

Lead and Lags

These are expressions used to describe the ways in which traders bring forward (leads) or delay (lags) payments for goods imported from abroad to prevent losses from exchange rate fluctuations. Thus, they are a form of 'hedging' or covering against the risk of exchange rates changing. Multinationals may be well placed to engage in such transactions.

Learning-by-doing

This is an expression used by economists to refer to the process whereby a firm's average costs fall as the cumulative output of the firm is increased. It is due to the firm becoming more experienced at producing the good and, as a result, finding ways of producing the good more efficiently.

Licensing Agreement

This is an agreement between a multinational company and a foreign company – which could be a subsidiary of the multinational – that involves the licensor granting the licensee the use of industrial property rights (e.g. a trade mark, knowledge about how to produce a particular product, etc.) in return for agreed royalties and fees.

Mercantilism

This refers to a school of economic thought dominant in the Middle Ages that advocated the accumulation of a large trade surplus as a primary objective of government interference in the economy. The term has come to be used more loosely to refer to any economic strategy that advocated the accumulation of a trade surplus either by restrictions on imports and/or subsidising of exports.

Minimum Efficient Scale (MES)

This corresponds to the lowest point on a firm's long-run average cost curve, that is, the point at which average costs are minimised.

Monopolistic Competition

This is a type of market structure characterised by the existence of many sellers of a product, but the product of each seller is differentiated from those of its rivals. As a result, in the eyes of the consumer, there is a difference between the product of one seller and another. This may take the form of subjective differences created by the use of brand names and advertising or there may exist physical differences between the product of one seller and another. In the latter case, these may be mere differences of style or appearance or there may be performance differences in the products of rival sellers.

Monopsony Power

This refers to market power on the buying side of the market that enables the buyer of a good to influence the market price of the good by buying more or less. In trade policy, a large importing nation may enjoy monopsony power and be able to impose an optimum tariff on foreign suppliers that forces them to supply the good at a lower price than before.

Most-Favoured Nation Principle

This principle states that a country agrees to refrain from discriminating against countries to which it has granted this status in the formulation and enforcement of its trade policy. It will treat equally all countries to which it extends this privilege. For example, any tariff imposed on imports from such a country will be no higher than equivalent tariffs imposed on imports from other countries but could be lower. This principle represents a central pillar of the GATT agreement.

Multilateralism

This is the name given to a situation where countries seek to balance their overall transactions with the world as a whole rather than seeking to balance their bilateral payments with every single trading partner.

Multinational Companies/Enterprises

The name given to any company/enterprise that owns, controls and manages production establishments in at least two countries.

National Treatment

This is an important principle of the GATT/WTO that requires all countries that are members of GATT/WTO to treat foreign producers of a particular good identically to domestic producers of the same good, taking no account of any differences in the way the good is produced. It is also an important principle of the General Agreement on Services and, therefore, should apply to government treatment of service providers.

New International Division of Labour

The name given to the process whereby different stages in the process of producing certain products are hived off and relocated in different countries so as to take advantage of differences among countries in factor costs and to exploit the economies of scale obtainable from greater plant specialization.

Newly Industrializing Countries (NICs)

This is the name given to a group of developing countries that have, in recent decades, achieved fast growth and rapid industrialization through expanding their exports of manufactured goods – often labour-intensive, light manufacturing consumer goods – to the markets of the developed countries. Supreme examples of such countries are the East Asian group of countries – Taiwan, Hong Kong, South Korea, and Singapore.

Newly Exporting Countries (NECs)

This is a term that has come to be used in recent years to refer to a second generation of newly industrialising countries that have followed in the wake of the NICs and achieved rapid economic growth through export expansion. Many of these are located in East Asia and include countries such as Thailand, Malaysia, Indonesia, the Philippines and the People's Republic of China.

New Protectionism

This is another rather loose term used by economists to refer to the protectionist tide that has occurred in recent decades and that has mainly taken the form of an increased resort to non-tariff interferences in trade. The resort to non-tariff devices for restricting imports is what distinguishes the current wave of protectionism from past periods of protection which have mainly involved higher tariffs.

Non-Tariff Barriers

This is a generic term for a wide variety of devices other than tariffs which intentionally or unintentionally interfere with the free flow of goods between countries. They include quantitative restrictions on trade, domestic subsidies, export subsidies, discriminatory public procurement policies, technical and health standards, customs procedures and delays, and so on.

Non-Separated (or Factor) Services

These are services that require production and consumption to take place at the same time and, therefore, cannot be sold across borders in the same manner as a product. This means that either the buyer must move to where the provider is located (provider-located services) or the provider must move to where the demander is located (demander-located service).

Offer Curves

This is an analytical tool used in trade theory to represent a country's demand for a product by expressing this in terms of the amounts of another product that it is prepared to offer in exchange at different prices. When trade takes place, the terms of trade must settle at the point at which the offer curves of the two countries intersect.

Offshore Assembly Processing

This is the name given to the process whereby the final assembly of a finished good takes place at an offshore site in an overseas country so as to take advantage of lower labour costs. Such a process has been encouraged by special tariff provisions whereby developed countries apply tariffs on the value-added rather than the final price of goods which have been assembled or processed in this way.

Oligopoly

An oligopoly is the name given to a market structure in which a relatively small number of firms account for a large share of total sales. Although these firms may still compete fiercely, such market structures often result in a high degree of price collusion, although most attempts at restricting competition are not long-lasting.

Orderly-Marketing Agreements

The name given to an agreement between an importing country and one or more exporting countries under which the exporting country or countries agree to limit the quantity of a certain product which they sell to the importing country over a stipulated period.

Openness

Openness is a term used by economists to refer to a country's willingness to trade with the rest of the world, as reflected in the ratio of trade (exports plus imports) to a country's GDP.

Pareto Efficiency

This is the point of optimal welfare, such that a country cannot make some consumers better off without at the same time making all other consumers equally worse off. In other words, it is a point at which resources are optimally allocated between alternative uses and consumer welfare is maximised.

Perfect Competition

This is a market in which there exist many buyers and sellers of the good, such that no one seller or buyer is able to influence the market price by selling/buying more or less. In other words, each seller and buyer is a price-taker, who can sell or buy as much as they like at the market price, but cannot alter the price. Other conditions for perfect competition to exist are no real or subjective differences in the product sold by rival sellers, perfect knowledge on the part of buyers and sellers and freedom of entry into and exit from the industry.

Portfolio Investment

This is the name given to the purchase by an individual, company, or financial institution of interest-bearing overseas securities – either government securities or company stocks and shares – but not involving the investor in acquiring control of the concern in which it is investing.

Positive Adjustment

This is a term first used by the OECD to distinguish government policies that promote adjustment in the face of increased import competition as opposed to policies that arc purely defensive and compensatory and that reduce the ability of countries to adjust. For example, a blanket subsidy given to a firm or an industry unable to compete with low-cost imports from abroad forestalls adjustment. Government assistance to enable workers to retrain promotes adjustment.

Product Life Cycle

This refers to the different stages through which products pass during their lifetime – namely, novelty, maturity and standardisation. As products pass through these stages, the nature of competition, the location of production and the direction of trade all change.

Predatory Pricing

This takes place when a dominant firm uses its superior financial resources to drive out rivals from a particular market by deliberately pricing below average cost. If the predator is successful in forcing competitors to leave the industry altogether, the aim will be to raise price well above average cost as and when the predator faces no more competition.

Preferential Trading Agreement

A preferential trading agreement is any agreement between two or more countries to grant preferential access (i.e. a lower rate of tariff than the rate applied to imports from other partners) to imports coming from members of the area.

Price Discrimination

This refers to the practice of a firm charging different prices for the same good to different consumers. In the context of trade, these consumers will be consumers in different countries.

Rationalised Product Industries

A term sometimes used to refer to industries that have reached the stage of maturity in their development but which have undergone a new phase of re-organization based on the redesign of the product, fragmentation of the production process, and greater plant specialization.

Rationalised Product Investments

This is the name frequently used to refer to direct investments abroad by multinational companies that aim to concentrate certain stages or processes of production in particular countries. Such investments tend to be trade-enhancing as opposed to investments that jump trade barriers and are therefore trade-inhibiting.

Real Exchange Rates

These are nominal exchange rates adjusted for inflation. For example, if the price level of a country rose 10% faster than the rest of the world, a nominal depreciation of its currency of 10% would leave the real exchange rate unchanged.

Regionalisation

This is a term used by economists to refer to the tendency for proportionately more trade to take place with countries belonging to the same region, rather than with countries belong to different regions.

Regional Trading Blocs

These are regional groupings of countries that reduce or eliminate tariffs on imports coming from other members of the group, but continue to apply tariffs on goods coming from the rest of the world.

Reciprocity

The principle of reciprocity applies to trade policy and means that, in international tariff negotiations, countries must offer tariff concessions in return for receiving concessions and not free ride. It is also sometimes used to mean that a country should apply the same treatment to imports of goods or services from another country as the latter applies to the exports of the former country.

Right of Establishment

This refers to the right of individuals or firms of one country to produce and sell services (e.g. banking or insurance) in another country in the same way as local persons or firms. Since such trade in services involves foreign investment abroad, the right of establishment is a key principle in ensuring free trade in services.

Separated (or Disembodied) Services

These are services in which the service has been separated or disembodied from its production, such that it can be transferred across borders to where the buyer is located without any need for the provider to move also. Such services can, therefore, be traded in much the same way as goods. Examples are books, musical recordings, films, computer software and scientific documents.

Services

These may be defined as any activity which changes either a person (e.g. education, hairdressing, entertainment) or a good (e.g. advertising, retailing) or both (e.g. banking and finance). Unlike manufacturing, the output of the services sector is an intangible output.

Splintering

This is a term used by economists to refer to the growing tendency for firms to buy-in services from specialist firms rather than perform these services in-house. This gives rise to the illusion that the service sector is becoming more important, whereas it is simply the result of activities being classified for statistical purposes in a different way to before.

Strategic Trade Policy

Strategic trade policy refers to the attempts of governments to promote the development of high-technology industries (e.g. the aerospace industry) through the use of subsidies. In such industries, firms act strategically, basing their decisions on how they think their rivals might react to any change they make. The aim of a subsidy granted to national producers of a high-technology product is to deter rivals from investing in that industry and, thereby, enabling the country to enjoy all the benefits accruing from expansion of the industry.

Subcontracting

Applied at an international level, this refers to an arrangement whereby a company – possibly a multinational company – subcontracts a company in another country to carry out some specific process or type of work or to supply a particular good rather than do the work itself.

Technology-Gap Trade

This refers to the temporary comparative cost advantage that a country enjoys as a result of the discovery of a new, cheaper method of producing a good. Once the process has been imitated by producers in other countries, however, the country ceases to be a net exporter of the product.

Terms of Trade

This can be defined as the ratio of a country's average export prices to average import prices. If average export prices rise faster than average import prices, the terms of trade of the country in question are said to have improved.

Transfer Pricing (or Price Manipulation)

This is the term used for the pricing policies used by multinational companies for selling goods or services from one unit of the company to another. Such prices may diverge from the prices used in equivalent arm's-length transactions.

Transformation (or Production Possibility) Curves

This is a tool used in the theory of trade to illustrate the changes that take place in production within a country, as the relative prices of goods change. In a simple two-commodity model, more of one good can only be obtained by having less of another, so that some units of one product are, in effect, transformed into extra units of another.

Trade-Related Investment Measures (TRIMs)

These are any form of restriction that governments may impose on foreign firms investing in their country, which create a distortion of trade. For example, any rules that state that a certain proportion of components and parts must be sourced locally implies a distortion of trade.

Trade-Related Intellectual Property Rights (TRIPs)

Intellectual property rights are knowledge that belongs to the citizens or firms of one country in the form of patents, copyright, trade marks, industrial designs or geographical indications. If these are copied by firms in another country without the permission of the owner and without making a payment to the owner for use of the know-how, the property rights of the owners are infringed.

Trade Creation

The most common usage of this term is in relation to customs unions and free trade areas. It refers to the replacement of high-cost domestic production of a good with lower cost imports from another member of the union/area.

Trade Diversion

This may occur when countries form a customs union/free trade area because the members of the union/area apply discriminatory tariffs on imports from non-members only. Goods that were previously imported from non-members may not be displaced by imports from member states, although non-member states can still produce these more cheaply.

Turnkey Operations

This refers to an agreement between a company in one country – usually an advanced industrialized country – and a company in another country under which the former designs, constructs, and commissions a plant and is paid partly with the future output generated by the new plant.

Vertical Disintegration

This is a term used for the growing tendency whereby multinational companies separate off various processes or stages in the production of a particular good and relocate these processes or stages at plants in other countries.

Vertical Differentiation

This refers to products belonging to the same industry but which differ in quality, such that consumers could agree on the order in which products should be ranked.

Vertical Foreign Direct Investment

This is the name given to direct investment abroad which involves setting up a new subsidiary or acquiring a controlling interest in a foreign company involved at a different stage of the production process; for example a raw material supplier or a distribution outlet.

Vertical Intra-Industry Trade

This refers to intra-industry trade in products that are vertically differentiated.

Voluntary Export-Restraints

These are agreements between an exporting and an importing nation under which the former agrees to restrain its exports of a certain product either to some fixed quantity or some share of the market.

Index